Subaru Owners Workshop Manual

1978
1600cc.

by J H Haynes

Member of the Guild of Motoring Writers

and B Gilmour

D1736828

Models covered

UK

Subaru Saloon, Hardtop, Coupe and Estate with 1595 cc engine

USA

Subaru Sedan, Coupe, Hardtop, Pick-up and Station Wagon with 66.4 cu in, 77.3 cu in, 83.1 cu in and 97 cu in engines

Covers all 4WD and MPV models including BRAT

ISBN 0 85696 729 7

ABCDE
FGHI.

Printed in England *(237–10F1)*

HAYNES PUBLISHING GROUP
SPARKFORD YEOVIL SOMERSET ENGLAND

distributed in the USA by

HAYNES PUBLICATIONS INC
861 LAWRENCE DRIVE
NEWBURY PARK
CALIFORNIA 91320
USA

Acknowledgements

Thanks are due to Fuji Heavy Industries Limited of Japan for the supply of technical information and certain illustrations, to Castrol Limited who supplied lubrication data, and to the Champion Sparking Plug Company who supplied the illustrations showing the various spark plug conditions. The bodywork repair photographs used in this manual were provided by Holt Lloyd Limited, who supply 'Turtle Wax', 'Dupli-color Holts' and other Holts range products.

Lastly, special thanks are due to all those people at Sparkford and Yeovil who helped in the production of this manual. Martin Penny and Brian Horsfall carried out the mechanical work, Les Brazier took the photographs, John Rose edited and Ian Robson planned the layout of the book. The supplementary information was written by John Mead and edited by Paul Hansford.

About this manual

Its aim

The aim of this manual is to help you get the best value from your car. It can do so in several ways. It can help you decide what work must be done (even should you choose to get it done by a garage), provide information on routine maintenance and servicing, and give a logical course of action and diagnosis when random faults occur. However, it is hoped that you will use the manual by tackling the work yourself. On simpler jobs it may even be quicker than booking the car into a garage and going there twice to leave and collect it. Perhaps most important, a lot of money can be saved by avoiding the costs the garage must charge to cover its labour and overheads.

The manual has drawings and descriptions to show the function of the various components so that their layout can be understood. Then the tasks are described and photographed in a step-by-step sequence so that even a novice can do the work.

Its arrangement

The manual is divided into thirteen Chapters, each covering a logical sub-division of the vehicle. The Chapters are each divided into Sections, numbered with single figures, eg 5; and the Sections into paragraphs (or sub-sections), with decimal numbers following on from the Section they are in, eg 5.1, 5.2, 5.3 etc.

It is freely illustrated, especially in those parts where there is a detailed sequence of operations to be carried out. There are two forms of illustration: figures and photographs. The figures are numbered in sequence with decimal numbers, according to their position in the Chapter – eg Fig. 6.4 is the fourth drawing/illustration in Chapter 6. Photographs carry the same number (either individually or in related groups) as the Section or sub-section to which they relate.

There is an alphabetical index at the back of the manual as well as a contents list at the front. Each Chapter is also preceded by its own individual contents list.

References to the 'left' or 'right' of the vehicle are in the sense of a person in the driver's seat facing forwards.

Unless otherwise stated, nuts and bolts are removed by turning anti-clockwise, and tightened by turning clockwise.

Vehicle manufacturers continually make changes to specifications and recommendations, and these when notified are incorporated into our manuals at the earliest opportunity.

Whilst every care is taken to ensure that the information in this manual is correct, no liability can be accepted by the authors or publishers for loss, damage or injury caused by any errors in, or omissions from, the information given.

Introduction to the Subaru

The Subaru, which is manufactured by Fuji Heavy Industries Ltd. of Japan, was first introduced in the United States in 1968 as a mini car, the Subaru 360. The 360 was followed by the FF-1 series, front engine, front wheel drive cars with a horizontally opposed flat four, liquid cooled engine, the 1100 and 1300G. The range included 2 door and 4 door Sedan and Station Wagon.

In 1972 the 1400 was introduced and the Coupe GL and GSR was added to the range. Automatic transmission was introduced in 1974.

With the introduction of the 4WD Station Wagon in 1975, Subaru became the only small 4WD vehicle on sale in the United States. Also added to the range was a Hardtop model and 5-speed transmission was available on Coupe and Hardtop models.

In 1976 the 1600 with a larger (97 cu in) engine was introduced. Automatic transmission being available on all models and a 5-speed transmission available on Hardtop and Coupe models.

1977 saw the introduction of the 4WD Open MPV (Multipurpose Passenger Vehicle), this being a pick-up version of the highly successful 4WD Station Wagon. Detail refinements to the range were also carried out and the 97 cu in engine became the standard power plant for all models.

Contents

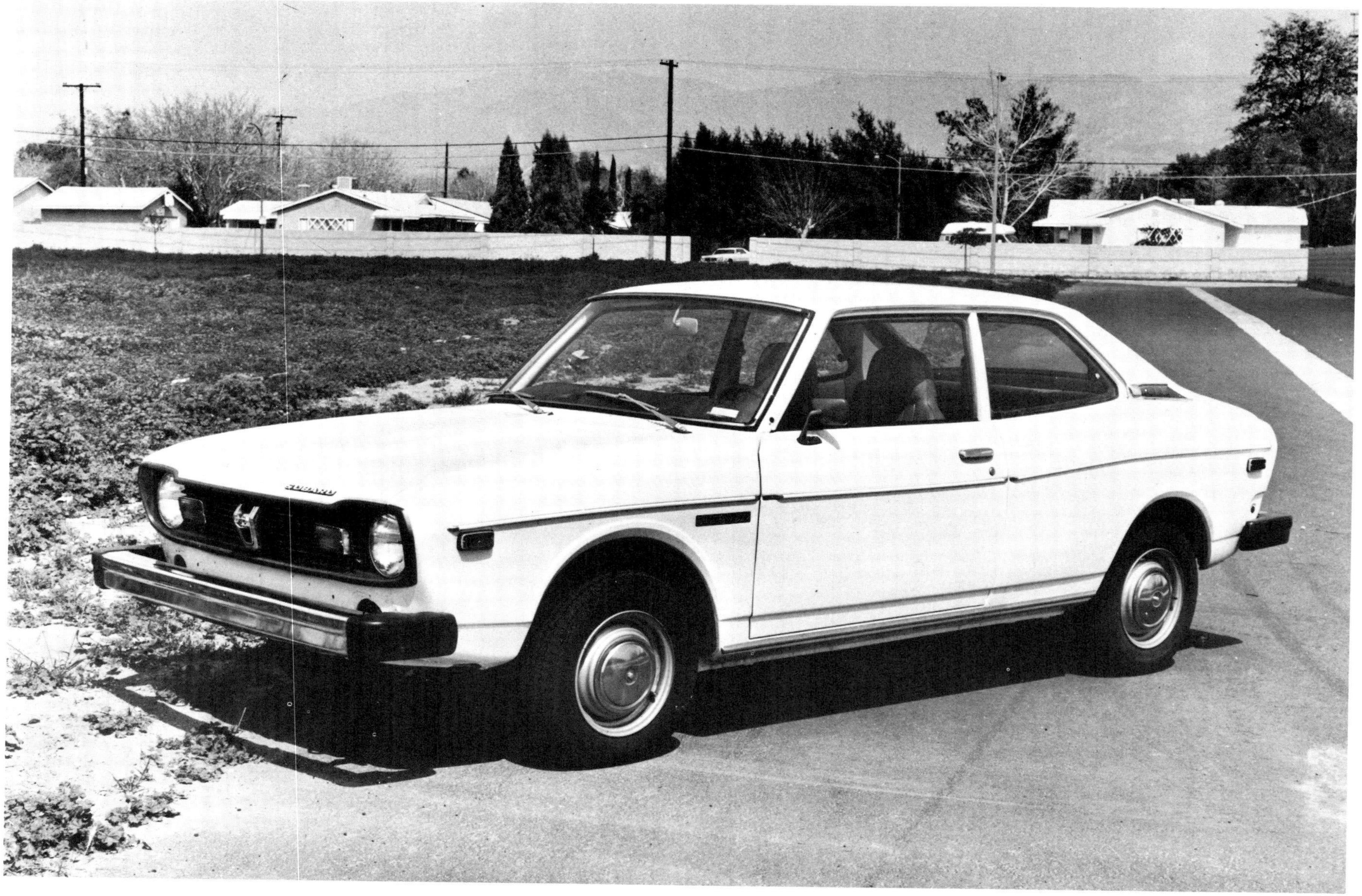

1976 1400 SUBARU (USA)

Buying spare parts and vehicle identification numbers

Buying spare parts

Spare parts are available from many sources, for example: Subaru garages, other garages and accessory shops, and motor factors. Our advice regarding spare part sources is as follows:

Officially appointed Subaru garages - This is the best source of parts which are peculiar to your car and are otherwise not generally available (eg. complete cylinder heads, internal gearbox components, badges, interior trim etc). It is also the only place at which you should buy parts if your car is still under warranty - non-Subaru components may invalidate the warranty. To be sure of obtaining the correct parts it will always be necessary to give the storeman your car's engine and chassis number, and if possible, to take the 'old' part along for positive identification. Remember that many parts are available on a factory exchange scheme - any parts returned should always be clean! It obviously makes good sense to go straight to the specialists on your car for this type of part for they are best equipped to supply you.

Other garages and accessory shops - These are often very good places to buy materials and components needed for the maintenance of your car (eg. oil filters, spark plugs, bulbs, fan belts, oils and greases, touch-up paint, filler paste etc). They also sell general accessories, usually have convenient opening hours, charge lower prices and can often be found not far from home.

Motor factors - Good factors will stock all of the more important components which wear out relatively quickly (eg. clutch components, pistons, valves, exhaust systems, brake cylinders/pipes/hoses/seals/ shoes and pads etc). Motor factors will often provide new or reconditioned components on a part exchange basis - this can save a considerable amount of money.

Vehicle identification numbers

Modifications are a continuing and unpublished process in vehicle manufacture, quite apart from major model changes. Spare parts manuals and lists are compiled upon a numerical basis, the individual vehicle numbers being essential to correct identification of the component required.

The *vehicle identification number plate* is located on top of the dashboard and is visible thru the windshield, see Fig. 1.

The die stamped *chassis serial number* is located on the firewall in the engine compartment, see Fig. 2.

The *engine number* is die stamped on the right-hand side of the crankcase (photo).

The engine number is die stamped on the crankcase

Vehicle identification number plate is on the dashboard

The vehicle chassis number is on the firewall

Tools and working facilities

Introduction

A selection of good tools is a fundamental requirement for anyone contemplating the maintenance and repair of a motor vehicle. For the owner who does not possess any, their purchase will prove a considerable expense, offsetting some of the savings made by doing-it-yourself. However, provided that the tools purchased are of good quality, they will last for many years and prove an extremely worthwhile investment.

To help the average owner to decide which tools are needed to carry out the various tasks detailed in this manual, we have compiled three lists of tools under the following headings: Maintenance and minor repair, Repair and overhaul, and Special. The newcomer to practical mechanics should start off with the 'Maintenance and minor repair' tool kit and confine himself to the simpler jobs around the vehicle. Then, as his confidence and experience grows, he can undertake more difficult tasks, buying extra tools as, and when, they are needed. In this way, a 'Maintenance and minor repair' tool kit can be built-up into a 'Repair and overhaul' tool kit over a considerable period of time without any major cash outlays. The experienced do-it-yourselfer will have a tool kit good enough for most repair and overhaul procedures and will add tools from the 'Special' category when he feels the expense is justified by the amount of use these tools will be put to.

It is obviously not possible to cover the subject of tools fully here. For those who wish to learn more about tools and their use there is a book entitled 'How to Choose and Use Car Tools' available from the publishers of this manual.

Maintenance and minor repair tool kit

The tools given in this list should be considered as a minimum requirement if routine maintenance, servicing and minor repair operations are to be undertaken. We recommend the purchase of combination spanners (ring one end, open-ended the other); although more expensive than open-ended ones, they do give the advantages of both types of spanner.

Combination spanners - 10, 11, 13, 14, 17 mm
Adjustable spanner - 9 inch
Engine sump/gearbox/rear axle drain plug key (where applicable)
Spark plug spanner (with rubber insert)
Spark plug gap adjustment tool
Set of feeler gauges
Brake adjuster spanner (where applicable)
Brake bleed nipple spanner
Screwdriver - 4 in long x ¼ in dia (plain)
Screwdriver - 4 in long x ¼ in dia (crosshead)
Combination pliers - 6 inch
Hacksaw, junior
Tire pump
Tire pressure gauge
Grease gun (where applicable)
Oil can
Fine emery cloth (1 sheet)
Wire brush (small)
Funnel (medium size)

Repair and overhaul tool kit

These tools are virtually essential for anyone undertaking any major repairs to a motor vehicle, and are additional to those given in the Maintenance and minor repair list. Inclded in this list is a comprehensive set of sockets.
Although these are expensive they will be found invaluable as they are so versatile - particularly if various drives are included in the set. We recommend the ½ in square-drive type, as this can be used with most proprietary torque wrenches. If you cannot afford a socket set, even bought piecemeal, then inexpensive tubular box spanners are a useful alternative.

The tools in this list will occasionally need to be supplemented by tools from the Special list.

Pliers - electricians side cutters
Pliers - needle nosed
Pliers - circlip (internal and external)
Cold chisel - ½ inch
Scriber (this can be made by grinding the end of a broken hacksaw blade)
Scraper (this can be made by flattening and sharpening one end of a piece of copper pipe)
Center punch
Pin punch
Hacksaw
Valve grinding tool
Steel rule/straight edge
Allen keys
Selection of files
Wire brush (large)
Jack (strong scissor or hydraulic type)
Jackstands
Sockets (or box spanners) to cover range 6 to 27 mm
Reversible ratchet drive (for use with sockets)
Extension piece, 10 inch (for use with sockets)
Universal joint (for use with sockets)
Torque wrench (for use with sockets)
'Mole' wrench - 8 inch
Ball pein hammer
Soft-faced hammer, plastic or rubber
Screwdriver - 6 in long x 5/16 in dia (plain)
Screwdriver - 2 in long x 5/16 in square (plain)
Screwdriver - 1½ in long x ¼ in dia (crosshead)
Screwdriver - 3 in long x 1/8 in dia (electricians)

Special tools

The tools in this list are those which are not used regularly, are expensive to buy, or which need to be used in accordance with their manufacturers instructions. Unless relatively difficult mechanical jobs are undertaken frequently, it will not be economic to buy many of these tools. Where this is the case, you could consider clubbing together with friends (or a motorists club) to make a joint purchase, or borrowing the tools against a deposit from a local garage or tool hire specialist.

The following list contains only those tools and instruments freely available to the public, and not those special tools produced by the vehicle manufacturer specifically for its dealer network. You will find occasional references to these manufacturers special tools in the text of this manual. Generally, an alternative method of doing the job without the vehicle manufacturers special tool is given. However, sometimes, there is no alternative to using them. Where this is the case and the relevant tool cannot be bought or borrowed you will have to entrust the work to a franchised garage.

Valve spring compressor
Piston ring compressor
Balljoint separator
Universal hub/bearing puller
Impact screwdriver
Micro and/or vernier gauge
Carburetor flow balancing device (where applicable)
Dial gauge
Stroboscopic timing light
Dwell angle meter/tachometer
Universal electrical multi-meter
Cylinder compression gauge
Lifting tackle
Trolley jack
Light with extension lead

Buying tools

For practically all tools, a tool factor is the best source since he will have a very comprehensive range compared with the average garage or accessory shop. Having said that, accessory shops often offer excellent quality tools at discount prices, so it pays to shop around.

Remember, you do not have to buy the most expensive items on the shelf, but it is always advisable to steer clear of the very cheap tools. There are plenty of good tools around, at reasonable prices, so ask the proprietor or manager of the shop for advice before making a purchase.

Care and maintenance of tools

Having purchased a reasonable tool kit, it is necessary to keep the tools in a clean and serviceable condition. After use, always wipe off any dirt, grease and metal particles using a clean, dry cloth, before putting the tools away. Never leave them lying around after they have been used. A simple tool rack on the garage or workshop wall, for items such as screwdrivers and pliers is a good idea. Store all normal spanners and sockets in a metal box. Any measuring instruments, gauges, meters, etc, must be carefully stored where they cannot be damaged or become rusty.

Take a little care when the tools are used. Hammer heads inevitably become marked and screwdrivers lose the keen edge on their blades from time-to-time. A little timely attention with emery cloth or a file will soon restore items like this to a good serviceable finish.

Working facilities

Not to be forgotten when discussing tools, is the workshop itself. If anything more than routine maintenance is to be carried out, some form of suitable working area becomes essential.

It is appreciated that many an owner mechanic is forced by circumstance to remove an engine or similar item, without the benefit of a garage or workshop. Having done this, any repairs should always be done under the cover of a roof.

Wherever possible, any dismantling should be done on a clean flat workbench or table at a suitable working height.

Any workbench needs a vise: one with a jaw opening of 4 in (100 mm) is suitable for most jobs. As mentioned previously, some clean dry storage space is also required for tools, as well as the lubricants, cleaning fluids, touch-up paints and so on which soon become necessary.

Another item which may be required, and which has a much more general usage, is an electric drill with a chuck capacity of at least 5/16 in (8 mm). This, together with a good range of twist drills, is virtually essential for fitting accessories such as fender mirrors and reversing lights.

Last, but not least, always keep a supply of old newspapers and clean, lint-free rags available, and try to keep any working area as clean as possible.

Spanner jaw gap comparison table

Jaw gap (in)	Spanner size
0.250	¼ in AF
0.275	7 mm AF
0.312	5/16 in AF
0.315	8 mm AF
0.340	11/32 in AF/1/8 in Whitworth
0.354	9 mm AF
0.375	3/8 in AF
0.393	10 mm AF
0.433	11 mm AF
0.437	7/16 in AF
0.445	3/16 in Whitworth/¼ in BSF
0.472	12 mm AF
0.500	½ in AF
0.512	13 mm AF
0.525	¼ in Whitworth/5/16 in BSF
0.551	14 mm AF
0.562	9/16 in AF
0.590	15 mm AF
0.600	5/16 in Whitworth/3/8 in BSF
0.625	5/8 in AF
0.629	16 mm AF
0.669	17 mm AF
0.687	11/16 in AF
0.708	18 mm AF
0.710	3/8 in Whitworth/7/16 in BSF
0.748	19 mm AF
0.750	¾ in AF
0.812	13/16 in AF
0.820	7/16 in Whitworth/½ in BSF
0.866	22 mm AF
0.875	7/8 in AF
0.920	½ in Whitworth/9/16 in BSF
0.937	15/16 in AF
0.944	24 mm AF
1.000	1 in AF
1.010	9/16 in Whitworth/5/8 in BSF
1.023	26 mm AF
1.062	1 1/16 AF/27 mm AF
1.100	5/8 in Whitworth/11/16 in BSF
1.125	1 1/8 in AF
1.181	30 mm AF
1.200	11/16 in Whitworth/¾ in BSF
1.250	1 ¼ in AF
1.259	32 mm AF
1.300	¾ in Whitworth/7/8 in BSF
1.312	1 5/16 in AF
1.390	13/16 in Whitworth/15/16 in BSF
1.417	36 mm AF
1.437	1 7/16 in AF
1.480	7/8 in Whitworth/1 in BSF
1.500	1 ½ in AF
1.574	40 mm AF/15/16 in Whitworth
1.614	41 mm AF
1.625	1 5/8 in AF
1.670	1 in Whitworth/1 1/8 in BSF
1.687	1 11/16 in AF
1.811	46 mm AF
1.812	1 13/16 in AF
1.860	1 1/8 in Whitworth/1 ¼ in BSF
1.875	1 7/8 in AF
1.968	50 mm AF
2.000	2 in AF
2.050	1 ¼ in Whitworth/1 3/8 in BSF
2.165	55 mm AF
2.362	60 mm AF

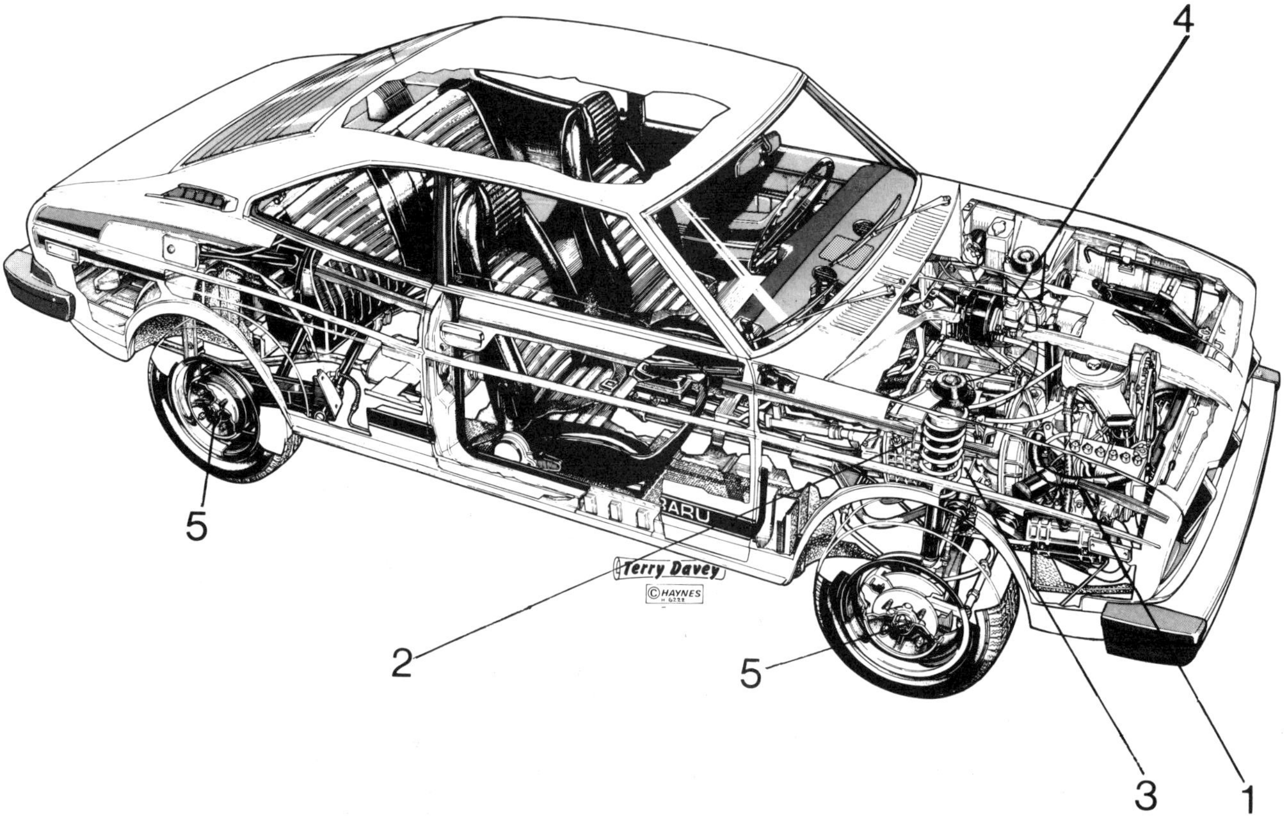

Recommended lubricants and fluids

Component or system	Lubricant type or specification	Castrol product
Engine (1)	SAE 20W/50 multigrade engine oil	GTX
Gearbox and differential (2)	API GL-4 or API GL-5, SAE 80 or SAE 90 hypoid gear oil	Hypoy
Automatic transmission	Dexron R type automatic transmission fluid	TQ Dexron R
Differential (auto trans) (3)	API GL-4 or API GL-5, SAE 80 or SAE 90 hypoid gear oil	Hypoy
4WD rear differential	API GL-4 or API GL-5, SAE 80 or SAE 90 hypoid gear oil	Hypoy
Braking system (4)	FMVSS-116 or DOT3 hydraulic fluid	Girling Universal Brake and Clutch Fluid
Wheel bearings (5)	General purpose lithium based grease	LM grease

Note: *The above are general recommendations only. Lubrication requirements vary from territory to territory and depend on the vehicle usage. If in doubt, consult the operator's handbook supplied with the car.*

Routine maintenance

Introduction

1 In the paragraphs that follow are detailed the routine servicing that should be performed on your vehicle. This work has the prime aim of doing adjustments and lubrication to ensure the least wear and most efficient function. But there is another important gain. By looking the car over, on top and underneath, you have the opportunity to check that all is in order.

2 Every component should be looked at, your gaze working systematically over the whole car. Dirt cracking near a nut or a flange can indicate something loose. Leaks will show. Electric cables rubbing, or rust appearing through the underneath paint will all be found before they bring on a failure on the road, or if not tackled quickly, a more expensive repair. Also it prevents the car becoming a danger to yourself or others because of an undetected defect.

3 The tasks to be done are in general those recommended by the maker. But we have also put in some additional ones which will help to keep your car in good order. For someone getting his service done at a garage it may be more cost effective to accept component renewal after a somewhat short life in order to avoid labour costs. For the home mechanic this tends not to be so.

4 When you are checking the car, and find something that looks wrong, look it up in the appropriate Chapter. If something seems to be working badly, look in the fault finding Section.

5 Always drive the car on a road test after a repair, and then inspect the repair is holding up all right, and check nuts or hose connections for tightness. Check again after about another 150 miles.

Every 250 miles or weekly - whichever comes first

Check radiator coolant level.
Check engine oil level.
Check battery electrolyte level.
Check tire pressures. Examine tread depth and for other damage.
Check operation of all lights.
Check windshield washer fluid level.
Check brake master cylinder reservoir hydraulic fluid level.
Check operation of windshield wipers and washers.

Every 3,000 miles or 3 months

Check engine oil.
Check automatic transmission fluid level.

Every 6,000 miles or 6 months

Renew engine oil filter.
Check level of transmission oil.
Examine engine and transmission for oil leaks.
Check level of differential gear oil (automatic transmission).
Lubricate pedal system and linkage.
Check level of rear differential gear oil (4WD vehicle).
Check manual linkage and inhibitor switch.
Lubricate the distributor cam.
Check disc brake pads for wear.
Check the hydraulic brake system for leaks.
Check steering linkage for security and wear.
Check the front suspension for wear or damage.
Rotate tires (to even out wear).
Check wheel nuts and hub nuts for tightness.
Check operation and efficiency of parking brake.
Check clutch and gearshift operation.
Check exhaust system for leaks and security.

Every 12,000 miles or 12 months

Adjust intake and exhaust valve clearances.
Check the drivebelt tension.
Inspect all cooling system hoses and connections.
Inspect all vacuum fittings, hoses and connections.
Check idling speed and adjust as necessary.
Check choke mechanism.
Renew the in-line fuel filter.
Check fuel filler cap (with relief valve) tank, pump and fuel lines.
Renew the air cleaner element.
Renew distributor breaker points.
Check ignition timing.
Renew spark plugs.
Check distributor cap, rotor and condenser (breakerless ignition).
Examine all emission control hoses.
Check air suction valve (air suction system).
Check carburetor float level.
Renew the hydraulic brake fluid.
Check shock absorbers for signs of leakage.
Check wheel alignment.
Lubricate hinge and locks of doors, hood and trunk lid.
Check front and rear bumper shock absorbers.

Every 24,000 miles or 2 years

Renew the coolant in the cooling system.
Check all ignition wiring.
Check air suction manifolds.
Inspect and renew EGR components as necessary.
Check all evaporative fuel vapor lines. Renew the one in the engine compartment.
Renew canister filter in fuel evaporative control system.
Change the transmission gear oil.
Change the automatic transmission fluid.
Change the differential gear oil (automatic transmission).
Change the rear differential gear oil (4WD vehicles).
Check the engine mountings for deterioration and security.

Checking the engine oil level

Checking the brake fluid level

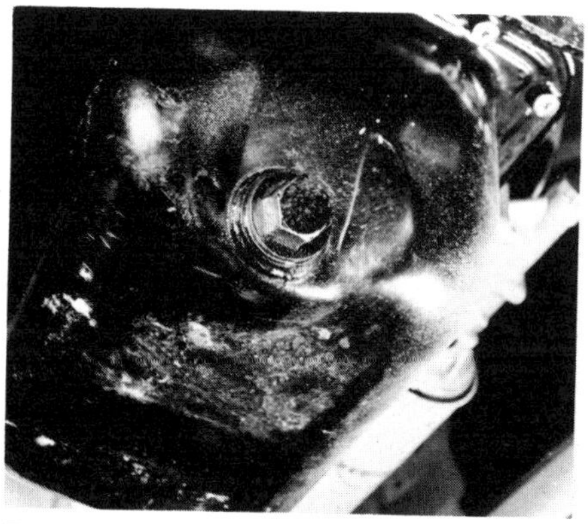
Engine oil pan drain plug

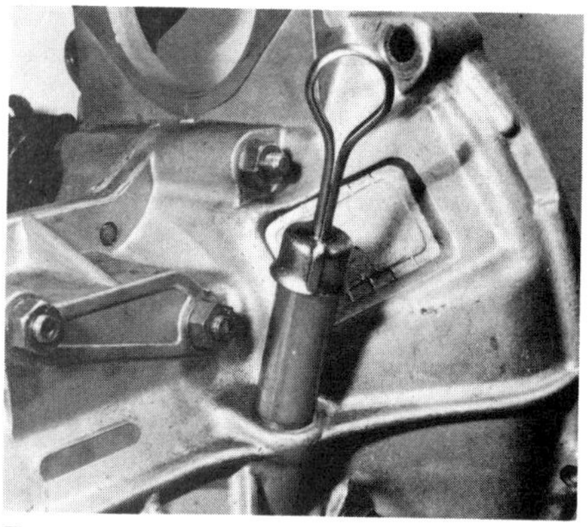
Transmission oil level dipstick

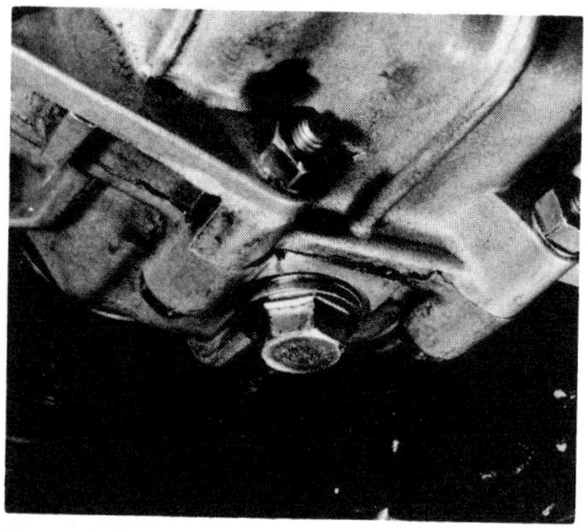
Transmission drain plug

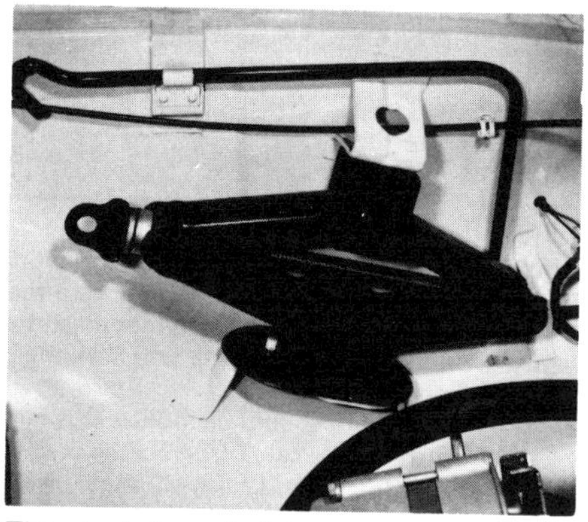
The wheel change jack is stowed on the left-hand front wheel apron

Front jacking-up point

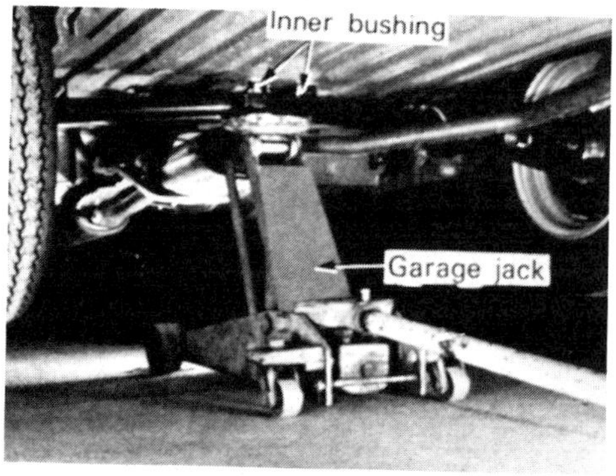

Rear jacking-up point

Front support points

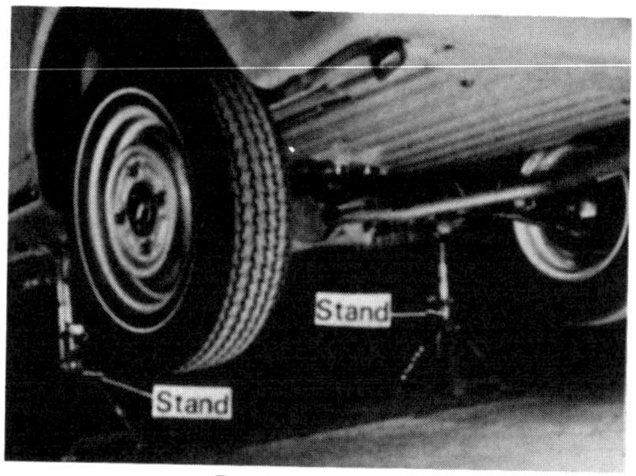

Rear support points

Renew the cups and dust seals of master cylinders and wheel cylinders.

Renew the rubber parts of the brake servo system.

Repack the front and rear wheel bearings with grease.

Check the headlight beams.

Every 48,000 or 4 years

Renew brake rubber hoses.

Renew brake servo system vacuum hose.

Other aspects of Routine Maintenance

Jacking-up

Always chock a wheel on the opposite side from the one being removed, in front and behind. Always support the car on jackstands as well as on the jack. Use only the jacking points shown in the associated illustrations.

Wheel nuts

These should be cleaned and lightly smeared with grease during work, to keep them moving easily. If the nuts are stubborn to undo due to dirt and overtightening, it may be necessary to loosen them with the wheels on the ground. When tightening the wheel nuts always use the wheel wrench supplied with the car to prevent overtightening. After refitting a wheel make a point later of checking the nuts again for tightness.

Safety

Whenever working, even partially, under the car, always use jack-stands, do not depend on the tire changing jack alone.

Always disconnect the battery before carrying out any work on the electrical system.

Take care when working on the fuel system, keep sparks or open flame away from gasoline.

Cleanliness

Whenever you do any work allow time for cleaning. When something is in pieces or components removed to improve access to other areas, give an opportunity for a thorough clean. This cleanliness will allow you to cope with a crisis on the road without getting yourself dirty. During bigger jobs when you expect a bit of dirt it is less extreme and can be tolerated at least whilst removing a component. When an item is being taken to pieces there is less risk of ruinous grit finding its way inside. The act of cleaning focuses your attention onto parts and you are more likely to spot trouble. Dirt on the ignition parts is a common cause of poor starting. Large areas such as the engine compartment, wheel aprons or firewall should be brushed thoroughly with a grease solvent and then carefully hosed down. Water in the wrong places, particularly the carburetor or electrical components will do more harm than dirt. Use kerosene and a small brush to clean the more inaccessible places.

Waste disposal

Old oil and cleaning kerosene must be destroyed. Although it makes a good base for a bonfire the practice is dangerous. It is also illegal to dispose of oil and kerosene down domestic drains. By buying your new engine oil in one gallon cans you can refill with old oil and take back to the local garage who have facilities for disposal.

Long journeys

Before taking the car on long journeys, particularly such trips as holidays, make sure that the car is given a thorough check in the form of the next service due, plus a full visual inspection well in advance so that any faults can be found and rectified in time.

Towing

Towing hooks are provided at the front and rear of the vehicle. Before towing the car, make sure the parking brake is released and the transmission is in neutral. Never turn the ignition key to the 'LOCK' position while the car is being towed.

When towing a vehicle with automatic transmission place the selector lever in 'N' position and do not exceed 20 mph (30 km/h). Vehicles with defective transmission should be towed with the front wheels off the ground.

Front towing hooks

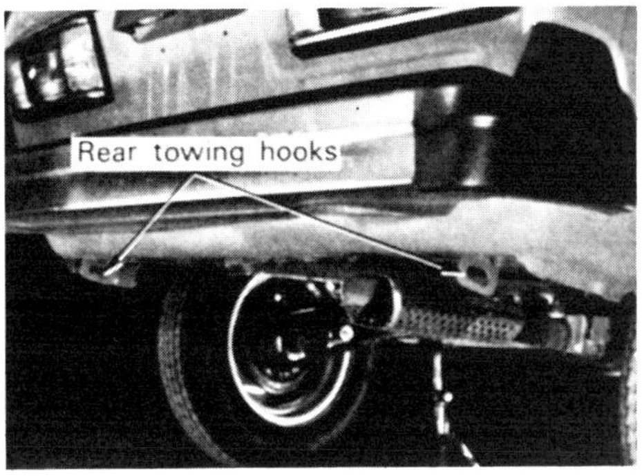

Rear towing hooks

Chapter 1 Engine

For modifications, and information applicable to later models, see Supplement at end of manual

Contents

Specifications

Engine model	EA61
Number of cylinders	Four, horizontally opposed.
Firing order	1 - 3 - 2 - 4
Type of cylinder liner	Wet
Bore	2.99 in (76.0 mm)
Stroke	2.36 in (60.0 mm)
Capacity	66.4 cu in (1088 cc)
Compression ratio	9 : 1
Pistons	
Type	Auto-thermic
Material	Aluminum
Diameter:	
Standard	2.9903 - 2.9915 in (75.955 - 75.985 mm)
0.25 oversize	3.0002 - 3.0012 in (76.205 - 76.235 mm)
0.50 oversize	3.0100 - 3.0112 in (76.455 - 76.485 mm)
Piston rings	
Ring end gap:	
Top ring	0.008 - 0.016 in (0.2 - 0.4 mm)
Second ring	0.008 - 0.016 in (0.2 - 0.4 mm)
Oil ring (rail only)	0.012 - 0.035 in (0.3 - 0.9 mm)
Ring side clearance in groove:	
Top ring	0.0014 - 0.0029 in (0.035 - 0.075 mm)
Second ring	0.0010 - 0.0025 in (0.025 - 0.065 mm)
Oil ring	Nil
Piston pin	
Diameter	0.7477 - 0.7480 in (18.992 - 19.00 mm)
Clearance in piston	0.0001 - 0.0002 in (0.003 - 0.005 mm)
Clearance in connecting rod	0.0002 - 0.0009 in (0.005 - 0.023 mm)

Crankshaft

Journal diameter:	
Standard	1.9665 - 1.9669 in (49.949 - 49.960 mm)
Undersize	1.9645 - 1.9649 in (49.899 - 49.910 mm)
Ovality limit	0.0012 in (0.3 mm)
Main bearing clearance	0.0008 - 0.0024 in (0.020 - 0.060 mm)
Clearance limit	0.0047 in (0.12 mm)
Thrust clearance (endfloat)	0.0016 - 0.0054 in (0.040 - 0.137 mm)
Thrust clearance limit	0.012 in (0.3 mm)

Crankpins

Diameter:	
Standard	1.771 - 1.772 in (44.989 - 45.000 mm)
Undersize	1.769 - 1.770 in (44.939 - 44.950 mm)
Ovality limit	0.0012 in (0.03 mm)

Connecting rods

Distance between centers	4.329 - 4.333 in (109.95 - 110.05 mm)
Large end side clearance	0.004 - 0.007 in (0.10 - 0.185 mm)
Side clearance limit	0.016 in (0.4 mm)
Large end bearing clearance	0.0012 - 0.0026 in (0.030 - 0.067 mm)
Bearing clearance limit	0.0047 mm (0.12 mm)

Camshaft

Thrust clearance	0.0008 - 0.0035 in (0.020 - 0.090 mm)
Thrust clearance limit	0.012 in (0.3 mm)
Diameter of journals	1.0218 - 1.0224 in (25.954 - 25.970 mm)

Camshaft gear

Backlash	0.0008 - 0.0020 in (0.02 - 0.05 mm)
Backlash limit	0.0059 in (0.15 mm)

Cylinder head

Material	Aluminum
Grinding limit of face	0.002 in (0.5 mm)

Valves

Clearance - cold:	
Intake valve	0.008 - 0.009 in (0.20 - 0.24 mm)
Exhaust valve	0.010 - 0.011 in (0.25 - 0.29 mm)
Timing:	
Intake valve	Opens 20° BTDC - Closes 60° ABDC
Exhaust valve	Opens 60° BTDC - Closes 20° ATDC
Valve head diameter:	
Intake valve	1.256 - 1.264 in (31.9 - 32.1 mm)
Exhaust valve	1.083 - 1.091 in (27.5 - 27.7 mm)
Valve stem diameter:	
Intake	0.3134 - 0.3140 in (7.960 - 7.975 mm)
Exhaust	0.3125 - 0.3134 in (7.938 - 7.960 mm)
Valve length - intake and exhaust	4.13 in (105 mm)
Clearance - valve stem to valve guide:	
Intake	0.0010 - 0.0022 in (0.025 - 0.055 mm)
Exhaust	0.0016 - 0.0030 in (0.040 - 0.077 mm)
Valve seat angle - intake and exhaust	45°

Valve springs

Free length:	
Inner	1.79 in (45.5 mm)
Outer	1.66 in (42.2 mm)

Valve lifter

Diameter	1.165 - 1.173 in (20.959 - 20.980 mm)
Diameter lifter hole in crankcase	0.8268 - 0.8276 in (21.000 - 21.021 mm)
Clearance limit	0.004 in (0.1 mm)

Cylinder liner

Inside diameter	2.991 - 2.993 in (75.985 - 76.015 mm)
Ovality limit	0.0004 in (0.01 mm)
Wear limit	0.006 in (0.15 mm)
Clearance between liner and piston	0.0006 - 0.0018 in (0.015 - 0.045 mm)
Protrusion allowance of liner	0.0024 - 0.0035 in (0.06 - 0.09 mm)

Lubrication system

Oil pump	Trochoid type
Oil filter	Disposable cartridge type
Relief valve opens	42.7 - 46.2 lb/in^2 (3.0 - 3.25 kg/cm^2)

By-pass valve opens	12.8 - 15.7 lb/in^2 (0.9 - 1.1 kg/cm^2)
Relief valve spring free length	1.84 in (46.8 mm)
Engine oil capacity	2.8 US qt (2.6 litre)

Engine model	EA62
Number of cylinders	Four, horizontally opposed
Firing order	1 - 3 - 2 - 4
Type of cylinder liner	Wet
Bore	3.23 in (82 mm)
Stroke	2.36 in (60 mm)
Capacity	1267 cc (77.3 cu in)
Compression ratio	9 : 1

Pistons

Type	Auto-thermic
Material	Aluminum
Diameter:	
Standard	3.2258 - 3.2270 in (81.935 - 81.965 mm)
0.25 oversize	3.2356 - 3.2368 in (82.185 - 82.215 mm)
0.50 oversize	3.2455 - 3.2466 in (82.435 - 82.465 mm)

Piston rings

Ring end gap:	
Top ring	0.008 - 0.020 in (0.2 - 0.5 mm)
Second ring	0.008 - 0.020 in (0.2 - 0.5 mm)
Oil ring (rail only)	0.008 - 0.047 in (0.2 - 1.2 mm)
Ring side clearance in groove:	
Top ring	0.0014 - 0.0029 in (0.035 - 0.075 mm)
Second ring	0.0010 - 0.0025 in (0.025 - 0.065 mm)
Oil ring	Nil

Piston pin

Diameter	0.7870 - 0.7874 in (19.992 - 20.000 mm)
Clearance in piston	0.0002 - 0.0005 in (0.005 - 0.013 mm)
Clearance in connecting rod	0.0002 - 0.0013 in (0.005 - 0.034 mm)

Crankshaft

Journal diameter:	
Standard - front and rear	1.9682 - 1.9688 in (49.955 - 49.970 mm)
Standard - center	1.9688 - 1.9692 in (49.969 - 49.980 mm)
0.05 undersize	1.9668 - 1.9672 in (49.919 - 49.930 mm)
0.25 undersize	1.9589 - 1.9594 in (49.719 - 49.730 mm)
Main bearing clearance:	
Front and rear	0.0004 - 0.0023 in (0.010 - 0.058 mm)
Center	0 - 0.0017 in (0 - 0.044 mm)
Clearance limit	0.0039 in (0.1 mm)
Ovality limit	0.0012 in (0.03 mm)
Thrust clearance (endfloat)	0.0016 - 0.0054 in (0.040 - 0.137 mm)
Thrust clearance limit	0.012 in (0.3 mm)

Crankpins

Diameter:	
Standard	1.7726 - 1.7730 in (44.989 - 45.000 mm)
0.05 undersize	1.7706 - 1.7710 in (44.939 - 44.950 mm)
0.25 undersize	1.7627 - 1.7632 in (44.739 - 44.750 mm)
Ovality limit	0.0012 in (0.03 mm)

Connecting rods

Distance between centers	4.3320 - 4.3360 in (109.95 - 110.05 mm)
Large end side clearance	0.0028 - 0.118 in (0.070 - 0.300 mm)
Side clearance limit	0.016 in (0.4 mm)
Large end bearing clearance	0.0012 - 0.0029 in (0.030 - 0.073 mm)
Bearing clearance limit	0.004 in (0.1 mm)

Camshaft

Thrust clearance	0.0008 - 0.0035 in (0.020 - 0.090 mm)
Thrust clearance limit	0.012 in (0.3 mm)

Diameter of journals:	
Front and center	1.0226 - 1.0232 in (25.954 - 25.970 mm)
Rear	1.4166 - 1.4172 in (35.954 - 35.970 mm)

Camshaft gear

Backlash	0.0008 - 0.0020 in (0.02 - 0.05 mm)
Backlash limit	0.0059 in (0.15 mm)

Cylinder head

Material	Aluminum
Grinding limit of face	0.02 in (0.5 mm)

Valves

Clearance - cold:	
Intake and exhaust	0.011 - 0.012 in (0.28 - 0.32 mm)
Valve timing:	
Intake valve opens	24° BTDC
Intake valve closes	64° ABDC
Exhaust valve opens	70° BBDC
Exhaust valve closes	18° ATDC
Valve head diameter:	
Intake	1.452 - 1.461 in (36.9 - 37.1 mm)
Exhaust	1.280 - 1.288 in (32.5 - 32.7 mm)
Valve stem diameter:	
Intake	0.3130 - 0.3136 in (7.950 - 7.965 mm)
Exhaust	0.3124 - 0.3130 in (7.935 - 7.950 mm)
Valve length - intake and exhaust	4.29 in (109 mm)
Clearance - valve stem to valve guide:	
Intake	0.0010 - 0.0022 in (0.025 - 0.055 mm)
Exhaust	0.0020 - 0.0032 in (0.050 - 0.080 mm)
Angle of contact surface - valve to valve seat	90° (included)

Valve springs

Free length:	
Inner	1.92 in (48.65 mm)
Outer	1.90 in (48.2 mm)

Valve lifter

Diameter	0.8252 - 0.8260 in (20.959 - 20.980 mm)
Diameter of lifter hole in crankcase	0.8268 - 0.8276 in (21.000 - 21.021 mm)
Clearance limit	0.004 in (0.1 mm)

Cylinder liner

Inside diameter	3.2302 - 3.2313 in (81.985 - 82.015 mm)
Ovality limit	0.008 in (0.2 mm)
Wear limit	0.006 in (0.15 mm)
Clearance between liner and piston	0.0008 - 0.0031 in (0.020 - 0.080 mm)
Protrusion allowance of liner	0.0028 - 0.0035 in (0.07 - 0.09 mm)

Lubrication system

Oil pump	Trochoid type
Oil filter	Disposable cartridge type
Relief valve opens	42.7 - 46.2 lb/in^2 (3.0 - 3.25 kg/cm^2)
By-pass valve opens	12.8 - 15.7 lb/in^2 (0.9 - 1.1 kg/cm^2)
Relief valve spring - free length	1.84 in (46.8 mm)
Engine oil - capacity:	
Without oil filter	3.5 US qt (3.3 liter)
With oil filter	3.8 US qt (3.6 liter)

Engine model	EA63
Number of cylinders	Four, horizontally opposed
Firing order	1 - 3 - 2 - 4
Type of cylinder liner	Wet
Bore	3.35 in (85 mm)
Stroke	2.36 in (60 mm)
Capacity	83.2 cu in (1361 cc)
Compression ratio	9 : 1

Pistons

Type	Auto-thermic
Material	Aluminum
Diameter:	
Standard	3.3445 - 3.3457 in (84.950 - 84.980 mm)
0.25 oversize	3.3543 - 3.3555 in (85.200 - 85.230 mm)
0.50 oversize	3.3642 - 3.3653 in (85.450 - 85.480 mm)

Piston rings

Ring end gap:	
Top ring	0.012 - 0.020 in (0.3 - 0.5 mm)
Second ring	0.012 - 0.020 in (0.3 - 0.5 mm)
Oil ring (rail only)	0.012 - 0.035 in (0.3 - 0.9 mm)
Ring side clearance in groove:	
Top ring	0.0014 - 0.0029 in (0.035 - 0.075 mm)
Second ring	0.0010 - 0.0025 in (0.025 - 0.065 mm)
Oil ring	Nil

Piston pin

Diameter	0.7870 - 0.7874 in (19.992 - 20.000 mm)
Clearance in piston	0.0002 - 0.0005 in (0.005 - 0.012 mm)
Clearance in connecting rod	0.0002 - 0.0016 in (0.005 - 0.040 mm)

Crankshaft

Journal diameter:	
Standard - front and rear	1.9667 - 1.9673 in (49.955 - 49.970 mm)
Standard - center	1.9672 - 1.9677 in (49.969 - 49.980 mm)
0.05 undersize	1.9653 - 1.9657 in (49.919 - 49.930 mm)
0.25 undersize	1.9574 - 1.9578 in (49.719 - 49.730 mm)
Main bearing clearance:	
Front and rear	0.0004 - 0.0020 in (0.01 - 0.05 mm)
Center	0 - 0.0014 in (0 - 0.036 mm)
Clearance limit	0.0039 in (0.1 mm)
Ovality limit	0.0012 in (0.03 mm)
Thrust clearance (endfloat)	0.0016 - 0.0054 in (0.040 - 0.137 mm)
Thrust clearance limit	0.012 in (0.3 mm)

Crankpins

Diameter:	
Standard	1.7711 - 1.7716 in (44.989 - 45.000 mm)
0.05 undersize	1.7692 - 1.7696 in (44.939 - 44.950 mm)
0.25 undersize	1.7613 - 1.7618 in (44.739 - 44.750 mm)
Ovality limit	0.0012 in (0.03 mm)

Connecting rods

Distance between centers	4.3287 - 4.3327 in (109.95 - 110.05 mm)
Large end side clearance	0.0028 - 0.0118 in (0.07 - 0.30 mm)
Side clearance limit	0.016 in (0.4 mm)
Large end bearing clearance	0.0012 - 0.0031 in (0.030 - 0.080 mm)
Bearing clearance limit	0.0047 in (0.12 mm)

Camshaft

Thrust clearance	0.0008 - 0.0035 in (0.020 - 0.090 mm)
Thrust clearance limit	0.012 in (0.3 mm)
Diameter of journals:	
Front and center	1.0218 - 1.0226 in (25.954 - 25.975 mm)
Rear	1.4155 - 1.4163 in (35.954 - 35.975 mm)

Camshaft gear

Backlash	0.0008 - 0.0020 in (0.02 - 0.05 mm)
Backlash limit	0.0059 in (0.15 mm)

Cylinder head

Material	Aluminum
Grinding limit of face	0.02 in (0.5 mm)

Valves

Valve clearance - cold:		
1972 - 1974	Intake	0.011 - 0.013 in (0.28 - 0.32 mm)
1972 Coupe	Intake	0.009 - 0.011 in (0.23 - 0.27 mm)
	Exhaust	0.011 - 0.013 in (0.28 - 0.32 mm)
1975	Intake	0.011 - 0.013 in (0.28 - 0.32 mm)
	Exhaust	0.013 - 0.015 in (0.33 - 0.37 mm)
1976	Intake	0.009 - 0.011 in (0.23 - 0.27 mm)
	Exhaust	0.013 - 0.015 in (0.33 - 0.37 mm)

Valve timing

Intake valve opens	24° BTDC
Intake valve closes	64° ABDC
Exhaust valve opens	70° BBDC
Exhaust valve closes	18° ATDC
Valve stem diameter:	
Intake	0.2130 - 0.3136 in (7.950 - 7.965 mm)
Exhaust	0.3124 - 0.3130 in (7.935 - 7.950 mm)
Clearance - valve stem to valve guide:	
Intake	0.0013 - 0.0025 in (0.035 - 0.065 mm)
Exhaust	0.0020 - 0.0032 in (0.050 - 0.080 mm)
Angle of contact surface - valve to valve seat	90° (included)

Valve springs

Free length:	
Inner	1.92 in (48.65 mm)
Outer	1.90 in (48.2 mm)
1972 Coupe - outer	1.80 in (45.7 mm)

Valve lifter

Diameter	0.8252 - 0.8260 in (20.959 - 20.980 mm)
Diameter of lifter hole in crankcase	0.8268 - 0.8276 in (21.000 - 21.021 mm)
Clearance limit	0.004 in (0.1 mm)

Cylinder liner

Inside diameter	3.3459 - 3.3471 in (84.985 - 85.015 mm)
Ovality limit	0.0004 in (0.01 mm)
Wear limit	0.0059 in (0.15 mm)
Clearance between liner and piston	0.0008 - 0.0019 in (0.020 - 0.049 mm)
Protrusion allowance of liner:	
1972 - 1974	0.0028 - 0.0035 in (0.07 - 0.09 mm)
1975 - 1976	0.0035 - 0.0043 in (0.09 - 0.11 mm)

Lubrication system

Oil pump	Trochoid type
Oil filter	Disposable cartridge type
Relief valve opens:	
1972 - 1974	42.7 - 46.2 lb/in^2 (3.0 - 3.25 kg/cm^2)
1975 - 1976	57 - 64 lb/in^2 (4.0 - 4.5 kg/cm^2)
By-pass valve opens	13 - 16 lb/in^2 (0.9 - 1.1 kg/cm^2)
Relief valve spring - free length:	
1972 - 1974	1.84 in (46.8 mm)
1975 - 1976	1.855 in (47.1 mm)
Engine oil - capacity	
Without oil filter	3.5 US qt (3.3 liters)
With oil filter	3.8 US qt (3.6 liters)

Engine model	EA71
Number of cylinders	Four, horizontally opposed
Firing order	1 - 3 - 2 - 4
Cylinder liner	Dry type
Bore	3.62 in (92 mm)
Stroke	2.36 in (60 mm)
Capacity	97 cu in (1596 cc)
Compression ratio	8.5 : 1

Pistons

Type	Auto-thermic
Material	Aluminum
Diameter:	
Standard	3.6205 - 3.6216 in (91.960 - 91.990 mm)
Service	3.6209 - 3.6213 in (91.970 - 91.980 mm)
0.25 oversize	3.6307 - 3.6311 in (92.220 - 92.230 mm)

Piston rings

Ring end gap:	
Top ring	0.012 - 0.020 in (0.3 - 0.5 mm)
Second ring	0.012 - 0.020 in (0.3 - 0.5 mm)
Oil ring (rail only)	0.012 - 0.035 in (0.3 - 0.9 mm)
Ring side clearance groove:	
Top ring	0.0016 - 0.0031 in (0.04 - 0.08 mm)
Second ring	0.0012 - 0.0028 in (0.03 - 0.07 mm)
Oil ring	Nil

Piston pin

Diameter	0.8265 - 0.8268 in (20.992 - 21.000 mm)
Clearance in piston	0.00004 - 0.00067 in (0.001 - 0.017 mm)
Clearance in connecting rod	0.0002 - 0.0015 in (0.005 - 0.040 mm)

Crankshaft

Journal diameter:	
Standard - front and rear	1.9667 - 1.9673 in (49.955 - 49.970 mm)
0.05 undersize	1.9648 - 1.9654 in (49.905 - 49.920 mm)
0.25 undersize	1.9569 - 1.9575 in (49.705 - 49.720 mm)
Standard - center	1.9671 - 1.9677 in (49.965 - 49.980 mm)
0.05 undersize	1.9652 - 1.9657 in (49.915 - 49.930 mm)
0.25 undersize	1.9573 - 1.9579 in (49.715 - 49.730 mm)
Main bearing clearance:	
Front and rear	0.0004 - 0.0020 in (0.01 - 0.05 mm)
Center	0 - 0.0014 in (0 - 0.36 mm)
Clearance limit	0.0039 in (0.1 mm)
Ovality limit	0.0012 in (0.03 mm)
Thrust clearance	0.0016 - 0.0054 in (0.040 - 0.137 mm)
Thrust clearance limit	0.012 in (0.3 mm)

Crankpins

Diameter:	
Standard	1.7715 - 1.7720 in (44.995 - 45.010 mm)
0.05 undersize	1.7695 - 1.7701 in (44.945 - 44.960 mm)
0.25 undersize	1.7616 - 1.7622 in (44.745 - 44.760 mm)
Ovality	0.0012 in (0.03 mm)

Connecting rods

Large end side clearance	0.0028 - 0.0130 (0.070 - 0.330 mm)
Side clearance limit	0.016 in (0.4 mm)
Large end bearing clearance	0.0008 - 0.0028 in (0.020 - 0.070 mm)
Bearing clearance limit	0.0047 in (0.12 mm)

Camshaft

Thrust clearance	0.0018 - 0.0045 in (0.045 - 0.115 mm)
Thrust clearance limit	0.012 in (0.3 mm)
Diameter of journals:	
Front and center	1.0218 - 1.0226 in (25.955 - 25.975 mm)
Rear	1.4155 - 1.4163 in (35.955 - 35.975 mm)
Clearance limit between journal and journal bore	0.0039 in (0.10 mm)

Camshaft gear

Backlash	0.0008 - 0.0020 in (0.020 - 0.050 mm)
Backlash limit	0.0059 in (0.15 mm)

Cylinder head

Material	Aluminum
Grinding limit of face	0.02 in (0.5 mm)

Valves

Valve clearance - cold:	
Intake	0.010 in (0.25 mm)
Exhaust	0.014 in (0.35 mm)
Valve timing:	
Intake valve opens	24° BTDC
Intake valve closes	64° ABDC
Exhaust valve opens	70° BBDC
Exhaust valve closes	18° ATDC
Valve stem diameter:	
Intake	0.3130 -.0.3136 in (7.950 - 7.965 mm)
Exhaust	0.3128 - 0.3134 in (7.945 - 7.960 mm)
Clearance valve stem to valve guide:	
Intake	0.0014 - 0.0026 in (0.035 - 0.065 mm)
Exhaust	0.0016 - 0.0028 in (0.040 - 0.070 mm)

Clearance limit:-	
Intake and exhaust	0.0059 in (0.15 mm)
Angle of contact surface - valve to valve seat	$90^\circ \pm {}^{1^\circ}_{0^\circ}$ (included)

Valve springs

Free length:	
Inner	1.915 in (48.65 mm)
Outer	1.008 in (48.20 mm)

Valve lifter

Diameter	0.8248 - 0.8256 in (20.949 - 20.970 mm)
Diameter of lifter hole in crankcase	0.8268 - 0.8276 in (21.000 - 21.021 mm)
Clearance limit	0.004 in (0.10 mm)

Cylinder liner

Inside diameter	3.6214 - 3.6226 in (91.985 - 92.012 mm)
Wear limit	0.0059 in (0.15 mm)
Ovality limit	0.004 in (0.01 mm)
Clearance between liner and piston	0.0004 - 0.0016 in (0.010 - 0.040 mm)
Liner reboring limit	0.0098 in (0.25 mm)

Lubrication system

Oil pump	Trochoid type
Oil filter	Disposable cartridge
By-pass valve opens	13 - 16 lb/in^2 (0.9 - 1.1 kg/cm^2)
Relief valve opens	57 - 64 lb/in^2 (4.0 - 4.5 kg/cm^2)
Relief valve spring - free length	1.855 in (47.1 mm)
Engine oil capacity:	
Without oil filter	3.5 US qt (3.3 liters)
With oil filter	3.8 US qt (3.6 liters)

Torque wrench settings

	lb f ft	kg f m
Connecting rod bolt:		
EA61, EA62, EA63A, EA63E	34 - 37	4.8 - 5.2
Connecting rod nut:		
EA63S, EA71	29 - 31	4.0 - 4.3
Crankshaft pulley bolt	39 - 42	5.4 - 5.8
Crankcase nuts - 10 mm	27 - 31	3.7 - 4.3
Crankcase bolts - 10 mm	29 - 34	4.0 - 4.8
Crankcase bolts - 8 mm	17 - 19	2.3 - 2.7
Flywheel bolts	31 - 33	4.2 - 4.6
Flywheel housing bolts	17 - 19	2.3 - 2.7
Cylinder head bolts (EA61)	31 - 34	4.2 - 4.8
Cylinder head nuts	37 - 42	5.1 - 5.9
Crankcase plug	60 - 70	8.3 - 9.7
Transmission to flywheel housing nuts	34 - 39	4.7 - 5.5

1 General description

1 The engine is of the horizontally opposed, four cylinder, oversquare, overhead valve type.

2 The crankcase is made of aluminum alloy and can be separated into right and left halves. The cylinder heads, also of aluminum alloy, employ bathtub type combustion chambers giving a high combustion efficiency. The crankshaft is a steel forging and is supported in three main bearings. The cylinder liners are of the wet type on 1100, 1300 and 1400 engines. The 1600 engine has dry type liners.

3 The pistons are of the slipper type made of aluminum alloy on an

Fig. 1.1. 1400 engine with 4-speed transmission

Fig. 1.2. 1400 engine with automatic transmission

elliptic, tapered shape, and each piston has two compression rings and one combination type oil ring.

4 The camshaft is short, its four cam lobes operating the intake and exhaust valves on both sides. The cam lobes are tapered so that the valve lifters are rotated. The camshaft is directly supported in the crankcase at three places without using bearings.

5 The lubrication system is of a full-flow, forced feed type. Incorporated in the trochoid type oil pump are oil relief and oil by-pass valves. The oil pump is driven directly by the camshaft, and is mounted on the outside of the crankcase, making for ease of inspection and maintenance. The oil flow in the engine is shown in Fig. 1.4. If the oil filter becomes clogged, the by-pass valve opens and allows the oil to by-pass the filter. The relief valve opens, when the oil pressure reaches a pre-set value, and the oil circulates back to the pump.

2 Major operations requiring engine removal

To carry out the following operations, the engine must be removed from the car.

a) Removal and refitting of the cylinder head.
b) Removal and refitting of connecting rods and pistons.
c) Removal and refitting of crankshaft and main bearings.
d) Removal and refitting of camshaft.
e) Removal and refitting of flywheel.
f) Removal and refitting of the crankshaft rear bearing oil seal.

3 Engine removal - general

1 On 1970 to 1972 models (FF - 1 1100 and 1300 G) the engine and transmission must be removed as an assembly. On models from 1972 onwards the engine can be removed as a separate unit or as an engine/transmission assembly.

2 It is easier if a hydraulic trolley jack is used in conjunction with two jackstands so that the car can be raised high enough to allow easy access underneath the car. It is essential to have a good hoist for lifting the engine out of the car.

4 Engine - removal (FF - 1 1100 and 1300 G 1972 - 1974)

1 Disconnect the cables from the battery terminals, negative terminal first.

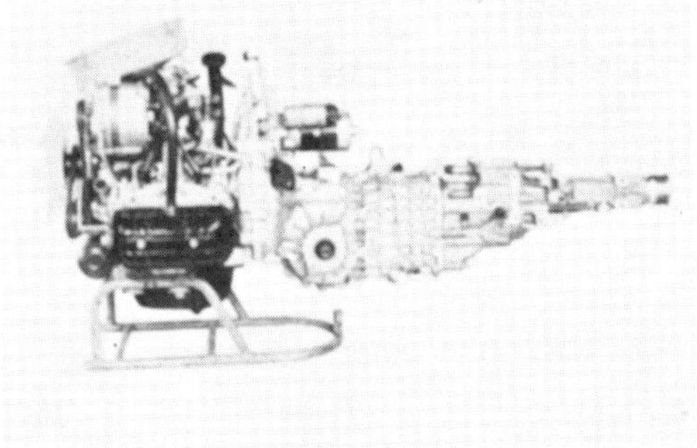

Fig. 1.3. 1400 engine/transmission - 4WD model

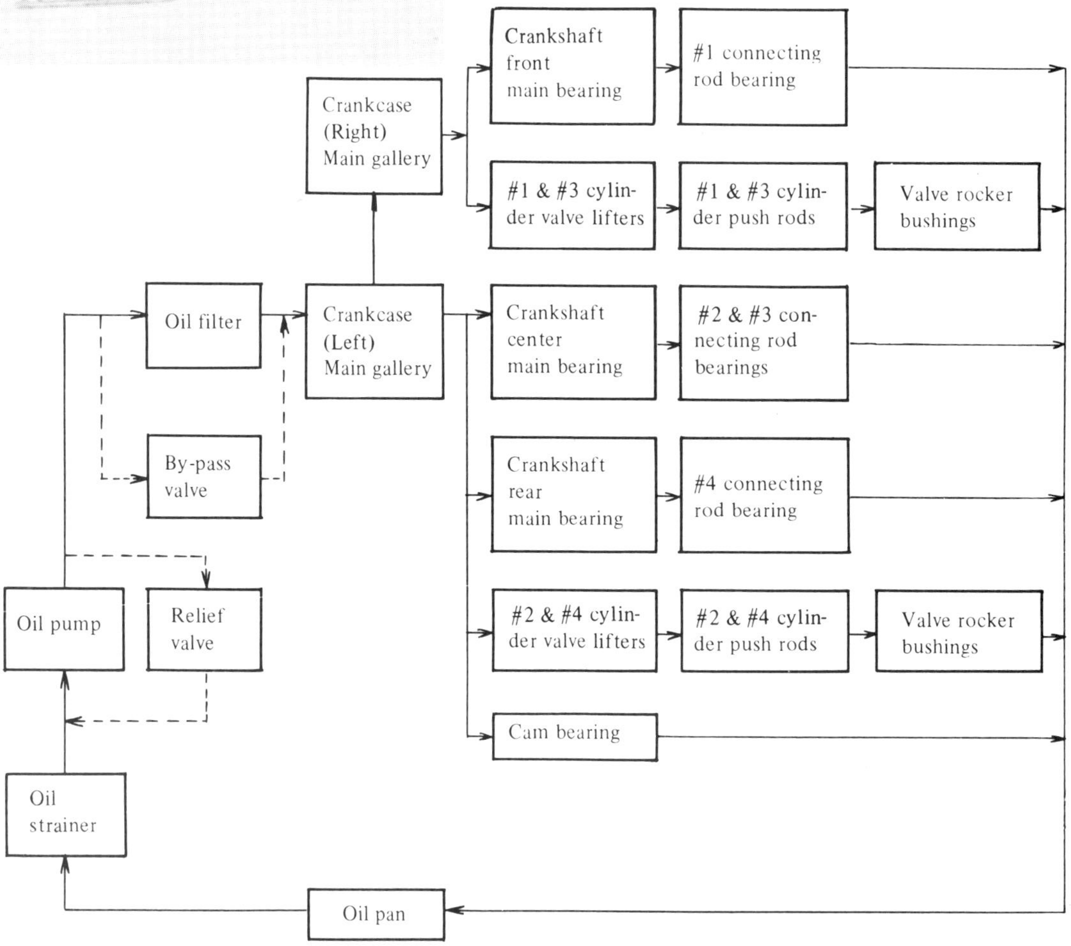

Fig. 1.4. Engine oil flow diagram

2 Remove the spare wheel from the engine compartment.
3 Disconnect the horn connector. Remove the nut securing the hood stay to the firewall, then the left and right-hand hinge mounting bolts, and lift off the hood. Leave the hinges attached to the hood.
4 Remove the two bolts attaching the front bumper to the bumper brackets and lift away the bumper.
5 Remove the two screws each side of the grille and remove the grille towards the front.
6 Remove the five bolts attaching the hood lock to the radiator support and move the lock to the side out of the way (leave it connected to the control cable).
7 Remove the ten bolts around the edge of the front skirt and remove it in a downward direction.
8 Disconnect the hose from the air cleaner and remove the air cleaner assembly. Cover the carburetor opening to prevent the entry of dirt.
9 Remove the clip which clamps the fuel delivery line and pull the hose off the fuel pump union. Have a container ready to collect the gasoline which will flow out. Plug the hose to prevent ingress of dirt.
10 Drain the cooling system as described in Chapter 2, Section 2.
11 Remove the three hoses between the radiator and the engine.
12 Disconnect the following wiring:

a) Alternator connectors.
b) The starter harness. Pull out the connector on the positive (+) side. Disconnect the negative (–) side when removing the starter.
c) Thermostat.
d) Oil pressure switch connector.
e) High tension cable at the coil.
f) The three blower motor connectors.
g) The distributor primary lead.
h) The two thermoswitch leads.

13 Remove the two nuts securing the starter motor to the transmission case and lift out the starter.
14 Remove the heater duct from the blower housing.
15 Disconnect the heater control cable by removing the circlip holding the inner cable and the nut holding the outer cable, then detaching the cables from the blower motor housing.
16 Remove the radiator and hood lock support bracket with the main radiator, sub-radiator, shroud, blower motor and expansion tank as an assembly. Do not separate the blower motor from the shroud as reassembly is difficult. To remove the assembly undo the two 8 mm bolts securing the blower housing, the four screws and two bolts which secure the radiator support bracket to the headlamp brackets (do not remove the centre bolt) and withdraw the assembly towards the front.
17 Disconnect the hoses and leads from the windshield washer pump. Remove the windshield washer reservoir by pulling it upwards out of its bracket.
18 To disconnect the double offset joints (DOJ), apply the parking brake, to lock the brake drums, and remove the three bolts which join the brake drum and DOJ. Lower the DOJ and the axle shaft.
19 Disconnect the brake lines each side and drain the brake fluid into a container. Do not re-use the fluid.
20 Disconnect the throttle cable by loosening the screw on the carburetor throttle lever, disconnecting the end of the outer cable and pulling the cable out.
21 Remove the nut attaching the choke cable to the choke lever, loosen the 6 mm bracket retaining nut and disconnect the choke cable.
22 Disconnect the speedometer cable from the speedometer head at the rear of the instrument cluster and pull it out from the engine compartment.
23 On cars with column gear shift disconnect the gear selector cable from the top of the transmission. Disconnect the parking brake cable at the car interior end, and arrange it so that it can be removed together with the transmission when pulling the engine forward.
24 On models fitted with floor gear shift disconnect the gear selector rod from inside the car. Disconnect the parking brake right and left-hand cables at the turnbuckle inside the car.
25 Remove the two bolts securing the clutch torque rod (ball stud) on the side crossmember.

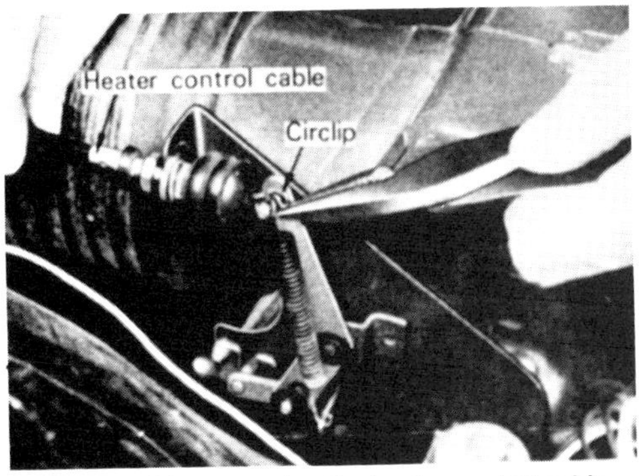

Fig. 1.5. Disconnecting the heater control cable

Fig. 1.6. Removing the radiator assembly (FF-1 models)

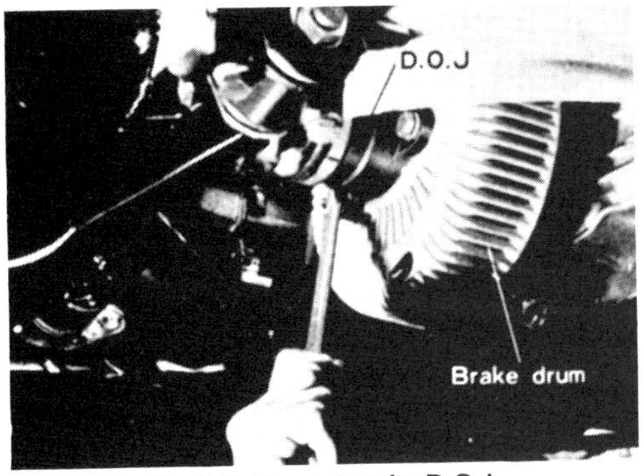

Fig. 1.7. Removing the D.O.J.

Fig. 1.8. Removing the torque rod securing bolts

26 Remove the bolts from the exhaust manifold flanges and separate the down pipes from the manifolds. Collect the gasket and insulator located between the flanges. Remove the bracket attaching the exhaust pipe to the body. Remove the bolts securing the exhaust pipe to the muffler hanger bracket and the tail pipe bracket and remove the exhaust pipe.
27 Disconnect the engine mounting by removing the nut from the shaft while holding the adjuster nut. Take out the washer, cushion, pipe and tube. Unscrew the two retaining bolts and remove the bracket.
28 Remove the left and right bolts from the rear mounting cushion located on the transmission case. Leave the cushion rubber attached to the transmission case. When removing the mounting rubber take care not to lose the adjuster washer.
29 Remove the nut, spring washer and plain washer from the front mounting. Leave the mounting rubber attached to the engine.
30 On sports sedans and station wagons remove the horizontal damper by unscrewing the front nut and pulling the shaft out rearwards. Take care not to lose any of the component parts, see Fig. 1.9.
31 Check that all the relevant parts have been removed or disconnected and that all cables and hoses are tucked out of the way where they will not get caught-up as the engine is removed.
32 Attach the lifting hoist to the front and rear engine lifting hooks and carefully raise the engine horizontally to such a height that the brake drums can pass the crossmember, then pull the engine carefully towards the front so that the exhaust manifolds do not get damaged by the front crossmember and torsion bars.
33 Remove the oil pan drain plug and collect the oil in a container.
34 Lower the engine/transmission assembly and support it so that it will not get damaged. If a suitable engine stand is not available rest the assembly on an old tire to prevent damage to the aluminium casing or oil pan.

5 Engine (without transmission) - removal (1972 - 77 models)

1 Open the hood, remove the securing bolts and lift off the hood.
2 Disconnect the ground cable from the negative (–) terminal of the battery. Remove the 8 mm bolt securing the ground cable to the intake manifold. Disconnect the cable from the manifold and leave it connected to the body.
3 Remove the spare wheel (if mounted in the engine compartment).
4 Remove the emission control system hoses from the air cleaner and remove the air cleaner. Cover the carburetor opening to prevent the entry of dirt.
5 Loosen the clip securing the fuel delivery hose to the carburetor and pull off the hose. On 1977 models remove the purge and vacuum hoses.
6 Drain the cooling system as described in Chapter 2, Section 2. Remove the oil pan drain plug and collect the oil in a suitable container. Refit the drain plug.
7 Disconnect the radiator inlet and outlet hoses, the heater inlet and outlet hoses, and on automatic transmission models, the oil cooler inlet and outlet hoses. Disconnect the radiator and oil cooler hoses from the radiator and the heater hoses from the pipes on the engine.
8 Disconnect the electrical wiring from the following:

a) Alternator connector
b) Two leads to the radiator fan motor and the lead to the thermoswitch at the connector.
c) The oil pressure switch.
d) The temperature switch.
e) The anti-dieseling valve.
f) Primary and secondary ignition leads.
g) Starter motor.
h) EGR vacuum solenoid.
j) EGR coolant temperature switch.
k) Automatic choke lead.
l) Inhibitor switch and downshift solenoid (automatic transmission models).

Not all models have all the above connections. 1977 models have a block connector for the oil pressure switch, anti-dieseling valve, distributor, thermometer and automatic choke leads. An additional block connector for full transistor ignition system is fitted on 1977 California models only.
9 Remove the two radiator mounting bolts, disconnect the ground lead from the top of the radiator and lift the radiator out.
10 On 4WD models, remove the engine fan from the pulley by loosening the alternator mounting bolts, removing the drive belt and the fan securing nut.
11 Remove the horizontal damper by removing the front nut from the damper and the nut on the body bracket. Pull the damper rearwards away from the engine lifting hook.
12 Remove the two nuts (10 mm) retaining the starter motor to the transmission casing and lift out the starter.
13 Disconnect the following cables and hoses:

a) Loosen the screw connecting the throttle cable to the throttle

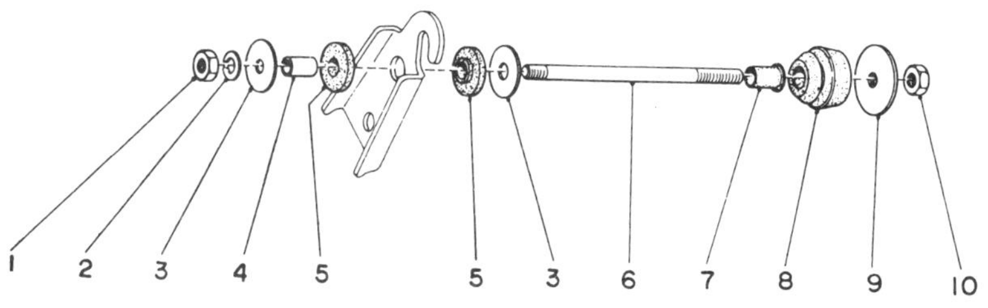

Fig. 1.9. Exploded view of horizontal damper

1	*Nut*	*6*	*Shaft*
2	*Spring washer*	*7*	*Tube*
3	*Washer (stopper)*	*8*	*Cushion*
4	*Pipe*	*9*	*Nut (adjuster)*
5	*Cushion*	*10*	*Nut*

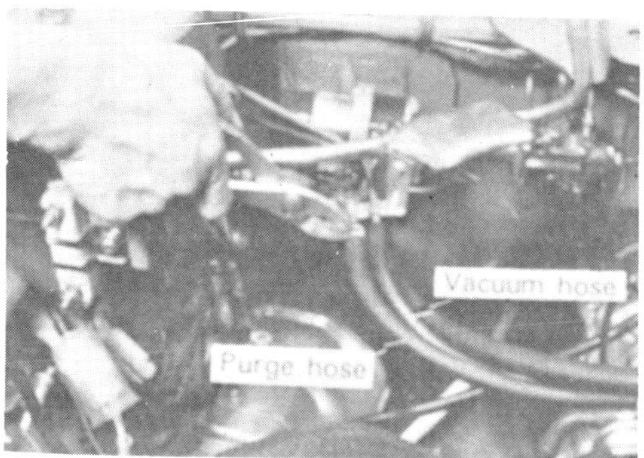

Fig. 1.10. Removing the purge and vacuum hoses (1977 models)

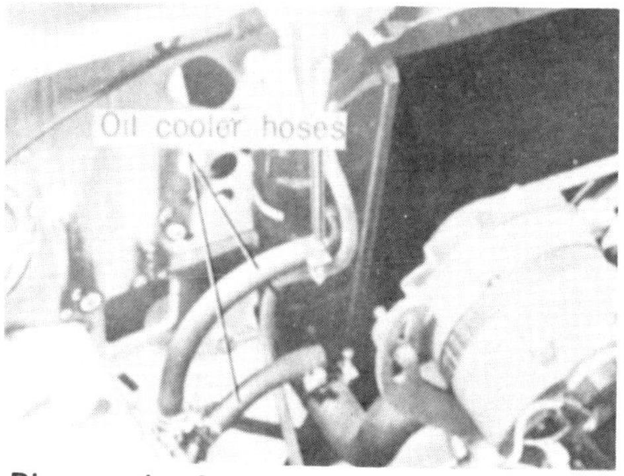

Fig. 1.11. Disconnecting the oil cooler hoses (automatic transmission)

5.1 Removing the hood securing bolts

5.3 On some models the spare wheel is mounted in the engine compartment

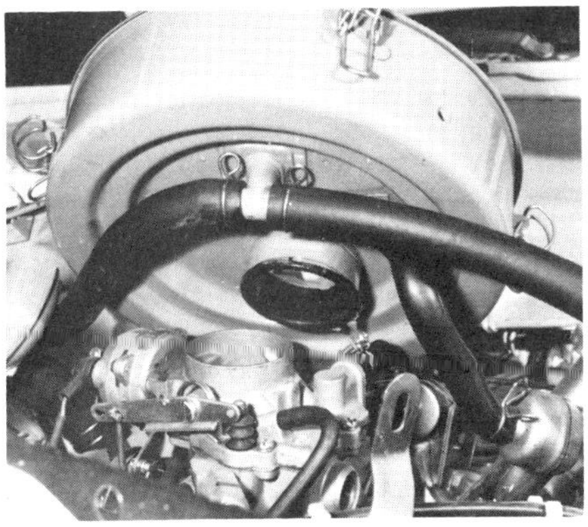
5.4 Removing the emission control hoses and air cleaner

5.5 Disconnect the fuel delivery hose

5.8a Disconnect the alternator leads

5.8b Disconnect the leads to the radiator fan motor ...

5.8c ... and the starter motor

5.9a Remove the radiator mounting bolts

5.9b Disconnect the ground lead from the top of the radiator and ...

5.9c ... lift the radiator out

5.11 Removing the horizontal damper

5.13a Disconnecting the throttle cable

lever of the carburetor. Remove the cable outer end and pull out the cable.

b) On 1972 - 73 models loosen the nut which secures the cable to the manual choke lever, loosen the retaining bracket nut and detach the choke cable.

c) Remove the return spring from the clutch release lever and the intake manifold, and remove the clutch cable from the lever (manual transmission).

d) Vacuum hose (automatic transmission) connected to the engine, from the vacuum pipe attached to the transmission.

e) Vacuum hose for the power brake unit (if fitted), at the check valve attached to the oil filler pipe.

14 On models with automatic transmission, disconnect the torque converter from the engine by rotating the crankshaft so that the four bolts (8 mm) securing the torque converter to the drive plate can be removed through the timing hole in the casing.
15 Remove the exhaust pipe to manifold bolts and the pipe support bracket from the transmission.
16 Remove the front mounting bolts. Leave the rubber cushions attached to the crossmember.
17 Remove the engine-to-transmission bolts. To remove the lower nuts, work from the engine compartment using a socket wrench and extension.
18 Check that all relevant parts have been removed or disconnected and that all cables and hoses are tucked out of the way where they will not get caught up when the engine is being removed.
19 Attach a suitable hoist to the lifting hooks and take the weight of the engine without lifting it. Position a jack under the transmission to support it while separating the engine from the transmission. Lift the engine slightly and pull it forward off the transmission input shaft. Take care not to put any strain on the input shaft. Do not lift the engine higher than necessary when removing it to avoid straining the DOJ. When separating the engine from the automatic transmission be sure to leave the torque converter on the transmission side.
20 Lower the engine and support it so that it will not get damaged. If an engine stand is not available, place it on an old tire to prevent damage to the oil pan.

6 Engine (with transmission) - removal (1972 - 77 models)

1 Carry out the operations given in Section 5, paragraphs 1 to 11 and 13.
2 Disconnect the speedometer cable from the transmission.
3 Disconnect the leads from the back-up light switch, and on 4WD models, the pilot light switch and drive selector switch from the transmission.
4 Drain the automatic transmission fluid by removing the drain plug from the oil pan. Take care when removing the plug, the oil will spurt forward so have the receptacle for the oil positioned correctly.
5 Remove the inlet and outlet oil cooler hoses, which are connected to the transmission, from the pipes attached to the body. Plug each pipe and hose end to prevent entry of dirt.
6 Remove the exhaust pipe by undoing the exhaust pipe to engine bolts and removing the pipe retaining bracket from the transmission.
7 Remove the heat insulating panel under the floor (if fitted), by undoing the seven retaining bolts.
8 Remove the two 8 mm bolts connecting the gear selector rod to the stay on the rear engine mounting and the shift lever joint and remove the selector rod. On automatic transmission models remove the pin joining the manual lever to the control rod.
9 On 4WD models disconnect the drive selector lever by pushing up the drive selector boot, removing the retaining bolt and lifting the lever out.
10 Attach a suitable hoist to the lifting hooks and take the weight of the engine without lifting it as the front and rear mountings are still attached.
11 Disconnect the rear mounting by undoing the two securing nuts (10 mm) located under the mounting rubber.
12 On 4WD models remove the drain plug and drain the gear oil into a container. Remove the four bolts, securing the propeller shaft to the companion flange of the rear differential, and pull the propeller shaft out of the transmission to the rear. Remove the stabilizer from the leading rods and rear crossmember. Undo the rear crossmember securing bolts and remove the crossmember.
13 Remove the engine front mounting by undoing the bolts securing the engine front mounting brackets to the engine.
14 Undo the clamps on the axle shaft boots, transmission end, push back the boots and, with a hammer and pin punch, tap out the spring pins which secure the axle shafts to the transmission output shafts.
15 To separate the axle shafts from the transmission push the engine as far as possible to one side and pull the axle shaft on the opposite side off the transmission output shaft, then push the engine to the other side and pull off the other axle shaft.
16 Check to make sure that all relevant parts have been removed or disconnected and that all cables, hoses and wiring are tucked out of the way where they will not get caught-up as the engine is removed.
17 Hoist the engine out of the engine compartment taking care not to damage the brake pipes with the rear end of the transmission as it is lifted clear of the firewall. Lower the engine and support it so that the oil pan does not get damaged.

7 Engine and transmission - separation

1 Remove the starter motor securing bolts and lift off the starter motor.
2 On automatic transmission models disconnect the torque converter from the engine by rotating the crankshaft, as necessary, and removing the four 8 mm bolts, through the timing hole in the crankcase, that attach the torque converter to the engine drive plate. Separate the transmission from the engine, leaving the torque converter on the transmission.
3 On manual transmission models remove the transmission to engine connecting bolts and withdraw the transmission from the engine, taking care not to put any strain on the main shaft or damage the clutch diaphragm spring.

8 Dismantling the engine - general

1 When the engine is removed from the car it, and particularly its accessories, are more vulnerable to damage. If possible mount the

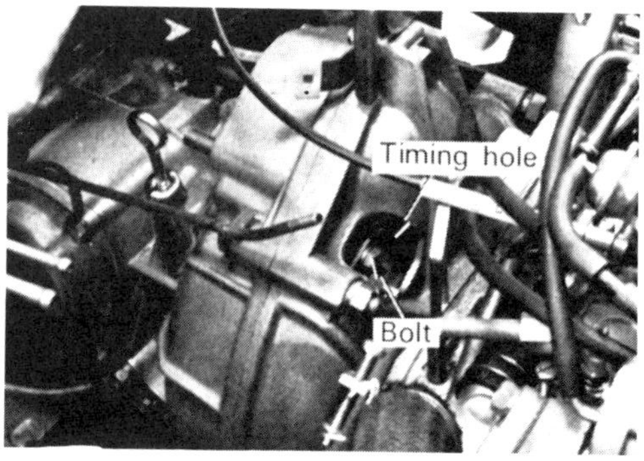

Fig. 1.12. Removing the torque converter to driveplate attaching bolts (automatic transmission)

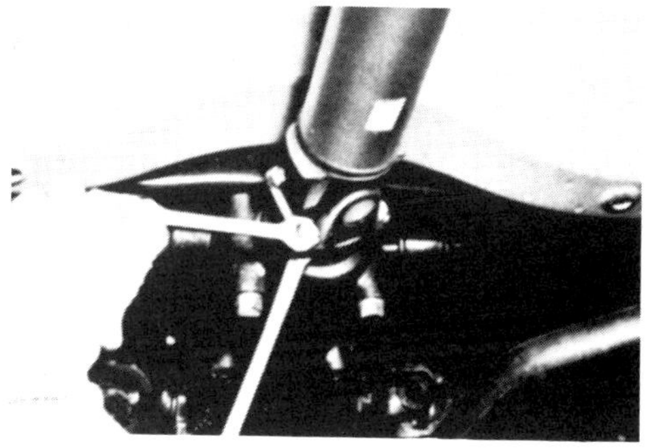

Fig. 1.13. Removing the propeller shaft - 4WD model

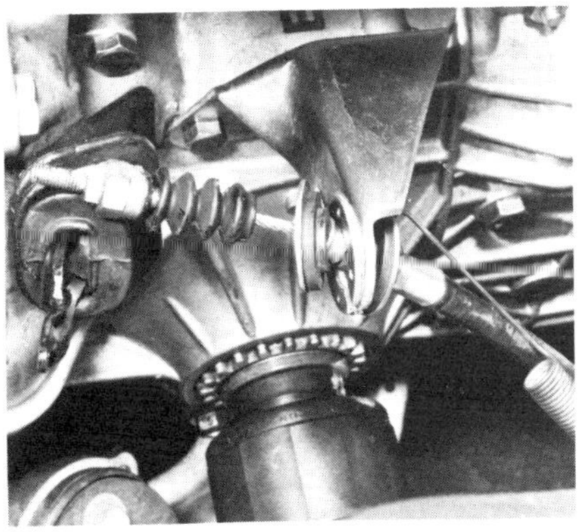

5.13b Disconnect the clutch cable from the clutch release fork

5.13c Disconnect the vacuum hose at the check valve on the oil filler pipe

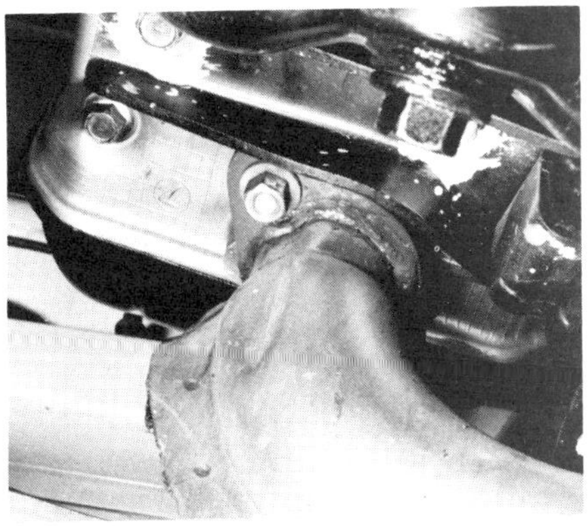

5.15 Remove the exhaust pipe to manifold bolts

6.2 Disconnect the speedometer cable from the transmission ...

6.3 ... and the leads from the back-up lamp switch

6.8 Remove the gear selector rod and stay attaching bolts

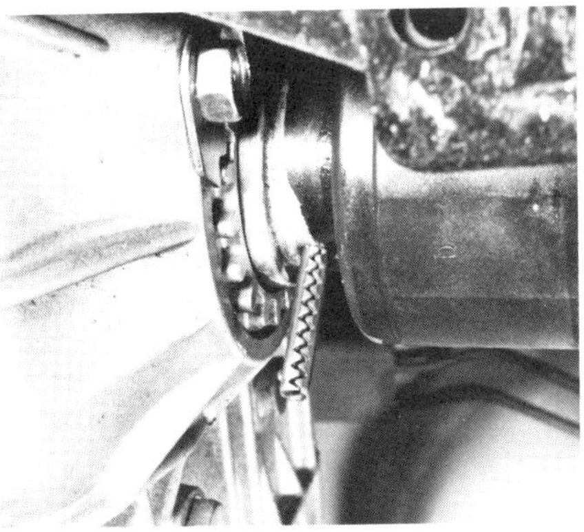

6.14 Remove the axle shaft retaining pins

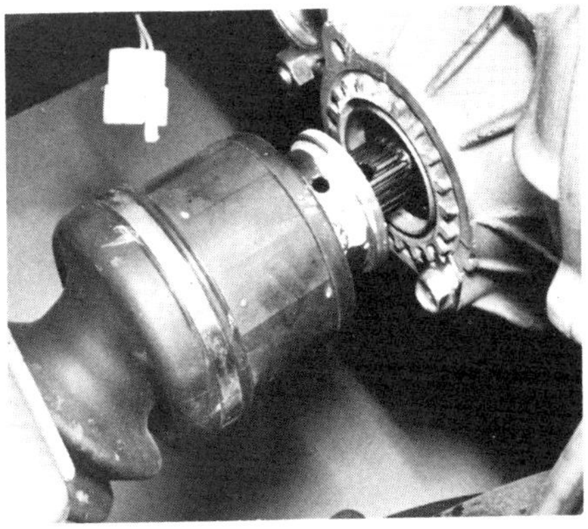

6.15 Pull the axle shaft off the transmission output shaft

6.17a Hoist the engine and pull it forward ...

6.17b ... then lift it out while tilting, so that the transmission clears the firewall

7.1 Removing the starter motor

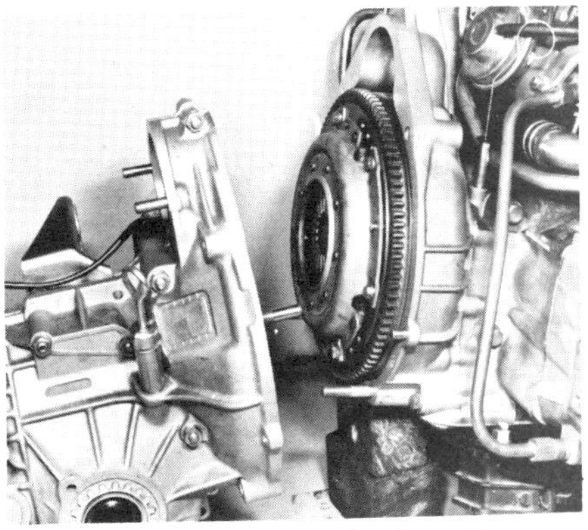

7.3 Separating the transmission from the engine

engine on a stand, or failing this, make sure it is supported in such a manner that it will not get damaged whilst undoing tight nuts and bolts.
2 Cleanliness is important when dismantling the engine to prevent exposed parts from contamination. Before starting the dismantling operations, clean the outside of the engine with kerosene, or a good grease solvent if it is very dirty. Carry out this cleaning away from the area in which the dismantling is to take place.
3 If an engine stand is not available carry out the work on a bench or wooden platform. Avoid working with the engine directly on a concrete floor, as grit presents a real source of trouble.
4 As parts are removed, clean them in a kerosene bath. However, do not immerse parts with internal oilways in kerosene as it is difficult to remove, usually requiring a high pressure air line. Clean oilways with nylon pipe cleaners.
5 It is advisable to have suitable containers to hold small items by their groups as this will help when reassembling the engine and also prevent possible losses.
6 Always obtain complete sets of gaskets when the engine is being dismantled. It is a good policy to always fit new gaskets in view of the relatively small cost involved. Retain the old gaskets when dismantling the engine with a view to using them as a pattern to make a replacement if a new one is not available.
7 When possible refit nuts, bolts and washers in their locations as this helps to protect the threads and will also be helpful when the engine is being reassembled as it establishes their location.
8 Retain unserviceable items until the new parts are obtained, so that the new can be checked against the old part to ensure that the correct item has been supplied.

9 Engine ancillaries - removal

Although the items listed may be removed separately with the engine installed (as described in the relevant Chapters) it is more appropriate to take them off after the engine has been removed from the car when extensive dismantling is being carried out.

Carburetor (can be removed together with the intake manifold).
Emission control system components.
Distributor.
Spark plugs.
Alternator.

10 Engine - dismantling

1 Remove the oil filler duct retaining bolts, and on later models, the support stay, and remove the filler duct.
2 Remove the water pump together with the water pipe elbow, water hose, water pipe, water by-pass hose and water by-pass pipe as a unit.
3 Loosen the crankshaft pulley bolt and using a suitable puller, remove the pulley. Restrain the crankshaft from turning when removing the pulley retaining bolt by wedging the flywheel.
4 Undo the four retaining bolts and remove the oil pump together with the oil filter as a unit.
5 Remove the clutch assembly as described in Chapter 5, Section 4.
6 Restrain the flywheel from turning and remove the flywheel securing bolts. Lift off the flywheel. On automatic transmission models remove the converter drive plate.
7 Remove the flywheel housing securing bolts and lift off the housing complete with crankshaft rear main bearing seal.
8 Remove the valve rocker covers and gaskets.
9 Remove the valve rocker assemblies and valve push rods. If the push rods are to be refitted, identify them so that they can be fitted in their original positions.
10 Loosen the cylinder head holding down nuts in the sequence indicated in Fig. 1.18. Remove the nuts and lift off the cylinder heads and gaskets. Mark the heads so that they can be refitted in the same positions.
11 Turn the engine on its side and remove the oil pan securing bolts. Remove the oil pan, oil pan gasket and the transmission cover plate

10.4 The oil pump and oil filter assembly

10.6a Remove the flywheel securing bolts ...

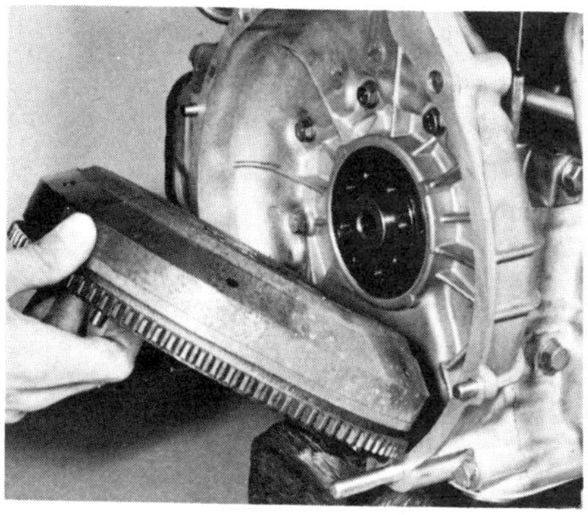
10.6b ... and lift off the flywheel

10.12 Do not remove the oil strainer unless it is defective

10.13a Removing the crankcase plug using a roadwheel nut in lieu of an Allen wrench

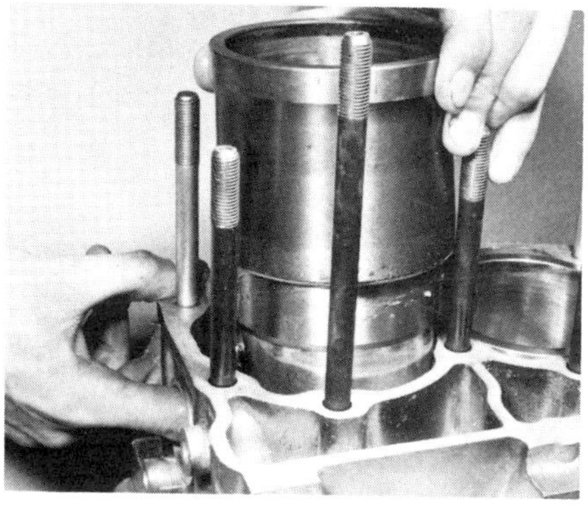
10.13b Lifting out the cylinder liner

(manual transmission only).

12 If necessary, remove the nut and bolt securing the oil strainer stay and drive out the oil strainer and stay as an assembly. Never remove the strainer unless it is really necessary as it is likely to be damaged while doing so. When refitting the strainer use a soft drift to tap in the pipe.

13 Remove the cylinder liners and pistons on 1100, 1300 and 1400 models as follows:

- *a) Remove the crankcase plugs, with an Allen wrench (14 mm across flats), which provides access for the removal of the piston pins.*
- *b) Remove the cylinder liners. Fig. 1.19 shows them being removed using a special tool, but on the engine we dismantled, the liners were removed by turning the crankshaft, and the pistons pushed the liners up enough to enable them to be withdrawn by hand. Remove the cylinder liner gaskets and keep the gaskets and liners of each cylinder together. Mark the flanges of the liners to ensure that they can be refitted in their original position.*
- *c) Working thru the crankcase plug holes, using long nosed circlip pliers, remove the piston pin circlips.*
- *d) Using a length of heavy gauge wire rod, with the end bent over, remove the piston pins. Keep the piston and pins together with their respective cylinders and mark the pistons to indicate their correct fitting position.*

14 Remove the pistons on 1600 models as follows:

- *a) Temporarily fit the crankshaft pulley bolt on the crankshaft front end to provide a means of turning the crankshaft.*
- *b) To remove the piston pin circlip on the rear side of Nos. 3 and 4 pistons, set the piston to bottom dead center by turning the crankshaft, and then insert long nosed pliers through the rear service holes to remove the circlips.*
- *c) Remove the piston pins, using a length of heavy gauge wire with the end bent over to pull the pin out thru the rear service hole.*
- *d) Remove the crankcase plugs from the front service holes with a 14 mm Allen wrench, then remove the circlips and piston pins from Nos. 1 and 2 pistons in the same way as described for Nos. 3 and 4 pistons.*
- *e) Keep the pistons and pins together and mark the pistons so that they can be refitted in their original position.*

10.13c Removing the piston pin circlip

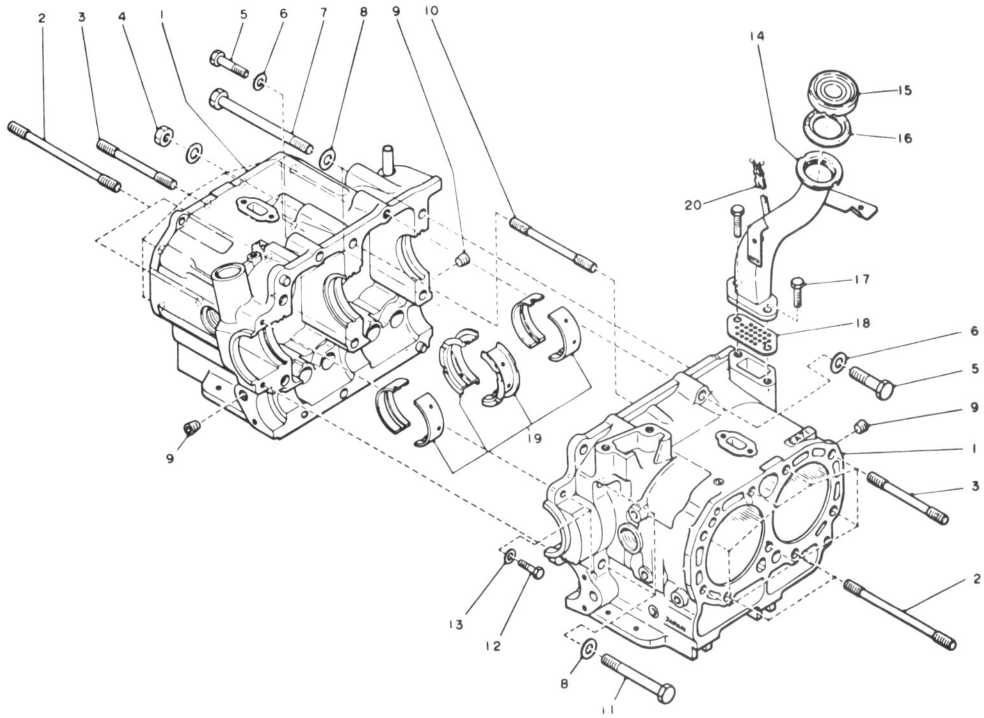

Fig. 1.14. Exploded view of crankcase - 1600 engine

1 Crankcase
2 Stud bolt
3 Stud bolt
4 Nut
5 Bolt
6 Washer
7 Bolt
8 Washer
9 Main gallery plug
10 Stud bolt
11 Bolt
12 Bolt
13 Washer
14 Oil filler duct
15 Oil filler cap
16 Gasket
17 Bolt
18 Air breather duct gasket
19 Crankshaft bearing
20 Supporter

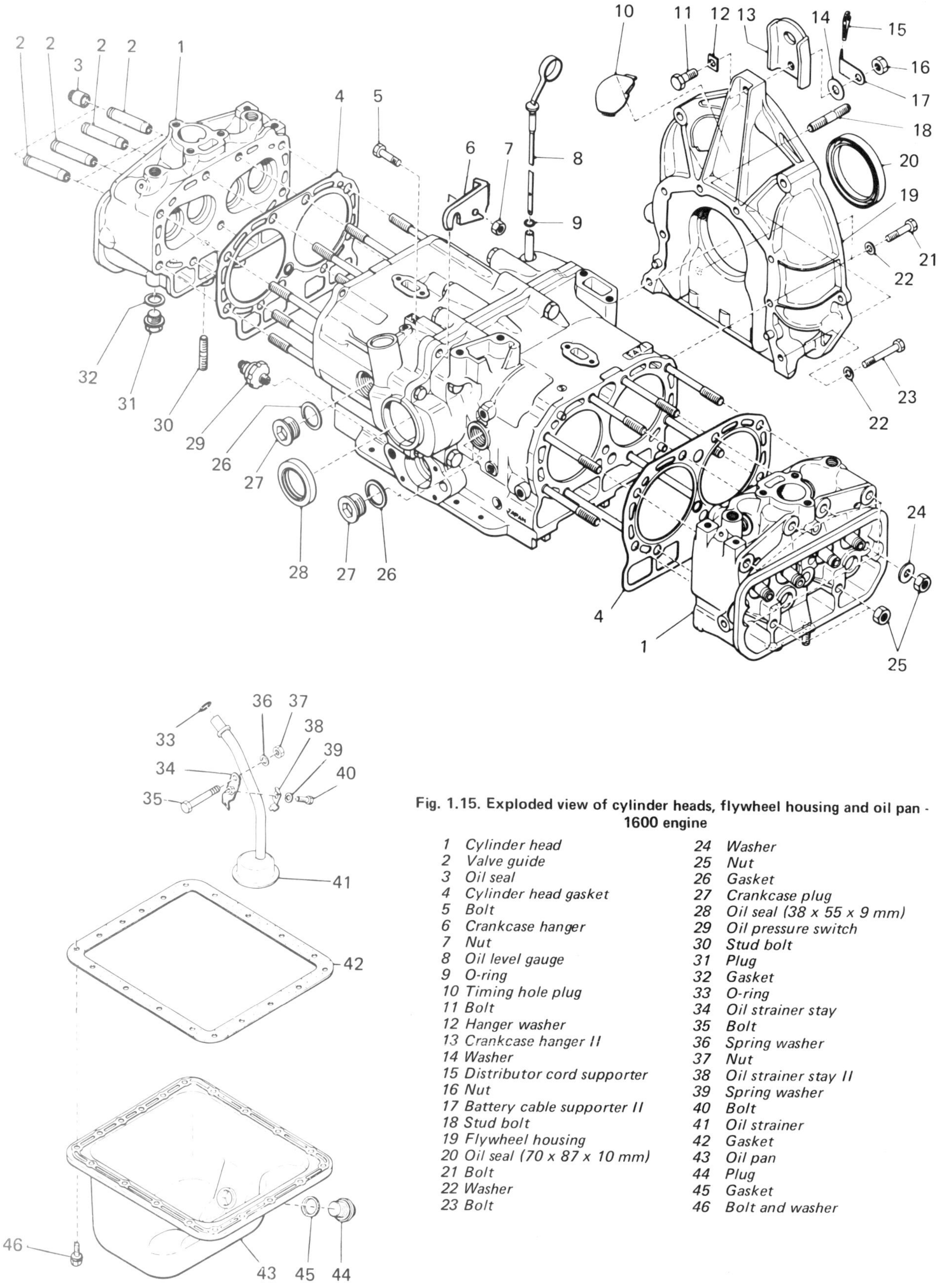

Fig. 1.15. Exploded view of cylinder heads, flywheel housing and oil pan - 1600 engine

1 *Cylinder head*
2 *Valve guide*
3 *Oil seal*
4 *Cylinder head gasket*
5 *Bolt*
6 *Crankcase hanger*
7 *Nut*
8 *Oil level gauge*
9 *O-ring*
10 *Timing hole plug*
11 *Bolt*
12 *Hanger washer*
13 *Crankcase hanger II*
14 *Washer*
15 *Distributor cord supporter*
16 *Nut*
17 *Battery cable supporter II*
18 *Stud bolt*
19 *Flywheel housing*
20 *Oil seal (70 x 87 x 10 mm)*
21 *Bolt*
22 *Washer*
23 *Bolt*
24 *Washer*
25 *Nut*
26 *Gasket*
27 *Crankcase plug*
28 *Oil seal (38 x 55 x 9 mm)*
29 *Oil pressure switch*
30 *Stud bolt*
31 *Plug*
32 *Gasket*
33 *O-ring*
34 *Oil strainer stay*
35 *Bolt*
36 *Spring washer*
37 *Nut*
38 *Oil strainer stay II*
39 *Spring washer*
40 *Bolt*
41 *Oil strainer*
42 *Gasket*
43 *Oil pan*
44 *Plug*
45 *Gasket*
46 *Bolt and washer*

Fig. 1.16. Exploded view of crankshaft and related parts - 1600 engine

1 Bolt
2 Washer
3 Crankshaft pulley
4 Drive belt
5 Distributor drive gear
6 Woodruff key
7 Crankshaft
8 Woodruff key
9 Needle bearing
10 Oil seal
11 Crankshaft gear
12 Flywheel (MT)
13 Starter ring gear
14 Bolt
15 Bolt
16 Drive plate (AT)
17 Connecting rod
18 Nut
19 Connecting rod bolt
20 Connecting rod bearing
21 Piston rings
22 Piston
23 Piston pin
24 Circlip

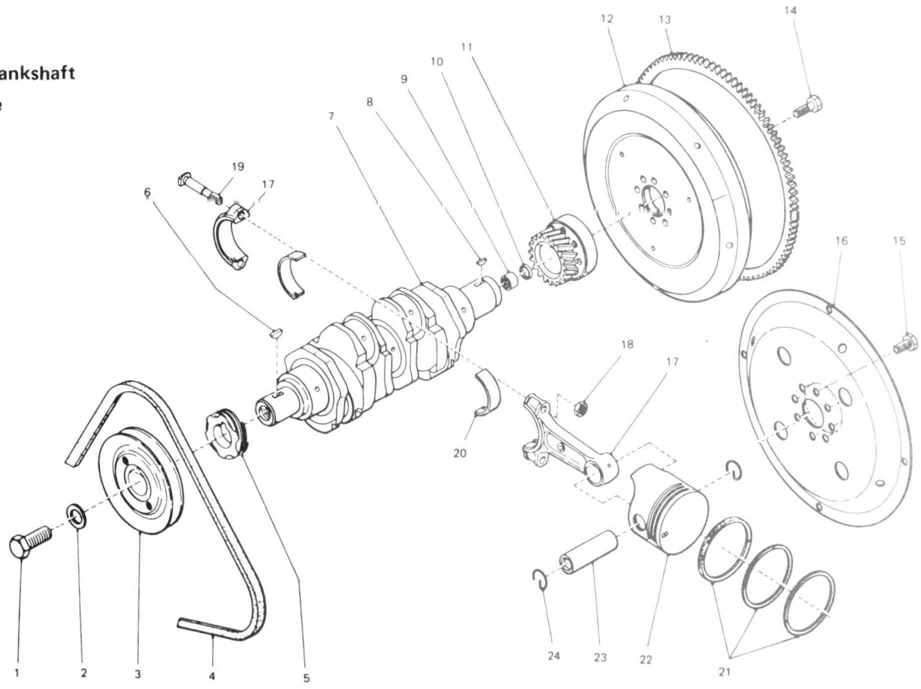

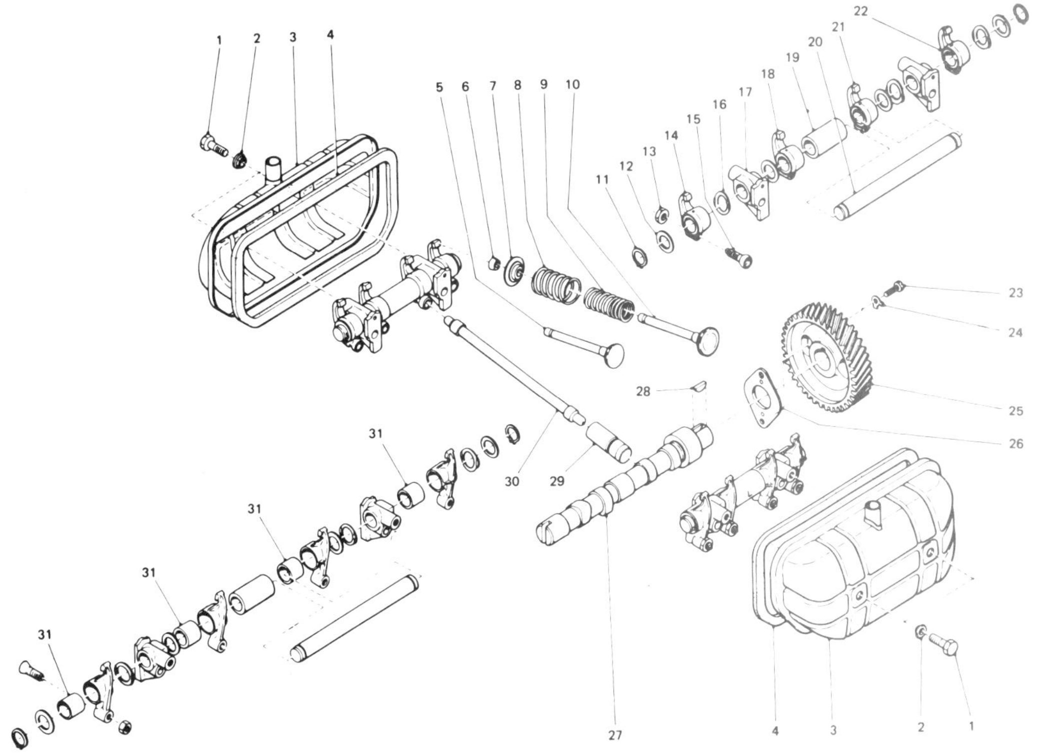

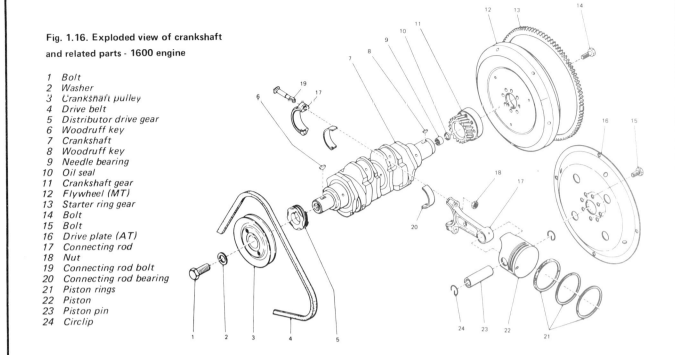

Fig. 1.17. Exploded view of valve mechanism - 1600 engine

1 Bolt
2 Valve rocker cover seal washer
3 Valve rocker cover
4 Valve rocker cover gasket
5 Exhaust valve
6 Valve spring retainer key
7 Valve spring retainer
8 Valve spring (outer)
9 Valve spring (inner)
10 Intake valve
11 Snap ring
12 Washer
13 Nut
14 Valve rocker arm
15 Valve rocker screw
16 Rocker shaft spring washer
17 Rocker shaft supporter
18 Valve rocker arm
19 Rocker shaft spacer
20 Valve rocker shaft
21 Valve rocker arm
22 Valve rocker arm
23 Bolt
24 Lock washer
25 Camshaft gear
26 Camshaft plate
27 Camshaft
28 Woodruff key
29 Valve lifter
30 Valve push rod
31 Valve rocker bushing

10.16 Fit a piece of rubber hose between the valve lifters to prevent them falling out when the crankcase halves are separated

f) The piston can be left in the cylinder until the crankcase halves are separated or it can be removed at this stage by turning the crankshaft gently so that the connecting rod pushes the piston out to some extent, then by fitting the piston pin in the connecting rod small end and again turning the crankshaft gently to push the piston further until it protrudes from the cylinder and can be pulled out.

15 Straighten the lockwashers on the camshaft securing bolts, working through the holes in the camshaft gear, and remove the bolts.
16 Remove the nuts, bolts or stud bolts (there are different arrangements, according to the year) bolting the crankcase halves together. Before separating the crankcase, pull the camshaft to the rear so that it does not interfere with the crankcase and wedge the valve lifters with spring clips or a piece of rubber hose to prevent them falling out.
17 Separate the crankcase halves. Remove the oil seal at the front of the crankshaft and lift out the crankshaft with the connecting rods and distributor gear as an assembly. Remove the connecting rods from crankshaft. Mark the caps and rods so that they can be refitted in their original positions.
18 Remove the camshaft and camshaft gear assembly.
19 Remove the valve lifters and keep them in order with their respective push rods so that they can be refitted in their original positions.
20 On 1600 engines remove the pistons from the cylinders if they were not removed at the same time as the piston pins.
21 Remove the crankshaft bearings. If they are to be refitted identify them so that they can be refitted in their original positions.
22 Unscrew and remove the oil pressure switch.

Fig. 1.18. Loosening sequence of cylinder head nuts

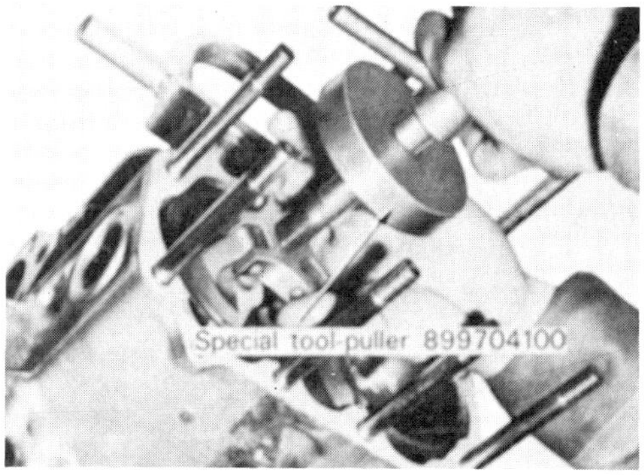

Fig. 1.19. Using a special tool-puller to remove the cylinder liner (not 1600 engines)

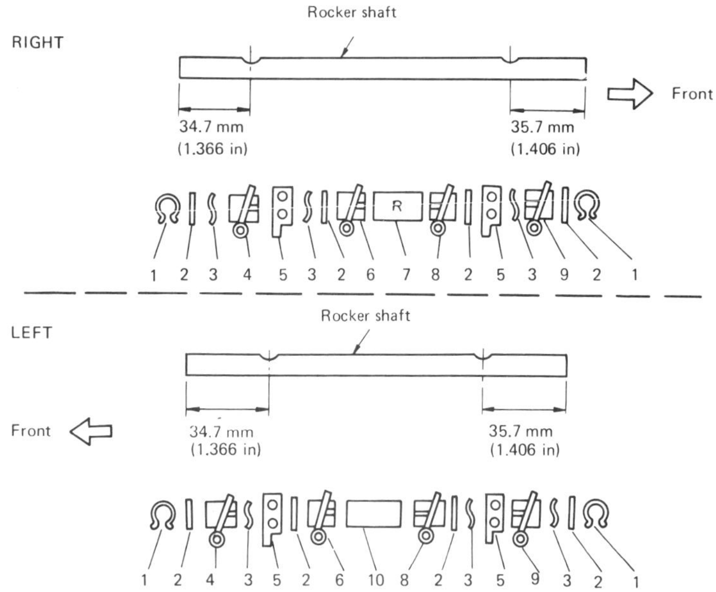

Fig. 1.20. Valve rocker assembly

1 Snap ring
2 Plain washer
3 Spring washer
4 Rocker arm IV (2 oil holes)
5 Support
6 Rocker arm II (1 oil hole)
7 Spacer (R)
8 Rocker arm I (1 oil hole)
9 Rocker arm III (2 oil holes)
10 Spacer

11 Valve rockers - dismantling, inspection and reassembly

Note: Pay special attention to the direction of the rocker shaft, the position of the spring washers, the difference between the rocker arms and the 'R' mark on the right-hand spacer.

1 Refer to Fig. 1.20. Remove the snap-ring and slide the parts off the shaft, taking care not to mix them up, so that they can be refitted in the same order.

2 Examine the rocker shaft and rocker bushings for wear. If the rocker arm surface that contacts the stem head is considerably worn, renew the rocker arm. If worn slightly in a stepped shape it can be corrected on a valve refacing machine. If the rocker arm bushing has to be renewed this requires special tools and is best left to your Subaru dealer.

3 Oil the parts and reassemble them on their respective shafts in the original order.

12 Valve lifters and pushrods - inspection and renovation

1 Check the valve lifters for wear and damage. Renew if defective.

2 Check the pushrods for signs of bending or damage. Correct or renew as necessary.

3 Ensure that the oil holes in the pushrods are not clogged, clean as necessary.

13 Camshaft and gear assembly - inspection and renovation

1 Examine the camshaft and gear for damage and wear. Measure the thrust clearance between the camshaft and camshaft plate, see Fig. 1.21. If it exceeds 0.012 in (0.3 mm), remove the cam gear and renew the plate.

2 Inspect the cam surfaces for wear. Renew the camshaft if noticeably worn, if it is only very slightly scored this can be corrected with a fine oilstone.

3 If the cam gear, camshaft or thrust plate have to be renewed, press the cam gear off the shaft. When refitting the cam gear on the shaft fit the Woodruff key on the camshaft and press the gear onto the shaft. The camshaft plate must be fitted with the side having no protrusion facing the cam journal and the cam gear with the side having a boss of 1.57 in (40 mm) facing the camshaft plate.

14 Crankcase - inspection

1 Check both halves of the crankcase for damage. Check the valve lifter holes for wear.

2 Ensure that all oil passages are clean.

3 Check that the stud bolts are not loose, bent or have damaged threads. Correct as necessary.

4 Check the crankcase surfaces that mate with the cylinder head for warping, using a straight edge and feeler gauge. If warping exceeds 0.002 in (0.05 mm) the surface will have to be refaced on a surface grinder. Maximum amount that can be ground off is 0.0157 in (0.4 mm).

15 Cylinder heads - dismantling, renovation and reassembly

1 Clean the dirt and oil off the cylinder heads. Remove the carbon from the combustion chamber and valve heads with a scraper or rotary wire brush.

2 Remove the valves by compressing the valve springs with a suitable valve spring compressor and lifting out the keepers. Release the valve spring compressor and remove the valve spring retainer, the springs and the valve. Mark each valve so that they can be refitted in the same location.

3 With the valves removed clean out any remaining carbon from the ports. Remove the intake valve oil seals.

4 Using a straight edge and feeler gauge check the cylinder heads for warpage. If the warpage exceeds 0.002 in (0.05 mm) take it to an engineering workshop and have the surface reground with a surface grinder (grinding limit 0.020 in (0.5 mm).

5 Examine the heads of the valves and the valve seats for pitting and

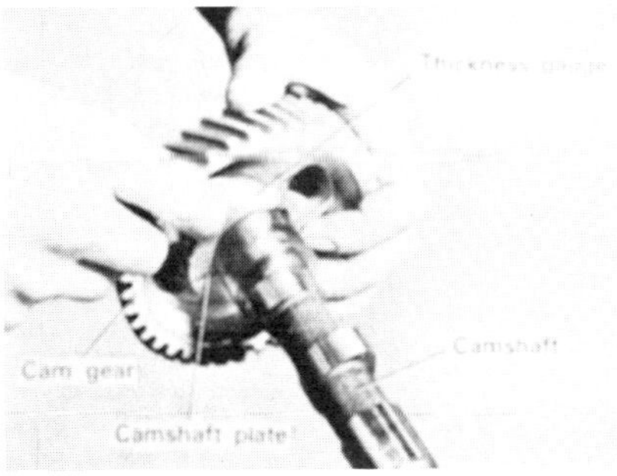

Fig. 1.21. Measuring the camshaft thrust clearance

11.0 The right-hand rocker spacer is marked with the letter 'R'

15.2 Compressing the valve spring with a valve spring compressing tool

15.9 Fit new oil seals on the intake valve guides

burning. If the pitting on valve and seat is slight it can be removed by grinding the valves and seats together with coarse, and then fine, valve grinding paste. If bad pitting has occurred the valves will have to be reground on a valve grinding machine and the seats will have to be re-cut with a valve seat cutter, both these operations are a job for your local Subaru dealer.

6 Check the valve guides with the valve stems to ensure that they are a good fit, the valve stem should move easily in the guides without side play. Renewal of worn guides requires special tools and should be left to your Subaru dealer.

7 When lapping-in slightly pitted valves and valve seats with carborundum paste proceed as follows: Apply a little coarse grinding paste to the valve seat and using a suction type valve grinding tool, lap the valve into its seats with a semi-rotary movement, lifting the valve from time-to-time. A light spring under the valve head will assist in this operation. When a dull matt even surface finish appears on both the valve and the valve seat, clean off the coarse paste and repeat the lapping operation with a fine grinding paste until a continuous ring of light grey matt finish appears on both valve and valve seat. Carefully clean off all traces of grinding paste. Blow through the gas passages with compressed air.

8 Check the valve springs for damage and renew if defective.

15.10a Fit the valve in the valve guide ...

15.10b ... then the inner and outer valve springs

15.10c Fit the valve spring retainer ...

15.10d ... and the retaining keepers

9 Press new oil seals on to the intake valve guides.
10 Fit the intake and exhaust valves with the inner and outer valve springs, valve spring retainers and keepers in the cylinder head, using a valve spring compressor to compress the springs. Take care not to damage the lip of the intake valve oil seals when fitting the intake valves. Fit the valve springs with the close coil side toward the cylinder head as shown in Fig. 1.22.
11 After fitting all the parts, tap the top of the valve springs lightly with a plastic hammer to ensure correct seating of the valve spring retainer keepers.

16 Cylinder liners and pistons - inspection and renovation

1 Check the cylinder liners for scoring or damage and wear. If the cylinder bores are worn this will result in excessive oil consumption and loss of power. A preliminary check for wear can be made by feeling the inside walls of the cylinders about 0.5 in (12.7 mm) from the top edge. If a ridge can be felt at any point then the bores should be measured with a cylinder bore gauge to ascertain the amount of wear. Measure the inner diameter in both the axial and thrust directions at the positions shown in Fig. 1.23. If wear exceeds the limits specified in Specifications at the beginning of this Chapter, the liner must be renewed, or rebored and oversize pistons fitted. **Note:** If any one of the cylinder liners require reboring all the others must be rebored at the same time.
2 If the same pistons are being refitted with only the rings being renewed, carefully clean the piston ring grooves with the aid of a broken piece of used ring. If the clearance of the rings in the grooves exceeds the figure in Specifications the pistons will have to be renewed.
3 Check the fit of the piston pin in the piston. It should be possible to push the pin in with thumb pressure at a temperature of 20°C (68°F).
4 Before fitting new rings to the pistons check the ring gap by placing each ring in the cylinder in which it will be fitted, and using a piston make sure the ring rests square in the bore near the bottom of the cylinder. Measure the gap between the ring ends with a feeler gauge and, if necessary, file the ends of the ring to obtain the specified dimension.
5 If new rings are to be fitted to the old pistons, then the top ring should be stepped so as to clear the ridge left above the previous top ring. If a normal but oversize ring is fitted it will hit the ridge and break. If stepped rings are not available, the ridge at the top of the cylinder can be removed with a ridge reamer. This is a job for a specialist and should be taken to an engineering workshop.
6 When fitting the rings on the piston ensure that the marks on the compression rings face upwards and that the oil rings consisting of two rails and a spacer are assembled correctly, refer to Fig. 1.24.

17 Crankshaft and main bearings - inspection and renovation

1 Examine the crankpin and main journal surfaces for signs of scoring or scratches. Measure the ovality of the journals at different positions with a micrometer. If more than 0.0012 in (0.03 mm) out of round, the crankpins will have to be reground. It will also have to be reground if the journals are scored or damaged in any way.
2 If it is necessary to regrind the crankshaft and fit new undersize bearings your Subaru dealer will be able to determine how much grinding is necessary and the size of new bearings required.
3 Inspect the individual crankshaft bearings for signs of flaking, pitting, scoring and wear. Unless the bearings have done a low mileage it is recommended that new bearings are fitted.
4 Measure the oil clearance of each crankshaft bearing by means of Plastigage as follows:

a) Wipe off all oil, dust, etc on the surface to be measured.
b) Fit the bearings in the crankcase halves and set the crankshaft in position.
c) Cut a piece of Plastigage to the bearing width and place it on the journal parallel with the crankshaft axis. Be careful not to put it on the oil hole or groove. Bolt the crankcase halves together and tighten the nuts to a torque of:

10 mm nuts	*29 - 35 lb f ft (4.0 - 4.8 kg fm)*
8 mm nuts	*17 - 20 lb f ft (2.3 - 2.7 kg fm)*
6 mm nuts	*3.3 - 4.0 lb f ft (0.45 - 0.55 kg fm)*

Do not rotate the crankshaft or turn the crankcase over while doing this work.
5 Remove the nuts and bolts, separate the crankcase halves and measure the Plastigage width with the scale printed on the Plastigage case. If the measurement is not within the specification, fit undersize bearings and renew or recondition the crankshaft.
6 Measure the thrust clearance of the crankshaft at the center bearing. If the clearance exceeds 0.0118 in (0.3 mm) renew the bearing.
7 Check the needle bearing in the rear end of the crankshaft (not on automatic transmission models), for free rotation and the bearing rollers for damage. Check the oil seal for damage and hardening.
8 Examine the crankshaft gear teeth and the oil seal contacting surface for wear or damage and renew as necessary.
9 Examine the distributor drive gear for wear or damage and check that the Woodruff key is a good fit. Renew as necessary.

Fig. 1.22. Fitted position of valve spring

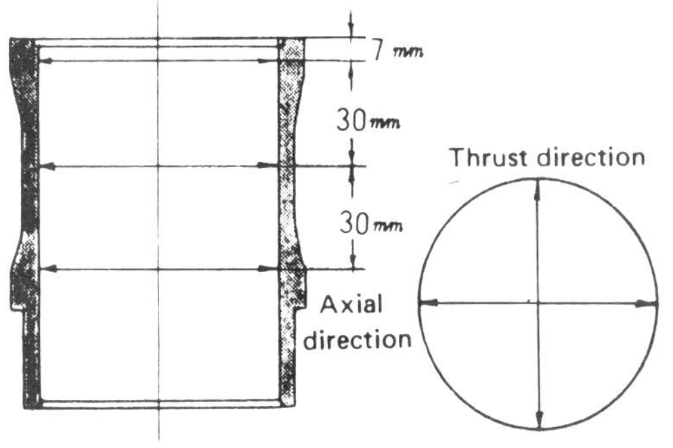

Fig. 1.23. Measuring the bore of the cylinder liner

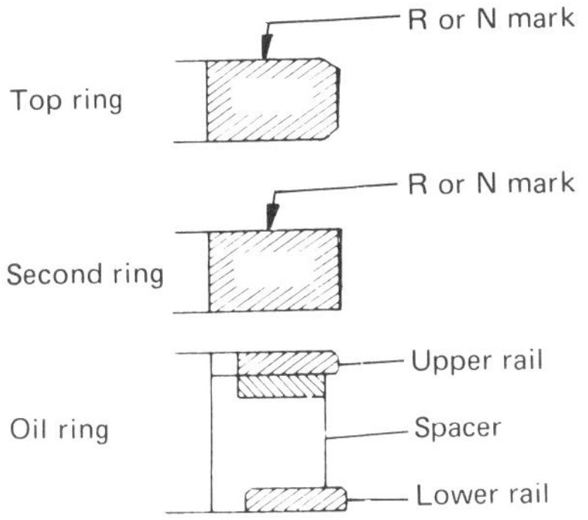

Fig. 1.24. Cross-section of piston rings

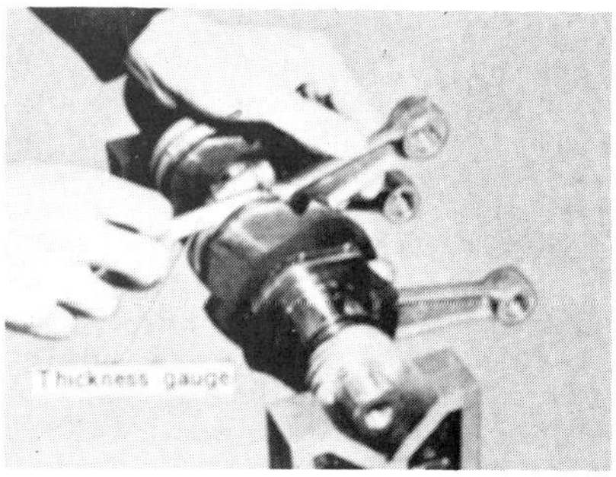

Fig. 1.25. Measuring connecting rod side clearance

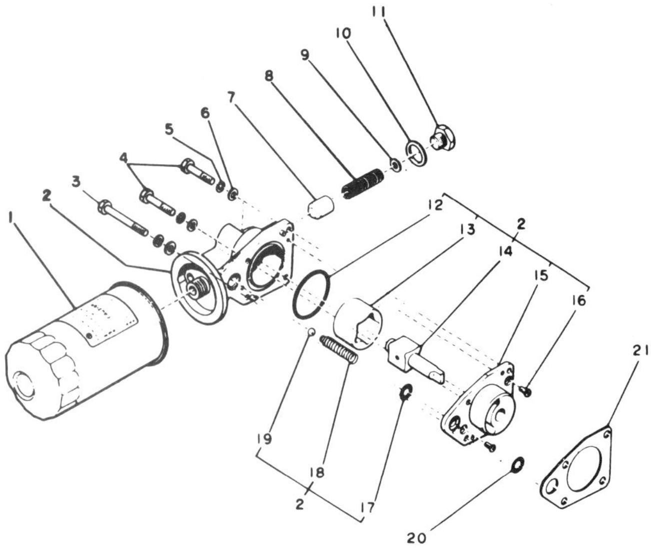

Fig. 1.26. Exploded view of oil pump

1	*Oil filter*	12	*'O' ring*
2	*Oil pump body*	13	*Rotor*
3	*Bolt (6 x 54 mm)*	14	*Gear complete*
4	*Bolt (6 x 32 mm)*	15	*Holder (oil pump)*
5	*Spring washer*	16	*Screw (4 mm)*
6	*Washer*	17	*'O' ring*
7	*Oil relief valve*	18	*Spring (bypass valve)*
8	*Spring (relief valve)*	19	*Ball*
9	*Washer (6 mm)*	20	*'O' ring*
10	*Washer (14.5 mm)*	21	*Gasket*
11	*Plug*		

18 Connecting rods - inspection and renovation

1 Examine the connecting rod bearing surfaces for pitting, scoring and wear. Fit the connecting rod to the crankpin and measure the side (thrust) clearance. Renew the connecting rod if the clearance exceeds 0.016 in (0.4 mm).
2 Measure the oil clearance using the same method as for the crankshaft bearings, see Section 17, paragraph 4. Tighten the connecting rod bolts and nuts to:

EA61, EA62, EA63	*36.2 ft lb (5 kg fm)*
EA63S, EA71	*30 ft lb (4.2 kg fm)*

If the oil clearance exceeds 0.0047 in (0.12 mm) replace the bearing with a new one of standard size or undersize and recondition or renew the crankshaft, as necessary.
3 Check the connecting rod for bend or twist, also the small end of the rod for wear or damage. Check that the piston pin is a push fit in the small-end. Renew as necessary.

19 Oil pump and filter - dismantling, inspection and reassembly

1 Unscrew the oil filter from the oil pump.
2 Remove the two screws securing the oil pump body holder and the oil pump body, and pull the rotor out. Remove the O-rings, and the by-pass ball valve and spring.
3 Remove the relief valve retaining plug and take out the relief valve spring, relief valve and washer.
4 Clean all the parts and check for wear and damage.
5 Measure the clearance between the pump drive gear and pump rotor. Renew both the drive gear and rotor as a set if the clearance exceeds 0.0079 in (0.2 mm).
6 Measure the side clearance between the pump body and rotor, if the clearance exceeds 0.0079 in (0.2 mm), renew the rotor and drive gear (as a set) or the pump body as necessary.
7 Using a straight edge and feeler gauge measure the endfloat of the rotor and drive gear as shown in Fig. 1.29. Renew the rotor and drive gear or pump body if endfloat exceeds 0.0098 in (0.25 mm).

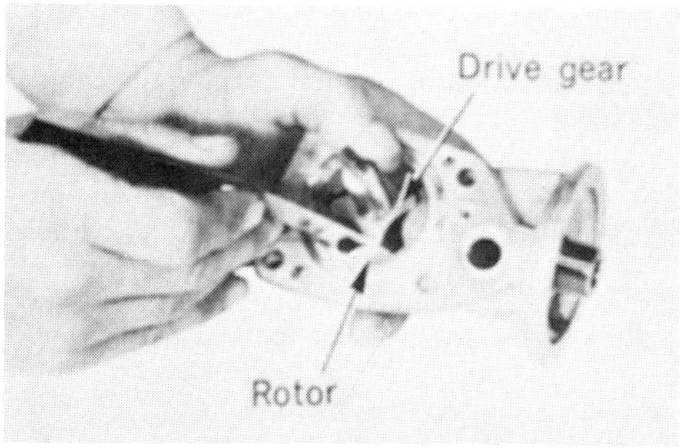

Fig. 1.27. Measuring the pump drive gear-to-rotor clearance

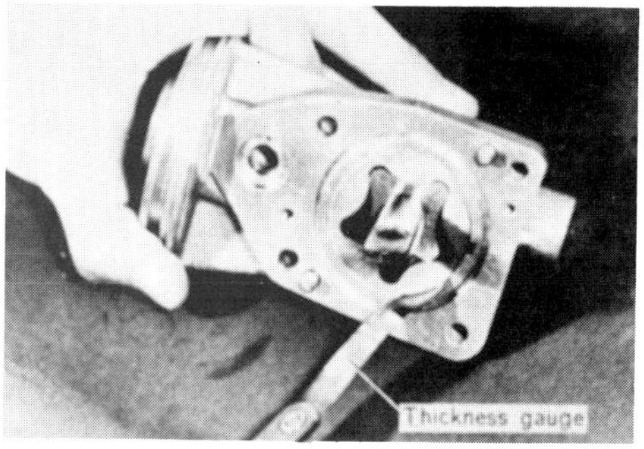

Fig. 1.28. Measuring the clearance between the pump body and rotor

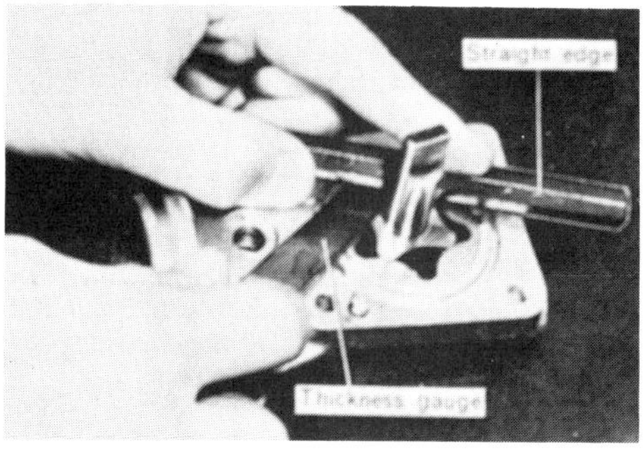

Fig. 1.29. Measuring the endfloat of rotor and drive gear

8 Reassembly is the reverse of dismantling. Always fit new washers, gaskets and O-rings. Oil all parts before assembly. When fitting the oil filter smear the rubber seal with engine oil and take care not to damage the seal when screwing on the filter. Tighten the filter by hand approximately one third of a turn after the rubber seal contacts the pump body. Do not over-tighten.

20 Flywheel ring gear - renewal

1 If the teeth on the starter ring gear are worn or broken then it will be necessary to remove the ring gear and fit a new one, or exchange the flywheel for a reconditioned unit.
2 Remove the old ring gear by drilling through it at the root of the gear teeth at two diametrically opposite points, being careful not to drill the flywheel. Drill as large a hole as possible then split the ring gear with a hammer and cold chisel.
3 Heat the new ring in an electric oven to about 200°C (392°F) and then quickly fit it to the flywheel before it has time to cool down.
4 Clamp it in position so that when it cools down it will be located in its correct position.
5 Take care not to overheat the ring gear or to heat it with a flame. If it is overheated, indicated by a light metallic blue color, the temper of the ring gear will be lost.

21 Engine reassembly - general

1 To ensure maximum life with minimum trouble from an overhauled engine, not only must every part be correctly assembled but everything must be spotlessly clean, all oilways must be clear, locking washers and spring washers must always be fitted where needed and all bearings and other sliding surfaces must be thoroughly lubricated during assembly.
2 Before assembly, renew any bolts, studs and nuts whose threads are in any way damaged and whenever possible use new spring washers.
3 When refitting parts which have been removed ensure that they are refitted in their original positions and directions. Oil seal lips should be coated with grease before fitting. A liquid gasket sealant should be used where specified to prevent leakage.
4 Apart from your normal tools, a supply of clean rags, an oil can filled with engine oil and a torque wrench are essential.

22 Engine - reassembly

1 Apply liquid gasket sealant to the threads of the oil pressure switch and fit the oil pressure switch in the crankcase. Use a new gasket and tighten the switch to 16 - 20 lb f ft (2.2 - 2.8 kg fm).
2 Fit the crankshaft bearing shells in the two halves of the crankcase. If the same bearings are being refitted ensure that they are located in their original positions.
3 Oil the connecting rod bearings and fit the connecting rods and caps, with the side having the mark as shown in Fig. 1.30 facing forward. Fit the stud bolts and lockwashers or bolts and nuts and

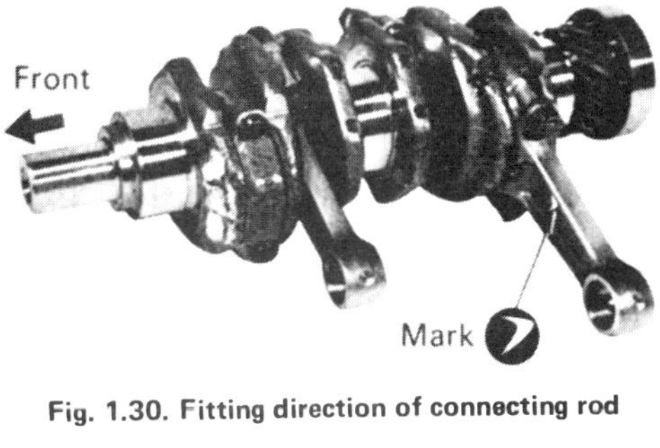

Fig. 1.30. Fitting direction of connecting rod

22.2 Fit the crankshaft bearing shells in the casing

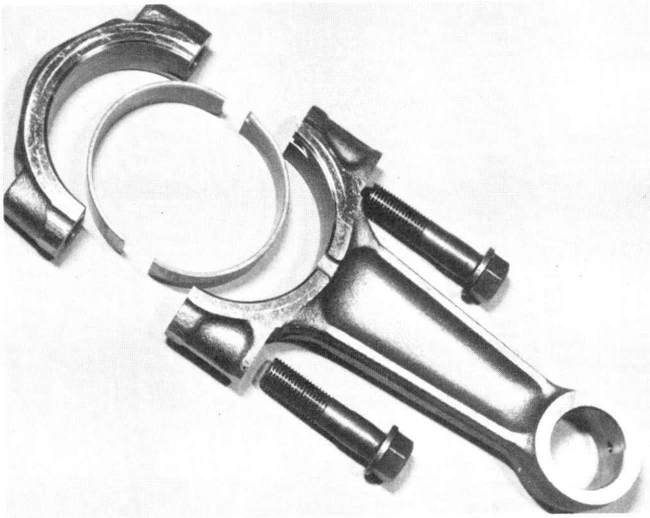

22.3a Connecting rod assembly

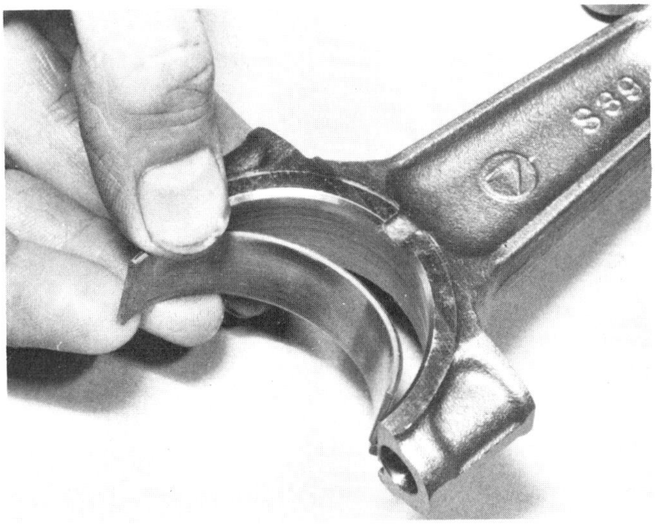

22.3b Fit the bearing shell in the connecting rod ...

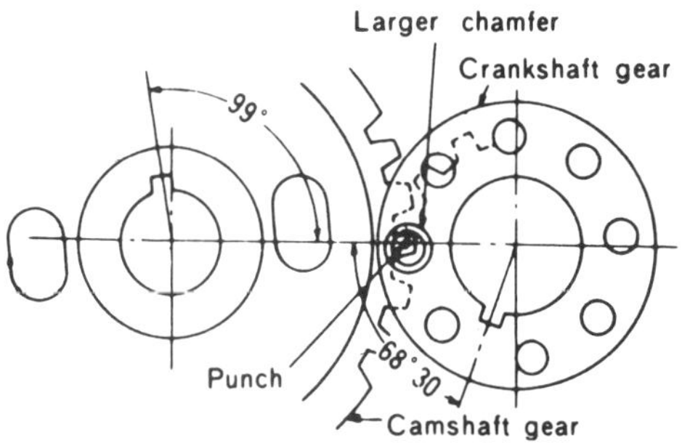

Fig. 1.31. Crankshaft and camshaft matching marks

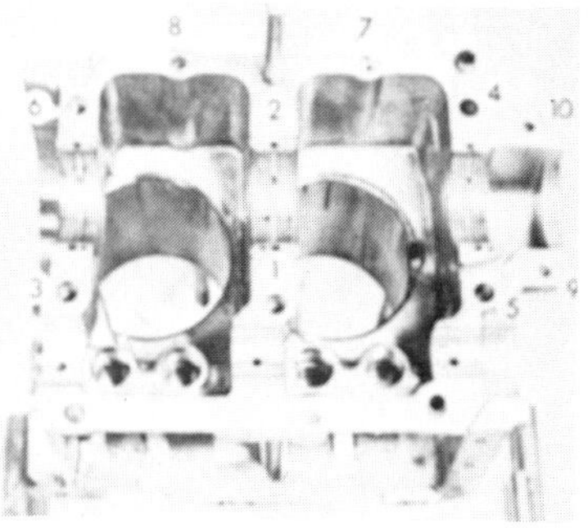

Fig. 1.32. Tightening sequence for crankcase bolts and nut

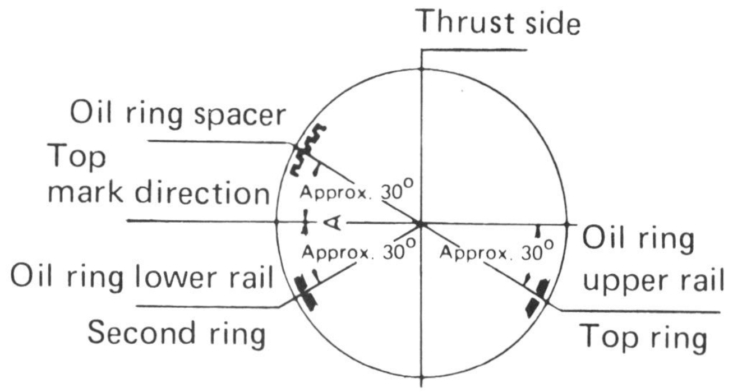

Fig. 1.33. Piston ring gap position

tighten to a torque of:

Engine	lb f ft	kg fm
EA61, EA62, EA63A and EA63E	*34 - 37*	*4.8 - 5.2*
EA63S, EA71	*29 - 31*	*4.0 - 4.3*

Make sure that each connecting rod has its own mating cap by checking their matching marks made at disassembly. Recheck the side clearance as described in Section 18, paragraph 1.

4 Apply oil to the valve lifters and fit them into the lifter holes in the crankcase halves.

5 Oil the crankshaft and camshaft bearing surfaces and fit the crankshaft and camshaft on the crankcase half with Nos. 2 and 4 cylinders (left-hand half). One of the bolt holes in the crankshaft gear has a larger chamfer than the others. Fit the crankshaft so that the punch mark on the camshaft gear can be seen through this bolt hole in the crankshaft flange, see Fig. 1.31.

6 Thoroughly clean the mating surfaces of both crankcase halves and apply a coat of liquid gasket sealant.

7 Fit spring clips or rubber hose between the valve lifters in the crankcase half having Nos. 1 and 3 cylinders, to prevent the lifters dropping out as the crankcase halves are fitted together.

8 Fit the securing bolts and nuts with a plain washer under each nut and tighten the nuts in the sequence shown in Fig. 1.32 to a torque of:

10 mm nuts	*29 - 35 lb f ft (4.0 - 4.8 kg fm)*
8 mm nuts	*17 - 20 lb f ft (2.3 - 2.7 kg fm)*
6 mm nuts	*3.3 - 4.0 lb f ft (0.45 - 0.55 kg fm)*

Fit the engine lifting hook at this time and also the fan stay on 4WD models.

9 Fit the camshaft plate lockwashers and securing bolts working through the holes in the camshaft gear. Bend over the tabs of the lockwashers to lock the bolts.

10 Fit the cylinder liners and pistons on 1100, 1300 and 1400 models as follows:

a) *Position the piston ring gaps as shown in Fig. 1.33. Insert the circlips into the rear side of the pistons.*
b) *Oil the piston and fit a piston ring band to compress the rings.*
c) *Fit the piston into its cylinder liner, as marked at disassembly. Push the piston into the liner as far as the piston pin boss to allow for the fitting of the piston pin when the liner and piston assembly is fitted in the crankcase.*
d) *Position the crankcase upright so that Nos. 2 and 4 cylinders face downwards.*
e) *Turn the crankshaft carefully until No. 3 connecting rod is at top dead center and fit the piston and liner with the cylinder liner gasket fitted under the liner. Align the small end of the connecting rod with the piston pin hole and working thru the service hole, push the piston pin into position and fit the retaining circlip using long nosed circlip pliers. Push the cylinder liner fully into the crankcase.*
f) *Repeat the same procedure for No. 1 cylinder.*
g) *Check the amount the cylinder liner protrudes above the*

22.3c ... then fit the connecting rod on the crankpin with the cap ...

22.3d ... and tighten the bolts with a torque wrench

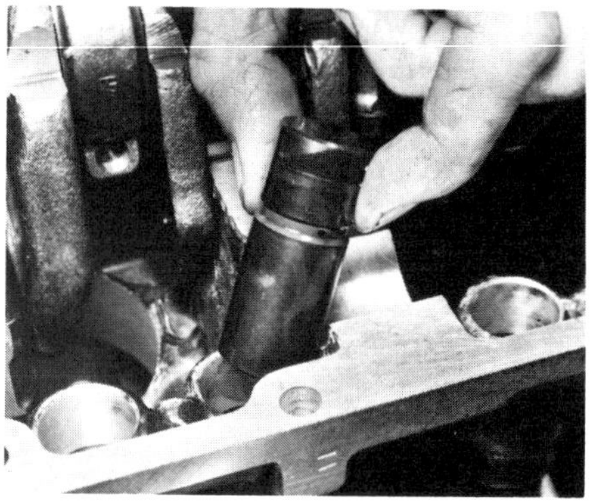

22.4 Fit the valve lifters in the crankcase

22.5a Place the crankshaft and ...

22.5b ... then the camshaft in position on the left-hand half casing

22.5c Punch mark on camshaft gear and chamfered hole on the crankshaft flange to be matched

22.7 Rubber hose wedged between the valve lifters

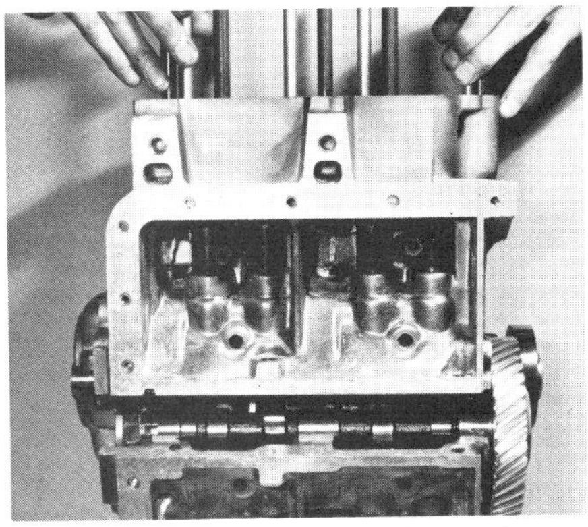

22.8a Fit the right-hand half casing on the left-hand half ...

22.8b ... and tighten the half casing securing bolts with a torque wrench

22.9 Fitting the camshaft plate securing bolt and lockwasher

22.10a Compress the piston rings with a piston ring band and fit the piston in the cylinder liner

22.10b Position the piston in the liner

22.10c Fitting the piston pin ...

22.10d ... and the piston pin retaining circlip

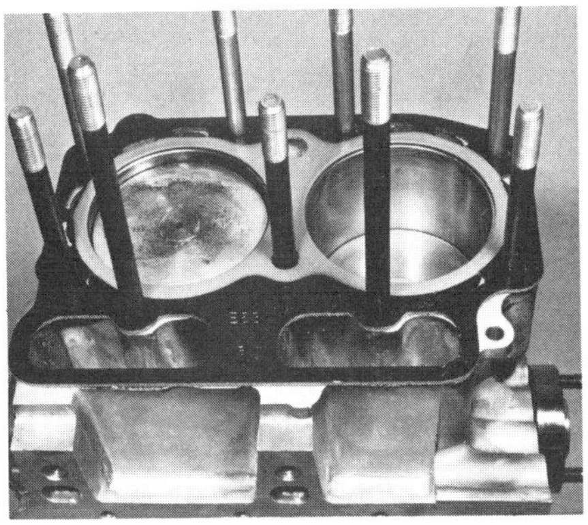

22.14a Fit the cylinder head gasket ...

crankcase surface. It should be as follows:

EA61	0.0024 - 0.0035 in (0.06 - 0.09 mm)
EA62	0.0028 - 0.0035 in (0.07 - 0.09 mm)
EA63	0.0035 - 0.0043 in (0.09 - 0.11 mm)

The cylinder liner gasket should be selected to obtain the specified protrusion. Gaskets are available in sizes ranging from 0.0404 to 0.0447 in (1.025 to 1.135 mm) in steps of 0.0004 in (0.01 mm). Gasket thickness required can be determined by measuring the depth of the cylinder liner hole in the crankcase and the height of the cylinder liner prior to fitting the liner. Cylinder liner gaskets are not the same for all engines, always specify which engine they are for.

h) Fit a device to keep the cylinder liners in position. A piece of suitable tubing placed over the stud between the cylinder liners and held in position with a cylinder head nut is sufficient. Then turn the crankcase upside down so that Nos. 1 and 3 cylinders face downwards and fit Nos. 4 and 2 pistons and liners, using the same procedure as described for Nos. 1 and 3.

11 Fit the pistons on 1600 models (EA71 engine) as follows:

a) Fit circlips into the piston pin bosses (inner side of piston) and position the piston ring gaps as shown in Fig. 1.33. Oil the pistons and rings and fit a piston ring band to compress the rings.

b) Carefully turn the crankshaft until No. 2 connecting rod is at bottom dead center, then insert the piston into the cylinder. Tap the piston with a hammer shaft to push it into the cylinder and free it from the piston ring band. If the same pistons are being refitted ensure that they are being located in their original positions.

c) Push the piston into the cylinder till the piston pin boss protrudes at the bottom. Align the piston pin hole and the small end of the connecting rod and, working thru the front service hole, fit the piston pin and retaining circlip using long nosed circlip pliers.

d) Fit No. 4 piston, piston pin and circlip into the cylinder in the same manner, working through the service hose on the flywheel housing side.

e) Repeat the above procedure for pistons Nos. 1 and 3.

12 Apply liquid gasket sealant to the crankcase plugs, fit new gaskets and tighten the plugs.

13 If the oil strainer was removed at disassembly, fit it with a new O-ring and using an aluminium drift, drive the pipe into the crankcase. Fit the oil strainer stays.

14 Position the crankcase with Nos. 1 and 3 cylinders facing downwards. Ensure that the crankcase and cylinder head faces are clean and fit the cylinder head gasket onto the crankcase. Fit the Nos. 2 and 4 cylinder head. Fit spacers on the two valve rocker shaft studs. Fit and tighten the cylinder head nuts in the sequence shown in Fig. 1.34.

Fig. 1.34. Tightening sequence of cylinder head nuts

22.14b ... and then the cylinder head

22.14c Fit spacers (a socket wrench will do) on the valve rocker shaft studs and tighten the cylinder head nuts with a torque wrench

22.15a Fit the valve push rods in their original positions ...

22.15b ... and then the valve rocker assembly

22.17a Press oil seal into the flywheel housing ...

22.17b ... and fit the flywheel housing to the crankcase

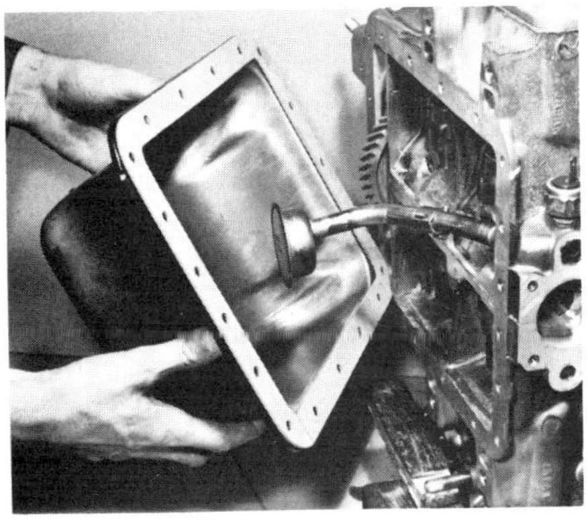
22.18 Fitting the crankcase oil pan

22.19a Fit the flywheel securing bolts

22.19b Restrain the flywheel from turning and tighten the bolts with a torque wrench

22.21 Fit the water pump and by-pass pipe

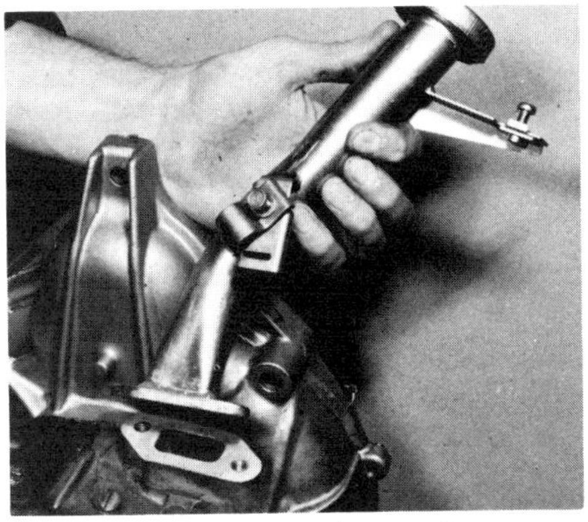
22.22 Fitting the oil filler duct on the crankcase

22.23a Insert a new O-ring on the oil pump ...

22.23b ... and fit the pump to the crankcase

22.24 Fit the distributor drive gear on the crankshaft ...

22.25 ... and then the crankshaft oil seal

22.26a Fitting the crankshaft pulley ...

22.26b ... washer and retaining bolt

22.27 Adjusting the valve clearance

Tighten the nuts in three stages as follows:

1st stage	*14 lb f ft (2.0 kg fm)*
2nd stage	*25 - 29 lb f ft (3.5 - 4.0 kg fm)*
3rd stage	*37 - 43 lb f ft (5.1 - 5.9 kg fm)*

Remove the spacers from the rocker shaft mounting studs.
15 Insert the valve pushrods in their original positions and fit the left-hand valve rocker. Fit and tighten the retaining nuts to 37 - 43 lb f ft (5.1 - 5.9 kg fm). Do not fit washers.
16 Invert the crankcase so that Nos. 2 and 4 cylinders face downwards, remove the cylinder liner retaining device and fit the No. 1 and 3 cylinder head in the same way as described for the No. 2 and 4 cylinder head.
17 Press the oil seal into the flywheel housing and fit the flywheel housing to the crankcase with the mating surface coated with liquid gasket. Make sure the mating surfaces are clean and free of oil and grease before applying the liquid gasket. Take care not to damage the oil seal when fitting the flywheel housing. Fit the engine rear lifting bracket.
18 Fit the crankcase oil pan and transmission cover plate and secure with bolts, spring washers and plain washers. Check the drain plug for tightness.

22.29 Fitting the distributor in the crankcase

22.31 Fitting the alternator mounting bracket

19 Fit the flywheel (manual transmission) or drive plate (automatic transmission) on the crankshaft. It can only be fitted in one position as two bolt holes are offset. Apply liquid sealant to the threads of the flywheel bolts then fit and tighten them to a torque of 30 - 33 lb f ft (4.2 - 4.6 kg fm).
20 Fit the clutch disc and clutch cover as described in Chapter 5, Section 6.
21 Fit the water pump, together with the water pipe elbow, water hose, water pipe, water by-pass hose and water by-pass pipe. Tighten the bolts gradually and evenly to prevent leakage from the joints.
22 Fit the oil filler duct on the crankcase together with the gasket and water by-pass pipe stay.
23 Using a new O-ring and gasket, fit the oil pump with the drive shaft engaged in the end of the camshaft.
24 Fit the distributor drive gear on the front of the crankshaft.
25 Fit the oil seal on the front end of the crankshaft. Oil the seal before fitting and take care not to damage it when pressing it in.
26 Fit the crankshaft pulley on the crankshaft and secure it with the retaining bolt tightened to 39 - 42 lb f ft (5.4 - 5.8 kg fm). Wedge the flywheel to restrain it from turning while tightening the bolt.
27 Adjust the intake and exhaust valve clearances when the engine is cold, coolant temperature between 20°C and 40°C (68° and 104°F). Clearances are important. If they should be too great the valves will not open as fully as they should. They will also open late and close early, this will affect engine performance. If the clearances are too small the valves may not close completely which would result in lack of compression and very soon, burnt-out valves and valve seats. To adjust the valves proceed as follows:

a) Set the piston of No. 1 cylinder at top dead center on compression stroke. To do this turn the engine over, use a wrench on the crankshaft pulley bolt, and with a finger over No. 1 cylinder spark plug hole to check that there is compression, bring the 'O' mark on the flywheel up to the pointer on the housing.
b) Insert a feeler gauge between the valve stem and the rocker arm to measure the clearance.
c) To adjust the clearance slacken the locknut and turn the adjusting screw until the specified clearance is obtained. Tighten the locknut while holding the adjuster. After tightening the locknut re-check the clearance.
d) Continue to check the other clearances, the order is 3 - 2 - 4 which is the firing order. To bring the No. 3 piston to TDC of its compression stroke, rotate the crankshaft 180°. Repeat for Nos. 2 and 4.
e) The valve clearances for the different models are specified in Specifications at the beginning of this Chapter.

28 Fit the valve rocker cover gasket, valve rocker cover, seal washers and securing bolts.
29 Fit the distributor and adjust the ignition timing as described in Chapter 4.
30 Fit the spark plugs and tighten to torque of 13 - 17 lb f ft (1.8 - 2.4 kg fm).
31 Fit the alternator mounting bracket on the crankcase and cylinder head.
32 Fit the intake manifold and carburetor assembly as described in Chapter 3.
33 Fit the alternator and adjust the drive belt tension as described in Chapter 10.
34 Engage the wiring harness on the support on the oil filler duct and to the clip on the water pipe. Connect the harness lead to the oil pressure switch.
35 Connect the EGR pipe (if so equipped) to the intake manifold and cylinder head.

23 Manual transmission - refitting to engine

1 If the engine and transmission was removed as a single unit the transmission must now be refitted to the engine.
2 Check that the clutch disc has been properly centralized with the spigot bearing in the crankshaft and offer up the transmission to the engine, holding it square to avoid putting any strain on the transmission main shaft. An assistant can help by turning the engine over slowly, using a wrench on the crankshaft pulley nut, to allow the splines of

the clutch disc and input shaft to line-up and engage. Push the transmission into place on the mounting studs.
3 Fit the securing nuts and tighten to 34 - 40 lb f ft (4.7 - 5.5 kg fm).
4 Fit the starter motor.

24 Automatic transmission - refitting to engine

1 Offer up the transmission with torque converter to the engine.
2 Fit the transmission to engine securing nuts.
3 Fit the four bolts that secure the torque converter to the drive plate, by working thru the timing hole in the engine casing and rotating the engine as necessary. Take care when fitting the bolts not to drop them into the housing.
4 Tighten the drive plate to converter bolts and the transmission to engine securing nuts.
5 Fit the starter motor.

25 Refitting the engine in the car

1 Refitting of the engine or engine/transmission in the car is the reverse of the removal procedure.
2 On FF-1 models before fitting the DOJ, fit the parking brake cable, and apply the brake. After the engine/transmission is fitted, top up the brake hydraulic system and bleed the brakes as described in Chapter 9.
3 When refitting the horizontal damper refer to Fig. 1.35 and adjust to dimension shown for FF-1 models. For adjustment of the horizontal damper on 1972 - 77 models refer to Fig. 1.36 and proceed as follows:

a) Tighten the nut (1) completely.
b) Turn the nut (6) until the clearance between washer (2) and rubber (3) is zero.
c) Fit the bushing (4) and then tighten the nut (5) to a torque of 7 - 10 lb f ft (0.9 - 1.4 kg fm).
d) For 4WD models, tighten the bolts at the stiffeners to the torque shown in Fig. 1.37.

4 When connecting the axle shafts to the transmission drive shafts, align the DOJ paint mark and the chamfered side of the drive shaft pin hole, and then fit a new spring pin.
5 Check that all the wiring and control cables are connected.
6 Fill the cooling system with coolant described in Chapter 2.

23.2 Assembling the transmission to the engine

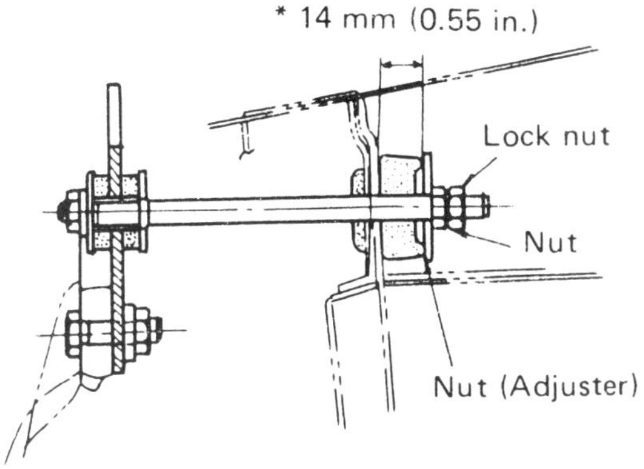

Fig. 1.35. Adjusting the horizontal damper (FF-1 models)

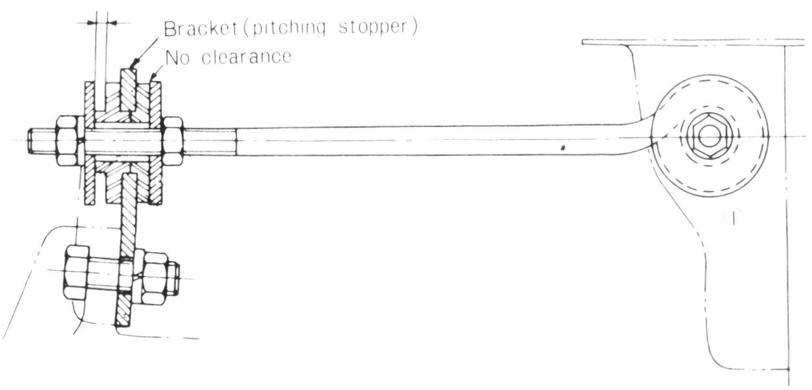

Fig. 1.36. Adjusting the horizontal damper (1972-1977 models)

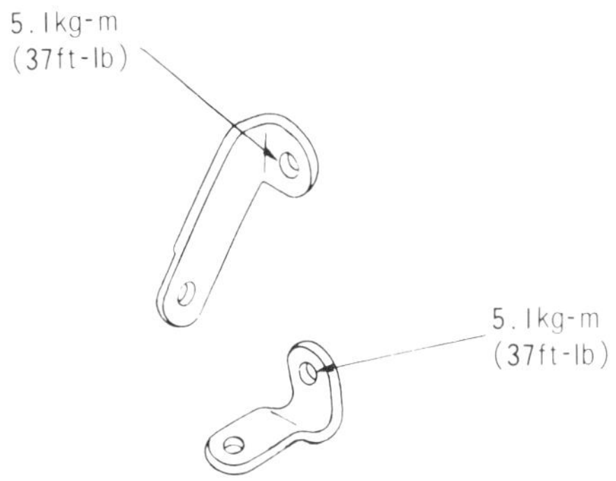

Fig. 1.37. Tightening the stiffeners (4WD models)

7 Refill the engine oil pan with the correct grade and quantity of oil.
8 Refill the transmission with gear oil, through the dipstick/filler tube, to the correct level.

26 Engine - initial start-up after major repair

1 Make a final visual check to see that everything has been connected and that no loose rags or tools have been left in the engine compartment.
2 Make sure that the battery is fully charged and that all lubricants, coolant and fuel are replenished.
3 Start the engine. As soon as the engine fires and runs, keep it going at a fast idle and bring it to normal operating temperature. As the engine warms up there will be odd smells and some smoke from parts getting hot and burning off oil deposits.
4 Check for water, fuel or oil leaks. Check the exhaust system for leaking exhaust gases.
5 When the engine has reached normal operating temperature, adjust the idling speed as described in Chapter 3.
6 Road test the car and check that the timing is correct and that the car runs smoothly. Do not race the engine. If new bearings have been fitted it should be treated as a new engine and run-in at reduced speed for the first 500 miles (800 km). After 500 miles change the engine oil.

27 Engine front mounting rubber (1972 - 77 models) - renewal

1 Disconnect the ground cable from the negative (—) terminal of the battery.
2 Remove the horizontal damper as described in Section 5.
3 Disconnect the exhaust pipe from the engine and the pipe support bracket from the transmission.
4 Unscrew the nut securing the front mounting rubber and heat insulating plate to the crossmember.
5 Hoist the engine to take the weight without straining other parts and remove the bolts attaching the mounting bracket to the engine.
6 Remove the engine mounting rubber, and spacer (4WD) by unscrewing the nut. Renew the mounting rubber.
7 After refitting the mounting rubber, with the spacer (4WD model) fitted between the mounting bracket and rubber, fit them to the engine and remount the engine on the crossmember. Tighten the nuts to 14 - 22 lb f ft (2 - 3 kg fm).
8 The front mounting is provided with a stopper plate, make sure that the mounting rubber is fitted correctly. When placing the mounting rubber on the crossmember make sure that the rubber is adjoining, but not on the stopper plate, see Fig. 1.38 and insert the heat insulating plate between the mounting rubber and crossmember.
9 Connect the exhaust pipe to the engine and fit the pipe support bracket to the transmission.
10 Refit the horizontal damper as described in Section 25.
11 Connect the battery ground cable to the negative (—) terminal of the battery.

28 Engine rear mounting rubber (1972 - 77 models) - renewal

1 Disconnect the ground cable from the battery negative (—) terminal.
2 Loosen the horizontal damper, disconnect the exhaust pipe from the engine and remove the exhaust pipe support bracket from the transmission.
3 Remove the nuts securing the rear mounting rubber to the rear crossmember. Disconnect the gear shift system.
4 Jack up the transmission as far as possible without applying stress to other parts. Unscrew the bolt attaching the rear mounting rubber to the mounting bracket and pull the bolt towards the right.
5 On 4WD models, unscrew the two bolts attaching the mounting rubber to the transmission casing.
6 Fit a new rear mounting rubber. Fit the bolt securing the rear mounting rubber to the mounting bracket and tighten it to 14 - 22 lb f ft (2 - 3 kg fm). On 4WD models, fit the rear mounting rubber to the transmission casing with two bolts. Don't forget to fit the plate between the left-hand mounting rubber and the casing, see Fig. 1.39.
7 Fit the mounting rubber securing bolts onto the holes in the rear crossmember and tighten the nuts to 14 - 22 lb f ft (2 - 3 kg fm).
8 Connect the exhaust pipe to the engine and fit the exhaust pipe support bracket to the transmission.
9 Adjust the horizontal damper as described in Section 25 and connect the ground cable to the battery terminal.

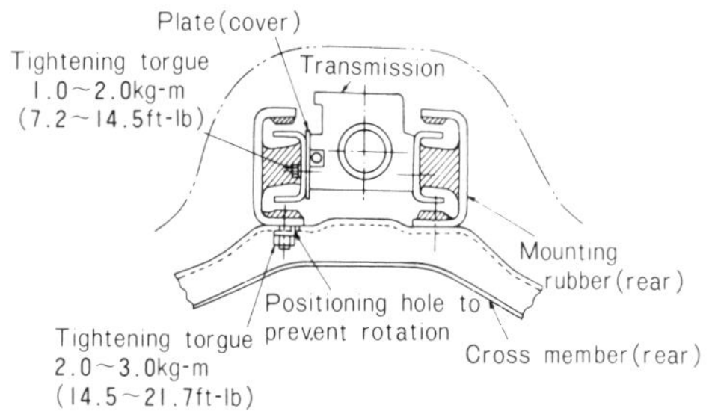

Fig. 1.38. Fitting the front mounting rubber

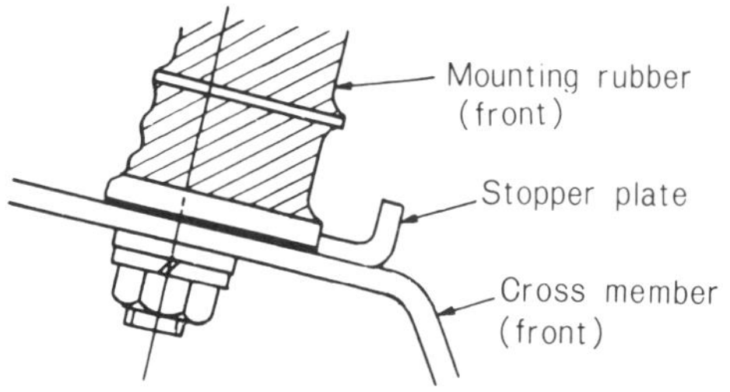

Fig. 1.39. Rear engine mounting rubber (4WD)

25.7 Do not forget to refill the engine oil pan

25.8a Transmission dipstick/filler tube

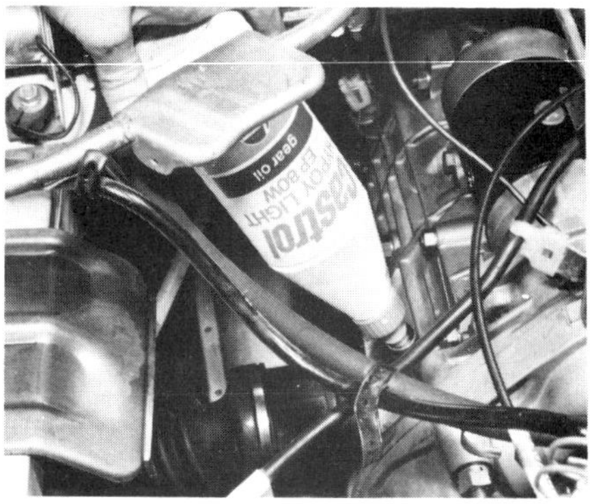

25.8b Replenish the transmission with hypoid gear oil

29 Fault diagnosis - engine

When investigating starting and uneven running faults do not be tempted into snap diagnosis. Start from the beginning of the check procedure and follow it thru. It will take less time in the long run. Poor performance from an engine in terms of power and economy is not normally diagnosed quickly. In any event the ignition and fuel systems must be checked first before assuming any further investigation needs to be made.

Symptom	Reason/s	Remedy
Engine will not turn over when starter switch is operated	Battery discharged Bad battery connections Bad connections at solenoid switch and/or starter motor	Check that battery is fully charged and that all connections are clean and tight.
	Starter motor jammed	Rock car back and forth with a gear engaged. If ineffective remove starter.
	Defective solenoid	Remove starter and check solenoid.
	Starter motor defective	Remove starter and overhaul.
Engine turns over normally but fails to fire and run	No spark at plugs	Check ignition system according to procedures given in Chapter 4.
	No fuel reaching engine	Check fuel system according to procedures given in Chapter 3.
	Too much fuel reaching the engine (flooding)	Slowly depress the accelerator pedal to floor and keep it there while operating starter motor until engine fires. Check fuel system if necessary as described in Chapter 3.
Engine starts but runs unevenly and mis-fires	Ignition and/or fuel system faults	Check the ignition and fuel systems as though the engine had failed to start.
	Incorrect valve clearances	Check and reset clearances.
	Burnt out valves	Remove engine and examine and overhaul as necessary.
Lack of power	Ignition and/or fuel system faults	Check the ignition and fuel systems for correct ignition timing and carburetor setting.
	Incorrect valve clearances	Check and reset the clearances.
	Burnt out valves	Remove engine and examine and overhaul as necessary.
	Worn out piston or cylinder bores	Remove engine and examine pistons and cylinder bores. Overhaul as necessary.
Excessive oil consumption	Oil leaks from crankshaft oil seals, rocker cover gasket, oil pump, drain plug gasket	Identify source of leak and repair as appropriate.
	Worn piston rings or cylinder bores resulting in oil being burnt by engine. Smoky exhaust is an indication	Fit new rings - or rebore cylinders and fit new pistons, depending on degree of wear.
	Worn valve guides and/or defective valve stem seals	Remove engine and recondition valve stem bores and valves and seals as necessary.
Excessive mechanical noise from engine	Wrong valve to rocker clearances	Adjust valve clearances.
	Worn crankshaft bearings	Inspect and overhaul where necessary.
	Worn cylinders (piston slap)	Inspect and overhaul where necessary.
Unusual vibration	Misfiring on one or more cylinders	Check ignition system.
	Loose mounting bolts	Check tightness of bolts and condition.
	Horizontal damper loose or incorrectly adjusted	Check and re-adjust as necessary.

Chapter 2 Cooling, heating and exhaust systems

Contents

Specifications

Cooling system type		
FF-1 models	Dual radiator with forced cooling water circulation	
All other models except 4WD	Electric fan and forced cooling water circulation	
4WD models	Electric fan plus engine driven fan and forced cooling water circulation	
Water pump	Centrifugal impeller type	
Radiator	Corrugated fin type	
Thermostat	Wax type	
Operating range	*Starts to open*	*Fully open*
1970-74	82°C (180°F)	92°C (197°F)
1975	82°C (180°F)	95°C (203°F)
1976-77	88°C (190°F)	100°C (212°F)
Valve opening pressure of filler cap	11.4 - 14.2 lb/in^2 (0.8 - 1.0 kg/cm^2)	
Thermoswitch operating range	*On*	*Off*
1972-75	90°-94°C (194°-201°F)	86°-90°C (154°-162°F)
1976-77	96°-100°C (205°-212°F)	92°-96°C (198°-205°F)
Coolant capacity	6.3 US quart (6 liters)	

1 General description

1 The cooling system on FF-1 1100 and 1300G models is of a dual-radiator sealed type and consists of a main radiator, sub-radiator and expansion tank. The sub-radiator is equipped with a small electric motor-driven fan. The system layout is shown in Fig. 2.1.
2 When the temperature of the coolant is below 82°C (179°F) the thermostat is closed, the coolant does not flow thru the main radiator but only to the sub-radiator and this shortens the engine warm-up time.
3 When the temperature of the coolant rises to 82°C (179°F) or above, the thermostat opens and the coolant flows thru into the main radiator and the cooling performance is rapidly increased. This is sufficient for normal driving and the temperature is kept between 82° and 92°C (179° and 198°F).
4 When the coolant temperature exceeds 92°C (198°F) because of driving conditions, the thermoswitch on the sub-radiator operates to start the motor-driven fan. This increases the cooling performance of the sub-radiator and the coolant temperature starts to fall. When the coolant temperature drops to 88°C (190°F) the thermoswitch operates to stop the fan and the temperature starts to rise again. Thus during heavy-load or slow-speed driving the temperature range of the coolant is maintained between 88° and 92°C (190° and 198°F).
5 In cold weather the sub-radiator may also be used as a heating source. The warm air sucked through by the motor-driven fan is ducted into the car interior, making the fitting of a separate heater unnecessary.
6 On all later models a single cross-flow type radiator, equipped with an electric motor-driven fan is employed. With this system, cooling ability at idling speed, and warming-up characteristics, are improved. Station Wagons with 4WD are equipped with an engine-driven fan in addition to the electric fan.
7 When the coolant temperature is under 82°C (190°F) coolant

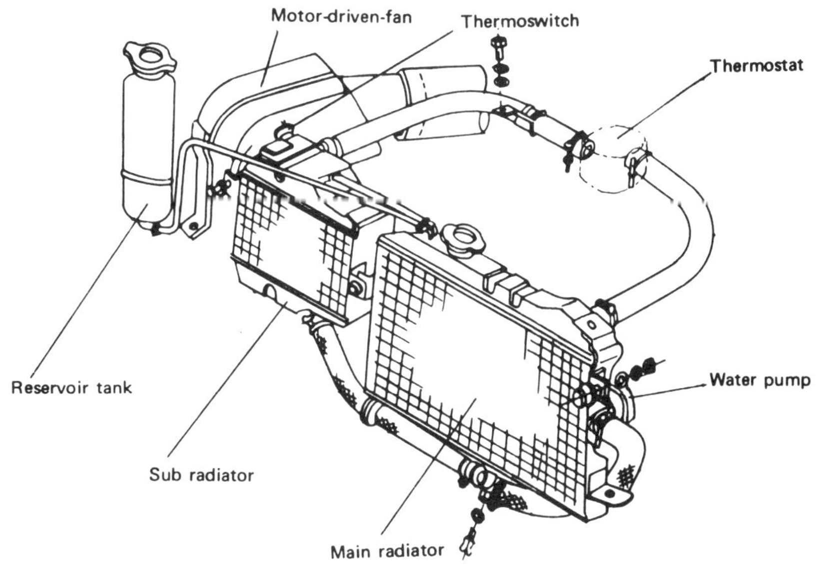

Fig. 2.1. Cooling system - FF-1 1100 and 1300G

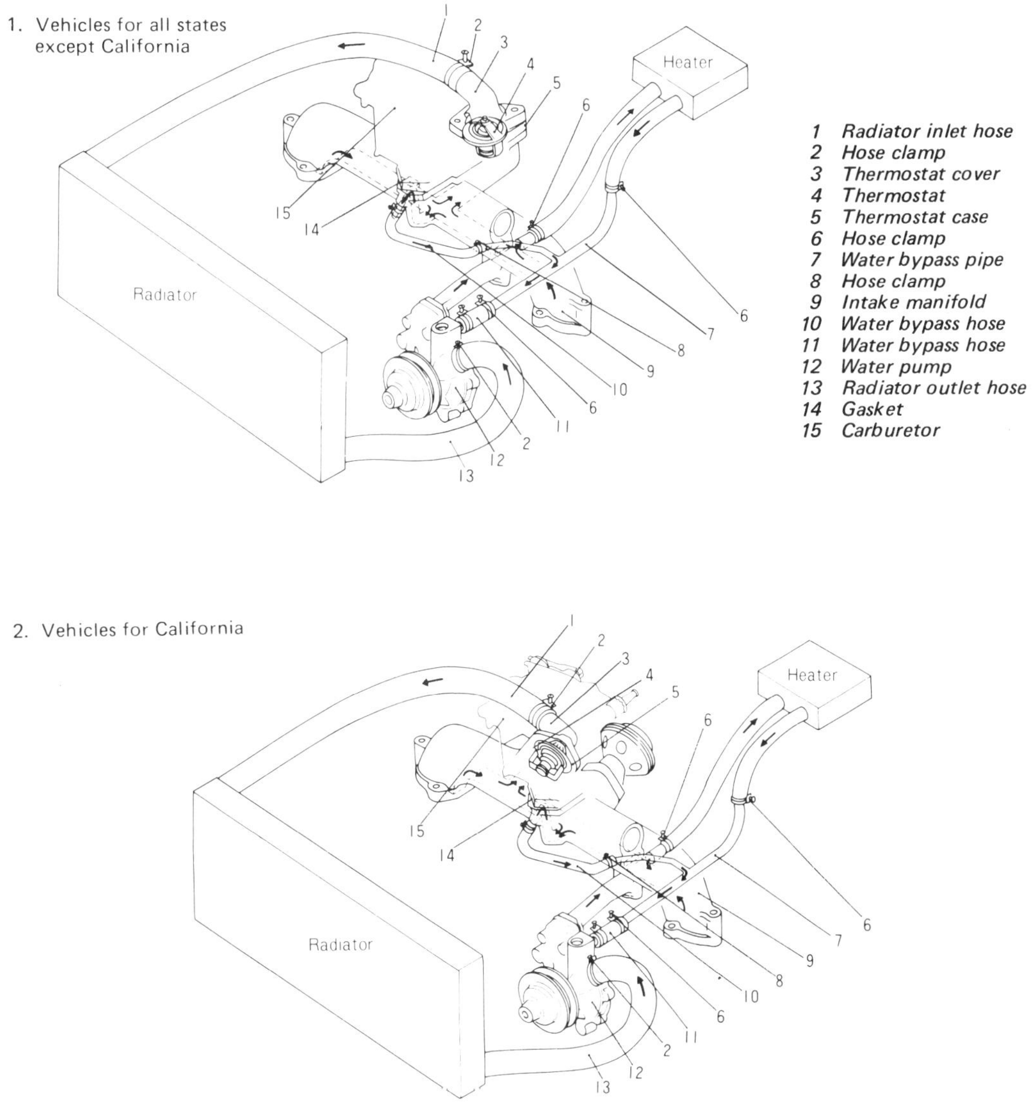

Fig. 2.2. Cooling system - later models

flows only thru the bypass, thus shortening the warm-up time.
When the coolant temperature exceeds 82°C (179°F) the thermostat opens and the coolant circulates thru the radiator.
8 When the coolant temperature exceeds 92°C (198°F) the thermo-switch operates to start the electric fan. This forced air cooling maintains the coolant temperature between 82°C (179°F) and 92°C (198°F). On 1977 models the operating temperature range is between 88° and 98°C (190° and 208°F).
9 On models equipped with automatic transmission an oil cooler is built into the radiator to cool the automatic transmission fluid. Heated oil circulating thru the torque converter returns to the oil cooler and is cooled by the coolant, thus maintaining the oil at an adequate temperature.
10 The heater serves as a converter. As the engine warms, water is circulated to absorb the heat given off by the engine. The heated water passes into the heater core which in turn combines heated air and fresh air which is released into the car interior by operation of the heater controls. The heater can also be used as a defroster by operating the shutter lever which directs heated air into the defrost nozzle.
11 If an air conditioning unit is fitted do not attempt to service any of the air conditioning components, have this work done by your Subaru dealer: if accidentally discharged, refrigerant can cause severe burns and may also result in damage to the air conditioning system.
12 The exhaust systems of early models have an exhaust manifold and a single muffler. On later models the exhaust pipe is connected directly to the cylinder heads and a pre-muffler is fitted in front of the main muffler.

2 Cooling system - draining

1 With the cooling system cold remove the radiator cap (and expansion tank cap on FF-1 models). The radiator cap on the FF-1 models is not a pressure/vacuum cap. Never remove it when the engine is hot. Always remove the expansion tank cap first, after depressing the release button on it to release the pressure from the cooling system.
2 If the coolant has been recently renewed and is to be re-used it should be collected in a container located under the radiator drain plug.
3 Unscrew the drain plug at the bottom of the radiator. Remove the drain plugs from the cylinder blocks.
4 When all the coolant has drained out, probe the drain orifices with a piece of wire to dislodge any rust or sediment which may block the drain hole and prevent complete draining.
5 To drain the expansion tank (FF-1 models), disconnect it from its mounting and hold it above the radiator. The coolant will drain into the radiator and thru the drain hole.

3 Cooling system - flushing

1 Even with proper use, the cooling system will gradually lose its efficiency as the radiator becomes choked with scale deposits from water and other sediment. To clear the system out, remove the radiator cap and drain plugs. Place a water hose pipe into the top of the radiator and flush thru for fifteen minutes.
2 Detach the bottom radiator hose and insert the hose pipe. Make a suitable connection by using different size hoses to step down the radiator outlet. Reverse flush the system for a further fifteen minutes. Cover the engine with polythene sheeting as water will flow out of the radiator cap orifice.
3 After flushing, close the drain holes, fit the bottom radiator hose and refill the system as described in Section 4.

4 Cooling system - filling

1 Set the heater control to the maximum heat position to prevent air locks from developing in the system.
2 Slowly fill the system with coolant.
3 On FF-1 models fill the radiator and the expansion tank till the level reaches the mark on the side of the expansion tank. On other models fill the radiator to the level plate inside the radiator.
4 After filling the system, run the engine for several minutes at fast idle, then check the level, top-up if necessary, and refit the cap.
5 After driving for a short time, check the coolant level again and, if necessary, top-up with coolant.

5 Radiator - removal and refitting

1 Drain the cooling system as described in Section 2.

FF-1 models main radiator

2 Remove the grille. Disconnect the sub-radiator outlet hose, the main radiator outlet hose and the clips from the main and sub-radiator inlet hoses.
3 Remove the main and sub-radiator mounting bolts and pull the

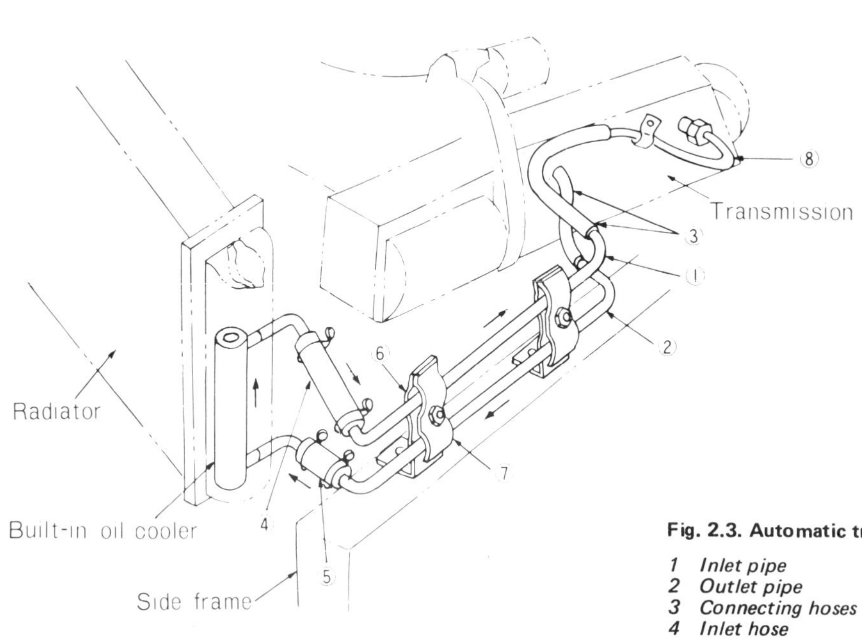

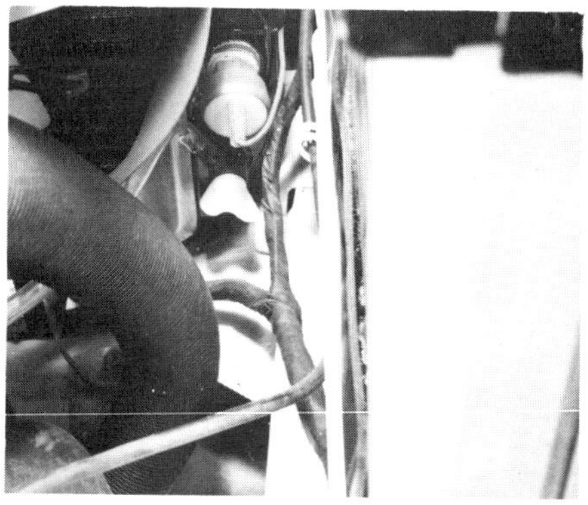

2.3 Radiator drain plug and thermoswitch

Fig. 2.3. Automatic transmission fluid cooling system

1 *Inlet pipe*
2 *Outlet pipe*
3 *Connecting hoses*
4 *Inlet hose*
5 *Outlet hose*
6 *Pipe bracket*
7 *Pipe bracket*
8 *Pipe assembly*

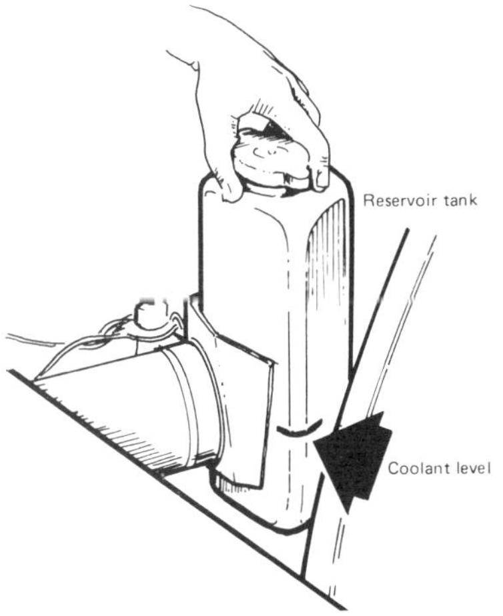

Fig. 2.4. Checking the coolant level - FF-1 models

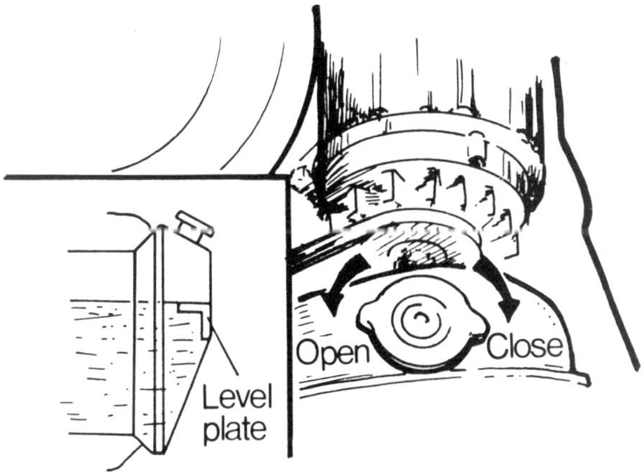

Fig. 2.5. Checking the coolant level - models except FF-1

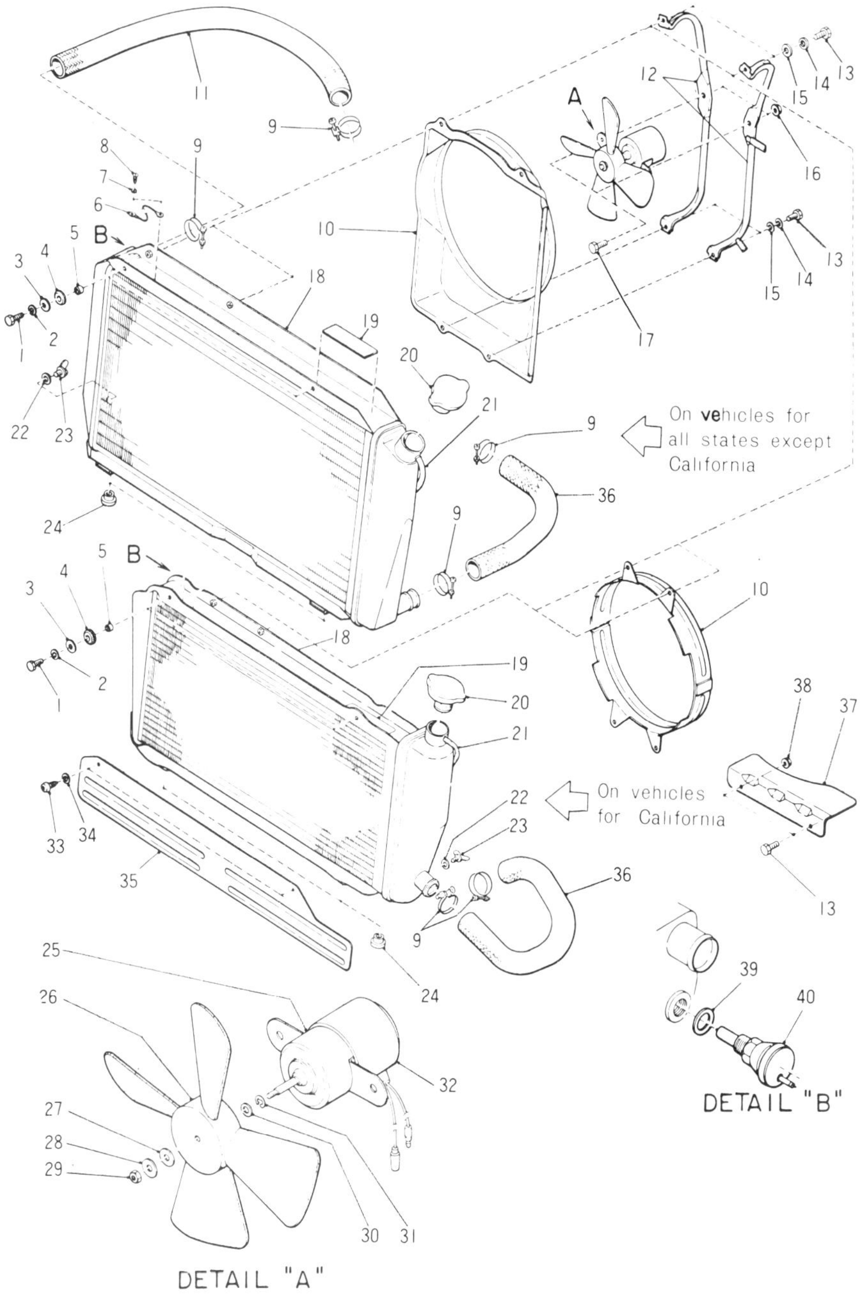

Fig. 2.6. Exploded view of coolant system - 1975 models

1 Bolt
2 Spring washer
3 Washer
4 Grommet
5 Spacer
6 Ground cord
7 Lock washer
8 Tapping screw
9 Hose clamp
10 Shroud
11 Radiator inlet hose
12 Stay (electric fan)
13 Bolt
14 Spring washer
15 Washer
16 Flange nut
17 Bolt
18 Radiator
19 Label
20 Radiator cap
21 Overflow tube
22 Gasket
23 Drain plug
24 Cushion (radiator)
25 Motor
26 Fan
27 Washer
28 Washer
29 Nut
30 Washer
31 Circlip
32 Motor cover
33 Tapping screw
34 Spring washer
35 Plate
36 Radiator outlet hose
37 Protector
38 Flange nut
39 Gasket
40 Thermoswitch

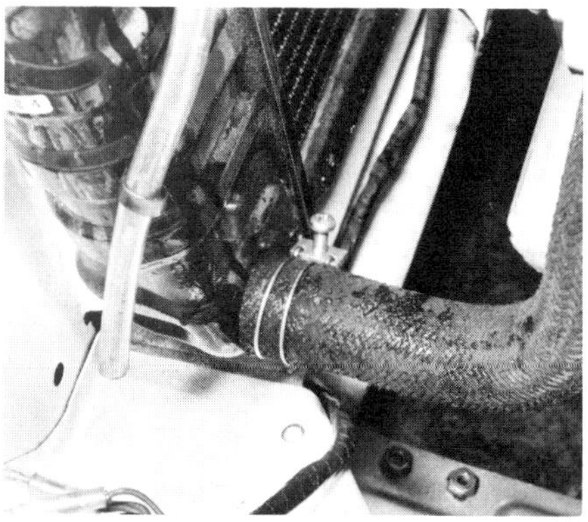

5.7 Disconnect the bottom radiator hose

5.9 Removing the radiator

7.4a Remove the thermostat cover ...

7.4b ... and take out the thermostat

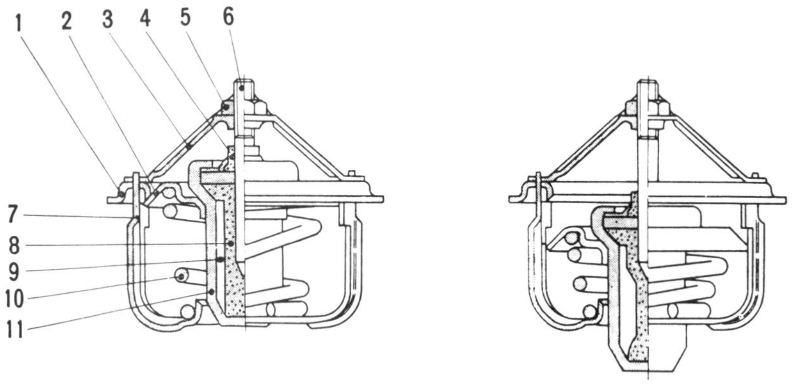

When valve is closed

When valve is opened

Fig. 2.7. Operating diagram of thermostat

1 Seat
2 Valve
3 Supporter
4 Cap
5 Nut
6 Shaft
7 Frame
8 Sleeve
9 Wax
10 Spring
11 Cover

1. Vehicles for all states except California

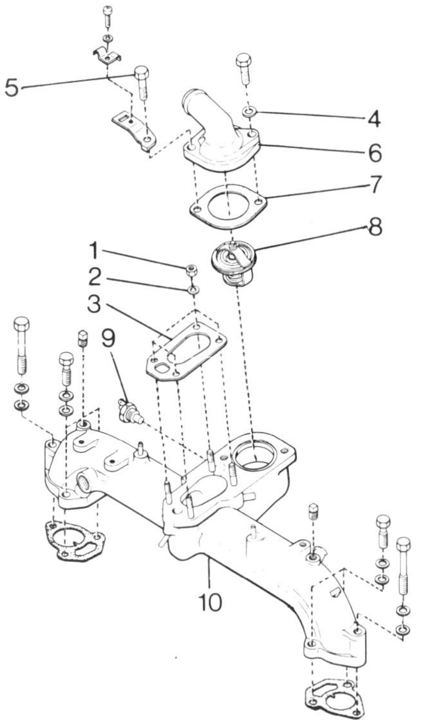

2. Vehicles for California

1 Nut
2 Spring washer
3 Gasket
4 Washer
5 Bolt
6 Thermostat cover
7 Gasket
8 Thermostat
9 Thermometer unit
10 Intake manifold

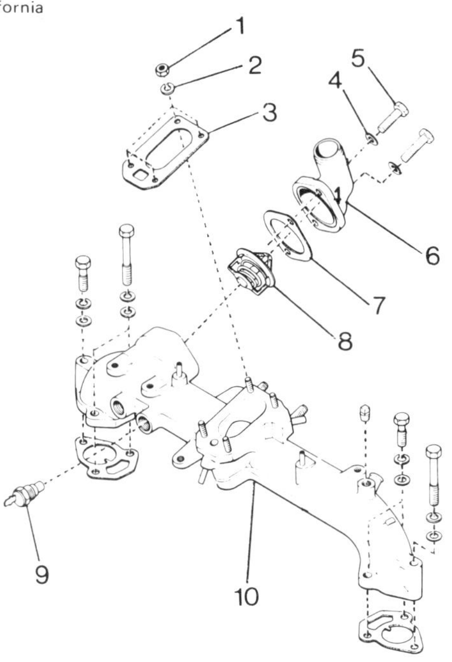

Fig. 2.8. Component parts of intake manifold and thermostat

radiator out and upwards.

F-1 models sub-radiator

4 Remove the front grille.
5 Remove the three bolts retaining the shroud and blower assembly.
6 Remove the sub-radiator mounting bolts and remove the shroud and sub-radiator as an assembly.

All models except FF-1

7 Loosen the hose clips and remove the inlet and outlet hoses from the radiator.
8 Disconnect the following wiring harness:

a) Thermostat and thermoswitch
b) Oil pressure switch
c) Fan motor
d) Secondary terminal of the distributor.

9 Remove the two radiator mounting bolts and lift the radiator out.
10 Separate the fan and motor assembly from the radiator by removing the four securing bolts.
11 Refitting the radiator/s is the reverse of the removal sequence. Fill the system as described in Section 4. Check that all hose joints are water-tight.

6 Radiator - cleaning and servicing

1 Clean the exterior of the radiator by hosing down the matrix with a strong jet of water to remove road dirt, dead flies, etc. Clean out the inside of the radiator by flushing, as described in Section 3.
2 Repair leaks by soldering or with a suitable sealing compound.
3 Inspect hoses for cracks, internal or external perishing and damage caused by over-tightening of the hose clips. Renew any suspect hoses. Examine the hose clips and renew them if they are rusted or distorted.

7 Thermostat - removal, testing and refitting

1 The wax pellet-type thermostat opens and closes its valve with the expansion of the sealed wax, see Fig. 2.7. The temperature characteristics of the thermostat are not changed due to pressure, therefore coolant system pressure can be increased, thereby raising the boiling point of the coolant.
2 Remove the spare wheel (if fitted in the engine compartment) and the air cleaner assembly as described in Chapter 3.
3 Lower the level of the coolant in the engine by opening the radiator drain tap. Collect the coolant in a container for re-use.
4 Remove the thermostat cover retaining bolts, lift off the cover and take out the thermostat. Discard the gasket.
5 If the valve is not closed completely at ambient temperature, a new thermostat is required.
6 To temperature test the thermostat, immerse it in a container of water with a thermometer. Increase the water temperature gradually and note the temperature at which the valve begins to open and that at which it is fully open. During the test, agitate the water to ensure even temperature distribution.
7 Compare the noted temperatures with those given in Specifications at the beginning of this Chapter and if they differ considerably the thermostat must be renewed.
8 Usually when the thermostat fails, it remains closed. This results in overheating, and if you are unable to renew it immediately you should remove it and run the car without it, but be sure to renew it as soon as possible as the engine will be operating below its optimum efficiency without it.
9 Refitting is the reverse of the removal sequence. Ensure that the thermostat is fitted the correct way round, refer to Fig. 2.8.

8 Water pump - removal and refitting

1 Drain the cooling system as described in Section 2.
2 Loosen the alternator mounting bolts to release the tension of the drivebelt and then remove the belt.
3 Disconnect the radiator outlet hose and the bypass hose from the water pump.
4 Unscrew the five securing bolts and remove the water pump.
5 Refitting is the reversal of the removal procedure. Adjust the drivebelt tension as described in Chapter 10, Section 8. Refill the cooling system as described in Section 4, run the engine and check that there is no abnormal noise.

9 Water pump - dismantling, inspection and reassembly

1 If the water pump is leaking or shows signs of excessive side movement of the shaft, or is noisy, it can be dismantled and serviced by renewal of defective parts. Before commencing any dismantling, check on availability of spare parts and of a press. You may consider it better to fit a reconditioned pump.

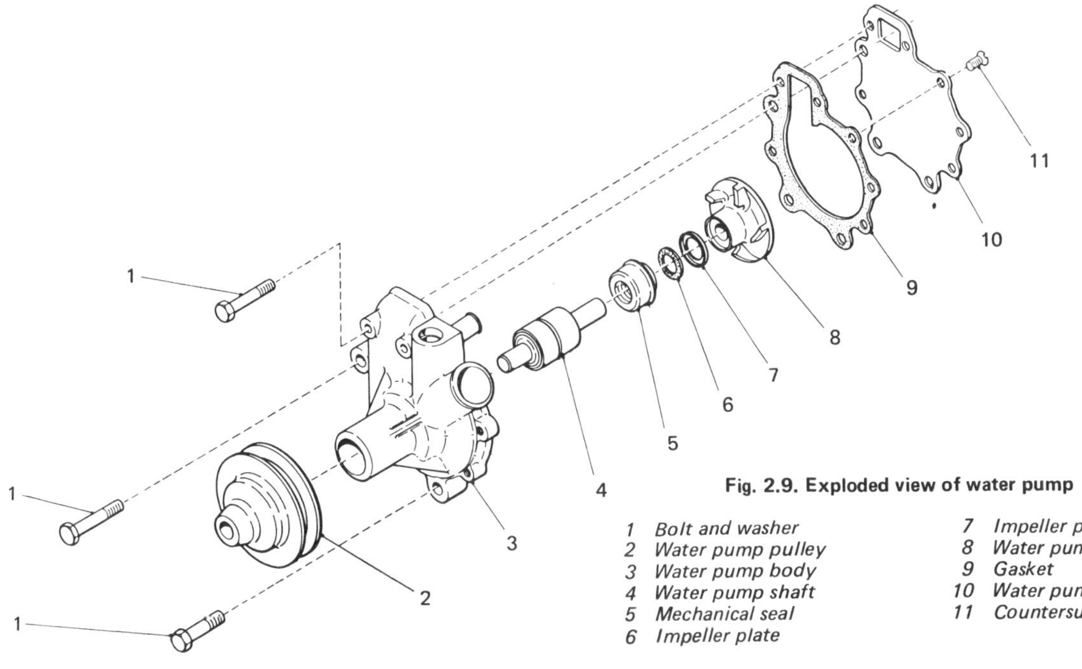

Fig. 2.9. Exploded view of water pump

1 Bolt and washer
2 Water pump pulley
3 Water pump body
4 Water pump shaft
5 Mechanical seal
6 Impeller plate
7 Impeller plate seat
8 Water pump impeller
9 Gasket
10 Water pump plate
11 Countersunk screw

Fig. 2.10. Checking the water pump plate for warp

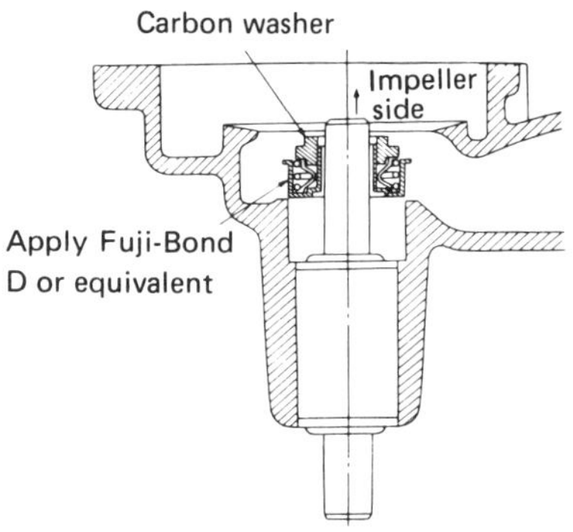

Fig. 2.11. Fitting the mechanical seal

Fig. 2.12. Checking the clearance between the impeller and pump body

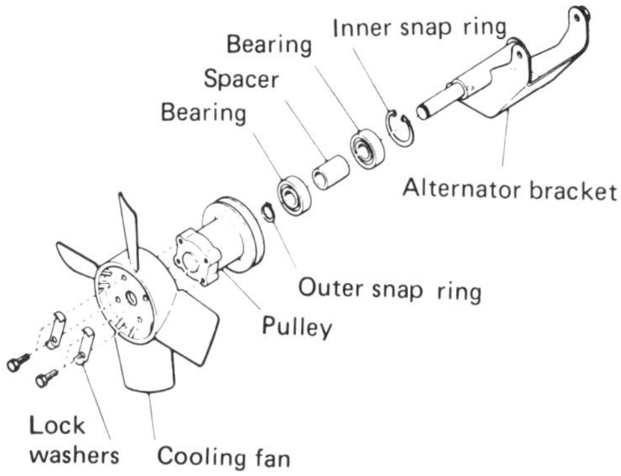

Fig. 2.13. Component parts of engine cooling fan (4WD)

2 Remove the four screws and detach the water pump plate and gasket.
3 Remove the water pump pulley.
4 Remove the shaft from the water pump body, together with the impeller and mechanical seal. Do not press the shaft or the bearings will be damaged, press on the bearing outer race.
5 Remove the impeller from the shaft.
6 Remove the mechanical seal from the shaft.
7 Clean all the disassembled parts thoroughly.
8 Inspect the pump shaft for wear and damage.
9 Inspect the carbon washer of the mechanical seal for wear and damage, and the spring for deterioration.
10 Inspect the impeller surface that contacts the mechanical seal for wear and damage.
11 Check the water pump plate for flatness; maximum warping must not exceed 0.008 in (0.2 mm).
12 Always renew the mechanical seal and gasket at reassembly.
13 Heat the pump body to approximately 90°C (194°F) before fitting the shaft into the pump body using a press. Do not press the shaft or the bearing will be damaged. Press the bearing outer race.
14 Apply liquid gasket sealant to the periphery of the mechanical seal and press the seal into the body with the carbon washer facing the impeller.
15 Smear a thin coat of silicone grease on the shaft surface and press the impeller onto the shaft to give an impeller-to-pump-body clearance of 0.020 to 0.028 in (0.5 to 0.7 mm). Measure the clearance with a feeler gauge as shown in Fig. 2.12.
16 Support the impeller end of the pump shaft and press on the pulley until the distance between the pump body surface, which mates with the plate, and the center of the belt groove of the pulley is 2.34 to 2.37 in (59.5 to 60.1 mm).
17 Apply liquid gasket sealant to both sides of the gasket and fit the plate and four securing screws.

10 Temperature gauge sender unit

1 The temperature sending unit, which is located in the intake manifold, consists of a thermistor, lead wire, spring, terminal plate and resin body, sealed in a threaded case with a hexagon nut.
2 The thermistor is a kind of semi-conductor like a transistor or diode. The thermistor is warmed by the coolant, and the resistance of the thermistor changes according to the coolant temperature. The current flowing in the temperature gauge is controlled by this resistance. Thus the needle on the gauge, which deflects in proportion to the current, indicates the coolant temperature. As the thermistor resistance also changes with voltage, a voltage regulator is provided to prevent error in the gauge reading due to voltage fluctuation.
3 To remove the sender unit, drain the coolant thru the radiator drain plug until the level falls below the intake manifold. To check this, unscrew the sender unit slightly and check if there is any leakage. When draining is sufficient, close the drain plug. Disconnect the wiring from the sender then unscrew it from the intake manifold.
4 When testing, do not apply battery voltage directly to the temperature gauge or sending unit as these two units are designed to be connected in series. If battery voltage is applied to one of them only the gauge or thermistor may be damaged.
5 The simplest way to test the sender unit is to attach temporary extension leads, one from the tag on top to the lead in the cable harness, the other from the metal part to the vehicle frame, and suspend the sender unit in a container of water which can be heated up to boiling point. Check that the gauge needle rises smoothly as the water temperature rises, finishing well up in the red when the water starts to boil. Do not forget that the boiling point of water in free air is considerably lower than that in a pressurised system.
6 When refitting the sender unit do not forget to top-up the cooling system.

11 Electric fan and motor - removal and refitting

1 Disconnect the wiring from the fan motor.
2 Remove the shroud and motor mounting stays securing bolts and lift out the shroud with the fan and motor assembly.
3 Refitting is the reversal of the removal procedure.

12 Electric fan and motor-servicing

1 Remove the rear cover by undoing the securing screws.
2 Pull the brushes out of their holder. If the brush length is less than 0.39 in (10 mm), they must be renewed.
3 Clean the commutator with a non-fluffy cloth moistened with gasoline. Clean the inside of the brush holder.
4 Check the nut retaining the fan on the motor shaft for tightness. Check the fan blades for damage.
5 Refit the rear cover.
6 If there is any abnormal vibration or noise when the fan is operating, renew the fan and/or motor as necessary.

13 Engine driven fan (4WD) - removal and refitting

1 Loosen the alternator mounting bolts and remove the drivebelt from the fan pulley.
2 Bend back the tabs on the lockplates, remove the four fan securing bolts and take off the fan.
3 Remove the inner snap-ring and the fan pulley.
4 Remove the outer snap-ring and pull off the bearings and spacer.
5 Refitting is the reverse of the removal sequence. Adjust the drive-belt tension as described in Chapter 10, Section 8.

14 Anti-freeze mixture

1 The cooling system should be filled with Subaru Coolant or water mixture (by volume) for the lowest atmospheric anticipated temperature according to the table in Fig. 2.14.
2 The coolant which has rust preventative qualities should be renewed every two years. Use distilled water when mixing the coolant. When topping-up the system this should be done with a mixture of the same proportions to the original in order to avoid dilution.
3 It is advisable to have the specific gravity of the coolant checked at your local dealer every six months.

15 Heater assembly (early models) - removal and refitting

1 Disconnect the ground lead from the negative (—) terminal of the battery.
2 Remove the instrument panel as described in Chapter 12.
3 Drain the cooling system as described in Section 2.
4 Disconnect the heater inlet and outlet hoses on the engine side.
5 Remove the securing screws and lift out the console.
6 Disconnect the electrical wiring from the fan motor and control switch.
7 Disconnect the shutter cable and remove the two air inlet control rods.
8 Remove the heater unit mounting bolts and lift the assembly to the side. Remove the grommet on the firewall at this time then remove the heater unit.
9 Refitting is the reverse of the removal procedure. Pull the heater knob to 'ON' and fill the cooling system as described in Section 4. Run the engine and check for coolant leaks.

16 Heater assembly (later models) - removal and refitting

1 Disconnect the negative terminal of the battery.
2 Drain the coolant as described in Section 2.
3 Disconnect the heater inlet and outlet hoses on the engine side.
4 Remove the console box securing screws and lift out the console.
5 Remove the luggage shelf, and the instrument cluster as described in Chapter 10.
6 Pull out the ventilator knob and remove the center ventilator grille.
7 Disconnect the heater cock cable and the shutter control rod.
8 Disconnect the wiring at the multi-connector.
9 Remove the heater unlt mounting bolts and lift out the heater assembly.
10 Refitting is the reverse of the removal procedure. When connecting the shutter control rod, loosen the screw which connects the air inlet shutter rod to the link and push the link down to the lowest position. Position the air outlet control at 'CIRC' and tighten the screw. To connect the heater cock cable position the knob at 'COOL', pull the heater cock lever towards the driver's side and connect the heater cock cable to the heater cock lever. Locate the heater cock knob in 'WARM' position, push the heater cock lever outwards and then secure the outer cable of the heater cock cable with the clamp.
11 Fill the cooling system as described in Section 4. Run the engine and check for coolant leaks. Check the operation of the heater controls.

Lowest atomospheric anticipated temperature	SUBARU coolant-to-* water ratio (Volume)	Specific gravity					Freezing point
		at 10°C (50°F)	at 20°C (68°F)	at 30°C (86°F)	at 40°C (104°F)	at 50°C (122°F)	
Above –15°C (5°F)	30 to 70	1.047	1.043	1.039	1.034	1.029	–17°C (1.4°F)
Below –15°C (5°F)	50 to 50	1.078	1.072	1.067	1.058	1.055	–36°C (–33°F)

Fig. 2.14. Coolant specification

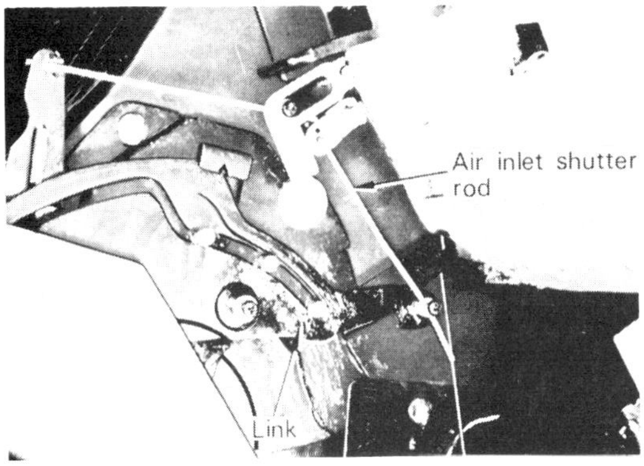

Fig. 2.15. Connecting the heater air inlet shutter rod

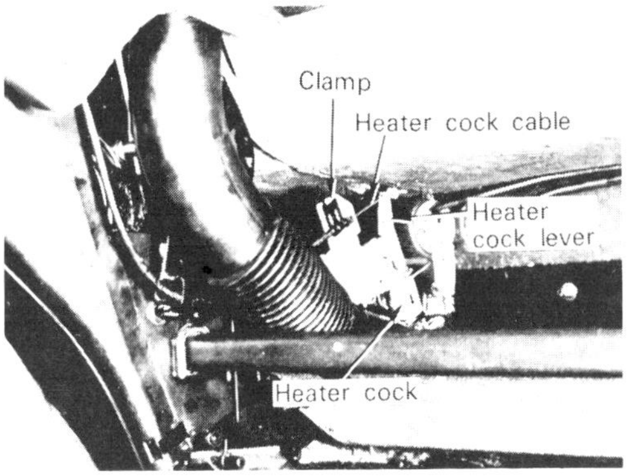

Fig. 2.16. Connecting the heater cock cable

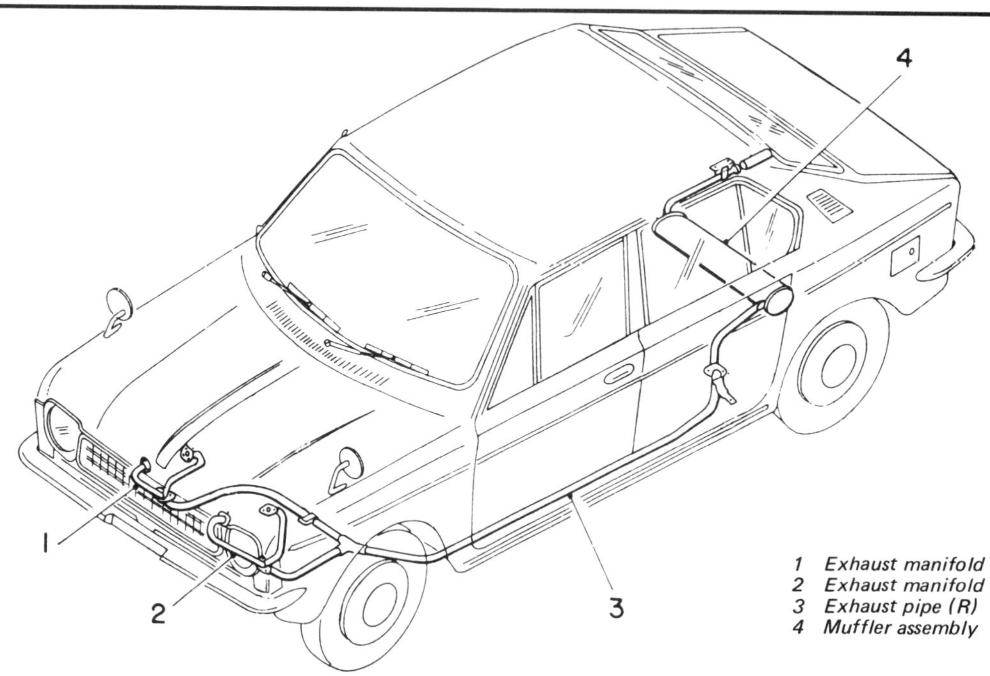

1 Exhaust manifold (RH)
2 Exhaust manifold (LH)
3 Exhaust pipe (R)
4 Muffler assembly

Fig. 2.17. Exhaust system (early models)

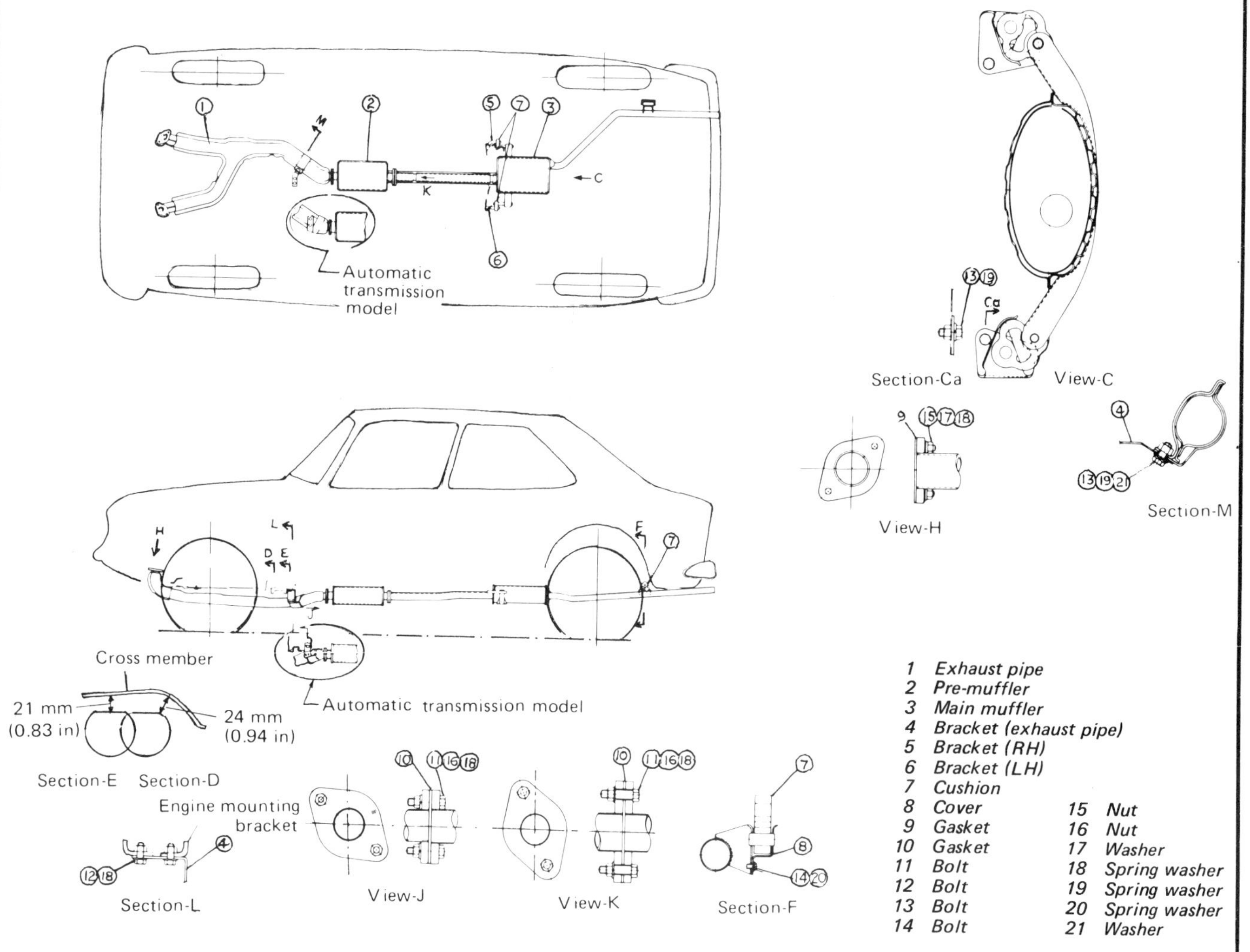

1 Exhaust pipe
2 Pre-muffler
3 Main muffler
4 Bracket (exhaust pipe)
5 Bracket (RH)
6 Bracket (LH)
7 Cushion
8 Cover
9 Gasket
10 Gasket
11 Bolt
12 Bolt
13 Bolt
14 Bolt
15 Nut
16 Nut
17 Washer
18 Spring washer
19 Spring washer
20 Spring washer
21 Washer

Fig. 2.18. Exhaust system (later models) - Sedan, Coupe and Hardtop

17 Exhaust system

1 The exhaust pipe is of double pipe construction. Some of the different system layouts used are shown in Figs. 2.17 to 2.19.

2 Removal and refitting is straightforward. When removing the system, it should be disconnected at the front first.

3 When a leak develops in the exhaust, short term repairs can be made, but this is usually the first sign of general deterioration and it is better to fit a new system complete.

4 When fitting a new exhaust use new clamps and flexible mountings.

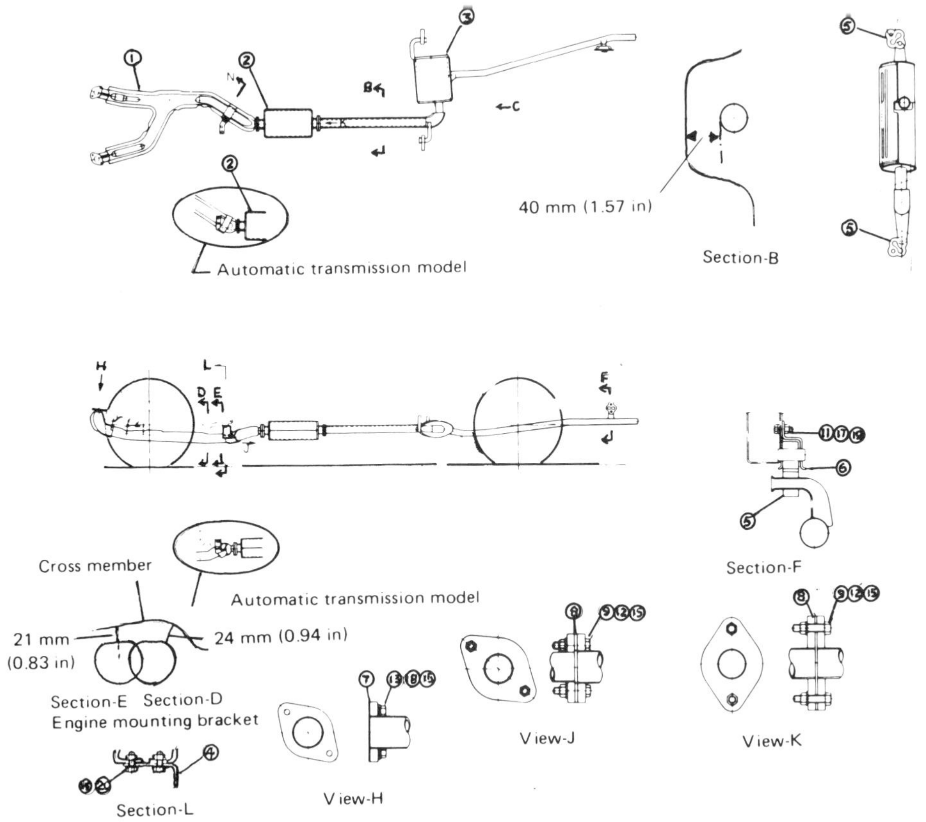
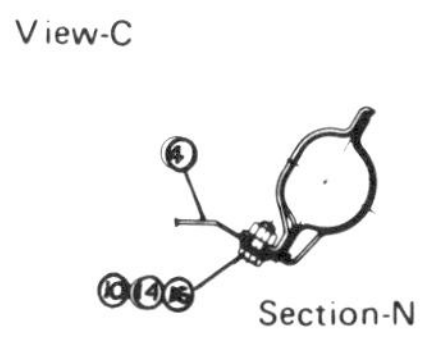

Fig. 2.19. Exhaust system (later models) - Station Wagon

1 Exhaust pipe
2 Pre-muffler
3 Main muffler
4 Bracket (exhaust pipe)
5 Cushion
6 Cover
7 Gasket
8 Gasket
9 Bolt
10 Bolt
11 Bolt
12 Nut
13 Nut
14 Washer
15 Spring washer
16 Spring washer
17 Spring washer
18 Washer
19 Nut
20 Bolt

18 Fault diagnosis - cooling systems

Symptom	Reason/s	Remedy
Overheating	Insufficient coolant	Replenish coolant, inspect for leakage and repair as necessary.
	Loose drivebelt	Adjust belt tension.
	Thermostat defective	Renew.
	Water pump defective	Repair or renew.
	Coolant passages blocked	Clean.
	Ignition timing incorrect	Adjust timing.
	Radiator blocked	Clean out by flushing.
	Incorrect fuel mixture	Adjust fuel mixture.
	Incorrect valve clearance	Adjust.
	Binding brakes	Adjust.
	Malfunction of thermoswitch and/or electric fan	Check and renew as necessary.
Over-cooling	Defective thermostat	Renew.
Loss of coolant	Leaking radiator or hoses	Repair or renew.
	Cylinder head gasket defective	Renew.
	Cylinder liner gasket defective	Renew.
	Leakage from intake manifold or cracked thermostat cover	Repair or renew.
	Radiator cap defective or wrong type fitted	Renew.
Noise	Defective drivebelt	Renew.
	Defective electric fan	Renew.
	Defective water pump bearing and/or mechanical seal	Renew.

Chapter 3 Carburetion; fuel and emission control systems

For modifications, and information applicable to later models, see Supplement at end of manual

Contents

Specifications

Fuel pump

Type	Electromagnetic
Discharge pressure	1.85 - 2.56 lb/in^2 (0.13 - 0.18 kg/cm^2)
Output	More than 7.4 US gal/h (28 l/h)

Fuel tank

Location	Behind rear seat back (except station wagon) Under rear floor (station wagon)

Capacity

	Sedan	Station Wagon
1970 - 71	11.8 US gal (45 litres)	9.5 US gal (36 litres)
1972 - 73	13.2 US gal (50 litres)	9.5 US gal (36 litres)
1974 - 77	13.2 US gal (50 litres)	11.8 US gal (45 litres)

Fuel filter type

In-line, disposable

Air cleaner type

Viscous, disposable paper element

Carburetors

Type ... **Hitachi DCG 286**

	Primary	Secondary
Bore diameter	1.024 in	1.102 in
Venturi diameter	0.32 in	0.28 in
Main jet	88	133
Main air bleed	60	80
Slow jet	43	60
Slow air bleed	200	60
Power jet		

Type ... Hitachi DCG 306 - 18

	Primary	Secondary
Bore	1.024 in	1.181 in
Venturi diameter	0.32 in	0.28 in
Main jet	95	155
Main air bleed	60	90
Slow jet	43	60
Slow air bleed	200	70
Power jet	45	

Type ... Hitachi DCG 306 - 12

	Primary	Secondary
Bore	1.024 in	1.181 in
Venturi diameter	0.32 in	0.28 in
Main jet	96	155
Main air bleed	60	90
Slow jet	43	60
Slow air bleed	200	70
Power jet	45	

Type ... Hitachi DCG 306W - 2

	Primary	Secondary
Bore	1.024 in	1.181 in
Venturi diameter	0.32 in	0.28 in
Main jet	88	130
Main air bleed	90	70
Slow jet	40	80
Slow air bleed	210	160
Power jet	45	

Type ... Hitachi DCJ 306 - 5

	Primary	Secondary
Bore	1.02 in	1.18 in
Venturi diameter	0.32 in	0.28 in
Main jet	93	155
Main air bleed	60	90
Slow jet	43	60
Slow air bleed	200	70
Power jet	45	
Choke mechanism	Automatic	

Type ... Hitachi DCJ 306 - 6

	Primary	Secondary
Bore	1.02 in	1.18 in
Venturi diameter	0.32 in	0.28 in
Main jet	93	155
Main air bleed	60	90
Slow jet	43	60
Slow air bleed	200	70
Power jet	35	

Type ... Hitachi DCJ 306 - 7

	Primary	Secondary
Bore	1.02 in	1.18 in
Venturi diameter	0.32 in	0.28 in
Main jet	103	155
Main air bleed	75	80
Slow jet	45	70
Slow air bleed	20	70
Power jet	45	

Type ... Hitachi DCJ 306 - 8

	Primary	Secondary
Bore	1.02 in	1.18 in
Venturi diameter	0.31 in	0.28 in
Main jet	103	155
Main air bleed	75	80
Slow jet	46	70
Slow air bleed	170	70

Power jet	45	
Type	**Hitachi DCJ 306 - 9**	
	Primary	**Secondary**
Bore	1.02 in	1.18 in
Venturi diameter	0.31 in	0.28 in
Main jet	95	135
Main air bleed	75	80
Slow jet	46	70
Slow air bleed	170	70
Power jet	45	

Idling speed

Engine EA61	600 - 700 rpm
EA62	700 - 800 rpm
EA63 (1972 - 73)	650 - 750 rpm
EA63 (1974)	700 - 800 rpm (at 800 - 900)
EA63 (1975)	750 - 850 rpm (at 850 - 950)
EA63 (1976)	850 - 950 rpm
EA71 (1977)	800 - 900 rpm (49 states) 850 - 950 rpm (California)

1 General description

The carburetors fitted to all Subaru engines are of the down-draft two barrel type, which are capable of supplying the correct air-fuel mixture under all operating conditions. Both the primary and secondary venturi are provided with a throttle valve.

The primary side of the carburetor consists of the main, acceleration and choke system. During normal driving the primary side satisfies all the requirements for the carburetor. The primary low-speed system is an economizer type which provides smooth acceleration and deceleration during light-load driving. It also provides stable idling speed.

The carburetors are provided with a coasting by-pass valve system for controlling exhaust emission during deceleration.

Icing of the throttle bore is prevented by utilizing hot coolant to preheat the throttle chamber.

The fuel system comprises a fuel tank at the rear of the car, an electrically operated fuel pump mounted on the firewall in the engine compartment and a disposable type fuel filter. The pump draws gasoline from the tank and delivers it to the carburetor. The gasoline level in the carburetor is controlled by a float operated needle valve. Gasoline flows past the needle valve until the float rises to a predetermined level and closes the needle valve. The fuel pump then free wheels under slight back pressure until the gasoline level drops in the carburetor float chamber and the needle valve opens.

Various arrangements of the emission control systems are used to control the amount of air pollution caused by the emission of carbon monoxide, hydrocarbons and nitrogen produced by the engine. Three types of emission control systems are used on Subaru models: crankcase emission control, exhaust emission control and fuel evaporation control.

2 Air cleaner element - renewal

1 The standard air cleaner comprises a body in which is housed a paper element type filter, a lid and connecting hoses. On models with a hot air control system a vacuum motor, temperature sensor and drain valve are incorporated in the body.

2 Every 12500 miles (20,000 km) the filter element should be renewed and the hot air control system (if fitted) inspected.

3 Release the clips securing the lid to the body, lift off the lid and remove the filter element.

4 Clean the inside of the air cleaner body and fit a new filter element.

5 Refit the lid and secure with the clips.

3 Fuel filter - renewal

1 The fuel filter is located in the tank to pump fuel line and is mounted on the firewall in the engine compartment. It should be renewed every 12500 miles (20,000 km).

2 Renew the filter by removing the clips and pulling the hoses off the filter. Pull the filter out of its holder, insert a new filter in the holder and refit the fuel hoses.

4 Fuel tank - description, removal and refitting

Sedan, Hardtop and Coupe

1 The fuel tank is located behind the backrest of the rear seat and varies in capacity according to the model. Filter tube, vent pipes and fuel lines are connected to the tank by flexible hoses. The fuel gauge unit is mounted on top of the tank.

2 Disconnect the ground cable from the battery negative (–) terminal.

3 Remove the backrest and cushion of the rear seat, and the rear luggage shelf.

4 Disconnect the delivery pipe from the delivery hose under the body and drain the gasoline into a clean container. Removing the filler cap will allow the tank to drain quicker. After draining blank off the delivery hose.

5 Loosen the securing clips and remove the fuel filter hose. Disconnect the air vent tube and evaporation tube from the fuel tank. Disconnect the lead from the fuel gauge unit.

6 Undo the support securing bolts on each side and the tank securing bolts, accessible from inside the car. Remove the tank by pulling it out of its support bracket.

7 Remove the five screws securing the fuel gauge unit to the top of the tank and lift out the assembly.

8 Clean the tank and check for signs of leakage, rust or damage.

9 Refitting is the reverse of the removal procedure. When fitting the fuel gauge unit apply sealing compound to both sides of the gasket.

Station Wagon and 4WD

10 The fuel tank is located underneath the rear floor. Filler tube, vent pipes and fuel lines are connected to the upper rear corners of the tank by flexible hoses. The fuel gauge unit is mounted on the rear left side of the tank.

11 Disconnect the ground cable from the battery negative (–) terminal.

12 Remove the drain plug from the bottom of the tank and drain the gasoline into a clean container. Remove the filler cap to speed up the draining process. After draining, refit the drain plug.

13 Slacken the hose clip and remove the fuel filler hose from the tank.

14 Loosen the five fuel tank retaining bolts and move the rear of the tank downwards. Now disconnect the evaporation tube and air vent tube from the top of the tank, and the lead to the fuel gauge unit from the side of the tank.

15 Remove the five retaining bolts and lower the tank from under the car.

16 Remove the five nuts securing the fuel gauge unit to the side of

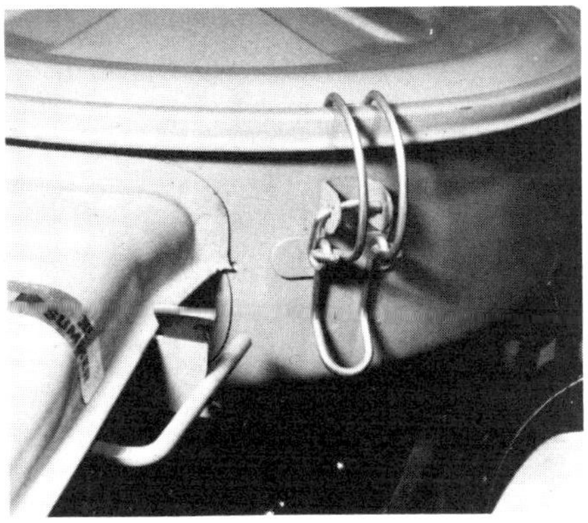

2.3a Release the lid securing clips

2.3b Lift out the air cleaner element

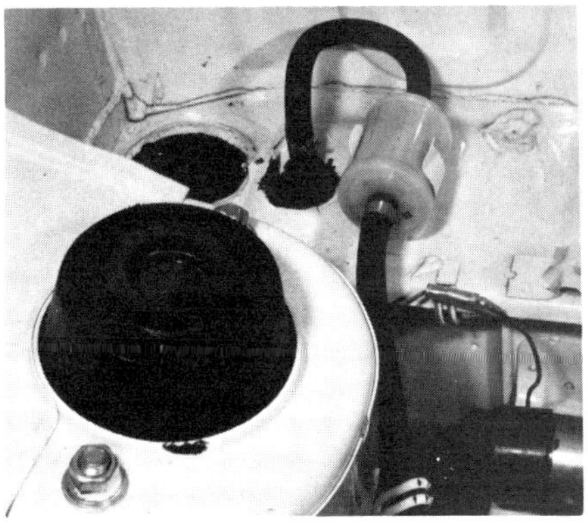

3.1 The fuel filter is mounted on the firewall

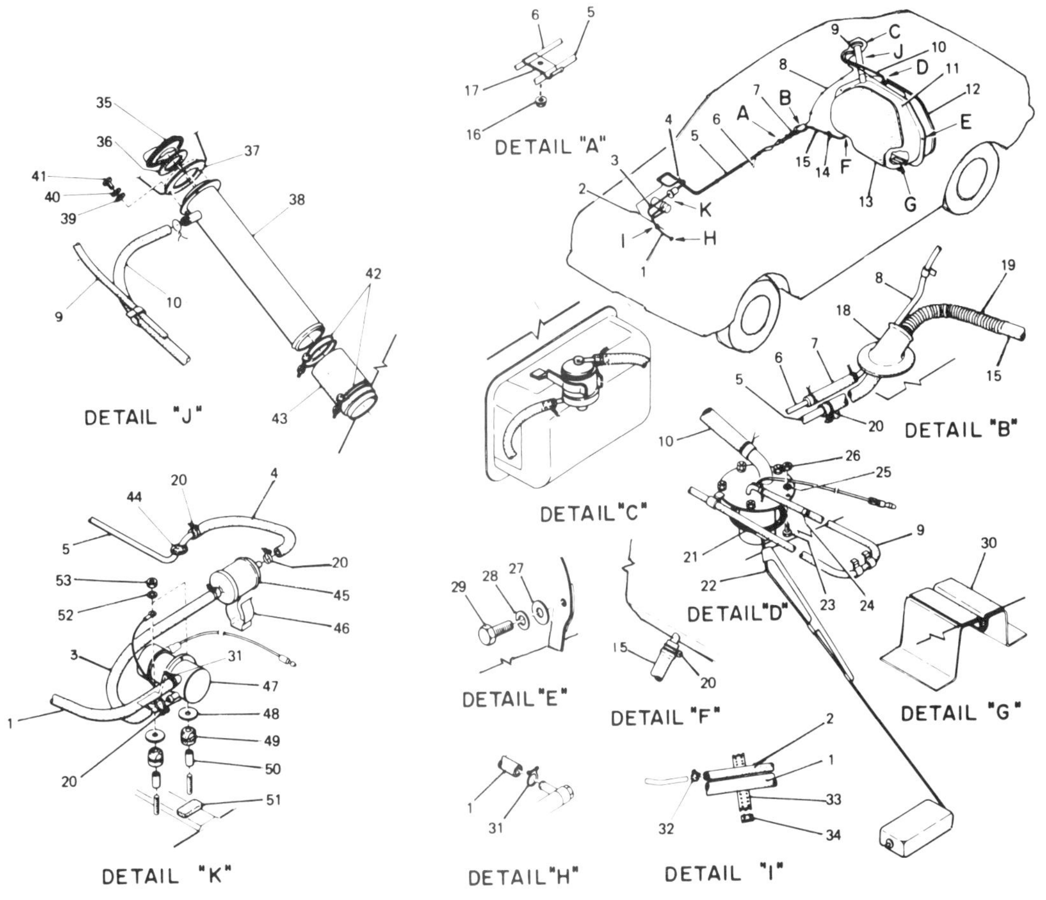

Fig. 3.1. Layout of fuel system (Sedan and Coupe)

1 Hose (pump-carburetor)
2 Tube A (evaporation)
3 Hose (strainer-pump)
4 Hose (pipe-strainer)
5 Pipe (delivery)
6 Pipe A (evaporation)
7 Tube (EEC joint)
8 Pipe B (evaporation)
9 Tube (air breather)
10 Tube (air vent)
11 Fuel tank
12 Insulator A (fuel tank)
13 Insulator B (fuel tank)
14 Grommet (air vent pipe)
15 Hose (tank-pipe)
16 Flange nut
17 Clip (fuel)
18 Grommet (delivery hose)
19 Spring (hose protector)
20 Clip (fuel)
21 Gasket (meter unit)
22 Fuel meter unit
23 Bolt
24 Orifice (air breather system)
25 Spring washer
26 Nut
27 Washer
28 Spring washer
29 Bolt
30 Cushion (fuel tank)
31 Clip (fuel system)
32 Clip
33 Band (air breather hose)
34 Fastener
35 Fuel filler cap
36 Packing (cap)
37 Packing
38 Fuel filler pipe
39 Washer
40 Spring washer
41 Screw
42 Clip
43 Fuel filler hose
44 Grommet
45 Fuel strainer
46 Holder
47 Fuel pump
48 Washer
49 Grommet
50 Spacer
51 Cushion (fuel pump)
52 Spring washer
53 Nut

4.1 The fuel tank is located behind the back seat

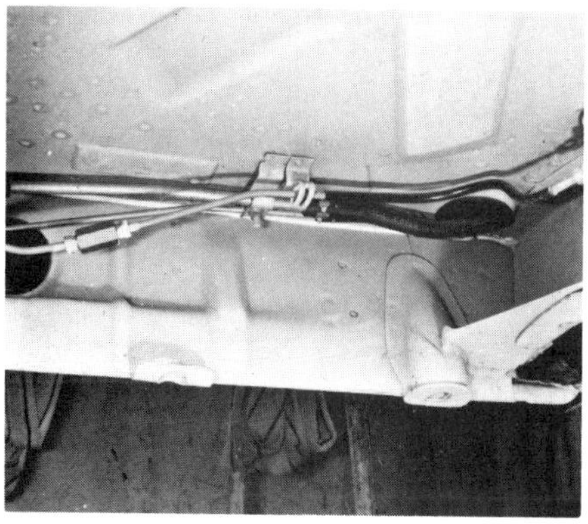

4.4 Disconnect the fuel delivery hose under the body

5.3 The fuel pump is mounted on the firewall

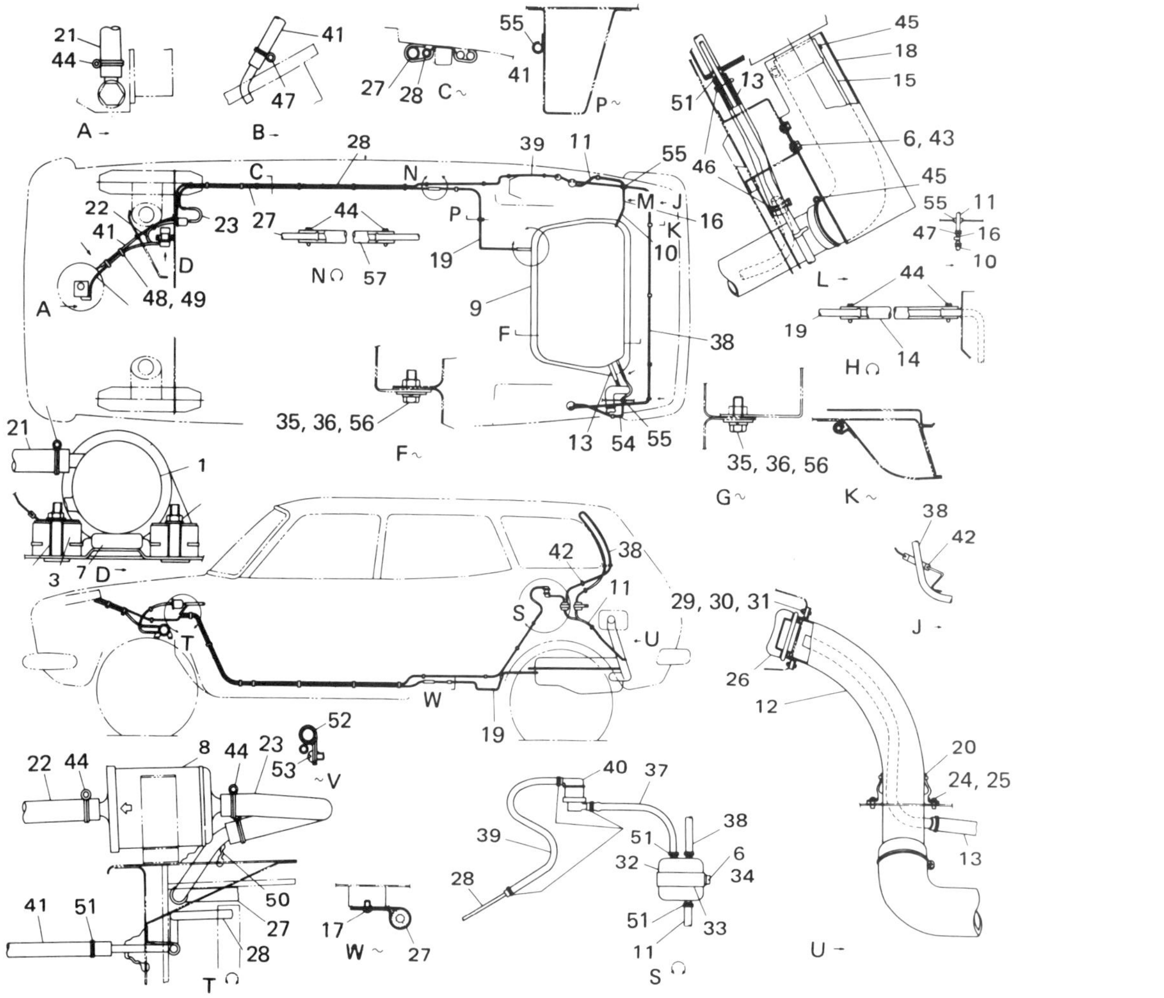

Fig. 3.2. Layout of fuel system (Station Wagon)

1 Fuel pump
2 Pipe (fuel pump)
3 Grommet (fuel pump)
4 Nut
5 Washer
6 Spring washer
7 Cushion
8 Fuel strainer
9 Fuel tank
10 Tube (air breather)
11 Tube (air breather)
12 Filler pipe
13 Hose (air vent)
14 Hose (delivery)
15 Hose (filler)
16 Pipe (air breather)
17 Tapping screw
18 Protector (filler hose)
19 Pipe (delivery) B
20 Grommet (floor)
21 Hose (pump to carburetor)
22 Hose (strainer to pump)
23 Hose (pump to strainer)
24 Tapping screw
25 Washer
26 Cap
27 Pipe (delivery) A
28 Pipe (evaporation)
29 Screw
30 Washer
31 Spring washer
32 Reserve tank
33 Clip (reserve tank)
34 Screw
35 Bolt
36 Washer
37 Tube (air breather)
38 Tube (air breather)
39 Tube (air breather)
40 Overflow limiter
41 Tube (evaporation) A
42 Grommet
43 Bolt
44 Clip (fuel system)
45 Clip (fuel system)
46 Clip (fuel system)
47 Clip (fuel system)
48 Band
49 Fastener
50 Boot
51 Lock wire
52 Clip (earth)
53 Tapping screw
54 Tube (air breather)
55 Grommet
56 Spring washer
57 Hose

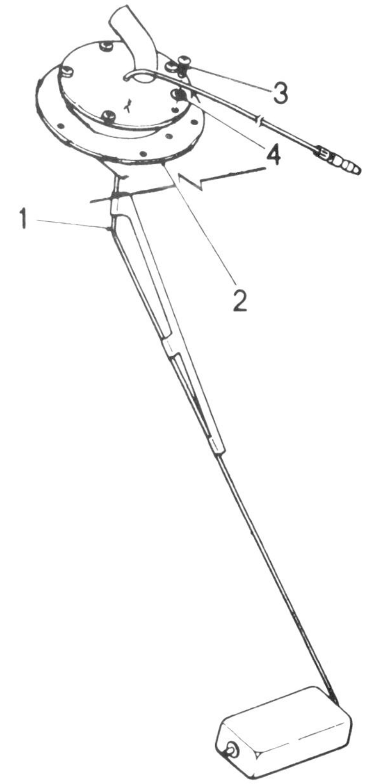

Fig. 3.3. Fuel gauge unit

1 Fuel gauge unit
2 Gasket
3 Screw
4 Spring washer

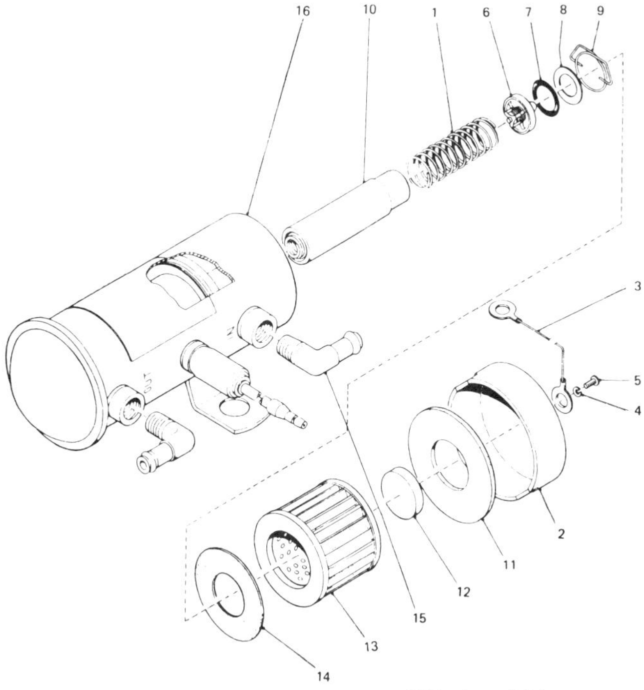

Fig. 3.4. Bendix type fuel pump (FF - 1 models)

1 Plunger spring
2 Cover
3 Grounding wire
4 Spring washer
5 Screw
6 Spring cap
7 O-ring
8 Washer
9 Spring retainer
10 Plunger sub assembly
11 Sediment bowl gasket
12 Cover magnet
13 Filter
14 Gasket
15 Elbow
16 Body (fuel pump)

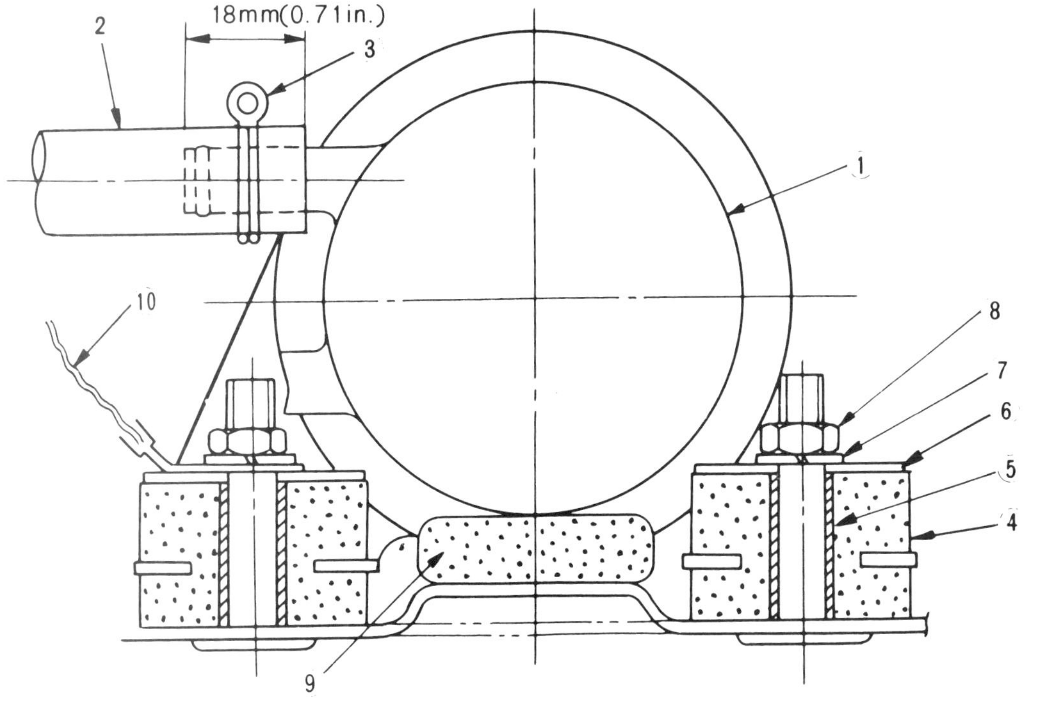

Fig. 3.5. Fuel pump mounting

1 Fuel pump
2 Fuel delivery hose
3 Clip
4 Grommet
5 Spacer
6 Washer
7 Spring washer
8 Nut
9 Cushion (fuel pump)
10 Grounding wire

the tank and lift out the assembly. Take care not to damage the gasket.
17 Clean the tank and check for signs of leakage, rust or damage.
18 Refitting is the reverse of the removal procedure. When fitting the fuel gauge unit, apply sealing compound to both sides of the gasket.

5 Fuel pump - description

On FF-1 1100 and 1300G sedans a Bendix type electromagnetic fuel pump is fitted, all other models employ a diaphragm electro-magnetic type.

The pumps are not repairable and must be renewed when defective. The Bendix type pump has a filter element which can be removed and cleaned or renewed as necessary.

The fuel pump is mounted on the right-hand side of the firewall in the engine compartment and is fitted in the fuel line between the in-line filter and the carburetor.

6 Fuel pump - removal and refitting

1 Remove the spare wheel, if fitted, from the engine compartment.
2 Remove the clamps and pull the fuel lines off the pump. Disconnect the electrical leads from the pump.
3 Remove the pump securing nuts and then the fuel pump.
4 Refitting is the reverse of the removal procedure. Fit the ground lead between the washers as shown in Fig. 3.5.

7 Fuel pump - testing

Having checked that the fuel lines are not kinked or blocked and that all connections are tight, the pump operation can be tested by disconnecting the fuel pipe at the carburetor inlet and with a suitable container in position to catch the ejected fuel, switch on the ignition. A steady pulsating supply of fuel should emerge from the delivery pipe.

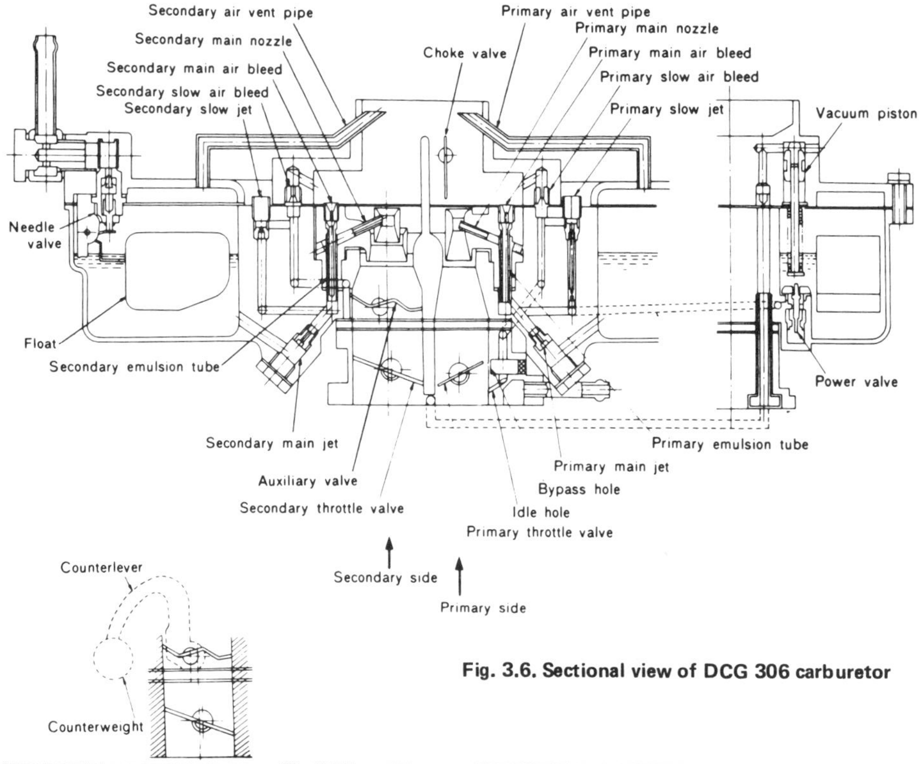

Fig. 3.6. Sectional view of DCG 306 carburetor

8.1 The carburetor fitted on the engine (1976 model)

8.8 The anti-dieseling valve is screwed into the float chamber casting

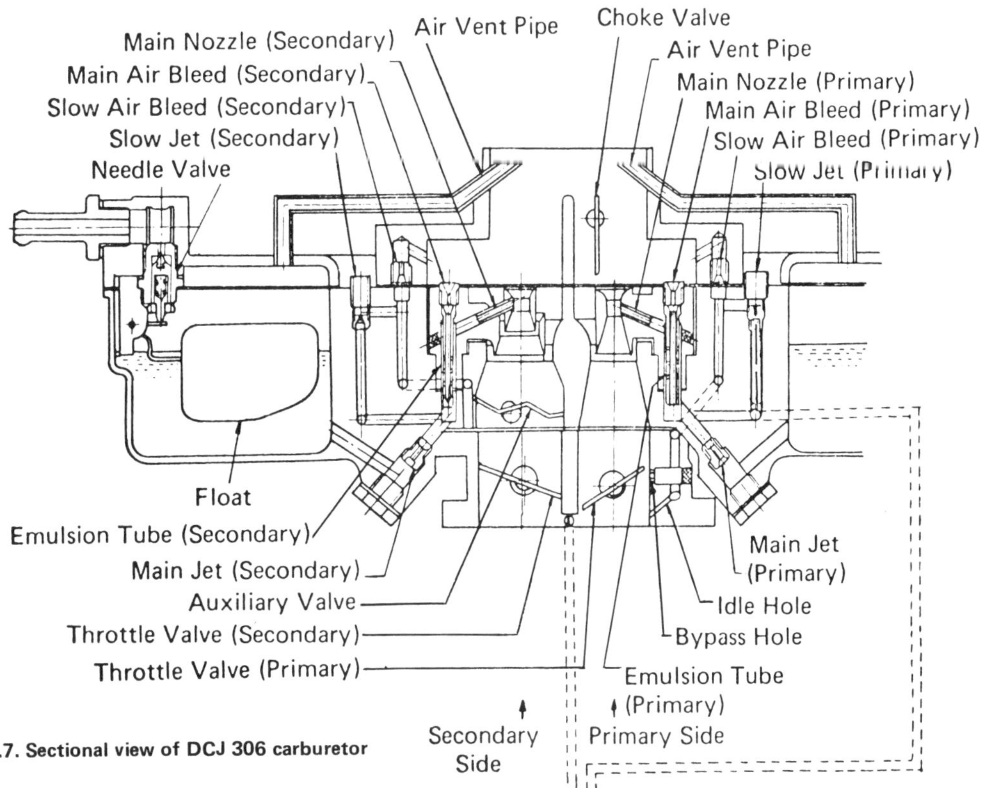

Fig. 3.7. Sectional view of DCJ 306 carburetor

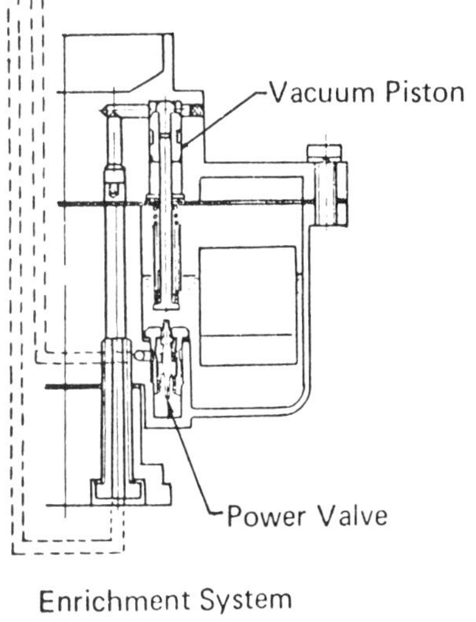

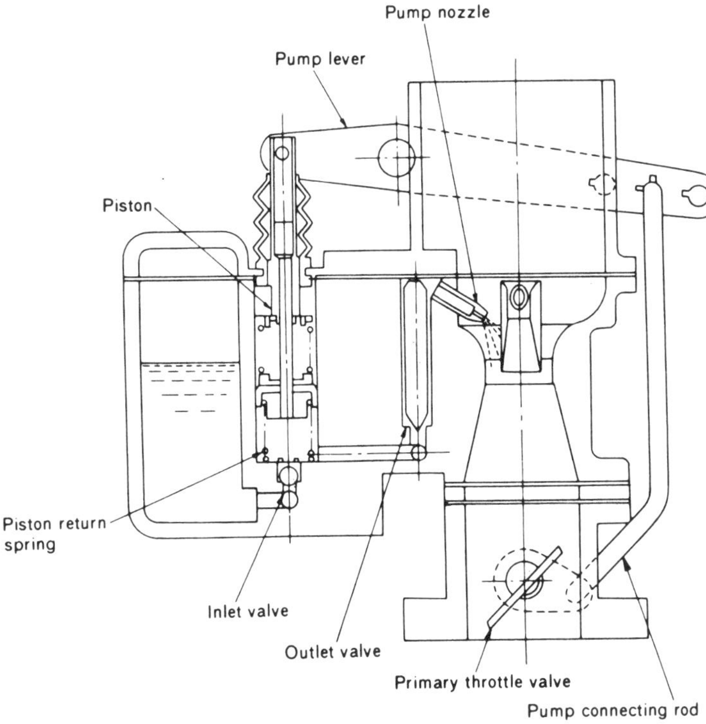

Fig. 3.8. Diagram of accelerator pump and linkage

8 Carburetor - description

The carburetor fitted to all models is of the Zenith-Stromberg two barrel type. The carburetor uses a progressive linkage between the primary and secondary systems. For optimum performance and fuel economy, the secondary system is used only at high engine speed. Normal low speed driving requirements are satisfied by the primary system.

The DCG 306 type carburetor fitted to 1970 - 73 models has a manually operated choke while the DCJ 306 carburetor, fitted to all models from 1974, has an automatic choke.

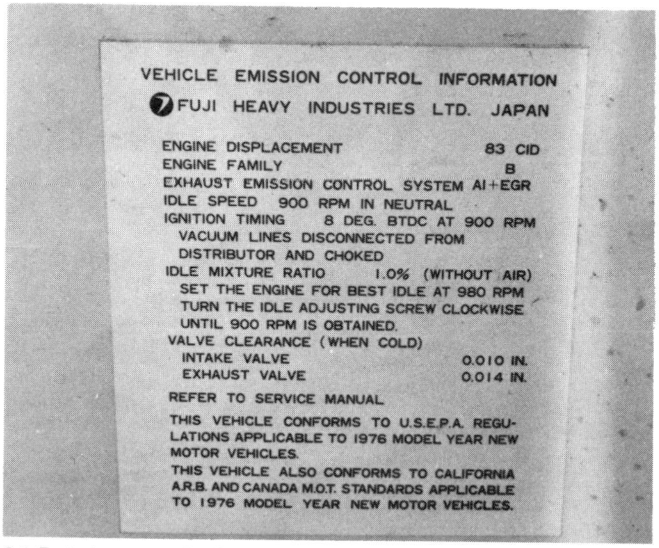

VEHICLE EMISSION CONTROL INFORMATION
FUJI HEAVY INDUSTRIES LTD. JAPAN
ENGINE DISPLACEMENT 83 CID
ENGINE FAMILY B
EXHAUST EMISSION CONTROL SYSTEM AI+EGR
IDLE SPEED 900 RPM IN NEUTRAL
IGNITION TIMING 8 DEG. BTDC AT 900 RPM
VACUUM LINES DISCONNECTED FROM
DISTRIBUTOR AND CHOKED
IDLE MIXTURE RATIO 1.0% (WITHOUT AIR)
SET THE ENGINE FOR BEST IDLE AT 980 RPM
TURN THE IDLE ADJUSTING SCREW CLOCKWISE
UNTIL 900 RPM IS OBTAINED.
VALVE CLEARANCE (WHEN COLD)
INTAKE VALVE 0.010 IN.
EXHAUST VALVE 0.014 IN.
REFER TO SERVICE MANUAL
THIS VEHICLE CONFORMS TO U.S.E.P.A. REGULATIONS APPLICABLE TO 1976 MODEL YEAR NEW MOTOR VEHICLES.
THIS VEHICLE ALSO CONFORMS TO CALIFORNIA A.R.B. AND CANADA M.O.T. STANDARDS APPLICABLE TO 1976 MODEL YEAR NEW MOTOR VEHICLES.

9.1 Emission control information label

10.1 Check the float level in the sight glass

The carburetor is conventional in operation and has a mechanically operated accelerator pump and a vacuum response type power system.

For idle and slow running, the fuel passes through the slow running jet, the primary air bleed and the secondary slow air bleed. The fuel is finally ejected from the by-pass and idle holes.

The accelerator pump is synchronized with the throttle valve. During periods of heavy acceleration, the pump which is of piston and valve construction, provides an additional metered quantity of fuel to

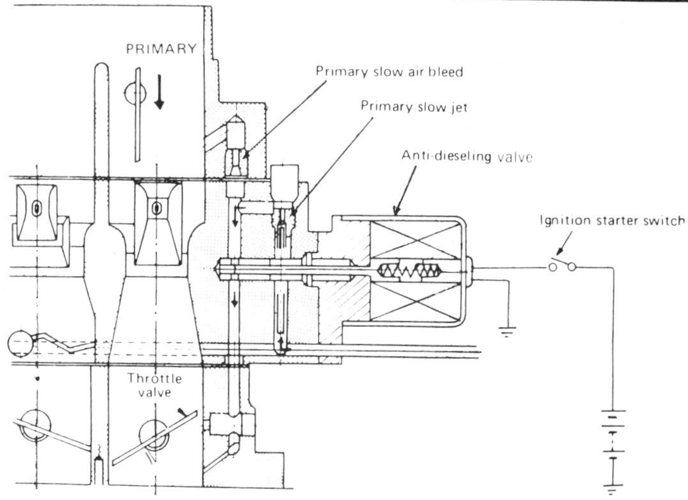

Fig. 3.9. Sectional view of anti-dieseling valve

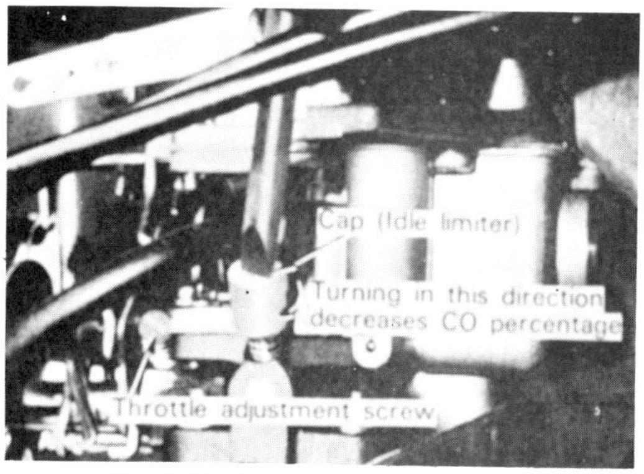

Fig. 3.10. Adjusting the idling speed

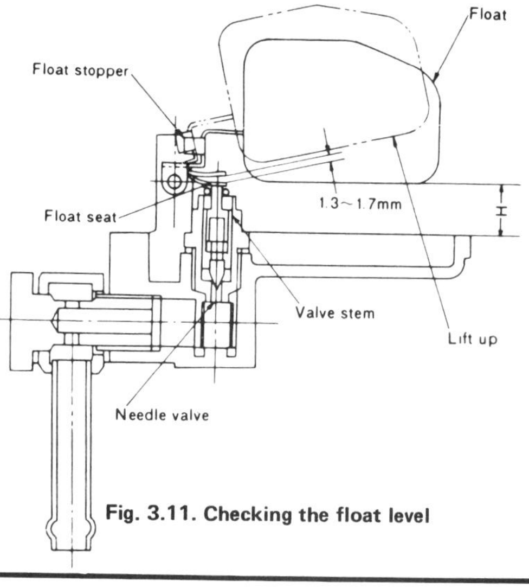

Fig. 3.11. Checking the float level

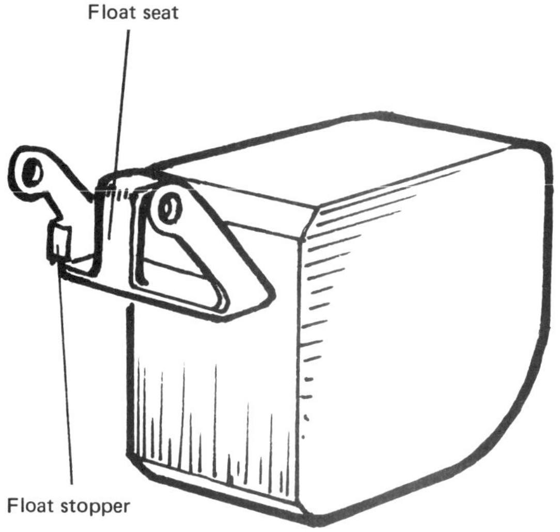

Fig. 3.12. Float adjustment position

enrich the normal mixture. The quantity of fuel metered can be varied according to operating climatic conditions by adjusting the stroke of the pump linkage.

The float chamber, which is common to both primary and secondary systems is supplied with fuel pumped by the electrically operated fuel pump. The fuel from the pump enters the float chamber thru a filter and needle valve which opens and closes according to the position of the float.

The power valve system utilizes the vacuum in the intake manifold to open or close the valve. During light load running the valve is closed, but is opened during full load running or acceleration, thus supplying more fuel.

The DCG 306 carburetor (1972 - 73 models) and DCJ 306 are equipped with an anti-dieseling valve to prevent engine dieseling by closing the primary slow passage as soon as the ignition is switched off. While the ignition is switched on, electric current flows to the switch from the battery, actuating the valve of the switch and keeping the primary slow passage open. On the other hand, when the ignition is switched off, the valve is pushed back by the return spring and the primary slow passage is closed.

9 Idling speed - adjustment

1 Adjust the engine idling speed to the figures given in Specifications at the beginning of this Chapter. CO percentage should be within the figure given on the emission data label under the hood. Make sure that ignition timing and valve clearances are correctly adjusted before carrying out this adjustment.
2 Run the engine to normal operating temperature and then set the throttle adjusting screw to obtain the specified engine speed. If the car is fitted with a tachometer then the engine speed can be set accurately. If an instrument is not available then the charge warning light can be used as a guide. This should be just going out at the correct idling speed.
3 The use of a CO meter is essential when adjusting the idle mixture adjusting screw. Turn the throttle adjusting screw and the idle mixture adjusting screw in or out as necessary to obtain the specified idle speed and CO percentage.
4 An idle limiter cap is fitted on the idle mixture adjusting screw on DCG 306 carburetors. It is used to limit the amount of CO in the exhaust gases by restricting the adjustment of the screw to ensure that the CO emission does not exceed the specified percentage.
5 As a temporary measure, the adjustment screws may be turned progressively, first one and then the other until the engine idles at the correct speed without any hunting or stalling. Turning the mixture screw clockwise weakens the mixture and counter-clockwise enriches the mixture.
6 On 1600 models with pumpless air injection emission control system, disconnect the air suction hose (silencer to air cleaner) from the silencer before carrying out the idling speed adjustment. The CO percentage should be as follows:

49 States	*1.5 ± 0.5*
California	*0.75 ± 0.25*

When checked, after adjustment, with the air suction hose refitted, the CO percentage should be:

49 States	*0.5 – 1.5*
California	*0.1 – 0.5*

10 Float level - adjustment

1 The fuel level in the carburetor can be checked thru the sight glass of the float chamber. A fuel level within a range of 0.006 in (1.5 mm) above or below the point mark on the sight glass is normal. If the fuel level is out of this range the float position must be adjusted.
2 Remove the choke chamber, as described in Section 16, and turn it upside down. If the clearance 'H' in Fig. 3.11 is not 0.413 in (10.5 mm) when the float seat comes in contact with the valve stem, adjust the level by bending the float seat.
3 Check that the clearance 'L' between the float seat and valve stem, with the float fully lifted, is between 0.051 - 0.067 in (1.3 - 1.7 mm). Adjust, if necessary, by bending the float seat.

11 Fast idle adjustment - manually operated choke

1 Ensure that the choke control is fully out. Remove the air cleaner and check that the choke butterfly valve is in the fully closed position.
2 Measure the clearance between the upper edge of the primary throttle valve and its bore 'G' in Fig. 3.13, with a wire gauge. It should be as specified in Specifications at the beginning of this Chapter.
3 Where adjustment is required, bend the choke connecting rod as necessary to obtain the correct clearance.
4 After adjustment, check the operation of the choke linkage.

12 Fast idle adjustment - automatic choke

1 When the choke is closed, the primary throttle valve is slightly opened from its fully closed position by the action of the fast idle cam and the linkage. At this time, the top of the cam adjusting lever rests on the fourth (highest) step of the fast idle cam.
2 Measure the clearance between the lower edge of the primary throttle valve and its bore, 'G' in Fig. 3.14. If the clearance is not as specified in Specifications at the beginning of this Chapter, adjust by means of the fast idle adjusting screw.

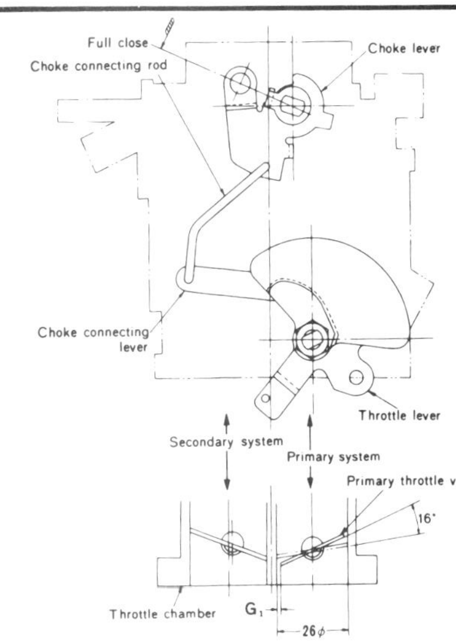

Fig. 3.13. Choke linkage adjustment

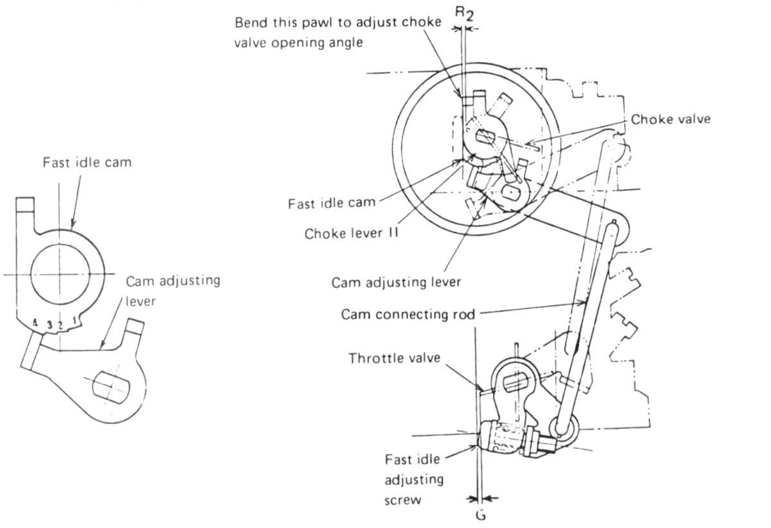

Fig. 3.14. Fast idle mechanism - automatic choke

13 Primary and secondary throttle interlock - adjustment

1 Actuate the primary throttle valve until the secondary throttle valve is just about to open. Measure the distance between the edge of the primary valve plate and the wall of the bore, this should be 0.24 in (6 mm), 'G2' in Fig. 3.15.
2 Adjust, if necessary, by bending the connecting rod.

14 Carburetor - removal and refitting

1970 - 73 models

1 Remove the spare wheel from the engine compartment.
2 Disconnect the blow-by hose from the air cleaner, remove the bracket bolts and lift off the air cleaner.
3 Disconnect the fuel hose from the nipple on the carburetor and pull off the distributor vacuum pipe (FF-1 models) or the servo diaphragm hose.
4 Disconnect the choke cable from the choke lever and the throttle cable. Disconnect the lead to the anti-dieseling valve (if fitted).
5 Disconnect the water by-pass hose.
6 Remove the four nuts and washers which secure the carburetor to the intake manifold, lift off the carburetor and discard the flange gasket.
7 Refitting is the reverse of the removal sequence, always use a new flange gasket.

1974 - 77 models

8 Remove the spare wheel, if located in the engine compartment.
9 Remove the air cleaner emission control hoses and the air cleaner, air intake hose and air pump inlet pipe, if fitted.
10 Disconnect the coolant hoses from the carburetor.
11 Remove the vacuum hoses from the servo diaphragm, automatic choke diaphragms, distributor, EGR valve and silencer, if so equipped.
12 Disconnect the fuel lines and the accelerator cable from the carburetor.
13 Disconnect the leads from the anti-dieseling valve and the automatic choke heater.
14 Remove the four nuts securing the carburetor to the intake manifold and lift off the carburetor. Cover the intake manifold port to prevent anything from dropping in.
15 Refitting is the reverse of removal sequence, always use a new gasket.

15 Carburetor - servicing (general)

1 As wear takes place in the carburetor an increase in fuel consumption and a falling off in performance will be evident. When a carburetor requires major repair it is recommended that an exchange rebuilt one is purchased. Because of the high degree of precision involved and the necessity to renew the casing when wear takes place round spindles and other moving parts, this is one time when it is better to buy a new component rather than to rebuild the old one.
2 Repair kits are available for servicing carburetors and providing care is taken the carburetor can be serviced by following the instructions in Sections 16 or 17, in conjunction with the exploded views in Figs. 3.16 and 3.17.
3 Efficient carburetion depends on careful cleaning to a great extent, therefore care must be taken to exclude all dirt, gum or water from the carburetor during servicing. Always make sure to have a clean area for dismantling and lay parts out separately to avoid similar looking parts from getting mixed up.
4 Never probe jets, fuel passages, or air bleeds with a wire or similar to clean them. Always blow them out with compressed air or air from a car tire pump. Use gasoline when cleaning the dismantled parts. Always use wrenches and screwdrivers of the correct size when dismantling the carburetor to avoid damage to jets and screws.

16 Carburetor (DCG 306) - dismantling and reassembly

1 The main jets and needle valves are accessible from the exterior of the carburetor. They should be unscrewed and removed.
2 Detach the choke chamber by removing the connecting rod, accelerator pump lever, return spring and the five securing screws.
3 The primary and secondary emulsion tubes are accessible after removing the main air bleeds.
4 Remove the accelerator pump cover, retaining the spring, piston and ball valve.
5 Separate the float chamber from the throttle housing by unscrewing and removing the three securing screws. Slide out the float pivot pin

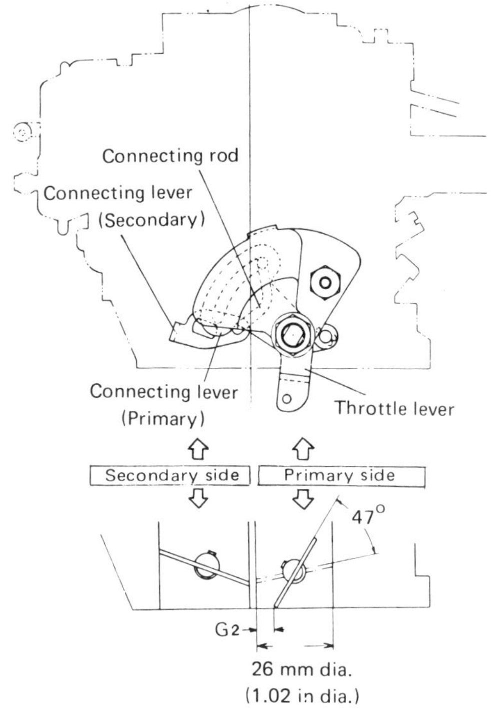

Fig. 3.15. Primary and secondary throttle interlock adjustment

14.13 Disconnect the leads from the anti-dieseling valve and the automatic choke heater

and remove the float.

6 Unless it is essential, do not dismantle the throttle butterfly valves from their spindles.

7 Take care when disconnecting the interlock rods that they are not bent or twisted, otherwise the settings and adjustments will be upset.

8 Inspect all the components for wear and the body and chamber castings for cracks. Clean the small gauze inlet filter and if corroded or damaged it should be renewed.

9 Check the ejection of fuel when the accelerator pump is operated.

10 Reassembly is the reverse of the dismantling procedure. Use all the items in the repair kit. When reassembling the carburetor check the float movement, see Section 10.

17 Carburetor (DCJ 306) - dismantling and reassembly

1 Remove the throttle return spring, the accelerator pump lever shaft and the pump lever.

2 Pull off the three cotter pins and remove the cam connecting rod and pump connecting rod.

3 Remove the diaphragm bracket, disconnecting the connecting rods at the main diaphragm and choke lever.

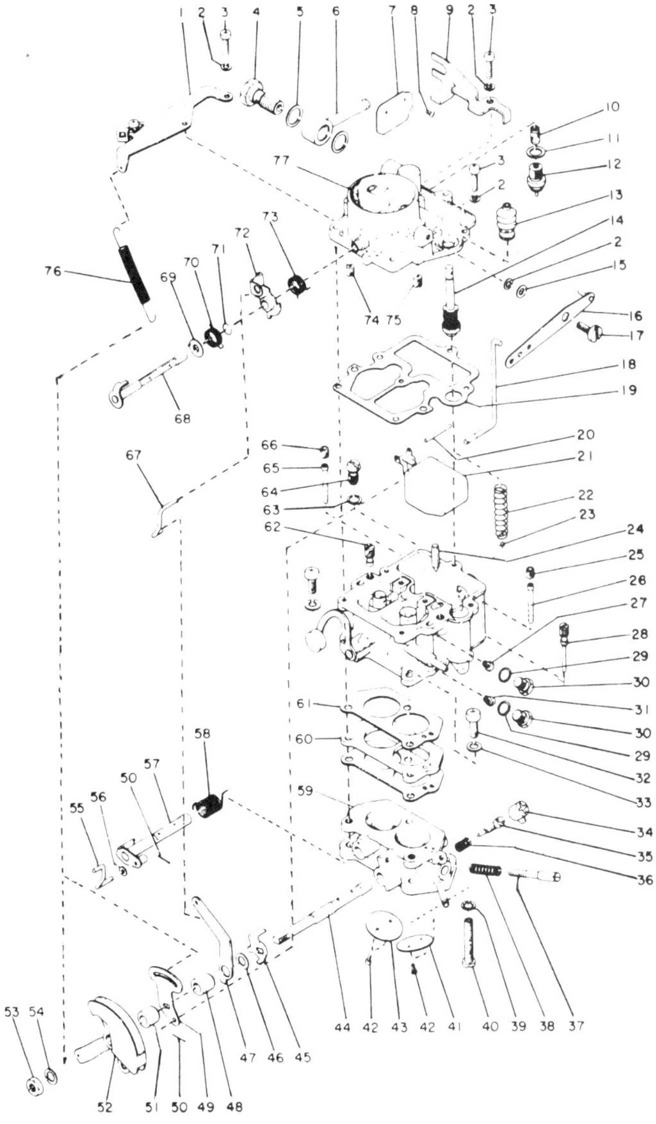

Fig. 3.16. Exploded view of DCG 306 carburetor

1 Hanger (spring)
2 Spring washer
3 Screw (pan head)
4 Bolt (filter)
5 Washer
6 Nipple
7 Valve (choke)
8 Screw
9 Nipple guide
10 Filter
11 Washer
12 Needle valve
13 Cover (pump)
14 Piston
15 Washer
16 Lever (pump)
17 Shaft (pump lever)
18 Connecting rod (pump)
19 Gasket (float chamber)
20 Shaft (float)
21 Float (carburetor)
22 Spring (piston return)
23 Ball
24 Weight (injector)
25 Air bleed
26 Emulsion tube (P)
27 Main jet
28 Slow jet
29 Washer
30 Plug (float chamber drain)
31 Main jet (S)
32 Screw (pan head)
33 Spring washer
34 Cap (idle limiter)
35 Screw (idle adjusting)
36 Spring (idle adjusting screw)
37 Screw (throttle adjust)
38 Spring (idle adjust screw)
39 Washer
40 Screw
41 Valve (throttle) (P)
42 Screw
43 Valve (throttle) (S)
44 Shaft (throttle) (P)
45 Plate (adjust)
46 Washer
47 Lever (connecting)
48 Sleeve
49 Connecting lever
50 Cotter pin
51 Sleeve (throttle)
52 Lever (throttle)
53 Nut
54 Spring washer
55 Connecting rod
56 Washer
57 Shaft S (throttle)
58 Spring (throttle)
59 Throttle chamber
60 Insulator
61 Gasket (throttle chamber)
62 Slow jet (S)
63 Washer
64 Power valve
65 Emulsion tube
66 Air bleed
67 Connecting rod (choke)
68 Shaft (choke)
69 Sleeve (A)
70 Spring (adjust screw)
71 Clip
72 Lever (choke)
73 Spring (choke)
74 Air bleed
75 Slow air bleed (P)
76 Spring (throttle return)
77 Choke chamber

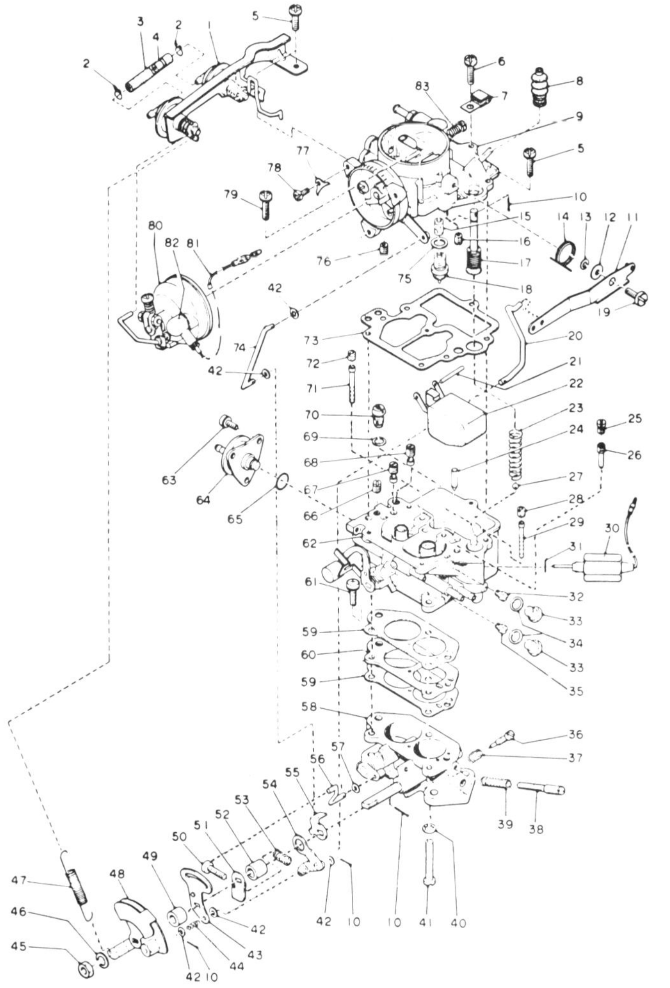

Fig. 3.17. Exploded view of DCJ 306 carburetor

1 Diaphragms and bracket
2 Clip
3 Rubber pipe
4 Orifice
5 Pan head screw
6 Screw
7 Cord stopper
8 Pump cover
9 Choke chamber
10 Cotter pin
11 Pump lever
12 Washer
13 Spring washer
14 Pump lever spring
15 Filter
16 Primary slow air bleed (No. 170)
17 Piston
18 Needle valve
19 Pump lever shaft
20 Connecting rod
21 Float shaft
22 Float
23 Piston return spring
24 Injector weight
25 Plug
26 Primary slow jet (No. 46)
27 Ball
28 Primary main air bleed (No. 75)
29 Primary emulsion tube
30 Anti-dieseling switch
31 Washer
32 Primary main jet
No. 103 ... DCJ 306 - 8
No. 135 ... DCJ 306 - 9
33 Float chamber drain plug
34 Washer
35 Secondary main jet
No. 155 ... DCJ 306 - 8
No. 135 ... DCJ 306 - 9
36 Idle mixture adjusting screw
37 Spring
38 Throttle adjusting screw
39 Spring
40 Washer
41 Screw
42 Washer
43 Connecting lever
44 Rod spring
45 Nut
46 Spring washer
47 Throttle return spring
48 Throttle lever
49 Sleeve
50 Screw
51 Fast idle lever A
52 Sleeve
53 Spring
54 Fast idle lever B
55 Adjusting plate
56 Connecting rod
57 Washer
58 Throttle chamber
59 Gasket
60 Insulator
61 Screw
62 Float chamber
63 Screw and washer
64 Servo diaphragm
65 O-ring
66 Bypass air bleed (No. 200)
67 Secondary slow jet (No. 70)
68 Bypass jet (No. 45)
69 Washer
70 Power valve
71 Secondary emulsion tube
72 Secondary main air bleed (No. 80)
73 Float chamber gasket
74 Connecting rod
75 Washer
76 Secondary slow air bleed (No. 70)
77 Spring washer
78 Pan head screw
79 Screw
80 Thermostat cover
81 Cord
82 Thermostat cord boot
83 Fuel enrichment screw and spring (high altitude models only)

17.6a Pull out the float shaft and remove the float ...

17.6b ... then remove the needle valve

4 Remove the screws securing the choke chamber and separate the choke chamber from the float chamber, disconnecting the cam connecting rod at its upper end. Take care not to damage the float.
5 Separate the float chamber and the throttle chamber by removing the securing screws. Take care not to damage the longest screw as it has a hole in it which is the vacuum passage for the power valve.
6 Dismantle the choke chamber by removing the three securing screws and taking off the thermostat cover. Remove the accelerator pump piston and pump cover. Pull out the float shaft and remove the float. Remove the needle valve.
7 To dismantle the float chamber, remove the piston return spring and inlet valve ball. Remove the outlet valve (injector weight). Remove the primary and secondary main air bleeds and take out the primary and secondary emulsion tubes. Keep the emulsion tubes apart so they will not get mixed up. Remove the primary slow jet plug and slow jet and the secondary slow jet. Remove the power valve. After removing the float chamber drain plugs take out the primary and secondary main jets. The servo diaphragm is removed by undoing the three securing screws. Remove the by-pass jet and by-pass air bleed.
8 Remove the throttle adjusting screw, idle mixture adjusting screw and their springs. Remove the nut on the throttle valve shaft and then remove the throttle lever, sleeve, connecting lever, fast idle lever A, sleeve, fast idle lever B, and adjusting plate.

9 Wash all the dismantled parts in clean gasoline. Inspect all the parts for wear, damage or corrosion.
10 Reassembly is the reverse of the removal procedure. Use all the items in the repair kit.

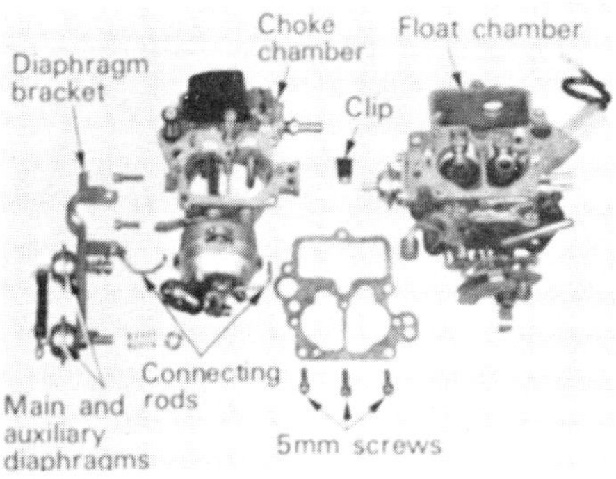

Fig. 3.18. Removing the choke chamber

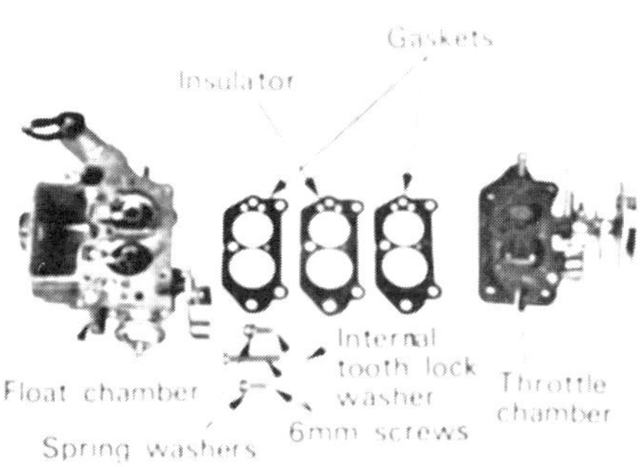

Fig. 3.19. Separating the float chamber and throttle chamber

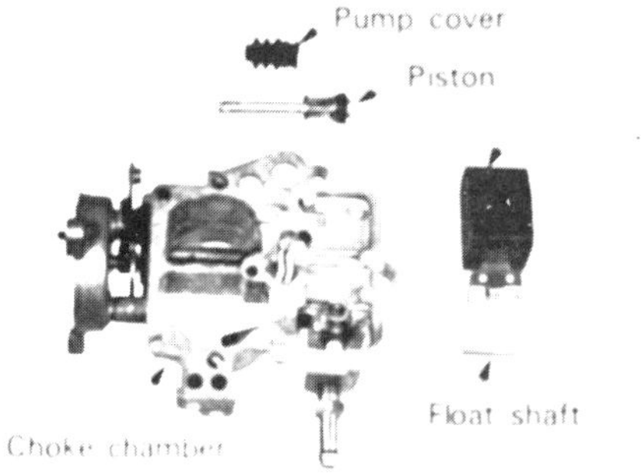

Fig. 3.20. Removing the piston and float

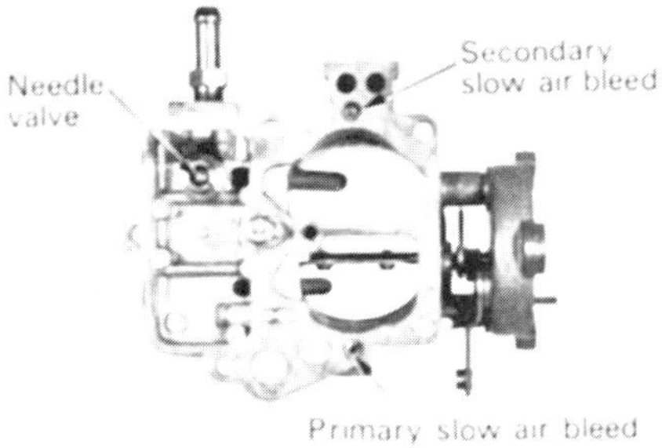

Fig. 3.21. Removing the needle valve and slow air bleeds

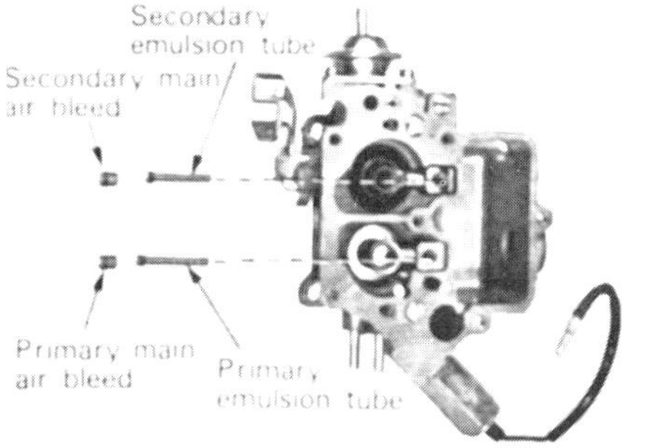

Fig. 3.22. Main air bleeds and emulsion tubes

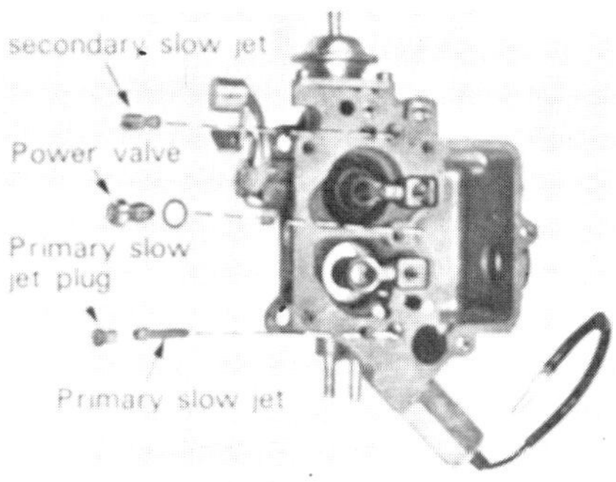

Fig. 3.23. Removing the slow jets and power valve

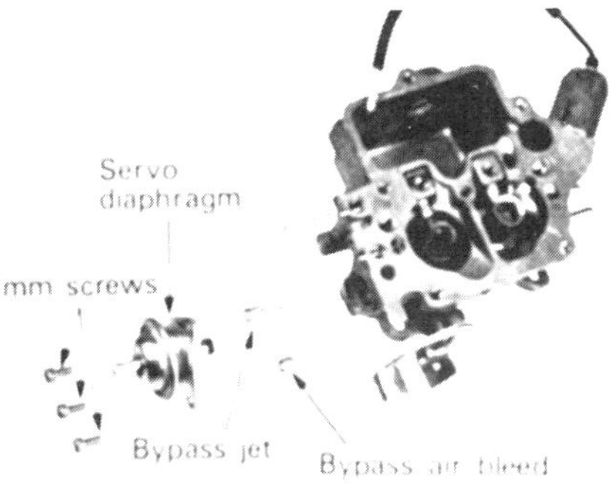

Fig. 3.24. Removing the servo diaphragm and bypass jet and air bleed

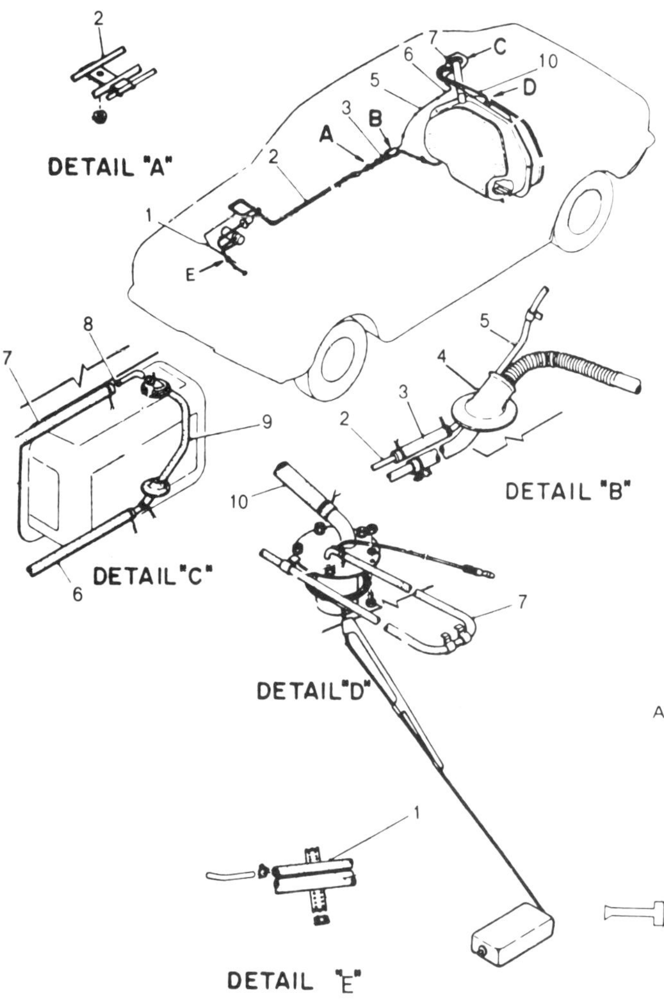

Fig. 3.25. Air vent and evaporation line - 1972 models

1 Evaporation tube (to air cleaner)
2 Evaporation pipe
3 Evaporation tube (connector)
4 Grommet
5 Evaporation pipe
6 Evaporation tube
7 Evaporation tube (tank-air breather valve)
8 Connector
9 Air breather hose assembly
10 Air vent tube

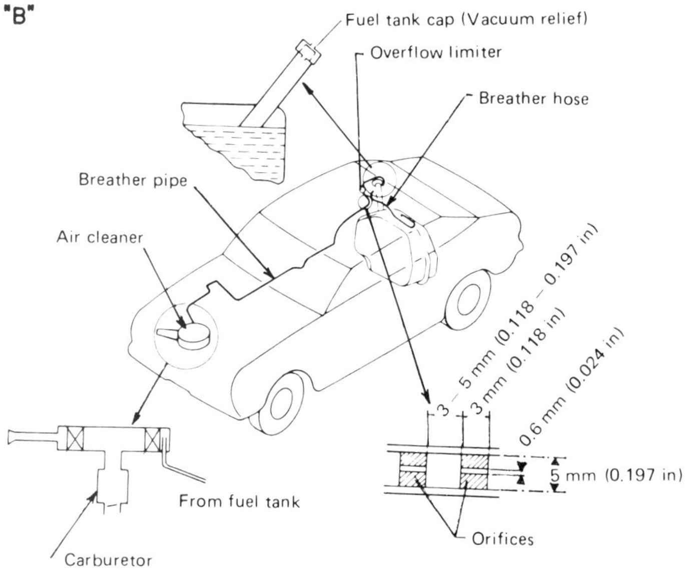

Fig. 3.26. Evaporative emission control system - 1976 Sedan, Coupe and Hardtop models

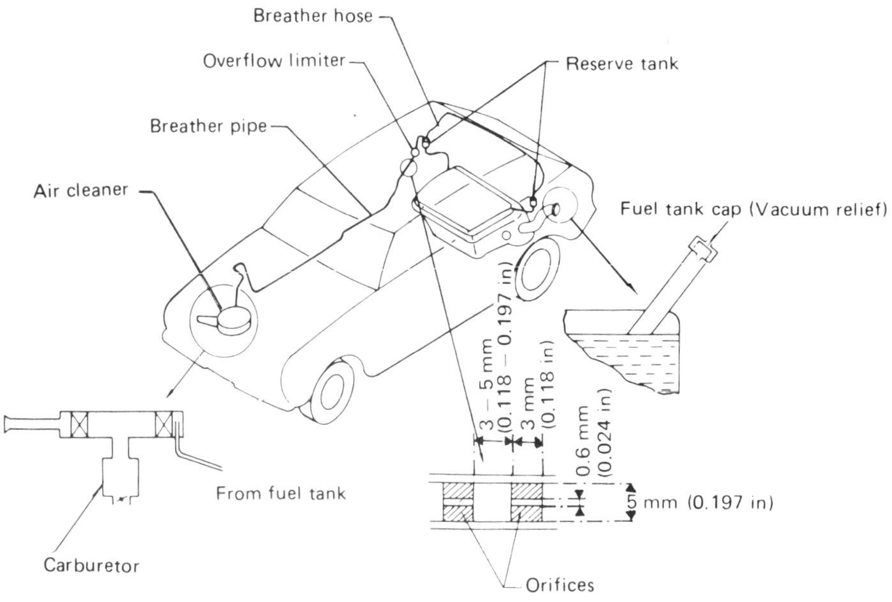

Fig. 3.27. Evaporative emission control system - 1976 - Station Wagon including 4WD

18 Evaporative emission control system - description

The evaporative emission control system is designed to prevent vapor from the tank escaping into the atmosphere. The system on Subaru vehicles vary with different year models.

1970 - 72 models

Gasoline vapor from the fuel tank is passed to the air cleaner where it is drawn into the combustion chamber and burnt. No absorbent is used and the system is easy to maintain. The system comprises the sealed fuel tank (and two reserve tanks on station wagons) and filler cap, air breather valve, hoses, pipes and air cleaner. When the engine is running the gasoline vapor is drawn into the engine. When the engine is stopped the vapor collects on the inner wall or the element of the air cleaner, and when the engine is started again the attached or condensed gas is drawn into the manifold together with fresh air.

1973 models

The air breather valve is replaced by a nylon tube on station wagons and an orifice on sedans. The filler cap is replaced by a vacuum relief cap.

1974 models

An overflow limiter is introduced in place of the orifice and nylon tube. The overflow limiter is located in the fuel vapor line and operates to prevent fuel from overflowing out of the tank. At the same time, it permits the flow of evaporative gas into the air cleaner and when pressure in the fuel tank decreases due to consumption of fuel, it vents the tank to fresh air from the air cleaner.

1976 models

Two orifices are added to the system, as shown in Figs. 3.26 and 3.27, which prevents fuel spillage.

1977 models

This system includes a canister, a check valve (49 States (high altitude) and California models) and a two-way valve (49 States (high altitude) models). Gasoline vapor from the fuel tank passes to the canister located in the engine compartment. When the engine is idling, the vapor is stored in the canister as the purge valve on the canister is closed by the manifold vacuum. During this time the gasoline vapor is absorbed by the activated charcoal in the canister. As the engine speed is increased the purge valve opens and the absorbed vapor is drawn into the intake manifold. While the purge valve is open, fresh air is sucked into the canister through the bottom filter, purging the absorbed vapor from the charcoal. When the engine is not running the purge valve is opened by the return spring but the vapor remains in the canister because there is no vacuum to draw it out.

The two reserve tanks (vapor separators) on station wagons, including 4WD, are to prevent liquid fuel from flowing to the air cleaner during fierce cornering.

19 Evaporative emission control system - servicing

1 Periodic preventative maintenance of the system should be carried out. Check all vinyl tubes, rubber hoses and metal pipes for damage, leakage, clogging and loose connections. Check the relief type filler cap by blowing into the relief valve housing. If air passes through with light pressure or fails to pass air at stronger pressure, it should be renewed.

2 Test the purge check valve (49 States (high altitude) and California models) to ensure that there is no air flow from the intake manifold side to the canister. Immerse the valve in water, as shown in Fig. 3.30 and check for air leaks. Connect a manometer to the check valve and measure the pressure at which the valve starts to open. Blow clean compressed air in the direction of the arrow mark on the check valve, it should start to open between 0.2 and 0.59 in Hg (2 and 15 mm). If

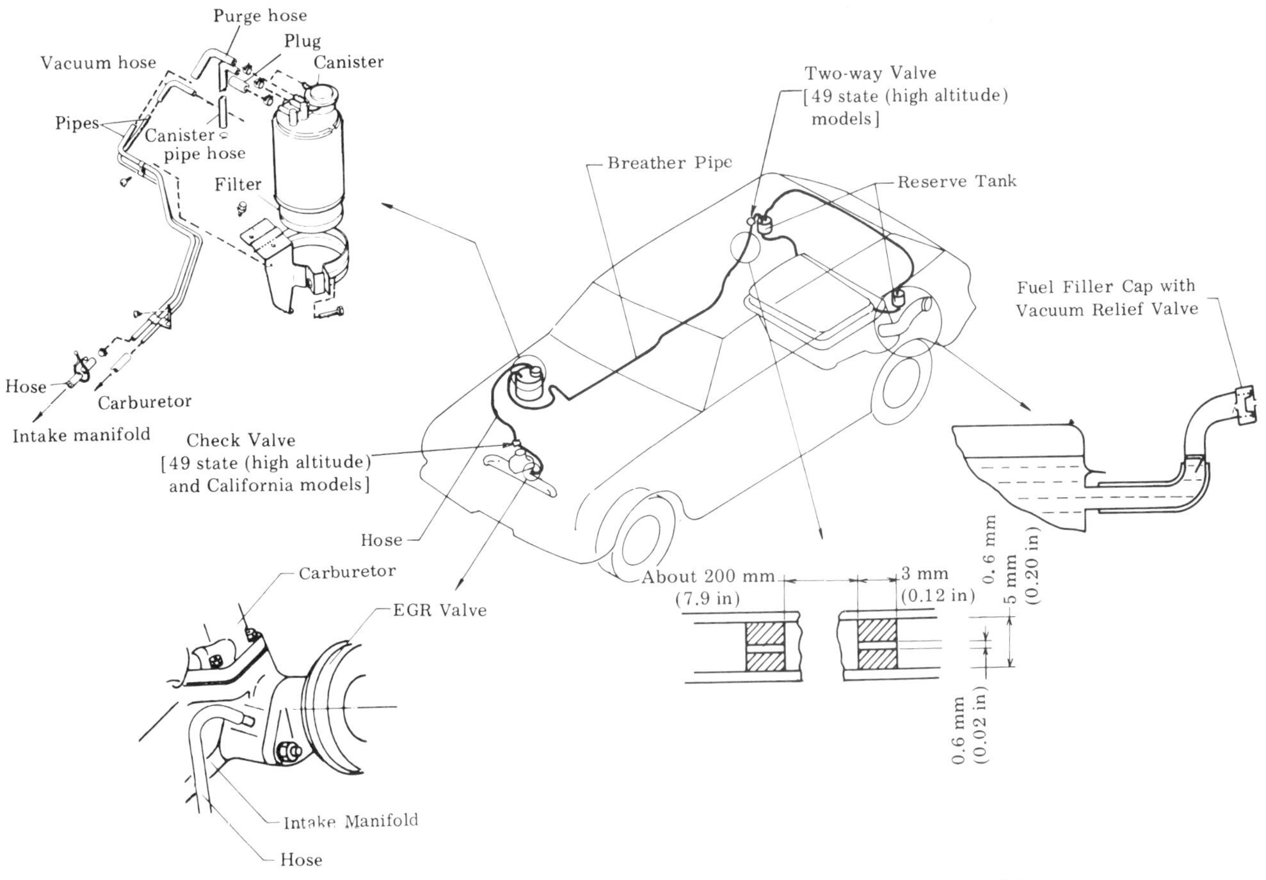

Fig. 3.28. Evaporative emission control system - 1977 - Sedan, Coupe and Hardtop models

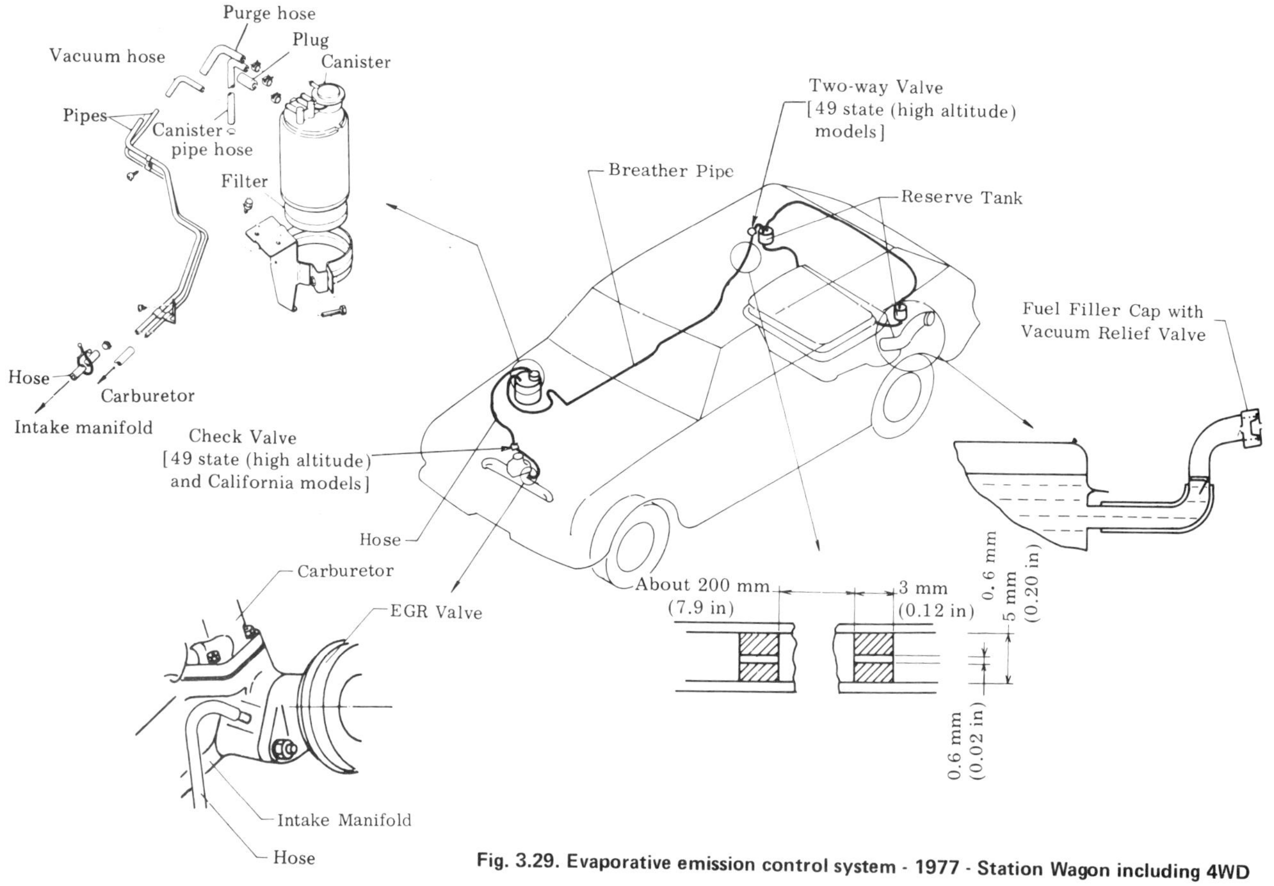

Fig. 3.29. Evaporative emission control system - 1977 - Station Wagon including 4WD

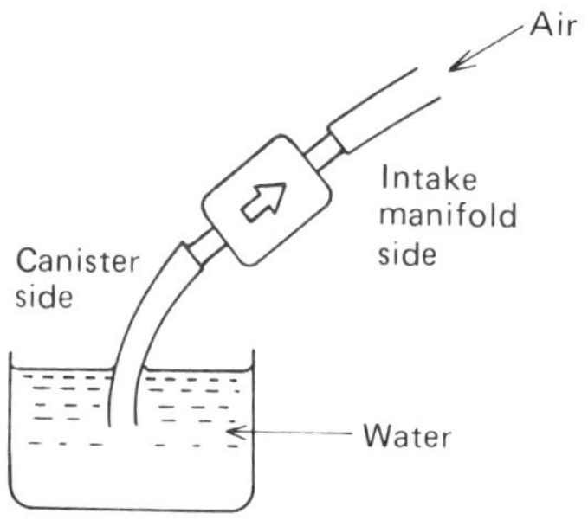

Fig. 3.30. Testing the purge check valve

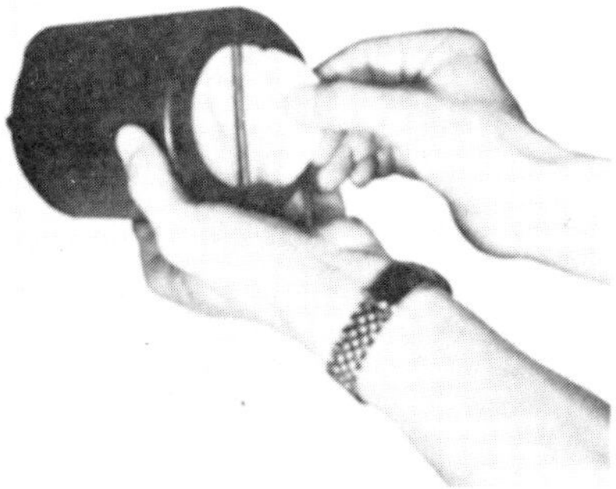

Fig. 3.31. Renewing the filter in the fuel evaporative system canister (1977 models)

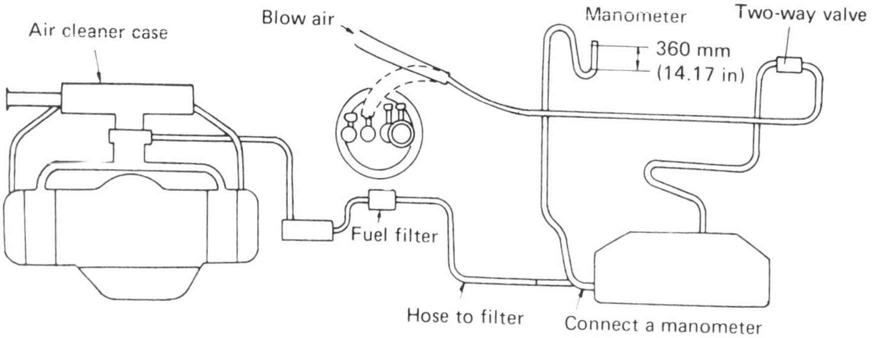

Fig. 3.32. Testing the fuel evaporative system

defective, renew the valve.

3 Check the canister case for cracks or damage. Ensure that the vacuum hose, purge hose, canister pipe hose and plug are securely connected to the canister. Renew the canister filter at the specified intervals as follows:

a) *Disconnect the vacuum hose, evaporation hose and purge hose from the canister.*
b) *Loosen the canister bracket clamp bolt and pull the canister upwards.*
c) *Pull the filter out carefully, otherwise it may tear and become difficult to get out (Fig. 3.31).*
d) *Insert a new filter and refit the canister into the bracket with the nipples facing outwards and reconnect the hoses.*

4 Carry out an airtight test of the system as follows:

a) *Drain the gasoline from the tank into a clean container.*
b) *Make sure the filler cap is properly fitted.*
c) *Disconnect the evaporation hose from the canister or air cleaner as appropriate.*
d) *Disconnect the fuel delivery hose from the pipe under the body and fit a manometer to the hose as shown in Fig. 3.32. The manometer should be capable of measuring up to 15.8 in (400 mm).*
e) *Blow compressed air thru the canister (or air cleaner) side of the evaporation hose into the tank until the manometer registers 14.2 in (360 mm). Adjust the air pressure to 2.13 lb/in^2 (0.15 kg/cm^2) or less.*
f) *Check that the manometer reading does not drop by more than 1.97 in (50 mm) from a height of 14.17 in (360 mm), in less than 5 minutes. If it does there is a leak which must be found and rectified.*

20 Crankcase emission control system - description

The sealed crankcase emission control system is adopted to prevent pollution of the atmosphere by blow-by gas emitted from the crankcase. In this system the blow-by gas is returned to the intake manifold, thru the air cleaner, for reburning.

The system consists of a sealed oil filler cap, rocker covers with an outlet connection, an air cleaner and connecting hoses as shown in Fig. 3.33.

Blow-by gas in the crankcase is drawn thru the rocker covers and the connecting hoses into the clean side of the air cleaner, from where it passes thru the carburetor into the intake manifold.

Periodic checks should be made for leaks, clogging or damage to the crankcase ventilation hoses. Check the oil filler cap to ensure that the gasket is not damaged and that the cap fits firmly on the filter tube.

21 Exhaust emission control system - description

The exhaust emission control systems employed on Subaru vehicles have changed considerably over the years as more stringent anti-pollution standards have been introduced.

On the FF-1 models an air injection system is used to reduce the amount of pollution of the atmosphere from exhaust gases.

The principle of operation is that clean filtered air is injected into the exhaust port of each cylinder where unburned carbon monoxide (C)) and hydrocarbons (HC) are present, a chemical reaction takes place which reduces the exhaust gases to an acceptable level.

A belt driven air pump supplies air, under pressure, to the air distributor manifolds which directs the air to each exhaust port. An anti-backfire valve is fitted between the intake manifold and delivery line to prevent backfiring in the exhaust system when the throttle is closed at high speed, and a coasting condition exists. This valve supplies the intake manifold with a certain amount of air which will burn completely in the combustion chamber and not in the exhaust manifold during these coasting conditions.

Check valves prevent hot exhaust gases flowing back into the air pump and hoses in the event of pump failure or when the anti-backfire valve is faulty.

Special engine modifications were introduced in 1972 to improve the air/fuel mixture, while the engine is decelerating, and the com bustion of the gases by retarding the ignition. When the vehicle is decelerating an increasing vacuum is created in the intake manifold. This vacuum is controlled through a vacuum valve and passes on to the carburetor, where a by-pass jet is opened and extra mixture is allowed to enter the venturi below the throttle butterfly valves.

The vacuum also passes to the distributor vacuum retarder and the ignition is retarded in order to improve the combustion in the cylinders.

Models from 1974 have automatic chokes in place of the manual choke. With the automatic choke an electric heating element speeds up the choke valve opening and reduces the CO emissions. The heating element is connected to a terminal on the voltage regulator.

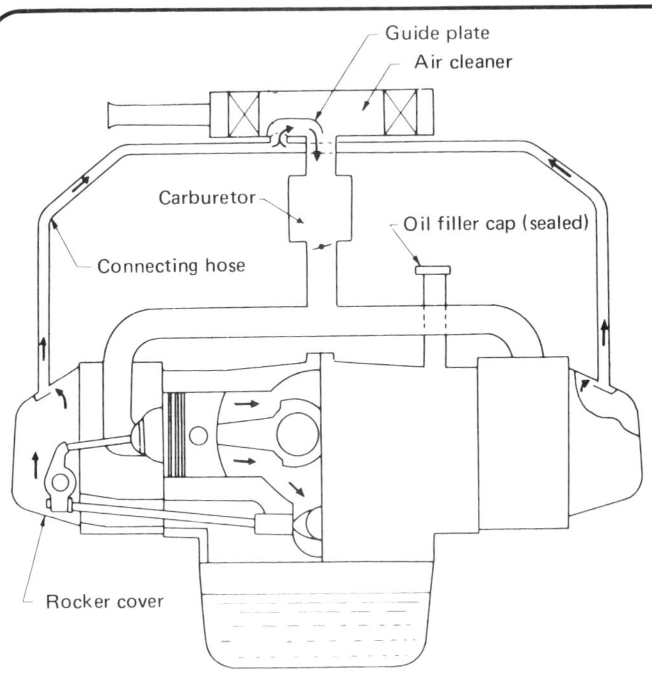

Fig. 3.33. Crankcase emission control system

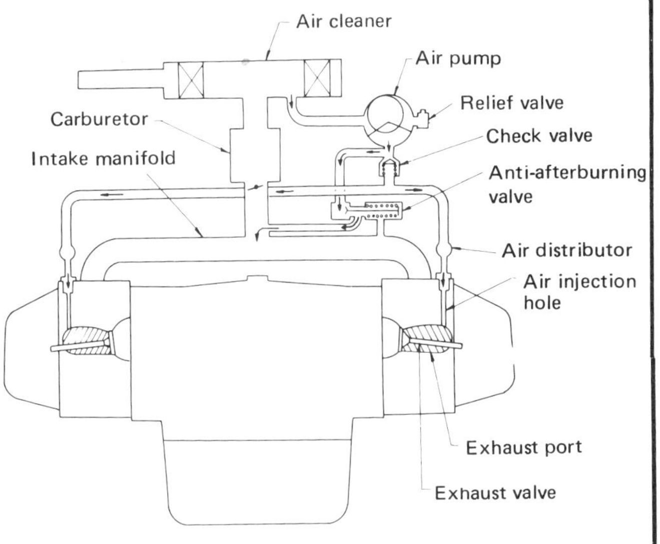

Fig. 3.34. Air injection system

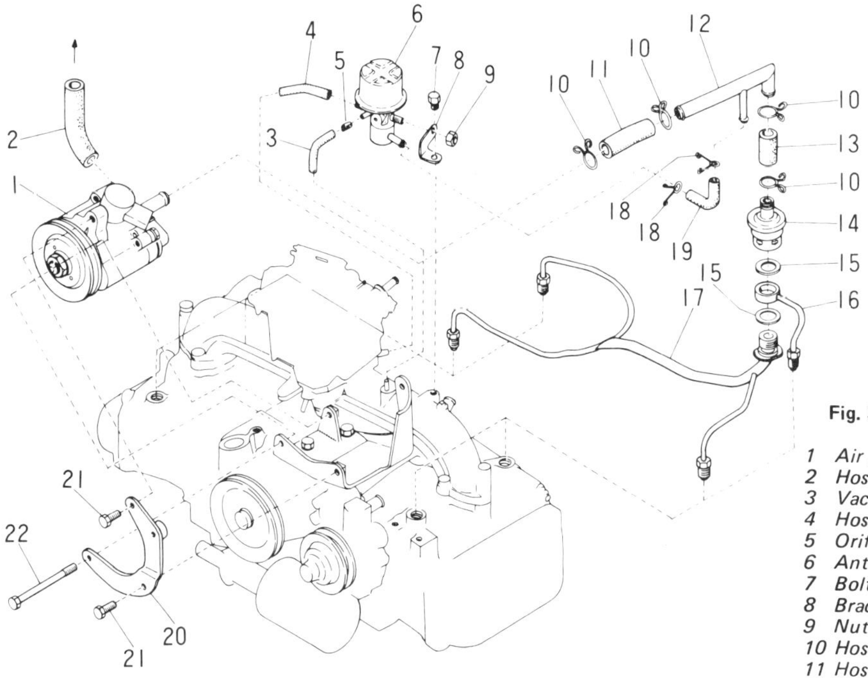

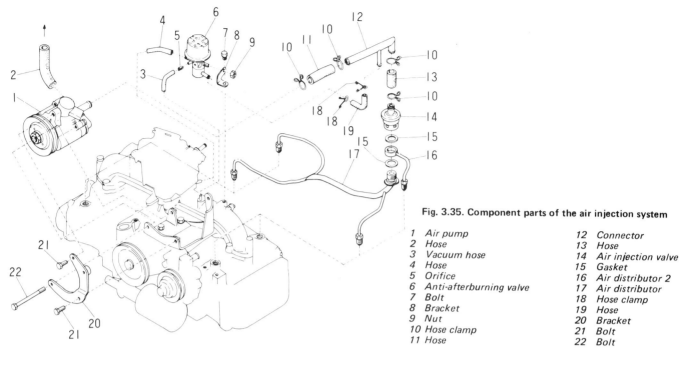

Fig. 3.35. Component parts of the air injection system

1	*Air pump*	*12*	*Connector*
2	*Hose*	*13*	*Hose*
3	*Vacuum hose*	*14*	*Air injection valve*
4	*Hose*	*15*	*Gasket*
5	*Orifice*	*16*	*Air distributor 2*
6	*Anti-afterburning valve*	*17*	*Air distributor*
7	*Bolt*	*18*	*Hose clamp*
8	*Bracket*	*19*	*Hose*
9	*Nut*	*20*	*Bracket*
10	*Hose clamp*	*21*	*Bolt*
11	*Hose*	*22*	*Bolt*

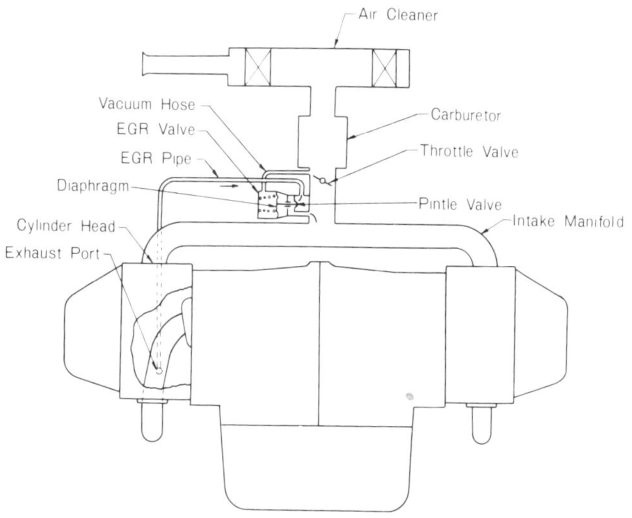

Fig. 3.36. EGR system

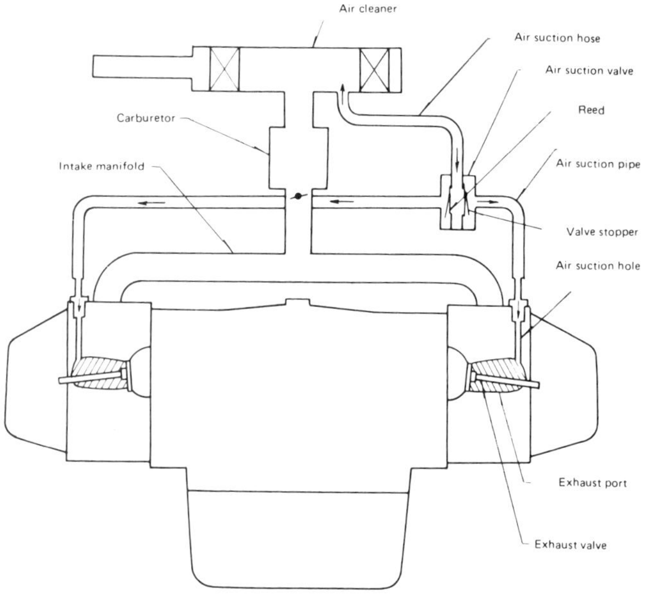

Fig. 3.37. Air suction system

From 1974 an exhaust gas recirculation system was added to models for California only. The purpose of the EGR system is to reduce NOx emission. After starting the engine, some of the exhaust gas from the exhaust port is recirculated thru the EGR control valve into the intake manifold in response to driving conditions. This lowers the combustion temperature and thus reduces the NOx level in the exhaust emissions.

In 1976 a different exhaust emission control system was adopted. This system is fundamentally composed of an air suction system and exhaust gas recirculation (EGR) system which does not use an air pump, catalyst or thermal reactor.

The air suction system reduces HC and CO emissions during low-speed, light-load engine operation by supplying secondary air into the exhaust ports. A feature of the system is that it automatically controls the amount of air to be supplied.

The operation principle is based on a utilisation of the negative pressure caused by exhaust gas pulsation and intake manifold pressure during valve overlap period. The gas pressure in each exhaust port is transmitted to the air suction valve thru the air suction hole and air suction pipe. When the pressure transmitted is negative, the reed of the air suction valve is opened towards the valve stopper and at the same time, fresh air is drawn from the clean side of the air cleaner, through the air suction hose and silencer, into the exhaust port. On the other hand when positive pressure reaches the air suction valve the reed is immediately closed to prevent the flow of exhaust gas. The fresh air sucked in is mainly used for oxidation of HC and CO in the exhaust passage and partly for fuel combustion in the cylinders.

The main components of the air suction emission control system are the silencer, which is fitted between the air suction valve and air cleaner to muffle the sound of air being admitted into the system; the air suction valve, described above; the vacuum control valve which controls the operation of the coasting by-pass system in the carburetor and the vacuum modulator which is used to simplify the routing of the vacuum hoses.

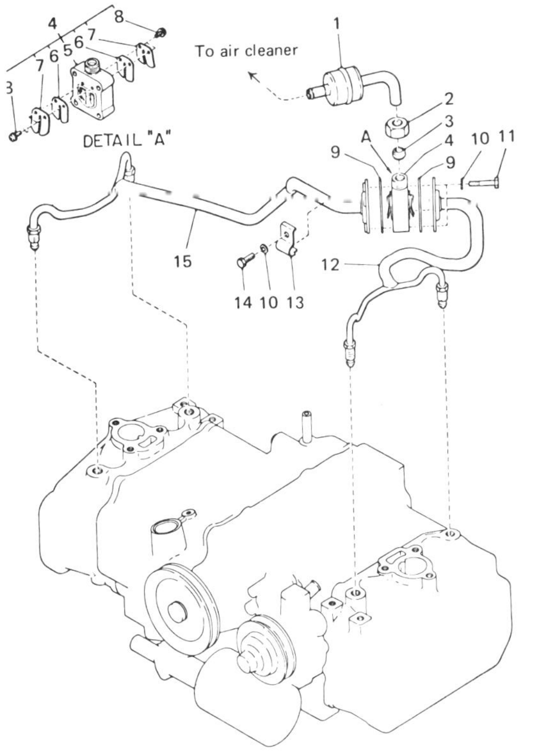

Fig. 3.38. Component parts of the air suction system

Silencer	9 *Gasket*
Sleeve nut	10 *Spring washer*
Tapered sleeve	11 *Bolt*
Air suction valve	12 *Air suction manifold II*
Valve body	13 *Clamp*
Reed valve	14 *Bolt (6 x 13 mm)*
Valve stopper	15 *Air suction manifold I*
Screw	

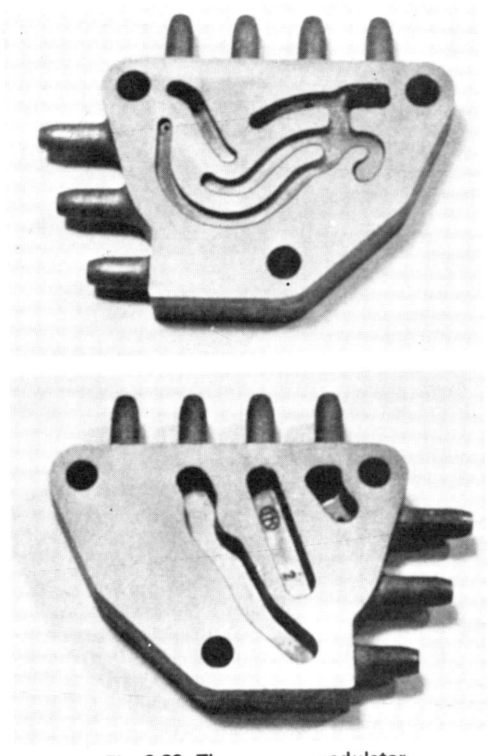

Fig. 3.39. The vacuum modulator

21.10 The EGR valve

21.11a The air suction system silencer

21.11b The air suction valve

22 Air pump - removal and refitting

Note: On 4WD vehicles remove the belt driven cooling fan.
1 Loosen the hose clips and remove the hoses from the pump.
2 Loosen the bolt on the adjusting arm and remove the belt.
3 Remove the mounting bolts and lift off the pump.
4 Refitting is the reverse of removal procedure. Tension the drivebelt so that the deflection is approximately 0.4 in (10 mm) with 22 lbs (9.5 kg) pressure.

23 Air pump - testing

1 Check that the drivebelt tension is correct; refer to Section 22.
2 Start the engine and run it until normal operating temperature is reached.
3 Check all clips for tightness and hoses for damage or leaks. Rectify any fault found.
4 Disconnect the air supply hose at the anti-backfire valve.
5 Connect a pressure gauge, using a suitable adaptor, to the air supply hose.
6 With the engine running at 2,000 rpm the air pump outlet pressure must be between 2.9 and 5.7 lb/in^2 (0.2 and 0.4 kg/cm^2).
7 Should the pressure be too low, check the air cleaner for clogging. If this does not rectify the fault, a new air pump must be fitted.

24 Check valve - testing

1 Start the engine and run until it reaches normal operating temperature.
2 Check all the hoses and connections for leaks. Rectify any faults.
3 With the engine stationary insert a suitable probe into the check valve and depress the plate. When released the valve plate should return on to its seating. If it sticks, renew the valve.
4 Start the engine and slowly increase its speed to approximately 1,500 rpm. Check for exhaust gas leakage at the check valve and if any is present the valve must be renewed as it is a sealed unit and cannot be repaired.

25 Anti-backfire (anti-afterburning) valve - checking

1 Disconnect the hose connecting the connector and anti-backfire valve at the connector side.
2 With the engine idling, confirm that the disconnected hose is not sucking air, if it is renew the anti-backfire valve.
3 Run the engine to approximately 3,000 rpm, then release the accelerator pedal sharply and check that the disconnected hose is drawing air.
4 If the hose does not draw air check the vacuum sensing hose on the anti-backfire valve for clogging or damage. If defective clean or renew, as necessary. If the vacuum sensing hose is in order, renew the anti-backfire valve.

26 Carburetor dashpot - checking and adjustment

1 Open the choke valve fully and check that the dashpot stroke is 0.24 ± 0.04 in (6 ± 1 mm). The stroke is the distance from the piston position where the carburetor throttle lever touches the piston tip of the dashpot to that for the idling position.
2 Check whether the carburetor returns to the idling position.
3 If the stroke is not as specified, adjust as follows:

a) Open the choke valve fully.
b) Release the locknut on the dashpot and screw the dashpot in clockwise until its piston end is lowered enough to move the end away from the carburetor lever.
c) Turn the dashpot counterclockwise to raise its piston until its end touches the carburetor lever. Then, turn the dashpot six more turns counterclockwise. (The screw pitch is 0.04 in (1 mm) so the stroke is 0.24 in (6 mm).
d) Tighten the locknut.

27 Exhaust gas recirculation (EGR) valve - servicing

1 Check the EGR valve every 2,400 miles (40,000 km). Check if the shaft moves upward when the engine speed is 3000 - 3500 rpm with no load.
2 If there is a malfunction, remove the valve and push the diaphragm upwards with a finger to confirm the operation. If the EGR valve is in order, check the vacuum lines for defects.
3 If the operation of the EGR valve is faulty it can be caused by two things, a defective diaphragm or a sticking valve. If the diaphragm is at fault the valve must be renewed, if sticking it must be cleaned.
4 After servicing the EGR valve, reset the switch of the EGR warning lamp.

28 Air suction valve - servicing

1 Check the reed valve for cracks.
2 Check the rubber seat part of the valve body for shrinkage, cracks or deformation.
3 Check that the contacting surfaces of the reed valve and the reed valve stopper are smooth.
4 The clearance between the reed valve and rubber seat must be less than 0.0079 in (0.2 mm) at the tip of the reed valve.
5 If the clearance is more than specified, dismantle the air suction valve and wash the valve body and the reed valve in gasoline.
6 If, after cleaning, the clearance still exceeds the specified limit renew the reed valve or air suction valve as necessary.

29 Hot air control system - description

The mechanically operated valve in the air cleaner is replaced by an automatic control system on 1977 models. The hot air system consists of the air cleaner, the air stove on the exhaust pipe and the air intake hose connecting the air cleaner and air stove. The control valve in the air cleaner maintains the air being drawn into the carburetor at 100 - 127°F (38 - 53°C) to reduce HC emission when the under hood temperature is below 100°F (38°C). In addition it also prevents carburetor icing and improves the warm-up time of the engine.

The air cleaner is fitted with the following devices:

a) A vacuum motor and air control valve which is actuated by intake manifold vacuum to admit hot air or cool air according to the under-hood temperature and intake manifold vacuum.
b) A temperature sensor which detects the intake air temperatures and opens or closes the vacuum passage between the intake manifold and vacuum motor.
c) The flame arrester which prevents flame from entering the crankcase through the crankcase ventilation hoses in the event of a backfire.
d) The air cleaner element which is the disposable type and should not be cleaned.
e) A rubber plate is provided in the bottom of the air cleaner to drain off any water which might be drawn up into the air cleaner through the hose from the air stove.

When the under hood temperature is low and the intake manifold vacuum is high, the sensor valve remains closed and establishes vacuum passage from the intake manifold to the vacuum motor diaphragm. In this condition, the vacuum actuates the diaphragm which opens the air control valve to introduce hot air into the air cleaner thru the intake hose from the air stove.

When the under hood temperature is low but the intake manifold vacuum is too weak it actuates the diaphragm, the sensor valve remains closed and the air control valve closes the hot air passage, allowing only the under-hood air (cool air) into the air cleaner thru its air horn.

When the under-hood air temperature is high, the sensor valve opens fully to break the vacuum passage between the intake manifold and the vacuum motor diaphragm. In this condition, the diaphragm return spring presses on the air control valve, to close the hot air passage, and the under-hood air (cool air) is admitted into the air cleaner thru the air horn.

When the under-hood air temperature is around 100°F (38°C), the sensor valve is partially opened and the opening of the air control

Fig. 3.40. Removing the air pump

Fig. 3.41. The anti-backfire valve

Fig. 3.42. Checking the dashpot

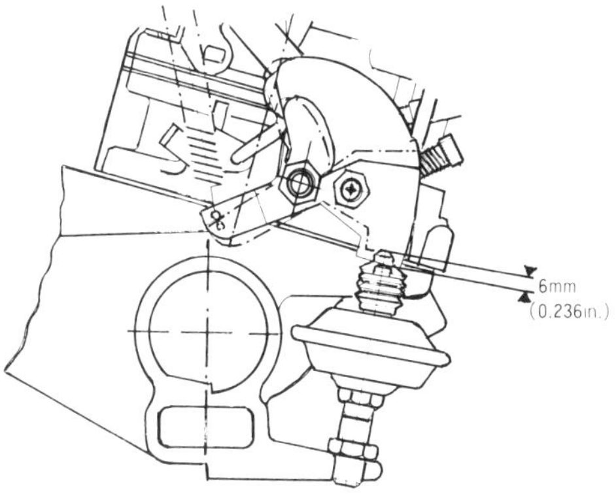

Fig. 3.43. Dashpot adjustment

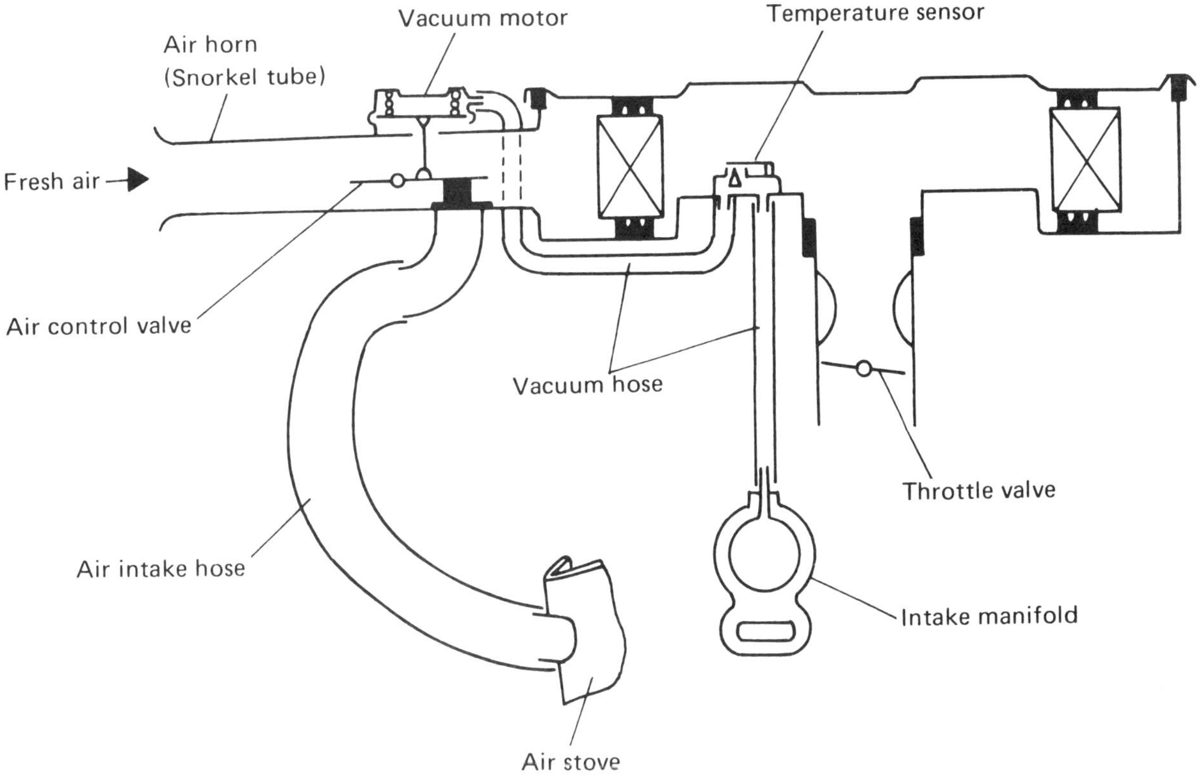

Fig. 3.44. Hot air control system

valve varies with the vacuum from the intake manifold. With the air control valve partially opened, cool air and hot air are sucked together and mixed, controlling the temperature of the air entering the air cleaner.

30 Temperature sensor and vacuum motor - removal and refitting

1 Using a pair of pliers, flatten the clip securing the vacuum hose to the sensor vacuum pipe and disconnect the hose from the sensor.
2 Remove the clip from the sensor vacuum pipe and remove the sensor from the air cleaner. Do not remove the gasket between the sensor and air cleaner, unless it is defective, as it is glued to the air cleaner.
3 Remove the three screws securing the vacuum motor to the air cleaner.
4 Disconnect the valve shaft, attached to the vacuum motor diaphragm at the air control valve, and remove the vacuum motor from the air cleaner.
5 Refitting is the reverse of the removal procedure.

31 Hot air control system - checking

1 In warm weather, it is difficult to detect faults in the hot air control system. In cold weather, however, malfunction of the system will result in insufficient automatic control of the intake air. Engine stalling, increase in fuel consumption and lack of power are indications of a faulty air control system and the system should be checked before looking at the carburetor.
2 Check the vacuum hose for cracks and the connections for tightness.
3 Check the vacuum motor, with the engine stationary, as follows:

a) Hold a mirror at the end of the air cleaner inlet and check the position of the air control valve. Its under-hood air inlet should be open and hot air inlet closed. Check the air control valve linkage.
b) Disconnect the motor vacuum inlet vacuum hose and connect a piece of tube to the inlet. Apply vacuum by sucking the tube, as shown in Fig. 3.46 and check the position of the air control valve. It should be the opposite of that described in (a) above.
c) With the hot air inlet open, as described in (b), pinch the vacuum hose with fingers so that air does not enter the vacuum motor. In this condition check that the air control valve maintains the under-hood air inlet in the closed position and the hot air inlet in the open position for more than 30 seconds. If the diaphragm spring actuates the control valve within 30 seconds renew the vacuum motor assembly.

4 Check the temperature sensor as follows:

a) With the engine stationary, check the position of the air control valve. The under-hood inlet should be open.
b) Start the engine and keep it idling. Check the position of the air control valve, the under-hood air inlet should be closed and the hot air inlet open.
c) Check that the air control valve gradually moves to open the under-hood air inlet as the engine warms up.

5 Check the rubber plate for sticking or deterioration.
6 Examine the air intake hose for damage and security of connections.

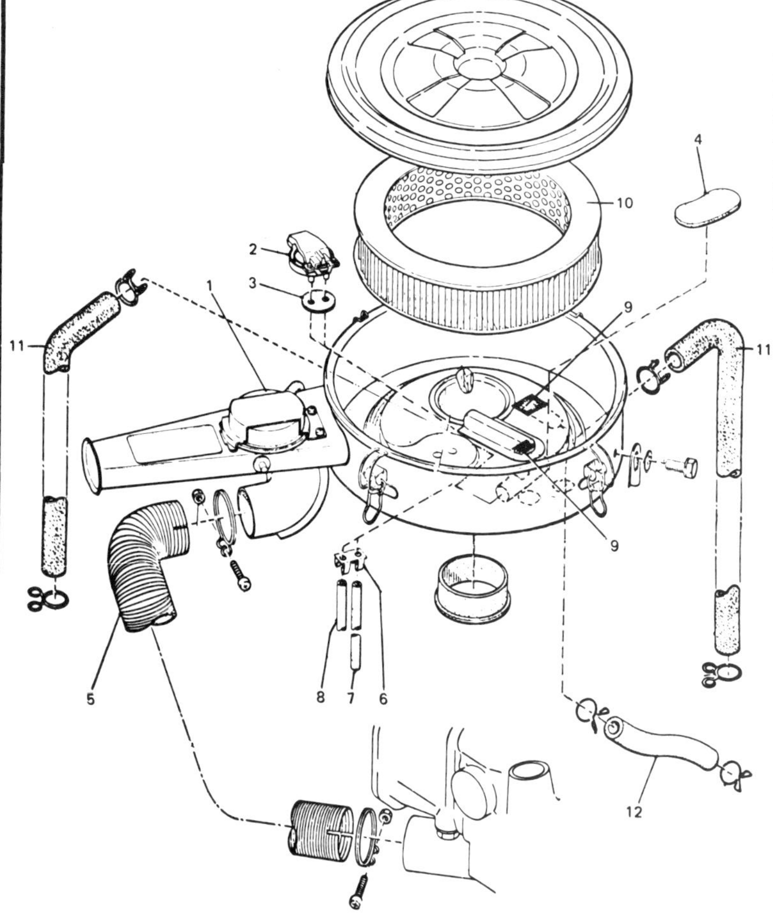

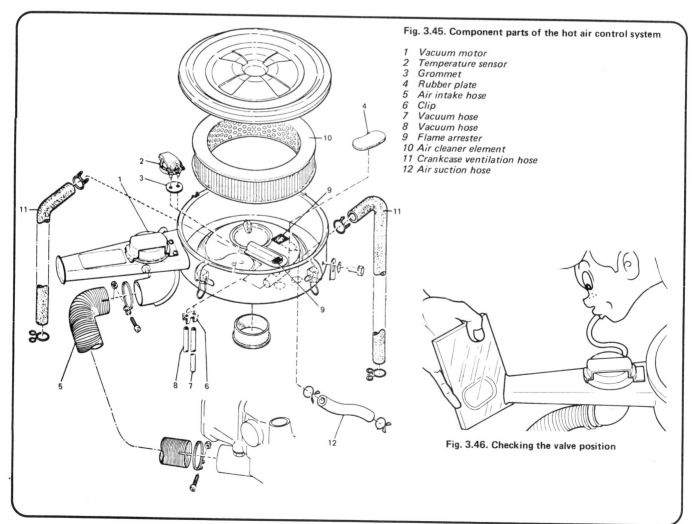

Fig. 3.45. Component parts of the hot air control system

1 Vacuum motor
2 Temperature sensor
3 Grommet
4 Rubber plate
5 Air intake hose
6 Clip
7 Vacuum hose
8 Vacuum hose
9 Flame arrester
10 Air cleaner element
11 Crankcase ventilation hose
12 Air suction hose

Fig. 3.46. Checking the valve position

32 Fault diagnosis

Symptom	Reason/s	Remedy
Excessive fuel consumption	Fuel leakage from carburetor, fuel pump or fuel lines	Trace source of leak and rectify.
	Float chamber flooding	Check and adjust float level.
	Clogged air bleed	Clean or renew.
	Incorrect main jet or slow jet	Renew as necessary.
	Defective power valve or vacuum leakage in power valve system	Check and repair or renew, as necessary.
	Choke valve maladjusted	Inspect and adjust linkage.
	Secondary throttle valve maladjusted	Inspect and adjust linkage.
Rough idling	Incorrect idle adjustment	Adjust.
	Damaged idle adjusting screw	Renew.
	Clogged idle hole, by-pass hole or slow system passage	Clean as necessary.
	Clogged slow jet	Clean.
	Clogged coasting by-pass jet	Clean.
	Worn throttle shaft	Renew.
	Leaking vacuum hoses	Renew.
Poor acceleration	Defective accelerator pump	Renew.
	Malfunction of accelerator inlet or outlet valve.	Renew.
	Defective power valve	Renew.
	Incorrect float level	Adjust float level.
Insufficient fuel delivery	Partially clogged fuel filter	Renew.
	Defective fuel pump	Renew
	Union joints on fuel pipes loose	Tighten and check for leaks.
	Split in fuel line on suction side of fuel pump	Locate and renew pipe or hose.
Difficulty in starting at low temperatures	Malfunction of choke valve and/or linkage	Adjust.
	Incorrect fast idle opening	Adjust.
	Incorrect adjustment of automatic choke	Adjust.
Poor high speed performance	Clogged main jet	Clean.
	Incorrect throttle valve opening	Adjust.
	Worn throttle valve shaft	Renew.
	Incorrect float level	Adjust float level.
Dieseling (running-on)	Anti-dieseling valve defective	Check and renew if necessary.
	Incorrect adjustment of dashpot	Re-adjust.
After burning in the exhaust system	Anti-backfire valve, hoses and connections faulty	Inspect and renew as necessary.
	Lack of air to anti-backfire valve	Check air pump and hoses. Renew as necessary.
	EGR valve defective	Check and clean or renew if necessary.

Chapter 4 Ignition system

For modifications, and information applicable to later models, see Supplement at end of manual

Contents

Specifications

Ignition system type

All models except California 1977	With breaker points
1977 models for California	Breakerless
System voltage	12 volt negative ground
Firing order	1 - 3 - 2 - 4

Spark plugs

1100 model	NGK B-6ES
1300 - 1400 - 1600 models	NGK BP-6ES
Gap	0.028 - 0.032 in (0.7 - 0.8 mm)

Coil

Breaker point ignition		
Make	Nippon Denso	Hitachi
Type No.	29700	C6R - 209
Breakerless ignition		
Make	Nippon Denso	Hitachi
Type No.	029700 - 4290	CIT - 26

Distributor

Breaker point type		
Make	Hitachi	Nippon Denso
Type No.	D414 - 60, D414 - 88, D412 - 83A, D410 - 65A	029100 - 3710
Rotation	Counterclockwise	
Points gap	0.018 - 0.022 in (0.45 - 0.55 mm)	0.016 - 0.020 in (0.40 - 0.50 mm)
Condenser capacity	0.22 UF ± 10%	
Breakerless type	*Manual transmission*	*Automatic transmission*
Make	Nippon Denso	Hitachi
Type No.	0.29100 - 4270	D4H6 - 01
Rotation	Counterclockwise	
Air gap	0.008 - 0.016 in (0.2 - 0.4 mm)	0.012 - 0.016 in (0.3 - 0.4 mm)
Ignition control unit	131100 - 0.790	E12 - 24

Ignition timing (vacuum disconnected)

Year	*Engine type*	*Degrees BTDC*	*at rev/min*
1970 and 1971	EA61	8°	850

1971	EA62	8°	750
	EA62 (sports)	12°	850
1972	EA62	6°	800
1973 - 1974	EA63	6°	800
1975 - 1976	EA63	8°	850 (manual transmission)
1976 - 1977	EA71	8°	900 (breakerless ignition)

Torque wrench setting

Spark plug	15 - 22 lb f ft	2 - 3 kg f m

1 General description

The ignition circuit consists of the ignition switch, coil, distributor, wiring, spark plugs and battery. A resistor is fitted in the circuit.

During starting, electrical current by-passes the resistor thereby connecting the ignition coil to the battery. This provides full battery voltage at the coil and keeps the ignition voltage as high as possible.

Low voltage current is supplied by the battery, or alternator, and flows thru the primary circuit, which consists of the ignition switch, resistor, primary winding of the ignition coil, distributor contact points, condenser and all connecting low tension wiring.

High voltage current is produced by the ignition coil and flows thru the secondary circuit, resulting in a high voltage spark between the electrodes of the spark plugs in the engine cylinders. This circuit consists of the secondary winding of the ignition coil, high tension wiring, distributor rotor and cap.

When the distributor contact points are closed, the primary current flows thru the primary winding of the coil and thru the contact points to ground.

When the contact points are opened by the rotating distributor cam, the magnetic field, built up in the primary winding of the coil, induces a high voltage in the secondary winding of the coil. This high voltage is produced every time the contact points open. The high voltage current flows thru the high tension wire to the distributor cap where the rotor arm distributes the current to the spark plug lead terminals in the distributor cap.

The spark is obtained when the high voltage current jumps the gap between the insulated electrode and the ground side electrode of the spark plug. This process is repeated for each power stroke of the engine.

The ignition is advanced and retarded automatically, both mechanically and by a vacuum device, to ensure that the spark occurs at the right instant for the particular load at the prevailing engine speeds. As the engine speed increases, centrifugal action of rotating weights pivoting against the tension of governor springs advances the contact breaker cam in relation to the distributor shaft and so advances the timing. The vacuum control is connected via a small bore pipe to the carburetor and according to the varying intake depression it advances or retards the ignition timing.

On early models an octane selector plate was fitted to provide a means of altering the timing according to the octane value of the fuel being used. When the octane value is high the ignition is advanced and when low the ignition is retarded.

A breakerless type of ignition is fitted to 1977 models for California. The distributor is equipped with a pick-up coil which electrically detects the ignition timing signal in place of the breaker points of the conventional distributor. An ignition control unit generates the signal required for the make and break of the primary current for the ignition coil.

When the ignition switch is turned on and the distributor reluctor rotates, the primary current flows thru the primary winding of the coil and thru the ignition control unit to ground. When the primary circuit is opened by the ignition control unit high voltage is induced in the secondary winding of the ignition coil. The high voltage current to the spark plugs is the same as for the breaker type ignition. The centrifugal advance and the vacuum advance and retard mechanism is also the same as those for the breaker point type.

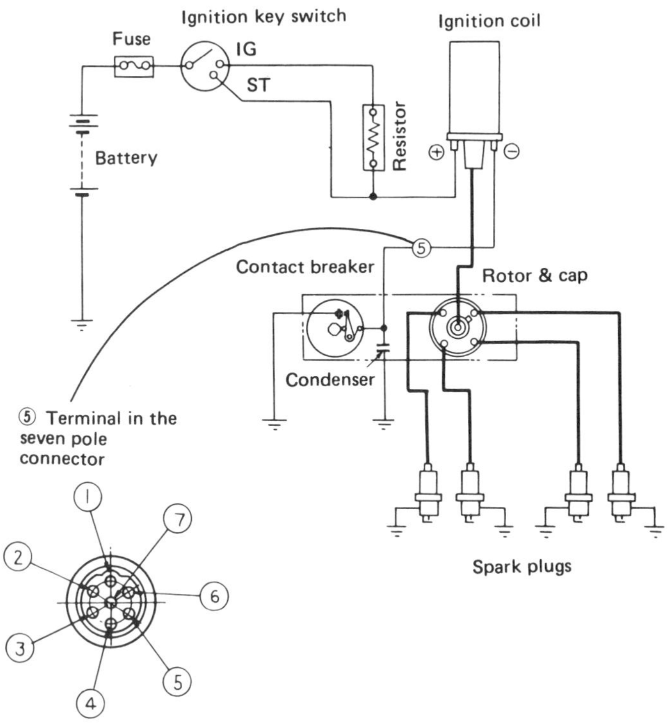

Fig. 4.1. Ignition circuit diagram - 1977 contact breaker type system

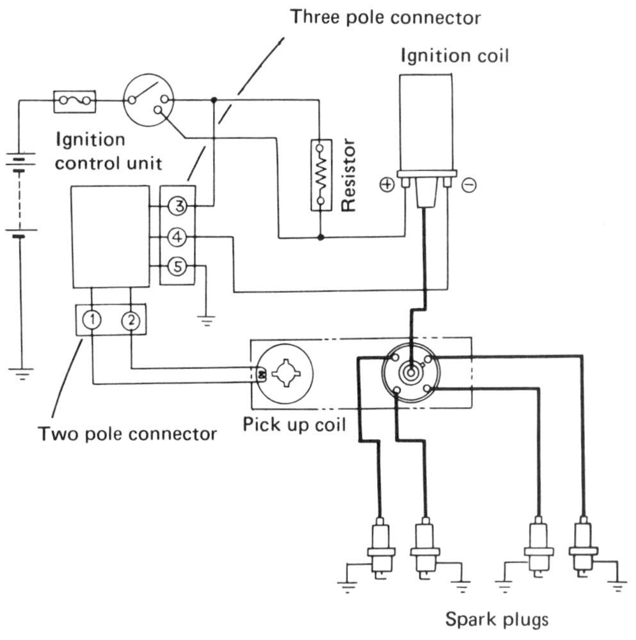

Fig. 4.2. Ignition circuit diagram - 1977 breakerless type system

2 Contact breaker points - adjustment

1 Release the two clips securing the distributor cap to the distributor body and lift off the cap. Clean the cap inside and out with a dry cloth. Check the condition of the four segments, it is unlikely that they will be badly burned or scored, but if they are the cap will have to be renewed.
2 Check that the carbon brush contact located in the top of the cap is unbroken and stands proud of the cap.
3 Check the contact spring on the top of the rotor arm, it must be clean and have enough tension to ensure good contact with the carbon brush.
4 Remove the dust cover, if fitted, and carefully prise open the contact breaker points to examine the conditions of the contact surfaces. If they are rough, pitted or dirty, it will be necessary to remove them for cleaning, resurfacing or for new points to be fitted.
5 If the points are in good condition measure the gap between the points. To do this turn the engine over until one cam lobe of the distributor shaft lifts the contact heel to its highest point.
6 Slacken the points securing screws and adjust the points gap, to the specified dimension given in Specifications at the beginning of this Chapter, by turning the adjusting screw.
7 Tighten the securing screws and re-check the gap.
8 Refit the rotor, dust cover and distributor cap.

3 Contact breaker points - removal and refitting

1 Remove the distributor cap, rotor arm and dust cover, if fitted.
2 Remove the contact breaker securing screws, disconnect the ground lead and lift out the contact set.
3 Fit a new contact set, but do not fully tighten the securing screws. Connect the electrical leads.
4 Adjust the points gap as described in Section 2.
5 Lubricate the cam surface, rubbing block, and arm pivot sparingly with high melting point grease.
6 Refit the dust cover, rotor and distributor cap.

4 Condenser (capacitor) - removal, testing and refitting

1 The condenser ensures that when the contact breaker points are open there is no arcing between the points which would cause severe pitting of the contact surfaces.
2 To test for an unserviceable condenser, switch on the ignition and separate the contact points by hand. If this action is accompanied by a blue flash then condenser failure is indicated. Difficult starting, misfiring after several miles running and badly pitted points are other indications of a faulty condenser.
3 The most reliable test, without special equipment, is to replace the suspect condenser with a new one.
4 To remove the condenser, undo the screw securing it to the distributor and disconnect the lead to the points. Refitting is the reverse of the removal procedure.

5 Distributor - removal and refitting

1 Disconnect the vacuum hose/s from the distributor.
2 Disconnect the primary lead, the spark plug leads and the lead to the ignition coil from the distributor. Identify the spark plug leads with tags.
3 If the distributor is to be refitted without the crankshaft having been moved, remove the distributor cap and mark the position of the rotor in relation to the distributor body.
4 On early models, fitted with an octane selector, note the position of the pointer on the selector scale and remove the retaining bolt. On later models mark the position of the distributor mounting plate in relation to the crankcase and remove the retaining bolt.
5 Remove the distributor and O-ring from the crankcase.
6 To refit the distributor align the rotor opposite the mark on the body, made at removal, and fit the O-ring and distributor in the crankcase. Take care not to damage the O-ring.

2.1 Release the distributor cap retaining clips

2.4 Check the condition of the contact points

5.4 Remove the distributor retaining bolt

5.5 Withdraw the distributor from the crankcase

5.7 Distributor mounting plate

7 Fit the octane selector pointer in its original position (early models) or align the marks made at removal, on the mounting plate and crankcase (later models) and fit the retaining bolt.
8 If the crankshaft is turned while the distributor is removed, the ignition timing will have to be reset as follows:

a) Remove the right-hand rocker cover. Turn the crankshaft to bring No. 1 piston to top dead center on compression stroke (both valves closed).
b) Fit the distributor, with O-ring, into the crankcase after aligning the distributor setting marks, see Fig. 4.3, taking care not to damage the O-ring.
c) On early models position the pointer on the octane selector midway between the 'A' and 'R'.
d) Fit the distributor retaining bolt.

9 Fit the distributor cap, primary lead, spark plug leads and lead to the coil. Connect the vacuum hose/s to the vacuum unit.
10 Adjust the ignition timing as described in Section 11.

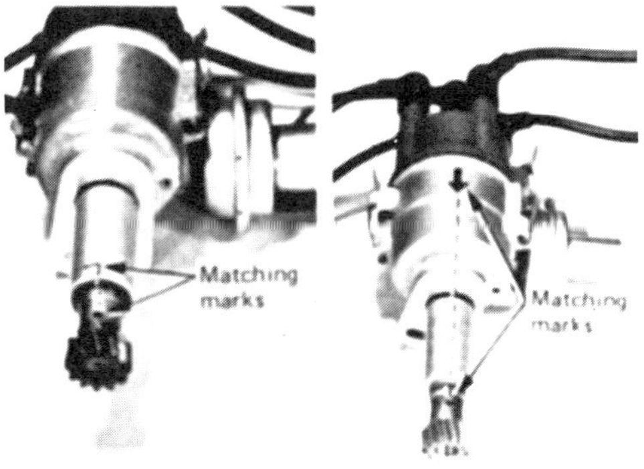

Fig. 4.3. Aligning the distributor setting marks

6 Distributor (contact breaker type) - dismantling, inspection and reassembly

1 Remove the distributor cap, rotor and, if fitted, the dust cover and dust cover packing.

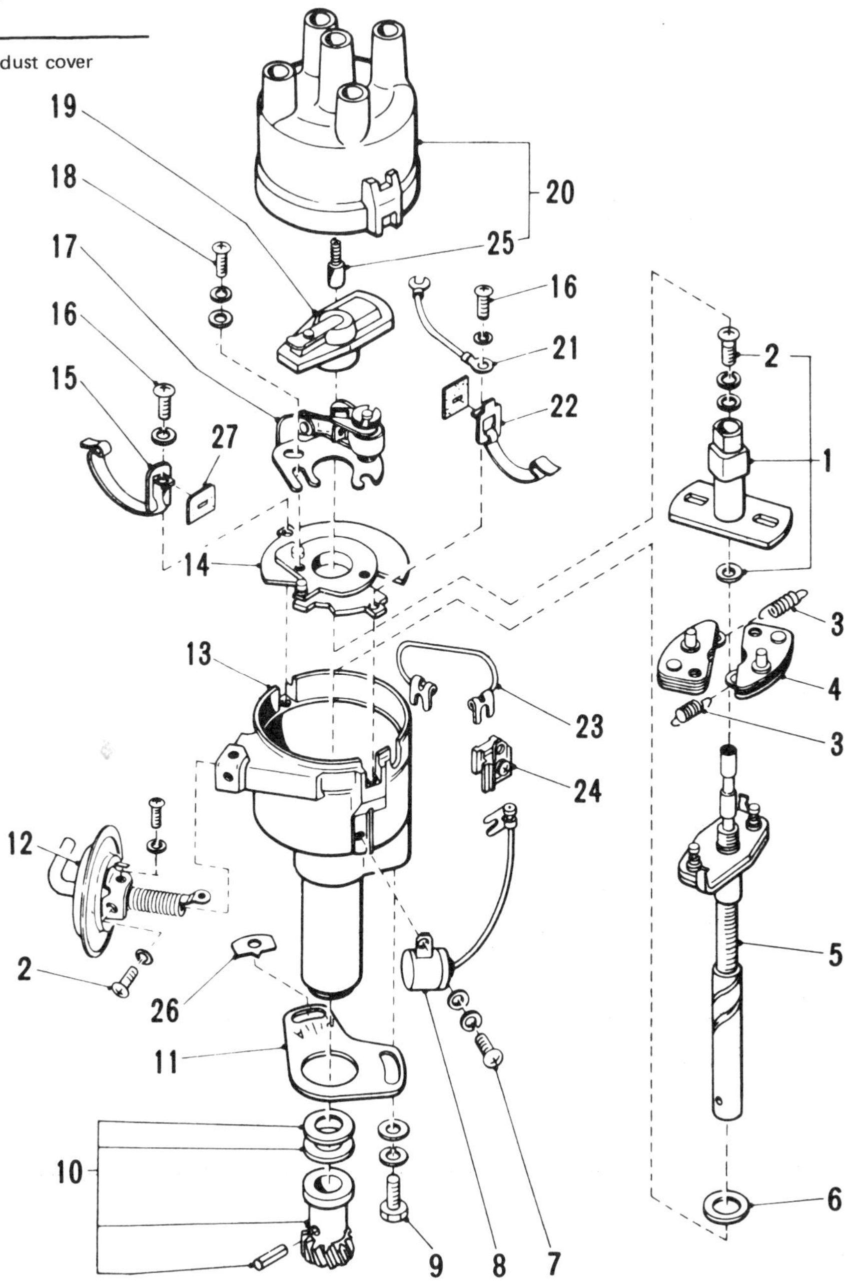

Fig. 4.4. Exploded view of Hitachi distributor; type No. D412-83A

1 Cam
2 Screw
3 Governor spring
4 Governor weight
5 Distributor shaft
6 Washer
7 Screw
8 Condenser
9 Bolt
10 Pinion
11 Plate
12 Vacuum control
13 Housing
14 Contact breaker plate
15 Clamp II
16 Screw
17 Contact set
18 Contact set screw
19 Rotor head
20 Cap
21 Ground wire
22 Clamp I
23 Lead wire
24 Terminal
25 Carbon point
26 Indicator
27 Seal II

2 Remove the nut, terminal and terminal insulator.
3 Unscrew the three securing screws and remove the contact breaker set, and damper spring, if fitted.
4 Remove the snap washer, securing screw, condenser and vacuum unit.
5 Remove the two screws securing the contact breaker plate and remove the plate. Remove the two governor springs, take care not to open the spring end too wide.
6 Remove the cam securing screw and remove the cam from the distributor shaft.
7 Drill the end of the pinion retaining pin, to remove the staking and then tap out the pin and remove the pinion.
8 Pull the shaft from the housing and remove the snap washers and governor weights
9 Clean all the disassembled parts and inspect for damage and wear. Check the diaphragm of the vacuum unit, by sucking the retard-side pipe and, if the plunger does not move, replace the vacuum unit with a new one. Inspect the cap and rotor for cracks, corrosion and burnt terminals. Check the spring action of the carbon brush. Inspect the surface of the contact points for burning and pitting. If pitting is slight correct with an oilstone, otherwise renew the contact points.
10 Reassembly is the reverse of dismantling. Lubricate the shaft, cam and the heel of the contact arm and damper spring lightly with high melting point grease. When fitting the pinion adjust the thrust clearance of the shaft, by selecting the correct thrust washers, to 0.006 - 0.019 in (0.15 - 0.5 mm). Washers are available in two thicknesses 0.004 and 0.012 in (0.1 and 0.3 mm).
11 Adjust the contact point gap and the damper spring gap to the dimension specified in Specifications at the beginning of this Chapter.
12 After assembly check the operation of the governor by holding the pinion and turning the rotor to the left. When the rotor is released it must return freely to its original position.

7 Distributor (breakerless Nippon Denso) - dismantling, inspection and reassembly

1 Remove the cap, rotor, dust cover and dust cover packing.
2 Remove the pick-up coil securing screws and remove the coil. Remove the vacuum unit attaching screw, pull the vacuum unit and turn it clockwise about 90° to remove it.
3 Remove the two securing screws and lift the pick-up base out of the housing.
4 Drill the end of the pinion retaining pin to remove the staking, then tap out the pin and remove the pinion and thrust washers.
5 Remove the governor shaft from the housing and remove the governor springs with long nosed pliers. Take care not to open the spring end too wide.
6 Disassemble the flyweight by removing the two snap washers. Remove the rubber cap and screw, then remove the cam and timing rotor from the governor shaft.
7 Clean all the disassembled parts and check for damage and wear. Check the diaphragm in the vacuum unit, and the cap and rotor as described for the breaker type distributor.

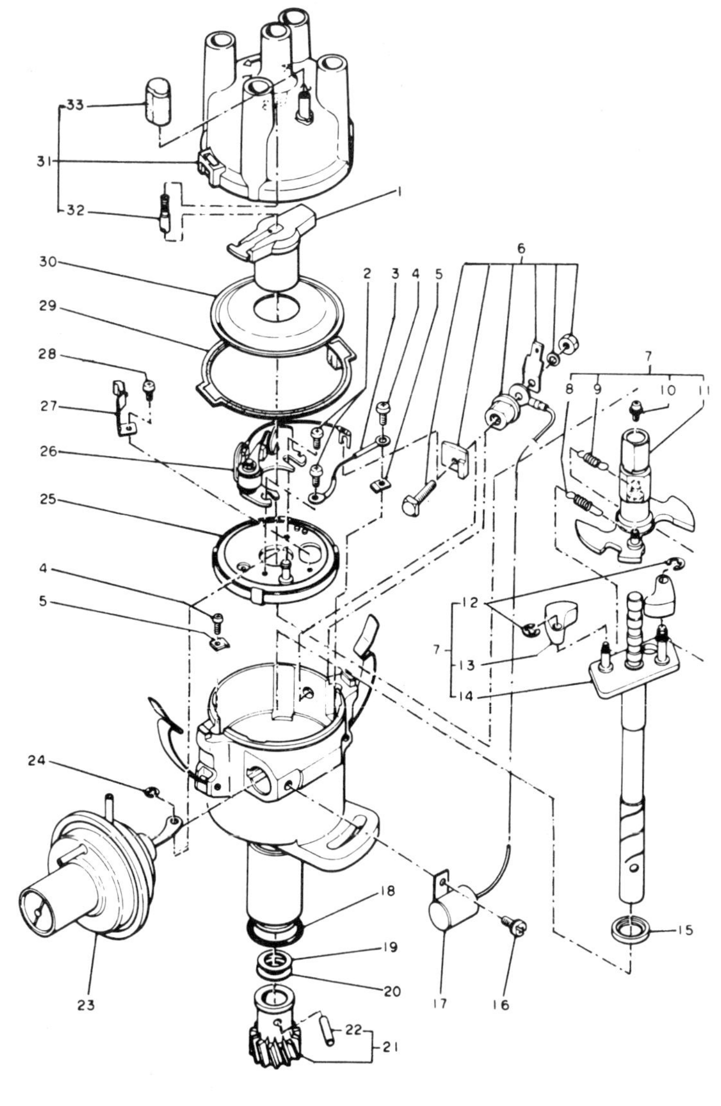

Fig. 4.5. Exploded view of Nippon Denso distributor; type No. 029100-3710

1 *Rotor (distributor)*
2 *Set screw (contact breaker)*
3 *Earth wire (distributor)*
4 *Screw (round head)*
5 *Plate*
6 *Terminal set*
7 *Shaft and governor assembly*
8 *Spring B (governor)*
9 *Spring A (governor)*
10 *Screw and washer*
11 *Cam assembly (distributor)*
12 *Clip (snap ring)*
13 *Weight (governor)*
14 *Shaft assembly (distributor)*
15 *Washer*
16 *Screw and washer*
17 *Condenser (distributor)*
18 *'O' ring*
19 *Thrust washer (0.1)*
20 *Thrust washer (0.3)*
21 *Pinion set (distributor)*
22 *Straight pin*
23 *Vacuum controller assembly*
24 *Clip (snap ring)*
25 *Plate complete (contact breaker)*
26 *Contact breaker set*
27 *Spring (damper)*
28 *Screw and washer*
29 *Packing (dust proof)*
30 *Cover (dust proof)*
31 *Cap assembly (distributor)*
32 *Carbon point (distributor)*
33 *Cap (rubber)*

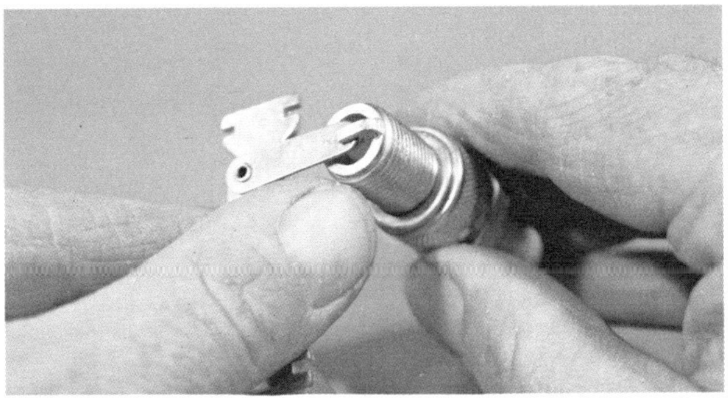

Measuring plug gap. A feeler gauge of the correct size (see ignition system specifications) should have a slight 'drag' when slid between the electrodes. Adjust gap if necessary

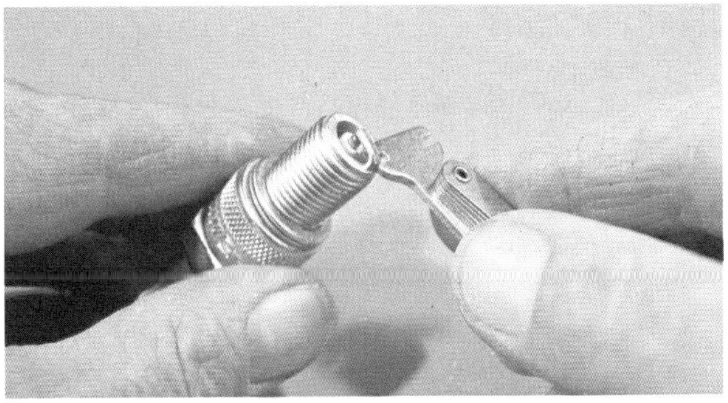

Adjusting plug gap. The plug gap is adjusted by bending the earth electrode inwards, or outwards, as necessary until the correct clearance is obtained. Note the use of the correct tool

Normal. Grey-brown deposits, lightly coated core nose. Gap increasing by around 0.001 in (0.025 mm) per 1000 miles (1600 km). Plugs ideally suited to engine, and engine in good condition

Carbon fouling. Dry, black, sooty deposits. Will cause weak spark and eventually misfire. Fault: over-rich fuel mixture. Check: carburettor mixture settings, float level and jet sizes; choke operation and cleanliness of air filter. Plugs can be re-used after cleaning

Oil fouling. Wet, oily deposits. Will cause weak spark and eventually misfire. Fault: worn bores/piston rings or valve guides; sometimes occurs (temporarily) during running-in period. Plugs can be re-used after thorough cleaning

Overheating. Electrodes have glazed appearance, core nose very white – few deposits. Fault: plug overheating. Check: plug value, ignition timing, fuel octane rating (too low) and fuel mixture (too weak). Discard plugs and cure fault immediately

Electrode damage. Electrodes burned away; core nose has burned, glazed appearance. Fault: pre-ignition. Check: as for 'Overheating' but may be more severe. Discard plugs and remedy fault before piston or valve damage occurs

Split core nose (may appear initially as a crack). Damage is self-evident, but cracks will only show after cleaning. Fault: pre-ignition or wrong gap-setting technique. Check: ignition timing, cooling system, fuel octane rating (too low) and fuel mixture (too weak). Discard plugs, rectify fault immediately

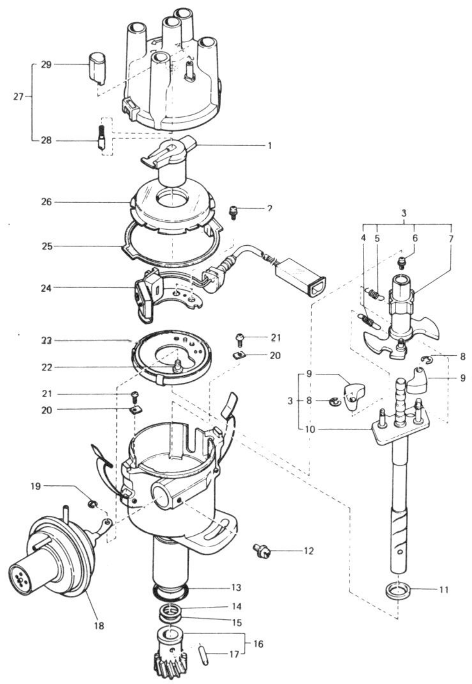

Fig. 4.6. Exploded view of Nippon Denso breakerless distributor for 1977 models with manual transmission

1 Distributor rotor
2 Screw and washer
3 Shaft and governor assembly
4 Governor spring B
5 Governor spring A
6 Screw and washer
7 Signal rotor sub assembly
8 Snap ring clip
9 Governor weight
10 Distributor shaft assembly
11 Washer
12 Screw and washer
13 'O' ring
14 Thrust washer (0.1)
15 Thrust washer (0.3)
16 Distributor pinion set
17 Straight pin (5 x 20)
18 Vacuum controller assembly
19 Snap ring clip
20 Plate
21 Round head screw
22 Screw and washer
23 Contact breaker plate complete
24 Pick-up coil set
25 Dust proof packing
26 Dust proof cover
27 Distributor cap assembly
28 Carbon point complete
29 Rubber cap

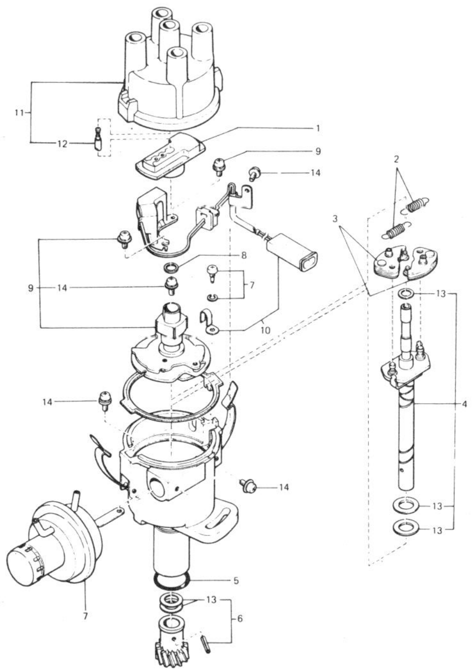

Fig. 4.7. Exploded view of Hitachi breakerless distributor for 1977 models with automatic transmission

1 Rotor
2 Governor spring set
3 Weight
4 Shaft and governor assembly
5 O-ring
6 Point set
7 Vacuum controller assembly
8 Dust proof packing
9 Contact breaker plate assembly
10 Pick up coil set
11 Cap
12 Carbon point
13 Thrust washer
14 Screw kit

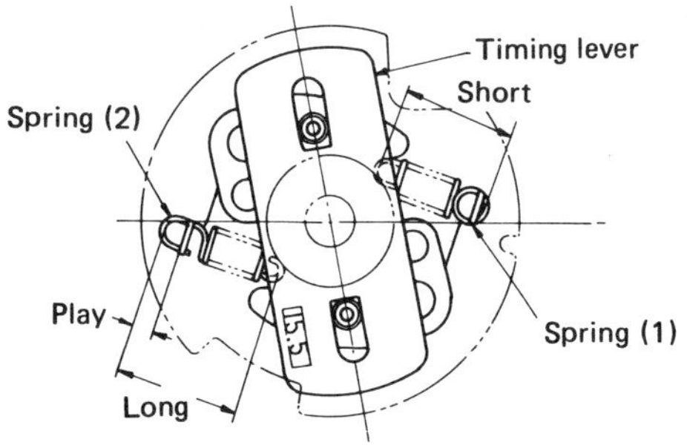

Fig. 4.8. Fitting the governor springs

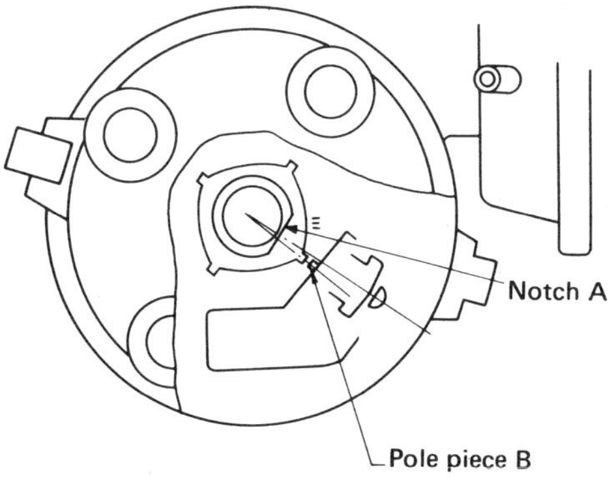

Fig. 4.9. Fitting the pinion on the shaft

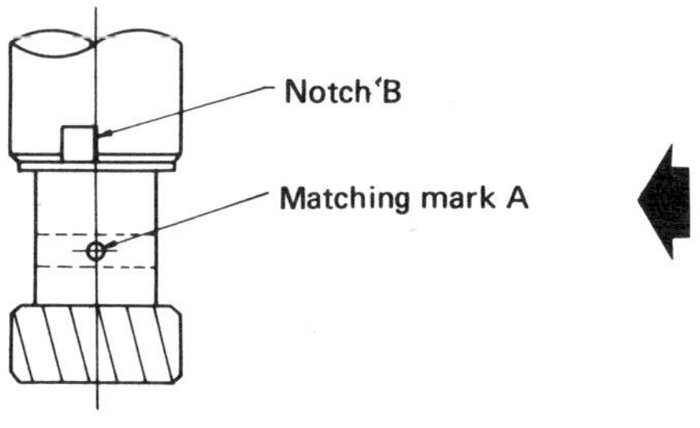

Fig. 4.10. Pinion to housing alignment marks

8 Assembly is the reverse of dismantling, however, pay attention to the following:

a) When assembling the cam, match the 15.5 mark on the cam plate and stopper thru the hole in the governor shaft. Pack high melting point grease into the inside of the cam.
b) When fitting the governor shaft in the housing coat the shaft with engine oil.
c) When fitting the spiral gear, adjust the clearance between the spiral gear and housing to 0.006 - 0.019 in (0.15 - 0.5 mm) with thrust washers. Thrust washers are supplied in two thicknesses 0.004 - 0.012 in (0.1 and 0.3 mm).
d) When fitting the pick-up coil base plate align the four clips of the base plate with the grooves in the housing.
e) After fitting the pick-up coil on the base plate adjust the air gap to 0.008 - 0.016 in (0.2 - 0.4 mm).

9 After assembly check the operation of the governor as described in Section 6, paragraph 12.

8 Distributor (breakerless - Hitachi) - dismantling, inspection and reassembly

1 Remove the cap and rotor head.
2 Remove the clamp holding the leads on the inside and outside of the housing and the pick-up coil securing screws and lift out the pick-up coil.
3 Remove the vacuum unit.
4 Drive out the pin securing the pinion, then remove the pinion and thrust washer.
5 Remove the pick-up base securing screws and withdraw the rotor assembly.
6 Remove the rubber cap on top of the rotor shaft, then the retaining screw, and remove the rotor shaft.
7 Remove the weights and springs, match mark the parts so that they can be refitted in the same positions.
8 Clean and inspect the parts as described in Section 7, paragraph 6.
9 Assembly is the reverse of dismantling. When fitting the springs and rotor shaft, fit the spring with the longer free length to the starter hole side of the timing lever as shown in Fig. 4.8. Align the notch on the pick-up base with the grooved end of the housing. When fitting the pick-up coil, adjust the air gap to 0.012 - 0.016 in (0.3 - 0.4 mm). To refit the pinion, position notch 'A' on the rotor shaft opposite the pole piece 'B', as shown in Fig. 4.9, and align the mark 'A' on the pinion with the notch 'B' at the lower end of the housing as shown in Fig. 4.10.
10 After assembly check the operation of the governor as described in Section 6, paragraph 12.

9 Ignition control unit - removal and refitting

The ignition control unit for breakerless ignition systems is located on the firewall, right-hand side, in the engine compartment. The only maintenance required is to keep the external surface clean and dry.
1 Disconnect the ground lead from the negative (—) terminal of the battery.
2 Note the connections and disconnect the wiring harness from the control unit.
3 Remove the two attaching bolts and remove the unit.
4 Refitting is the reverse of removal. Be sure to connect the wiring correctly. Failure to do so will damage the unit.

10 Coil - general

The ignition coil is an oil-filled type. The coil case is filled with oil which provides good insulating and heat - radiating characteristics.

The coil has a greater ratio between the primary and secondary windings to step up the battery voltage to the high voltage required to generate a spark at the spark plugs.

Coil testing is normally done during tests applied to the ignition system in the course of fault diagnosing. The testing involves checking that current flows through the primary windings and that the secondary windings deliver a high voltage.

11 Ignition timing - checking and adjusting

The ignition timing marks on the flywheel are graduated in steps of 2° from 0° to 16°, and can be seen thru a hole in the flywheel housing.
1 Remove the plastic cover from the flywheel housing.
2 Disconnect the vacuum hose/s from the vacuum unit to prevent the vacuum advance and retard operating while checking the ignition. Plug the end of the vacuum hoses. On early models ensure that the octane selector is set midway between 'A' and 'R'.
3 Clean the timing scale on the flywheel and mark the specified timing degree line and the tip of the pointer with quick drying white paint or with chalk.
4 Run the engine to normal operating temperature and check that the idling speed is correct.
5 Connect a stroboscope timing light between No. 1 spark plug and the No. 1 spark plug lead.
6 Start the engine and point the stroboscope at the white painted marks. They will appear stationary and if the timing is correct they will be in alignment.
7 If they are not directly opposite each other, adjust by loosening the 6 mm bolt on the mounting plate of the distributor and turning the distributor housing one way or the other until the marks line up. The timing is advanced when the distributor housing is turned clockwise and is retarded when turned counterclockwise. Tighten the bolt and recheck the timing.
8 If the engine speed is now increased the white mark on the flywheel will move away from the fixed pointer indicating that the centrifugal advance is operating. If the vacuum hoses are unplugged and reconnected to the vacuum unit the operation of the vacuum unit can be checked by revving up the engine and watching the timing marks.
9 Remove the timing light and reconnect the HT lead to the spark plug. Refit the plastic cover on the flywheel housing.
10 On distributors with contact breaker points the timing can be adjusted, though not so accurately, by setting the engine to the timing position as above and turning the distributor housing until the points just begin to open. This can be checked by connecting a test lamp between the distributor primary terminal and a good ground and switching on the ignition. When the points open, the test lamp will come on.
11 On breakerless ignition systems the only method of checking the timing is with a stroboscopic timing light.

12 Octane selector (1970 - 1973 models) - adjustment

The octane selector provides a means of adjusting the ignition

11.3 Clean the flywheel timing scale markings

timing, to the octane value of the gasoline being used. The selector consists of a scale on the distributor mounting plate and a pointer secured by the distributor retaining bolts.
1 Position the scale so that the pointer is midway between the 'A' and 'R' on the scale.
2 With the engine at normal operating temperature drive the car at 14 mph (20 kmh) in top gear on a level road.
3 Sudden acceleration should produce a slight knocking noise from the engine which should disappear as speed increases.
4 If the knocking is loud or if it doesn't stop as the speed increases, loosen the retaining bolt and turn the distributor to retard the timing. If there is no knocking, advance the timing until a slight knocking can be heard under the conditions described in paragraphs 2 and 3 above.
5 Don't forget to tighten the retaining bolt after each adjustment.

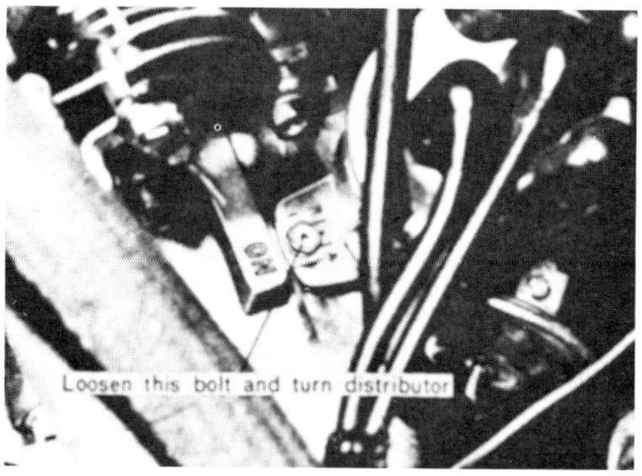

Fig. 4.11. Adjusting the octane selector - 1972 - 73 models

13 Spark plugs and leads

See page 83 for spark plug illustrations.
1 The correct functioning of the spark plugs is vital for the proper running and efficient operation of the engine.
2 At intervals of 6000 miles (10000 km) the plugs should be removed, examined, cleaned and if worn excessively, renewed. The condition of the spark plug can tell much about the general condition of the engine.
3 If the insulator nose of the spark plug is clean and white, with no deposits, this is indicative of a weak mixture, or too hot a plug (a hot plug transfers heat away from the electrodes slowly - a cold plug transfers heat away quickly).
4 If the insulator nose is covered with hard black looking deposits, then this is indicative that the mixture is too rich. Should the plug be black and oily then it is likely that the engine is fairly worn as well as the mixture being too rich.
5 If the insulator nose is covered with light tan to greyish brown deposits, then the mixture is correct, and it is likely that the engine is in good condition.
6 If there are any traces of long brown tapering stains on the outside of the white portion of the plug, then the plug will have to be renewed, as this shows that there is a faulty joint between the plug body and the insulator, and compression is being allowed to leak away.
7 Plugs should be cleaned by a sand blasting machine, which will free them from carbon more completely than cleaning by hand. The machine will also test the condition of the plugs under compression. Any plug that fails to spark at the recommended pressure should be renewed.
8 The spark plug gap is of considerable importance, as, if it is too large or too small the size of the spark and its efficiency will be seriously impaired. The spark plug gap should be set to 0.028 - 0.032 in (0.7 - 0.8 mm).
9 To set it, measure the gap with a feeler gauge, and then bend open, or close, the outer plug electrode until the correct gap is achieved. The center electrode should never be bent as this may crack the insulation and cause plug failure, if nothing worse.
10 When refitting the plugs, remember to use new washers and refit the leads from the distributor cap in the correct firing order which is 1, 3, 2, 4, No. 1 cylinder being the right-hand front one.
11 The plug leads require no maintenance other than being kept clean and wiped over regularly. At intervals of 6000 miles (10000 km) however, pull each lead off the plug in turn and remove it from the distributor cap. Water can seep down these joints giving rise to a white corrosive deposit which must be carefully removed from the end of each cable. At the same time, check that the suppressor connections are in good condition. If cracked or damaged they should be renewed.

14 Fault diagnosis - ignition system

There are two general symptoms of ignition faults. Either the engine will not fire, or the engine is difficult to start and misfires. If it is a regular misfire the fault is almost certain to be in the secondary (high tension) circuit. If the misfiring is intermittent, the fault could be in either the secondary or primary (low tension) circuits. If the engine stops suddenly, or will not start, it is most likely that the fault is in the primary circuit. Detail investigations and the explanation and remedial action in respect of symptoms of ignition malfunction are described in the following sub-sections.

Engine fails to start

1 If the engine fails to start and the car was running normally when it was last used, first check that there is gasoline in the fuel tank. If the engine turns over normally on the starter motor and the battery is evidently well charged, then the fault may be in either the primary or secondary circuits. Check the secondary circuit first.
Note: If the battery is known to be fully charged, the charge light comes on, and the starter motor fails to turn the engine check the tightness of the leads on the battery terminals and also the security of the ground lead to its connection on the body. It is possible for the leads to have become loose, even if they look and feel secure. If one of the battery terminals gets very hot when trying to operate the starter motor this is a sure indication of a faulty connection.
2 One of the commonest reasons for bad starting is wet or damp spark plug leads and distributor. Remove the distributor cap. If condensation is visible, dry the cap, inside and out, with a dry cloth and also wipe over the high tension leads. Refit the cap.
3 If the engine still does not start, check that current is reaching the spark plugs by disconnecting each plug lead in turn, at the spark plug end, and hold the end of the lead about 0.2 in (5 mm) away from the crankcase. Spin the engine on the starter motor. Sparking between the end of the lead and the crankcase should be regular with a strong blue spark. (Hold the lead with rubber to avoid electric shocks). If current is reaching the plugs, remove and clean them, and reset the gap. The engine should now start.
4 If there is no spark at the plug leads take off the high tension lead from the center of the distributor cap and hold it to the crankcase as before. Spin the engine on the starter motor once more. A rapid succession of blue sparks between the end of the lead and the crankcase indicates that the coil is in order and that the distributor cap is cracked, the rotor arm faulty, or that the carbon brush in the top of the distributor cap is not making good contact with the spring on the rotor arm. Possibly the points are in poor condition. Clean them and reset the gap as described in Section 2.
5 If there are no sparks from the end of the lead from the coil, check the connections at the coil end of the lead. If it is in order start checking the primary circuit.
6 Use a 12V voltmeter or a 12V bulb and two lengths of wire. With the ignition switch on and the points open, test between the primary lead to the coil (it is marked +) and ground. No reading indicates a break in the supply from the ignition switch. Check the connections at the switch to see if any are loose, if they are, refit them and the engine should start. A reading indicates a faulty coil or condenser, or broken lead between the coil and the distributor.
7 Disconnect the condenser lead from the points assembly and with the points open, test between the moving point and ground. If there is now a reading, then the fault is in the condenser and a new one is required.
8 With no reading from the moving point to ground, take a reading between ground and the negative (—) terminal on the coil. A reading here indicates a broken wire, which will have to be renewed, between the coil and distributor. No reading confirms that the coil has failed and must be renewed, after which the engine should start. Remember to fit the condenser lead to the points assembly. For these tests it is sufficient to separate the points with a piece of dry paper while testing with the points open.

Engine misfires

9 If the engine misfires regularly, run it at a fast idling speed. Disconnect each plug lead in turn and listen to the note of the engine. Hold the plug lead with a dry cloth or with a rubber glove as protection against a shock from the high tension voltage.

10 No difference in engine running will be noticed when the lead from a defective circuit is removed. Removing the lead from one of the good cylinders will accentuate the misfire.

11 Disconnect the lead from the spark plug in the defective circuit and hold the end of it about 0.2 in (5 mm) away from the crankcase. If the sparking is strong and regular then the spark plug is defective. The insulation may be cracked, or the electrodes may have burned away giving too wide a gap for the spark to jump, or carbon deposits may have closed the gap. Either renew the plug or clean it and reset the gap.

12 If there is no spark at the end of the plug lead, or if it is weak and intermittent, check the high tension lead from the distributor to the plug. If the insulation is cracked or perished, renew the lead. Check the connection at the distributor cap.

13 If there is still no spark, examine the distributor cap carefully for tracking. This can be recognised by a very thin black line running between two or more segments, or between a segment and some other part of the distributor. These lines are paths which now conduct electricity across the cap thus letting it run to ground. The only answer is a new distributor cap.

14 Apart from the ignition timing being incorrect, other causes of misfiring have already been dealt with under the sub-section dealing with the failure of the engine to start.

15 If the ignition is too far retarded, it should be noted that the engine will tend to overheat, and there will be quite a noticeable drop in power. If the engine is overheating and the power is down, and the ignition timing is correct, then the carburetor should be checked as it is likely that this is where the fault lies.

Chapter 5 Clutch

Contents

Specifications

Type	Dry, single disc type	
	All models except 1600 and 4WD vehicles	*1600 and 4WD vehicles*
Clutch disc facing size		
Outer diameter x inside diameter x thickness	7.09 x 4.92 x 0.12 in (180 x 125 x 3.2 mm)	7.87 x 5.12 x 0.14 in (200 x 130 x 3.5 mm)
Material	Woven asbestos	
Total friction area	20.5 sq in x 2 (132 sq cm x 2)	28.2 sq in x 2 (182 sq cm x 2)
Minimum allowable depth of rivet head from facing surface	0.012 in (0.3 mm)	
Maximum allowable facing run-out	0.0197 in (0.5 mm)	0.028 in (0.7 mm)

Torque wrench settings	**lb f ft**	**kg f m**
Clutch assembly retaining bolt		
1100, 1300 and 1400 models	7.2	1.0
1600 and 4WD vehicles	11.6	1.6

1 General description

1 The clutch is a single dry plate type and is cable operated from the clutch pedal. The clutch disc facings are of woven asbestos. The clutch cover assembly is a diaphragm spring type.
2 When the clutch pedal is depressed the clutch springs are compressed which releases the pressure plate pressure, thereby freeing the driven plate (disc), which is splined to the gearbox input shaft. When the clutch driven plate is freed there is no drive from the engine to the gearbox, and when engaged, drive is transmitted from the engine to the gearbox. Fig. 5.1. shows a cross-section thru the clutch.
3 The clutch release bearing is grease-sealed and no additional lubrication is required. If the release bearing is not being renewed at overhaul take care not to wash the bearing in cleaning fluid.
4 Adjustment of the release fork end play is by means of the spherical nut located at the end of the release fork.

2 Clutch cable - removal and refitting

1 Remove the spring clip and washer at the pedal end and disconnect the clutch cable from the clutch pedal.
2 Remove the return spring from the end of the clutch release fork.
3 Slacken off the locknut and adjusting nut at the end of the clutch release fork.
4 Remove the retaining clip and clamp securing the clutch cable to the support bracket, the two rubber grommets and washers. Release the cable from the bracket. Remove the spring support.
5 Withdraw the cable through the firewall into the engine compartment.
6 Refitting is the reverse of the removal sequence. After fitting

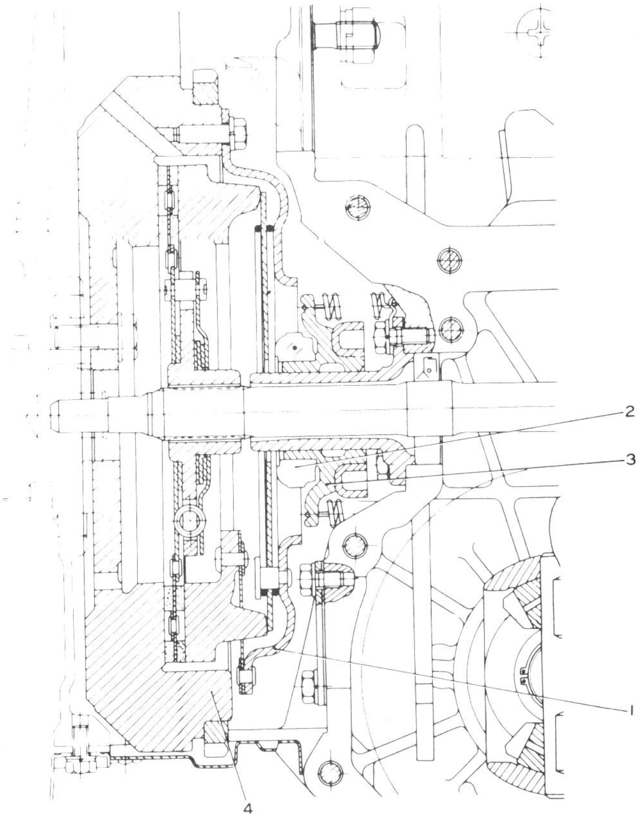

Fig. 5.1. Cross-section thru clutch

1 *Clutch cover*
2 *Clutch release bearing*
3 *Release bearing holder*
4 *Flywheel*

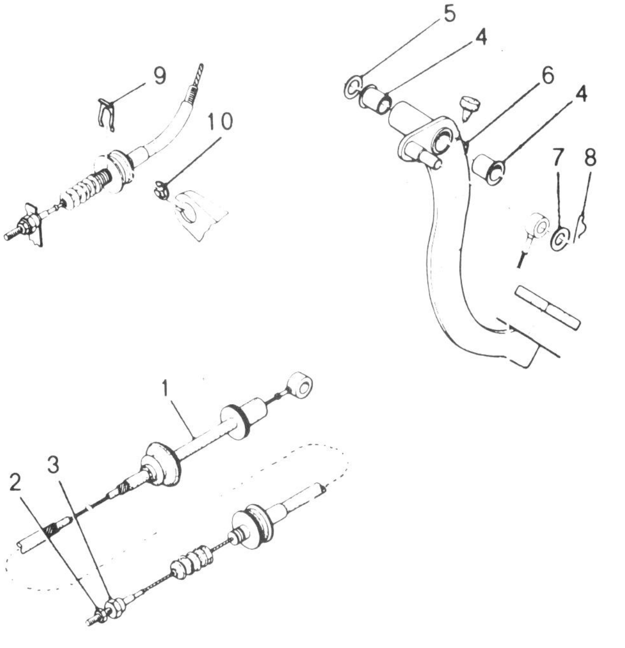

Fig. 5.2. Clutch cable and pedal assembly

1 *Clutch cable assembly*
2 *Nut*
3 *Nut (clutch cable)*
4 *Bushing (pedal)*
5 *Washer (pedal)*
6 *Clutch pedal complete*
7 *Washer*
8 *Snap pin*
9 *Clamp*
10 *Clip (retainer)*

2.2 Unhook the clutch return spring from the release fork

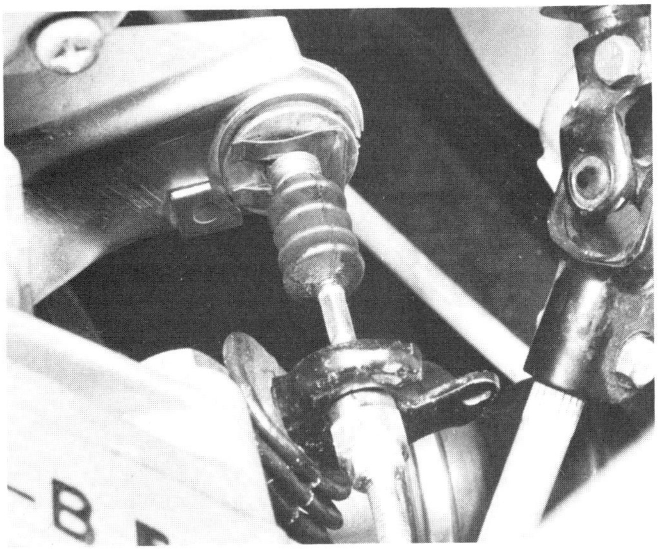

2.3 Slacken off the locknut and adjusting nut at the clutch release fork

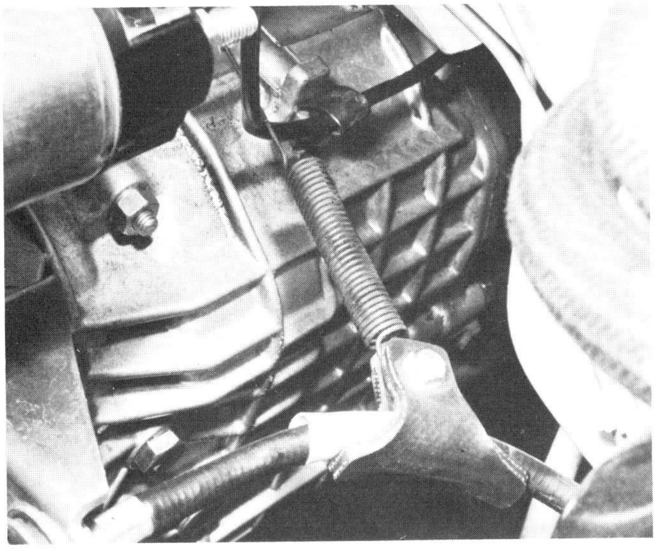

2.4 Remove the spring support from the clutch cable

adjust the clutch free play as described in Section 3.

3 Clutch free play - adjustment

1 To adjust the clutch play, remove the release fork spring attached to the clutch release fork.
2 Slacken the locknut and turn the spherical nut so that the play at the fork end is 0.142 to 0.181 in (3.6 to 4.6 mm). Take care not to twist the cable during adjustment.
Note: The clutch pedal free play is 0.94 to 1.18 in (24 to 30 mm) if the play at the release fork is correctly adjusted.
3 After completion of adjustment, tighten the locknut and fit the spring on the clutch release fork. Depress the clutch pedal and check the clutch operation.

4 Clutch - removal

1 Remove the engine/transmission for FF-1 1100 and 1300G models and separate the engine from the transmission as described in Chapter 1, Sections 4 and 7. For models from 1972 onwards remove the engine as described in Chapter 1, Section 5.
2 Restrain the flywheel from turning and slacken the cover assembly retaining bolts, working in a progressively diagonal sequence, so that the diaphragm spring pressure is released evenly to prevent any distortion.
3 When all the spring pressure on the bolts has been released, remove the bolts, clutch cover assembly and clutch disc. Take care not to contaminate the clutch disc facings with oil or grease.

5 Clutch - inspection and renovation

1 Do not dismantle either the clutch cover assembly or the clutch disc. Before inspection clean the parts, except the disc, with a suitable cleaning solvent to remove dirt and grease.
2 Examine the clutch disc facings for wear and contamination by oil. If the linings are dark in colour this indicates oil contamination caused by oil leaking past the crankshaft rear seal or the gearbox seal. An oil contaminated disc must be renewed. Check that depth of facing to rivet head is not less than 0.0118 in (0.3 mm). Check that there are no loose or broken damper springs or rivets on the disc and that the splines of the hub are in good condition.
3 Examine the friction faces of the flywheel and clutch pressure plate for scoring, caused by the heads of the rivets on the clutch disc, as a result of excessive wear of the facings. If there is deep scoring of the flywheel it will have to be machined (this is specialist work) or renewed. Scoring on the pressure plate or broken pressure spring necessitates the renewal of the complete clutch cover assembly.
4 Whenever the engine is removed for any reason, always examine the clutch operating mechanism and renew any worn parts as described in Section 7.

6 Clutch - refitting

1 Apply a light smear of molybdenum disulphide grease to the transmission main driveshaft splines. Slide the clutch disc on the main driveshaft several times. Remove the disc and clean off the excess grease pushed off by the disc hub.
2 Position the clutch disc, raised boss away from flywheel, and fit the clutch cover assembly to the flywheel. Fit the clutch cover to the flywheel so that there is a gap of at least 120° between the 'O' marks on the flywheel and clutch cover (the 'O' marks indicate the direction of residual unbalance). Fit the six retaining bolts and screw them in evenly just enough to grip the clutch disc but not enough to prevent it being moved.
3 Before tightening the retaining bolts it is necessary to line-up the center of the clutch disc with the pilot bearing in the crankshaft. This is easily done if you have a transmission main driveshaft available or a mandrel with the same spigot and spline diameter as the main driveshaft. It can also be aligned by eye, but this is not so reliable. If the clutch disc is not centered correctly, it will be impossible to fit the engine and transmission together and the main driveshaft may get damaged while attempting to do so.
4 With the clutch disc correctly positioned, proceed to tighten the retaining bolts in a progressive and even manner to a torque of 11.6 lb f ft (1.6 kg f m) for 1600 and 4WD vehicles, 7.2 lb f ft (1.0 kg f m) for all other models.

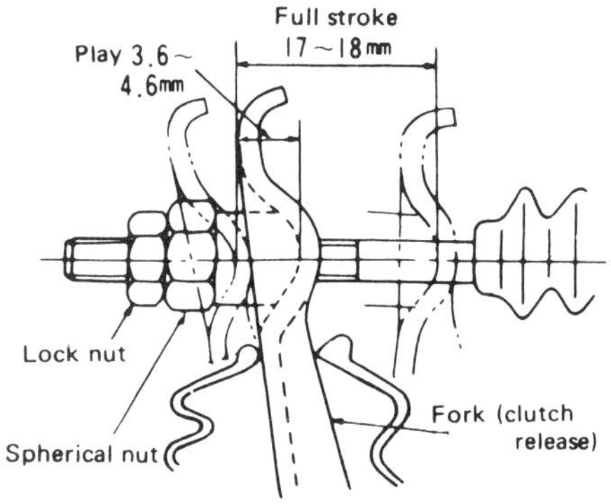

Fig. 5.3. Clutch free play adjustment

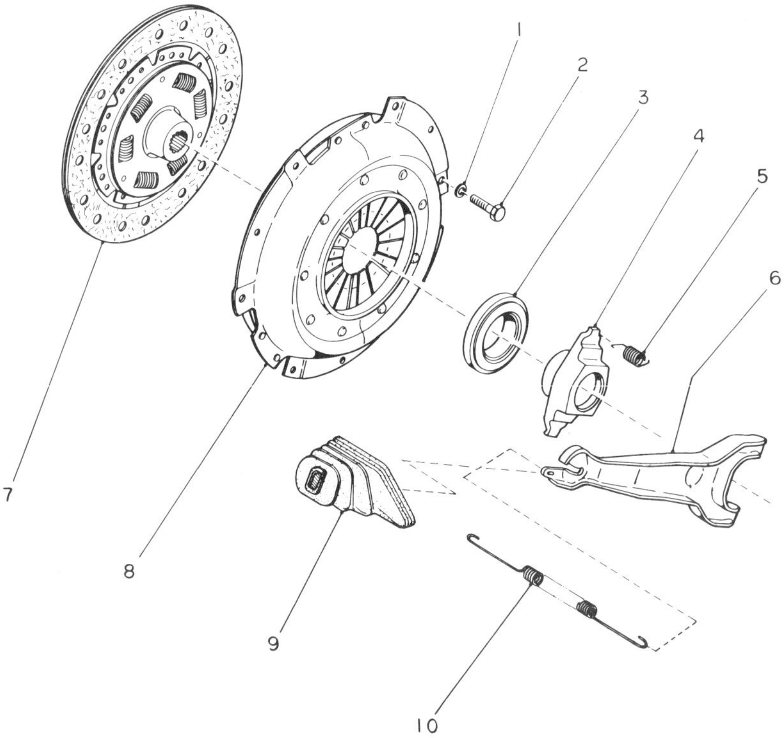

Fig. 5.4. Component parts of the clutch

1 Spring washer
2 Bolt
3 Clutch release bearing
4 Release bearing holder
5 Spring
6 Clutch release fork
7 Clutch disc complete
8 Clutch cover complete
9 Clutch release fork sealing
10 Release fork spring

5 Remove the centralising tool.
6 Refit the transmission and install the engine/transmission as described in Chapter 1.

7 Clutch release bearing and fork - removal, inspection and refitting

1 Refer to Chapter 1 and remove the engine or engine/transmission as appropriate.
2 Disconnect the return springs from the release bearing holder.
3 Remove the release bearing and holder as an assembly from the release bearing guide.
4 Remove the clutch release fork and fork seal.
5 Check the release bearing by rotating the bearing while applying pressure in the thrust direction, it should rotate smoothly. Check the contacting surface of the bearing holder with the release fork for wear or damage.
Note: This bearing is grease-sealed, do not wash with gasoline or any solvent when servicing the clutch.
6 Check the release fork and release bearing guide for worn fork pivot and contact point with release bearing holder. Check the guide shank for wear and damage.
7 When renewing the release bearing use a press to remove the bearing into the holder, do not apply pressure to the outer race.
8 Lubricate the following points with a light coat of multi-purpose grease:

a) Inner groove of release bearing sleeve.
b) Contact surfaces of fork, fork ball pin and guide.
c) Transmission main driveshaft.

Use a small amount of grease only, if too much is applied it will get on to the friction plates when warm, resulting in contaminated clutch disc facings.
9 Fit the clutch release fork seal on the front of the transmission. Insert the clutch release fork. Fit the release bearing holder and retain it with the two return springs.

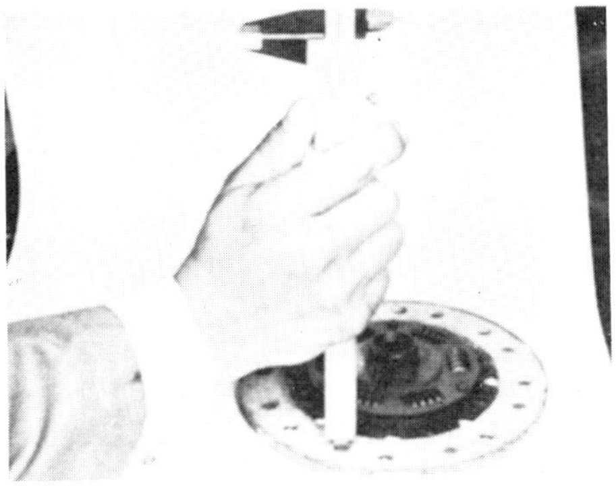

Fig. 5.5. Measuring facing wear

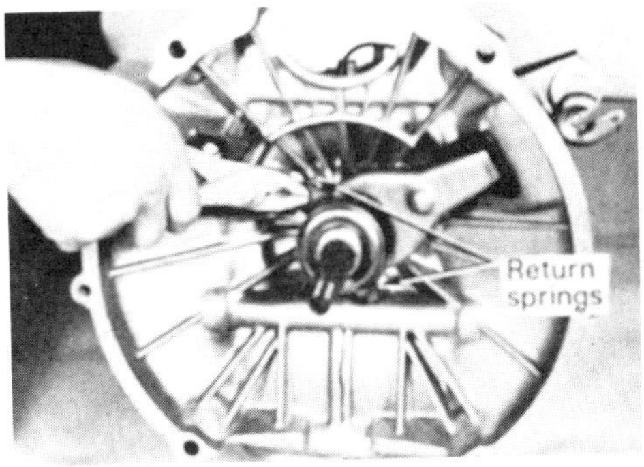

Fig. 5.6. Disconnecting return springs

6.2 Make sure the disc is fitted the right way round

6.3 Clutch release bearing and holder assembly

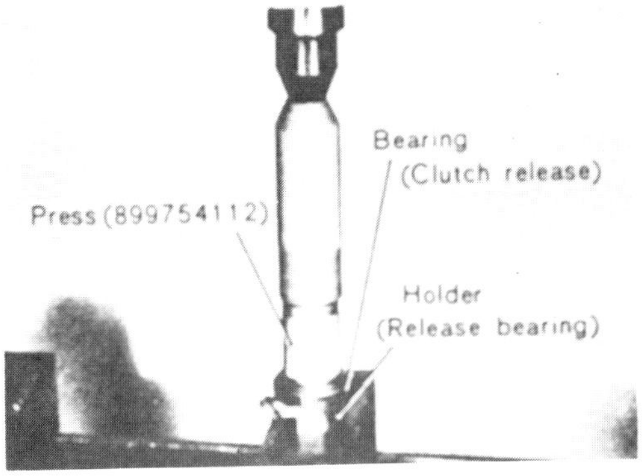

Fig. 5.7. Pressing a new release bearing into the holder

10 Refer to Chapter 1 and refit the engine or engine/transmission as appropriate.
11 Adjust the clutch release fork end play as described in Section 3.

8 Pilot bearing - renewal

1 Remove the clutch cover assembly as described in Section 4.
2 Remove the oil seal and pilot bearing from the end of the crankshaft.
3 Before fitting a new pilot bearing thoroughly clean the bearing hole in the crankshaft.
4 Use an aluminium mandrel when fitting the new bearing.
5 Pack the needle bearing with grease and fit a new oil seal.
6 Refit the clutch cover assembly as described in Section 6.

9 Clutch pedal - removal and refitting

The removal and refitting of the clutch pedal is described in Chapter 9, Section 16.

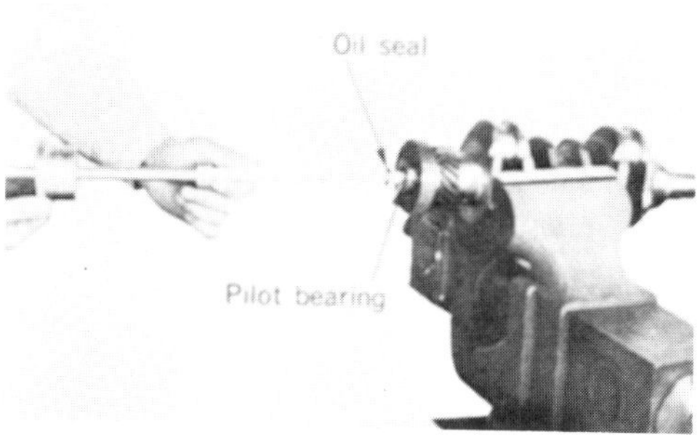

Fig. 5.8. Removing the pilot bearing

Fig. 5.9. Fitting the pilot bearing and oil seal

10 Fault diagnosis - clutch

Symptom	Reason/s	Remedy
Clutch slips	No release fork end play	Adjust.
	Clutch disc facings contaminated with oil	Renew clutch disc.
	Worn clutch disc facings	Renew clutch disc
Clutch drags	Excessive clutch release fork free play	Adjust.
	Worn clutch disc hub splines	Renew clutch disc.
	Seized pilot needle bearing	Renew.
Clutch judder	Hardened clutch disc facings	Roughen surface with emery cloth or renew clutch disc.
	Clutch disc facings contaminated	Renew clutch disc.
	Warped pressure plate or flywheel	Correct or renew as necessary.
	Loose disc rivets	Renew clutch disc.
	Loose engine mountings	Tighten or renew mounting.
Clutch noisy - clutch disengaged	Loose clutch disc hub	Renew clutch disc.
	Broken damper springs	Renew clutch disc.
Clutch noisy - clutch engaged	Worn, dry or broken release bearing	Renew release bearing.
	Broken or worn pilot needle bearing	Renew pilot bearing.

Chapter 6 Transmission

For modifications, and information applicable to later models, see Supplement at end of manual

Contents

Specifications

EA61 engine

	Sedan	Station Wagon
Type	4 forward speeds and 1 reverse	
Gear ratios		
1st	3.545 : 1	4.000 : 1
2nd	2.176 : 1	2.312 : 1
3rd	1.480 : 1	1.480 : 1
4th	1.033 : 1	1.033 : 1
Reverse	4.100 : 1	4.100 : 1

Reduction gear

Type of gear	Hypoid
Reduction ratio	4.125 : 1

Differential gear

Type and number of gears	Straight bevel gears - Pinion 2, side 2
Drive pinion/crown wheel backlash	0.0039 - 0.0059 in (0.10 - 0.15 mm)

Transmission mainshaft collar thrust and clearance	0 - 0.0079 in (0 - 0.02 mm)

Engine EA62, EA63A and EA63S

	EA62, EA63A	EA63S
Type	4 forward speed and 1 reverse	
Gear ratios		
1st	3.666 : 1	3.307 : 1
2nd	2.176 : 1	2.176 : 1
3rd	1.480 : 1	1;480 : 1
4th	1.033 : 1	1.033 : 1
Reverse	4.100 : 1	4.100 : 1

Reduction gear

Type of gear ...	Hypoid gear
Reduction ratio ...	3.889 : 1

Differential gear

Type and number of gears ...	Straight bevel gears - Pinion 2, side 2
Drive pinion/crown gear backlash ...	0.0039 - 0.0059 in (0.10 - 0.15 mm)

Transmission mainshaft collar thrust clearance ...	0 - 0.0079 in (0 - 0.02 mm)

Engine EA63AF6, EA63EF3 (4 wheel drive)

Type ...	4 forward speed and 1 reverse

Gear ratio

	EA63AF6	**EA63EF3**
1st ...	3.666 : 1	4.090 : 1
2nd ...	2.157 : 1	2.312 : 1
3rd ...	1.464 : 1	1.464 : 1
4th ...	1.029 : 1	1.029 : 1
Reverse ...	4.100 : 1	4.100 : 1

Reduction gear (front drive)

Type of gear ...	Hypoid
Reduction ratio ...	4.125 : 1

Differential gear

Type ...	Straight bevel gears - Pinion 2, side 2

Reduction gear (rear drive) (4 wheel drive)

1st reduction	
Type of gear ...	Helical gear
Reduction ratio ...	1.060 : 1
Final reduction	
Type of gear ...	Hypoid gear
Reduction ratio ...	3.900 : 1

Differential gear (Rear)

Type and number of gears ...	Straight bevel gears - Pinion 2, side 2
Drive pinion/crown gear backlash ...	0.0039 - 0.0059 in (0.10 - 0.15 mm)

Transmission mainshaft collar thrust clearance ...	0 - 0.0079 in (0 - 0.02 mm)

Engine EA63AP4

Type ...	5 forward speeds and 1 reverse

Gear ratios

1st ...	3.307 : 1
2nd ...	2.157 : 1
3rd ...	1.518 : 1
4th ...	1.156 : 1
5th ...	0.942 : 1
Reverse ...	4.100 : 1

Final reduction gear

Type of gear ...	Hypoid gear
Reduction ratio ...	4.125 : 1

Differential gear

Type and number of gears ...	Straight bevel gears - Pinion 2, side 2
Drive pinion/crown gear backlash ...	0.0039 - 0.0059 in (0.10 - 0.15 mm)

Transmission mainshaft collar thrust clearance ...	0 - 0.0079 in (0 - 0.02 mm)

Note: *Details of transmission units used in later models will be found in Chapter 13.*

Automatic transmission

Torque converter type ...	3 element, single stage, 2 phase
Transmission type ...	3 forward speeds with full automatic control and 1 reverse

Gear ratios

	Engine EA63AT5	**EA71AT, EA71AT4, EA71AT5 and EA71AT6**
1st ...	2.355 : 1	2.600 : 1
2nd ...	1.439 : 1	1.505 : 1
3rd ...	1.000 : 1	1.000 : 1
Reverse ...	2.086 : 1	2;167 : 1

Reduction gear

Type of gear	Hypoid	
Reduction ratio	4.125 : 1	3.700 : 1
Fluid	Automatic transmission fluid	

Final reduction gear lubricant

Final reduction gear lubricant	Hypoid gear oil

Torque wrench settings

	lb f ft	kg f m
Mainshaft locknut	58	8
Drive pinion locknut	58	8
Drive pinion bearing flange bolt	22	3
Differential crown gear bolts	42 - 49	5.8 - 6.8
Casing joining bolts		
8 mm	18	2.5
10 mm	29	4.0
Transmission cover bolts	18	2.5
Back-up lamp switch	13	1.8
Rear wheel carrier (4WD)		
Front mounting bolts	58 - 72	8 - 10
Rear mounting nuts	43 - 51	6 - 7
Rear drive shaft locknut (4WD)	58	8
Transfer casing bolts (4WD)	19	2.7
Rear casing bolts (4WD)	27	3.8
Rear differential pinion shaft flange nut (4WD)	123 - 145	17 - 20

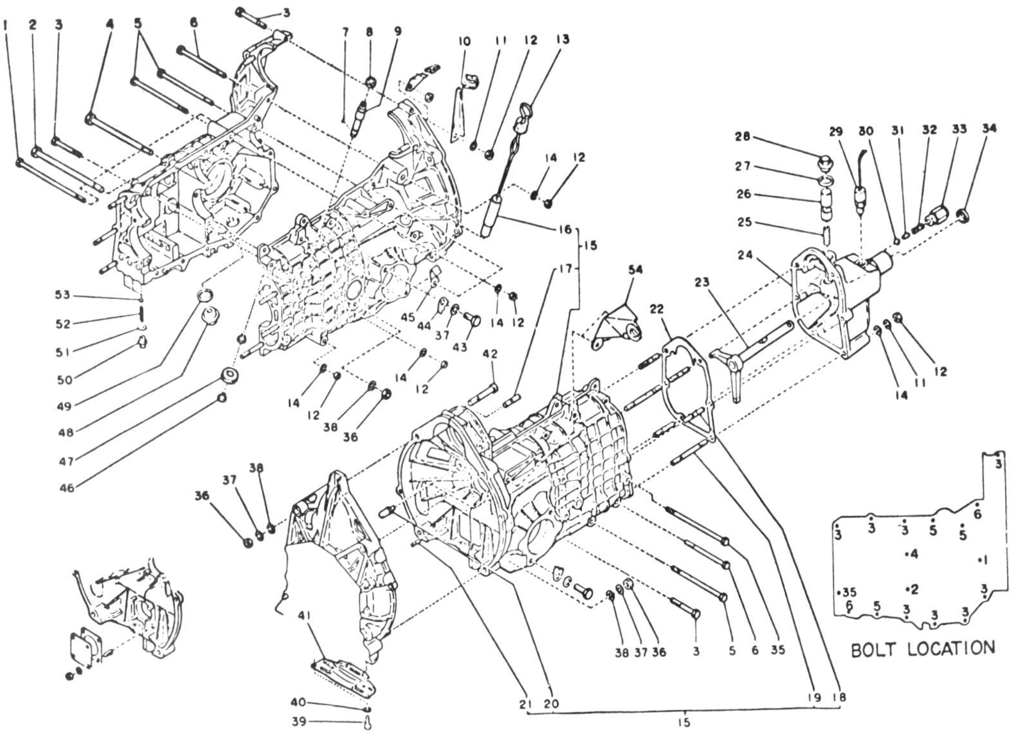

Fig. 6.1. Exploded view of 4-speed transmission casing assembly

1 *Bolt (8 x 163 x 13)*
2 *Bolt (10 x 168 x 18)*
3 *Bolt (8 x 62 x 18)*
4 *Bolt (10 x 152 x 18)*
5 *Bolt (8 x 122 x 21)*
6 *Bolt (8 x 110 x 18)*
7 *Woodruff key*
8 *Oil seal*
9 *Shaft (speedometer)*
10 *Bracket*
11 *Washer*
12 *Nut*
13 *Oil gauge*
14 *Washer*
15 *Transmission case assembly*
16 *Oil gauge guide*
17 *Stud bolt*
18 *Stud bolt (8 x 48 x 20)*
19 *Stud bolt (8 x 91 x 20)*
20 *Pivot (clutch release fork)*
21 *Stud bolt*
22 *Gasket (rear cover)*
23 *Shifter arm*
24 *Rear cover*
25 *Spring (reverse return)*
26 *Shaft (reverse accent)*
27 *Gasket (aluminium)*
28 *Plug*
29 *Neutral switch (newly added)*
30 *Ball*
31 *Straight pin*
32 *Spring (reverse accent)*
33 *Back-up lamp switch*
34 *Oil seal*
35 *Bolt (8 x 152 x 18)*
36 *Nut*
37 *Spring washer*
38 *Washer*
39 *Bolt*
40 *Spring washer*
41 *Cover II*
42 *Bolt (10 x 88 x 20)*
43 *Bolt*
44 *Lock plate (oil seal holder)*
45 *Clip (back-up lamp cord)*
46 *Snap ring*
47 *Speedometer driven gear*
48 *Oil drain plug*
49 *Gasket*
50 *Plug (shifter rail)*
51 *Gasket (aluminium)*
52 *Spring (shifter fork rail)*
53 *Ball*
54 *Clutch cable bracket*

1 General description

The manual transmission is of a four or five forward speed fully synchronized type with a sliding mesh reverse speed. Because of the front engine and front wheel drive system the differential is unified with the transmission, and is housed in the same aluminum casing which also serves as the clutch housing. The case can be split into two halves which are connected together by means of thru bolts.

The transmission and differential are lubricated by the same oil, and one filler/dipstick port and one drain plug are provided.

The hypoid gear, used in the differential is light in weight and compact in size, with quiet rotation due to the large tooth contact area.

The transmission gear shift is of a remote control floor shift type. It consists of a hand lever, a linkage connecting the hand lever to the transmission, and a bracket assembly which supports the linkage.

From 1975 a transfer for rear wheel drive for 4WD models is incorporated on the rear cover. The transfer is provided with a rear driveshaft for transmitting drive to the rear wheels, through the propeller shaft and rear differential. The rear roadwheels rotate with the drive pinion at a gear ratio of 1 : 1, while the rear driveshaft is equipped with a claw clutch for four wheel drive shifting. The claw clutch employs a conventional type synchromesh system to ensure that there is no damage to the gears when shifting to four wheel drive while the car is in motion.

Optional automatic transmission is available on most models.

Since hypoid gears are used for the final reduction, the gear oil must contain extreme-pressure additives, so use the correct hypoid gear oil always.

2 Transmission - removal

1 To remove the transmission from the car, it is necessary to remove the engine. The procedure for removal of engine and transmission as a unit is described in Chapter 1.
2 Separation of the transmission from the engine is described in Chapter 1, Section 7.

3 Rear differential carrier (4WD) - removal and refitting

1 Drain the gear oil from the differential carrier.
2 Chock the front wheels, jack up the rear of the car and support it on jackstands.
3 Remove the exhaust pipe and muffler.
4 Remove the propeller shaft and rear axle shafts as described in Chapter 7.
5 Support the differential carrier with a jack and remove the two

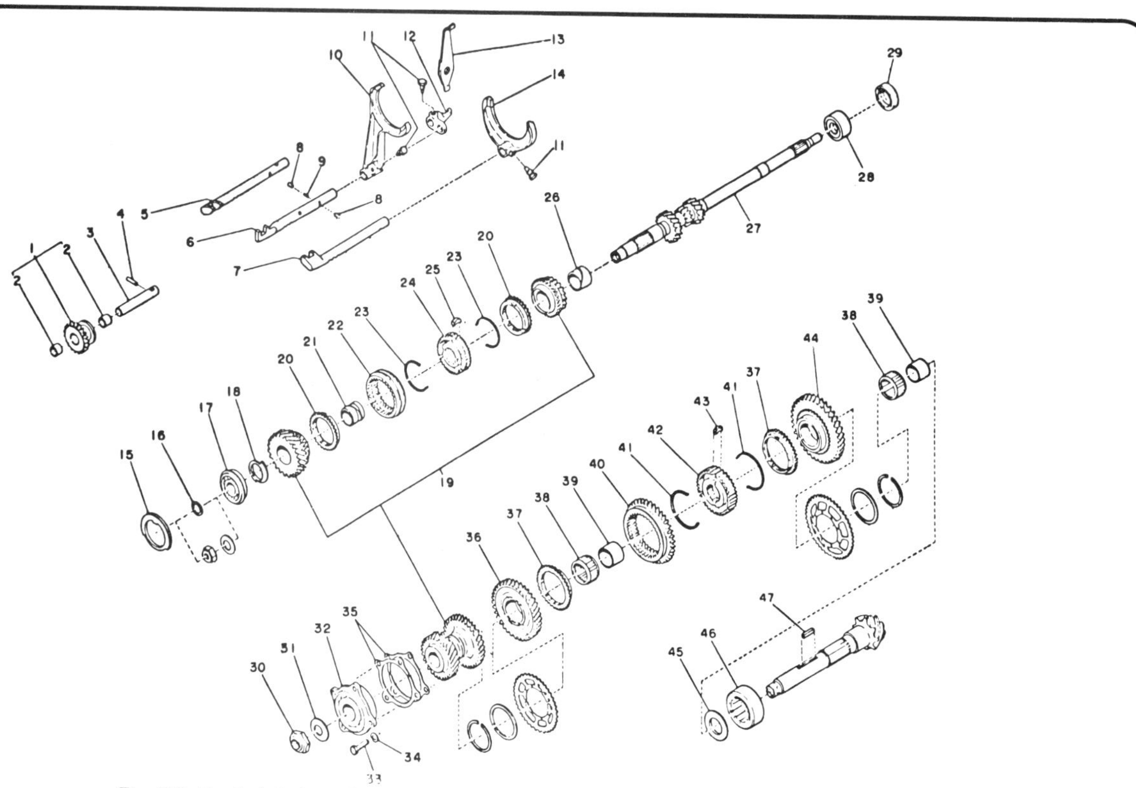

Fig. 6.2. Exploded view of 4-speed transmission gears and selector mechanism

1 Gear complete
2 Bushing (reverse idler gear)
3 Shaft (reverse idler gear)
4 Knock pin
5 Rail (reverse shifter)
6 Rail (shifter fork)
7 Rail 2 (shifter fork)
8 Plunger 2 (shifter rail)
9 Plunger (shifter rail)
10 Fork (shifter)
11 Set screw (shifter fork)
12 Arm (reverse shifter rail)
13 Lever complete (reverse shifter)
14 Fork 2 (shifter)
15 Collar 2 (transmission main shaft)
16 Snap ring (newly adopted)
17 Ball bearing (22 x 58 x 25)
18 Collar (transmission mainshaft)
19 Gear set
20 Ring (synchronizer)
21 Bushing (top drive gear)
22 Sleeve (synchronizer)
23 Spring (synchronizer hub)
24 Hub (synchronizer)
25 Insert (synchronizer hub)
26 Bushing (third drive gear)
27 Shaft (transmission main)
28 Needle bearing (22 x 42 x 20)
29 Oil seal (20 x 40 x 10)
30 Lock nut (drive pinion)
31 Lock washer (drive pinion)
32 Ball bearing (25 x 70 x 30)
33 Bolt (8 x 28 x 23)
34 Spring washer
35 Shim (drive pinion)
36 Gear (second driven)
37 Ring 2 (synchronizer)
38 Needle bearing (37 x 42 x 23.8)
39 Race (needle bearing in)
40 Gear (reverse driven)
41 Spring 2 (synchronizer hub)
42 Hub 2 (synchronizer)
43 Insert 2 (synchronizer hub)
44 Ring 3 (synchronizer)
45 Spacer (drive pinion)
46 Roller bearing (37.2 x 67 x 22)
47 Key

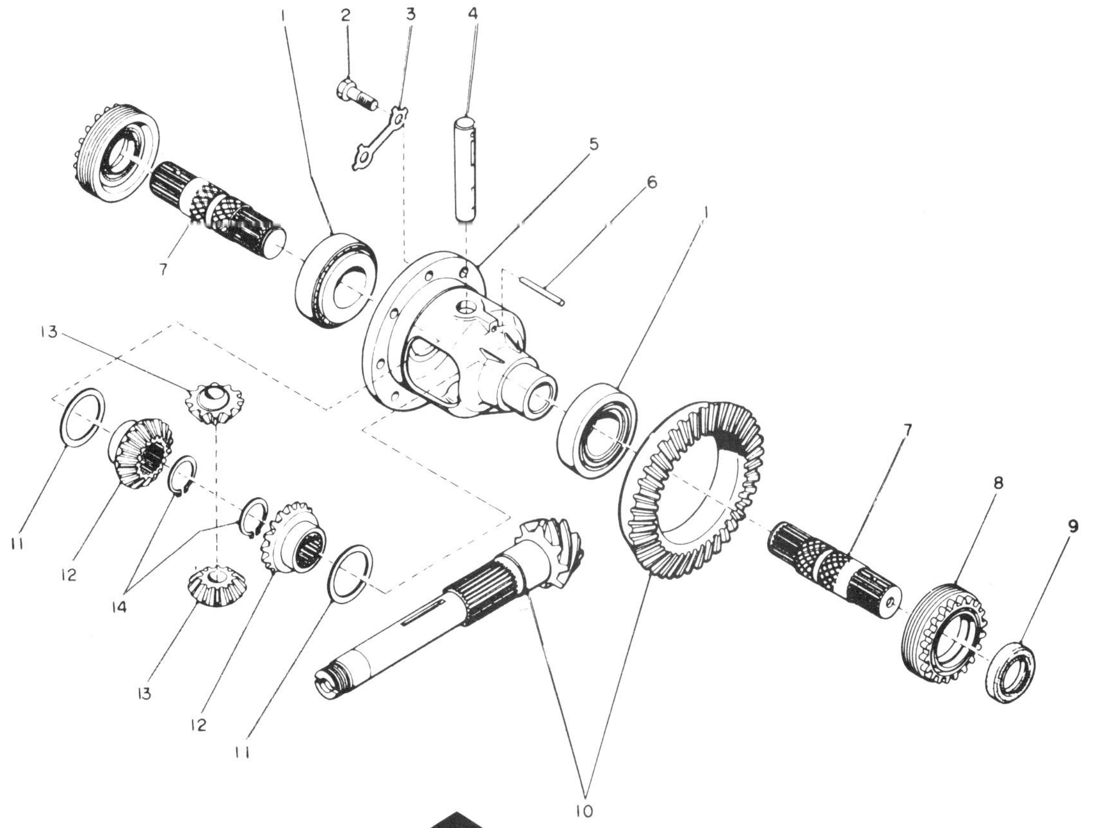

Fig. 6.3. Exploded view of differential unit

1. *Roller bearing (35 x 72 x 18.25)*
2. *Bolt (10 x 21 x 13)*
3. *Lock washer (crown gear)*
4. *Shaft (differential pinion)*
5. *Case (differential)*
6. *Straight pin (4 x 44)*
7. *Shaft (axle drive)*
8. *Holder (axle shaft oil seal)*
9. *Oil seal (27 x 45 x 9)*
10. *Pinion and crown gear set*
11. *Washer (35.1 x 45 x 0.950)*
12. *Gear (differential SD)*
13. *Pinion (differential)*
14. *Snap ring (outer - 26)*

Fig. 6.4. 4WD transmission

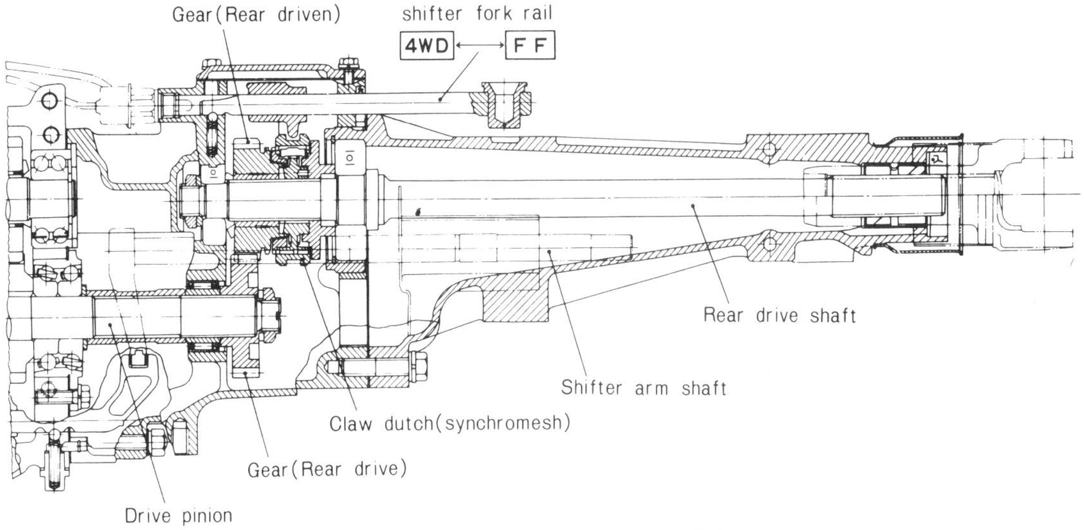

Fig. 6.5. Cross-section of 4WD transmission

nuts securing the carrier to the mounting member.
6 Disconnect the carrier mounting bracket and lower the jack. Remove the carrier from under the car.
7 Refitting is the reverse of removal procedure. Tighten the front mounting bolts to 58-72 lb f ft (8-10 kg f m) and the rear mounting nuts to 43-51 lb f ft (6-7 kg f m). Fill the differential carrier with gear oil.

4 Transmission - dismantling (general)

Before dismantling the transmission decide first if it is worthwhile from an economic point of view. If it is in generally poor condition then the cost of new parts could be greater than an exchange unit. Other points to consider are that access to a press will be necessary when dismantling the mainshaft and special gauge equipment is required when adjusting the drive pinion position in the casing.

Drain off all the oil and clean the exterior of the casing with a grease solvent.

As assemblies are dismantled lay the parts out in the order in which they are removed, to assist at reassembly, particularly when dismantling the mainshaft.

The photographs used in this Chapter are of a 1976 1400 model four speed transmission, and there are slight variations between models of different years.

5 Transmission - dismantling

1 Remove the clutch release fork and release bearing holder as described in Chapter 5, Section 7.
2 Remove the six securing nuts and take off the transmission cover. Remove the four bolts retaining the drive pinion.
3 Wrap vinyl tape round the splines of the driveshafts from the oil seal to the end of the shaft. This is to prevent damage to the oil seals as the casing is separated into two parts. This is important if you are separating the casing of a newly assembled transmission for any reason, in the case of transmissions which have been in use for some time it is recommended that new seals are fitted at assembly.
4 Remove the seventeen bolts clamping the transmission case together and separate the casing into the right half and left half. The case will easily separate if the two areas around the knock pins (dowels) are tapped with a plastic hammer.
5 Lift out the drive pinion, if necessary lever it up with a hammer shaft. Remove the shims from the drive pinion to prevent them being damaged.
6 Remove the transmission mainshaft.
7 Remove the differential assembly. Take care not to mix up the right-hand and left-hand sides of the roller bearings outer race. Identify them with labels.
8 Remove the three shifter rail spring plugs and collect the springs and balls.
9 Unscrew the shifter fork set screws and remove the shifter forks for 4th/3rd and 1st/2nd gears as well as the shifter fork rails. When pulling out a rail, keep the other rails in neutral position and take care not to drop the shifter rail plungers. To remove the 4th/3rd rail turn it thru 90° and then pull it out.
10 Unscrew the shifter fork securing set screw and remove the reverse shifter rail arm and shifter rail.
11 Unscrew the two attaching bolts from the transmission casing, then remove the oil seal holder lock plate and the driveshaft oil seal holder from each half of the transmission casing. Remove the 'O' rings from the oil seal holders.
12 Remove the circlip retaining the speedometer driven gear and pull the gear out. Then remove the speedometer shaft by tapping it out using a drift. The oil seal will come out with the shaft.
13 Pull out the knock pin and then remove the reverse idler gearshaft, reverse idler gear and the shift lever.

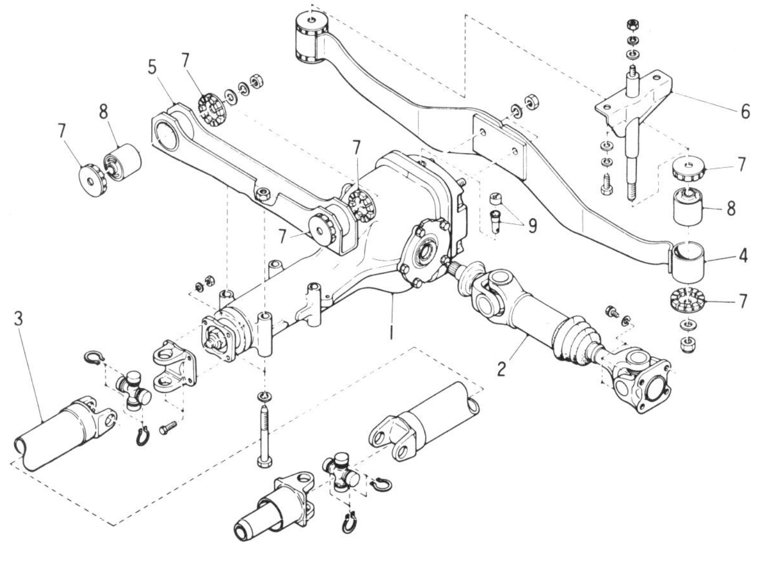

Fig. 6.6. Component parts of the rear drive system (4WD)

1 Differential assembly
2 Drive shaft assembly
3 Propeller shaft assembly
4 Mounting member
5 Mounting bracket
6 Bracket
7 Stopper
8 Bushing
9 Breather cap

Fig. 6.7. Removing the drive pinion

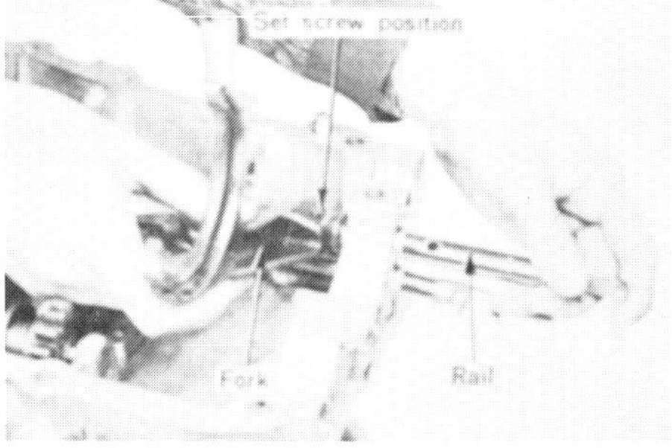

Fig. 6.8. Removing the shifter forks and rails

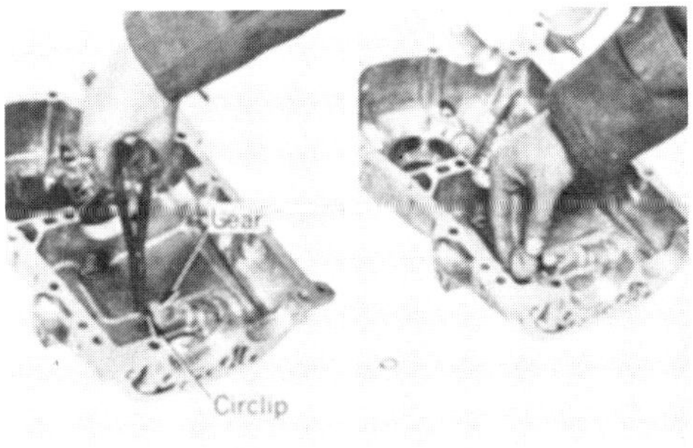

Fig. 6.9. Removing the speedometer driven gear and shaft

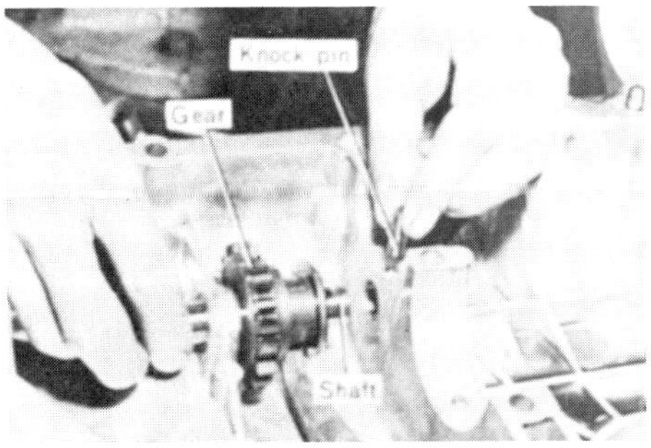

Fig. 6.10. Removing the reverse idler gear, shaft and shaft lever

5.2 Removing the pinion shaft retaining bolts

5.5 Lifting out the drive pinion

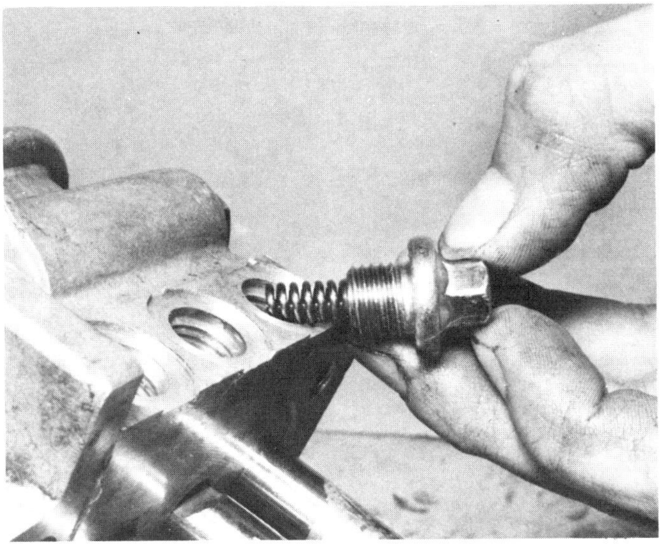

5.8 Removing the shifter rail spring retaining plugs

5.11 Oil seal holder and lockplate

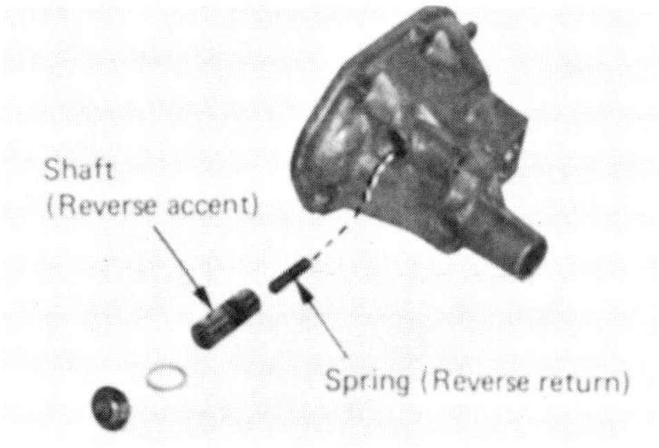

Fig. 6.11. Dismantling the transmission cover

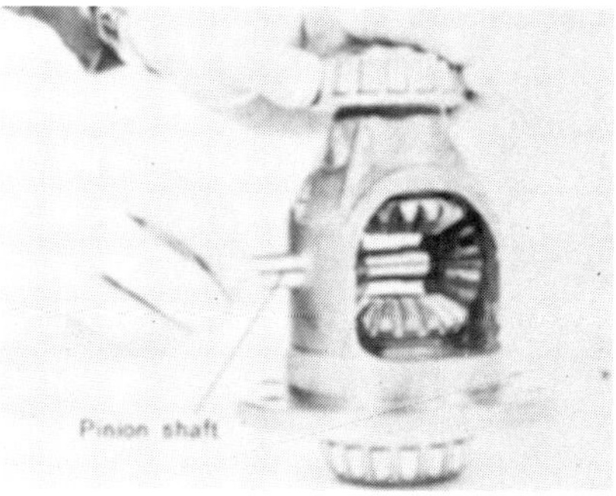

Fig. 6.12. Removing the differential pinion shaft

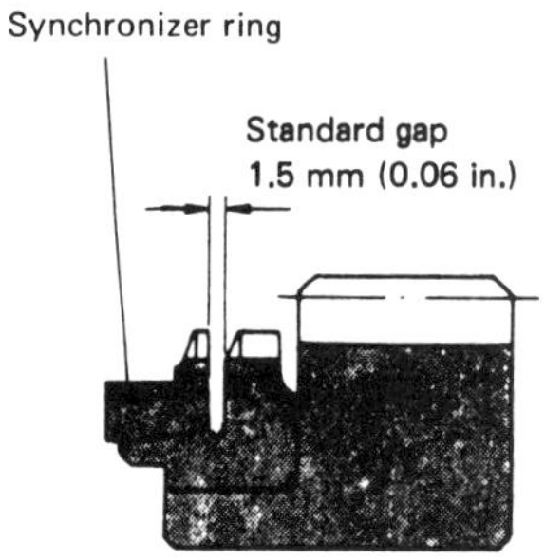

Fig. 6.13. Inspecting the synchronizer ring

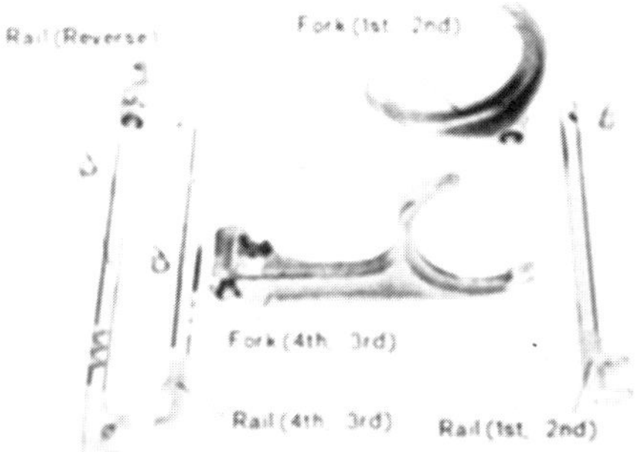

Fig. 6.14. Check the gear shift rails and forks for wear

11.3a Fitting the 3rd drive gear

11.3b ... and the assembled synchronizer ring and hub

11.4 Fit the 4th drive gear bushing

11.5a Fit the 4th drive gear and synchronizer ring ...

11.5b ... and then the mainshaft collar

11.6a Press on the ball bearing ...

6 Mainshaft - dismantling

1 Secure the mainshaft in a vise with suitable packing to prevent damage to the gears.
2 Remove the locknut (models to 1973) or snap-ring. In the case of the locknut relieve the staking before unscrewing it. Discard both the locknut and snap-ring and always fit new ones at reassembly.
3 Remove the ball bearing, mainshaft collar, 4th drive gear, synchronizer hub, 4th drive gear bushing and 3rd drive gear with a press.
4 The 3rd drive gear bushing should be left on the shaft if it is in good condition. If it requires renewing, cut a groove on it with a machine grinder and drive it off with a chisel. Once it has moved a little it can be removed with a press.

7 Drive pinion - dismantling

1 Using suitable packing to prevent damage to the gears, hold the 4th/3rd gears in a vise and remove the locknut after relieving the staking. The gears should be supported after removing the locknut, to prevent the ball bearings from dropping out, as some of the bearings are not a press fit on the drive pinion.
2 Remove the ball bearing (25 x 70 x 30) and 4th/3rd driven gears using a press and then take off the 2nd driven gear and needle bearing.
3 Remove the 1st driven gear, needle bearing race, synchronizer hub and needle bearing with a press. Remove the key from the drive pinion shaft before removing the needle bearing race.
4 Using the press remove the needle bearing race, drive pinion spacer and roller bearing.

8 Transmission cover - dismantling

1 Unscrew and remove the back-up lamp switch and then remove the reverse accent spring, ball and straight pin.
2 Remove the plug in the upper part of the cover and then take out the reverse accent shaft and reverse return spring.

9 Differential unit - dismantling

1 Remove the right and left-hand snap-rings and withdraw the axle driveshafts. Identify the shafts so that they can be refitted in the same positions.
2 Straighten the crown gear lockwasher, unscrew the eight securing bolts and lift the crown gear out of the case.
3 Drive out the differential pinion shaft retaining pin towards the crown gear position with a parallel pin punch. Pull out the differential pinion shaft and remove the differential pinions, side gears and washers.
4 Do not remove the roller bearings unless they are defective. If they have to be renewed use a puller to remove the bearings.

10 Transmission components - inspection

1 Clean all the parts thoroughly with a grease solvent and dry with compressed air.
2 Check all the bearings for cracked, pitted or worn balls. Examine the bearing cages for damage and corrosion. Lubricate the bearings with gear oil and rotate to check if the rotation is smooth or if unusual noises are emitted. The pinion end bearing rotation may be felt to be a little heavier than the others as preloading is applied to this bearing.
3 Renew any gears with cracked or damaged teeth, excessive wear or pitted tooth surface. Renew if the cone bearing synchronizer ring is rough or damaged.
4 Renew the synchronizer ring and hub if the contacting surface of the synchronizer hub insert is worn in steps or excessively worn. Renew the ring if the inner surface or tooth surface is damaged or unevenly worn. Renew the ring if the clearance between the surfaces of ring and cone facing each other is very small when the ring is forced against the cone of the gear, see Fig. 6.13.
5 Check the gearshift rails for wear or damage, if slightly bent, straighten them. Renew the forks if damaged or worn.
6 Examine the differential gears for excessive or uneven wear, pitted tooth surfaces or cracked teeth. If the crown gear is defective it must be renewed as a matched set with the drive pinion. Examine the axle driveshaft journals and splines for wear and damage, and renew as necessary.
7 Renew all oil seals and gaskets. Before reassembly lubricate all parts with gear oil.

11 Mainshaft - reassembly

1 Press on the 3rd drivegear bushing, if it was removed when dismantling.
2 Assemble three synchronizer inserts, synchronizer sleeve and two synchronizer springs on the hub so that the spring cut-ends are 120° apart and the synchronizer hub is fitted with the end of the spline having the narrower tooth width is on the 3rd gear side (see Fig. 6.16). **Note:** There are two kinds of inserts the short one is for the 3rd/4th synchronizer, while the longer one is for 1st/2nd synchronizer.
3 Fit the 3rd drivegear and the assembled synchronizer ring and hub. It may be necessary to use a press.
4 Press on the 4th drivegear bushing.
5 Fit the 4th drivegear, synchronizer ring and transmission mainshaft collar, taking care to align the insert with the synchronizer ring groove. Match the oil groove end of the 4th drivegear bushing with the large notch of the mainshaft collar, as shown in Fig. 6.17.
6 Press on the ball bearing. For transmissions 1970-73 fit the lock-

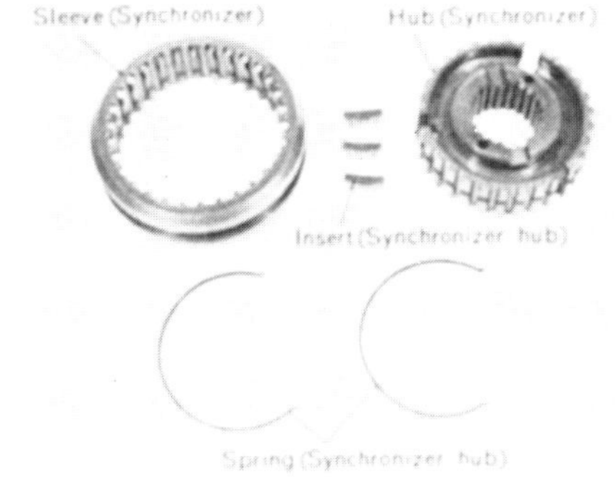

Fig. 6.15. Synchronizer hub assembly

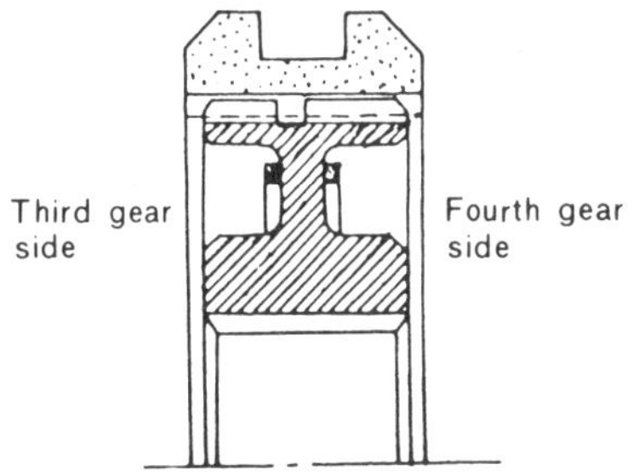

Fig. 6.16. Synchronizer hub fitting direction

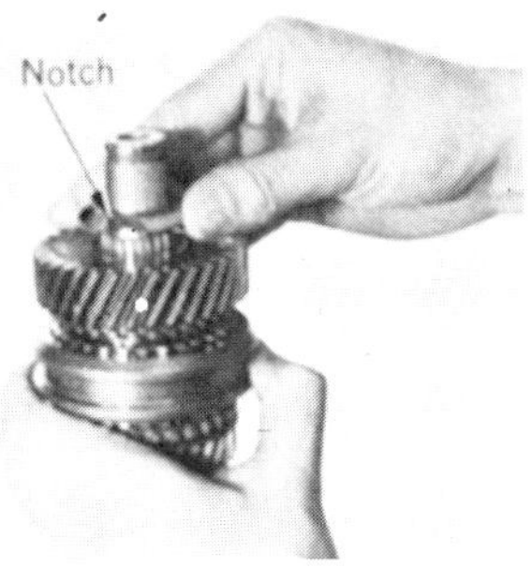

Fig. 6.17. Aligning the oil groove and notch of collar

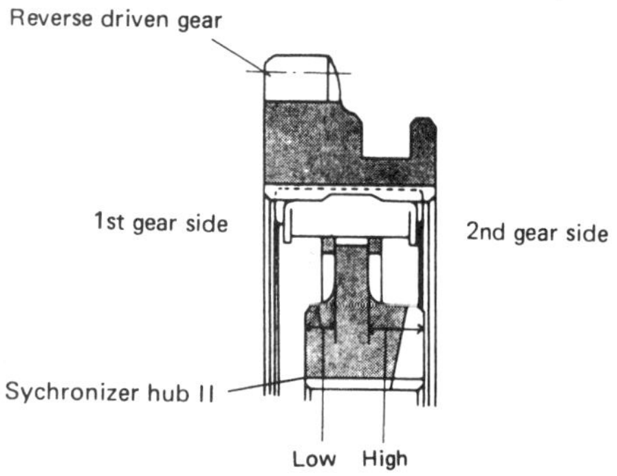

Fig. 6.18. Assembling the 1st/2nd synchronizer hub

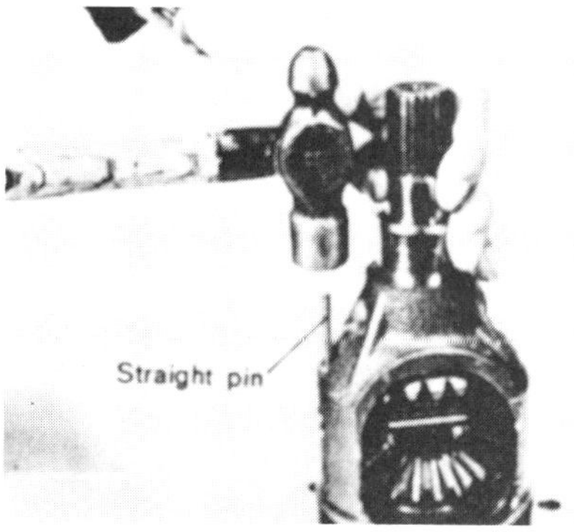

Fig. 6.19. Driving in the differential pinion shaft retaining pin

11.6b ... and then fit the snap ring

12.1 Press fit the roller bearing and drive pinion spacer

12.3a Fit the needle bearing and 1st driven gear ...

12.3b ... and then the assembled synchronizer rings and hub

12.4a Fit the needle bearing and the 2nd driven gear

12.4b Insert the key in the drive pinion groove

12.5a Press the 4th/3rd gear onto the drive pinion ...

12.5b ... and then the ball bearing

12.6 Fitting the drive pinion lockwasher and locknut

nut, tighten it to 58 lb f ft (8 kg f m) and then stake it. From 1974 a snap-ring is fitted in place of the locknut. Always fit a new snap-ring. Snap-rings are supplied in thickness from 0.095 in (2.42 mm) to 0.1059 in (2.69 mm) in steps of 0.0011 in (0.03 mm) and one at 0.1122 in (2.85 mm). Select a suitable snap-ring so that the axial play is 0-0.002 in (0-0.05 mm).

12 Drive pinion - reassembly

1 Fit the roller bearing and then the drive pinion spacer, using a press.
2 Assemble the three synchronizer inserts, reverse driven gear and two springs on the synchronizer hub, so that the spring cut-ends are 120° apart and the reverse driven gear with its toothed side and the hub having the smaller boss, are facing the same direction, see Fig. 6.18.
3 Press on the needle bearing race. Fit the needle bearing, 1st driven gear and the assembled synchroniser rings and hub. Ensure that the synchronizer ring groove is in line with the inserts.
4 Press on the needle bearing race and fit the 2nd driven gear. Insert the key into the groove on the pinion.
5 Press on the 3rd/4th driven gear and then the ball bearing. Some ball bearings may be fitted without having to press them on but this does not affect their operation.
6 Fit the drive pinion lockwasher and locknut. Tighten the locknut to 58 lb f ft (8 kg f m) and lock the nut by staking in two places.

13 Differential unit - reassembly

1 Fit the differential side gears and differential pinions together with the washers in the differential case and then insert the differential pinion shaft.
2 Using a dial gauge, measure the backlash between the gears and pinions and adjust by using appropriate thickness of washers to obtain a backlash of 0.0020 - 0.0059 in (0.05 - 0.15 mm). Washers are supplied in thicknesses from 0.0364 - 0.0413 in (0.925 - 1.050 mm) in steps of 0.001 in (0.025 mm).
3 Align the differential pinion shaft with the holes in the casing, insert the locking pin from the crown wheel side and, using a parallel pin punch, drive the pin in until it is just below the level of the casing and then stake the casing to retain the pin.
4 Fit the roller bearings on the casing with a press. If refitting the same bearings ensure they are fitted in the correct location and matched to the outer races.
5 Fit the crown gear on the casing and secure it with the lockwashers and bolts. Tighten the bolts to 42-49 lb f ft (5.8-6.8 kg f m) and then bend over the lockwashers.
6 Fit the axle driveshaft and secure with snap-rings. Measure the clearance between the differential pinion shaft and the end of the axle driveshafts. The clearance should be 0-0.0079 in (0-0.2 mm), adjust, if necessary, by selecting correct thickness of snap-ring.

14 Drive pinion - adjustment

1 The drive pinion has to be adjusted in relation to the crown gear of the differential unit as they are a matched set. The match marks on the drive pinion and crown gear are shown in Fig. 6.22. The three lower digits on the drive pinion end face is the match number for the three digit number on the crown gear, the top number is for shim adjustment. The second number on the crown gear indicates the backlash value in millimeters.
2 A special gauge is required, see Fig. 6.23. Adjust the gauge by loosening the two bolts and setting the scale so that it indicates 0.5 when the plate end and the scale are on the same level.
3 Place the drive pinion in the left-hand casing, without shims, and secure it with two bolts tightened to 22 lb f ft (3 kg f m). Position the gauge by fitting the pins of the gauge in the dowel holes in the transmission casing.
4 Slide the gauge scale with fingertips and read the value at the point where it matches with the end face of the drive pinion. The thickness of shim required is determined by adding the value indicated on the drive pinion to the value indicated on the gauge (add if the figure on the drive pinion is prefixed by a plus (+) sign and subtract if prefixed by a minus (—) sign). Select one to three shims from the range of shims available to obtain the required thickness.

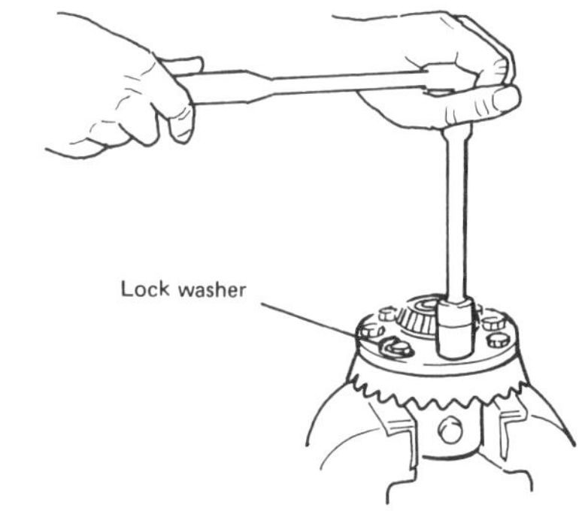

Fig. 6.20. Fitting the differential crown gear

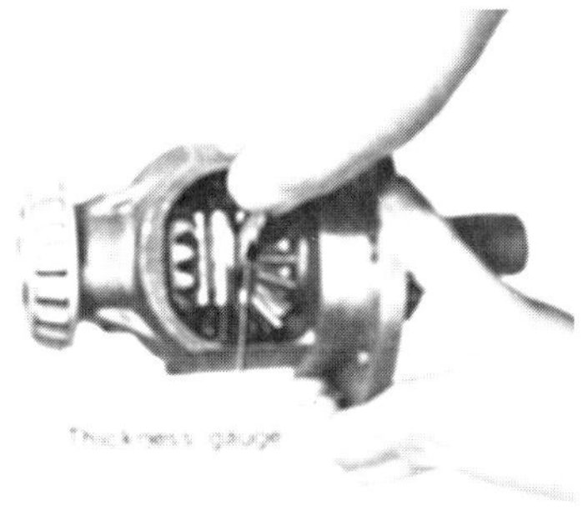
Fig. 6.21. Measuring the clearance between the differential pinion shaft and the end of the axle drive shaft

Fig. 6.22. Crown gear and drive pinion match marks

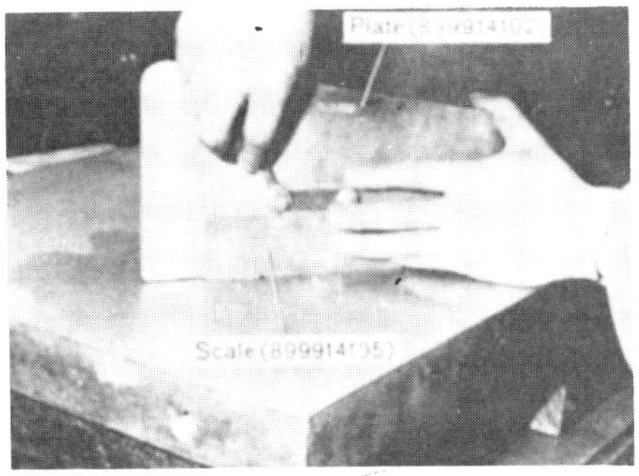
Fig. 6.23. Adjusting the drive pinion setting gauge

15.1 Axle shaft oil seals fitted in casing

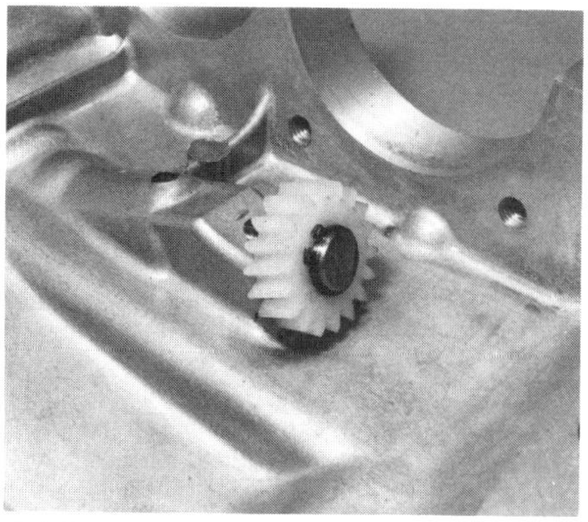

15.2 Fit the speedometer driven gear and snap ring

15.3a Assemble the reverse shift lever ...

15.3b ... and the reverse idler gear and shaft ...

15.3c ... then the securing pin

15.4 Tightening the reverse shifter fork set screw

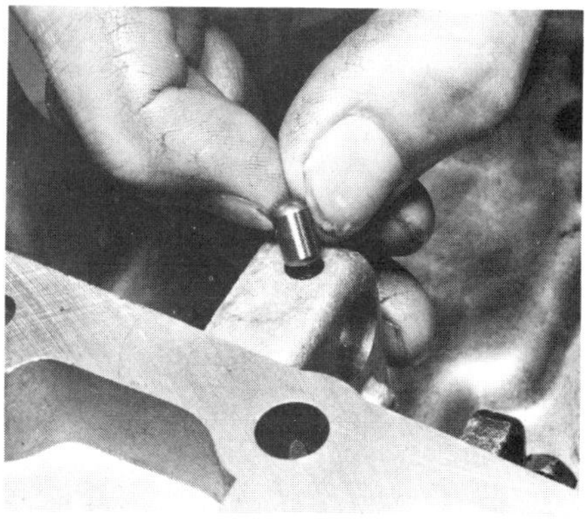

15.6 Insert the plunger in the casing

15.7a Fit the needle bearing on the mainshaft

15.7b Placing the mainshaft in position on the casing with the 3rd/4th gear fork

15.8 Fitting the differential unit in the casing

15.9a Fitting the shims on the drive pinion

15.9b The drive pinion assembly fitted in the casing

15 Transmission - reassembly

1 Fit new oil seals into the axle shaft oil seal holders, then screw the holders into the transmission casing, the one marked 'R' to the right-hand half and the one marked 'L' in the left-hand half of the casing, as far as the end of the thread but not fully into their final positions.
2 Fit the outer snap-ring and washer onto the speedometer shaft and insert them in the casing. Fit the speedometer driven gear on the shaft and retain with the snap-ring. Drive in the speedometer oil seal, use a socket wrench as a drift.
3 Fit the reverse shift lever into the left-hand casing, the reverse idler gear and shaft and secure in position with a lock pin.
4 Position the reverse shifter rail arm to the end of the reverse shifter lever. Fit the shifter rail and tighten the shifter fork set screw. Insert the shifter fork rail ball and spring in the casing and then fit the gasket and plug.
5 When fitting the reverse shifter rail arm check that the clearance between the reverse idler gear and wall of the casing is 0.059 - 0.079 in (1.5 - 2.0) mm), as shown in Fig. 6.24. Three different shifter rail arms are supplied, marked 1, 2 and 3. Number 1 reduces the clearance, 2 is the standard and 3 increases the clearance.
6 Fit the 1st/2nd gear shifter plunger in the hole in the casing.
7 Fit the needle bearing on the mainshaft and place the mainshaft assembly in the casing, ensuring that the hole in the needle bearing outer race is located on the dowel pin in the casing.
8 Wrap the splines of the right and left-hand axle driveshafts with vinyl tape, to prevent damage to the oil seals and fit the differential unit into the casing.
9 Fit the shims, selected in Section 4, on the drive pinion and fit the drive pinion assembly in position in the casing ensuring that the hole in the roller bearing outer race is located on the dowel in the casing.
10 Insert the plunger, fit the 3rd/4th gear fork on the shifter rail, then fit the rail in the casing and tighten the setscrew.
11 Insert the 1st/2nd gear shifter rail plunger in the hole in the casing and fit the shifter fork and rail. Tighten the setscrews. Insert the shifter rail spring and ball in the casing, then fit the gasket and plug.
12 Fit the mainshaft oil seal, locate it against the face of the casing. When fitting the right-hand casing be careful not to let the oil seal tilt and get damaged.
13 Remove all grease or oil from the joint faces of both halves of the casing. Apply liquid gasket sealant to the mating faces and fit the right-hand casing to the left-hand.
14 Remove the outer race of the roller bearing in the right-hand casing and align the case so that the drive pinion is not caught up in between. Check that the speedometer gear is in mesh, if not, turn the speedometer shaft with a screwdriver. Fit the outer race of the roller bearing in the right-hand casing.

Fig. 6.24. Checking the reverse idler gear to casing clearance

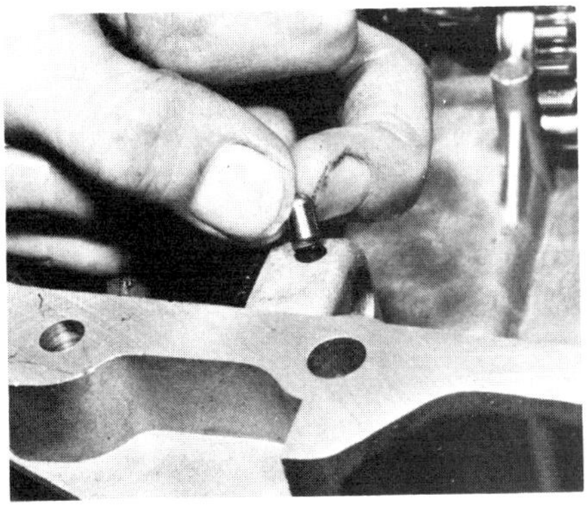

15.10a Insert the plunger ...

15.10b ... and then fit the 3rd/4th gear fork and shift rail

15.11a Fitting the 1st/2nd gear shifter rail and fork

15.11b Fitting the shifter rail ball ...

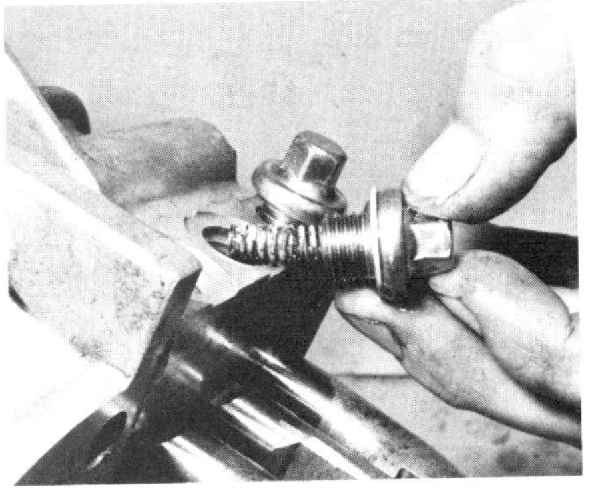

15.11c ... spring and plug

15.14 Removing the outer race of the roller bearing

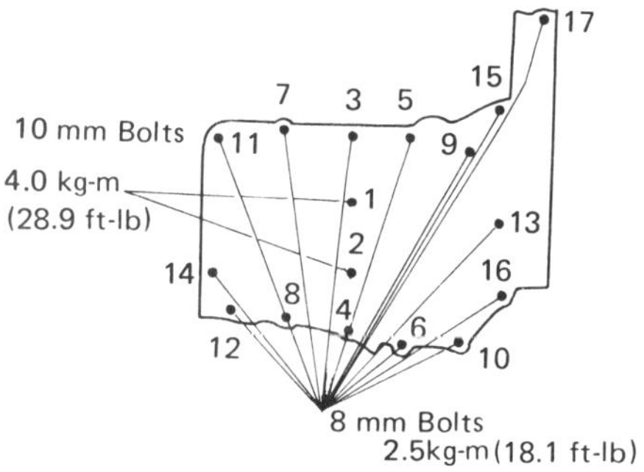

Fig. 6.25. Tightening sequence and torque for transmission case clamping bolts

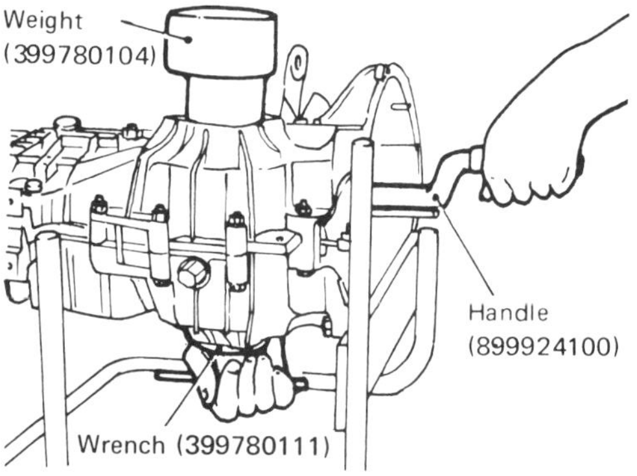

Fig. 6.26. Adjusting the pre-load on the differential roller bearings

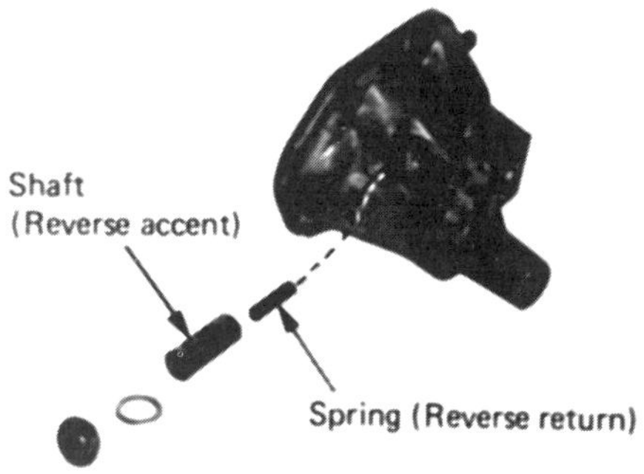

Fig. 6.27. Assembling the transmission cover

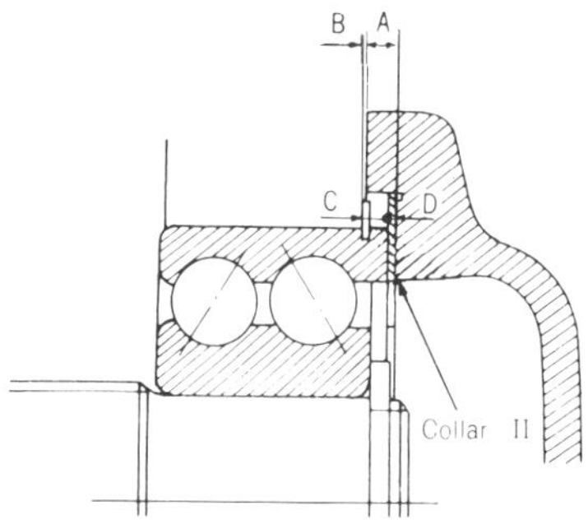

Fig. 6.28. Transmission cover to bearing end clearance

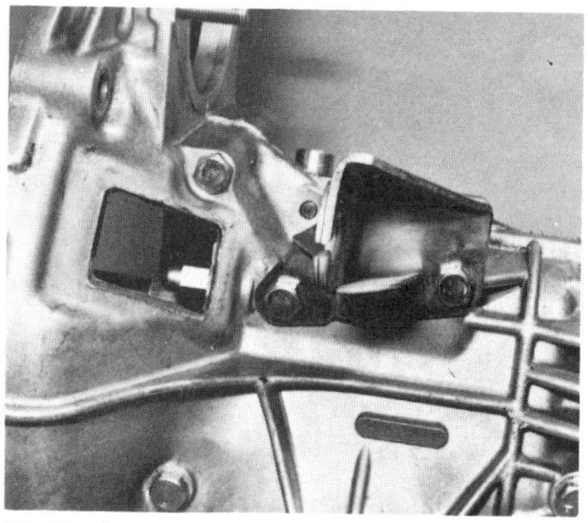

15.15a Attach the clutch cable bracket ...

15.15b ... and back-up lamp lead clip to the casing

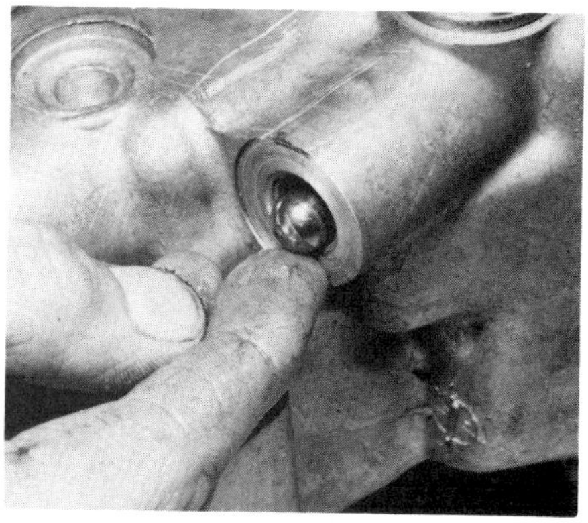

15.21a Inserting the ball ...

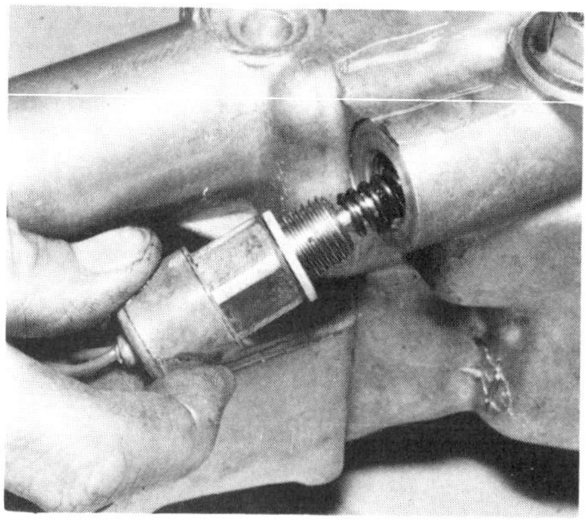

15.21b ... then the spring, washer and back-up lamp switch

15.23a Fit the shifter arm in the transmission cover

15.23b Shift rails in position for fitting the transmission cover

15 Attach the clutch cable bracket and back-up lamp lead clip to the casing, fit the casing joining bolts and tighten them to the specified torque and in the sequence shown in Fig. 6.25.
16 Fit the drive pinion bearing flange to the casing with the securing bolts tightened to 22 lb f ft (3 kg f m).
17 To adjust the pre-load on the roller bearings a handle for turning the mainshaft and a special pre-loading weight (Subane 39978 0104) is required. With the left-hand casing at the bottom place the bearing holder weight on the outer race of the bearing in the right-hand casing. Screw the axle shaft oil seal holder into the left-hand casing. Engage the 4th gear and while turning the mainshaft screw the holder in until a slight resistance is felt. This is the contact point of the crown gear and drive pinion. Remove the weight and screw in the drive shaft holder on the upper side and stop at the point where a slight resistance is felt. At this point the backlash between the crown wheel and drive pinion is zero.
18 Fit the driveshaft holder lock plate. Loosen the holder at the bottom by 1½ notches of the lock plate and screw in the holder at the top by the same amount to obtain a nominal backlash. The notch of the lock plate moves by half a notch if the plate is turned upside down. Screw the holder at the top in by ½ to 1 notch in order to apply pre-load to the taper roller bearing. Temporarily tighten both lock plates and index mark both the holders and lock plates for later re-adjustment.
19 Turn the mainshaft a number of times and then insert the probe of a dial gauge, suitably mounted, through the inspection hole in the front of the casing (models to 1974) or thru the drain plug hole on later models, so that it contacts the tooth surface at right angles and check whether the backlash is as specified according to the masking on the crown gear, refer to Section 14 and Fig. 6.22. To reduce backlash, loosen the holder in the upper (right-hand half) casing and screw in the holder on the lower (left-hand half) casing by the same amount. To increase backlash, loosen the holder in the bottom (left-hand) casing and screw in the holder on the upper (right-hand) casing to the same amount.
20 After checking the backlash, note the index marks on the holder lock plate and holder (both sides) then loosen the driveshaft holder until the O-ring groove appears. Fit the O-ring and screw the holder back into the same position. Tighten the holder lock plates and remove the vinyl tape from the axle driveshafts.
21 Fit the reverse return spring, accent shaft, aluminum washer and plug in the transmission cover, also the ball, pin, spring, aluminum washer and back-up lamp switch. Tighten the plug to 25 lb f ft (3.5 kg f m) and the switch to 13 lb f ft (1.8 kg f m).
22 When fitting the transmission cover adjust the bearing end clearance to 0 - 0.0079 in (0 - 0.2 mm) for models to 1974 and 0 - 0.0118 (0 - 0.3 mm) from 1975. To determine the thickness of collar required, measure the cover and casing with a depth gauge at the points showing in Fig. 6.28. (A + B) – (C + D) should be within the clearance range.
23 Fit the shifter arm in the transmission cover and bolt the cover to the casing. Tighten the bolts to 18 lb f ft (2.5 kg f m).
24 To adjust the selectors, insert an appropriate bar through the 0.315 in (8 mm) hole of the shifter arm and engage 4th gear. Move the shifter arm from 4th to 2nd and reverse position. The arm will move lightly towards 2nd but heavily to the reverse side because of the return spring, and the arm will come into contact with the stopper at the end. Adjust to equalize the movement by removing the plug on the cover and charging the thickness of aluminum gasket. Three thicknesses of gasket are available.
25 Fit the clutch release bearing holder and release fork as described in Chapter 5, Section 7.

16 Transmission (5-speed) - dismantling

1 Remove the clutch release fork and release bearing holder as described in Chapter 5, Section 7. Remove the six securing nuts and

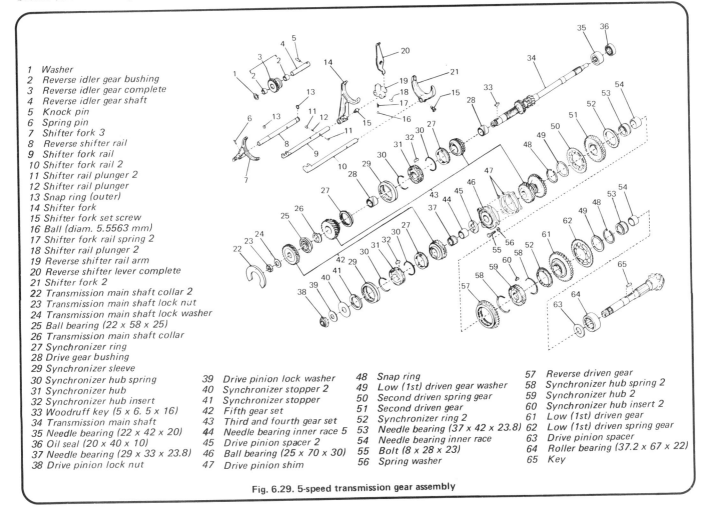

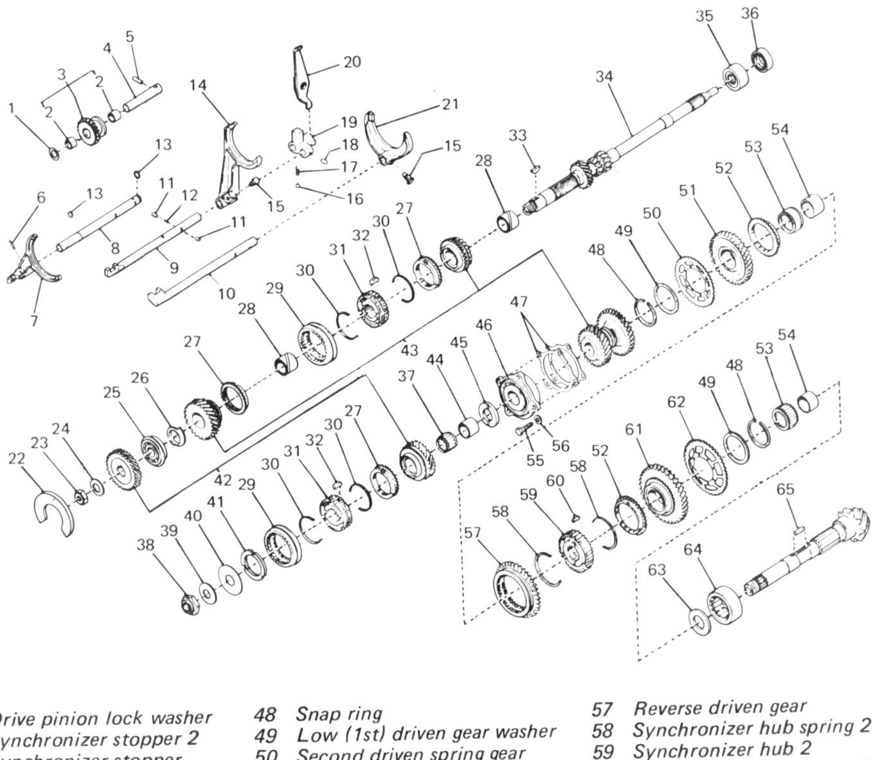

1 Washer
2 Reverse idler gear bushing
3 Reverse idler gear complete
4 Reverse idler gear shaft
5 Knock pin
6 Spring pin
7 Shifter fork 3
8 Reverse shifter rail
9 Shifter fork rail
10 Shifter fork rail 2
11 Shifter rail plunger 2
12 Shifter rail plunger
13 Snap ring (outer)
14 Shifter fork
15 Shifter fork set screw
16 Ball (diam. 5.5563 mm)
17 Shifter fork rail spring 2
18 Shifter rail plunger 2
19 Reverse shifter rail arm
20 Reverse shifter lever complete
21 Shifter fork 2
22 Transmission main shaft collar 2
23 Transmission main shaft lock nut
24 Transmission main shaft lock washer
25 Ball bearing (22 x 58 x 25)
26 Transmission main shaft collar
27 Synchronizer ring
28 Drive gear bushing
29 Synchronizer sleeve
30 Synchronizer hub spring
31 Synchronizer hub
32 Synchronizer hub insert
33 Woodruff key (5 x 6. 5 x 16)
34 Transmission main shaft
35 Needle bearing (22 x 42 x 20)
36 Oil seal (20 x 40 x 10)
37 Needle bearing (29 x 33 x 23.8)
38 Drive pinion lock nut
39 Drive pinion lock washer
40 Synchronizer stopper 2
41 Synchronizer stopper
42 Fifth gear set
43 Third and fourth gear set
44 Needle bearing inner race 5
45 Drive pinion spacer 2
46 Ball bearing (25 x 70 x 30)
47 Drive pinion shim
48 Snap ring
49 Low (1st) driven gear washer
50 Second driven spring gear
51 Second driven gear
52 Synchronizer ring 2
53 Needle bearing (37 x 42 x 23.8)
54 Needle bearing inner race
55 Bolt (8 x 28 x 23)
56 Spring washer
57 Reverse driven gear
58 Synchronizer hub spring 2
59 Synchronizer hub 2
60 Synchronizer hub insert 2
61 Low (1st) driven gear
62 Low (1st) driven spring gear
63 Drive pinion spacer
64 Roller bearing (37.2 x 67 x 22)
65 Key

Fig. 6.29. 5-speed transmission gear assembly

take off the transmission cover.
2 Drive out the spring pin on the 5th gear shifter fork with a parallel pin punch. Relieve the staking on the pinion shaft nut.
3 Engage two gears at once to lock the mainshaft from turning and remove the pinion shaft nut.
4 Remove the synchronizer hub and 5th gear shifter fork.
5 Remove the 5th driven gear, needle bearing inner race, needle bearing and drive pinion spacer. Remove the three bolts securing the pinion assembly to the transmission case.
6 Refer to Section 5. Follow the instructions given in paragraphs 3 - 9 and 11 - 13.
7 To remove the reverse idler gear shaft, take out the lock pin, then remove the shaft, reverse idler gear and reverse shifter lever. Remove the outer snap-ring and take off the shifter rail arm from the reverse shifter rail, then collect the ball and spring.

17 Mainshaft (5-speed transmission) - dismantling

1 Secure the mainshaft in a vise with suitable packing to prevent damaging the gear teeth.
2 Relieve the staking and remove the locknut.
3 Using a press remove the 5th drive gear. Remove the Woodruff key.
4 Press off the ball bearing and 4th driven gear.
5 Disassemble the synchroniser hub, 3rd drive gear and 4th drive gear bushing.
6 To eliminate backlash noise of the 1st and 2nd gears, sub-gears are used on the 1st and 2nd driven gears. Remove the outer snap-ring, 1st driven gear washer and spring, and 2nd driven gear spring. Use snap-ring expander pliers to remove the snap-rings.
7 The remainder of the dismantling procedure is the same as for the 4-speed transmission mainshaft, refer to Section 6.

18 Drive pinion and differential unit (5-speed transmission) - dismantling

1 After the removal of the 5th driven gear, needle bearing and spacer, as described in Section 17, the dismantling procedure for the drive pinion is the same as for the 4-speed transmission, refer to

Fig. 6.30. Driving out the spring pin of the 5th gear shifter fork

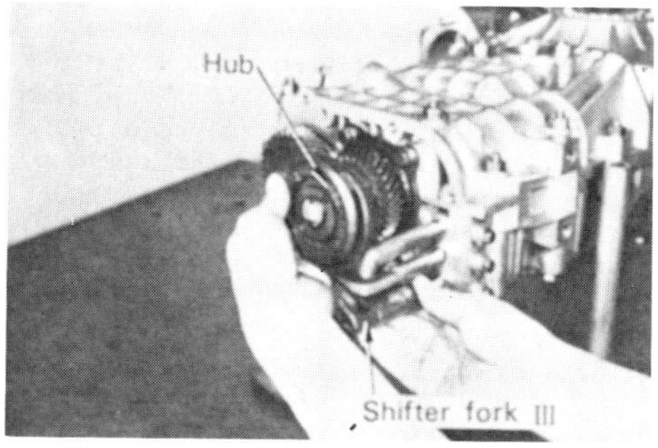

Fig. 6.31. Removing the synchronizer hub and 5th gear shifter fork

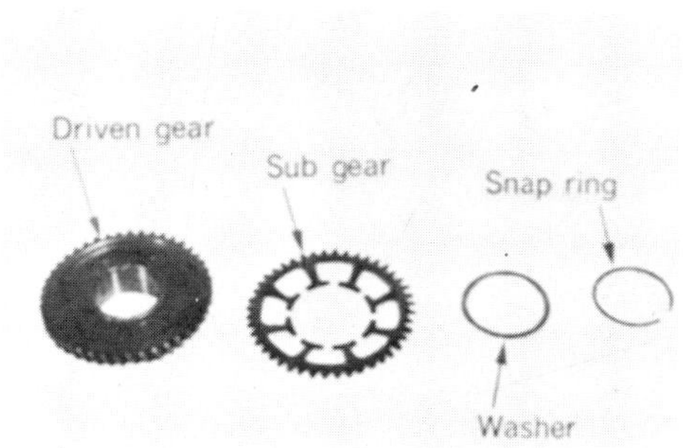

Fig. 6.32. 1st/2nd driven gear assembly

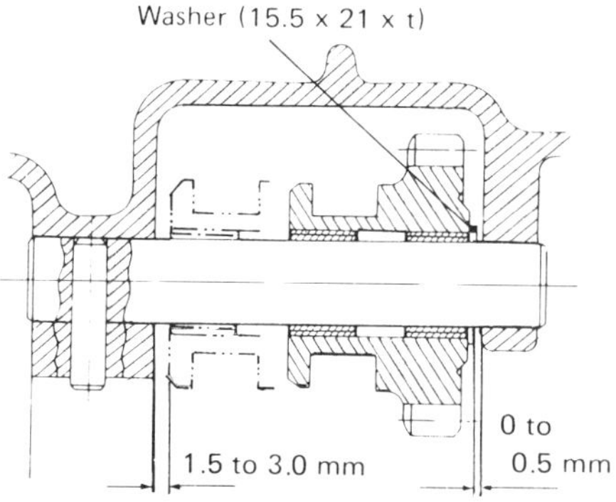

Fig. 6.33. Checking the reverse idler gear to casing wall clearance

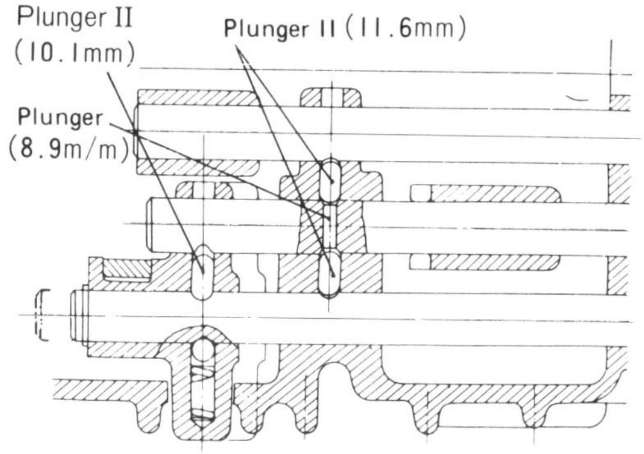

Fig. 6.34. Fitting the 1st/2nd shift rail plungers

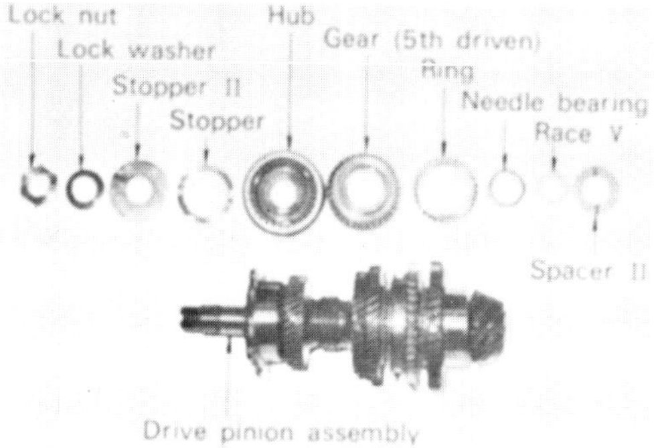

Fig. 6.35. Assembling the 5-speed gear

Section 7. For the dismantling procedure of the differential unit refer to Section 9.

19 Components (5-speed transmission) - inspection

1 Inspect the 1st/2nd gear spring for broken, damaged or excessive worn tooth surface. Renew if a leg is damaged. Fit the gear and rotate with finger-tip, renew if it rotates too lightly. Check that the clearance between the driven gear and the sub-gear is between 0.004 - 0.020 in (0.1 - 0.5 mm). Renew if necessary.
2 Refer to Section 10 for inspection instructions for all other component parts.

20 Mainshaft (5-speed transmission) - reassembly

1 Except for the assembly of the 1st/2nd driven gears follow the instructions in Section 11, paragraphs 1 - 5. For assembly of 1st/2nd gears, fit the gear springs (sub-gears) and washers to the 1st and 2nd gears and then fit the retaining snap-rings.
2 Press on the ball bearing. Fit the Woodruff key, 5th drive gear, lock-washer and locknut. Stake the locknut after tightening it to 58 lb f ft (8 kg f m).

21 Drive pinion and differential unit (5-speed transmission) - reassembly

1 Follow the instructions for assembling the drive pinion in Section 12, paragraphs 1 - 5.
2 Fit the spacer, needle bearing race, needle bearing, 5th driven gear, synchronizer stoppers, lockwasher and locknuts in this order. Tighten the locknut to 58 lb f ft (8 kg f m).
3 Adjustment of the drive pinion position and selection of adjusting shims is the same as described for 4-speed transmission in Section 14.
4 Do not stake the locknut at this stage.
5 For reassembly of the differential unit follow the instructions in Section 13.

22 Transmission (5-speed) - reassembly

1 Refer to Section 15 and follow the instructions in paragraphs 1 and 2.
2 Put the 1st/2nd shifter rail spring and ball in the reverse shifter rail arm then fit the reverse shifter rail. Fit the outer snap-ring.
3 Fit the reverse shifter fork rail spring, ball and gasket in the left-hand casing then fit and tighten the plug to 14.5 lb f ft (2 kg f m).
4 When fitting the reverse shift lever, check that the gap between the reverse idler gear and casing wall is 0.06 - 0.118 in (1.5 - 3.0 mm). Adjustments is by selection of one of three different reverse shift levers supplied. After fitting the reverse shift lever, set it to the neutral position and fit a suitable washer out of fine thicknesses so that the gap between the washer and the case walling is 0 - 0.02 in (0 - 0.5 mm) refer to Fig. 6.33.
5 Put the 1st/2nd gear shift rail plungers into the hole in the casing and the reverse shifter rail arm. Insert the correct plunger, referring to Fig. 6.34 for plunger location.
6 Fit the mainshaft assembly in the left-hand half of the transmission casing.
7 Insert the 3rd/4th shifter rail plunger and fit the shifter fork and shifter fork rail, then tighten the setscrew.
8 Fit the pinion drive assembly, with previously selected shims, on the casing.
9 Insert the 1st/2nd shifter rail plunger into the hole in the casing and fit the 1st/2nd gear shifter fork and rail, then tighten the setscrew.
10 Push the shifter rail spring and ball in the casing and fit the gasket and plug.
11 Refer to Section 15 and follow the instructions in paragraphs 12 - 20.
12 Undo the drive pinion locknut and remove the lockwasher, stoppers, and synchronizer hub.
13 Fit the 5th gear shifter fork to reverse shifter rail with a spring pin and assemble the synchronizer hub, stoppers and drive pinion lockwasher.
14 Fit the drive pinion locknut, engage two gears to lock the main-shaft from turning, then tighten the drive pinion locknut to 58 lb f ft (8 kg f m). Stake the locknut to prevent it from working loose.
15 Select the mainshaft collar as described in Section 15, paragraph 22.
16 Fit the rear cover assembly and tighten the attaching bolts to 18 lb f ft (2.5 kg f m).
17 Fit the clutch release bearing holder and release fork as described in Chapter 5, Section 7.

23 4WD transmission - dismantling

1 Remove the four securing bolts and lift off the top cover.
2 Drive out the straight pin, with a parallel pin punch, pull out the reverse shifter rail and remove the shifter fork, ball and spring. When pulling out the rail be careful that the ball does not fly out and get lost.
3 Undo the six bolts and remove the rear casing, if necessary tap it with a plastic hammer to free it.
4 Release the staking on the drive pinion locknut. Engage two gears at once, to lock the shaft from turning, and remove the drive pinion locknut. Withdraw the rear shaft drive gear from the drive pinion.
5 Remove the six securing nuts and take off the transfer casing, if necessary, tap it with a plastic hammer to free it from the main casing. Remove the needle bearing, collar and washer from the drive pinion.
6 Release the staking on the rear drive shaft locknut and remove the locknut and washer. Remove the ball bearing, spacer and rear shaft driven gear using a press.
7 Remove the synchronizer sleeve, hub and spacer from the rear drive shaft.
8 Remove the inner snap-ring from the casing with a screwdriver and drive the rear shaft out of the casing, with a soft metal drift.
9 Using a press, remove the ball bearing from the rear drive shaft.
10 Take the 'O' ring out of the shifter arm and then remove the shifter arm.
11 Remove the back-up lamp switch from the transfer casing assembly and then take out the reverse accent spring ball and pin.
12 Remove the plug from the casing and take out the reverse accent shaft and reverse turn spring.
13 Drive the needle bearing out of the transfer casing with a soft metal drift.
14 Remove the rear extension oil seal from the rear casing assembly.
15 For the remainder of the dismantling procedure refer to Sections 5, 6, 7 and 8.

24 Components (4WD transmission) - inspection

1 If there is excessive wear or scoring of the rear extension case bushing it must be renewed. To remove the bushing, cut it with a hacksaw blade and pull it out towards the rear. When pressing in the rear bushing ensure that the oil hole lines up with the groove in the casing. The bushing should be reamer finished to 1.38 - 1.3815 in (35 - 35.039 mm).
2 Follow the procedure in Section 10 for the inspection of the remaining transmission ports.

25 4WD transmission - reassembly

1 Assemble the main transmission unit as described in Sections 5, 6, 7 and 8, except for the following:

a) The rear cover assembly is not fitted.
b) The drive pinion is assembled by fitting the ball bearing, washer, collar needle bearing, rear shaft drive gear, lockwasher and locknut. The locknut is not staked at this stage.

2 Remove the locknut, lockwasher and rear shaft drive gear from the drive pinion.
3 Press fit the needle bearing in the transfer casing with the marked side of the bearing flush with the casing.
4 Insert the reverse return spring and accent shaft into the transfer casing, then fit the adjusting aluminum washer and the plug, tightened to 25 lb f ft (3.5 kg f m).
5 Fit the ball, reverse accent spring, pin, aluminum washer and back-up lamp switch, tightened to 13 lb f ft (1.8 kg f m).

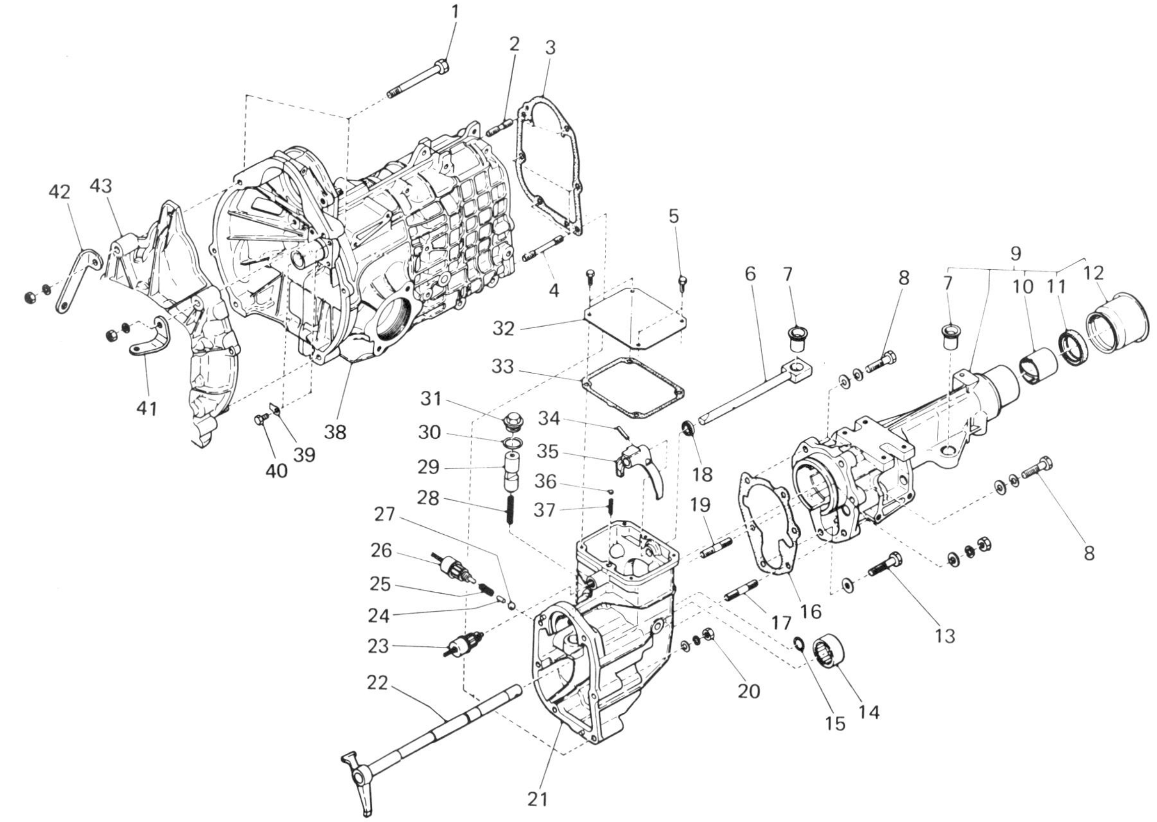

Fig. 6.36. 4WD transmission casing assembly

1 Bolt (10 x 96 x 28)
2 Stud bolt (8 x 48 x 20)
3 Transmission cover gasket
4 Stud bolt (8 x 48 x 20)
5 Bolt and washer
6 Shifter fork rail 3
7 Change rod bushing
8 Bolt
9 Transmission case 4
10 Rear extension bushing
11 Extension oil seal
12 Transmission cover 4
13 Bolt
14 Needle bearing (32 x 42 x 20)
15 'O' ring (13 x 1.9)
16 Transmission case gasket
17 Stud bolt
18 Oil seal (12 x 22 x 5)
19 Stud bolt
20 Nut
21 Transmission case 3
22 Shifter arm complete
23 Back-up lamp switch assembly (4WD selector)
24 Straight pin (6 x 11.5)
25 Reverse accent spring
26 Back-up lamp switch assembly
27 Ball (diam. 10.3188 mm)
28 Reverse return spring
29 Reverse accent shaft
30 Aluminium gasket
31 Plug (22 x 8)
32 Transmission case cover 3
33 Transmission case gasket 3
34 Straight pin (5 x 22)
35 Shifter fork 3
36 Ball (diam. 6.350)
37 Shifter rail spring
38 Transmission case assembly
39 Release spring bracket
40 Bolt
41 Stiffener 2
42 Stiffener
43 Flywheel housing complete

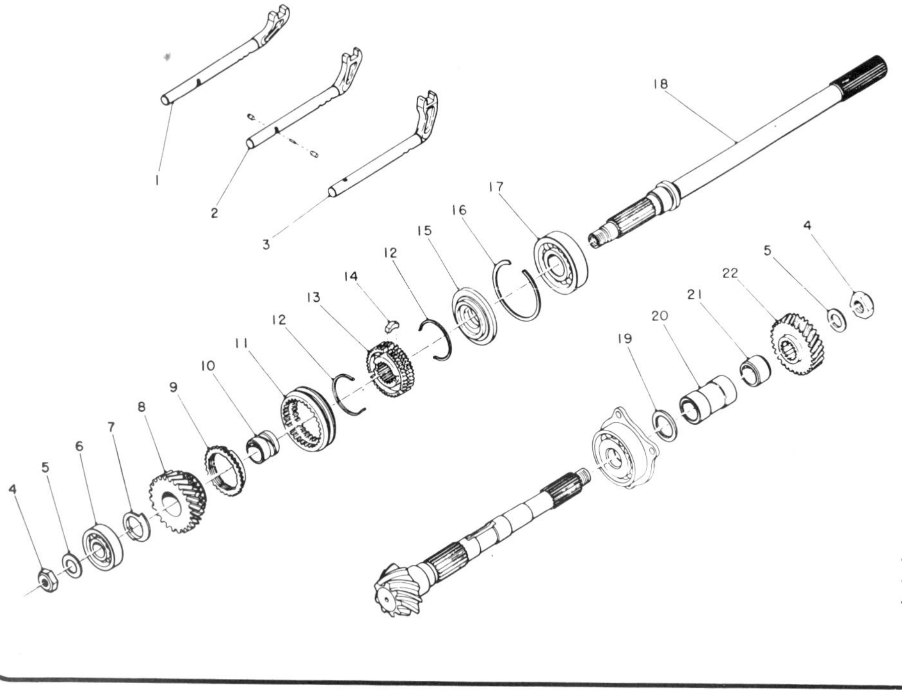

Fig. 6.37. 4WD transmission gear assembly

1 Shifter fork rail 2
2 Shifter fork rail
3 Reverse shifter rail
4 Transmission main shaft lock nut
5 Transmission main shaft lock washer
6 Ball bearing
7 Transmission main shaft collar
8 Rear shaft driven gear
9 Synchronizer ring
10 Rear shaft driven gear bushing
11 Synchronizer sleeve
12 Synchronizer hub spring
13 Synchronizer hub
14 Synchronizer hub insert
15 Rear drive spacer
16 Snap ring
17 Ball bearing (30 x 72 x 19)
18 Rear drive shaft
19 Washer (25.2 x 38 x 3.2)
20 Drive pinion collar
21 Needle bearing race 5
22 Rear shaft drive gear

6 Fit the shifter arm on the transfer case.
7 Press the rear ball bearing onto the rear drive shaft, then drive the shaft into the rear transfer casing and fit the snap-ring in the groove in the casing.
8 Assemble the three synchronizer inserts, synchronizer sleeve and two synchronizer springs on the synchronizer hub, so that the smallest spline is on the rear drive spacer side, see Fig. 6.40.
9 Fit the rear drive spacer, synchronizer hub assembly, rear shaft drive gear sleeve, synchronizer ring, rear shaft driven gear and transmission main shaft spacer to the rear drive shaft.
10 Press the ball bearing onto the rear drive shaft, fit the lockwasher and locknut. Tighten the locknut to 58 lb f ft (8 kg f m) and stake it in four places.
11 Determine the thickness of collar required to adjust the end clearance of the transfer casing as described in Section 15, paragraph 22.
12 Fit the washer, drive pinion collar and needle bearing race on the above pinion.
13 Fit the transfer case to the main transmission unit, using a new gasket, and tighten the securing nuts to 19 lb f ft (2.7 kg f m).
14 Fit the rear shaft drive gear, lockwasher and locknut on the drive pinion. Tighten the locknut to 58 lb f ft (8 kg f m).
15 Fit a new 'O' ring into the groove in the shifter arm.
16 Ensure all the parts are well lubricated with gear oil, use a new gasket and fit the rear casing to the transfer casing. Be careful not to damage the shifter arm 'O' ring. Before tightening each bolt make sure that the shifter arm moves smoothly. Tighten the bolts to 27 lb f ft (3.8 kg f m).
17 Fit the shifter fork, insert the shifter fork rail spring and the ball (coated with grease to make it stick) in the transfer casing and then fit the shifter fork rail. Drive in the straight pin. After the pin has been fitted check the operation of the shifter fork rail.
18 Use a new gasket and fit the top cover on the transfer casing and secure it with four bolts.

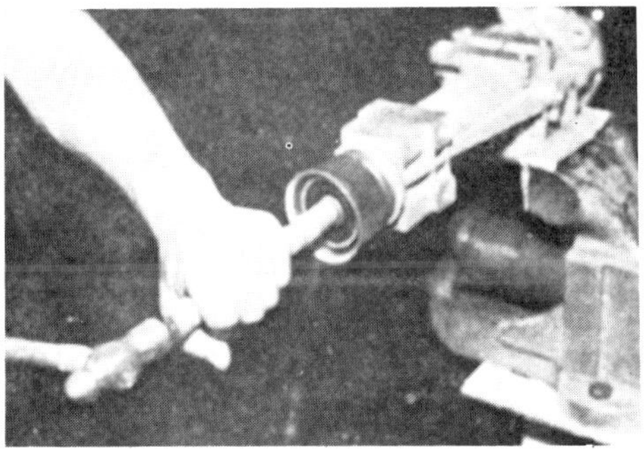

Fig. 6.38. Removing the rear drive shaft

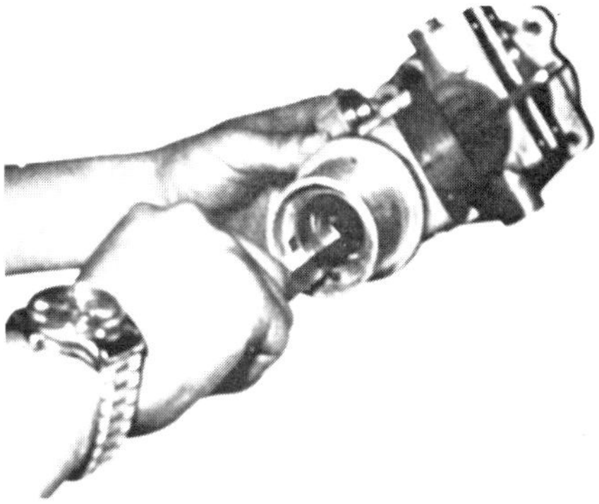

Fig. 6.39. Removing the bush from the rear casing

26 Rear differential servicing (4WD) - general

A number of special tools and a selection of adjusting washers, shims and pre-load spacers are required for the dismantling, reassembly

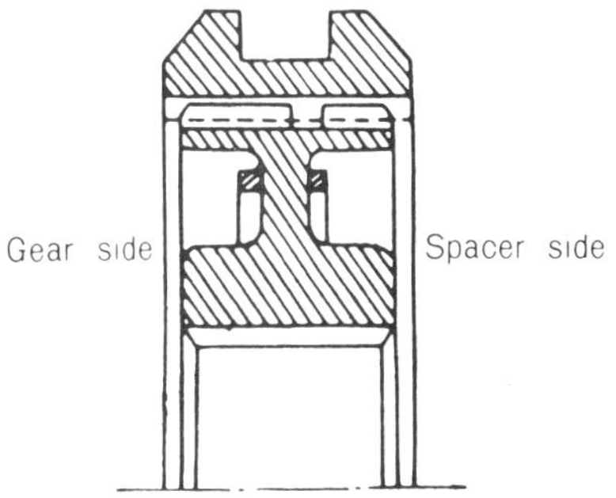

Fig. 6.40. Assembling the synchronizer hub

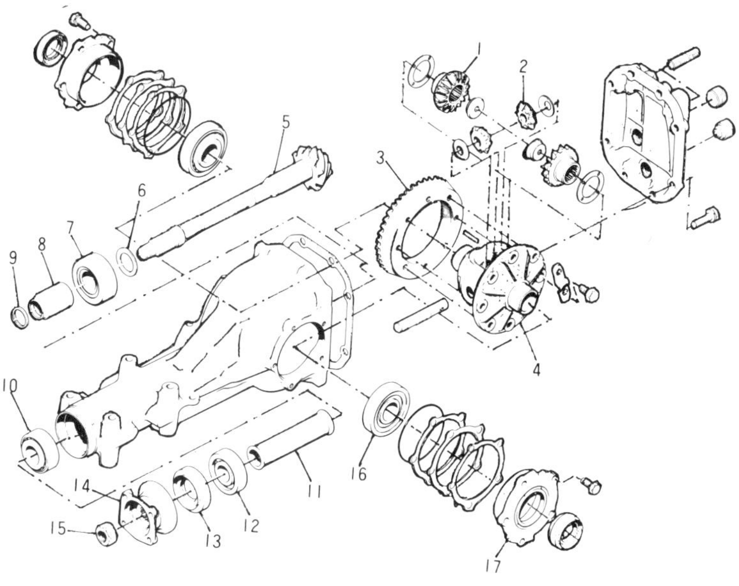

Fig. 6.41. Rear differential - 4WD

1 Side gear
2 Pinion mate gear
3 Drive gear
4 Differential case
5 Drive pinion
6 Pinion height adjusting washer
7 Rear bearing
8 Preload adjusting spacer
9 Preload adjusting washer
10 Front bearing
11 Spacer
12 Pilot bearing
13 Oil seal
14 Companion flange
15 Pinion nut
16 Side bearing
17 Side bearing retainer

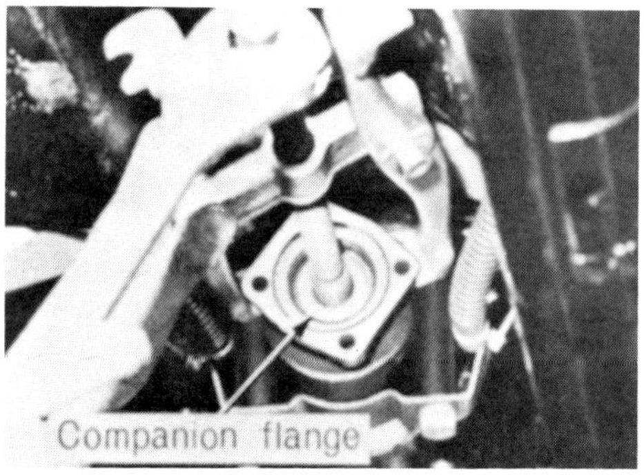

Fig. 6.42. Removing the differential pinion shaft flange

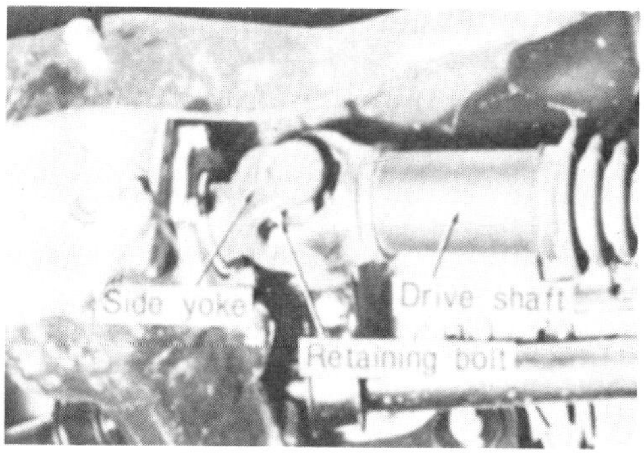

Fig. 6.43. Removing the drive shaft side yoke

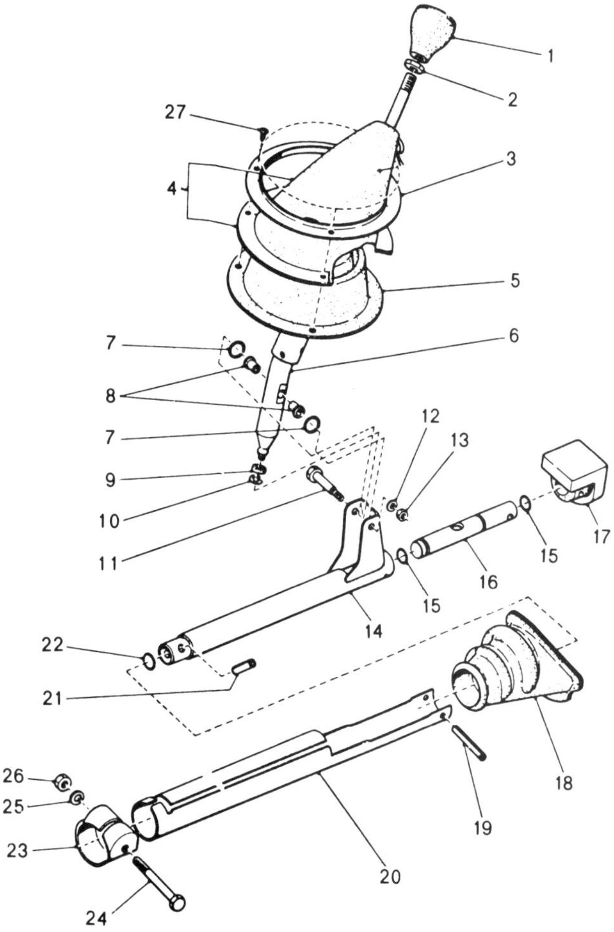

Fig. 6.44. Gear shift system (early models)

1 Shift lever knob
2 Nut
3 Plate
4 Boot assembly
5 Boot
6 Shift lever
7 O-ring
8 Bushing
9 Bushing
10 Clip
11 Bolt
12 Spring washer
13 Nut
14 Rod complete
15 O-ring
16 Shaft
17 Dynamic damper
18 Boot (gear shift stay)
19 Spring pin
20 Gear shift stay
21 Spring pin
22 O-ring
23 Bracket (gear shift stay)
24 Bolt
25 Spring washer
26 Nut
27 Tapping screw

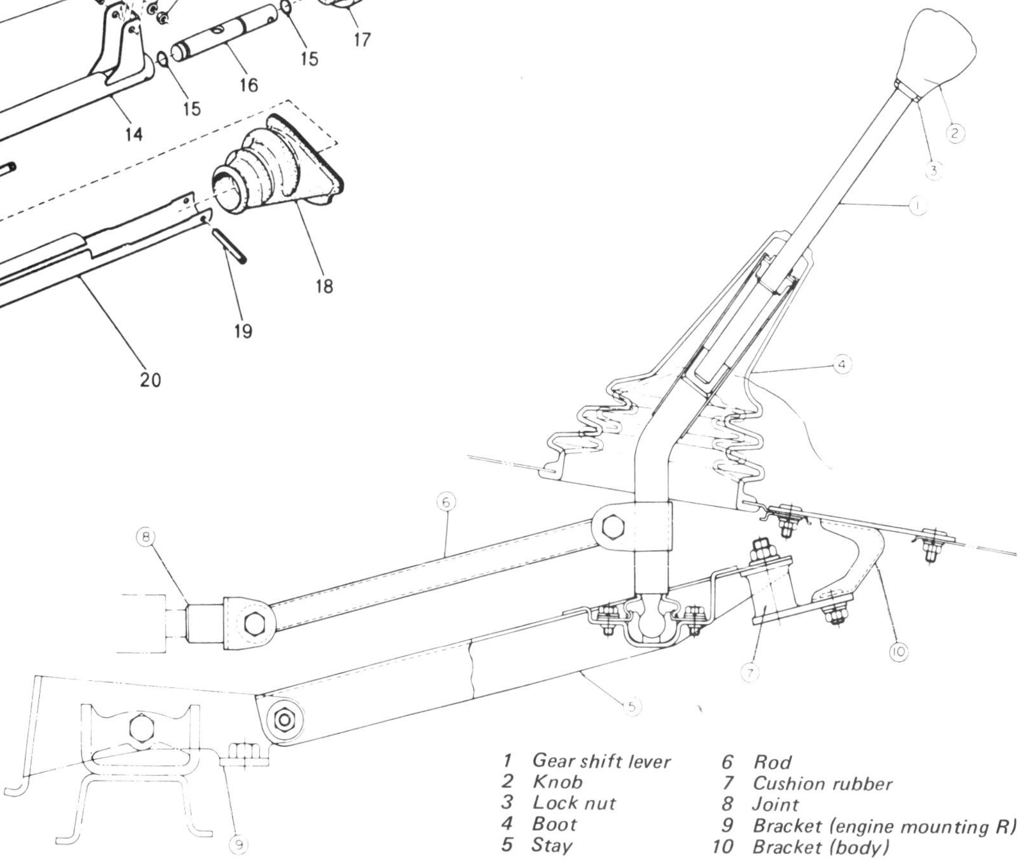

1 Gear shift lever
2 Knob
3 Lock nut
4 Boot
5 Stay
6 Rod
7 Cushion rubber
8 Joint
9 Bracket (engine mounting R)
10 Bracket (body)

Fig. 6.45. Gear shift system 1976 (except for automatic transmission and 4WD)

and adjusting of the rear differential unit. It is therefore recommended that servicing by the owner mechanic be limited to renewing the pinion and side oil seals as described in Section 27.

Should the differential develop a defect requiring dismantling, the rear differential carrier unit can be removed as a complete assembly, as described in Section 3, and taken to your local Subaru dealer for repair.

27 Rear differential oil seals (4WD) - renewal

1 Chock the front wheels, jack up the rear of the car and support it on jackstands.
2 Drain the gear oil into a suitable container.

Pinion oil seal

3 Remove the propeller shaft attaching bolts and separate the propeller shaft from the differential unit pinion shaft.
4 Remove the pinion shaft flange retaining nut. Fit two bolts temporarily in the flange and use a lever to restrain the flange from turning while undoing the nut.
5 Use a puller to pull off the flange and then remove the oil seal.
6 Apply grease to the lips of the new seal and fit it in the casing.
7 Fit the pinion shaft flange and retaining nut. Tighten the nut to 123 - 145 lb f ft (17 - 20 kg fm) then lock it by staking.

Side oil seals

8 Loosen the drive shaft side yoke retaining bolt and pull the side yoke out of the carrier.
9 Remove the oil seal by levering it out with a screwdriver.
10 Grease the lips of the new seal and drive it in, using a suitable drift.
11 Renew the side yoke, retaining bolt O-ring and reassemble in the reverse sequence to dismantling. Don't forget to fill with gear oil, capacity 1.7 US pt (0.8 liter).

28 Gear shift assembly - removal and refitting

1 Move the front seats to their fully back position.
2 Jack up the car and support it on jackstands.
3 Unscrew the gear shift lever knob after loosening the locknut. Undo the console retaining screw and remove the console.
4 Remove the boot from the tunnel. On early models the boot is secured with three screws, later model boots are glued to the tunnel.
5 Disconnect the exhaust pipes from the engine and remove the pipe retaining bracket from the transmission casing. There is no need to remove the rear part of the exhaust system. Remove the heat insulating panel, if fitted.
6 On models to 1974 remove the shift lever mounting bolt and take out the O-rings and bushings. Remove the gear shift stay by loosening it from the bracket on the transmission, pulling the stay to the rear and driving out the spring pin. Separate the rod assembly from the transmission and lift out the shift lever.
7 On later models remove the rubber cushion connecting the rear of the stay to the body and the through bolt connecting the stay to the engine mounting bracket. Remove the bolt connecting the shift rod to the joint and pull the gear shift lever down.
8 Inspect all the linkage components for wear and distortion. Pay special attention to cracks in the boot and wear of the bushings.
9 Refitting is the reverse of the removal procedure. Apply grease to the bushings and sliding surface of the spacers. Always fit new O-rings. Fit the shift lever knob so that the shifting pattern is in the correct direction.

29 Automatic transmission - general

The automatic transmission replaces the conventional clutch and gearbox and is bolted onto the engine in the same way. It consists of three basic parts: the torque converter, three-speed gearbox and differential. The differential is installed between the torque converter and the gearbox. Since hypoid gears are used for the final reduction system, a hypoid gear oil different from the ordinary automatic transmission oil must be used for proper lubrication. For this reason, the final reduction system is separated with oil seals from that part of

28.7 Disconnecting the gear shift stay from the engine mounting

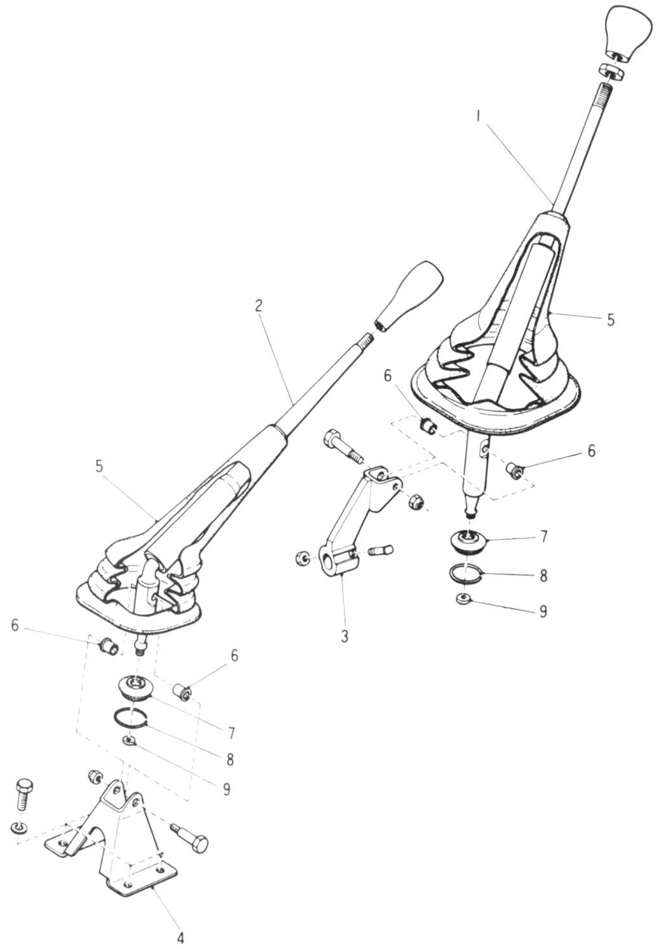

Fig. 6.46. Gear shift system - 4WD models

1	*Gear shift lever*	*6*	*Bushing*
2	*Drive selector*	*7*	*Dust seal*
3	*Bracket*	*8*	*Clip*
4	*Bracket*	*9*	*Bushing*
5	*Boot*		

the system where automatic transmission oil is used.

Because of the complexity of this type of transmission it is recommended that the owner should not attempt to dismantle it himself. If the system is suspect or there is a failure, your local Subaru dealer should be consulted. He has the special equipment required for fault diagnosing and rectification. Do not remove the unit from the car before consulting your dealer as most testing for faults have to be carried out with the unit in the car.

Removal of the transmission necessitates the removal of the engine, and the instructions for the removal and refitting of the unit as an engine/transmission assembly are described in Chapter 1.

The floor mounted selector lever has six positions. Position 'P' locks the transmission for parking, 'R' is reverse, 'N' is neutral, 'D' is the normal driving position, '2' prevents the engagement of top gear, while if '1' is selected the car will not move out of 1st gear. Position '1' is normally used to provide engine braking on steep downhill sections of road.

It is not possible to push or tow-start the car. If the car has to be towed for any reason, the speed must be kept below 30 mph and the selector in 'N' position. If there is a suspected fault in the transmission, the car should not be towed unless the driving wheels are raised, to prevent the possibility of the transmission suffering extensive damage.

30 Automatic transmission - checking the fluid level

1 Use only automatic transmission fluid (Castrol TQ Dexron or equivalent). The capacity is 5.92 - 6.34 US qts (5.6 - 6.0 liters). A dipstick is provided in the tiller tube which is located in the engine compartment.

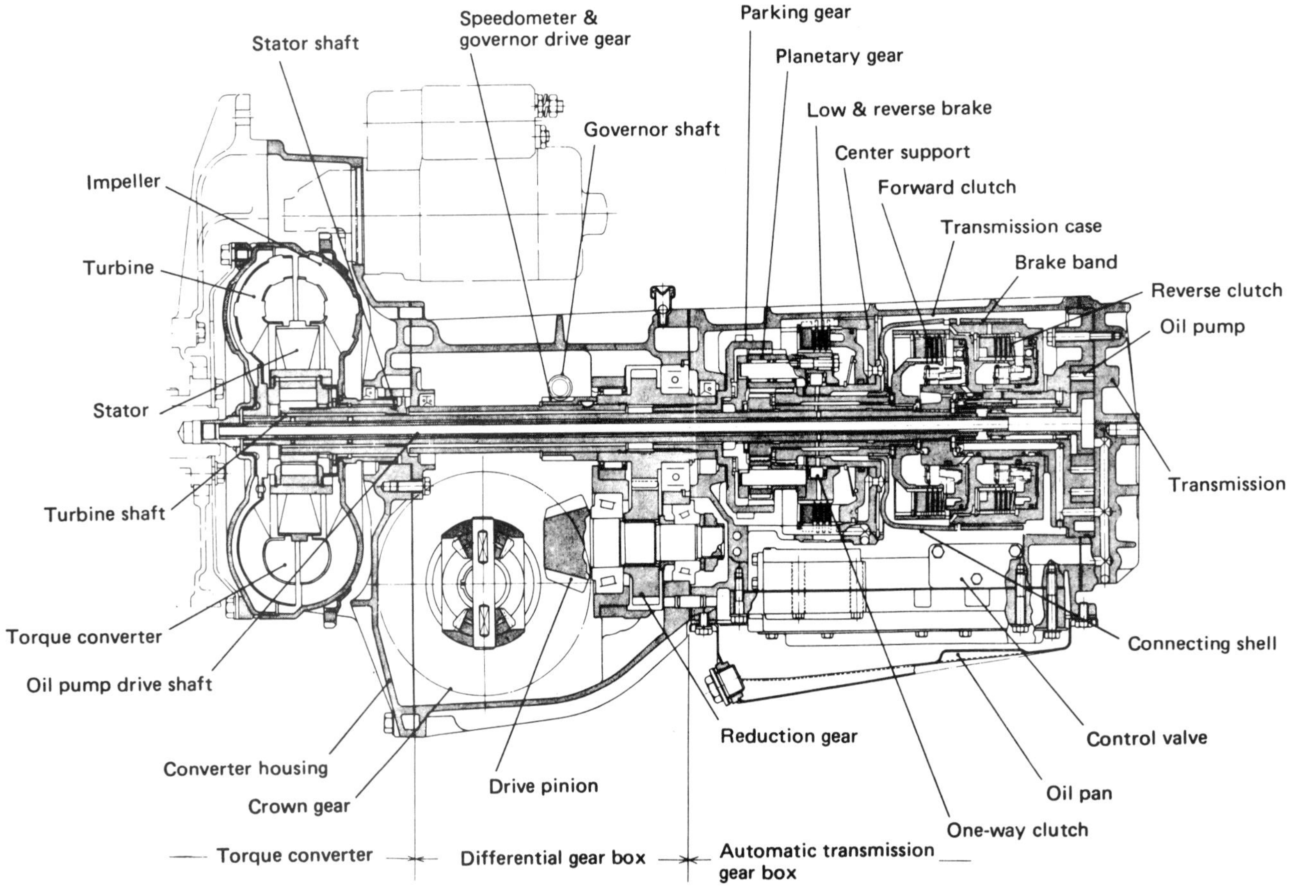

Fig. 6.47. Cross-section view of M41A automatic transmission

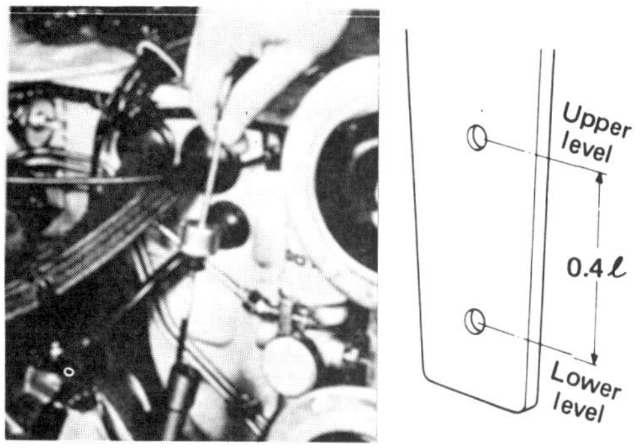

Fig. 6.48. Checking the automatic transmission fluid level

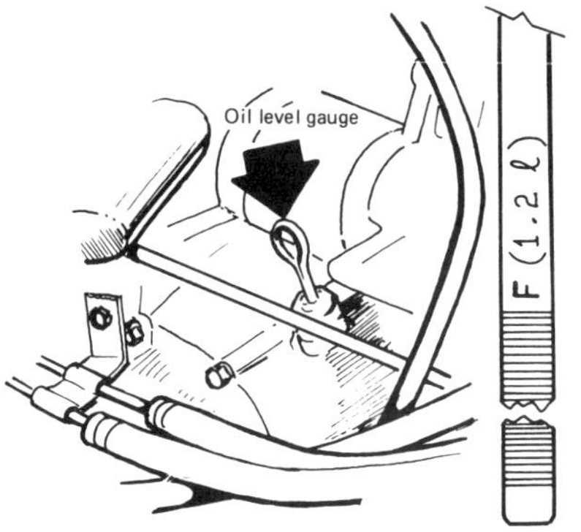

Fig. 6.49. Checking the differential gear oil level (automatic transmission models)

2 To check the fluid level, the transmission fluid should be warmed up until the fluid is in the temperature range 140 - 176°F (60 - 80°C), this will normally be attained after 3 to 6 miles running.
3 With the car stationary, on level ground and engine kept idling, and the selector in the 'P' position, remove the dipstick, clean it with a nylon cloth then refit and remove again to note the level. The level must be maintained between the upper and lower level marks on the dipstick. The difference between the upper and lower marks on the dipstick corresponds to 0.422 US qt (0.4 liter).
4 If it becomes necessary to frequently top-up the fluid level it is an indication of a leak in the transmission. Immediate remedial action is necessary to prevent damage to the transmission.
5 Change the fluid every 25000 miles (40,000 km).

31 Differential gear oil (automatic transmission) - checking the level

1 Because of the different type of lubricant used in the differential, the unit is separated from the automatic transmission by an oil seal fitted between the two.
2 Always use the correct hypoid type gear oil. The capacity of the differential is 0.9 - 1.3 US qts (0.8 - 1.2 liters).
3 The level dipstick is in the filler tube, always maintain the level between the upper and lower level marks. The difference between the upper and lower marks corresponds to 0.422 US qt (0.4 liters). When checking the gear oil always have the car on level ground.

32 Automatic transmission - stall test

1 Testing and adjusting the automatic transmission calls for specialized skill and experience as well as special testing equipment, therefore the owner is advised to have this work carried out by the Subaru dealer.
2 One test which the owner may carry out, if he suspects that there is slip or loss of drive power. A tachometer must be fitted to the engine, in a position where it can be seen from the driving seat, and the engine and transmission fluid must be at normal operating temperature.
3 Chock the wheels and apply the parking brake. Shift the selector lever into the 'D' position and slowly depress the accelerator fully. The engine speed should become stable at 2,100 rpm. Do not maintain the test for more than 10 seconds or overheating will result. If the engine rpm is too high then the torque converter oil supply should be suspect, or slippage of the clutches and bands in the automatic transmission can be assured. If the rpm is below 1800 then the engine is not delivering full power or there is a slipping one-way clutch in the torque converter.
4 If the stall test indicates a fault, consult your local Subaru dealer.

33 Fault diagnosis - transmission

Symptom	Reason/s	Remedy
Gears are difficult to mesh	Worn, damaged or burred chamfer of gears	Dismantle and renew.
	Incorrect contact between synchronizing ring and gear cone or wear	Dismantle and renew
Jumps out of gear when coasting or accelerating	Worn shifter fork or broken shifter fork rail spring	Dismantle and renew.
	Excessive clearance between splines of synchronizer hub and synchronizer sleeve	Dismantle and renew.
Noisy	Insufficient or incorrect lubricant	Check and replenish as necessary.
	Worn or damaged gears and bearings	Dismantle and renew as necessary.
	Crown gear and drive pinion worn or maladjusted	Dismantle and renew or adjust as necessary.
Noisy engagment of gears	Clutch fault	Check operation of clutch

Chapter 7 Axle shafts, driveshafts and propeller shaft

For modifications, and information applicable to later models, see Supplement at end of manual

Contents

Specifications

Front axle shaft joints (All models)

Outer end	Constant velocity joint
Inner end	Double offset joint

Rear axle driveshafts (4WD models)

Outer end joint	Universal joint
Inner end joint	Universal joint with sliding ball spline
Standard distance between centers of spiders	13.15 in (334 mm)
Sliding resistance of ball spline	44 lb (20 kg) maximum

Propeller shaft

Type	Two universal maintenance free type joints
Distance between joints	49.9 in (1115 mm)

Torque wrench settings

	lb f ft	kg f m
Front hub nut (1970 - 1971)	87 - 101	12 - 14
Front hub nut (1972 - 1977)	145 - 181	20 - 25
Control arm attaching bolts	72 - 87	10 - 12
Driveshaft flange bolts	14 - 19	1.9 - 2.6
Propeller shaft flange bolts	13 - 18	1.8 - 2.5

1 General description

Power is transmitted to the front wheels by two axle shafts which are carried by knuckle arms attached to the bottom of the struts. Each shaft is supported on two ball bearings, mounted back to back with a spacer in between, and is splined to the wheel hub.

A constant velocity joint (CVJ), fitted at the outer end of the axle shaft and a double offset joint (DOJ) at the inner end, ensures a smooth drive to the front road wheels.

The front wheel toe-in must be checked after completion of repair work on the front wheels and axle shafts.

On vehicles with 4WD, the drive is transmitted via a propeller shaft, with two maintenance free universal joints, to the rear axle differential. From these the drive to the rear road wheels is transmitted by two driveshafts with universal joints at each end, one of which is splined to the shaft to allow for side movement.

The driveshafts are attached to the companion flanges of the rear hub spindle by four bolts.

2 Front axle shaft - removal and refitting

FF-I 1100 and 1300 G models

1 Apply the parking brake. Loosen the road wheel nuts. Jack-up the car and support it on jackstands, then remove the wheel.

2 Straighten the lock plate on the hub nut, then remove the hub nut and lockplate.

3 Remove the three attaching bolts and separate the double offset joint (DOJ) from the front brake drum.

4 Remove the splash guard from the wheel well by removing the securing bolt.

5 Turn the steering to full lock on the side from which the axle shaft is being removed then push the axle shaft towards the engine to remove it from the hub. Now pull the axle shaft away from the engine and remove it out through the wheel well.

6 Refitting is the reverse of the removal procedure. Tighten the hub nut to 87 - 101 lb f ft (12 - 14 kg f m).

1300, 1400 and 1600 models

7 Remove the brake drum or brake disc assembly as described in Chapter 9.

8 On cars with drum brakes remove the back plate securing bolts and tie the back plate to the suspension without disconnecting the hydraulic brake hose. Disconnecting the support bracket attaching the brake hose to the suspension strut will provide enough free movement of the brake hose.

9 Drive the spring pin, which connects the axle shaft to the differential driveshaft, out of the axle shaft, using a pin punch and a hammer. Discard the spring pin, always use a new one when refitting the axle shaft.

10 Remove the self locking nuts which secure the ends of the control arm to the stabilizer bar and the crossmember inner pivot.

11 Pull the control arm from the stabilizer bar by swinging the link forward and separate the control arm from the crossmember by levering it to the rear.

12 Disengage the axle shaft from the differential driveshaft by pulling the front suspension assembly outwards. Take care not to damage the rubber boots on the double offset joint and constant velocity joint.

13 Withdraw the axle shaft from the housing. Do not hammer on the end of the axle shaft to remove it as the splines will get damaged. If it proves very stubborn use a puller as shown in Fig. 7.5 to free it.

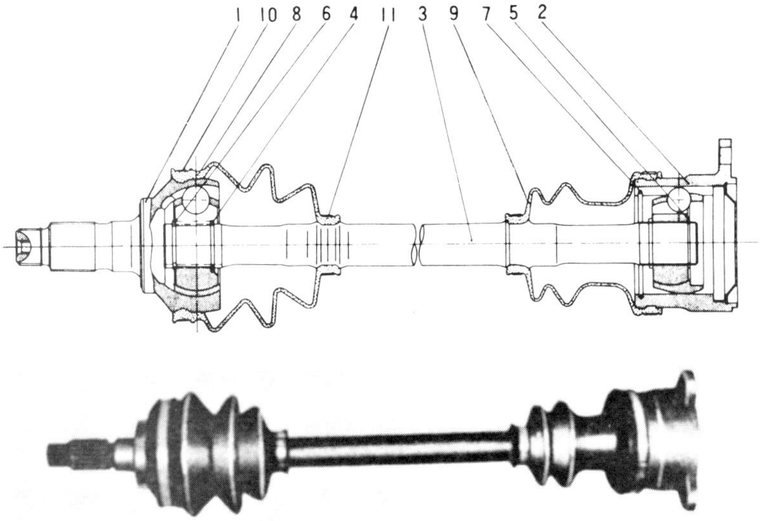

Fig. 7.1. Front axle shaft FF-1 1100 and 1300G models

1 CVJ (constant velocity joint)
2 DOJ (double offset joint)
3 Axle shaft
4 Snap ring
5 C-type snap ring
6 Circlip
7 Circlip
8 Boot (on CVJ side)
9 Boot (on DOJ side)
10 Band
11 Band

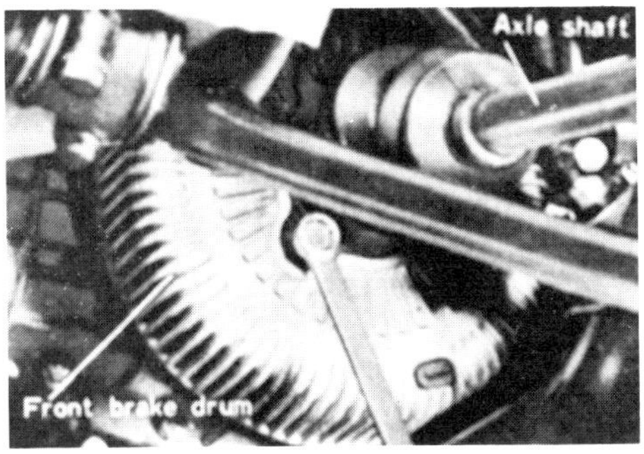

Fig. 7.2. Disconnecting the axle shaft - DOJ

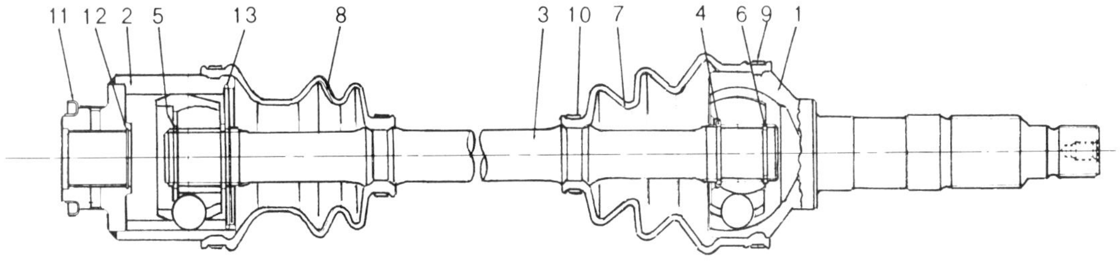

Fig. 7.3. Front axle shaft - 1300, 1400 and 1600 models

1 CVJ assembly
2 DOJ assembly
3 Axle shaft
4 Snap-ring
5 Snap-ring
6 Circlip
7 CVJ boot
8 DOJ boot
9 Band
10 Band
11 Baffle plate
12 Sealing plate
13 Circlip (DOJ)

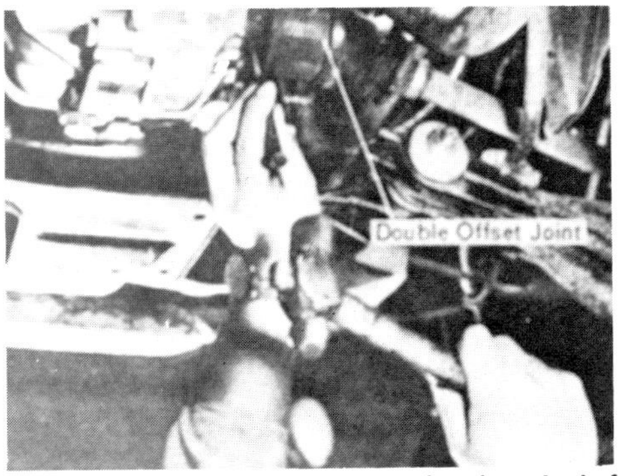

Fig. 7.4. Driving out the spring pin connecting the axle shaft to the differential driveshaft

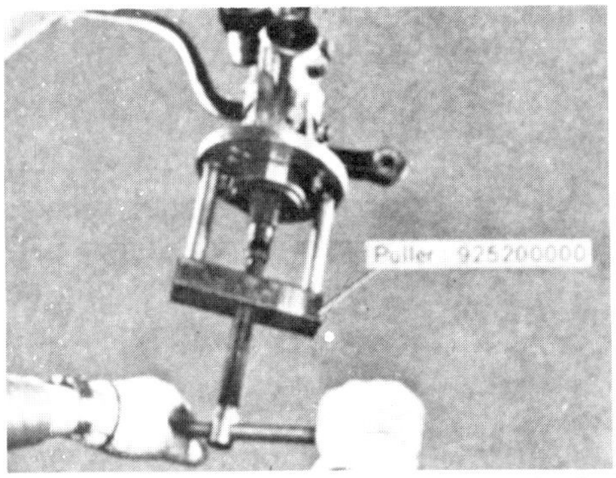

Fig. 7.5. Removing the axle shaft from the knuckle housing

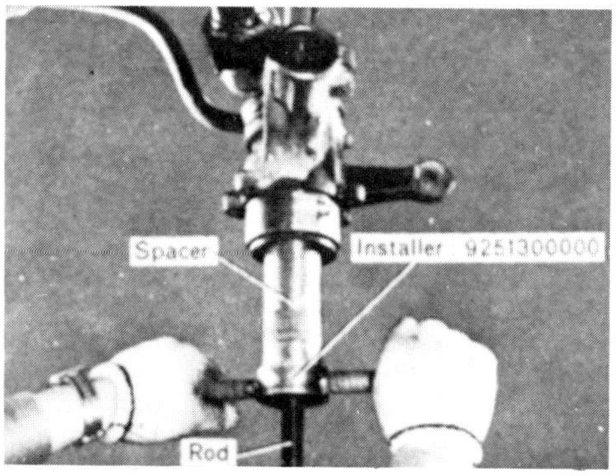

Fig. 7.6. Pulling the axle shaft into the housing

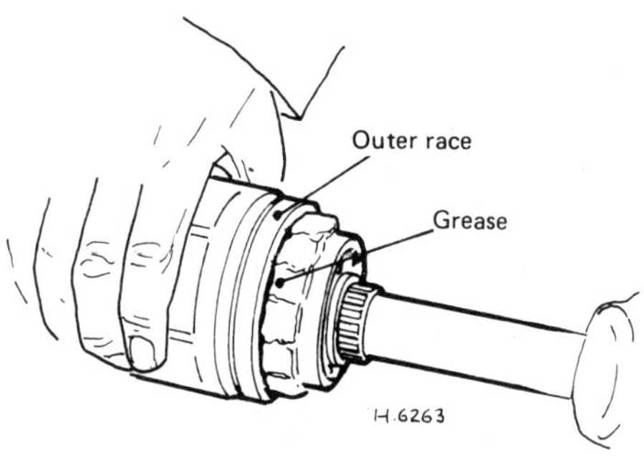

Fig. 7.7. Removing the outer race of the DOJ

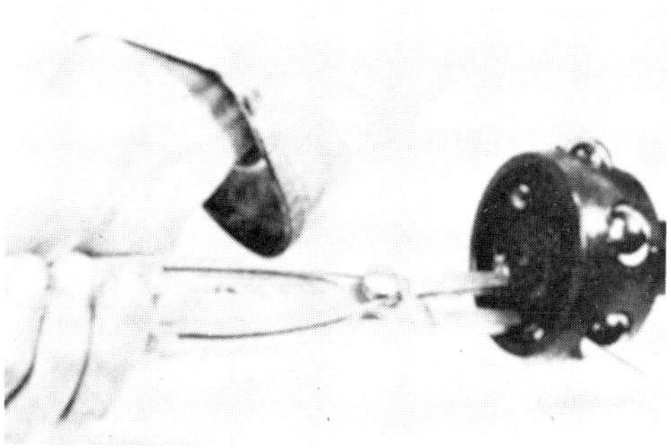

Fig. 7.8. Removing the snap-ring which retains the inner race

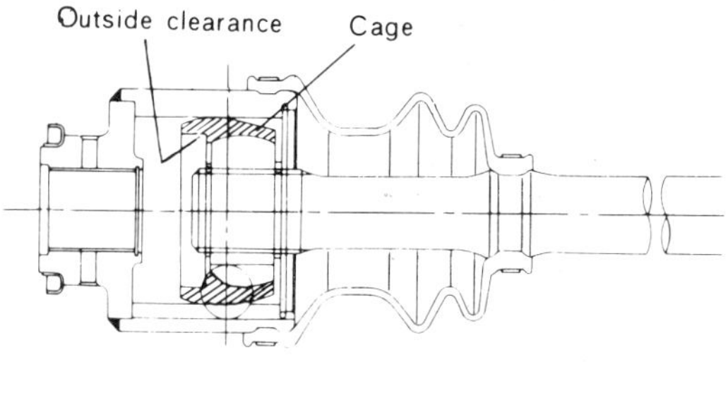

Fig. 7.9. Locating the ball cage on the shaft

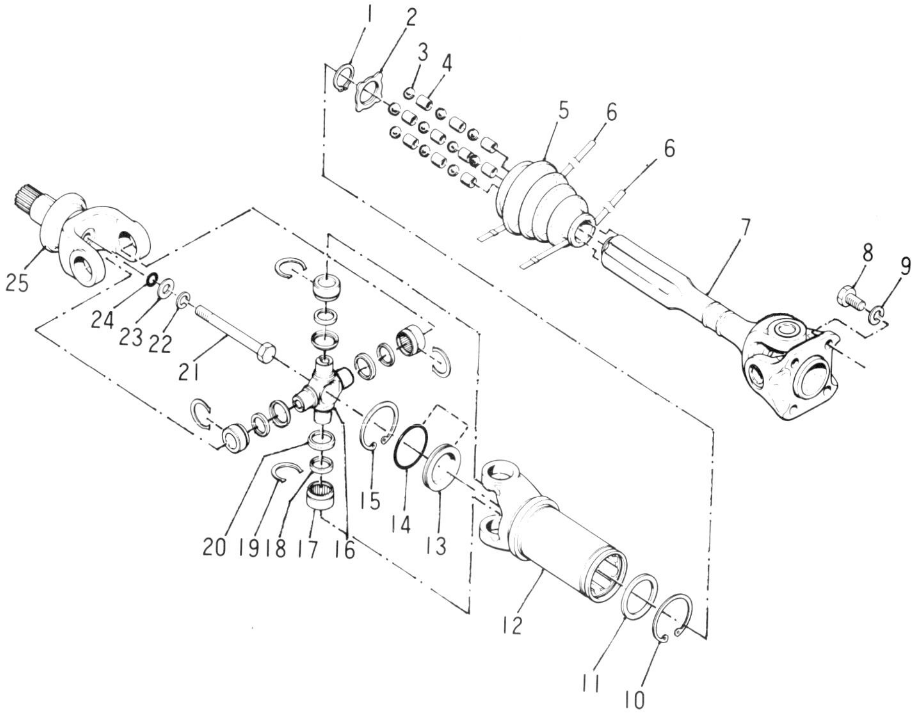

Fig. 7.10. Exploded view of rear axle driveshaft (4WD)

1 Snap-ring
2 Stopper
3 Ball
4 Ball spacer
5 Rubber boot
6 Boot band
7 Yoke
8 Bolt
9 Spring washer
10 Snap-ring
11 Stopper
12 Sleeve yoke
13 Plug
14 O-ring
15 Snap-ring
16 Spider
17 Bearing race
18 Oil seal
19 Snap-ring
20 Dust cover (oil seal)
21 Bolt
22 Spring washer
23 Washer
24 O-ring
25 Side yoke

14 For refitting the front axle shaft, Subaru supply a special tool for pulling the axle shaft into the housing, as shown in Fig. 7.6, but a piece of rod threaded at both ends and a suitable length of tubing to use as a spacer will do the job. Screw the rod into the end of the axle shaft, insert it into the housing, taking care not to damage the seals, splines or bearings. Fit the spacer and a nut on the rod and pull the axle shaft into the housing.
15 Fit the brake assemblies as described in Chapter 9.
16 On 1972 - 1973 models, fit the spacer, lockwasher and hub nut to 145 - 181 lb f ft (20 - 25 kg f m) and bend over the lockwasher to lock the nut.
17 On 1974 - 1977 models, fit the spacer, conical spring washer and hub nut. Tighten the nut to 174 lb f ft (24 kg f m) and lock it by staking the flange part of the nut into the groove on the axle shaft.
18 Connect the DOJ end of the axle shaft to the differential driveshaft and fit a new spring pin.
19 Fit the washer and bushing on the end of the stabilizer bar. Fit the control arm link to the stabilizer and fit the remaining washer and bushing, secured temporarily with a self locking nut.
20 Fit the control arm into the inner pivot of the crossmember and fit the bushing and washer, temporarily tighten the self locking nut.
21 Fit the road wheels, remove the jackstands and lower the car to the ground.
22 With the weight of the car on the suspension, tighten the self locking nuts connecting the control arm to the crossmember and the control arm to the stabilizer bar 72 - 87 lb f ft (10 - 12 kg f m).

3 Axle shaft - dismantling, inspection and reassembly

1 Place the axle shaft in a vise equipped with soft jaw grips. Remove the band type clamps which secures the rubber boots to the DOJ and CVJ's, and slide the boots back from the joints.
2 Remove the circlip which secures the outer race of the DOJ and withdraw the outer race.
3 Wipe the grease from the ball cage and remove the ball bearings. Turn the cage approximately half a turn and withdraw it from the inner race.
4 Remove the 'C' type snap-ring, using suitable type pliers, and remove the inner race, tap it lightly with a soft faced hammer, if necessary.
5 Remove the rubber boots from the shaft.
6 Clean all the dismantled parts in kerosene, and examine all the parts for wear, damage and corrosion. Examine the cage which fits between the inner and outer races for wear in the ball cage windows and for cracks. Examine the balls and ball tracks for wear or pitting. If wear is excessive then all the parts must be renewed as a matched set.
7 The CVJ cannot be dismantled, and if there is excessive wear in the joint, the axle shaft must be renewed.
8 If the rubber boots show any signs of deterioration, it is recommended that they be renewed, as most of the troubles with DOJ and CVJ's are caused by faulty boots allowing the ingress of dirt and moisture.
9 Reassembly is the reverse of the dismantling procedure. When fitting the cage onto the shaft locate it with the clearance, as shown in Fig. 7.7, to the outside. Before fitting the clamps on the rubber boots pack the joints with 2.1 - 2.8 oz (60 - 70 g) of grease (molitex No. 2).

4 Rear axle driveshafts (4WD) - removal and refitting

1 Jack-up the rear of the car and support it with jackstands.
2 Rotate the rear wheel to position the driveshaft for access to the retaining bolts on the wheel side and remove the bolts.
3 Remove the driveshaft assembly by withdrawing it from the differential.
4 Refitting is the reverse of the removal sequence. Tighten the retaining bolts to 14 - 19 lb f ft (1.9 - 2.6 kg f m).

5 Rear axle driveshaft (4WD) - dismantling

1 Secure the drive shaft in a vise and remove the rubber band securing the rubber boot. Pull back the boot.
2 Remove the snap-ring and stopper, then disassemble the ball spline. This will be made easier if an air hole is made through the grease with a piece of wire.
3 To dismantle the universal joint, remove the snap-rings which retain the bearings for the spider.
4 Drive the spider as far as it will go in one direction; this will make the bearing stick out of the yoke.
5 Repeat the process in the opposite direction. You will find that the spider can now be taken out of the yoke.
6 Drive out the bearings with a drift.

6 Rear axle driveshaft (4WD) - inspection and reassembly

1 Clean all the parts thoroughly with a cleaning solvent. Check for signs of wear, damage or corrosion.
2 If the ball spline portion of the driveshaft is worn or damaged, renew the driveshaft assembly.
3 Check the needle bearings of the universal joints for wear and blueing. Check that their rubber seals are undamaged. If the yokes are damaged or the bearings are a loose fit in them, renew the complete assembly.
4 Reassembly is the reverse of the dismantling procedure. Before reassembling, apply grease to the needle bearings, sleeve yoke oil groove (8 places) and to the position indicated in Fig. 7.11, (approx. 1.23 oz (35 g)).
5 Fit the rubber boots with the driveshaft at standard length of 13.5 in (334 mm) between centers of the spiders.
6 Using a spring balance check the sliding resistance of the ball spline, it should not exceed 44 lb (20 kg).

7 Propeller shaft (4WD) - removal and refitting

1 Drain the transmission oil.
2 Jack-up the rear of the car and support it with jackstands. Chock the front wheels.
3 Remove the bolts connecting the propeller shaft to the rear differential flange.
4 Lower the rear of the propeller shaft slightly and pull it rearwards out of the transmission rear extension, taking care not to damage the transmission rear oil seal.

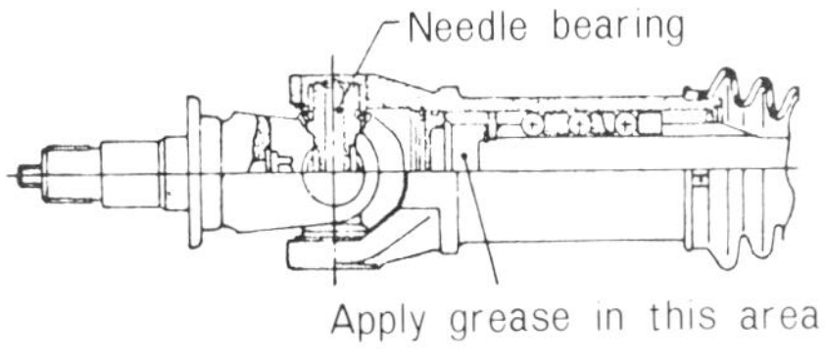

Fig. 7.11. Apply grease to the driveshaft

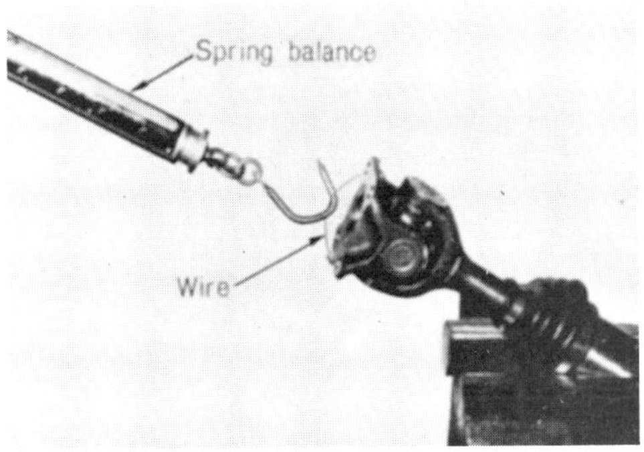

Fig. 7.12. Checking the sliding resistance of the driveshaft ball spline

5 Refitting is the reverse of the removal sequence. Apply grease to the splines and outside of the sleeve yoke. Tighten the flange yoke to companion flange bolts to 13 - 18 lb f ft (1.8 - 2.5 kg f m).

8 Propeller shaft (4WD) - dismantling, inspection and reassembly

1 The universal joints of the propeller shaft are dismantled in the same way as described for the driveshaft universal joints in Section 5.
2 After disassembly clean all the parts in grease solvent. Examine the component parts for wear and damage. If the shaft surface is dented or cracked it must be renewed.
3 Renew the shaft if the run-out exceeds 0.024 in (0.6 mm) when rotating it with both ends supported.
4 Reassembly is the reverse of the dismantling sequence. Since this type of joint is maintenance free, pack the bearings with grease at assembly. Adjust the free play of the spider by fitting selective snap-rings so that the play does not exceed 0.0008 in (0.02 mm), see Fig. 7.14. Snap-rings are supplied in thickness of 0.0787 - 0.0843 in (2.0 - 2.14 mm) in steps of 0.0008 in (0.02 mm). Always fit the same thickness of snap-ring on each side.

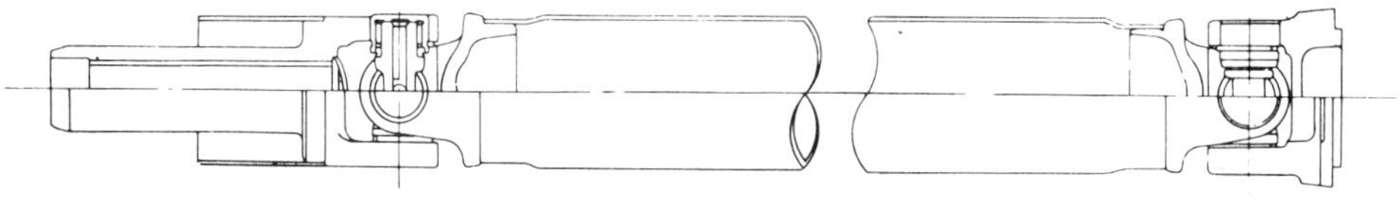

Fig. 7.13. Propeller shaft (4WD)

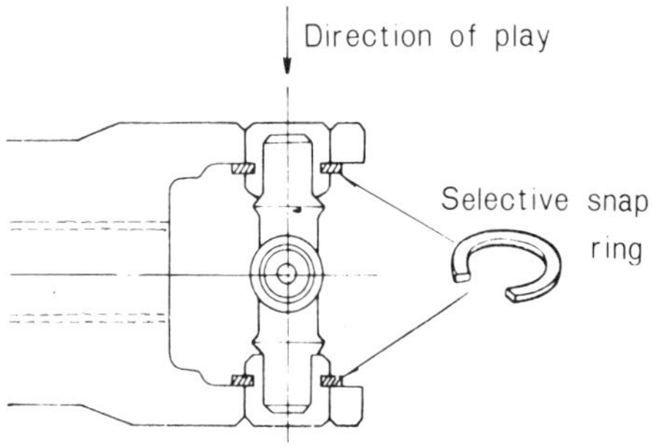

Fig. 7.14. Adjusting the free play of the spider by fitting selective snap-rings

9 Fault diagnosis - axle shafts, driveshafts and propeller shaft

Symptom	Reason/s	Remedy
All models		
Knocking sound when front wheels are turned on full lock	Worn DOJ and/or CVJ's	Renew.
4WD models		
Abnormal noise from rear axle and driveshaft	Wear or seizure of ball spline	Renew.
	Worn universal joint needle bearings	Renew.
Vibration	Worn universal joint needle bearings	Renew.
	Propeller shaft out of balance due to bend or twist	Renew.
	Propeller shaft securing bolts loose	Tighten.
Tapping noise when starting or when changing from drive to over-run and vice versa	Worn splines of sleeve yoke	Renew.
	Drive and/or propeller shaft securing bolts loose	Tighten.
	Worn universal joint needle bearings	Renew.

Chapter 8 Steering, wheels and tires

Contents

Specifications

FF - 1 1100 and 1300G (1970 - 72)

Type	Rack and pinion
Steering gear ratio	18.43 : 1 (Sports sedan 14.5 : 1)
Steering wheel play	0.39 - 1.18 in (10 - 30 mm) along circumference
Steering angle	
Inner	36° 20'
Outer	34° 20'
Pinion and rack backlash	Less than 0.0039 in (0.1 mm)
Pinion operating torque	1.6 lb f ft (0.22 kg fm) maximum
Wheel alignment: toe-in	0.04 - 0.2 in (1 - 5 mm) (Sports sedan 0 - 0.16 in (0 - 4 mm))

1300, 1400 and 1600 models (1972 - 77)

Type	Rack and pinion
Steering gear ratio	19.2 : 1
Turns - lock to lock	3.8 (4WD 3.2)
Minimum turning radius	15.8 ft (4.8 m) (4WD 18 ft (5.4 m))
Steering angle	
Inner	36° (4WD 31°)
Outer	35° (4WD 30°)
Tie-rod axial play	Less than 0.01 in (0.3 mm)
Rack stroke	2.87 in (73 mm)
Rack and pinion backlash	Nil
Pinion operating torque	1.6 lb f ft (0.22 kg fm) maximum

Wheel alignment

Toe-in (except 4WD models)	0.08 - 0.32 in (2 - 8 mm)
Toe-in - 4WD models	0.24 - 0.47 in (6 - 12 mm)

Wheels

Type and size	
1970 - 72	Disc WDC4 - J - 13
1973 - 77	Disc WDC 4½J - 13

Tire pressures ... Refer to tire inflation pressure label on the edge of driver's door

Torque wrench settings

	lb f ft	kg fm
Steering wheel nut	21 - 29	2.8 - 4.0
Universal joint bolt	21 - 23	2.8 - 3.2
Flexible coupling bolt	5	0.7
Steering column mounting bolt	12 - 14	1.6 - 2.0
Steering gearbox mounting bolt	33 - 40	4.5 - 5.5
Tie-rod end castle nut	18 - 22	2.5 - 3.0
Ball joint assembly	47 - 54	6.5 - 7.5
Cap securing bolt	6 - 8	0.8 - 1.2
Pinion nut	6 - 8	0.8 - 1.2
Wheel nut	40 - 50	5.5 - 7.5

1 General description

All models are fitted with a simple and reliable rack and pinion type steering. The steering wheel is splined to the steering shaft, which is connected to the steering gearbox pinion via a universal joint, torque rod and flexible rubber coupling. The collapsible steering column prevents the steering from being driven towards the driver in a front end collision.

The pinion teeth mesh with those machined in the rack so that rotation of the pinion moves the rack from one side of the housing to the other. Backlash is automatically adjusted to zero therefore no maintenance is required.

Located at each end of the rack are tie-rods, fitted with balljoints which provide for the adjustment of the front wheel toe-in. The tie-rods are connected to the steering knuckle arms.

A steering lock mechanism is incorporated with the ignition-starter switch. The ignition key cannot be pulled out of the switch except in the 'steering locked' position.

2 Steering system - inspection

1 The steering gear and linkage is easy to check and a lot of trouble, including ones own safety, can be avoided by frequent inspection of the steering system for wear.

2 Assuming that the suspension and wheel bearings have been checked and found in good order, the steering check involves tracing the amount of free movement between the steering wheel and the road wheels. If the rim of the steering wheel can be moved more than 2 inches (50 mm) without visible movement at the front road wheels this indicates that there is excess tire wear in the system or the steering gearbox mounting bolts are loose.

3 Have an assistant rock the steering wheel while you check throughout the system to discover where the fault lies. The most usual cause of excessive steering play is worn tie-rod ball joints, these can be renewed quite easily as described in Section 10.

4 If the play is in the steering gearbox this is more serious, as the backlash is automatically adjusted to take-up normal wear, and the gearbox will have to be removed for overhaul or renewal.

3 Steering column and wheel - removal and refitting

1100 and 1300G models (1970 - 72)

1 Disconnect the ground lead from the battery negative (—) terminal.

2 Disconnect the horn, turn signal, dimmer switch and stop switch at the connectors under the instrument panel. Remove the back-up light switch lead and gearshift cotter pin.

3 Remove the left-hand luggage shelf. Remove the two master cylinder mounting bolts and move the master cylinder away from the steering column.

4 Remove the two (upper) rubber coupling bolts and separate the steering shaft from the steering box.

5 Remove the two steering column securing bolts and draw the steering column and wheel assembly from the toe-board into the car.

6 Refitting is the reverse of the removal sequence.

1300, 1400 and 1600 models (1972 - 77)

7 Loosen the universal joint pinch bolt.

8 Disconnect the horn, turn signal, ignition-starter switch and dimmer switch lead at their connectors under the instrument panel.

9 Remove the steering column mounting bolts and pull the assembly from the hole in the toe-board.

10 Refitting is the reverse of removal. Before finally tightening the universal joint bolt ensure that the pinion shaft and steering shaft are in line. Tighten the universal joint bolt to 21 - 23 lb f ft (2.8 - 3.2 kg fm) and the steering column mounting bolts to 12 - 14 lb f ft (1.6 - 2 kg fm).

4 Steering column and wheel - dismantling, inspection and reassembly

1 Remove the three screws securing the horn bar and press it down

3.7 Loosen the steering universal joint pinch bolt

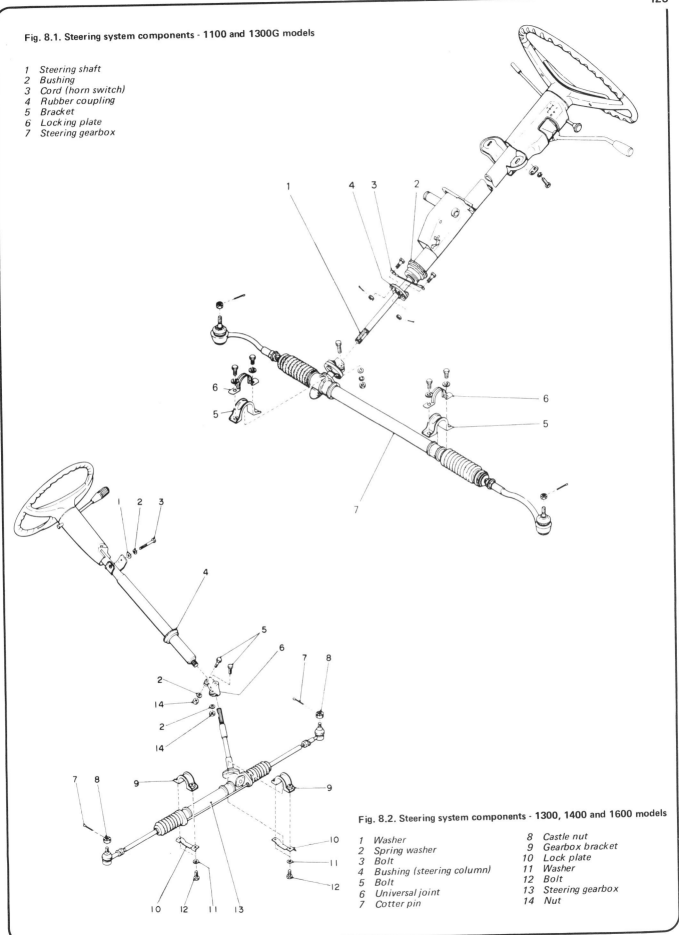

Fig. 8.1. Steering system components - 1100 and 1300G models

1 Steering shaft
2 Bushing
3 Cord (horn switch)
4 Rubber coupling
5 Bracket
6 Locking plate
7 Steering gearbox

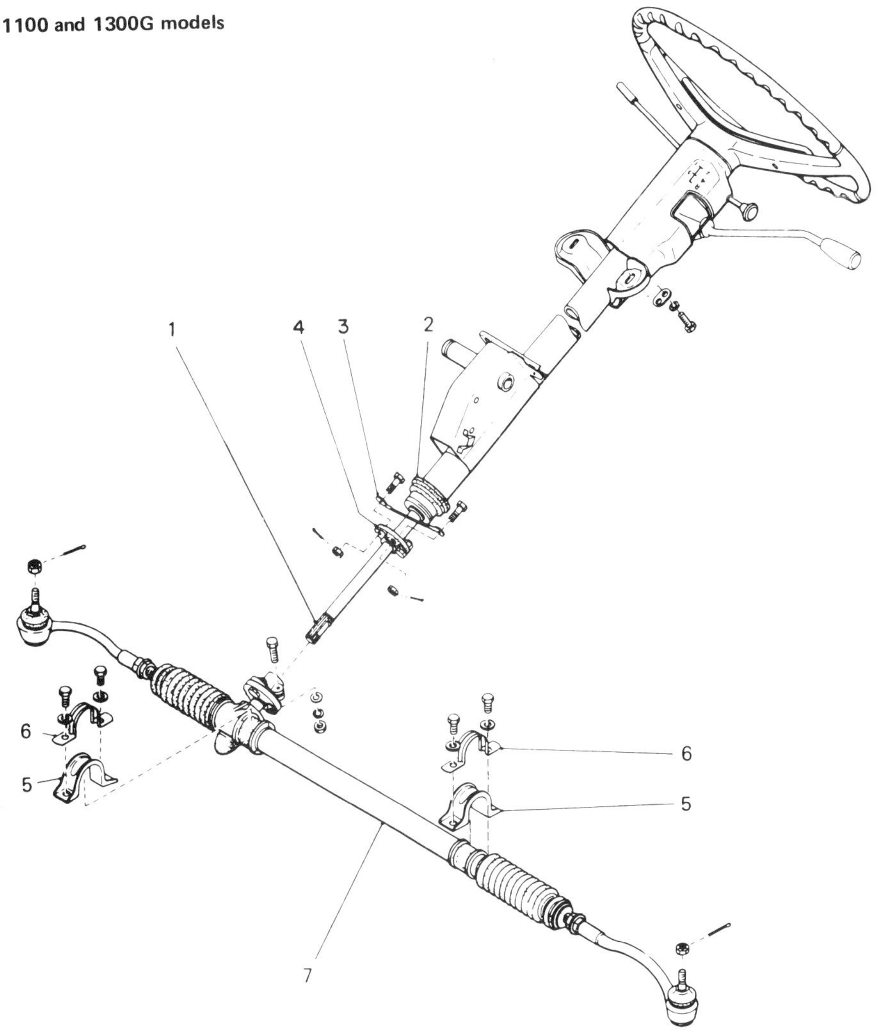

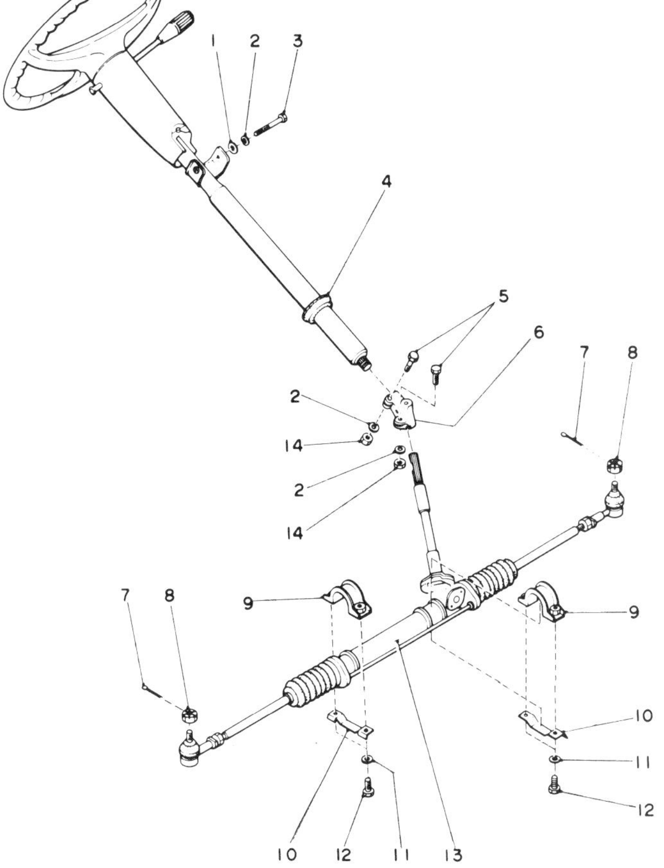

Fig. 8.2. Steering system components - 1300, 1400 and 1600 models

1 Washer
2 Spring washer
3 Bolt
4 Bushing (steering column)
5 Bolt
6 Universal joint
7 Cotter pin
8 Castle nut
9 Gearbox bracket
10 Lock plate
11 Washer
12 Bolt
13 Steering gearbox
14 Nut

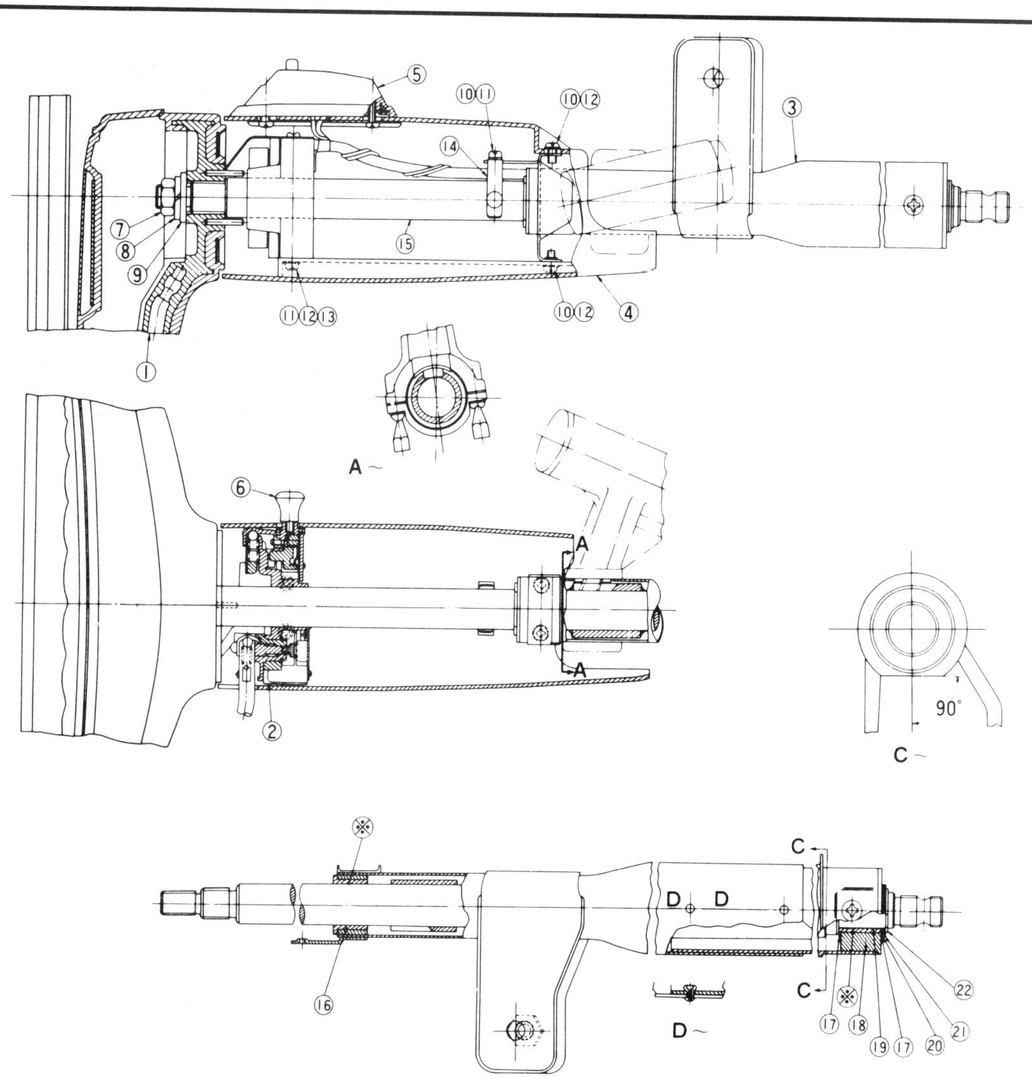

Fig. 8.3. Steering column and wheel assembly

1 *Steering wheel*
2 *Combination switch*
3 *Steering column*
4 *Column cover*
5 *Illumination light*
6 *Hazard knob*
7 *Nut*
8 *Spring washer*
9 *Washer*
10 *Screw*
11 *Spring washer*
12 *Washer*
13 *Tapping screw*
14 *Brush*
15 *Steering shaft*
16 *Bearing*
17 *Rubber washer*
18 *Housing*
19 *Bearing*
20 *Spacer*
21 *Spacer*
22 *Snap-ring*
⊛ *Grease*

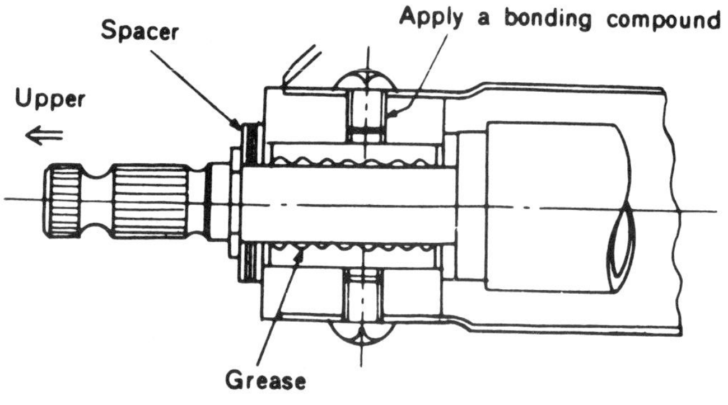

Fig. 8.4. Adjusting steering shaft endfloat

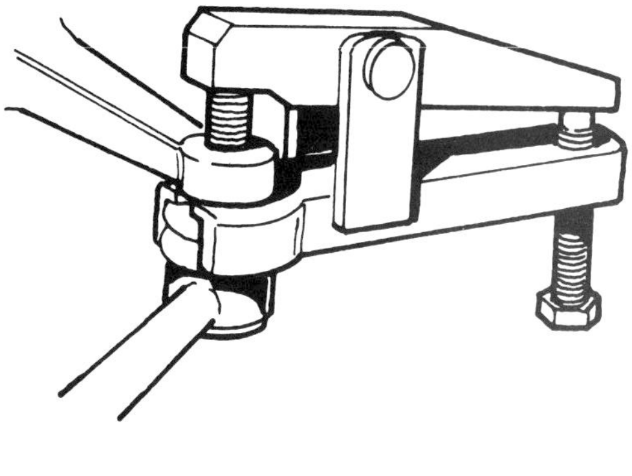

Fig. 8.5. Removing the tie-rod balljoint from the knuckle arm

and to the side to remove.
2 Remove the steering wheel retaining nut and pull the steering wheel off the steering shaft.
3 Refer to Fig. 8.3. Remove the snap-ring and take out the spacer, washer and rubber washer. Remove the screws attaching the steering column to the housing.
4 Drive out the housing with a screwdriver and pull the steering shaft out of the steering column.
5 Clean all the parts and inspect them for wear or damage. Do not wash the bearings in grease solvent.
6 Reassembly is the reverse of the removal sequence. Apply grease on the inner and outer surfaces of the upper and lower bearings. Apply a bonding compound (such as Loctite) on the screws which secure the steering column and the bearing.
7 Insert the steering shaft into the steering column from the bottom end. Check the endfloat of the shaft. If it exceeds 0.01 in (0.3 mm) add a spacer as shown in Fig. 8.4.
8 Check the clearance between the steering wheel and the column cover. If the clearance is not within 0.04 - 0.12 in (1 - 3 mm) loosen the cover securing screws and adjust the column cover.

5 Steering gearbox (except 4WD model) - removal and refitting

1 Jack up the front of the car and support it on jackstands. Remove the front wheels.
2 Pull out the cotter pin, unscrew the castle nut and remove the tie-rod end ball joint from the knuckle arm of the housing. For this you will need a ball joint separator of which there are several types, one shown in Fig. 8.5.
3 Remove the parking brake cable hanger from the tie-rod.
4 Pull out the cotter pins, then remove the rubber coupling connecting bolts and disconnect the pinion with gearbox from the steering shaft.
5 Undo the lockplate tabs and remove the gearbox bracket to crossmember retaining bolts. Pull the steering gearbox from the cross-member out towards the right-hand side, taking care not to damage the gearbox boots. (On left-hand drive vehicles the steering gearbox is removed, towards the left-hand side). Remove the gearbox brackets.
6 Refitting is the reverse of the removal procedure. Tighten the steering gearbox bracket to crossmember bolts to 33 - 40 lb f ft (4.5 - 5.5 kg fm) and the rubber coupling castellated nuts to 5 lb f ft (0.7 kg fm). Tighten the tie-rod end nuts to 18 - 22 lb f ft (2.5 - 3.0 kg fm). Check the front wheel toe-in, refer to Section 9.

6 Steering gearbox (4WD model) - removal and refitting

1 Removal and refitting of the steering gearbox on 4WD models is the same as for other models except that it is necessary to raise the engine slightly to allow the gearbox to clear the engine.
2 The additional operations are as follows:

a) Remove the fan guard on the top of the radiator.
b) Remove the horizontal damper as described in Chapter 1.
c) Loosen the front engine mounting nuts to the last few threads, do not remove them.

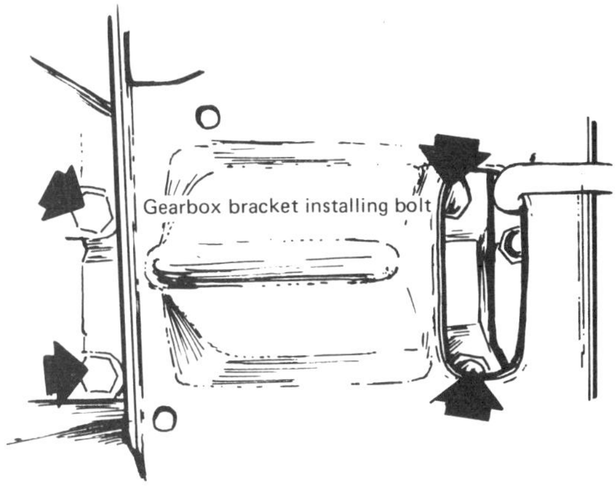

Fig. 8.6. Steering gearbox bracket to crossmember bolts

5.2 Disconnect the tie-rod ball joint

5.4 Remove the rubber coupling bolts

5.5 Steering gearbox and bracket

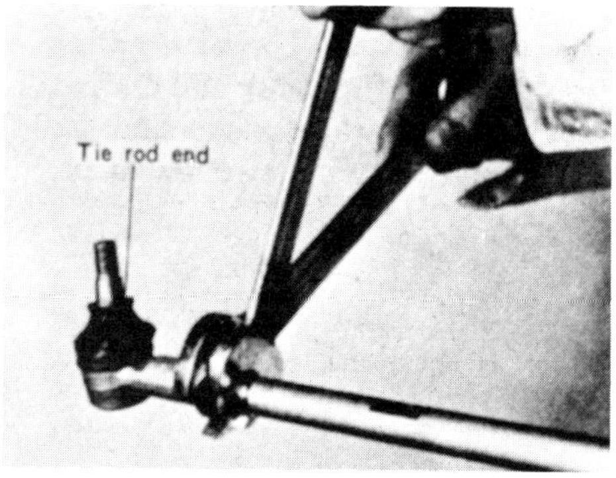

Fig. 8.7. Removing the tie-rod end balljoints

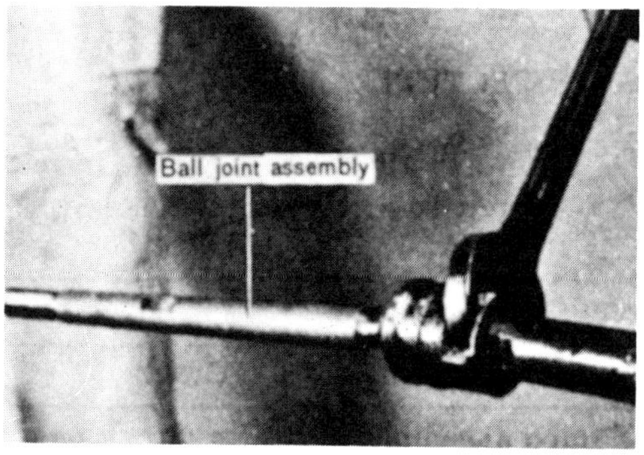

Fig. 8.8. Unscrewing the balljoint assembly from the rack

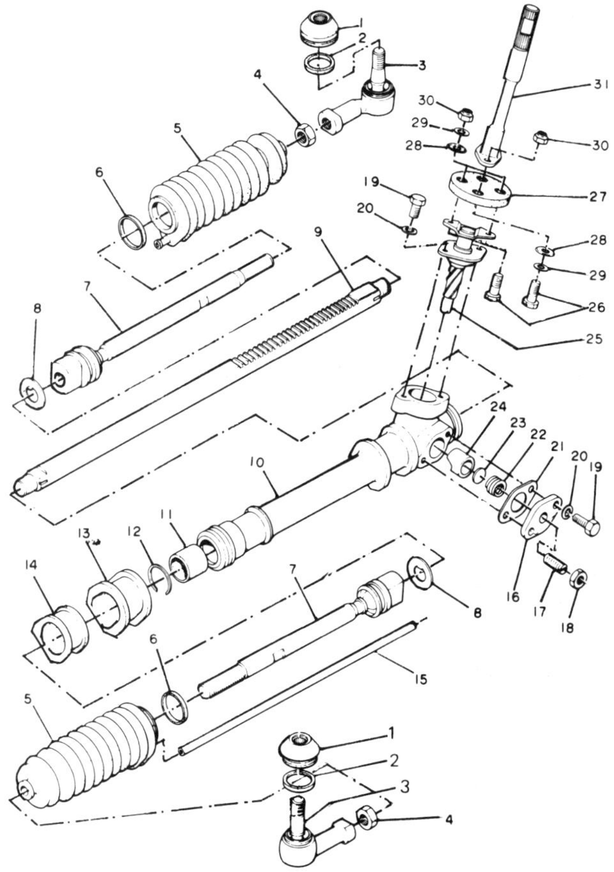

Fig. 8.9. Exploded view of steering gearbox (1972-77 models)

1 *Dust seal*
2 *Snap-ring*
3 *Tie rod end*
4 *Lock nut*
5 *Boot*
6 *Snap-ring (boot)*
7 *Balljoint assembly*
8 *Lock washer*
9 *Rack*
10 *Gearbox unit*
11 *Bushing A*
12 *Clip*
13 *Adapter A*
14 *Adapter B*
15 *Air vent tube*
16 *Cap (steering gearbox)*
17 *Adjusting screw*
18 *Lock nut*
19 *Bolt*
20 *Spring washer*
21 *Packing*
22 *Spring (sleeve)*
23 *Plate (sleeve)*
24 *Sleeve*
25 *Pinion*
26 *Bolt*
27 *Rubber coupling*
28 *Washer*
29 *Washer*
30 *Self lock nut*
31 *Shaft*

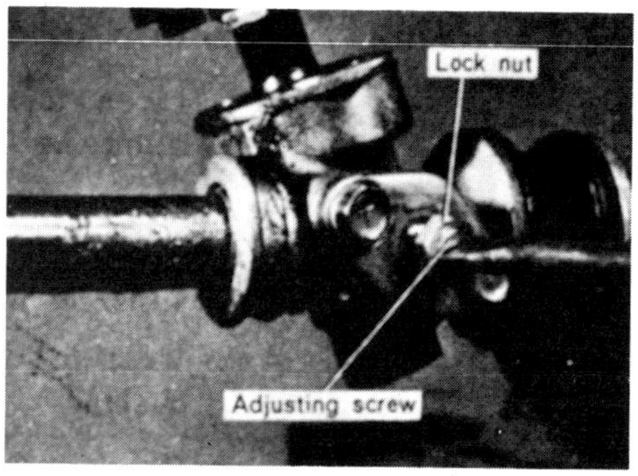

Fig. 8.10. Removing the backlash adjusting screw

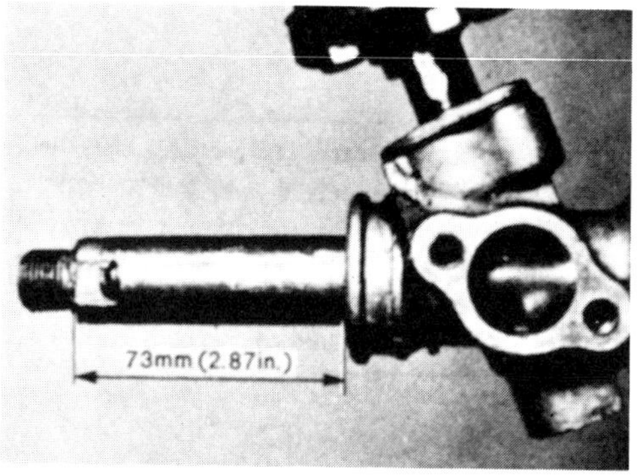

Fig. 8.11. Positioning the rack in the steering gearbox casing

d) Fit a hoist to the engine and raise it until it is stopped by the mounting nuts. This should be sufficient to allow the steering gearbox to be pulled out. Do not raise the engine higher as the DOJ boot and clip may get damaged.

3 When refitting the steering gearbox refer to Chapter 1, Section 25, for correct adjustment of the horizontal damper and tightening of the engine mounting bolts.

7 Steering gearbox (1972 - 77 models) - dismantling, inspection and reassembly

1 Secure the gearbox in a vise, taking care not to damage the casing, loosen the locknut and unscrew the tie-rod ends. Mark their position on the tie-rod so that they can be refitted in approximately the same position.
2 Pull the air vent tube out of the boots, remove the snap-rings on the end of the boots and pull out the boots.
3 Straighten the tab on the lockwasher and unscrew the ball joint assemblies from the rack.
4 Loosen the locknut on the gearbox adjusting screw and remove the adjusting screw.
5 Undo the gearbox cap securing bolts and remove the cap, packing, spring (sleeve) and plate (sleeve).
6 Remove the pinion retaining bolts and pull the pinion out from the rack. Remove the rack from the casing.
7 Clean all the parts and examine them for wear and damage. Check the rubber coupling for cracks and deterioration of the rubber, also the rubber boots and air vent tube. If water is found in the steering gearbox, the oil seal on the pinion, the rubber boots or the air vent tube must be suspect. Renew parts as necessary.
8 Apply grease to the teeth and sliding part of the rack and insert it into the gearbox casing.
9 Position the rack end 2.87 in (73 mm) from the end of the gearbox casing. Grease the pinion and fit it to mesh with the rack. Fit the pinion retaining bolts and tighten them to 6 - 8.5 lb f ft (0.8 - 1.2 kg fm).
10 Fit the sleeve, plate and spring, packing, cap and securing bolts.
11 To adjust the backlash, after the cap securing bolts are tightened to 6 - 8 lb f ft (0.8 - 1.2 kg fm), screw the adjusting screw fully in until it touches the inside plate and then back-off the screw 1/8th of a turn (45°) and lock it with the locknut. This adjustment leaves a clearance of 0.006 in (0.16 mm) between the end of the screw and the plate, see Fig. 8.13. Apply sealing compound on the adjusting screw and the cap securing bolts.
12 Fit the lockwasher on the threaded part of the rack end and screw in the ball joint. Bend over the tab of the lockwasher to lock the ball joint.
13 Fit the boots onto the gearbox and secure the boot end with the snap-ring (or rubber ring) and insert the air vent tube into the boots while aligning it with the embossed mark on the gearbox casing. When fitting the air vent tube be careful not to get grease, oil or water on the tube.
14 Screw on the tie-rod end and tighten the locknut finger tight. (To be tightened fully after adjustment of toe-in).
15 Check the operation of the pinion. The maximum torque required to rotate it must not exceed 1.6 lb f ft (0.22 kg fm).

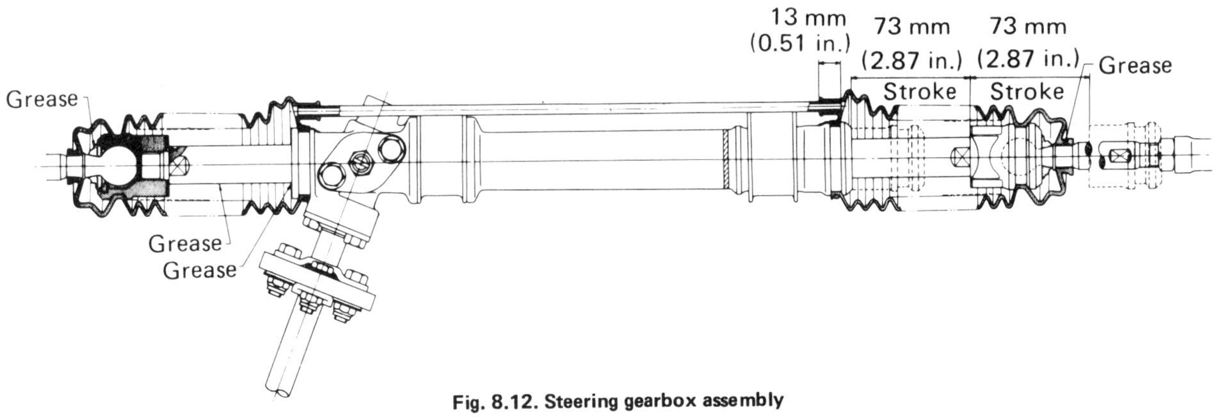

Fig. 8.12. Steering gearbox assembly

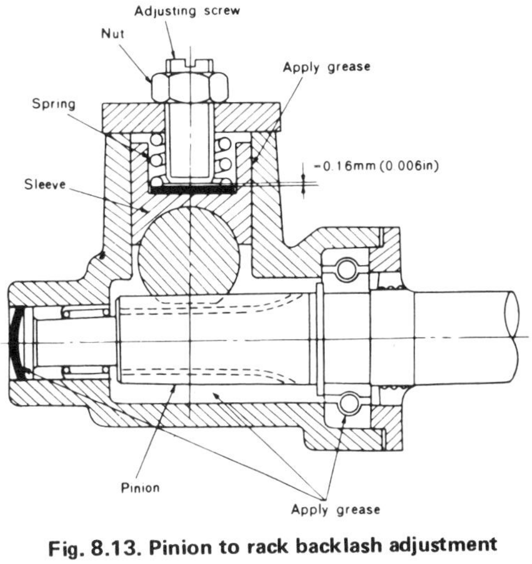

Fig. 8.13. Pinion to rack backlash adjustment

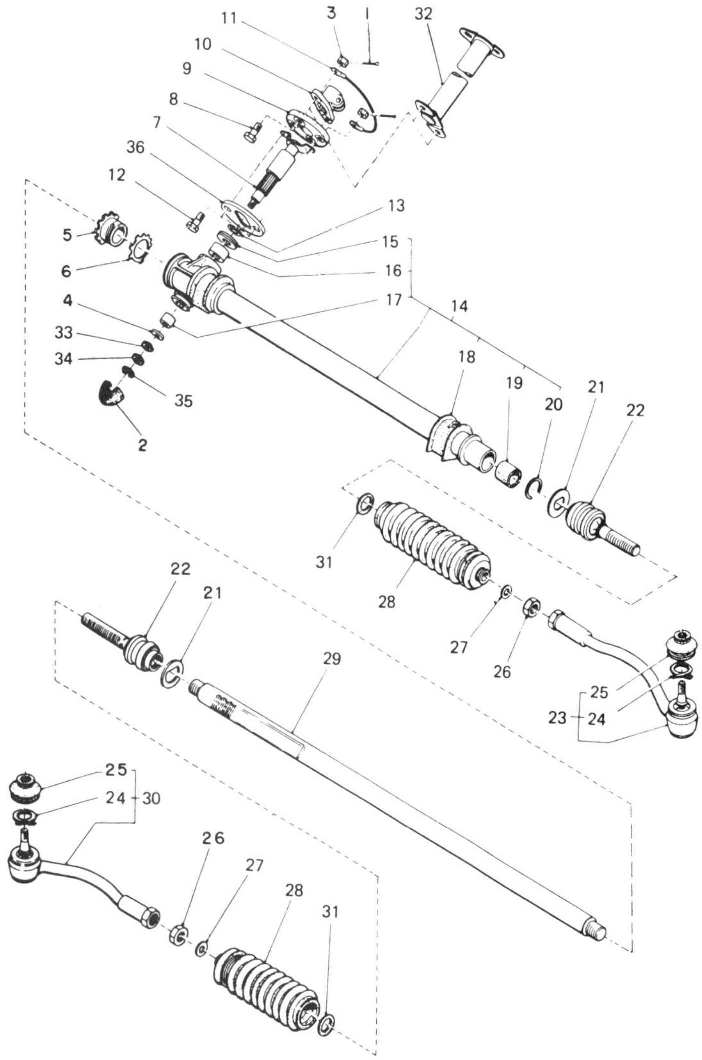

Fig. 8.14. Exploded view of steering gearbox (FF-1 1100 and 1300G models)

1 Cotter pin
2 Boot
3 Castle nut
4 Thrust washer
5 Bearing
6 Lock washer
7 Pinion assembly
8 Screw
9 Rubber coupling
10 Joint
11 Grounding wire
12 Screw
13 Thrust washer
14 Steering gearbox
15 Oil seal
16 Bushing
17 Bushing
18 Adaptor
19 Bearing
20 Clip
21 Lock washer
22 Balljoint assembly
23 Tie-rod assembly (LH)
24 Snap-ring
25 Dust seal
26 Nut
27 Snap-ring
28 Boot
29 Rack
30 Tie-rod assembly (RH)
31 Snap-ring
32 Shaft (steering)
33 Wave washer
34 Washer
35 Clip

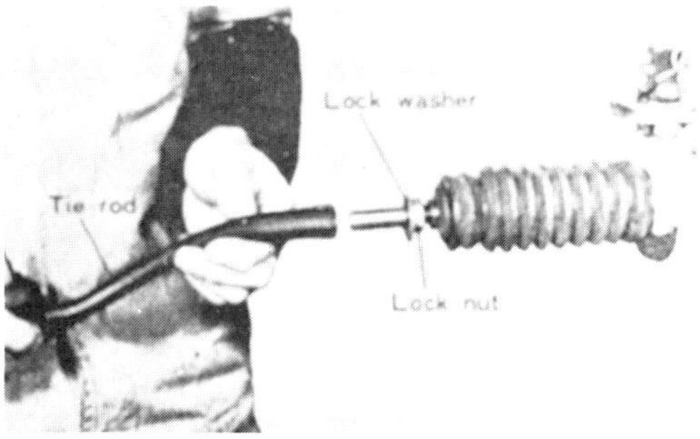

Fig. 8.15. Removing the tie-rod

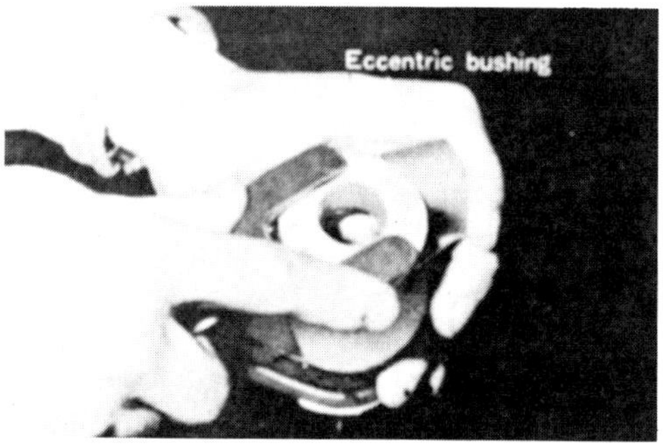

Fig. 8.16. Unscrewing the eccentric bushing

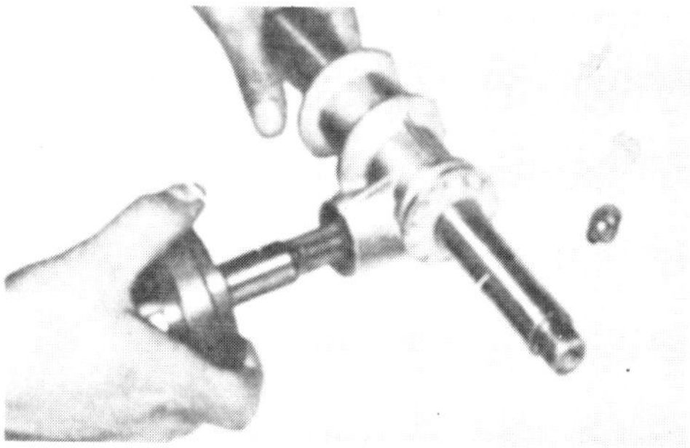

Fig. 8.17. Fitting the pinion

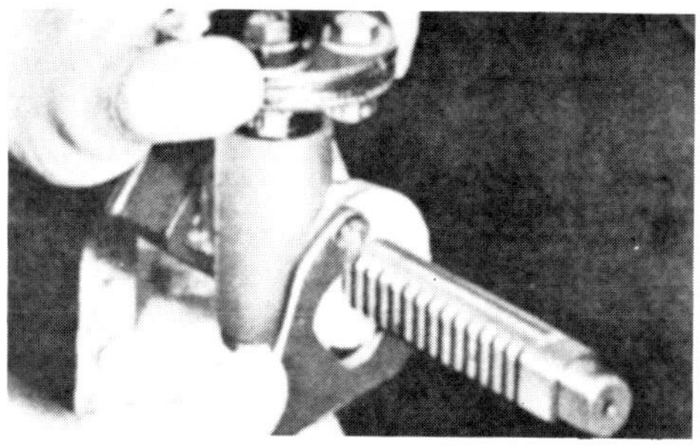

Fig. 8.18. Adjusting the backlash

8 Steering gearbox (FF - 1 1100 and 1300G models) - dismantling, inspection and reassembly

1 Secure the gearbox in a vise, taking care not to damage the casing, and undo the lockwashers and locknuts, then unscrew the tie-rods.
2 Loosen the three snap-rings and remove the rubber boots. Straighten the lockwashers and remove the ball joints from the rack.
3 Remove the pinion boot, cotter pin and castellated nut and withdraw the pinion. Remove the rack.
4 Straighten the lockwasher on the right-hand side and remove the threaded eccentric bushing. When the left-hand side clip has been taken off, remove the bearing.
5 Clean all the parts and examine them for wear and damage, renew parts as necessary.
6 Press the bearing in the gearbox pipe side and secure with a clip. Fit the lockwasher into the casing groove, screw in the nylon bearing, and after it is fully in match the bearing groove with the casing groove and tighten it temporarily. Grease the rack and pinion.
7 Fit the rack in the casing and then the pinion. Fit a thrust washer on the flange end of the pinion and at the nut end. Fit the castellated nut and cotter pin and then the rubber boot. Check that the pinion turns freely but without chattering.
8 Adjust the backlash by turning the eccentric bushing until there is no free play of the rack. Be careful not to overtighten the eccentric bushing, if there is backlash in excess of 0.0039 in (0.1 mm) after tightening, renew parts as necessary. Lock the eccentric bushing with the lockwasher.
9 Fill the ball joint assembly with grease and screw it onto the rack and tighten to 50 - 57 lb f ft (7 - 8 kg fm). Lock by bending over the tab of the lockwasher.
10 After the left and right ball joints have been locked determine the mid position of the rack and mark the gearbox casing and pinion with white paint.
11 Fit the rubber boots and secure with clips.
12 Fit the locknut and washer on the ball joint and screw on the tie-rod and tighten the locknut.
13 Check the operation of the pinion. The maximum torque required to rotate it must not exceed 1.6 lb f ft (0.22 kg fm).

9 Steering geometry - checking and adjustment

1 Unless the front suspension has been damaged, the castor angle and camber angle will not alter, provided there is no excessive wear or looseness in the suspension system. The toe-in setting, however, can vary more frequently and can pass unnoticed, if, for example a tie-rod is bent.
2 Toe-in of the front wheels must always be checked whenever the steering tie-rods have been disturbed. Indications of incorrect wheel alignment (toe-in) are uneven tire wear on the front wheels and erratic steering particularly when turning.
3 To check toe-in accurately requires optical alignment equipment, so this job must be left to the local Subaru dealer or a service station with the necessary equipment.
4 When the toe-in setting is found to have altered from its original setting, the steering system must be examined to ascertain the cause, and rectification carried out, before adjusting the toe-in to the correct measurement.

10 Tie-rod ends - renewal

1 It is not necessary to jack up the car when renewing tie-rod ends, but the increase in height above ground level may make it more convenient to do so.
2 Remove the cotter pin and undo the castellated nut until it is level with the end of the threads. This protects the threads while releasing the ball joint from the knuckle arm.
3 Separate the ball joint from the knuckle arm, using a ball joint separator, see Fig. 8.5.
4 Slacken the tie-rod end ball joint locknut, mark the position of the tie-rod end on the tie-rod and then unscrew the tie-rod end.
5 When fitting the new tie-rod end screw it onto the same position on the tie-rod as the old one and tighten the locknut.
6 Fit the ball joint stud into the knuckle arm and secure it with the nut, tightened to 18 - 22 lb f ft (2.5 - 3.0 kg fm). Fit the cotter pin.
7 Check the front wheel toe-in, see Section 9.

11 Wheels and tires

1 To provide equal, and obtain maximum wear from all the tires they should be periodically rotated. If the tires are maintained at the same positions for a long period, uneven wear results. They should be rotated as shown in Fig. 8.20.
2 Do not mix bias-ply and radial tires on the car as the basic design differences can cause unusual, and in certain conditions, very dangerous handling and braking characteristics. If in an emergency you have to use two different types, make sure the radials are on the rear wheels and drive particularly carefully until the tires can be rationalised, which should be at the earliest possible opportunity.
3 Check the tires regularly for signs of uneven wear or damage, and always maintain them at the correct pressure.
4 Wheels are not normally subject to servicing problems but when tires are renewed or changed the wheels should be balanced to reduce vibration and wear. If a wheel is suspected of damage caused by impact, have it checked for balance and true running at the earliest opportunity.
5 When fitting wheels do not overtighten the nuts. The maximum manual torque applied by using the wheel wrench, supplied with the car, is adequate. It also prevents difficulties when the same wrench has to be used to remove the wheels.

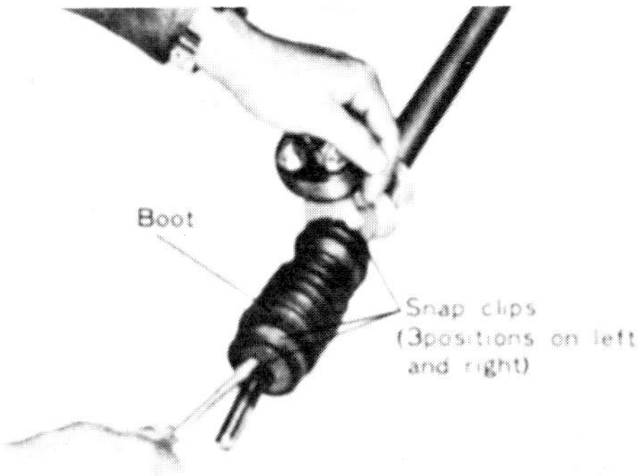

Fig. 8.19. Fitting the rubber boot

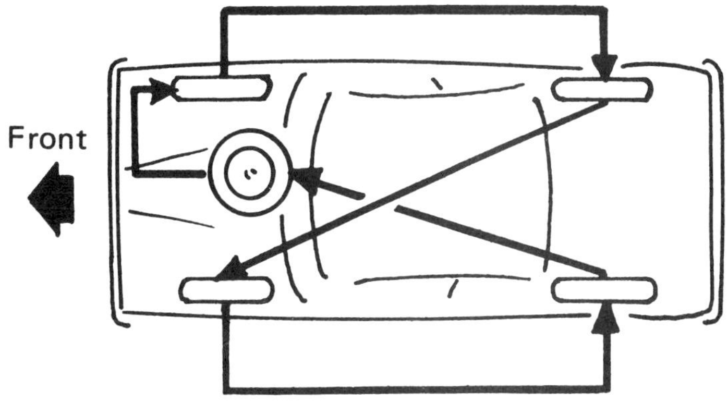

Fig. 8.20. Tire rotation

12 Fault diagnosis - steering, wheels and tires

Before diagnosing faults from the following chart check that the trouble is not caused by:

a) Brakes binding
b) Mixture of radial and bias-ply tires fitted
c) Incorrect tire pressures
d) Misalignment of the bodyframe
e) Faults in the suspension, see Chapter 11

Symptom	Reason/s	Remedy
Excessive 'free play' at the steering wheel	Wear in steering gearbox	Remove, dismantle and renew parts, as necessary.
	Worn tie-rod ends	Renew.
	Flexible coupling worn	Renew.
	Universal joint worn	Renew.
Car difficult to steer in a straight line - 'wanders'	As above	As above.
	Wheel alignment incorrect	Check front wheel toe-in.
Steering stiff and heavy	Wear or seizure in the steering gearbox	Remove, dismantle and renew, as necessary.
	Incorrect tire pressures	Check.
	Wheel alignment incorrect	Check front wheel toe-in.
Vibration and wheel wobble - 'shimmying'	Road wheels out of balance	Balance wheels.
	Road wheels out of true	Check for damage.
	Wheel alignment incorrect	Check front wheel toe-in.

Chapter 9 Brakes

For modifications, and information applicable to later models, see Supplement at end of manual

Contents

Specifications

Brake type

Front:	
Sedan and Station Wagon	Duo-servo drum brakes
Coupe and Hardtop	Disc brake
Rear:	
All models	Leading-trailing shoe drum type
Parking brake	Mechanical - on front wheels

Front brakes

Drum inside diameter:	
Standard	9.00 in (228.6 mm)
Serviceable limit	9.08 in (230.6 mm)
Disc thickness:	
Standard	0.39 in (10 mm)
Serviceable limit	0.33 in (8.5 mm)
Minimum shoe lining thickness:	
Primary	0.04 in (1.0 mm)
Secondary	0.06 in (1.5 mm)
Minimum pad thickness	0.06 in (1.5 mm)

Rear brakes

Drum inside diameter:	
Standard	7.09 in (180 mm)
Serviceable limit	7.17 in (182 mm)
Minimum shoe lining thickness	0.06 in (1.5 mm)

Wheel cylinders

Front drum	0.9374 in (23.81 mm)
Front disc	2.1248 in (53.97 mm)
Rear:	
Sedan and Station Wagon	0.6248 in (15.87 mm)
Station Wagon and 4WD from 1975	0.6874 in (17.46 mm)

Master cylinder inner diameter

Tandem	0.750 in (19.05 mm)
Single	0.750 in (19.05 mm)

Parking brake lever

1970-73

Normal stroke ...	7-9 notches
Stroke limit ...	12 notches

1974-77

Normal stroke ...	6 notches
Stroke limit ...	9 notches

Brake servo unit

Type ...	M45 (Master Vac)
Effective diameter ...	4.50 in (114.3 mm)
Stroke ...	More than 1.38 in (35 mm)

Torque wrench settings

	lb f ft	kg f m
Wheel cylinder nuts ...	5.8 - 7.2	0.8 - 1.0
Backplate bolts ...	22 - 34	3.0 - 4.8
Master cylinder nut ...	5 - 8	0.7 - 1.2
Brake pipe connections ...	11 - 14	1.5 - 2.0
Brake drum retaining nut (1970-71) ...	116 - 130	16 - 18
(1972-73) ...	145 - 181	20 - 25
(1974-77) ...	160 - 188	22 - 26

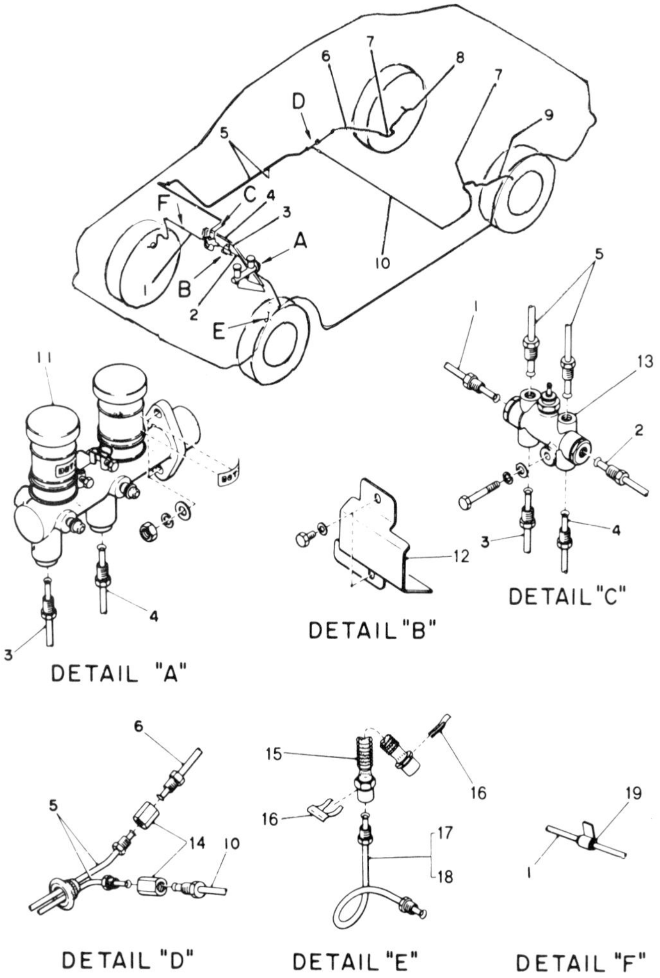

Fig. 9.1. Hydraulic system layout - Sedan

1 Brake pipe
2 Brake pipe
3 Brake pipe
4 Brake pipe
5 Brake pipe
6 Brake pipe
7 Brake hose (R)
8 Brake pipe (RH)
9 Brake pipe (LH)
10 Brake pipe (joint A - brake hose LH)
11 Master cylinder assembly
12 Protector (brake pipe)
13 Switch valve (fail indicator)
14 Connector (2-way)
15 Brake hose (F)
16 Clamp (brake hose)
17 Brake pipe (RH)
18 Brake pipe (LH)
19 Tube (brake pipe)

1 General description

1 The braking system is a four wheel, hydraulically operated, drum brake type on Sedans and Station Wagons. On Coupe and Hardtop models from 1972, the front wheel brakes are disc type with servo assistance. From 1975 the servo unit is also fitted to 4-door Sedans and Station Wagons.

2 The servo unit (Master Vac) is located between the brake pedal and the master cylinder and increases the braking effect by utilizing the pressure difference between the intake manifold and atmosphere. Its main advantage is that more braking effort is achieved with less pedal pressure. **Note:** It is inoperative when the engine is not running, ie. when the car is being towed.

3 The hydraulic system is a single circuit type on early FF-1 1100 and 1300G models: 1300, 1400 and 1600 models have a dual circuit layout with a primary and secondary system. The primary circuit serves the front right and rear left brakes, the secondary the front left and rear right. In the event of a failure in one system the other will still provide a braking effort. Do not keep running on one circuit, get the failed circuit rectified as soon as possible as this is a very important safety factor.

4 The master cylinder is a tandem type, in normal operation the primary piston compresses the fluid in the primary chamber, and the resultant pressure rise forces the secondary piston forward increasing the pressure in the secondary chamber. As the secondary piston is free, both pressures across the secondary piston become the same.

5 If the primary system fails and there is no rise in the primary chamber when the pushrod moves forward, the primary piston comes into contact with the spring retainer and actuates the secondary piston thus operating the secondary brake system.

6 If the secondary system fails and there is no rise in the secondary chamber when the pushrod moves forward, the secondary piston reaches the cylinder inner end, and the primary piston compresses the fluid in the primary chamber thus operating the primary system.

7 The parking brake system is a front wheel mechanically operated type. The parking brake lever is located between the front seats. The lever is connected to the front brake assemblies by cables and an equalizer is fitted to ensure equal application of both left and right brakes.

2 Bleeding the hydraulic system

1 Whenever the hydraulic system has been overhauled, a part renewed, or the level in the reservoir has become too low, air will have entered the system. This will cause some or all of the brake pedal travel to be used up in compressing the air rather than pushing fluid into the wheel cylinders or against the caliper pistons. If only a little air is present the pedal will have a 'spongy' feel, but if an appreciable amount has entered the system, the pedal will offer very little resistance to foot pressure and the brakes will not be very effective.

2 To overcome this, brake fluid must be pumped thru the hydrau-

lic system until all the air has been passed out in the form of air bubbles in the fluid. Bleed the brakes on all four wheels, beginning with the wheel furthest away from the master cylinder.

3 Before beginning to bleed the air from the system check the level of fluid in the reservoirs and top up if necessary. During the bleeding procedure make periodic checks of the brake fluid level.

4 Clean round the cap on the bleed screw, remove the cap and ensure that the bleed screw itself is clean. Dirt in the hydraulic brake system can result in the brakes becoming completely ineffective.

5 Fit a piece of transparent plastic tubing over the bleed screw and place the other end in a glass bottle or jar containing brake fluid, the end of the tube being immersed in the fluid. This is essential to avoid air being sucked back into the system as the bleeding procedure is carried out.

6 Loosen the bleeder screw and have an assistant pump the brake pedal up and down. The correct method is to depress the pedal slowly as far as it will go, pause a little, then release it quickly.

7 At first, air bubbles will be present in the fluid passing thru the tube, but after a time it will be completely free of them. When this is so, press the pedal down and tighten the bleed screw while it is kept depressed.

8 Remove the tube from the bleed screw and refit the cap. Apply the same procedure to the other wheels.

9 When the bleeding is complete, check the level of the brake fluid in the reservoir and top-up as necessary. Do not re-use any of the fluid pumped out during the bleeding of the system.

3 Front brakes - adjustment

1 All models equipped with front drum brakes are fitted with automatic adjusters and no manual adjustment of the front brake is necessary.

2 The front disc brakes fitted to Coupe and Hardtop models require no adjustment as hydraulic pressure maintains the correct brake pad-to-disc relationship at all times.

4 Rear drum brakes - adjustment

1 Apply the parking brake and chock the front wheels. Jack up the rear of the car and support it on jackstands.

2 Depress the brake pedal several times to centralise the brake shoes.

3 Loosen the lock nut on the adjusting wedge and turn the wedge

Fig. 9.2. Hydraulic system layout - Coupe

1 *Brake pipe*
2 *Brake pipe (RH)*
3 *Brake pipe (3-way connector - joint A)*
4 *Brake pipe*
5 *Brake hose (R)*
6 *Brake pipe (RH)*
7 *Brake pipe (LH)*
8 *Brake pipe (joint A - brake hose) (LH)*
9 *Brake pipe*
10 *Brake pipe*
11 *Protector (brake pipe)*
12 *Master cylinder assembly*
13 *Master vac assembly*
14 *Cotter pin (master cylinder)*
15 *Bracket complete*
16 *Head pin*
17 *Tube (brake pipe)*
18 *Connector (2-way)*
19 *Connector (3-way)*
20 *Brake hose (F)*
21 *Clamp (brake hose)*
22 *Brake pipe*
23 *Brake pipe*
24 *Bracket complete (LH)*
25 *Bracket complete (RH)*
26 *Brake hose*
27 *Gasket*
28 *Union bolt (wheel cylinder)*
29 *Spring pin*
30 *Clip (fuel system)*
31 *Vacuum hose*
32 *Check valve assembly*
33 *Vacuum hose*
34 *Fastener*
35 *Band (air breather hose)*
36 *Bolt (vacuum hose joint)*

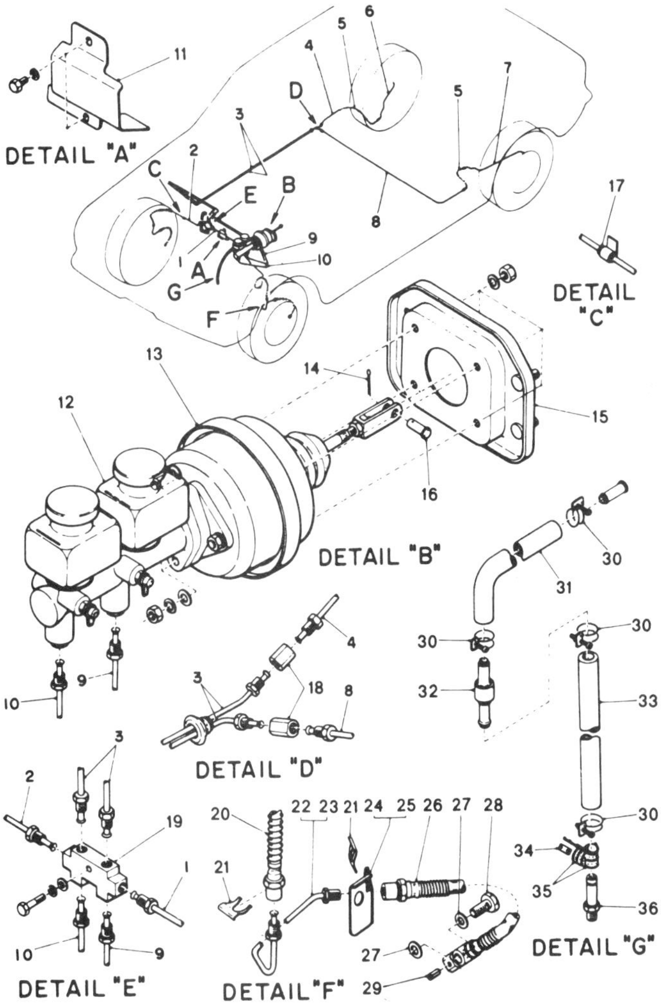

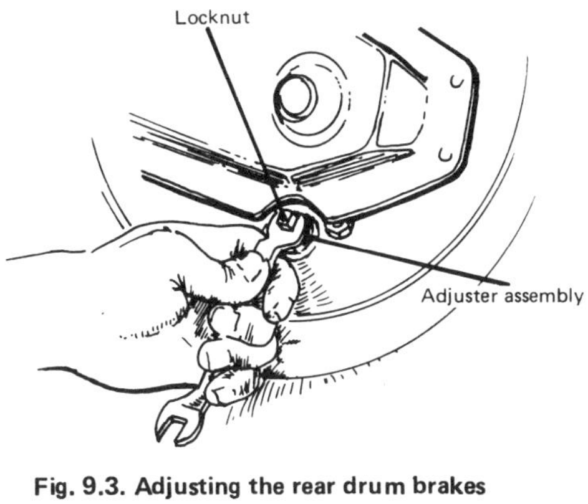

Fig. 9.3. Adjusting the rear drum brakes

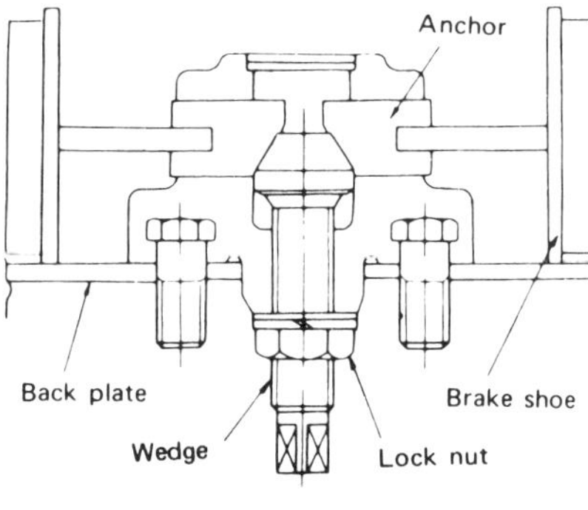

Fig. 9.4. Rear drum brake adjusting mechanism

Fig. 9.5. Exploded view of front drum brake - FF-1 models

1 *Back plate (F)*
2 *Wheel cylinder (F)*
3 *Lock washer*
4 *Nut*
5 *Brake shoe (F)*
6 *Lever assembly (F)*
7 *Strut*
8 *Spring (strut)*
9 *Automatic adjuster*
10 *Cable*
11 *Cable guide*
12 *Lever (automatic adjuster)*
13 *Spring (automatic adjuster)*
14 *Spring (front shoe return)*
15 *Spring (front shoe hold down)*
16 *Cup (front shoe hold down)*
17 *Pin (front shoe hold down)*
18 *Nut*
19 *Spring washer*
20 *Cover (brake drum)*

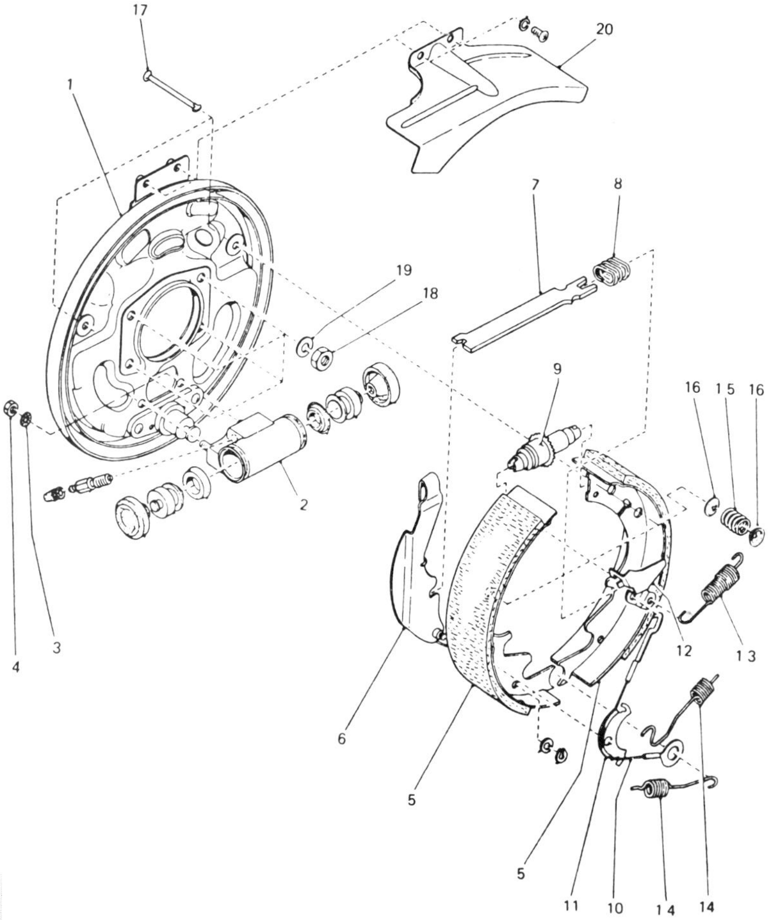

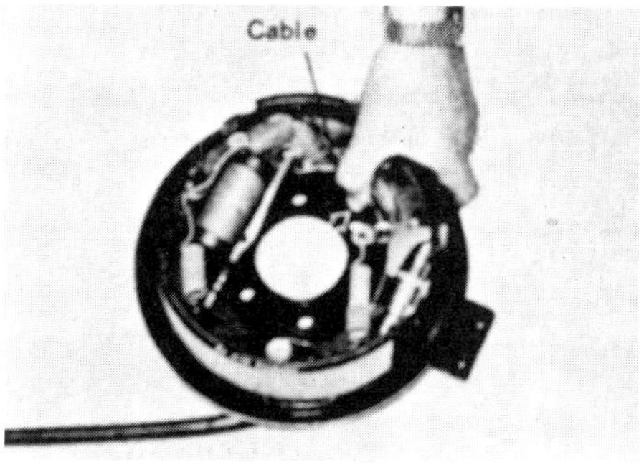

Fig. 9.6. Removing the automatic adjuster - front drum brakes

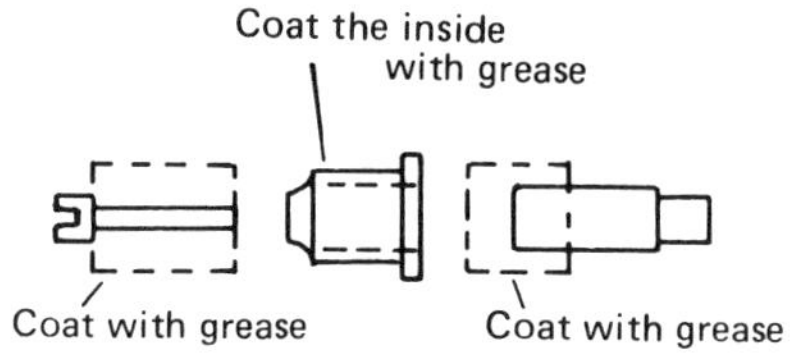

Fig. 9.7. Lubricating the automatic adjuster

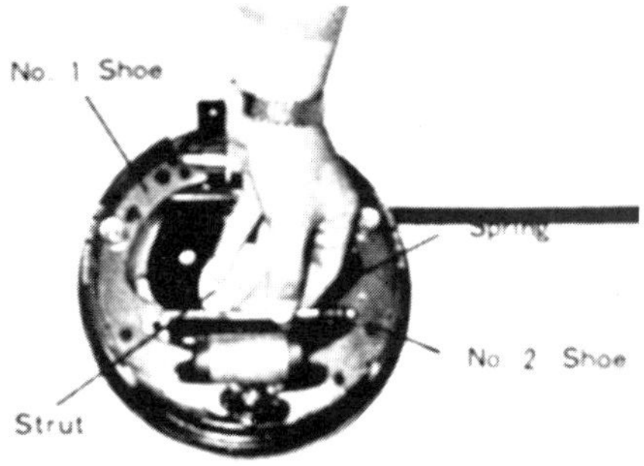

Fig. 9.8. Fitting the parking brake strut

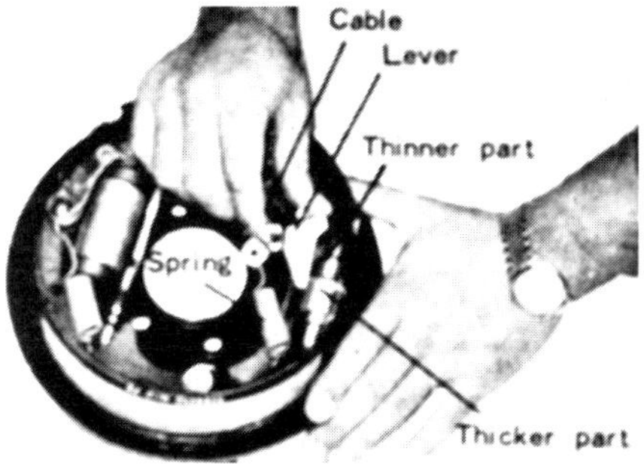

Fig. 9.9. Fitting the cable lever and automatic adjuster

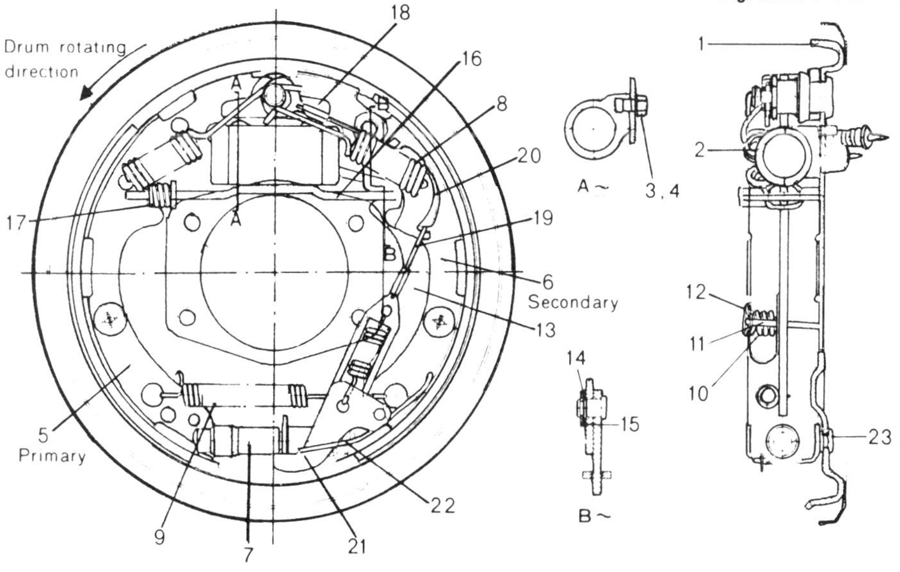

Fig. 9.10. Front drum brake mechanism - 1300, 1400, 1600 models

1 *Back plate*
2 *Wheel cylinder*
3 *Spring washer*
4 *Nut*
5 *Brake shoe (primary)*
6 *Brake shoe (secondary)*
7 *Automatic adjuster*
8 *Spring (shoe return, upper)*
9 *Spring (shoe return, lower)*
10 *Spring (shoe hold down)*
11 *Pin (shoe hold down)*
12 *Cup (shoe hold down)*
13 *Lever (parking brake)*
14 *Spring washer*
15 *Retainer*
16 *Strut*
17 *Spring (strut)*
18 *Stopper (brake shoe)*
19 *Adjuster cable*
20 *Cable guide*
21 *Adjuster lever*
22 *Adjuster spring*
23 *Plug*

clockwise until the wheel is locked. Now turn the wedge back 180° from the locked position. The wheel should now be free to rotate and the shoe to drum clearance will be 0.004 - 0.006 in (0.1 - 0.15 mm).
4 Tighten the adjusting wedge lock nut and then repeat this procedure for the other wheel.
5 Remove the jackstands and lower the car. Road test the car.

5 Front brake shoes - removal and refitting

After high mileage it will be necessary to fit new brake shoes. Always fit a complete set of four shoes, never renew shoes on one side only.

FF-1 1100 and 1300G models

1 Chock the rear wheels, jack up the front of the car and support it on jackstands. Remove the front wheels.
2 Loosen the three bolts on the double offset joint (DOJ) side, and separate the DOJ from the drum.
3 Remove the drum cover attached to the brake assembly.
4 Remove the interior part of the parking brake cable assembly into the engine compartment.
5 Remove the cotter pin from the brake drum retaining nut. Undo the nut and withdraw the drum in parallel with the splined shaft. Do not depress the pedal while the drum is removed.
6 Undo and remove the brake line from the rear of the backing plate. Plug the end of the line.
7 Remove the four backplate retaining bolts and withdraw the brake assembly.
8 Before dismantling the brake assembly, take note of the positions of the various parts. It is a good idea to dismantle the assembly on one side only at a time, in this way you can refer to the assembly on the other side for correct location of parts at reassembly.
9 At this stage, check that the automatic adjuster movement is correct by pulling the cable.
10 Lift the automatic adjuster cable by pulling it to the shoe side and release it from the hole in the shoe. Remove the automatic adjuster assembly from the shoe.
11 Remove the shoe return spring and cable from the anchor pin.
12 Remove the shoe set spring to free the shoe. Then disconnect the parking brake cable from the shoe.
13 Remove the parking brake shoe strut.
14 Examine the brake shoes for wear or damage. If the brake lining is worn down to less than 0.07 in (1.7 mm) on any shoe then all the front shoes must be renewed.
15 Clean the automatic adjuster and grease its threads. Remove all surface grease. Check the adjusting lever contacting surface, if worn renew the lever. If there is any sign of oil on the linings they must

Fig. 9.11. Front drum brake shoe assembly

be renewed.
16 Examine the brake drum inside surface, if it is scored it must be machine shimmed professionally or renewed.
17 When refitting the brake shoes, make sure that the brake linings do not get contaminated with oil or grease.
18 Fit the primary shoe on the backing plate and secure it with its spring. Attach the parking brake lever and cable to the secondary shoe and fit the shoe and set spring.
19 Very lightly smear the backplate surface with grease where it contacts the brake shoes.
20 Fit the parking brake strut between the two shoes as shown in Fig. 9.8. Fit the shoe return spring and automatic adjuster cable on the anchor pin. First fit the No 1 shoe return spring, the cable, and then fit the cable guide on the No 2 shoe. Now fit the No 2 shoe return spring.
21 Adjust the automatic adjusting screw so that the shoes will be positioned approximately 2.28 in (58 mm) apart.
22 Fit the adjuster spring and the automatic adjuster, make sure that the lever engages correctly with the starwheel.
23 Measure the outside diameter of the shoes and the inside diameter of the brake drum. The clearance between the shoes and the drum should be 0.012 - 0.024 in (0.3 - 0.6 mm). Move the adjuster as necessary, to obtain the correct clearance.
24 The remainder of the refitting procedure is the reversal of removal. Tighten the backplate bolts to 30 lb f ft (4.2 kg f m) and the brake drum retaining nut to 116 - 130 lb f ft (16 - 18 kg f m).

1300, 1400 and 1600 models

25 Repeat the operations at paragraph 1 above.

26 Unbend the tabs of the lockwasher or relieve the axle shaft nut staking with a chisel, according to the year model, and remove the axle shaft nut. Release the parking brake.
27 Using a suitable puller, remove the brake drum.
28 Remove the automatic adjuster spring, use a screwdriver, and then remove the automatic adjuster lever.
29 Remove the shoe return spring (lower) and automatic adjuster. Remove the parking brake cable end from the parking brake lever. Using a box wrench undo the clamp nut, remove the washer and pull the parking brake cable out.
30 Remove the shoe return springs (upper) from the anchor pin and the automatic adjuster cable. Remove the shoe set springs and lift off the brake shoes.
31 Refitting is the reverse of removal procedure. Inspection of the parts is the same as for FF-1 models except that the minimum lever thickness is:

Primary shoe	-	0.04 in (1.0 mm)
Secondary shoe	-	0.06 in (1.5 mm)

and the brake shoe-to-drum clearance is 0.004 - 0.010 in (0.1 - 0.25 mm).

32 Tighten the axle shaft nut to:

1972 - 73	-	145 - 181 lb f ft (20 - 25 kg f m)
1974 - 77	-	160 - 188 lb f ft (22 - 26 kg f m).

6 Front disc brake pads - removal and refitting

1 Chock the rear wheels, jack up the front of the car and support it on jackstands. Remove the roadwheels and release the parking brake.
2 Disconnect the parking brake cable by removing the outer cable clip.
3 Remove the four pins from the locking blocks and drive the locking blocks out with a parallel pin punch. When one is removed the other comes out easily.
4 Lift away the caliper and tie it up to the suspension with a piece of wire or cord so that it does not hang on the brake hose.
5 Remove the disc pads, mark them so that they can be refitted in the same positions if they are not being renewed.
6 Measure the brake pads and renew them if the lining thickness is less than 0.06 in (1.6 mm). Always renew all four front brake pads at the one time to avoid uneven braking.
7 Before fitting either new linings or the original ones, clean round

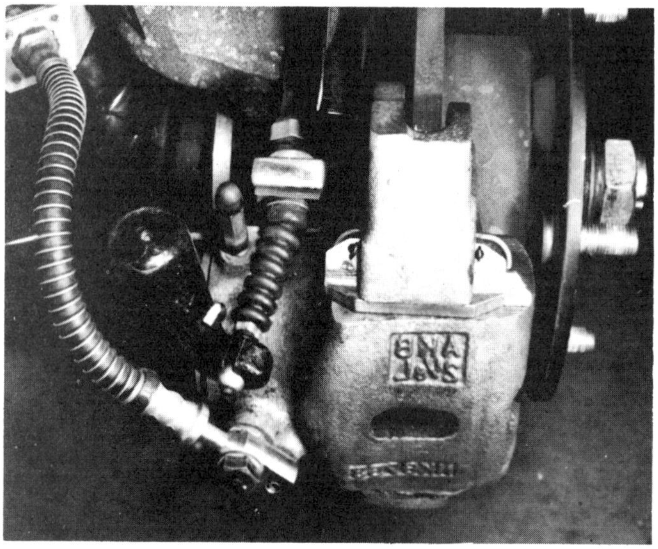

6.2 Disconnect the parking brake cable

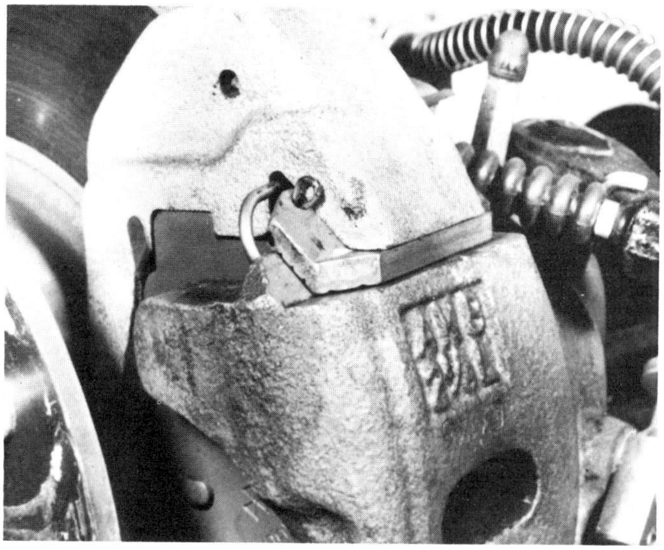

6.3a Remove the pins from the locking blocks ...

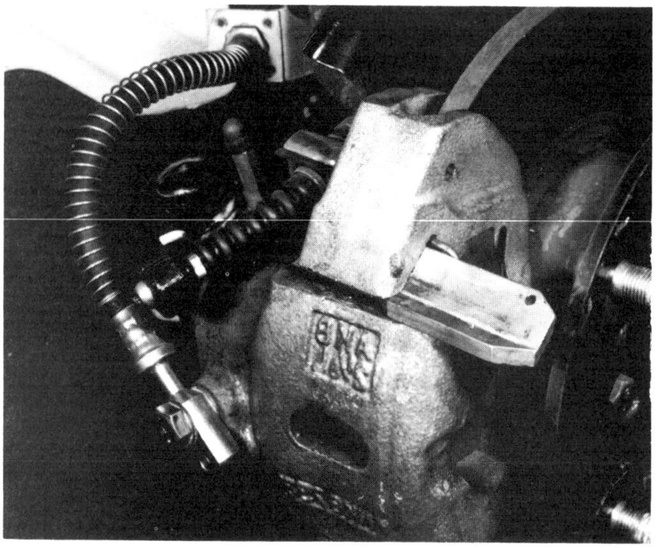

6.3b ... and remove the locking blocks

6.4 Lift away the caliper

the hydraulic fluid reservoir filter cap, unscrew the cap and remove a little of the fluid to prevent overflow as the piston is pushed into the caliper cylinder bore, as described in the following paragraph.

8 Before fitting the brake pads, return the piston to the bottom of the caliper cylinder bore by turning it clockwise with a screwdriver.

9 Refitting is the reverse of the removal procedure. Top-up the fluid level in the hydraulic reservoir. Road test the car, operating the brakes several times to adjust the pad to disc clearance.

7 Disc brake caliper unit - removal and refitting

1 Remove the brake pads as described in Section 6.

2 Disconnect the brake pipe from the caliper body.

3 Remove the caliper unit securing bolts and withdraw the caliper bracket.

4 Refitting is the reverse of the removal procedure.

8 Disc brake caliper - dismantling, inspection and reassembly

1 Clean the outside of the caliper before dismantling.

2 Remove the piston rubber boot from the caliper body and piston, do not use a metal tool to do this.

3 To remove the piston from the body apply an air line to the caliper and blow the piston out.

4 Remove the piston seal.

5 Inspect the cylinder bore and the piston for signs of scoring and pitting. If the cylinder bore is scored a complete new caliper assembly will be required.

6 To reassemble, wet the piston seal with fresh brake fluid and carefully fit in position. Next wet the piston with brake fluid, fit it in the

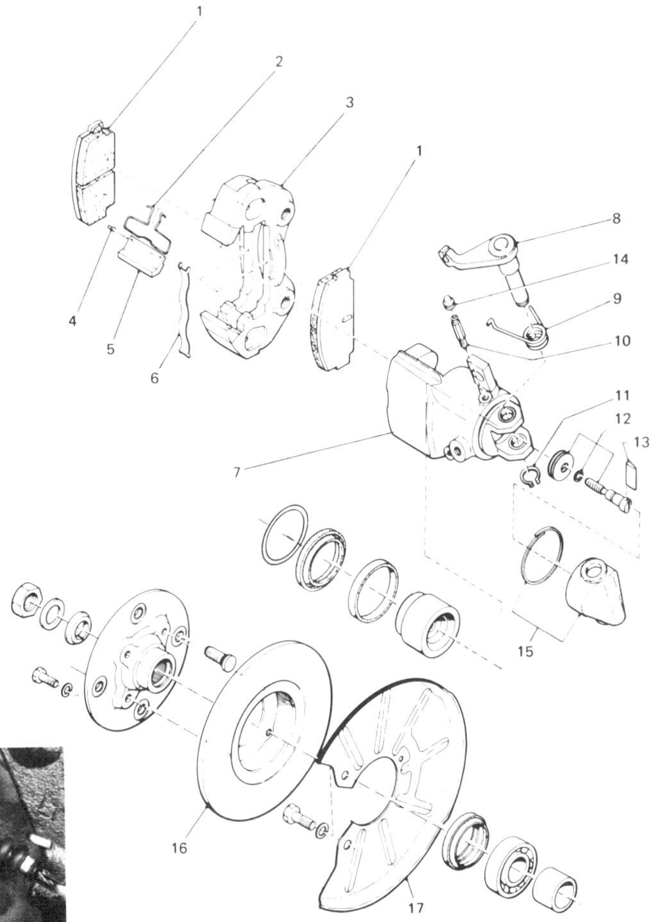

Fig. 9.12. Exploded view of disc brake

1 Pad (disc brake F)
2 Spring (caliper)
3 Bracket (mounting)
4 Pin (caliper)
5 Stopper (plug)
6 Spring pad
7 Caliper body
8 Lever and spindle assembly
9 Spring (parking brake lever return)
10 Bleeder screw (wheel cylinder)
11 Retaining spring
12 Spindle assembly
13 Connecting link
14 Cap (air bleeder)
15 Lever cap assembly
16 Brake disc (F)
17 Cover (disc)

6.5 Remove the disc pads

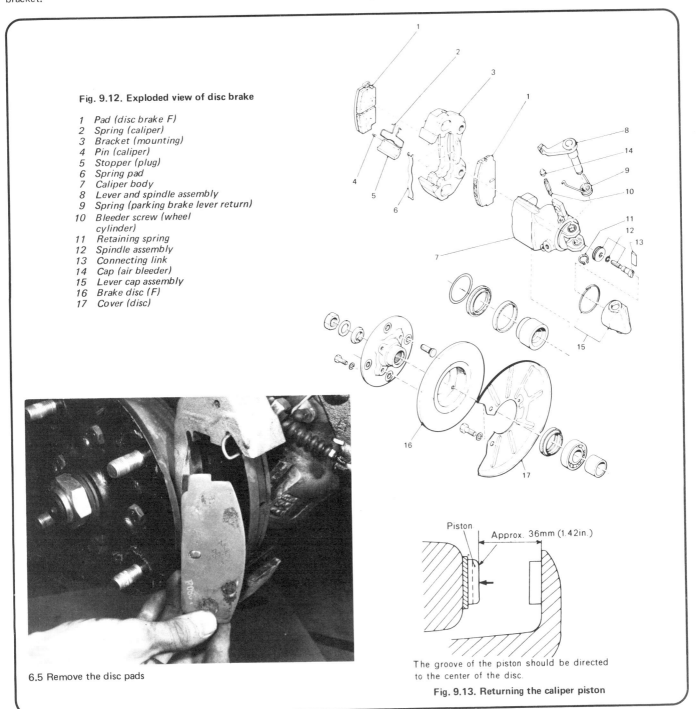

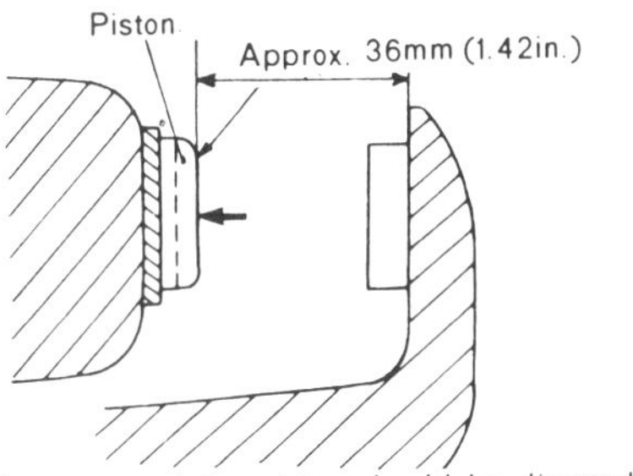

The groove of the piston should be directed to the center of the disc.

Fig. 9.13. Returning the caliper piston

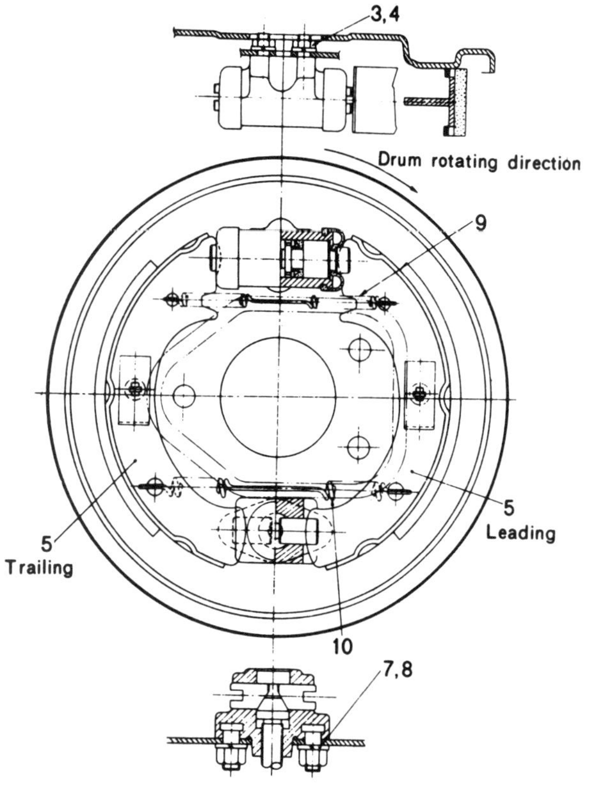

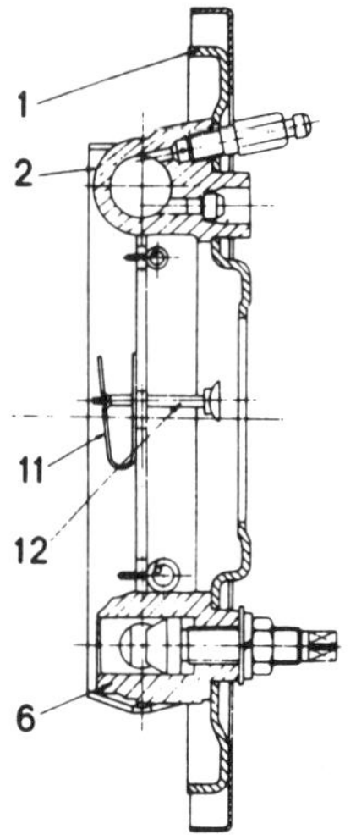

Fig. 9.14. Rear brake mechanism

1 Back plate
2 Wheel cylinder
3 Spring washer
4 Nut
5 Brake shoe
6 Adjuster
7 Spring washer (adjuster)
8 Nut (adjuster)
9 Spring (shoe return, upper)
10 Spring (shoe return, lower)
11 Spring (shoe hold down)
12 Pin (shoe hold down)

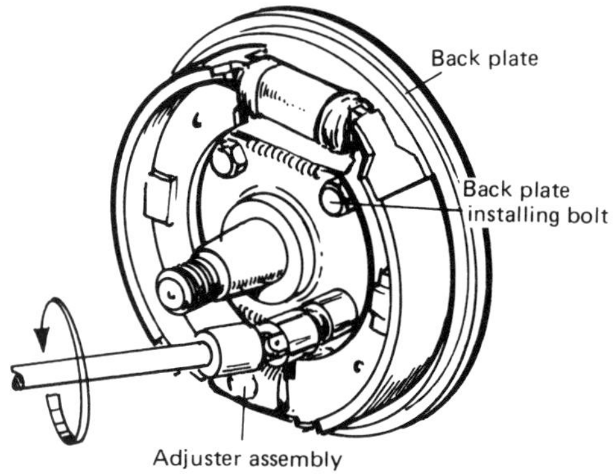

Fig. 9.15. Removing the backplate and shoe assembly

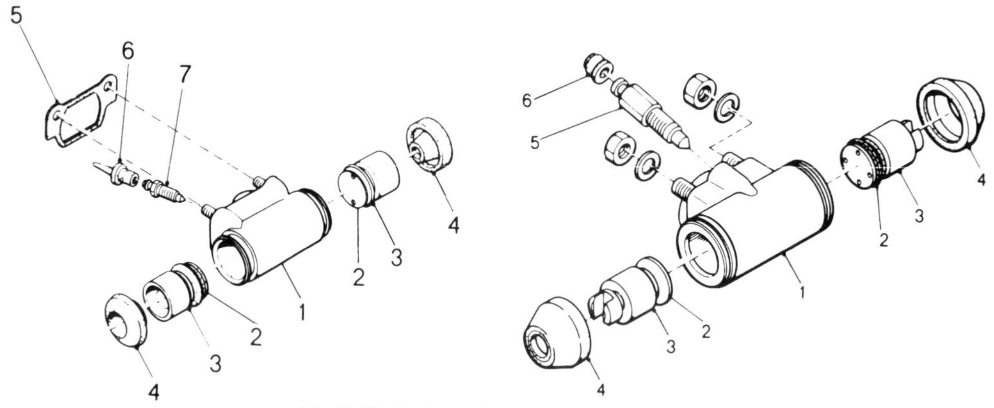

Fig. 9.16. Exploded view of wheel cylinders

FRONT
1 Wheel cylinder body
2 Cup
3 Piston
4 Boot
5 Seal (wheel cylinder)
6 Bleeder cap
7 Bleeder screw

REAR
1 Wheel cylinder body
2 Cup
3 Piston
4 Boot
5 Bleeder screw
6 Bleeder cap

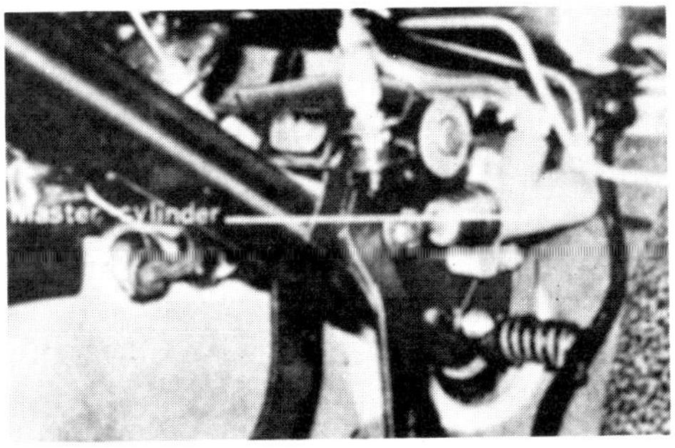

Fig. 9.17. Master cylinder removal - FF-1 models

bore and push it in until the rubber boot can be fitted to the piston and caliper body.

9 Front brake disc - removal and refitting

1 Remove the caliper unit as described in Section 7.
2 Remove the hub retaining nut and using a puller remove the hub and disc assembly from the axle shaft.
3 Remove the four attaching bolts and separate the disc from the hub.
4 Examine the condition of the discs. If the disc is scored it can be resurfaced by machining the faces. The thickness when new is 10 mm (0.39 in). The disc must be renewed when the thickness of the disc is less than 8.5 mm (0.33 in).
5 Refitting is the reverse of the removal procedure.

10 Rear brake shoes - removal and refitting

1 Chock the front wheels and jack up the rear of the car. Support it on jackstands and remove the rear wheels.
2 Remove the three cap securing bolts, the cap and the bearing retaining plate.
3 Remove the cotter pin and undo the castle nut, taking care not to damage the bearing seal. Using a suitable puller, remove the brake drum.
4 Undo the backplate securing bolts and remove the brake assembly.
5 Using a pair of pliers remove the shoe retaining springs. Remove the anchor end of the shoe first by pulling it outwards, then remove the cylinder end of the shoe and take the shoes off the backplate.
6 Inspect the shoes for excessive wear of the linings and for contamination with oil or grease. If the linings have oil on them or they are worn below the minimum permissible thickness, the brake shoes must be renewed. Always renew all four shoes of the rear brakes at the same time to avoid uneven braking: Brake shoe linings must not be less than:

0.067 in (1.7 mm) on FF-1 1100 and 1300G models
0.057 in (1.5 mm) on 1300, 1400 and 1600 models.

7 If the brake drum is scored, correct the surface by having it skimmed professionally. The maximum inside diameter must not exceed 7.17 in (182 mm).
8 Assemble the shoes and springs. The upper spring is thinner than the lower spring.
9 Lightly smear the part of the backplate that contacts the brake shoes with grease, taking care not to get any grease on the linings.
10 Refit the shoe and spring assembly, first to the wheel cylinder, then to the anchor pin and secure both shoes with the shoe retaining spring.
11 Measure the diameter at three positions round the shoes and adjust to 7.079 in (179.8 mm) with the adjuster wedge.
12 Refit the drum and adjust the brakes as described in Section 4. Road test the car.

11 Wheel cylinders - removal and refitting

1 Remove the brake drums and shoes as described in Section 5 for front drum brakes and Section 10 for rear brakes.
2 Disconnect the hydraulic brake pipe from the wheel cylinder and plug the end of the pipe.
3 Unscrew the two attaching nuts and remove the wheel cylinder. On front brakes remove the gasket.
4 Refitting is the reverse of removal procedure. Bleed the brakes as described in Section 2. Road test the car.

12 Wheel cylinders - servicing

1 Remove the rubber boots from both ends of the wheel cylinder and push out the piston assemblies. The rear wheel cylinders have a spring fitted in the center.
2 Inspect the bore of the wheel cylinder, if it is step-worn or scored, renew the wheel cylinder. Renew the rubber cups on the pistons. Renew the rubber boots if they are cracked or hardened. Replacement parts are supplied as a wheel cylinder repair kit.
3 Before reassembly clean all the parts in fresh brake fluid. Reassemble the wheel cylinder and refit it on the car in the reverse of the removal procedure. Bleed the hydraulic system as described in Section 2 and road test the car.

13 Master cylinder - removal and refitting

FF-1 1100 and 1300G

1 Disconnect the brake pipe at the three-way connector. Drain the brake fluid into a container, avoid spillage, as brake fluid is harmful to paintwork. Disconnect the reservoir to master cylinder pipe.
2 Remove the pushrod cotter pin and take out the pushrod pin.
3 Remove the master cylinder mounting bolts and remove the master cylinder from the mounting bracket on the steering column.
4 Refitting is the reverse of the removal procedure. Bleed the brakes as described in Section 2.

1300, 1400 and 1600 models

5 Disconnect the brake pipes from the master cylinder and collect the fluid in a container to prevent damage to paintwork.
6 Remove the nuts securing the master cylinder to the pedal bracket and pull the master cylinder assembly forward and out.
7 Refitting is the reverse of removal. Bleed the brakes as described in Section 2.
8 On models fitted with a servo unit (Master Vac) the master cylinder is mounted on the front of the servo unit which is attached to the firewall.

14 Master cylinder - dismantling, inspection and reassembly

FF-1 1100 and 1300G

1 Remove the boot from the cylinder body, loosen the clip and remove the connecting tube and nipple. Remove the brake pipe union.
2 Remove the retaining ring and washer, pull out the piston assembly, primary cup and return spring.
3 Remove the check valve and valve seat. If the cup and valve seat are difficult to get out use an air line and blow them out.
4 Examine all the parts for wear or damage. If the bore of the master cylinder is scored the master cylinder must be renewed. Always renew the rubber cup and boot, replacement parts are supplied as master cylinder repair kits. Renew the reservoir if damaged.
5 Before reassembly clean all the parts with fresh brake fluid and ensure that no dust or foreign matter contaminates any of the parts, absolute cleanliness is most important.
6 Reassembly is the reverse of the dismantling procedure.

1300, 1400 and 1600 models

7 Remove the boot from the body. Remove the retaining ring and washer.
8 Remove the stop pin and gasket.
9 Pull out the primary and secondary piston assemblies and remove the return spring.
10 Remove the screw, retainer, return spring and secondary cup.
11 Remove the check valve cap and take out the check valve and

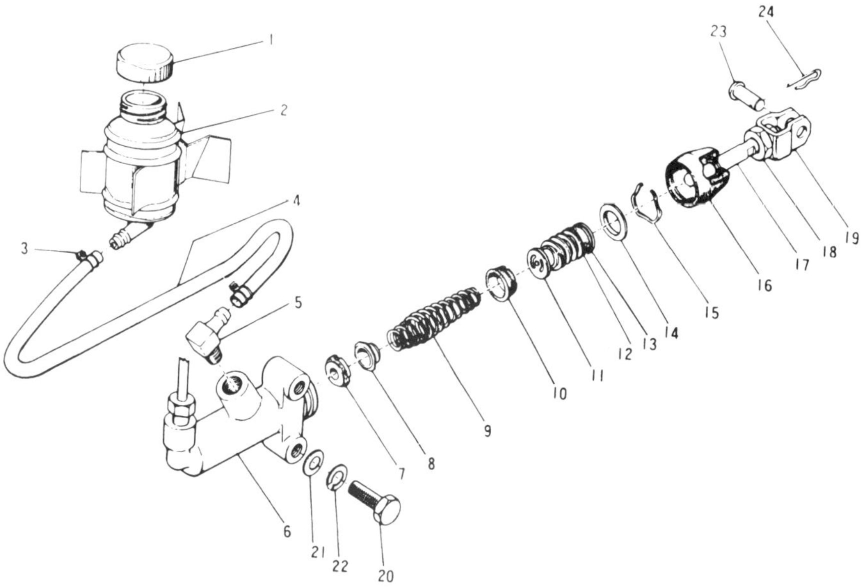

Fig. 9.18. Exploded view of master cylinder - early FF-1 models

1 *Cap (fluid tank)*
2 *Brake fluid tank*
3 *Clip*
4 *Connecting tube*
5 *Nipple*
6 *Cylinder body*
7 *Valve seat*
8 *Check valve*
9 *Return spring*
10 *Primary cup*
11 *Spacer*
12 *Secondary cup*
13 *Piston*
14 *Stop washer*
15 *Stop ring*
16 *Boot*
17 *Push rod*
18 *Nut*
19 *Yoke*
20 *Bolt*
21 *Washer*
22 *Spring washer*
23 *Pin*
24 *Cotter pin*

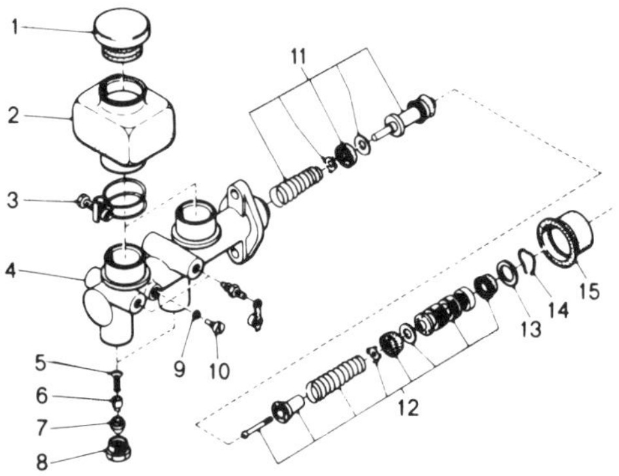

Fig. 9.19. Exploded view of tandem master cylinder

1 *Cap (reservoir)*
2 *Brake fluid reservoir*
3 *Band (reservoir)*
4 *Cylinder*
5 *Check valve spring*
6 *Check valve*
7 *Tube sheet*
8 *Check valve cap*
9 *Gasket*
10 *Stopper (secondary piston)*
11 *Secondary piston assembly*
12 *Primary piston assembly*
13 *Washer (piston stop)*
14 *Ring (piston stop)*
15 *Boot*

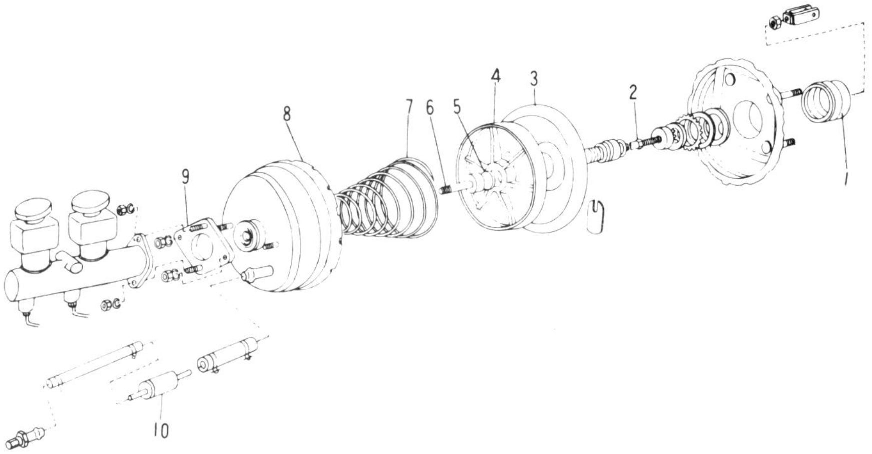

Fig. 9.20. Exploded view of servo unit

1 *Rear shell*
2 *Valve rod and plunger*
3 *Diaphragm*
4 *Diaphragm plate (power piston)*
5 *Reaction disc*
6 *Push rod*
7 *Diaphragm return spring*
8 *Front shell*
9 *Flange*
10 *Check valve*

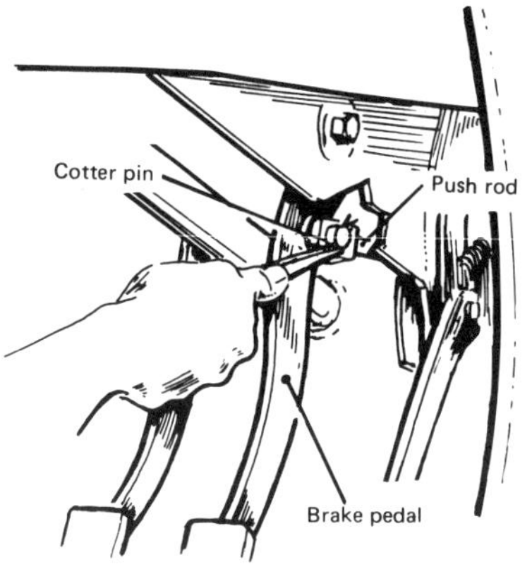

Fig. 9.21. Disconnecting the servo unit pushrod from the brake pedal

check valve spring.
12 Examine all the parts for wear and damage. If the cylinder bore is scored, renew the master cylinder. Renew the rubber cup, check valve and rubber boot. Replacement parts are supplied as a repair kit.
13 Check the free length of the return springs, they should be:

Primary	-	2.32 in (59 mm)
Secondary	-	1.99 in (50.5 mm).

14 Reassembly is the reverse of the dismantling procedure.

15 Servo unit - removal and refitting

The servo unit (Master Vac) is fitted into the brake system on some early models, and as standard on later models. It is fitted in series with the master cylinder to provide assistance to the driver when the brake pedal is depressed. The servo unit and hydraulic master cylinder are connected together so that the servo unit piston rod acts as the master cylinder pushrod. Another pushrod connects the brake pedal to the servo unit piston.
1 Disconnect the pushrod from the brake pedal by removing the cotter pin and withdrawing the clevis pin.
2 Disconnect the vacuum hose from the servo unit.
3 Remove the master cylinder as described in Section 13.
4 Remove the servo unit securing nuts from the passenger compartment and from the engine compartment side and lift out the servo unit.
5 If the operation of the servo unit is suspect have it serviced by your local Subaru dealer.
6 Refitting is the reverse of the removal procedure. Ensure that the arrow mark on the check valve is facing towards the engine.

16 Flexible brake hoses - general

1 Inspect the condition of the flexible hydraulic brake hoses leading from under the front wheel aprons to the wheel connections, and also the hoses to the rear wheels. If they are swollen, damaged or chafed, they must be renewed.
2 Remove the hose after unscrewing the brake pipe joint nut and then loosening the hose attaching nut. Refitting is the reverse of removal. When fitting the hose, do not allow it to come in contact with other parts, where it is likely to chafe through. Ensure that it has no kinks or tight bends.
3 After refitting bleed the brakes as described in Section 2.

17 Steel brake pipes - general

1 If the pipe is cracked or dented it must be renewed. When fitting new pipes use the old pipe as a pattern to bend it to the right shape. Do not make any sharp bends in the pipe.
2 When refitting the pipes ensure they are well supported by clips or brackets and that they do not chafe against other parts.
3 After refitting bleed the brakes as described in Section 2.

18 Brake fail indicator switch - general

1 In order to warn the driver should a failure of one brake circuit occur, a brake fail switch is fitted in the hydraulic system at the connector on the firewall.
2 If the hydraulic pressure fails in either of the circuits the indicator switch operates and illuminates the brake fail warning lamp on the instrument panel.

19 Brake pedal and stop lamp switch - removal and refitting

FF-1 1100 and 1300G models

1 Loosen the clamp bolts on the clutch cable, remove the clip and disconnect the clutch cable.
2 Remove the left-hand luggage shelf.
3 Remove the clip, washers, bushing and rod from the clutch pedal

15. Servo unit, master cylinder and hydraulic fluid reservoirs

18.1 The brake fail indicator switch is fitted in the connector center connection

Fig. 9.22. Brake and clutch pedal assembly - FF-1 models

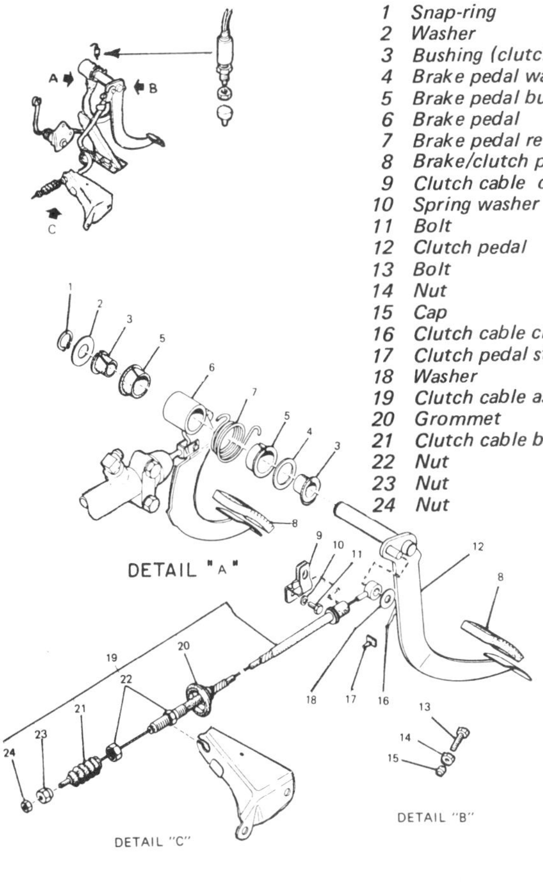

1 *Snap-ring*
2 *Washer*
3 *Bushing (clutch pedal)*
4 *Brake pedal washer*
5 *Brake pedal bushing*
6 *Brake pedal*
7 *Brake pedal return spring*
8 *Brake/clutch pedal pad*
9 *Clutch cable clamp*
10 *Spring washer*
11 *Bolt*
12 *Clutch pedal*
13 *Bolt*
14 *Nut*
15 *Cap*
16 *Clutch cable clip*
17 *Clutch pedal stopper*
18 *Washer*
19 *Clutch cable assembly*
20 *Grommet*
21 *Clutch cable boot*
22 *Nut*
23 *Nut*
24 *Nut*

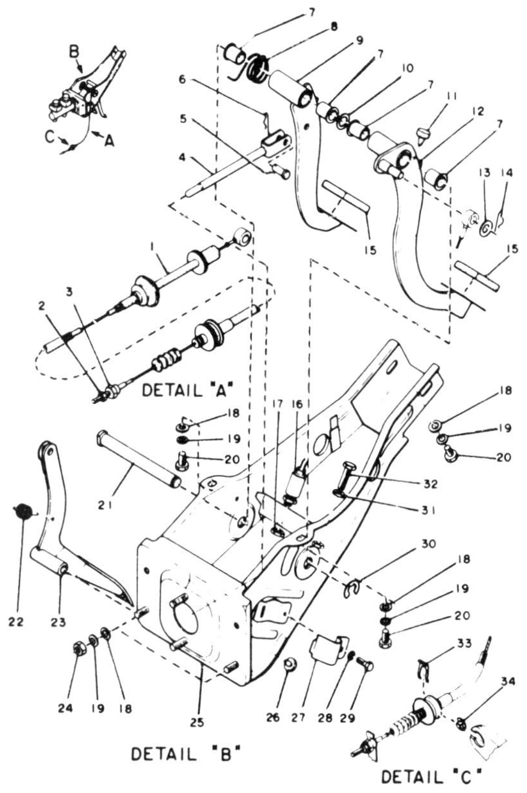

Fig. 9.23. Pedal and bracket assembly - 1300, 1400 and 1600 models

1 *Clutch cable*
2 *Lock nut*
3 *Clutch cable adjusting nut*
4 *Push rod*
5 *Pin*
6 *Cotter pin*
7 *Bushing*
8 *Brake pedal return spring*
9 *Brake pedal*
10 *Washer*
11 *Stopper*
12 *Clutch pedal*
13 *Washer*
14 *Snap-pin*
15 *Pad*
16 *Stop light switch*
17 *Nut*
18 *Washer*
19 *Spring washer*
20 *Bolt*
21 *Shaft*
22 *Accelerator pedal return spring*
23 *Accelerator pedal*
24 *Nut*
25 *Pedal bracket assembly*
26 *Stopper (clutch pedal)*
27 *Bracket (clutch cable)*
28 *Spring washer*
29 *Bolt*
30 *Circlip (retainer)*
31 *Nut*
32 *Bolt*
33 *Clamp*
34 *Circlip (retainer)*

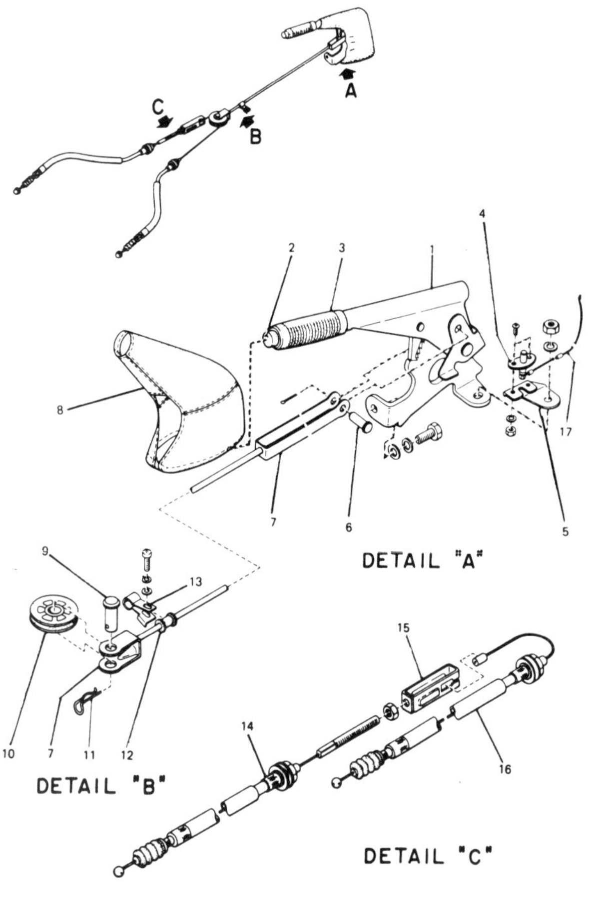

Fig. 9.24. Parking brake system - FF-1 models

1 *Lever assembly*
2 *Button*
3 *Grip*
4 *Switch (parking brake)*
5 *Bracket (warning light switch)*
6 *Clevis pin*
7 *Rod assembly*
8 *Boot (parking brake lever)*
9 *Pin (parking brake pulley)*
10 *Pulley (parking brake)*
11 *Clip (parking brake)*
12 *Bushing (parking brake rod)*
13 *Clip (parking brake rod)*
14 *Parking brake cable*
15 *Turn buckle*
16 *Parking brake cable*
17 *Cord (parking brake switch)*

assembly. Loosen the snap-rings on the clutch pedal shaft and remove the washers and bushings.
4 Pull out the clutch pedal shaft from the brake pedal.
5 Remove the steering column mounting bolts, push the steering column to the right and withdraw the clutch pedal from the bracket to the left-hand side.
6 Remove the brake stop light switch. Unhook the brake pedal return spring and withdraw the brake pedal from the bracket.
7 Examine all the parts for wear and damage. Renew defective parts.
8 Refitting is the reverse of the removal sequence. Depress the pedal to check the stroke: for disc brakes it should be 5.18 in (134 mm) and drum brakes 4.80 in (122 mm). Adjust the stop light switch position so that the pedal free play is 0.3 - 0.5 in (8 - 12 mm) at the pad center.

1300, 1400 and 1600 models

9 Disconnect the accelerator cable at the carburetor end.
10 Remove the master cylinder retaining nuts and at the same time remove the nuts securing the pedal bracket to the firewall.
11 For cars equipped with a servo brake unit, disconnect the pushrod from the brake pedal, remove the master cylinder securing nuts and the servo unit nuts. Separate the master cylinder from the servo unit and remove the servo, taking care not to damage the master cylinder.
12 Remove the luggage shelf.
13 Disconnect the accelerator cable end from the pedal.
14 Remove the snap pin and washer and disconnect the clutch cable from the clutch pedal.
15 Remove the steering column mounting bolts. Disconnect the stop light switch at the connector.
16 Remove the pedal bracket mounting bolts, front bolt first, and remove the pedal bracket assembly.
17 To disassemble the pedal bracket, remove the accelerator return spring, take out the circlip and remove the accelerator pedal. Take off the circlip, pull out the brake and clutch pedal shaft and collect both pedals. Remove the stop light switch.
18 Refitting is the reverse of the removal procedure. Grease the shaft and bushings. If the pedals have too much side play on the shaft, add another washer. Adjust the clutch pedal position by means of the clutch pedal adjusting bolt so that the clutch pedal is on the same level as the brake pedal.
19 Adjust the position of the stop light switch so that the free play of the brake pedal is as follows:

Drum and disc type	-	0.24 - 0.55 in (6 - 14 mm)
With servo unit	-	0.20 - 0.43 in (5 - 11 mm)

When adjusting the position of the stop light switch, disconnect the wiring to avoid twisting it.

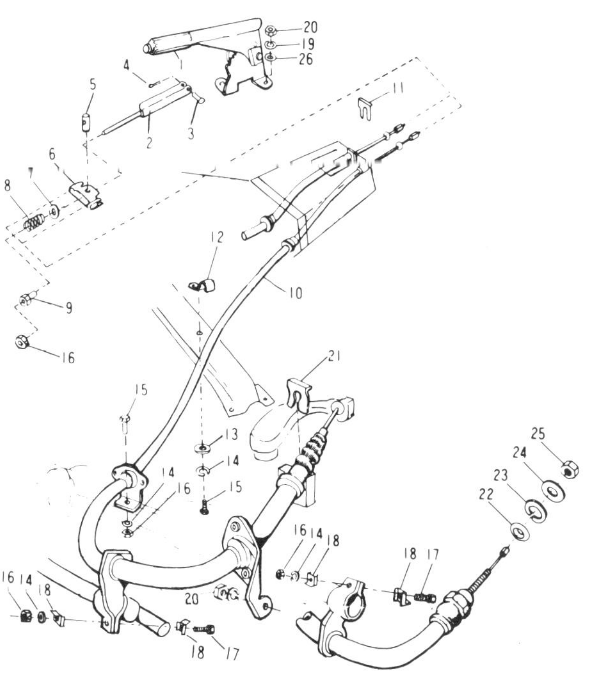

Fig. 9.25. Parking brake system - 1300, 1400 and 1600 models

1 *Lever assembly (parking brake)*
2 *Rod complete (parking brake)*
3 *Clevis pin*
4 *Cotter pin*
5 *Pin*
6 *Equalizer*
7 *Washer*
8 *Spring*
9 *Adjuster (parking brake)*
10 *Parking brake cable assembly*
11 *Clamp*
12 *Clamp*
13 *Washer*
14 *Spring washer*
15 *Bolt*
16 *Nut*
17 *Bolt*
18 *Washer (parking brake)*
19 *Spring washer*
20 *Nut*
21 *Clamp*
22 *O ring*
23 *Spring washer*
24 *Washer*
25 *Nut*
26 *Washer*

20 Parking brake cable - removal and refitting

FF-1 1100 and 1300G models

1 Loosen the cable turnbuckle and separate the right and left side of the cable.
2 Remove the clip, guide, pulley and cable.
3 Undo the attaching nut and remove the cable from the bracket.
4 Remove the cable boot from the engine compartment. Disconnect the cable from the brake lever and the backplate and then withdraw the cable.
5 Refitting is the reverse of the removal procedure.

1300, 1400 and 1600 models

6 Chock the rear wheels and jack up the front of the car. Remove the front roadwheels.
7 Release the parking brake and remove the brake drums, refer to Section 5 (drum type brakes).
8 Remove the parking brake cover and console box, loosen the cable adjusting nut and remove the cable end from the equalizer.
9 Remove the cable end tightening clip and the service hole attachment on the tunnel. Remove the cable clamp from the crossmember.
10 Remove the cable bracket from the control arm link and the cable hangers from the tie-rods.
11 Disconnect the cable end from the parking brake lever after removing the secondary brake shoe, refer to Section 5.
12 Remove the cable end nut, washer and spring washer from the

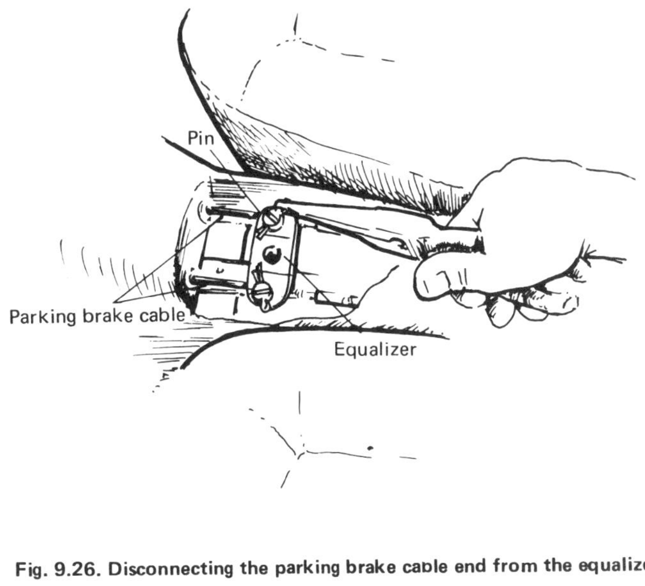

Fig. 9.26. Disconnecting the parking brake cable end from the equalizer

inside of the backplate and pull the parking brake cable out from the backplate (drum brakes).
13 On models with disc brakes, pull the brake hose clamp out and remove the parking brake cable end from the lever and spindle assembly.
14 Pull the parking brake cable assembly from the engine compartment together with the grommet from the body.
15 Refitting is the reverse of the removal procedure. Always fit a new grommet. Fit the parking brake cable hangers on the chamfered part of the tie-rods.

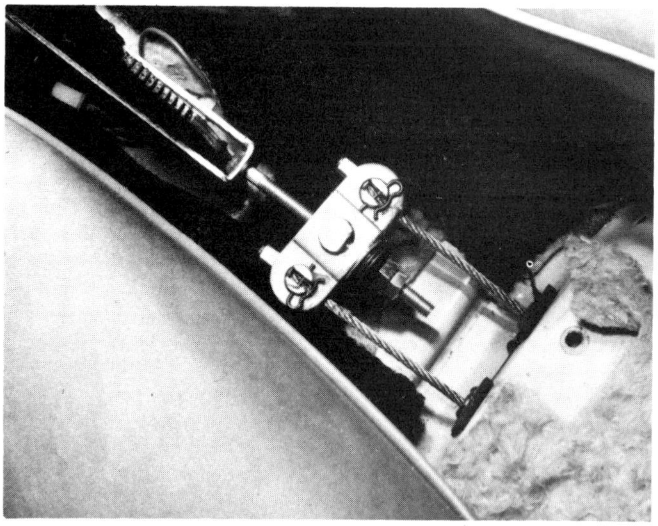
21.2 Adjust the parking brake by turning the turnbuckle

21 Parking brake - adjustment

1 Operate the parking brake lever two or three times.
2 Loosen the cable locknut at the turnbuckle, and adjust the length of the cable by turning the turnbuckle, so that it takes 7-9 notches of the lever to apply the brake on 1970-73 models, and 6 notches on 1974-77 models.
3 Tighten the locknut and recheck the operation of the parking brake lever.

Fig. 9.27. Removing the parking brake cable end nut from the backplate

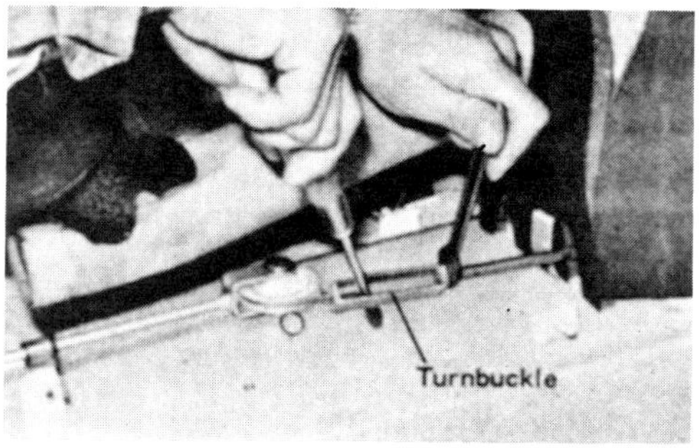

Fig. 9.28. Adjusting the length of the parking brake cable

22 Fault diagnosis

Symptom	Reason/s	Remedy
Brake grab	Contaminated with oil or grease	Renew brake shoes or pads.
	Scored drums or discs	Correct or renew.
Brake drag	Faulty master cylinder	Remove and service.
	Blocked reservoir vent	Clean.
	Seized wheel cylinder or caliper	Remove and service.
	Parking brake incorrectly adjusted	Re-adjust.
	Blocked or swollen pipe lines	Renew as necessary.
Excessive pedal effort required	Pads or shoes not bedded in	Operate brake repeatedly until corrected.
	Oil or grease on pads or linings	Renew.
	Scored disc or brake drums as a result of worn linings	Correct or renew discs or brake drums. Renew pads and brake shoes.
	Faulty servo unit (if so equipped)	Remove and rectify.
Brake pedal feels hard	Glazed surfaces of friction material	Renew brake shoes or pads.
	Rust on disc surfaces	Clean surface with emery cloth or by shimming.
	Seized caliper or wheel cylinder	Remove and service.
Excessive pedal travel	Low reservoir fluid level	Top-up as necessary.
	Air in the system	Bleed the system.
	Worn pads and brake shoe linings	Renew.
	Automatic adjuster faulty	Remove and service.
Pedal creep during sustained pressure	Fluid leak	Trace and rectify.
	Internal fault in master cylinder	Remove and service.
Pedal 'spongy'	Air in the system	Bleed the system.

Chapter 10 Electrical system

For modifications, and information applicable to later models, see Supplement at end of manual

Contents

Specifications

Battery

Type	NS40 - 1	NS 50	N50Z
Capacity	32AH	50AH	60AH
Voltage	12		
Ground	Negative		

Alternator

Make and type	Hitachi LT170 - 75
Nominal output	12V/30A
Polarity ground	Negative
Direction of rotation (viewed from pulley end)	Clockwise
Rotor coil resistance	4.5 ohms
Stator coil resistance	0.18 ohms per phase
Brush:	
Length new	0.75 in (19 mm)
Minimum length	0.47 in (12 mm)
Spring pressure	7.1 - 13.4 oz (200 - 380 g)
Make and type	Hitachi LT135 - 20
Nominal output	12V/35A
Polarity ground	Negative
Direction of rotation (viewed from pulley end)	Clockwise
Rotor coil resistance	4.0 ohms
Stator coil resistance	0.2 ohms
Brush:	
Length new	0.57 in (14.5 mm)
Minimum length	0.28 in (7 mm)
Spring pressure	9.0 - 12.2 oz (255 - 345 g)

Make and type	Hitachi LT150 - 21
Nominal output	12V/50A
Polarity ground	Negative
Direction of rotation (viewed from pulley end)	Clockwise
Rotor coil resistance	4.0 ohms
Stator coil resistance	0.2 ohms
Brush:	
Length new	0.75 in (19 mm)
Minimum length	0.47 in (12 mm)
Spring pressure	9.0 - 12.2 oz (255 - 345 g)

Regulator

Make	Hitachi
Type	Tirril type with charge relay
Voltage regulator:	
Regulating voltage	14 to 15V
Yoke gap	0.035 in (0.9 mm)
Core gap	0.024 - 0.039 in (0.6 - 1.0 mm)
Point gap	0.012 - 0.016 in (0.3 - 0.4 mm)
Charge relay:	
Releasing voltage	8 - 10V (at A terminal)
Yoke gap	0.035 in (0.9 mm)
Core gap	0.032 - 0.039 in (0.8 - 1.0 mm)
Point gap	0.016 - 0.024 in (0.4 - 0.6 mm)

Fuses

Type	Cartridge				
Rating	30A	25A	20A	15A	10A
Number of fuses:					
1970		2	1		2
1972	1	1	1		5
1974	1	1	2	3	1

Starter motor

Make	Nippon Denso
Type	Magnetic switch type
Nominal output	0.8 KW (manual transmission) 1.0 KW (automatic transmission)
Voltage	12V
Rating	30 seconds
Starting current at 60°F (20°C)	470 A or less
Direction of rotation (viewed from pulley end)	Counterclockwise
No load:	
Voltage	11V
Current	50 A or less
Revolutions	5000 rpm or more
Load:	
Voltage	9.5V
Current	240 A or less
Torque	5.1 ft lb (0.7 kg m) (manual transmission) 5.8 ft lb (0.8 kg m) (automatic transmission)
Revolutions	1100 rpm or more (manual transmission) 1200 rpm or more (automatic transmission)
Pinion travel	0.35 - 0.51 in (9 - 13 mm)
Brush length:	
Standard	0.75 in (19 mm)
Minimum	0.47 in (12 mm)
Brush spring tension	1.32 - 3.40 lb (0.6 - 1.38 kg)

Commutator

Standard	1.53 in (38.8 mm)
Wear limit	0.008 in (0.2 mm)
Ellipticity limit	0.016 in (0.4 mm)
Depth of mica	0.020 - 0.032 in (0.5 - 0.8 mm)
Depth limit of mica	0.008 in (0.2 mm)
Armature shaft:	
Outer diameter	0.4893 - 0.4899 in (12.425 - 12.440 mm)
Clearance between shaft and bearing	0.037 -
Wear limit	0.0079 in (0.2 mm)
Thrust clearance	0.0020 - 0.0024 in (0.05 - 0.06 mm)
Thrust clearance limit	0.032 in (0.8 mm)

Windshield wiper motor

Indicated voltage	12V
Test voltage	13V

No-load current:	
Low	2A
High	3A
No-load revolutions:	
Low	50 ± 5 rpm
High	70 ± 7 rpm
Difference between low and high	15 rpm or more
Lock current	18 A
Lock torque:	
Low	8.7 ft lb (1.2 kg m)
High	8.0 ft lb (1.1 kg m)
Wiping system	Tandem motion type
Wiping angle	Driver's side 81° Passenger side 101°

Windshield washer

Motor:	
Type	Direct current, magnetic type
Output	12V - 35W
Current	Less than 3A
Test voltage	13.5V
Maximum operating period	20 seconds
Pump:	
Type	Centrifugal type
Pumping pressure	Above 0.5 kg/cm^2 (7 psi)
Flow	Above 100 cc/10 sec (6.1 cu in/10 sec)
Nozzle - hole diameter	1 mm

Horn

Sedan and Coupe:	
Diameter	3.74 in (95 mm)
Current (max)	3A at 12V
Basic frequency	Low tone - 350 Hz High tone - 405 Hz
Station Wagon:	
Diameter	4.13 in (105 mm)
Current (max)	4A at 12V
Basic frequency	310 Hz

Bulbs

Headlamp	12V - 50W/40W
Front combination lamp:	
Turn signal light	12V - 23W
Clearance light	12V - 8 W
Rear combination lamp:	
Stop and tail light	12V - 23W/8W
Turn signal light	12V - 23W
Back-up light	12V - 23W
Side marker lamp:	
Front	12V - 8W
Rear	12V - 8W
Dome light	12V - 8W
Instrument cluster light	12V - 3.4W
Instrument panel light	12V - 2W
License plate lamp	12V - 7.5W
Warning and indicator lights:	
Oil pressure	12V - 3.4W
Charge	12V - 3.4W
High beam	12V - 3.4W
Turn signal	12V - 3.4W
Seat belt	12V - 3.4W
Brake failure and parking brake	12V - 3.4W
Rear window defogger	12V - 1.7W
Door ajar	12V - 3.4W

1 General description

The electrical system is of the 12 volt type and the major components comprise, a 12 volt battery of which the negative terminal is grounded, an alternator which is belt driven from a pulley on the front of the crankshaft and a starter motor which is mounted on the transmission casing and the rear of the engine.

The battery supplies the power required to operate the starter motor, which places a heavy demand on it. The battery also provides the current for the ignition, lighting and other electrical circuits, and provides a reserve of electricity when the current consumed by the electrical equipment exceeds that being produced by the alternator. It is kept fully charged by the alternator, the output of which is controlled by the voltage regulator.

When fitting electrical accessories to cars with a negative ground system it is important, if they contain silicone diodes or transistors, that they are properly connected, otherwise serious damage may be caused to the components concerned. Items such as radios, tape recorders, electronic tachometers and automatic headlight dipping,

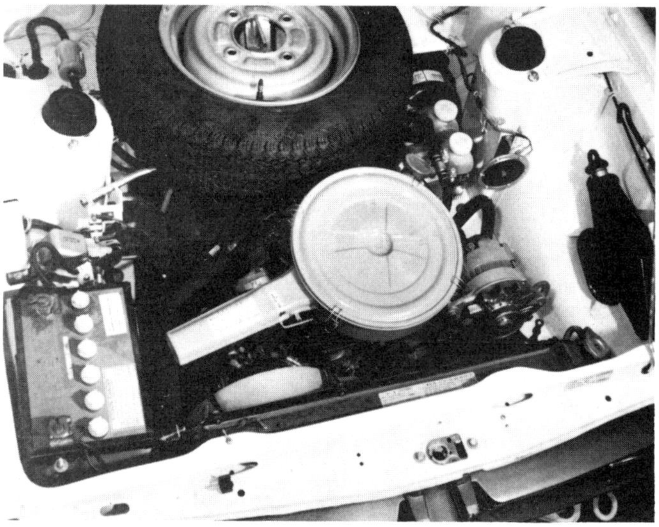

2.1 The battery is mounted on the front right-hand side in the engine compartment

etc, should all be checked for correct polarity.

2 Battery - removal and refitting

1 The battery is housed in the engine compartment at the front right-hand side.
2 Disconnect the negative terminal first and then the positive.
3 Remove the battery hold-down clamp and carefully lift the battery from its carrier. Hold the battery vertical to ensure that none of the electrolyte is spilled.
4 Refitting is the reverse of the removal sequence. Smear the terminal with petroleum jelly (vaseline) to prevent corrosion. Never use mineral grease. Always connect the negative lead first.

3 Battery - maintenance and inspection

1 Normal weekly battery maintenance consists of checking the electrolyte level of each cell to ensure that the separators are covered by ¼ inch of electrolyte. If the level has fallen, top up the battery using distilled water only. Do not overfill. If the battery is overfilled or any electrolyte spilled, immediately wipe away excess as electrolyte attacks and corrodes any metal it comes into contact with very rapidly.
2 As well as keeping the terminals clean and covered with petroleum jelly, the top of the battery, and especially the top of the cells, should be kept clean and dry. This helps to prevent corrosion and ensures that the battery does not become partially discharged by leakage through dampness and dirt.
3 Once every three months remove the battery and inspect the battery securing nuts, battery clamp plate, tray and battery leads for corrosion (white fluffy deposits on the metal which are brittle to touch). If any corrosion is found, clean off the deposits with ammonia and paint over the clean metal with an anti-rust, anti-acid paint.
4 At the same time inspect the battery case for cracks. If found, clean and plug it with a proprietary compound. If leakage through the crack has been excessive then it will be necessary to refill the appropriate cell with fresh electrolyte as described later. Cracks are frequently caused at the top of the battery case by pouring in distilled water in the middle of winter *after* instead of *before* a run. This gives the water no chance to mix with the electrolyte and so the former freezes and splits the battery case.
5 If the topping-up becomes excessive and the case has been inspected for cracks that could cause leakage, but none are found, the battery is being overcharged and the voltage regulator will have to be checked and reset.
6 With the battery on the bench at the three monthly interval check, measure the specific gravity with a hydrometer to determine the state of charge and condition of the electrolyte. There should be very little variation between the different cells and, if a variation in excess of 0.025 is present, it will be due to either:

a) Loss of electrolyte from the battery at some time caused by spillage or a leak, resulting in a drop in the specific gravity of the electrolyte when the deficiency was replaced with distilled water instead of fresh electrolyte.
b) An internal short circuit caused by buckling of the plates or similar malady pointing to the likelihood of total battery failure in the near future.

7 The specific gravity of the electrolyte for fully charged conditions at the electrolyte temperatures indicated, is listed in Table A. The specific gravity of a fully discharged battery at different temperatures of the electrolyte is given in Table B.

Table A
Specific gravity - battery fully charged.

1.268 at 100°F or 38°C electrolyte temperature
1.272 at 90°F or 32°C electrolyte temperature
1.276 at 80°F or 27°C electrolyte temperature
1.280 at 70°F or 21°C electrolyte temperature
1.284 at 60°F or 16°C electrolyte temperature
1.288 at 50°F or 10°C electrolyte temperature
1.292 at 40°F or 4°C electrolyte temperature
1.296 at 30°F or -1.5°C electrolyte temperature

Table B
Specific gravity - battery fully discharged.

1.098 at 100°F or 38°C electrolyte temperature
1.102 at 90°F or 32°C electrolyte temperature
1.106 at 80°F or 27°C electrolyte temperature
1.110 at 70°F or 21°C electrolyte temperature
1.114 at 60°F or 16°C electrolyte temperature
1.118 at 50°F or 10°C electrolyte temperature
1.122 at 40°F or 4°C electrolyte temperature
1.126 at 30°F or -1.5°C electrolyte temperature

4 Battery - electrolyte replenishment

1 If the battery is in a fully charged state and one of the cells maintains a specific gravity reading which is 0.025 or less than the others and a check of each cell has been made with a voltage meter to check for short circuits (a four to seven second test should give a steady reading of between 1.2 and 1.8 volts), then it is likely that electrolyte has been lost from the cell with the low reading at some time.
2 Top-up the cell with a solution of 1 part sulphuric acid to 2.5 parts of water. If the cell is already fully topped-up draw some electrolyte out of it with a pipette.
3 When mixing the sulphuric acid and water **NEVER ADD WATER TO SULPHURIC ACID** - always pour the acid slowly onto the water in a glass container. **IF WATER IS ADDED TO SULPHURIC ACID IT WILL EXPLODE.**
4 Continue to top-up the cell with the freshly made electrolyte and then recharge the battery and check the hydrometer readings.

5 Battery - charging

1 It is a good idea to occasionally have the battery fully charged from an external source at a rate of 3.5 to 4 amps, particularly after heavy loading.
2 Continue to charge the battery at this rate until no further rise in specific gravity is noted over a four hour period.
3 Alternatively, a trickle charger, charging at the rate of 1.5 amps can be safely used overnight.
4 Special rapid 'boost' charges which are claimed to restore the power of the battery in 1 to 2 hours are not to be recommended unless they are thermostatically controlled as they can cause serious damage to the battery plates through overheating.
5 While charging the battery note that the temperature of the electrolyte should never exceed 100°F (37.8°C).

6 Alternator - general description

1 The use of alternators for generating the current required to operate the car electrical systems is now more commonplace. Their main advantage over the dynamo type of generator is that they provide a high output for lower revolutions and are light in weight/output ratio.
2 The alternator generates alternating current and this current is rectified by diodes into direct current which is the current required for battery storage.
3 The alternator output is controlled by a voltage regulator and a charge relay operates the charge warning lamp to indicate whether or not the alternator is charging the battery.

7 Alternator - safety precautions

1 If there are indications that the charging system is malfunctioning in any way, care must be taken to diagnose faults properly, otherwise damage of a serious and expensive nature may occur to parts which in fact were quite serviceable.
2 The following basic requirements must be observed at all times:

a) All alternator systems use a negative ground. Even the simplest mistake of connecting a battery the wrong way round could burn out the alternator diodes in a few seconds.
b) Before disconnecting any wiring in the system the engine ignition should be switched off. This will minimise accidental short circuits.
c) The alternator must never be run with the output wire disconnected.
d) Always disconnect the battery from the car's electrical system if an external charging source is being used.
e) Do not use test wire connections that could move accidentally and short circuit against nearby terminals. Short circuits will not blow fuses - they will blow diodes or transistors.
f) Always disconnect the battery cables and alternator output lead before carrying out any electric welding work on the car.
g) When checking the circuit between individual terminals, or when testing silicone diodes for continuity, never use a high voltage tester (such as a megger) as the diodes will be damaged. Use an ordinary tester.
h) When using an extra battery as a starting aid, always connect it in parallel.

8 Alternator - removal and refitting

1 Disconnect the ground lead from the negative terminal of the battery.
2 Disconnect the wiring from the rear of the alternator.
3 Remove the adjusting arm bolt, slacken the pivot bolt and remove

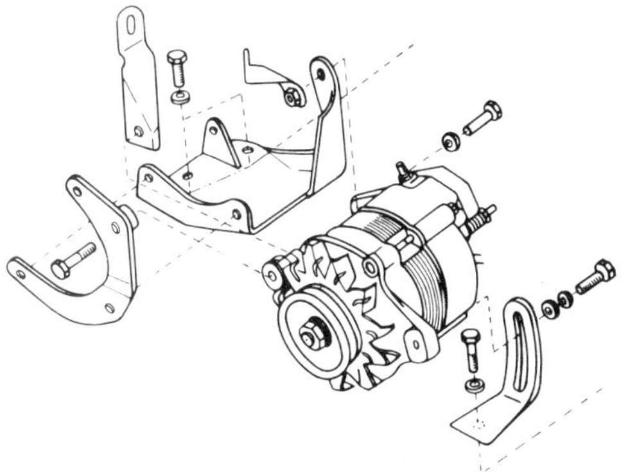

Fig. 10.1. Alternator and mounting bracket

8.2 The alternator is mounted on the front left-hand side of the engine

8.3a Slacken the alternator pivot bolt

8.3b Removing the alternator

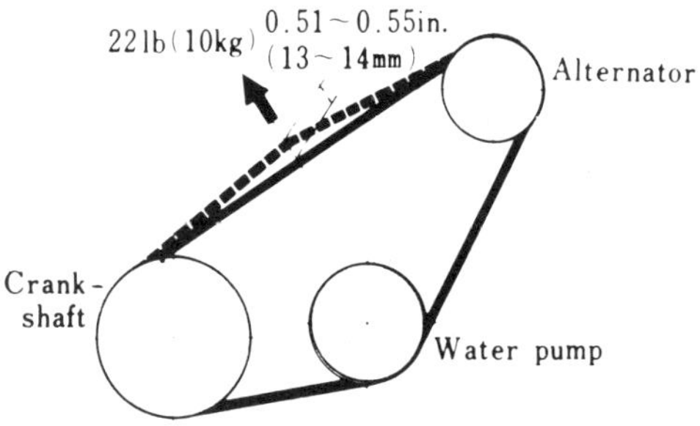

Fig. 10.2. V-belt tension adjustment (except 4WD)

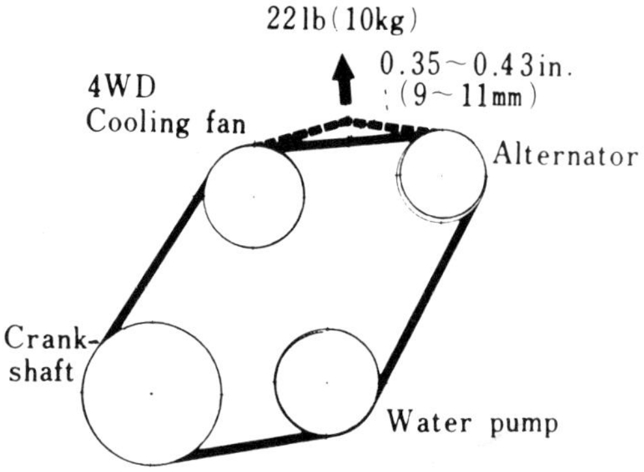

Fig. 10.3. V-belt tension adjustment for 4WD

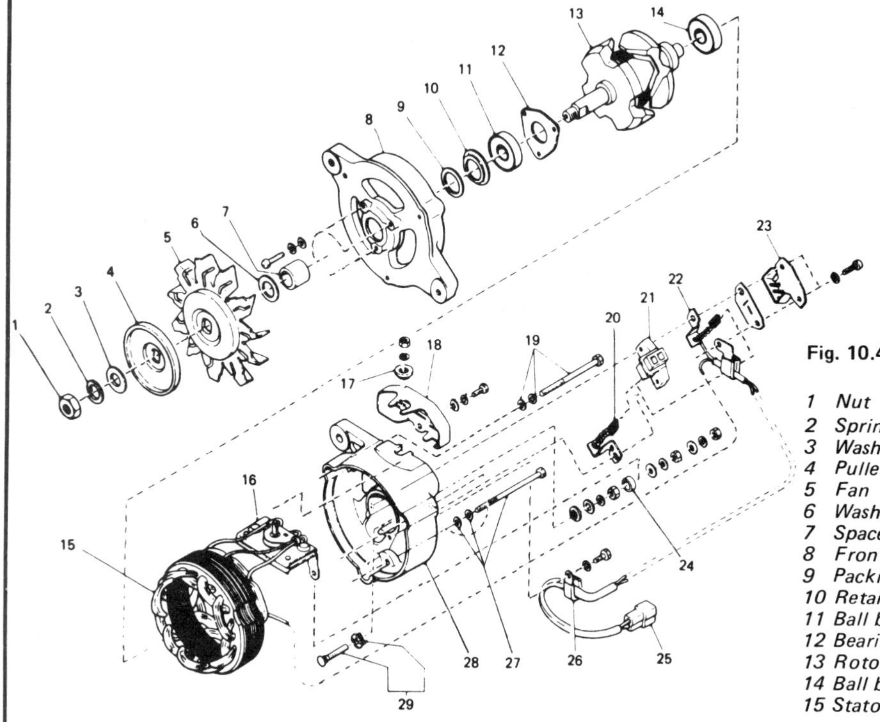

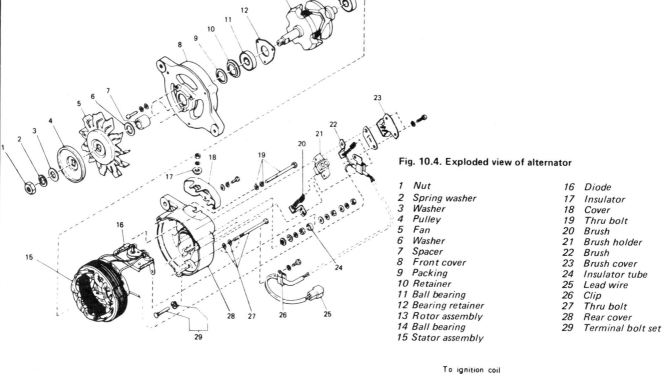

Fig. 10.4. Exploded view of alternator

1 Nut
2 Spring washer
3 Washer
4 Pulley
5 Fan
6 Washer
7 Spacer
8 Front cover
9 Packing
10 Retainer
11 Ball bearing
12 Bearing retainer
13 Rotor assembly
14 Ball bearing
15 Stator assembly
16 Diode
17 Insulator
18 Cover
19 Thru bolt
20 Brush
21 Brush holder
22 Brush
23 Brush cover
24 Insulator tube
25 Lead wire
26 Clip
27 Thru bolt
28 Rear cover
29 Terminal bolt set

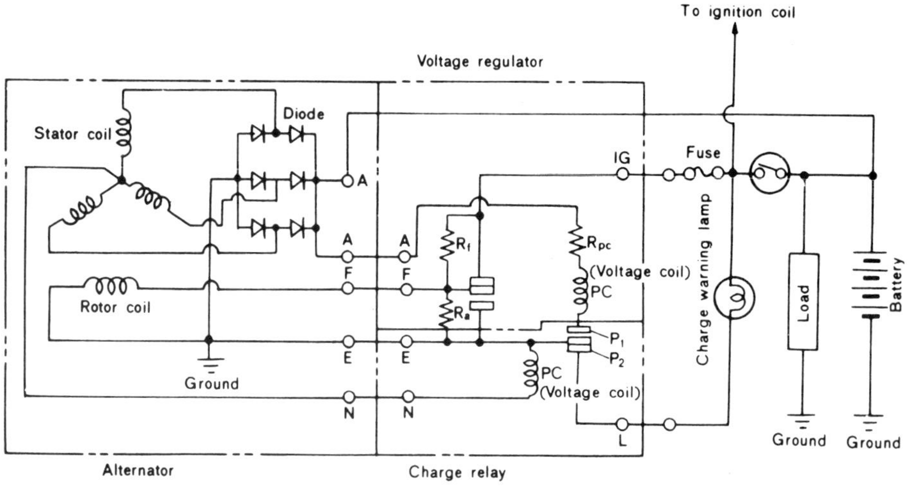

Fig. 10.5. Charging circuit (early models)

the drivebelt from the pulley. Remove the pivot bolt and lift out the alternator.

4 Refitting is the reverse of the removal sequence. Adjust the drivebelt tension by pivoting the alternator upwards on the pivot bolt, then tightening the adjusting arm bolt and the pivot bolt. For correct tension of belt refer to Figs. 10.2 and 10.3.

9 Alternator - testing and repair

Due to the specialist knowledge and equipment required to test and repair an alternator, it is recommended that if the performance is suspect, the car be taken to an automobile electrician who will have the equipment needed for such work.

10 Voltage regulator and charge relay - general description

The voltage regulator has two sets of contact points, lower and upper, which control the alternator voltage. An armature plate between the two sets of contacts, moves upwards, downwards or vibrates. When closed the lower contacts complete the field circuit to ground, and the upper contacts when closed complete the field circuit to ground thru a resistance (field coil) and thereby produce the alternator output.

The charge relay is similar in construction to the voltage regulator. It operates the charge warning lamp to indicate whether or not the alternator is charging the battery. When the upper contacts are closed, the charge warning lamp is on.

If the regulator or charge relay is suspect, have it checked by an automobile electrician.

10.1 The voltage regulator is mounted on right-hand wheel apron next to the ignition coil

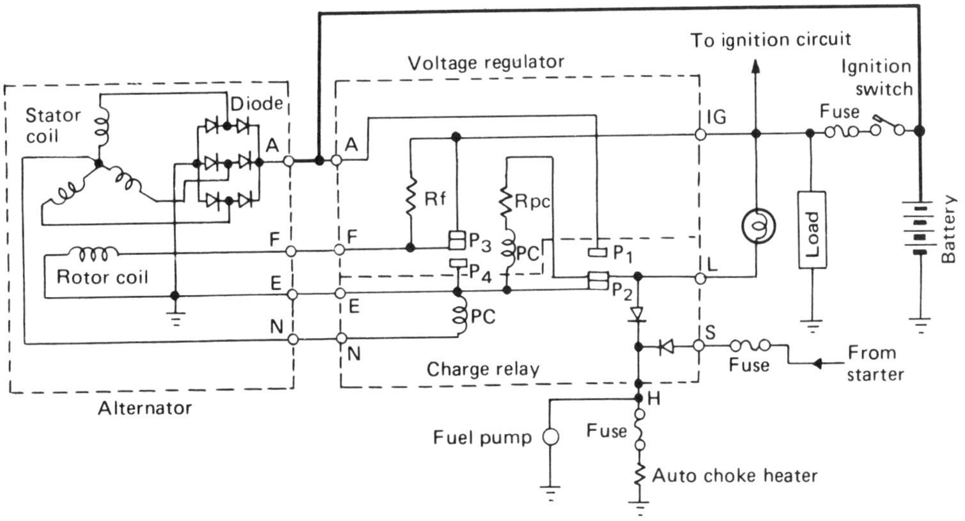

Fig. 10.6. Charging circuit (1977 models)

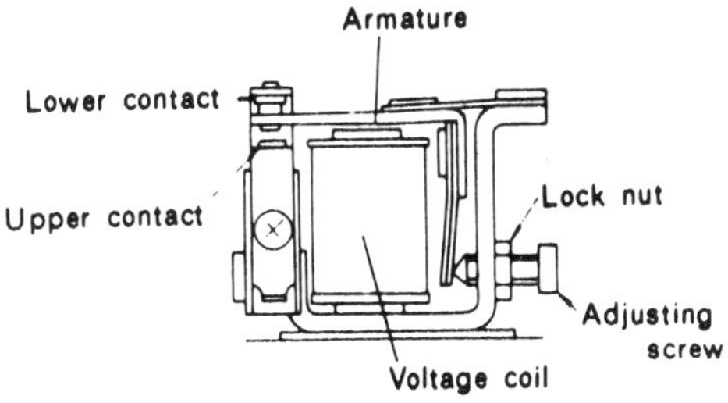

Fig. 10.7. Voltage regulator

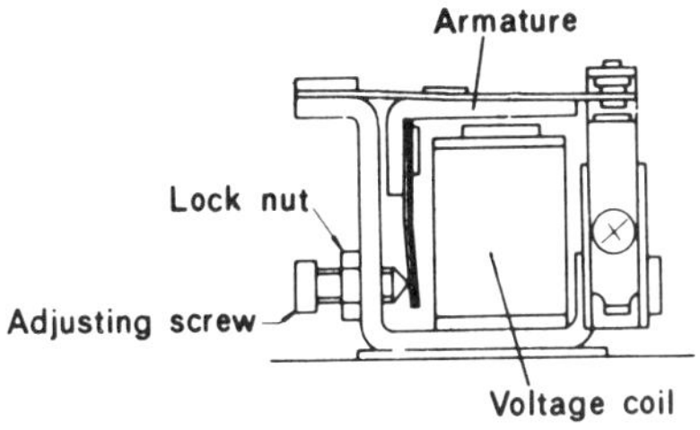

Fig. 10.8. Charge relay

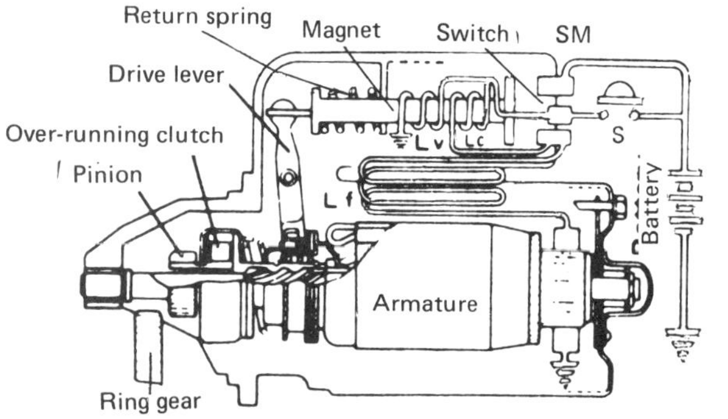

Fig. 10.9. Starter motor static condition

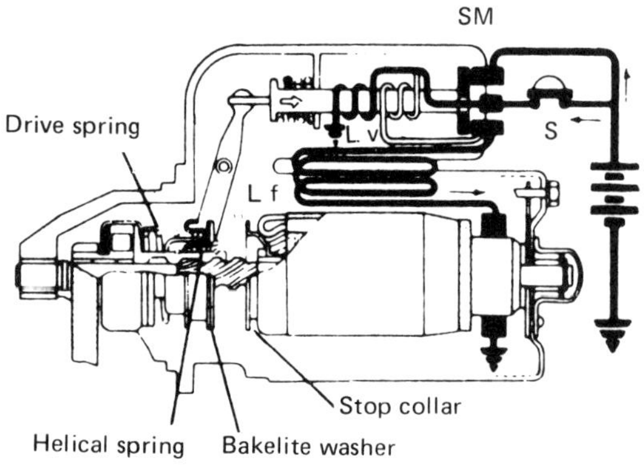

Fig. 10.10. Starter motor operating condition

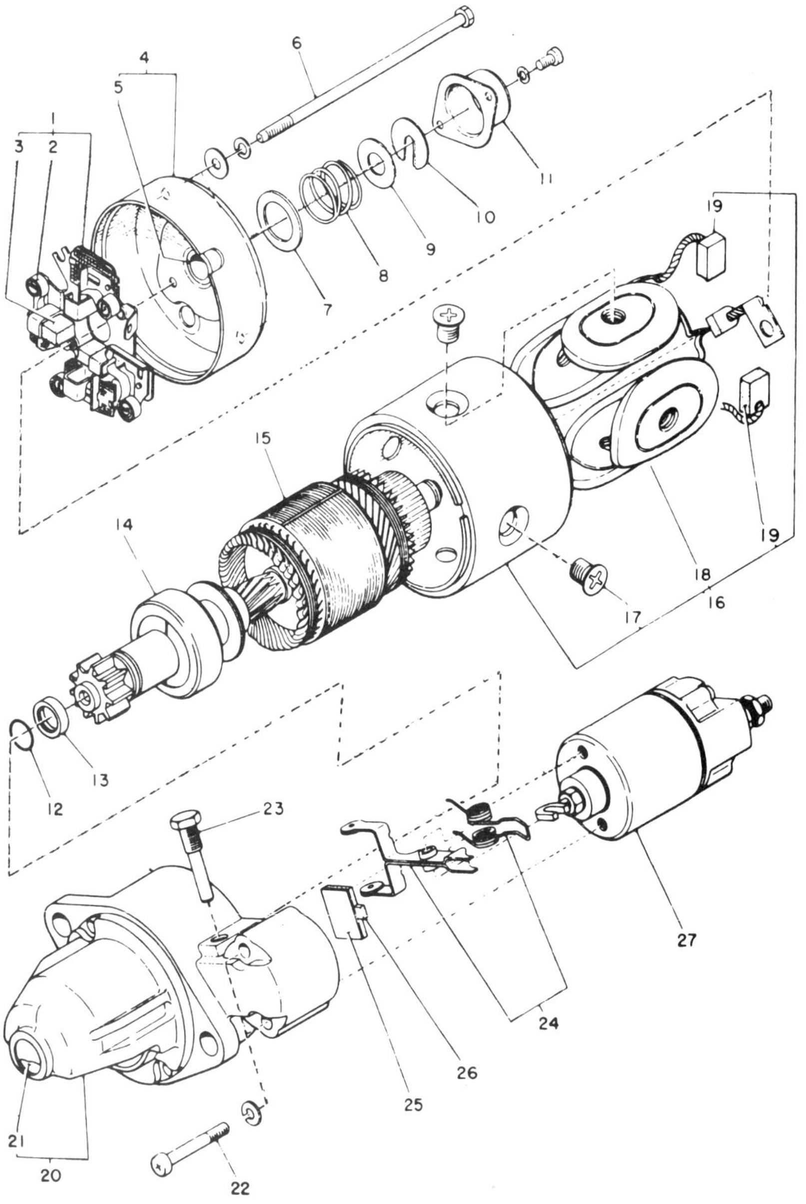

Fig. 10.11. Exploded view of starter motor (manual transmission vehicles)

1 *Brush holder plate complete*
2 *Spring (brush holder)*
3 *Brush (starter)*
4 *Frame complete (commutator)*
5 *Bushing*
6 *Thru bolt*
7 *Rubber parts*
8 *Spring*
9 *Washer*
10 *Lock plate*
11 *Cap (end frame)*
12 *Snap ring*
13 *Collar (pinion stop)*
14 *Over running clutch complete*
15 *Armature complete*
16 *Yoke complete*
17 *Screw (pole core)*
18 *Field coil complete*
19 *Brush (starter)*
20 *Housing complete*
21 *Bushing (housing)*
22 *Screw*
23 *Bolt (lever set)*
24 *Drive lever complete*
25 *Plate*
26 *Rubber parts*
27 *Magnet switch complete*

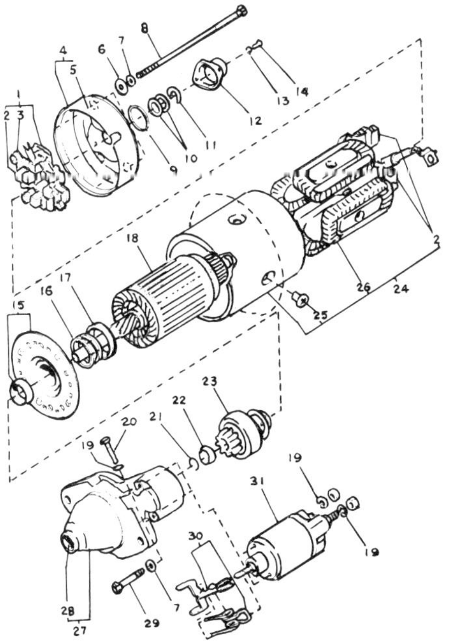

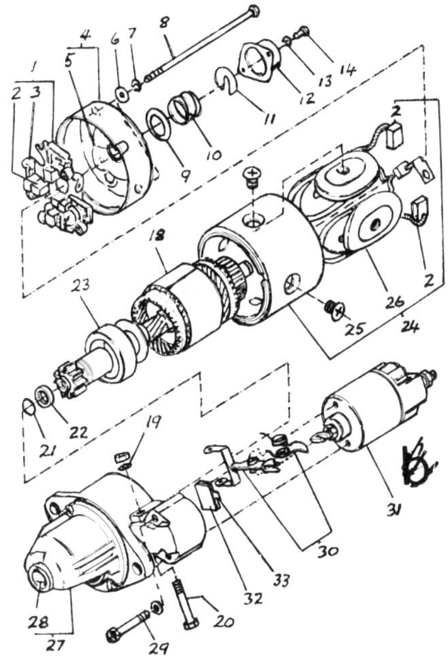

Fig. 10.12. Exploded view of starter motor (automatic transmission vehicles and California)

1 Brush holder plate complete
2 Starter brush
3 Brush holder spring
4 Commutator frame complete
5 Bushing
6 Washer (6.4 x 17.2)
7 Spring washer
8 Thru bolt
9 Starter seal
10 Starter washer (10) spring
11 Starter lock plate
12 End frame cap
13 Spring washer
14 Pan head screw
15 Plain bearing complete
16 Starter brake spring
17 Starter spring holder
18 Starter armature complete
19 Spring washer
20 Lever set bolt
21 Snap ring
22 Pinion stop collar
23 Over running clutch complete
24 Starter yoke complete
25 Pole core screw
26 Starter field coil complete
27 Starter housing complete
28 Housing bushing
29 Screw
30 Drive lever complete
31 Magnet switch complete
32 Plate
33 Rubber part

11 Starter motor - general description

1 The starting system consists of the battery, ignition starter switch, starter motor and solenoid. Current is supplied from the battery and the solenoid completes the circuit to operate the starter.
2 Fig. 10.9 shows the static condition and Fig. 10.10 shows the operating condition with the starter mounted on the engine. When the switch 'S' is turned on, current flows from the battery to the pull-in coil 'Lc' and hold-in coil 'Lv'. The drive lever is shifted and the pinion meshes with the flywheel ring gear before the main switch 'SM' closes. When the main switch closes current flows from the battery thru the heavy cable as shown in Fig. 10.10.
3 A large torque is generated and the pinion is advanced further by the spiral splines in the clutch for deeper gear meshing. Also, current to the pull-in coil 'Lc' is interrupted and the drive lever is held by the hold-in coil 'Lv'.
4 At the time the switch 'S' is opened, the main switch 'SM' is still closed; therefore current flows to the hold-in coil 'Lv' thru the pull-in coil 'Lc'. In this case the magnetic lines of both coils oppose each other and so the forces are cancelled and the pinion is disengaged from the ring gear by the return spring. However, the armature tends to continue to rotate, so in order to stop the armature it is equipped with a stopper. The bakelite washer of the overrunning clutch is pressed against the stopper by the return spring, causing a braking action.

12 Starter motor - testing on the car

1 If the starter motor fails to operate then check the condition of the battery by switching on the headlamps. If they glow brightly for several seconds and then gradually dim, the battery is in a discharged condition.
2 If the headlamps continue to remain bright and it is obvious that the battery is in good condition, then check the tightness of the battery connections, particularly the ground lead from the battery terminal to its connection on the engine. Check all connections from battery to solenoid switch and the heavy cable to the starter for cleanliness and security.
3 If the starter motor still fails to turn, check the solenoid by connecting a voltmeter or test lamp across the main cable connections on the starter side of the solenoid and ground. When the switch is operated there should be a reading, or lighted bulb, if not the solenoid switch is faulty. If it is established that the solenoid is not faulty and 12 volts are getting to the starter then the fault must be in the starter motor and it will have to be removed for examination. Before this is done, however, make sure that the pinion has not jammed in mesh with the ring gear. To release the pinion engage a low gear, and with the ignition switch off, rock the car backwards and forwards to release the pinion from the ring gear. If the pinion remains jammed the starter motor must be removed.

13 Starter motor - removal and refitting

1 Remove the spare wheel, if fitted in the engine compartment.
2 Disconnect the ground lead from the negative terminal of the battery.
3 Disconnect the leads from the starter.
4 Remove the two nuts securing the starter to the transmission casing and pull out the starter.
5 Refitting is the reverse of the removal sequence. Ensure that the contact surfaces of the mounting faces are clean.

14 Starter motor - dismantling, servicing and reassembly

1 Servicing operations should be limited to renewal of brushes, renewal of solenoid, the servicing of the starter drive gear and cleaning the commutator.
2 The major components of the starter should normally last the life of the unit and in the event of failure, a factory exchange replacement should be obtained.
3 Access to the brushes is obtained by removing the end frame cap, lock plate, washer, spring and rubber seal, then removing the two

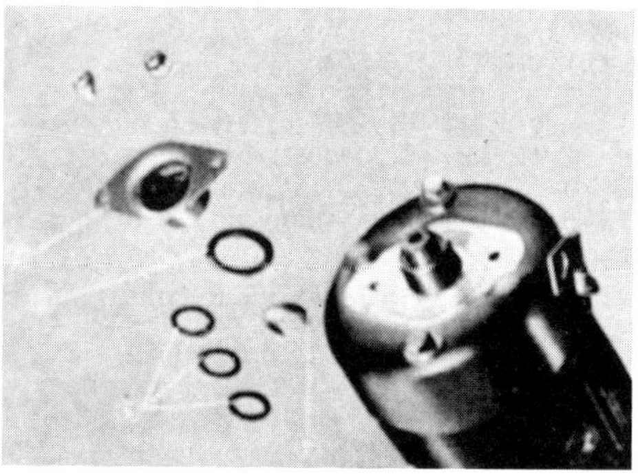

Fig. 10.13. Removing the end frame cap

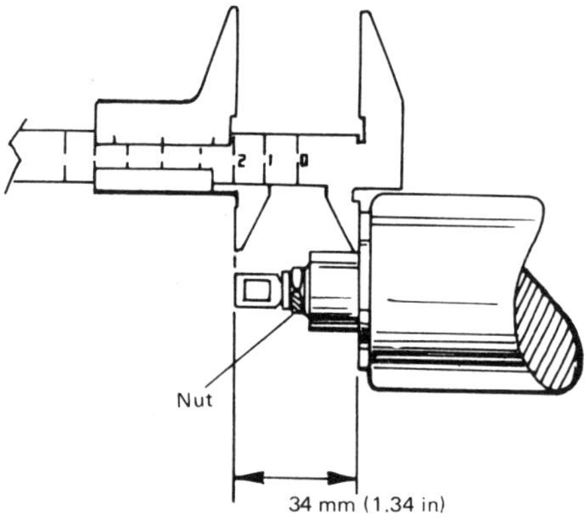

Fig. 10.14. Adjusting the stud bolt length

Fig. 10.15. Separating the yoke from the housing

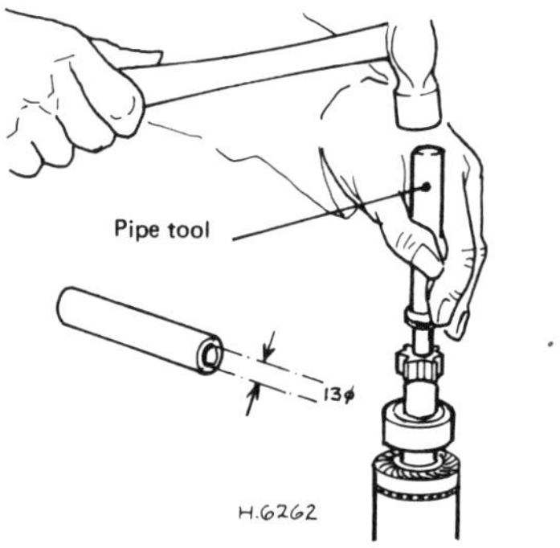

Fig. 10.16. Removing the pinion stop collar

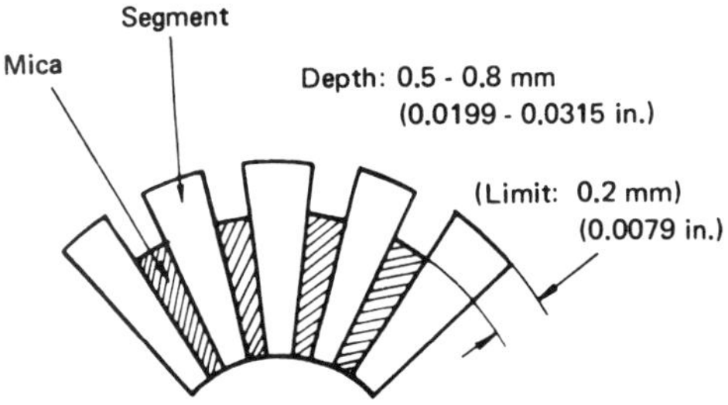

Fig. 10.17. Undercut dimension of the commutator

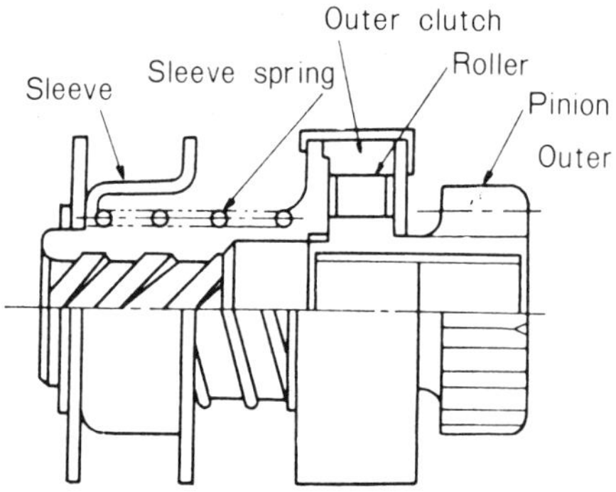

Fig. 10.18. Cut-away view of over-running clutch

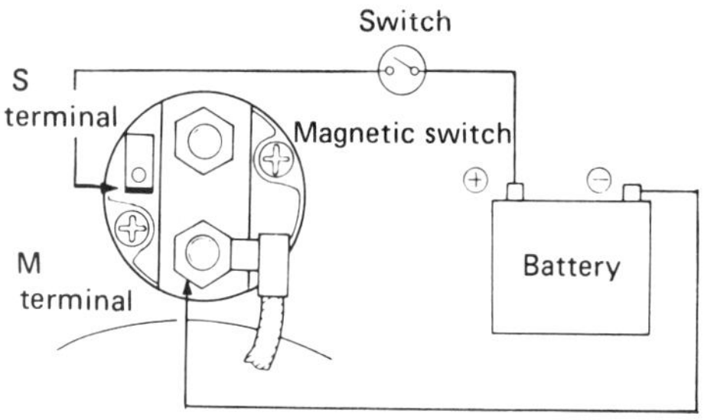

Fig. 10.19. Solenoid (magnet switch) assembly test circuit

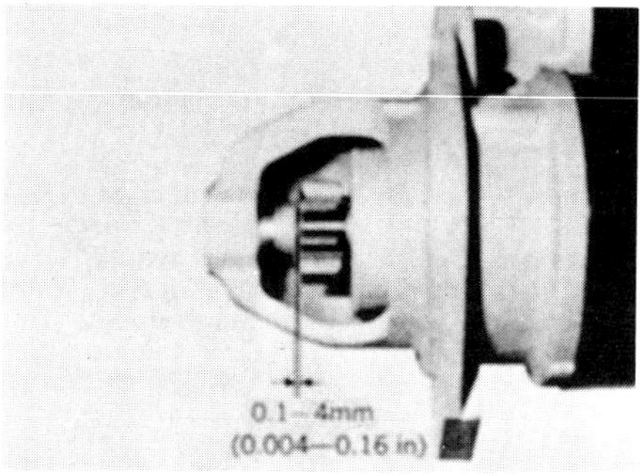

Fig. 10.20. Clearance between pinion and pinion stop collar

through bolts and pulling the frame towards the rear.
4 Move each brush holder spring to the side and pull the brushes from their holders.
5 Measure the overall length of the brushes and where they are below the minimum length, as given in the Specifications at the beginning of this Chapter, they must be renewed.
6 Ensure each brush slides freely in its holder. Clean any accumulated carbon dust or grease from the holder with a gasoline moistened rag.
7 Disconnect the lead from the starter motor to the solenoid 'M' terminal.
8 Remove the two screws securing the solenoid to the starter and lift off the solenoid.
9 Refitting the solenoid is the reverse of the removal sequence but the length of the plunger must be checked and, if necessary, adjusted. To do this, depress the plunger fully and measure the distance between the end of the plunger and the face of the solenoid body, see Fig. 10.14. If necessary, readjust the solenoid stud bolt length to obtain the correct dimension.
10 The commutator can be cleaned by holding a piece of non-fluffy cloth moistened with gasoline against it as it is rotated by hand. If, on inspection, the mica separators are found to be level with the copper segments then they must be undercut to between 0.020 and 0.032 in (0.5 and 0.8 mm).
11 Remove the brushes and solenoid as previously described. Separate the yoke from the housing, tapping it with a plastic mallet, if necessary, to free it. Take care not to damage the field coils of the yoke on the armature as the yoke is removed.
12 Remove the drive lever pin (or bolt) and remove the armature from the housing together with the overrunning clutch and drive lever.
13 The pinion stop collar is fitted on the armature shaft with a snap-ring. Tap the pinion stop collar, back off the pinion stop collar towards the overrunning clutch using a suitable piece of tubing over the armature shaft, and remove the snap-ring, the pinion stop collar and overrunning clutch.
14 Clean the component parts prior to inspection for wear or damage. Do not use grease-dissolving cleaning solvent for the overrunning clutch, armature, solenoid and field coils.
15 Undercut the mica separators using an old hacksaw blade ground to suit. The commutator can be polished with a piece of fine glass paper, if very rough it will need skimming on a lathe.
16 Inspect the pinion and screw sleeve of the overrunning clutch. The screw sleeve must slide freely along the armature shaft splines. Inspect the pinion teeth, if excessive wear is found, renew the clutch and check the flywheel ring gear.
17 Reassembly is the reverse of the removal sequence. When fitting the pinion stop collar ensure that the snap-ring is located in its groove. At assembly lightly oil the sliding surface of the overrunning clutch, the drive lever, commutator shaft bushing and grease the end frame cap.
18 After assembly check the clearance between the pinion and the pinion stop collar with the solenoid connected to the battery as shown in Fig. 10.20, If necessary, adjust the length of the solenoid stud bolt to obtain the dimension shown in Fig. 10.14.

15 Windshield wipers and washers - description

The windshield wiper motor is of the two-speed type. On FF-1 models it is mounted in the compartment behind the firewall and on later models it is mounted on the front of the firewall. The wiper spindle is interlocked by a linkage of a rod and crank to the output spindle of the motor.

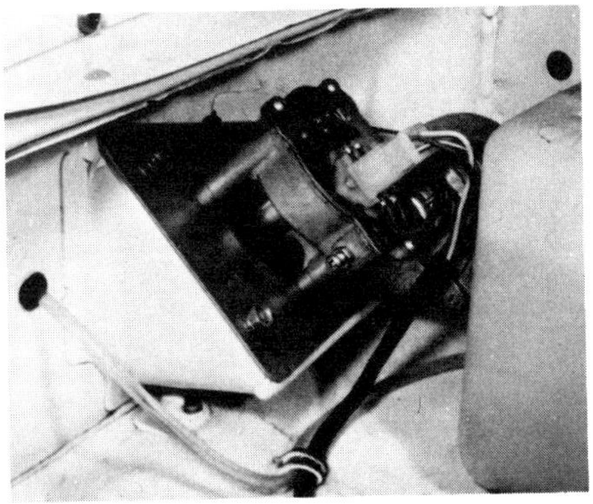

15.1 The windshield wiper motor is mounted on the firewall

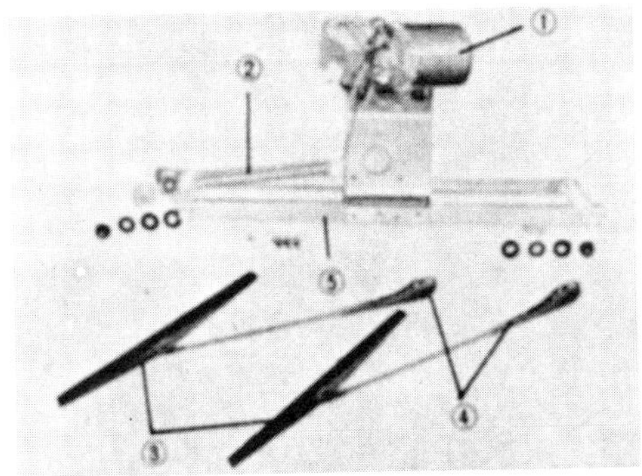

Fig. 10.21. Windshield wiper components (FF - 1 models)

1 Motor
2 Link
3 Blade
4 Arm
5 Frame

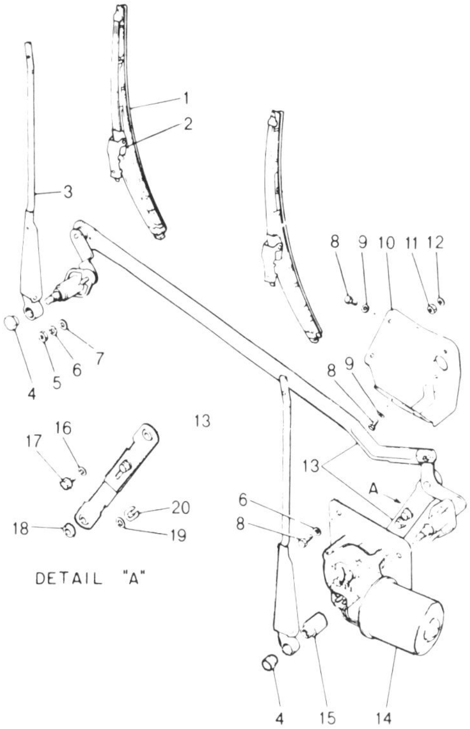

Fig. 10.22. Windshield wiper components (later models)

1 Wiper blade
2 Wiper blade clip
3 Wiper arm
4 Special nut
5 Nut
6 Spring washer
7 Washer
8 Bolt (6 x 16 mm)
9 Spring washer
10 Bracket
11 Nut
12 Spring washer
13 Link assembly
14 Wiper motor
15 Cap
16 Spring washer
17 Flange bolt
18 Packing
19 Washer
20 Clip

The electrically operated windshield washer unit (motor, reservoir and pump) is located in the engine compartment on the left-hand side in front of the firewall.

A combined wiper/washer switch is fitted. The switch operates the wipers in two stages and the washer is operated by holding the knob in against its spring. It should not be held in the 'ON' position for more than 30 seconds at a time.

At two yearly intervals, or earlier if the windshield is not being wiped effectively, renew the wiper blades.

Never operate the washer without liquid in the reservoir.

16 Windshield wiper arm and blade - removal and refitting

1 Before removing a wiper arm, turn the windshield wiper switch on and off to ensure that the arms are in their normal parked position parallel with the bottom of the windshield.

2 To remove the arm, pivot the arm back, undo the arm securing nut and lift the arm off the spindle.

3 When refitting the arm, position it so that it is in the parked position and fit the securing nut.

4 The blade is removed from the arm by depressing the retaining spring and pulling it out. To refit the blade just press it into the arm.

17 Windshield wiper mechanism - fault diagnosis

1 Should the windshield wipers fail, or operate very slowly, check the terminals for loose connections and make sure the insulation of the external wiring is not broken or cracked. If this is in order then check the current the motor is taking by connecting a 1 - 20 volt ammeter in series in the circuit and switch on the wipers. Consumption should be less than 2.5 amps on high speed for FF-1 models and 2 and 3 amps respectively for later models.

2 If no current is flowing check that the fuse has not blown. The correct rating is 10 amps. If it has blown, check the wiring of the motor and other electrical circuits serviced by the same fuse for short circuits. If the fuse is not blown check the wiper/washer switch.

3 If the motor takes a high current it is an indication that there is an internal fault or partially seized linkage.

4 The motor can be dismantled and overhauled, but it is recommended that a faulty motor be taken to an automobile electrician or replaced with a new unit.

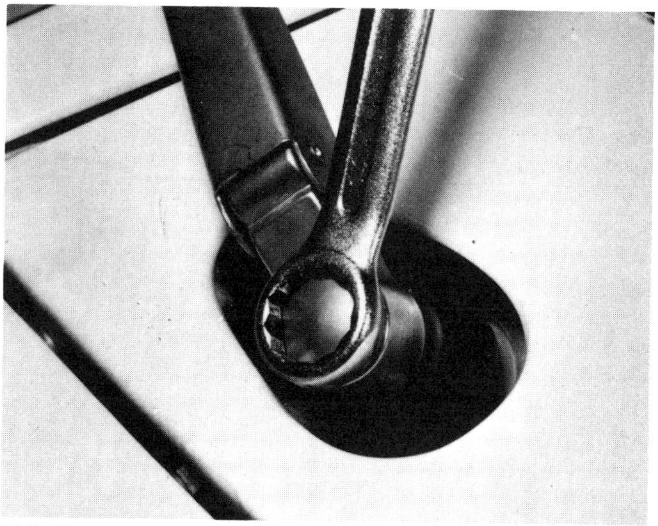

16.2a Remove the windshield wiper arm securing nut ...

16.2b ... and lift the wiper arm off

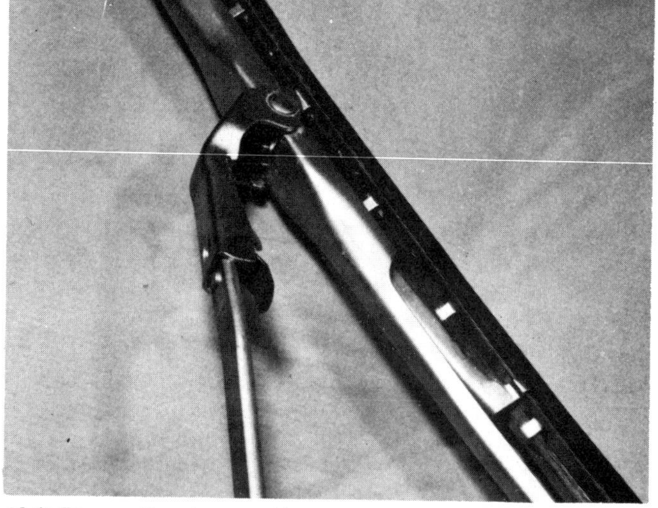

16.4a Remove the wiper arm blade by depressing the retaining spring ...

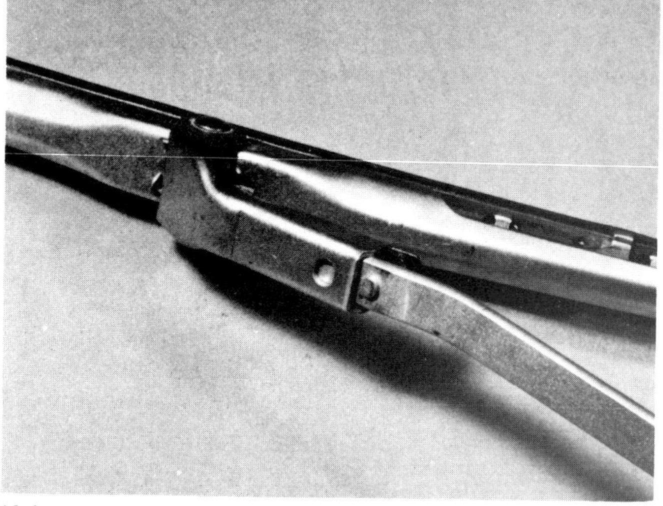

16.4b ... and then pull the blade out

18 Wiper motor and linkage - removal and replacement

FF-1 models

1 Disconnect the wiring from the wiper motor and loosen the speedometer installing spring.
2 Remove the wiper arms complete with blades.
3 Remove the wiper shaft retaining nut, rubber cap, packing and washer.
4 Undo both wiper motor securing bolts and remove the wiper motor.
5 Refitting is the reverse of removal.

Models from 1972 onwards

6 Disconnect the wiper motor wiring.
7 Remove the wiper arms and blades.
8 Remove the six cowl panel securing screws and lift off the panel.
9 Remove the two wiper link mounting nuts and the four wiper bracket mounting bolts.
10 Remove the windshield washer reservoir by pulling it upwards.
11 Remove the three wiper motor mounting bolts and pull out the wiper motor and link assembly. Separate the motor and link by removing the securing clip, see Fig. 10.24.
12 Refitting is the reverse of the removal sequence. If necessary adjust the link by loosening the flange bolts so that the center, 'a' in Fig. 10.25 is aligned with the body center line.
Note: From 1976 the wiper link to motor connection changed to a simpler type using plastic to eliminate rattling noises. After fitting adjust the wiper link as follows:

a) Refer to Fig. 10.26. If the distance 'a' is longer than 'b' adjust the link to make them equal by loosening the adjusting bolts and increasing the length of rod 'A'.
b) If 'a' is shorter than 'b', decrease the length of rod 'A' to make them equal.
c) To obtain the link positions of 'a' and 'b', turn the wiper switch to OFF with the ignition switch at 'ACC' position.

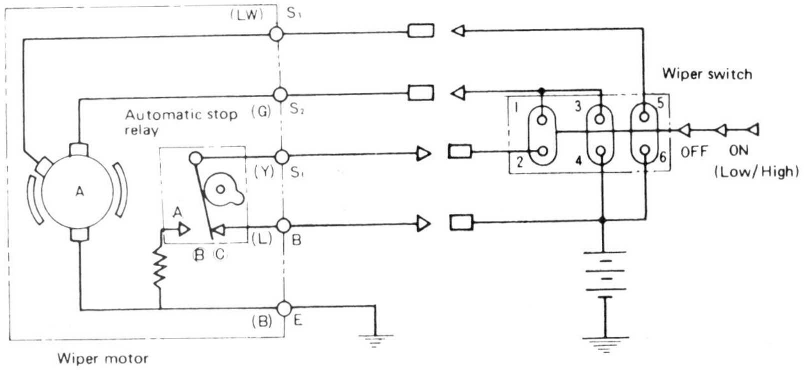

Fig. 10.23. Windshield wiper wiring diagram

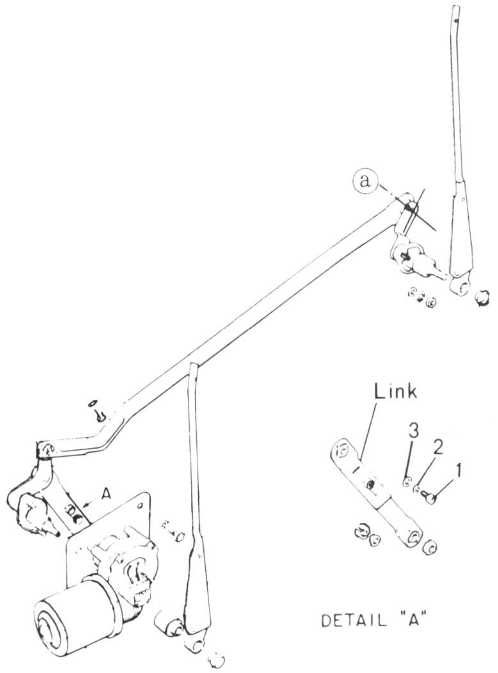

Fig. 10.25. Adjusting link mechanism

1 Flange bolt
2 Spring washer
3 Washer

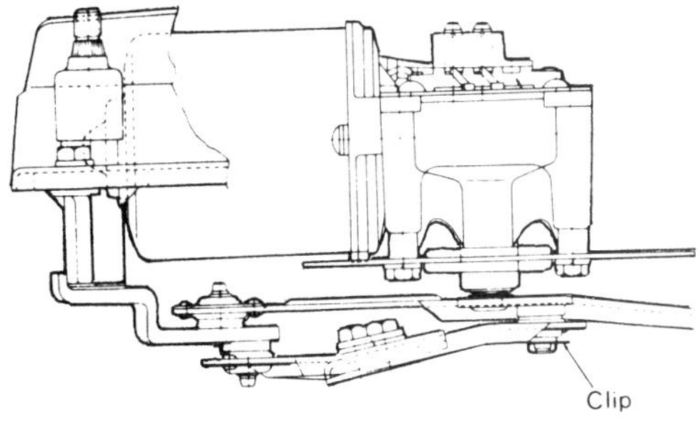

Fig. 10.24. Removing the securing clip

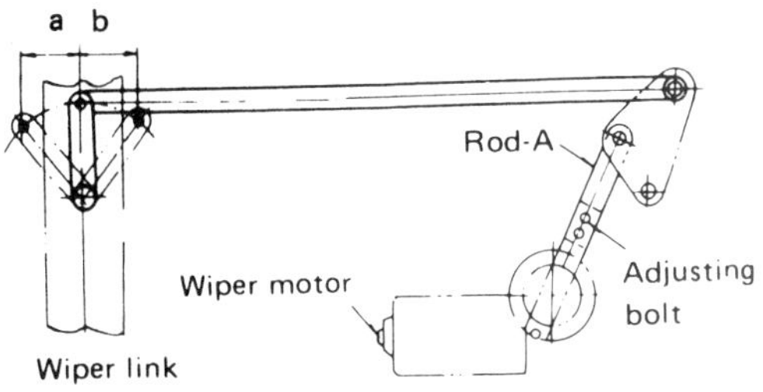

Fig. 10.26. Wiper link adjustment (from 1976)

19 Rear window wiper (4WD only) - removal and refitting

1 Remove the inner trim of the back door.
2 Disconnect the wiring to the wiper motor.
3 Remove the three bolts securing the wiper motor bracket to the door panel.
4 Remove the wiper arm and the shaft retaining nut.
5 Remove the clip joining the link and motor.
6 Refitting is the reverse of the removal procedure.

20 Rear window washer - tank and pump

A long pipe connects the rear washer nozzle and tank giving a considerable fall. To prevent flow from the pipe to the tank a check valve is provided at the tank side of the pipe. Should the tank be completely emptied before refilling the pump may become air-locked. If this happens compress the tank lightly to expel the air from the pump.

21 Instrument cluster - removal and refitting

1 This Section describes the removal of the instrument cluster. Removal of the instrument panel is described in Chapter 12.

FF-1 models

2 Disconnect the ground lead from the battery negative terminal.
3 Disconnect the speedometer cable by reaching behind the instrument panel and loosening the securing nut.
4 Pull the instrument wiring connector downwards to disconnect it from the socket.
5 Loosen the cluster retaining springs and pull the assembly forward out of the instrument panel.
6 Refitting is the reverse of removal.

All other models

7 Disconnect the ground lead from the negative terminal of the battery.
8 Disconnect the side ventilation duct by loosening the clamp.

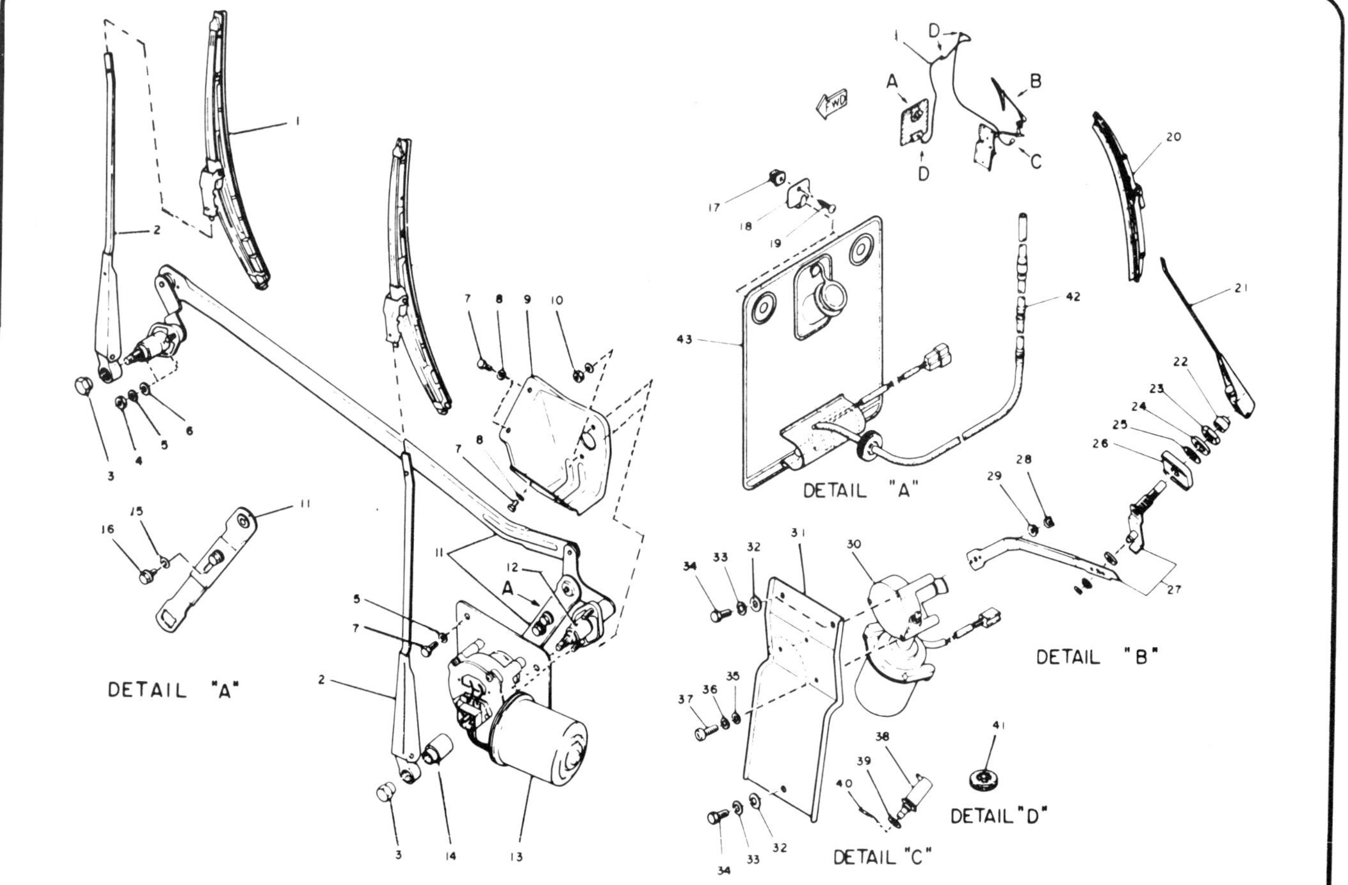

Fig. 10.27. Front and rear wiper components (4WD)

1 Wiper blade
2 Wiper arm
3 Special nut
4 Nut
5 Spring washer
6 Washer
7 Bolt
8 Washer
9 Bracket (wiper)
10 Flange nut
11 Wiper link
12 Sleeve unit
13 Wiper motor
14 Cap (wiper)
15 Washer
16 Flange bolt
17 Nut
18 Hanger (washer tank)
19 Screw (pan head)
20 Wiper blade
21 Wiper arm
22 Cap (wiper)
23 Nut (wiper)
24 Washer (wiper)
25 Rubber (cushion A)
26 Rubber (cushion B)
27 Wiper link
28 Stopper
29 Washer
30 Wiper motor
31 Bracket
32 Washer
33 Spring washer
34 Bolt
35 Washer
36 Spring washer
37 Screw (pan head)
38 Nozzle
39 Gasket
40 Clip (wiper washer nozzle)
41 Grommet
42 Hose (rear washer)
43 Washer tank (rear)

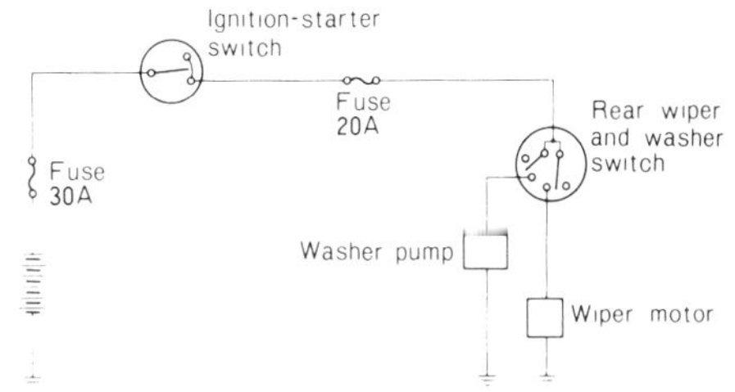

Fig. 10.28. Rear window wiper and washer pump diagram (4WD)

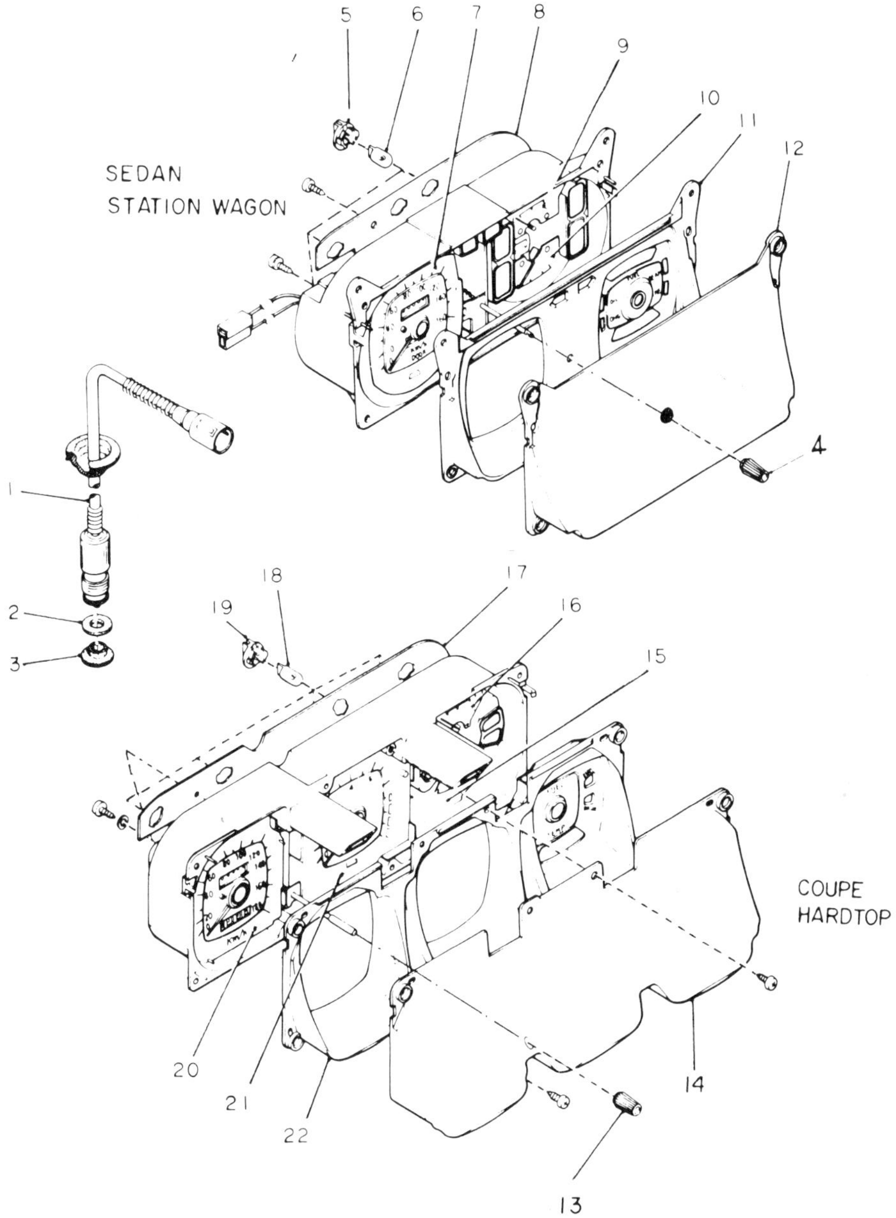

Fig. 10.29. Disassembled view of instrument cluster (later models)

1 *Speedometer cable*
2 *Washer*
3 *Washer*
4 *Knob (trip meter)*
5 *Socket*
6 *Bulb*
7 *Speedometer*
8 *Printed wiring plate*
9 *Fuel meter*
10 *Thermometer*
11 *Window plate*
12 *Front acrylic*
13 *Knob (trip meter) ... California models*
14 *Front acrylic*
15 *Thermometer*
16 *Fuel meter*
17 *Printed wiring plate*
18 *Bulb*
19 *Socket*
20 *Speedometer*
21 *Engine tachometer*
22 *Window plate*

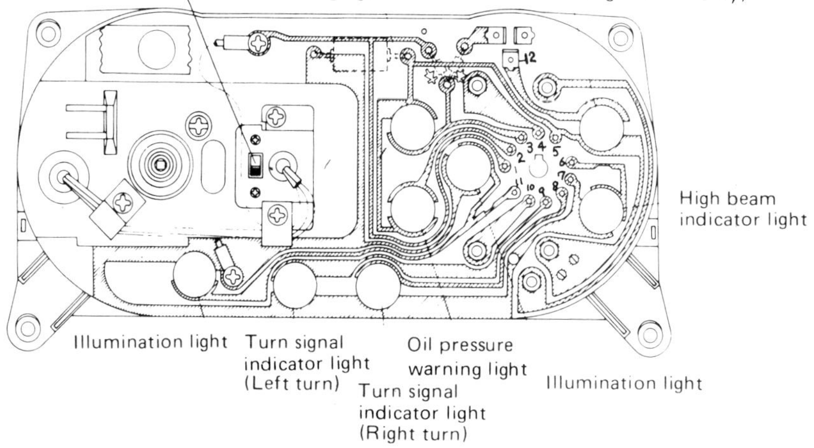

Fig. 10.30a. View of back of instrument cluster (later models) - Sedan, Station Wagon, and 4WD

1 *EGR warning light reset switch*
2 *Oil pressure warning light*
3 *Charge warning light*
4 *Thermometer*
5 *Ignition switch*
6 *High beam indicator light*
7 *Ground*
8 *Turn signal indicator light (right)*
9 *Turn signal indicator light (left)*
10 *Fuel meter*
11 *Illumination light*
12 *4WD indicator light*

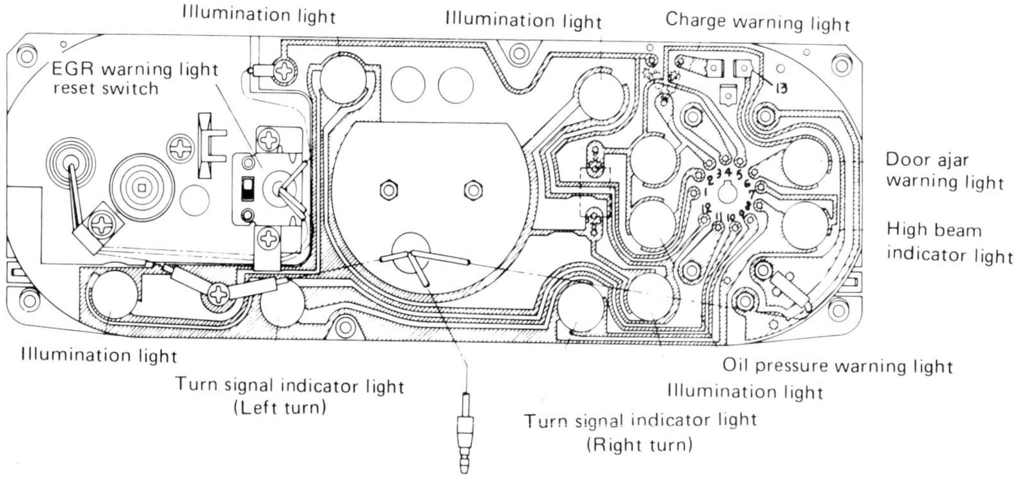

Fig. 10.30b. View of back of instrument cluster (later models) - Coupe and Hardtop

1 *EGR warning light reset switch*
2 *Oil pressure warning light*
3 *Charge warning light*
4 *Thermometer*
5 *Ignition switch*
6 *Door switch*
7 *High beam indicator light*
8 *Ground*
9 *Turn signal indicator light (right)*
10 *Turn signal indicator light (left)*
11 *Fuel meter*
12 *Illumination light*
13 *Door switch*

9 On Coupe models, working from under the dash, disconnect the rear window defogger switch leads and tachometer lead. Loosen the trip odometer reset knob setscrew and remove the knob.
10 Disconnect the speedometer cable and the junction block.
11 Loosen the retaining screws and remove the cluster from the instrument panel.

22 Speedometer cable - removal and refitting

1 Disconnect the speedometer cable from the transmission.
2 Disconnect the other end of the cable from the speedometer by pressing on the end of the retaining hook, refer to Fig. 10.31, and pulling the cable out of the speedometer.
3 Loosen the cable securing clip, remove the grommet and pull the cable into the engine compartment.
4 Refitting is the reverse of removal.

23 Horn - general

1 The horn is mounted in the engine compartment. On later sedan and coupe models two horns are fitted, a high tone and a low tone. Station wagons have only one horn.
2 If the horn does not operate check the fuse. If the fuse is in order check that there is current at the horn connections using a test lamp. If not, examine the wiring and switch contacts.
3 The volume of sound can be adjusted by loosening the locknut and turning the adjusting nut, see Fig. 10.33, counterclockwise to increase the volume and clockwise to decrease the volume.

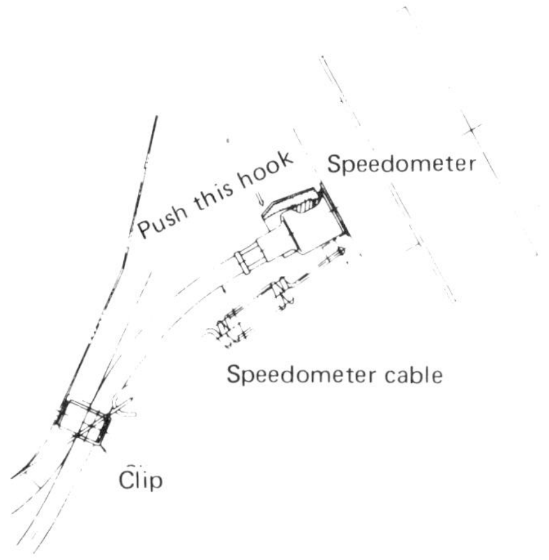

Fig. 10.31. Disconnecting the speedometer cable from the speedometer

23.1 The horn is mounted in the engine compartment

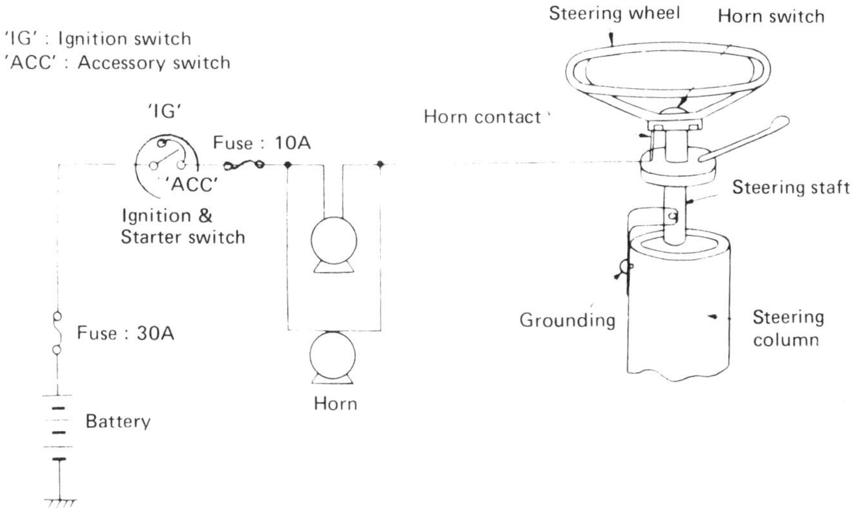

Fig. 10.32. Horn wiring diagram

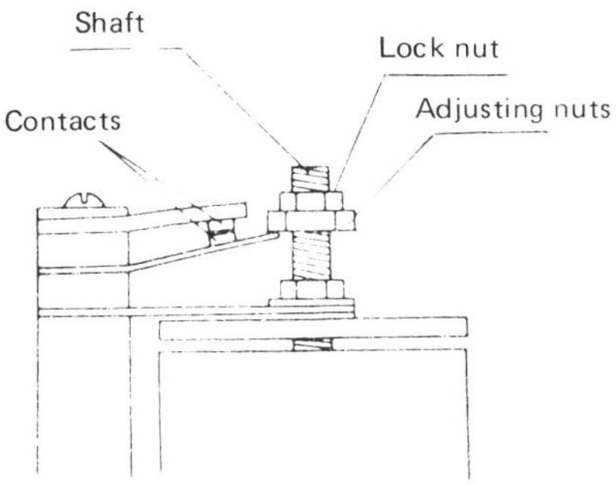

Fig. 10.33. Adjusting the horn contacts

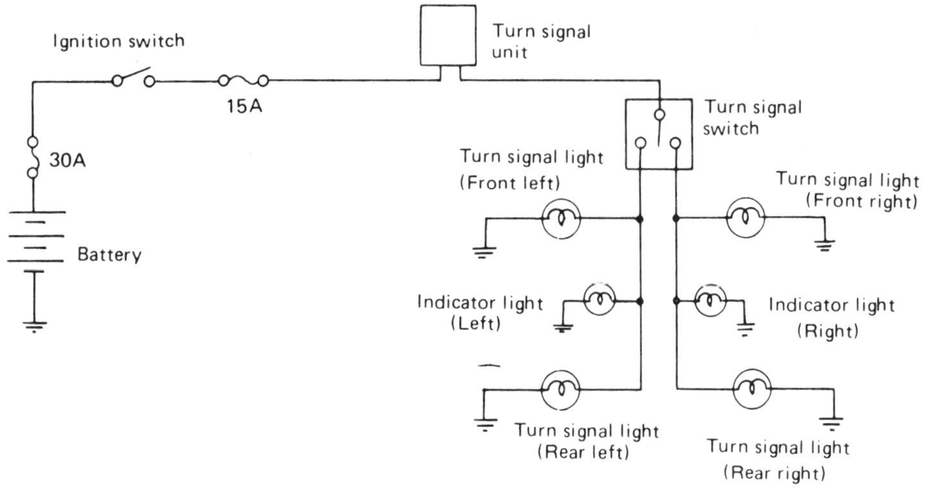

Fig. 10.34. Turn signal wiring diagram - all models except Station Wagon

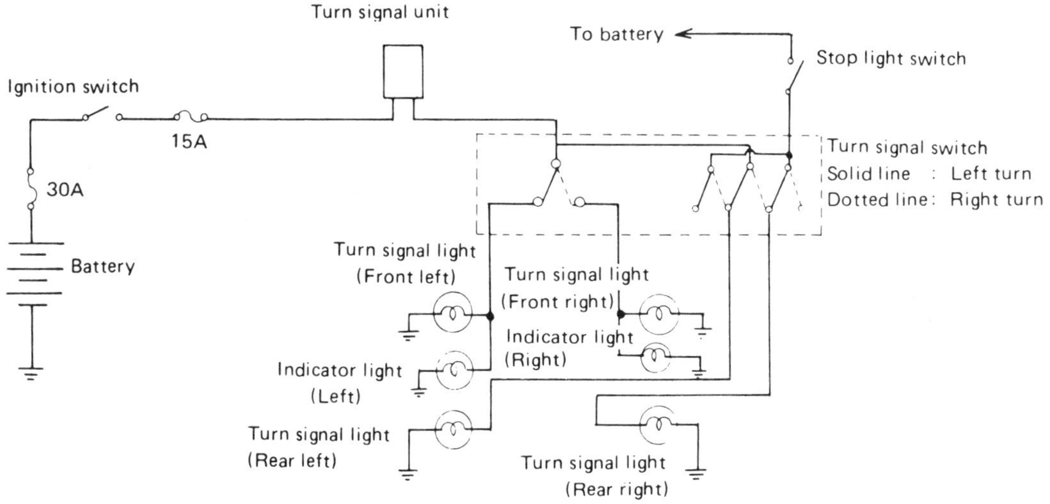

Fig. 10.35. Turn signal wiring diagram for Station Wagon

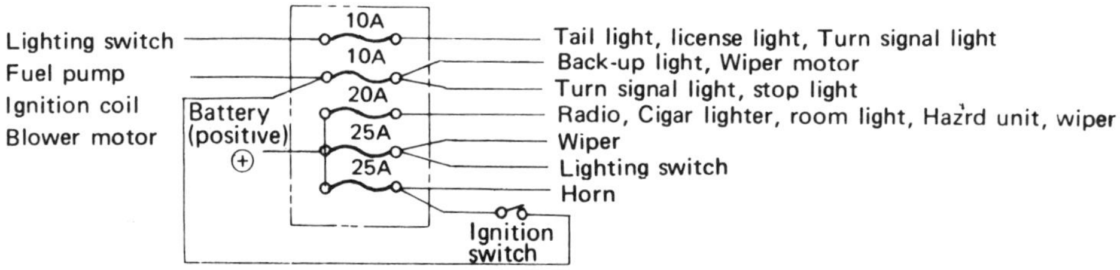

Fig. 10.36. Fuse circuit - 1970

24.1 The turn signal unit and the hazard warning unit are mounted under the instrument panel

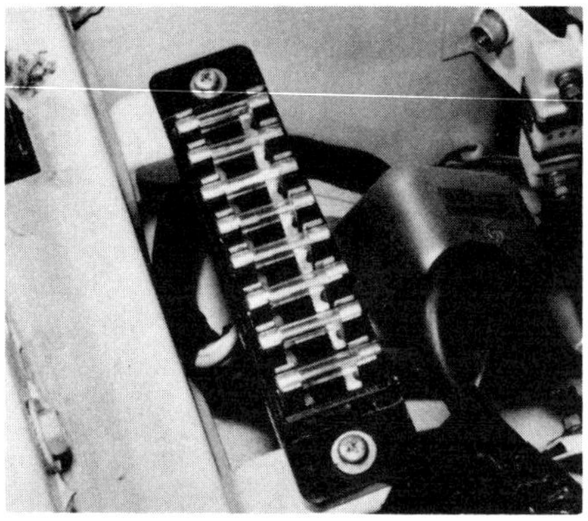

26.1 The fuse box with the cover removed

27.1 Removing the headlamp cover

24 Turn signal unit - general

1 The turn signal unit is mounted underneath the instrument panel. It is removed from the holder by pulling it upwards.
2 Always use the correct bulbs in the turn signal lamps. If bulbs other than those listed in the Specifications at the beginning of this Chapter are used, the intermitting time will be incorrect due to the different current load.
3 When either of the front or rear turn signal lamps are blown the intermittent flashes become uneven and the sound operation disappears. Thus the bulb failure is indicated both visually and audibly.

25 Hazard warning system - description

1 The system comprises a switch and hazard unit. When the switch is actuated all the turn signal lamps illuminate simultaneously as a warning to other drivers that the vehicle is stationary and causing a hazard.
2 The hazard unit is mounted underneath the instrument panel and is removed by pulling it upwards from its holder.

26 Fuses

1 The amperage of each fuse is marked on the cover of the fuse box, which is mounted on the left front fender inside the engine compartment of FF-1 models. Later models have it mounted on the right-hand front wheel arch under the hood.
2 The accessories and circuits protected by the individual fuses are shown in Figs. 10.36 to 10.38
3 If a fuse blows always establish the cause before fitting a new one. To trace the cause of a blown fuse, disconnect each of the switches, lamps, etc, fed by the fuse, in turn until the fault is located. Intermittent short-circuits are almost invariably due to wiring and connector faults.
4 Always uses fuses of the correct amperage and never be tempted to use a piece of wire in place of a blown fuse as this could cause a fire or at least result in serious damage to electrical components.

27 Headlamp - removal and refitting

1 Remove the headlamp cover by loosening the three retaining screws.

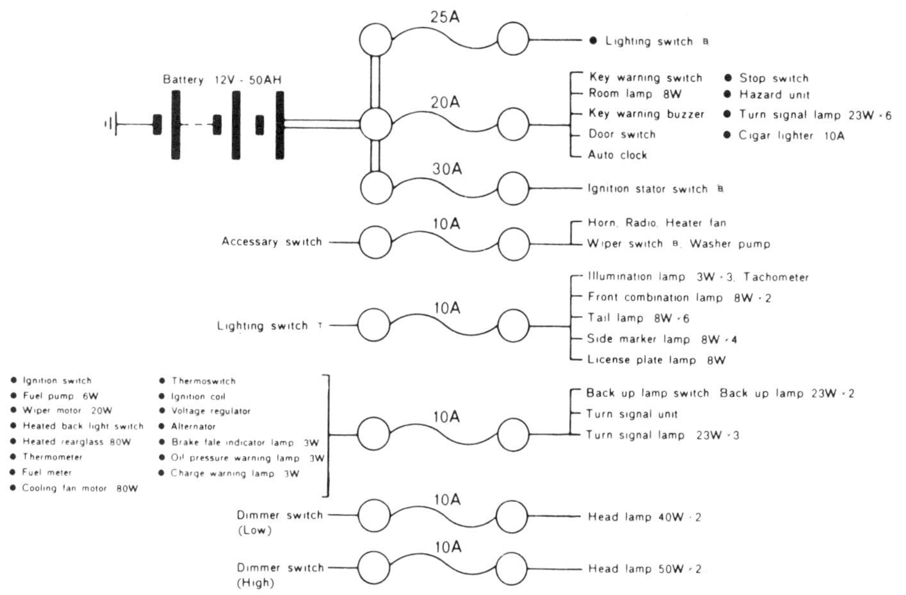

Fig. 10.37. Fuse circuit - 1972

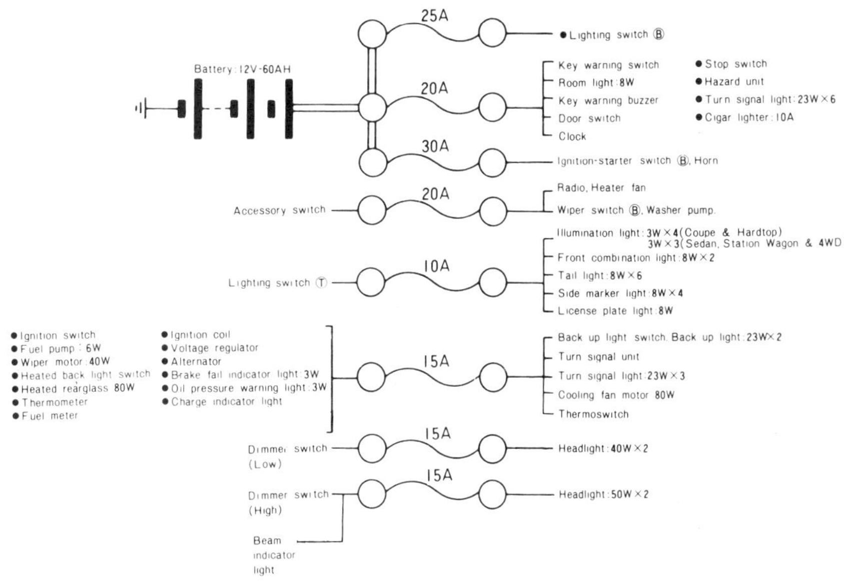

Fig. 10.38. Fuse circuit - 1975

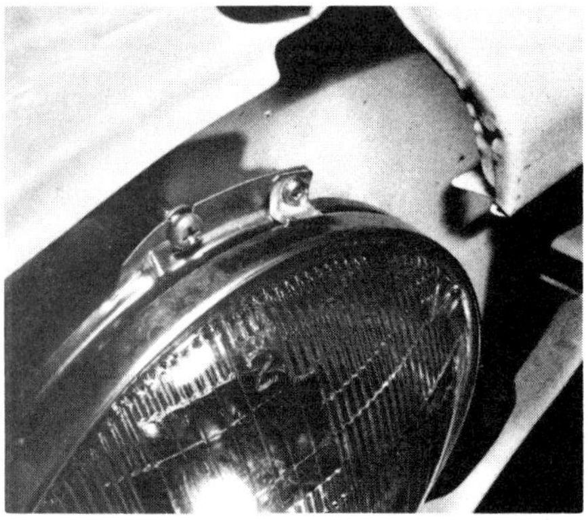

27.2a Remove the headlamp retaining screws ...

27.2b ... and disconnect the socket at the back of the lamp

29.1 Remove the lens from the front combination lamp ...

29.2 ... and then renew the bulb

30.1 Remove the lens securing screws, take off the lens

30.2 ... and renew the bulb

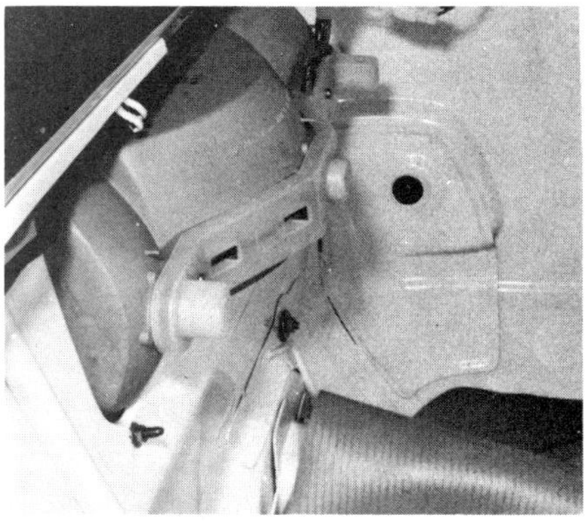

31.2a Remove the rear combination lamp securing screws

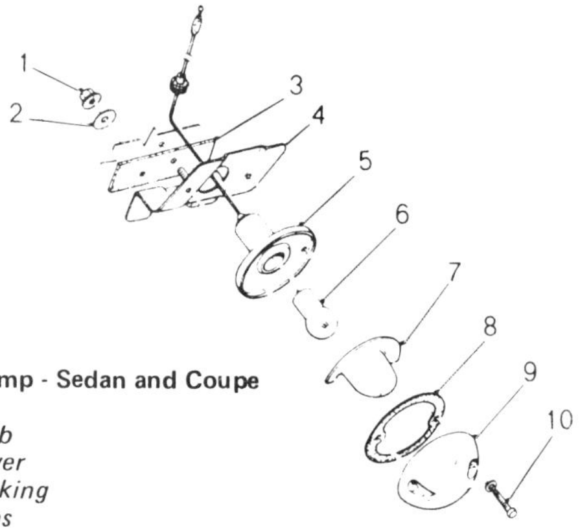

Fig. 10.39. Exploded view of license plate lamp - Sedan and Coupe

1 Flange nut
2 Washer
3 Packing
4 Bracket
5 Receptacle
6 Bulb
7 Cover
8 Packing
9 Lens
10 Screw

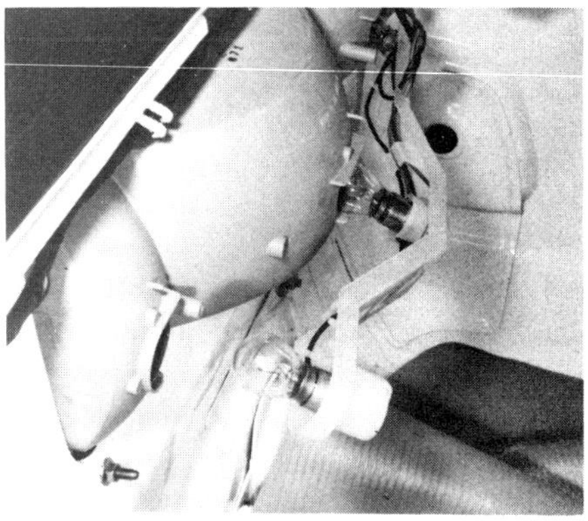

31.2b Pull out the cover assembly and renew the bulbs

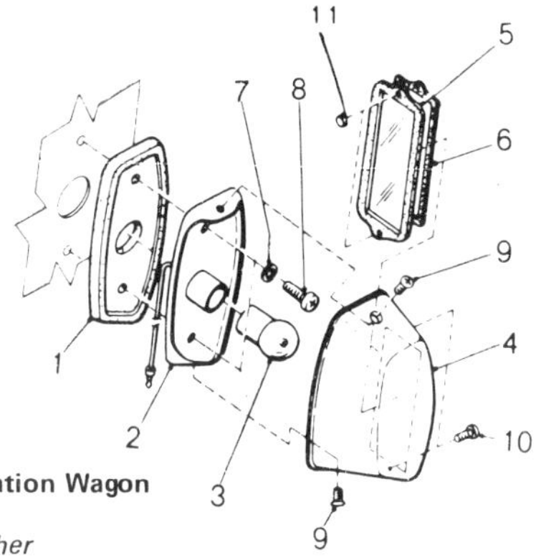

Fig. 10.40. Exploded view of license plate lamp - Station Wagon

1 Base
2 Socket
3 Bulb
4 Glove
5 Lens
6 Packing
7 Spring washer
8 Screw
9 Screw
10 Screw
11 Nut

2 Remove the headlamp retaining ring and disconnect the socket from the back of the headlamp.
3 Disconnect the headlamp holding spring then remove the headlamp. Do not disturb the setting of the headlamp beam adjusting screws.
4 Refitting is the reverse of removal.

28 Headlamp - adjustment

Adjustment of the headlamp beam requires special equipment and this should be left to a service station with the appropriate equipment.

29 Front combination lamp - bulb renewal

1 Undo and remove the screws securing the lens and retaining ring. Remove the retaining ring and lens.
2 Remove the bulb by pushing it in and turning it counterclockwise to release the bayonet connection.
3 Refitting the bulb is the reverse of the removal sequence. Check that the seal is in good order and that the lens fits snugly.

30 Side reflex - reflector and marker lamp - bulb renewal

1 Remove the lens securing screws and lift off the lens.
2 Remove the bulb by turning it counterclockwise while pushing it in to release the bayonet connection.
3 Refitting is the reverse of removal. Ensure the seal is in good condition.

31 Rear combination lamp - bulb renewal

Sedan and Coupe
1 Access to the rear combination lamp bulbs is from inside the trunk.
2 Remove the two rear cover retaining screws and lift off the cover. Remove the defective bulb from the cover.

Station Wagon
3 Remove the rear combination lamp assembly from the body by undoing the six retaining screws.
4 Remove the bulb from its holder.
5 Refitting is the reverse of removal.

32 License plate lamp - removal and refitting

Sedan and Coupe
1 Disconnect the wiring from the license plate lamp.
2 Loosen the two nuts, which secure the license plate lamp, from inside the trunk and remove the lamp assembly.
3 Loosen the securing nut and remove the license plate lamp from the cover.

Station wagon
4 Disconnect the wiring from the license plate lamp.
5 Undo the two screws which secure the license plate lamp assembly and remove the assembly from the body.
6 Undo the securing nut and remove the license plate lamp from the cover.
7 Refitting is the reverse of the removal sequence.

33 Interior lamp and bulb - removal and refitting

1 Remove the lens by turning it until the 'OEW' mark comes near the lever, and then pull it down.
2 The bulb is removed by pulling it from the holder.
3 To remove the lamp undo the two securing screws and disconnect the wiring.
4 Refitting is the reverse of removal sequence.

34 Combination switch - removal and refitting

1 The combination switch is fitted on the steering column and comprises the turn signal, hazard switch, headlamp beam control switch, windshield wiper switch and windshield washer switch.
2 Remove the steering wheel as described in Chapter 9.
3 Remove the hazard switch knob.
4 Undo the two combination switch retaining screws and remove the switch from the steering column.
5 Refitting is the reverse of the removal sequence.

35 Lighting switch - removal and refitting

1 Disconnect the ground cable from the battery negative terminal.
2 With a small screwdriver loosen the switch knob securing screw. Unscrew the switch knob.
3 Undo the locknut, disconnect the wiring at the socket and remove the switch from the panel.
4 Refitting is the reverse of the removal sequence.

36 Fuel and coolant temperature gauges - general description

The fuel gauge circuit comprises a tank sender unit, located in the fuel tank, and the fuel gauge. The sender unit has a float attached and this rides on the surface of the gasoline in the tank. At the end of the float arm is a contact and rheostat which controls the current flowing to the fuel gauge.

The coolant temperature gauge circuit comprises a meter and thermal transmitter which is fitted with a thermistor element which converts coolant temperature variations to a resistance. This therefore controls the current flowing to the meter.

The fuel gauge and coolant temperature gauge are provided with a bi-metal arm and heater coil. When the ignition is switched on, current flows and heats the coil. This heat eases the bi-metal arm to curve and this moves the needle.

Because a slight variation may occur on the fuel or coolant temperature gauges due to a fluctuation in voltage, a voltage regulator is used to supply a constant voltage and thus provide more consistent readings.

If both the fuel gauge and coolant temperature gauge are faulty then the voltage regulator must be suspect.

37 Fuel and coolant temperature gauges - removal and refitting

1 Remove the instrument cluster as described in Section 21.
2 Undo the printed circuit board securing screws and remove the printed circuit board.
3 To remove the gauges from the printed circuit board undo the three nuts securing the fuel gauge and the two nuts securing the temperature gauge.
4 Refitting the gauges is the reverse of the removal sequence.

38 Heated rear window - general

1 The heater element of the rear window is controlled by a switch and indicator light. On Coupe and Hardtop models the indicator light is located beside the rear window defogger switch and on Sedan and Station Wagon models it is fitted in the switch.
2 The system is wired in conjunction with the ignition switch to prevent the heater being left on when the vehicle is parked.
3 A break in the heating element can be repaired by your local Subaru dealer, using a conductive silver paint (Dupont 4817), thus saving you the expense of a new window.

39 EGR Warning light (California model only)

1 A switch, which is interlocked to the odometer, is actuated at every 2500^{+200}_{-250} miles to light up the EGR warning light.

40.1 The oil pressure switch fitted beside the oil pump

2 When the warning light comes on the EGR system must be serviced as described in Chapter 3, and the next switch knob changed over to turn off the warning light.
3 The EGR warning light reset switch is located on the back of the instrument cluster.

40 Oil pressure warning light

1 A switch is fitted in the engine lubrication system so that with the ignition switched on, a warning lamp on the instrument panel will light when the engine is not running or if necessary, when the oil pressure is below 2.85 lb/in^2 (0.3 kg/cm^2).

41 Brake failure warning and parking brake pilot lamp

1 The brake failure warning lamp is activated if the brake fluid pressure in one brake line is less than that of the other brake line while the ignition switch is turned on.
2 The parking brake pilot lamp is activated if the parking brake lever is not fully released while the ignition is switched on.
3 The parking brake switch is fitted at the bottom of the parking brake lever, refer to Chapter 9.

42 Seat belt/ignition interlock system - operation

The seat belt and ignition interlock system controls the starter motor and a warning lamp and buzzer.

The car cannot be started until the seat belts are fastened in the correct order. The driver (and front seat passenger) get into the car, close the door and then fasten their seat belts. If the seat belts are not fastened, or if they are fastened before the driver gets into the seat, the car will not start and the warning lamp and buzzer will operate. This prevents the belts being permanently fastened and stowed behind the seats. The sequence is independent for the driver and passenger.

In the event of a failure in the seat belt and ignition interlock system and for convenience when servicing the car, a by-pass switch is provided. The push button type switch is located on the firewall under the hood. If there is a failure in the interlock system and the engine cannot be started in the normal manner, the driver turns the key to 'IGNITION' position, then opens the hood and pushes the by-pass switch button. This allows one start of the engine. If the ignition is switched off the procedure must be repeated.

43 Seat belt/ignition interlock system - description and servicing

1 The seat belt/ignition interlock system comprises the following components: an interlock unit located under the driver's seat, two front seat switches, two seat belt buckle switches, a starter relay, a by-pass switch, a warning buzzer and a warning light. The location of the different components are shown in Fig. 10.41.
2 Repair of the seat belt/ignition interlock components is by renewal of defective items. Special test equipment is required for testing the system and this job should be left to your local Subaru dealer who will have the necessary equipment.
3 If the warning light bulb blows, it can be renewed after removing the instrument cluster as described in Section 21.

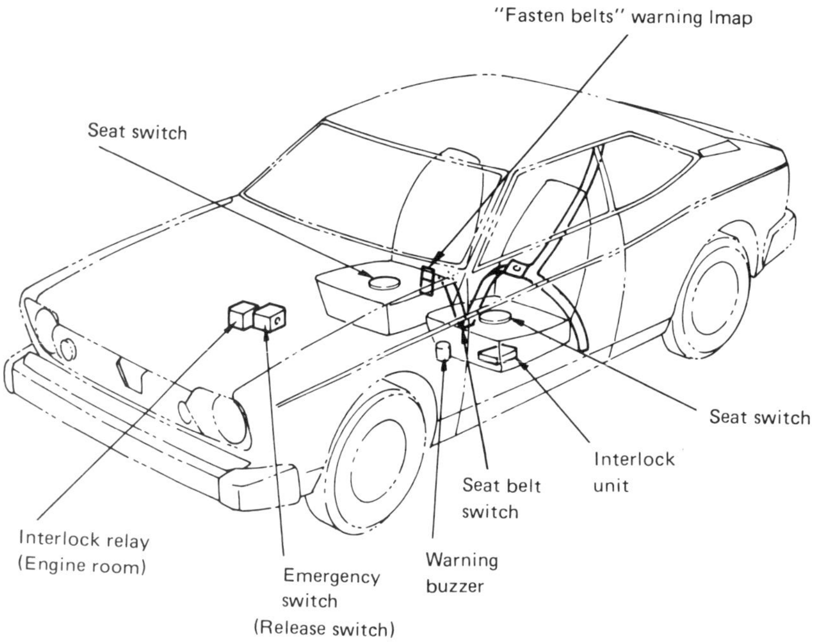

Fig. 10.41. Seat belt interlock system - 1974 models

44 Fault diagnosis

Symptom	Reason/s	Remedy
Starter motor fails to turn engine	Battery discharged Battery connections or ground lead loose Loose or broken connections in starter motor circuit Starter motor switch or solenoid faulty Failure in seat belt/ignition interlock system	Charge battery. Check and tighten leads. Check and rectify. Test and renew as necessary. Operate by-pass switch button, if starter turns have interlock system tested.
Starter motor turns engine very slowly	Battery charge low Starter brushes badly worn, sticking or brush wires loose Loose wires in starter motor circuit	Charge battery. Examine brushes, renew as necessary, secure brush wires. Check and tighten as necessary.
Starter motor operates without turning engine	Starter motor pinion sticking Pinion or flywheel gear teeth broken or worn	Remove starter and clean starter drive. Renew flywheel ring gear and/or starter drive pinion.
Starter motor noisy or excessively rough engagement	Pinion or flywheel ring gear teeth broken or worn Starter drive main spring broken Starter motor mounting bolts loose	Renew flywheel ring gear and/or starter drive pinion. Renew spring. Tighten mounting bolts.
Battery does not hold charge for more than a few days	Battery defective externally Electrolyte too weak or level too low Alternator drive belt slipping Alternator not charging properly Short in lighting circuit causing battery drain	Fit new battery. Top up electrolyte level. Check belt for wear and renew/adjust as necessary. Have charging system checked by specialist. Trace and rectify.
Charge light fails to go out, battery runs flat in a few days	Alternator drive belt loose or broken Fault in charging system	Check belt and renew and adjust as necessary. Have charging system checked by a specialist.
Horn operates all the time	Horn push grounded or stuck down	Disconnect ground lead from battery. Check and rectify fault.
Horn fails to operate	Blown fuse Wiring loose, broken or disconnected Defective horn	Check and renew if blown. Check for cause of fuse failure. Check all wiring and connections. Renew horn.
Horn emits intermittent or insufficient sound	Wiring loose or dirty connections Horn incorrectly adjusted	Clean and tighten as necessary. Adjust horn to obtain correct sound.
Lights do not come on	If engine not running, battery discharged Bulb filament burnt out Wiring loose, broken or disconnected Light switch faulty	Charge battery. Renew bulb. Check all connections and wiring. Rectify or renew switch.
Lights come on but fade out	If engine not running battery charge low	Charge battery.
Lights work erratically	Battery terminals and ground connections loose Lights not grounded properly Light switch faulty	Tighten connections. Examine and rectify. Renew switch.
Windshield wipers fail to work	Blown fuse Wiring loose, broken or disconnected Wiper motor faulty Wiper linkage jammed	Check and renew fuse. Check wiring, tighten loose connections. Remove for overhaul. Check and rectify.
Windshield wiper arms move sluggishly	Wiper motor faulty Wiper mechanism sticking or worn	Remove for overhaul. Check and rectify or renew as necessary.
Fuel gauge shows full all the time	Wiring between tank sender and gauge broken or disconnected	Check and rectify.
Fuel gauge gives no reading	Fuel tank empty Wiring between sender unit and gauge grounded. Fuel tank sender unit defective Fuel gauge faulty	Fill fuel tank. Check wiring for grounding. Check and rectify or renew as necessary. Renew gauge.

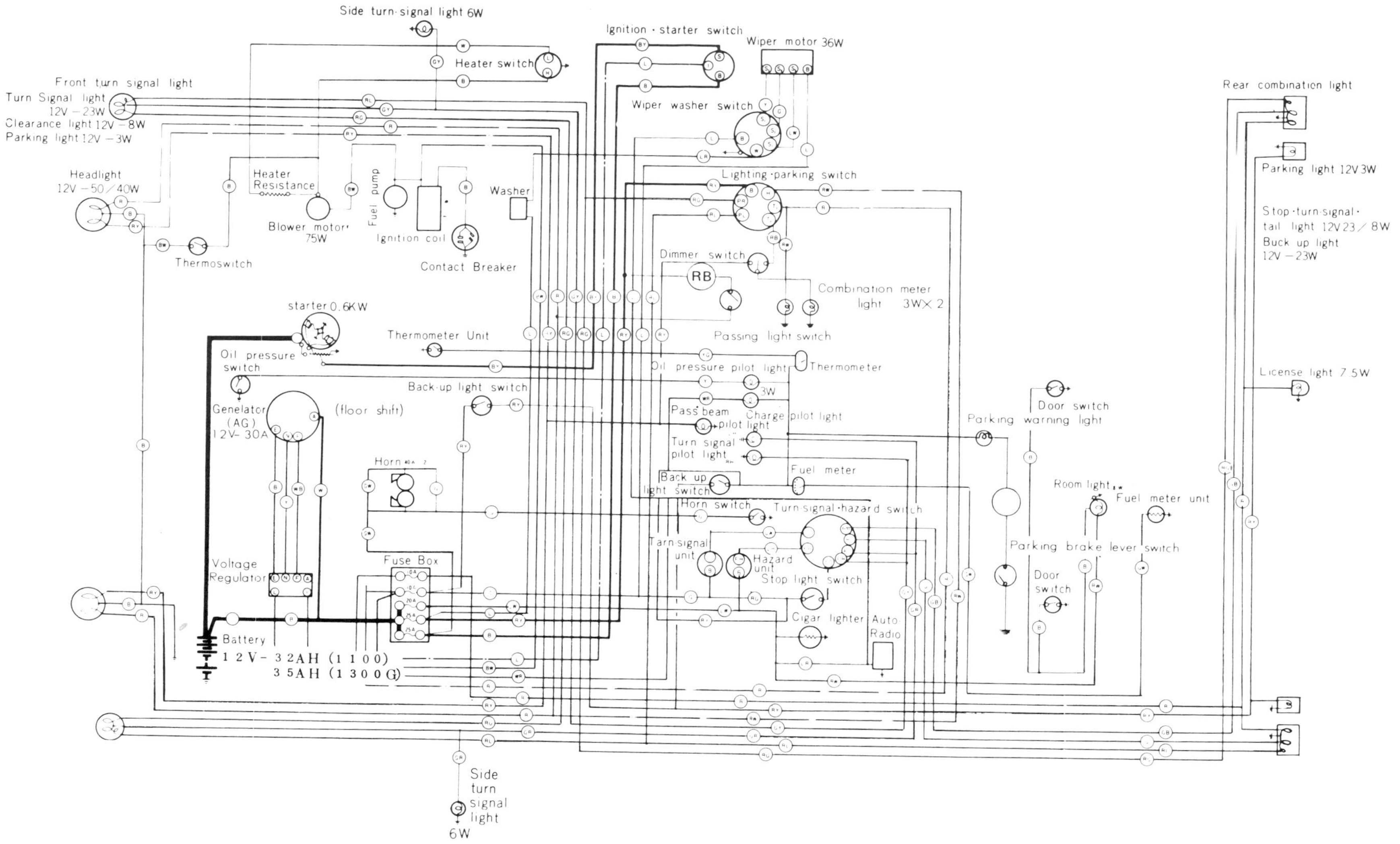

L Blue	LW Blue-white	LR Blue-red			Symbol	Safety Current
R Red	RW Red-white	RG Red-green	RY Red-yellow	RB Red-black		53
G Green	GW Green-white	GR Green-red	GY Green-yellow			16
Y Yellow	YR Yellow-red	YG Yellow-greer				11
W White	WB White-black	WR White-red				9
B Black	BW Black-white	BY Black-yellow				7
Color Code of Electric Wires					Wire Used	

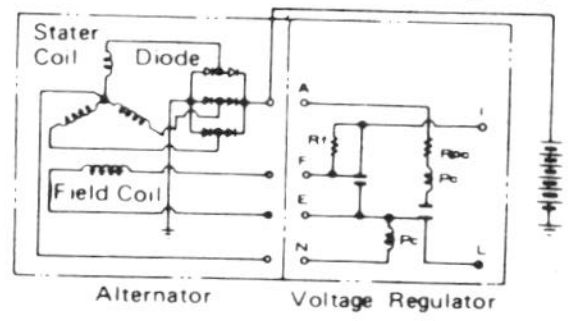

Fig. 10.42. Wiring diagram - 1970 Sedan and Station Wagon

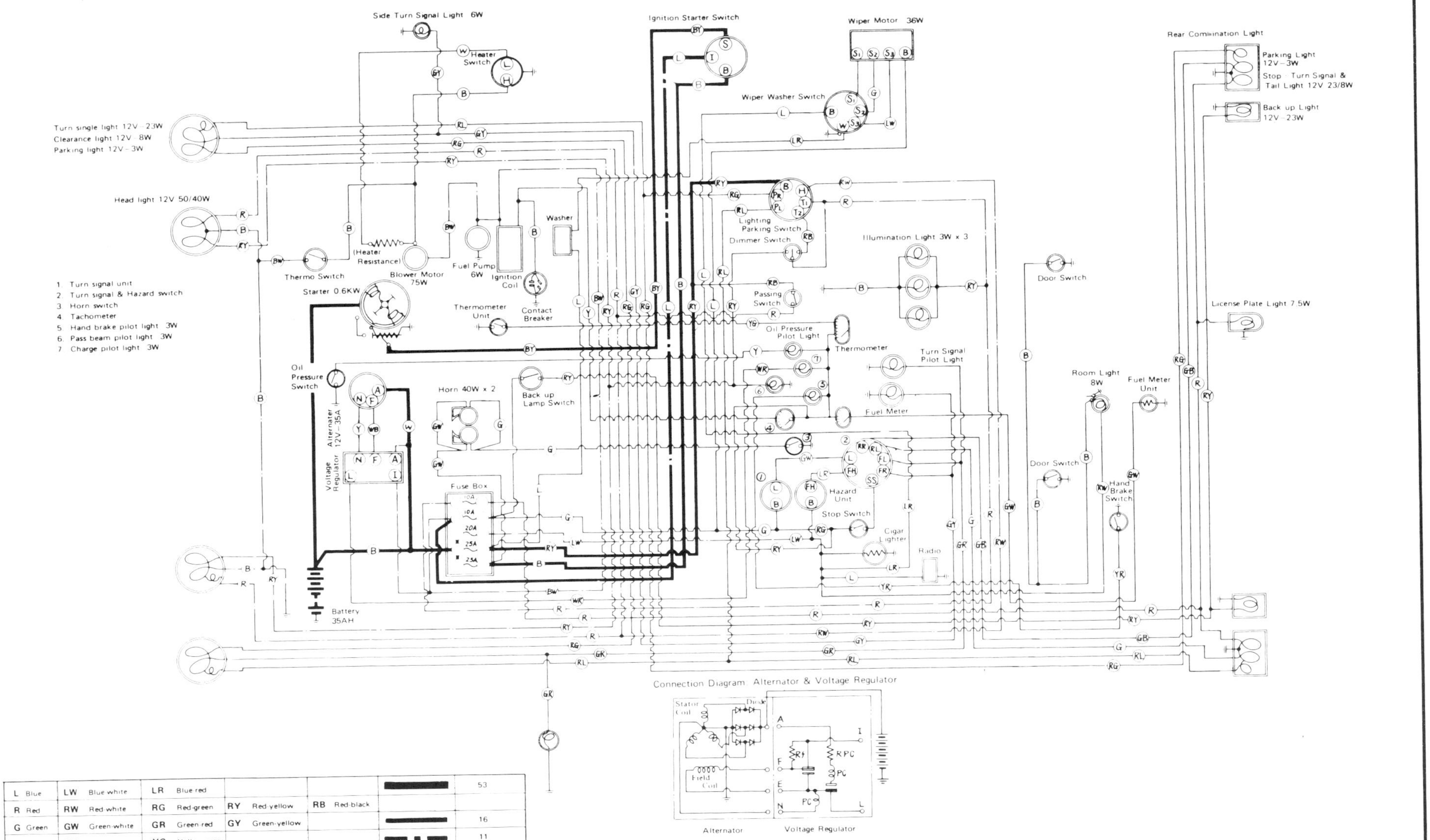

L	Blue	LW	Blue white	LR	Blue red				
R	Red	RW	Red white	RG	Red-green	RY	Red-yellow	RB	Red-black
G	Green	GW	Green-white	GR	Green-red	GY	Green-yellow		
Y	Yellow	YR	Yellow-red	YG	Yellow-green				
W	White	WB	White-black	WR	White-red				
B	Black	BW	Black white	BY	Black-yellow				

Color Code of Electric Wires

Symbol	Safety Current
	53
	16
	11
	9
	7

Wire Used

Fig. 10.43. Wiring diagram - 1970 Sports Sedan

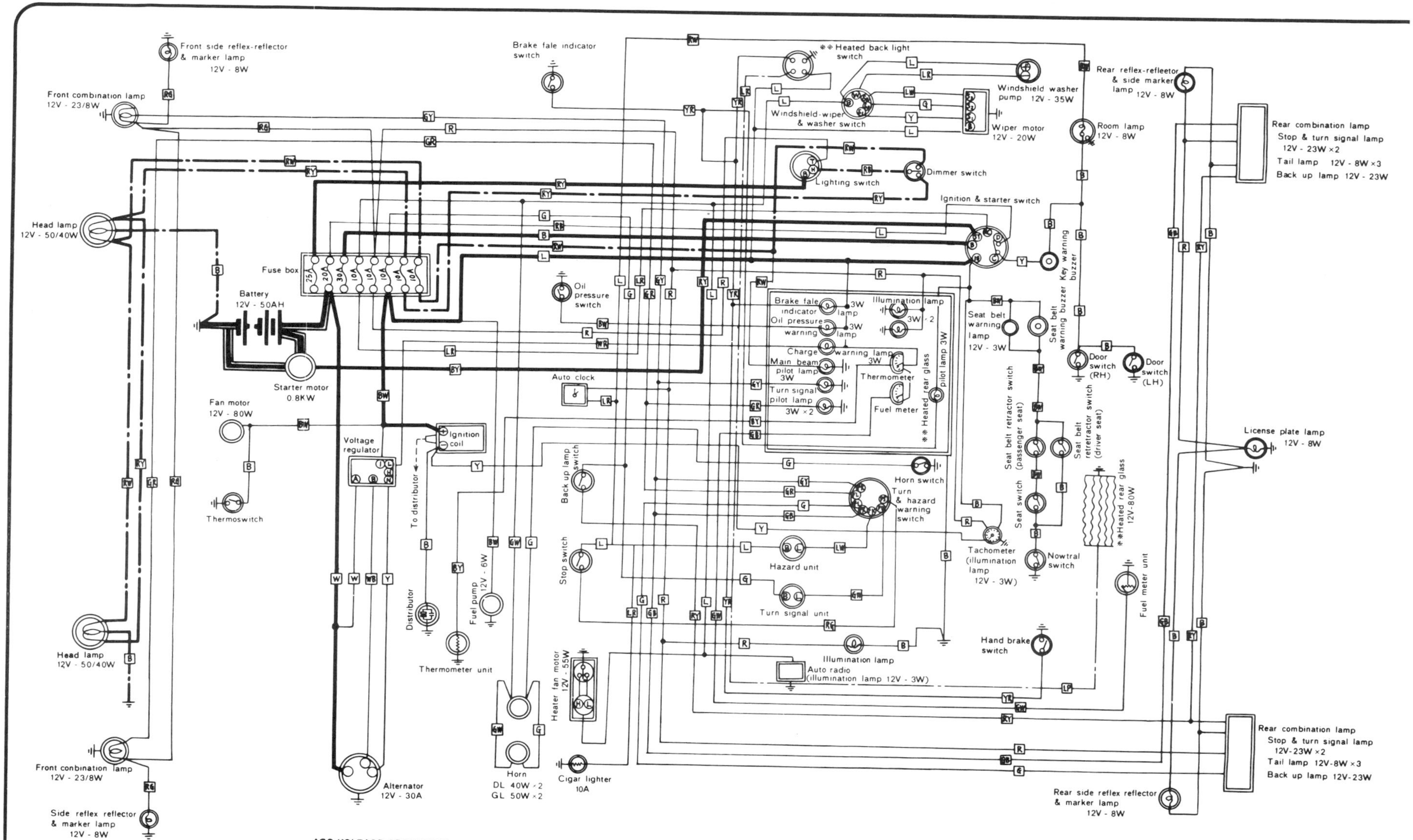

AL	AV20	▬	20.61	84A
	3	▬	3.297	34A
	2	▬	2.091	25A
	1.25	▬ ▬	1.287	19A
	0.85	— - —	0.8846	15A
	AV0.5	——	0.5629	11A
			Section area	Allowable current
Wiring cord used				

ACG-VOLTAGE REGULATOR

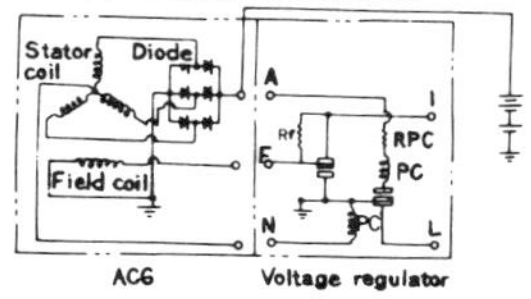

LIGHTING SWITCH

Cord color / Terminal / Switch	RY	RW	R	
	B	H	T	P
OFF				
I	o		o	o
II	o	o	o	o

IGNITION/STARTOR SWITCH

Terminal / Switch	B	IG	ST	ACC	C	D
LOCK					o	o
OFF					o	o
ACC	o			o	o	o
ON	o	o		o	o	o
START	o	o	o		o	o

WINDSHIELD WIPER & WASHER SWITCH

Terminal / Cord color / Switch	S_1	S_2	B	S_3	W	Ground	
	Y	G	L	LW	LR	—	Washer
OFF	o	o			o	o	Turning
I		o	o		o	o	Turning
II			o	o	o	o	Turning

TURN & HAZARD SWITCH

	Terminal / Switch	SS	RR	RL	FU	FR	FL	FH
Turn signal switch	R	o		o				
			o		o	o		
	N	o	o	o				
	L	o	o					
				o	o		o	
Hazard switch	OFF							
	ON		o	o		o	o	o

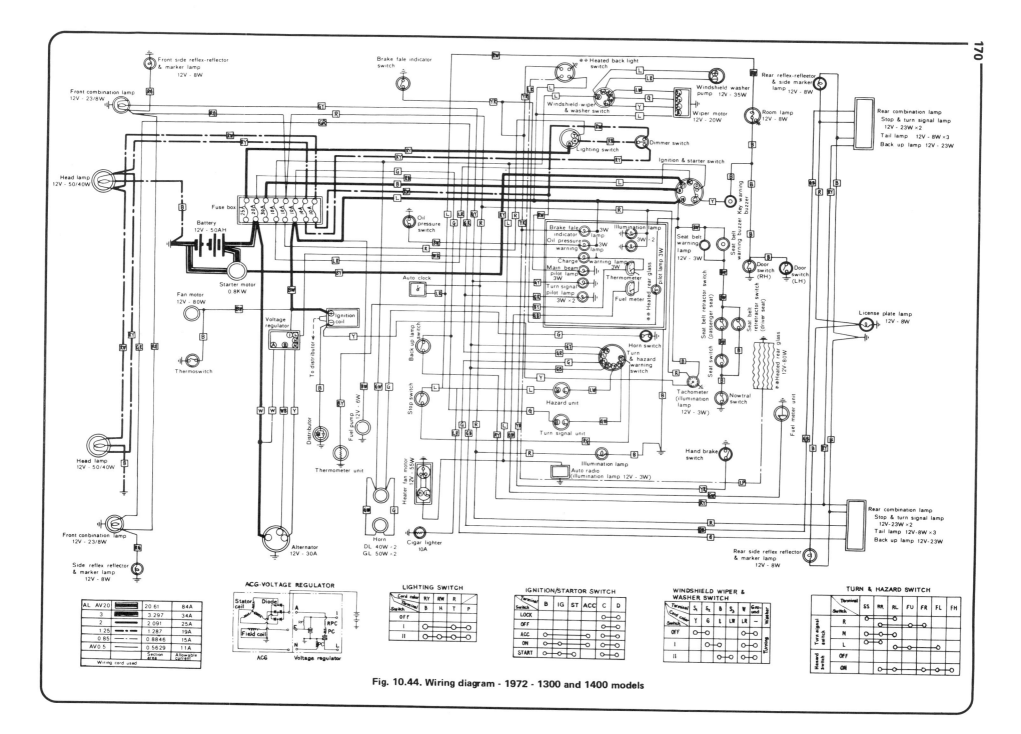

Fig. 10.44. Wiring diagram - 1972 - 1300 and 1400 models

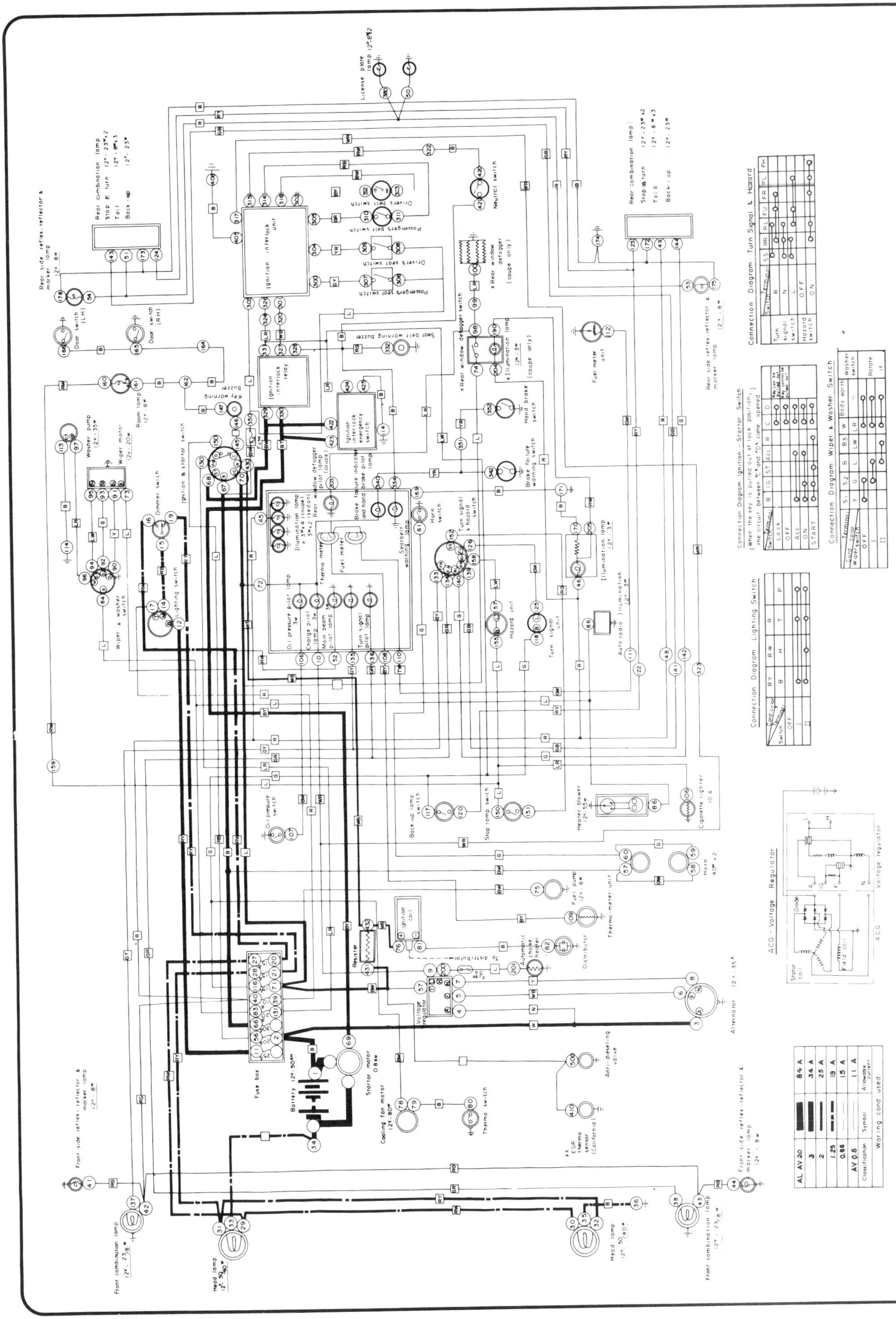

Fig. 10.45. Wiring diagram - 1974 Sedan and Coupe

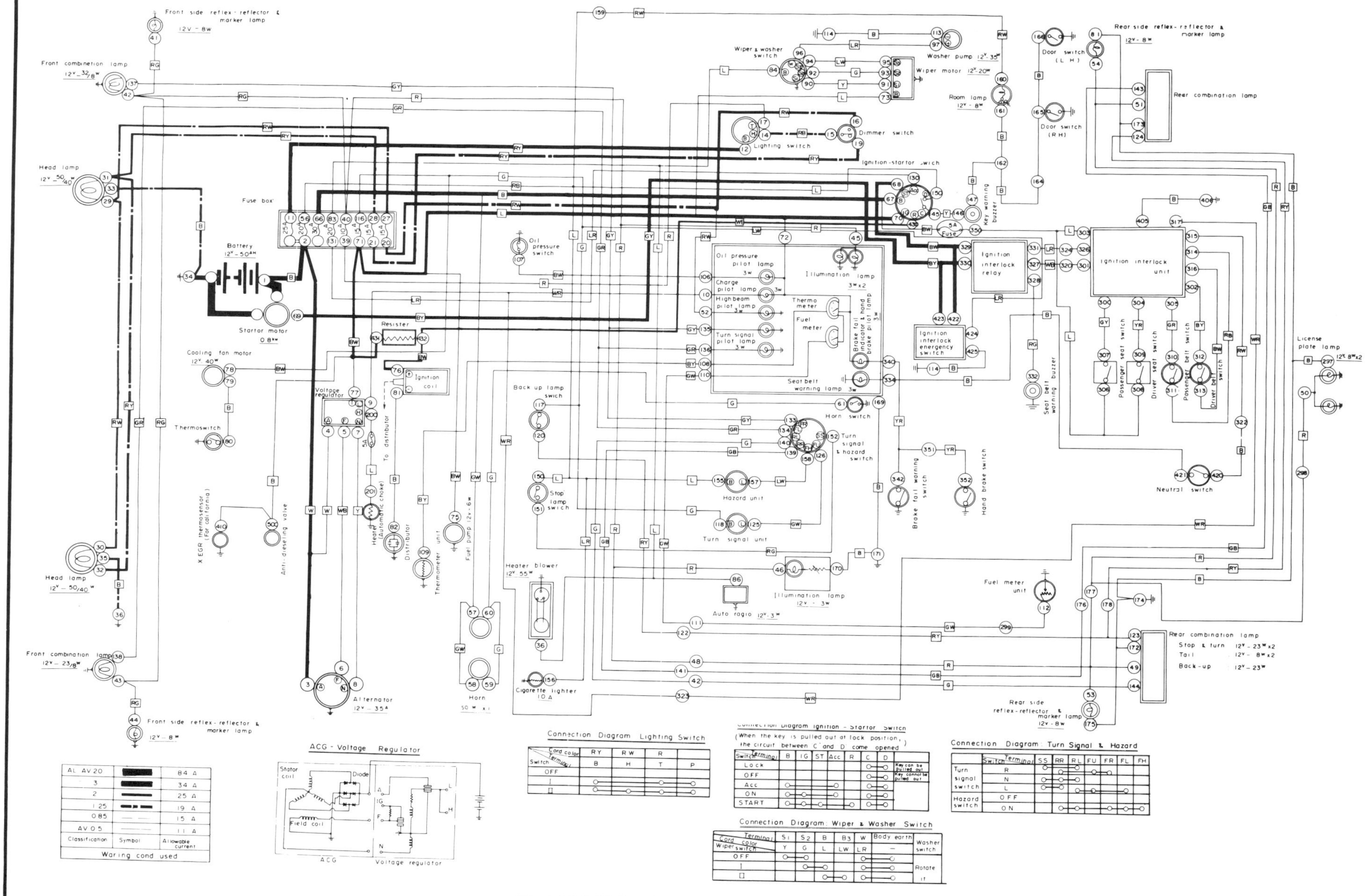

AL AV 20	[symbol]	84 A
3	[symbol]	34 A
2	[symbol]	25 A
1.25	[symbol]	19 A
0.85	[symbol]	15 A
AV 0.5	[symbol]	11 A
Classification	Symbol	Allowable current
Waring cond used		

Fig. 10.46. Wiring diagram - 1974 Station Wagon

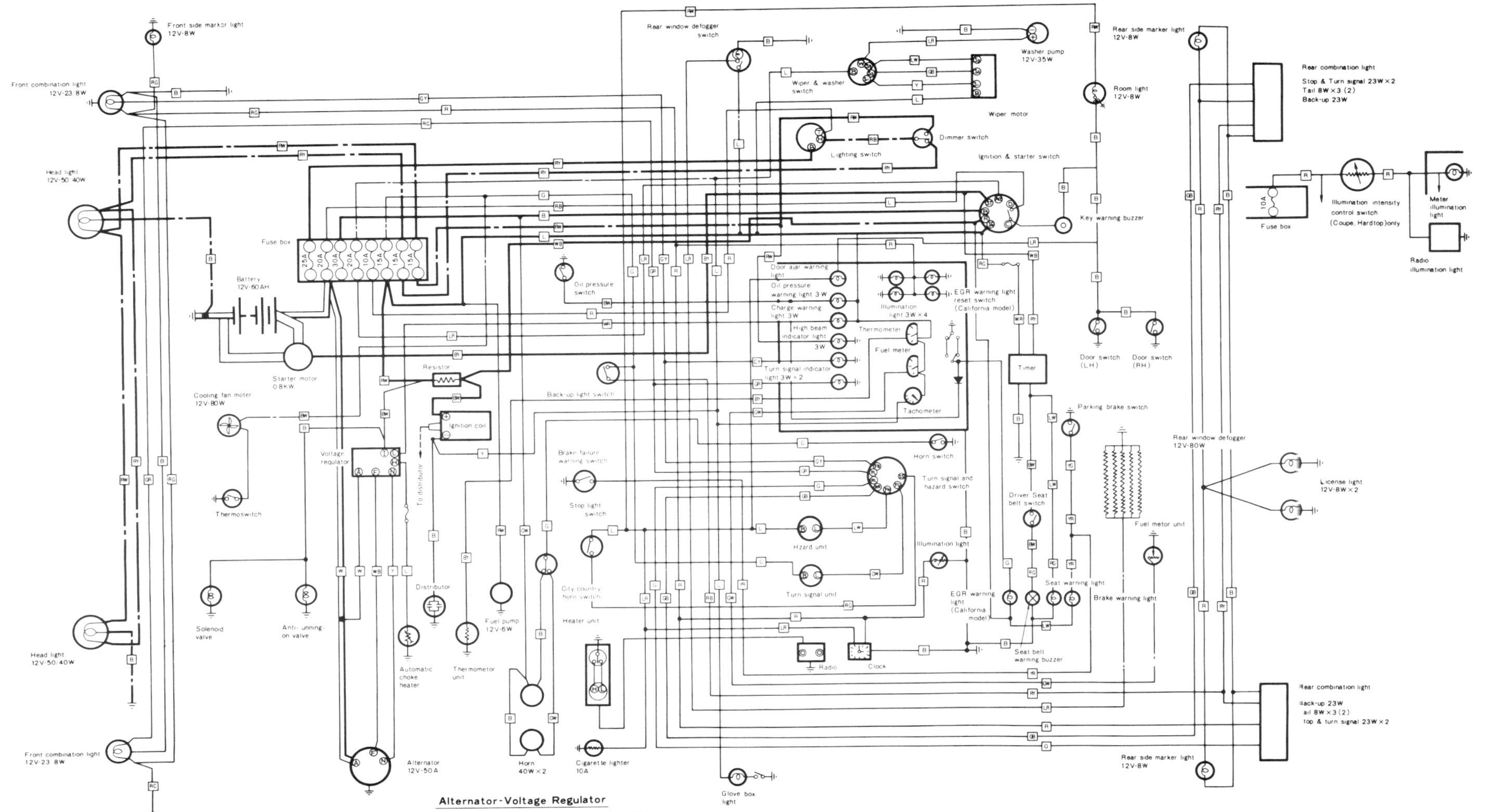

Alternator-Voltage Regulator

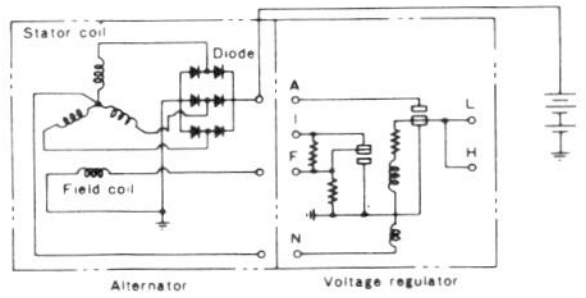

Wiring cord used	
Mark	Allowable current(A)
	84
	34
	25
	19
	15
	11

L Blue	LW Blue-white	LR Blue-red		
R Red	RW Red-white	RG Red-green	RY Red-yellow	RB Red-black
G Green	GW Green-white	GR Green-red	GY Green-yellow	
Y Yellow	YR Yellow-red	YG Yellow-green		
W White	WB White-black	WR White-red		
B Black	BW Black-white	BY Black-yellow		

Color Code of Electric Wires

Fig. 10.47. Wiring diagram - 1975 Sedan, Coupe, Hardtop and Station Wagon (manual transmission)

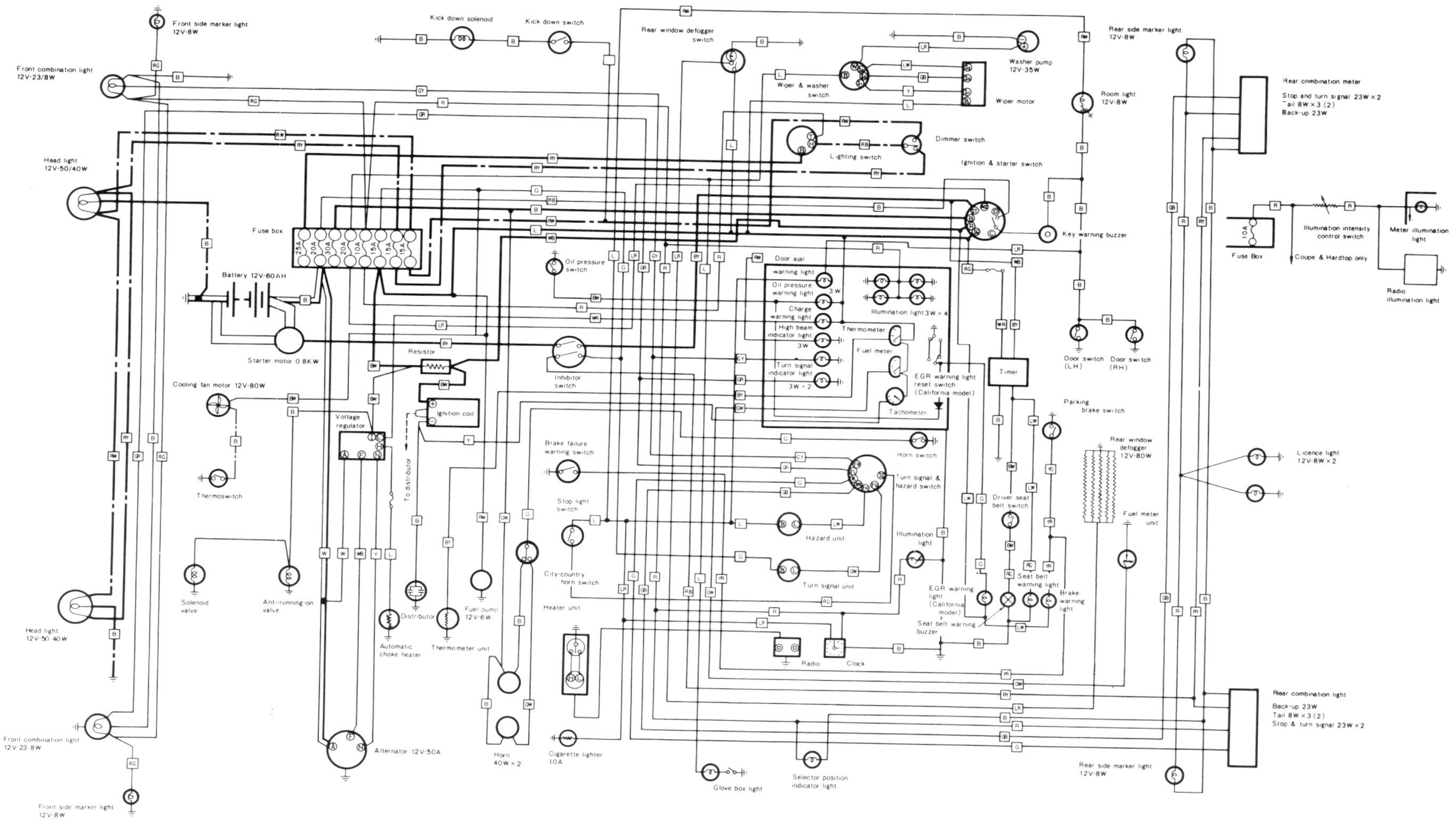

Wiring cord used	
Mark	Allowable current (A)
	84
	34
	25
	19
	15
	11

Alternator-Voltage Regulator

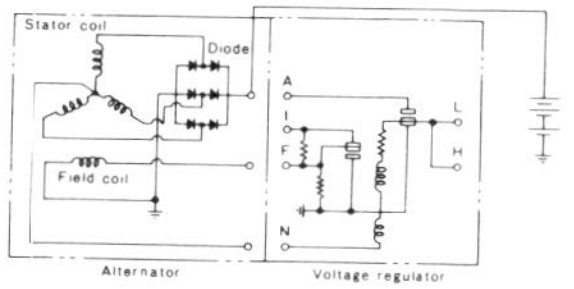

L Blue	LW Blue-white	LR Blue-red		
R Red	RW Red-white	RG Red-green	RY Red-yellow	RB Red-black
G Green	GW Green-white	GR Green-red	GY Green-yellow	
Y Yellow	YR Yellow-red	YG Yellow-green		
W White	WB White-black	WR White-red		
B Black	BW Black-white	BY Black-yellow		

Color Code of Electric Wires

Fig. 10.48. Wiring diagram - 1975 Sedan, Coupe, Hardtop and Station Wagon (automatic transmission)

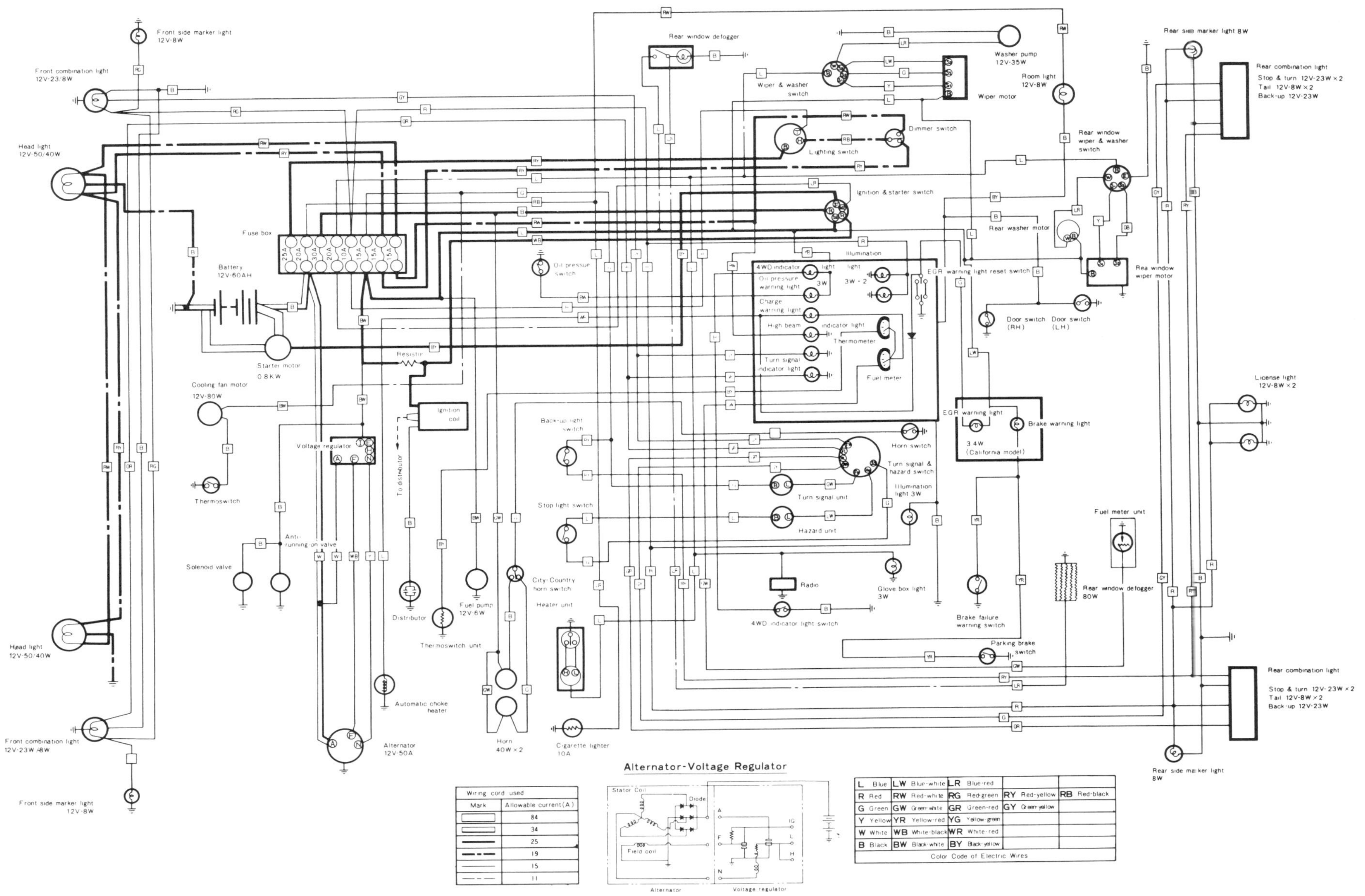

Fig. 10.49. Wiring diagram - 1975 4WD Station Wagon

Wiring cord used	
Mark	Allowable current (A)
	84
	34
	25
	19
	15
	11

L Blue	LW Blue-white	LR Blue-red		
R Red	RW Red-white	RG Red-green	RY Red-yellow	RB Red-black
G Green	GW Green-white	GR Green-red	GY Green-yellow	
Y Yellow	YR Yellow-red	YG Yellow-green		
W White	WB White-black	WR White-red		
B Black	BW Black-white	BY Black-yellow		

Color Code of Electric Wires

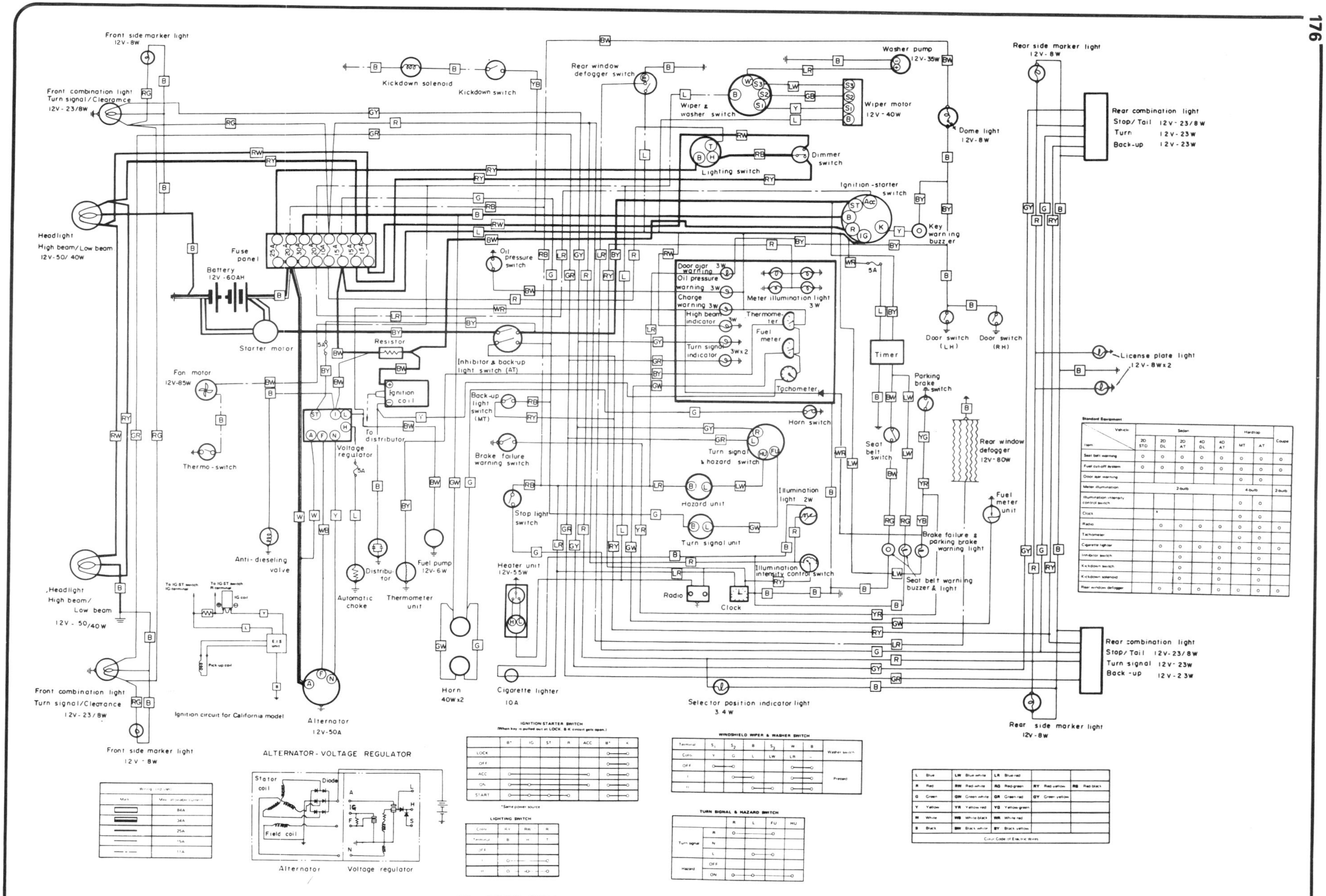

Fig. 10.50. Wiring diagram - 1977 Sedan, Coupe and Hardtop

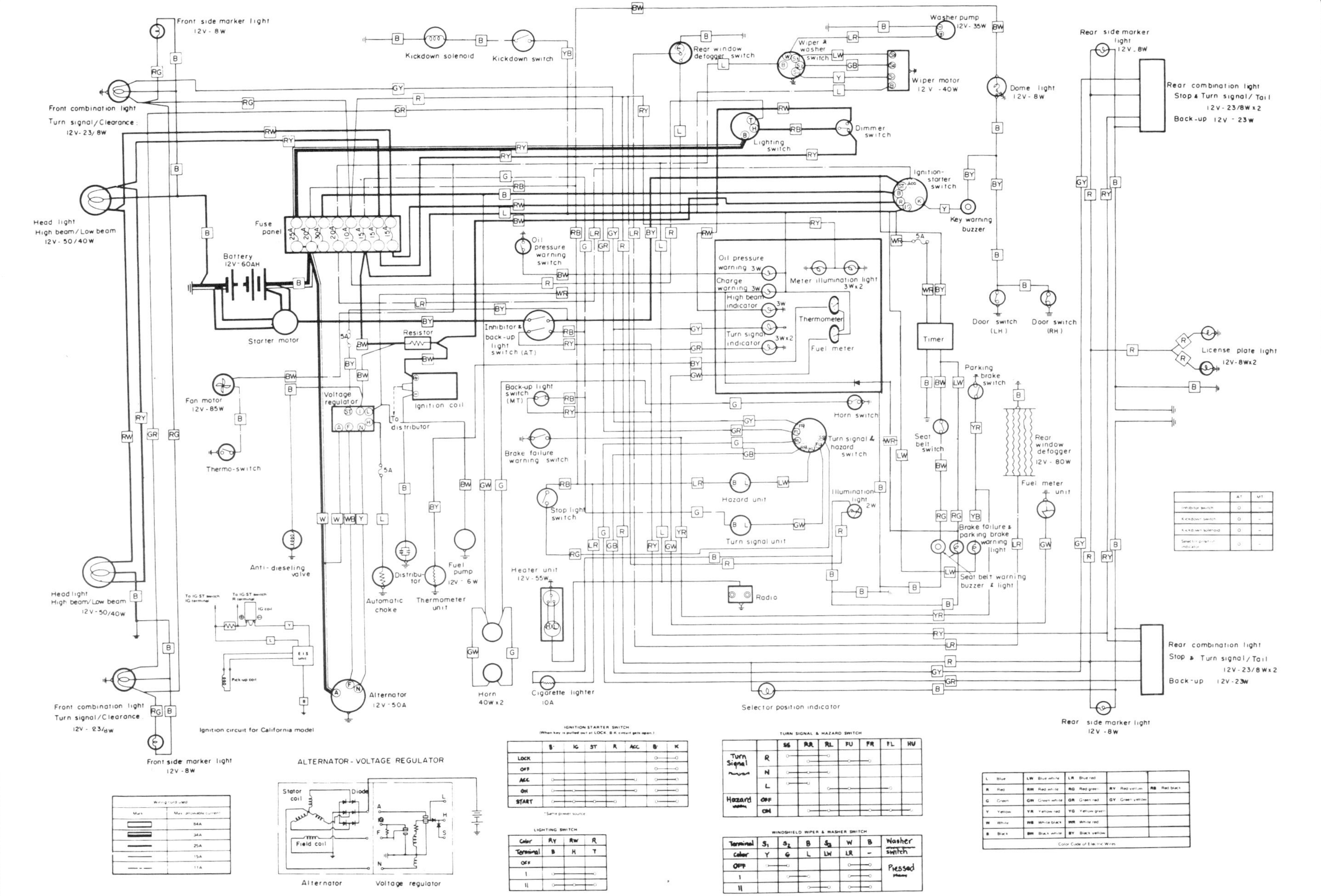

Fig. 10.51. Wiring diagram - 1977 Station Wagon

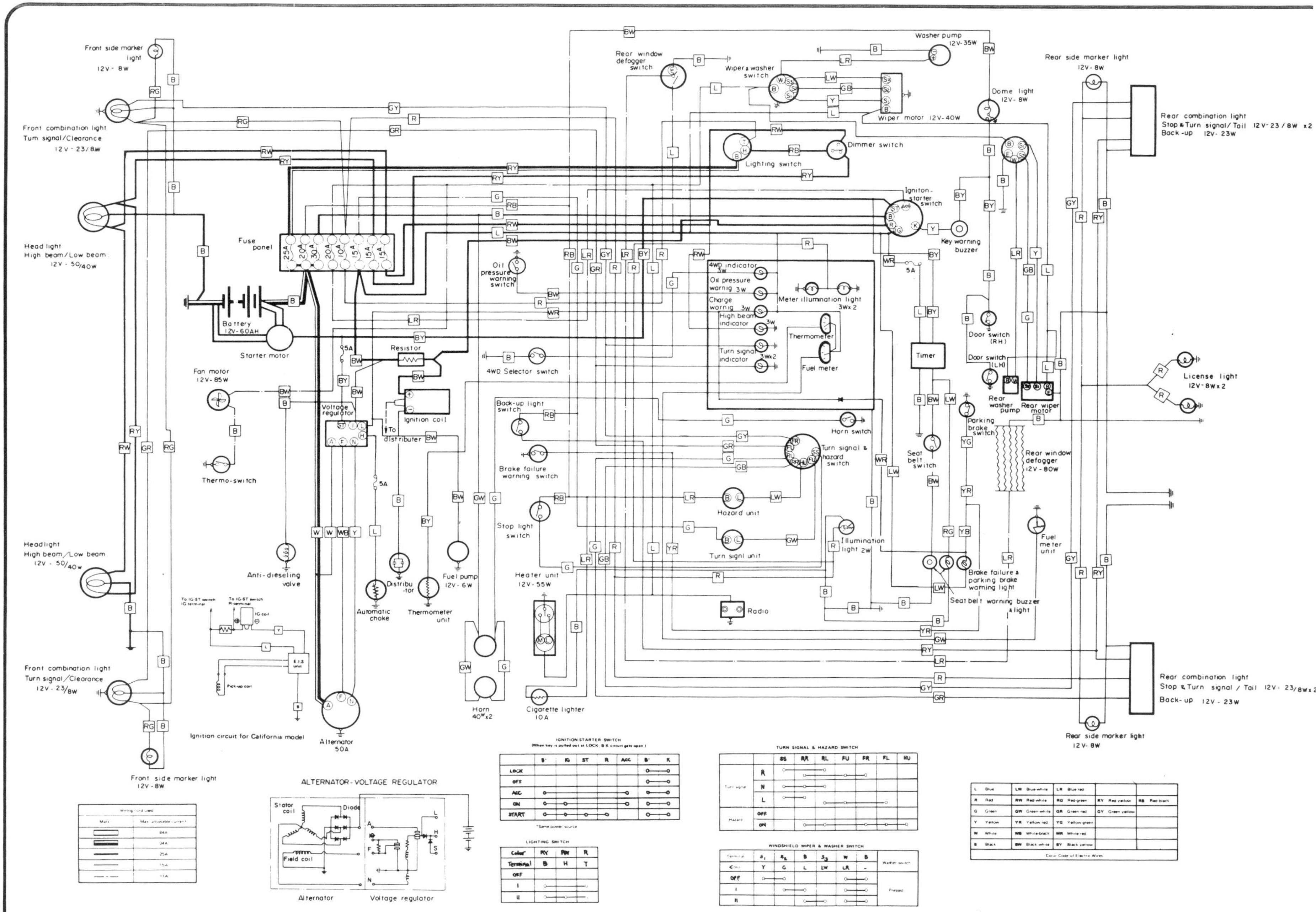

Fig. 10.52. Wiring diagram - 1977 4WD Station Wagon

Chapter 11 Suspension and axles

For modifications, and information applicable to later models, see Supplement at end of manual

Contents

Specifications

FF-1 1100 and 1300G models

Front suspension

Type	Wishbone independent type
Spring	Torsion bar

Rear suspension

Type	Semi-trailing arm type
Spring	Torsion bar

Shock absorbers

Front and rear	Oil damper - cylindrical double action

Wheel alignment

	Sedan	Sports Sedan
Front axle:		
Toe-in	5 mm (0.2 in)	5 mm (0.2 in)
Camber	1° 50′	1° 51′
Caster	2°	2°
King pin angle	-2° 20′	-1° 45′
Rear axle:		
Toe-in	0 - 0.20 in (0 - 5 mm)	0 - 0.20 in (0 - 5 mm)
Camber	1° 0′	0° 40′

1300, 1400 and 1600 models

Front suspension

Type	McPherson strut type	
Coil spring:	1972 - 74	1975 - 77
Diameter	4.13 in (105 mm)	4.13 in (105 mm)
Free length	15.4 in (390 mm)	13.48 in (342 mm)

Rear suspension

Type	Semi-trailing arm type
Spring	Torsion bar

Shock absorbers

Front and rear	Cylindrical double action	
Front stabilizer:	1972 - 74	1975 - 77
Diameter	0.87 in (22 mm)	0.79 in (20 mm)

Wheel alignment (1972 - 74)

Front axle:		
Toe-in	0.08 - 0.32 in (2 - 8 mm)	
Camber	1° 30'	
Caster	0° 45'	
King pin angle	12° 55'	
Rear axle:	Sedan	Station Wagon
Toe-in	0.04 - 0.20 in (1 - 5 mm)	0.08 - 0.24 in (2 - 6 mm)
Camber	1°	1° 30'

Wheel alignment (1975 - 77)

Front axle:	Sedan - Coupe - Hardtop	Station Wagon DL	4WD
Toe-in	0.08 - 0.32 in (2 - 8 mm)		0.24 - 0.47 in (6 - 12 mm)
Camber	1° 50' $\pm$ 30'		2° 30' $\pm$ 30'
Caster	45' $\pm$ 45'		
Rear axle:			
Toe-in	0.04 - 0.20 in (1 - 5 mm)	0.08 - 0.24 in (2 - 6 mm)	
Camber	$1^{\circ}\,{}^{+30'}_{-45'}$	1° 30' $\pm$ 30'	1° 50' $\pm$ 30'

Torque wrench settings

	lb f ft	kg f m
FF-1 110 and 1300G models		
Lower control arm to body bolt	26 - 32	3.5 - 4.50
Lower control arm shaft bolt	33 - 43	4.5 - 6.0
Front suspension mounting bolt	58 - 72	8 - 10
Lower arm castle nut	33 - 54	4.5 - 7.5
Rear suspension outer bracket bolt	44 - 65	6 - 9
Torsion bar lock bolt	26 - 32	3.5 - 4.5
Front hub to CVJ	87 - 101	12 - 14
Upper arm ball stud nut	116 - 133	16 - 18.5
Knuckle upper and lower balljoint nut	44 - 65	6 - 9
Front drum to axle shaft nut	116 - 133	16 - 18.5
Rear drum bearing nut	80 - 144	11 - 20
Front drum to DOJ	42 - 54	5.7 - 7.5
1300, 1400 and 1600 models		
Front suspension and axle		
Strut to knuckle	22 - 29	3 - 4
Strut to body	22 - 29	3 - 4
Control arm to crossmember	73 - 86	10 - 12
Stabilizer to leading rod	13 - 16	1.8 - 2.2
Tie-rod end to knuckle	18 - 22	2.5 - 3
Front hub nut (1972 - 73)	160 - 188	22 - 26
Front hub nut (1974)	174	24
Front hub nut (1975 - 77)	145 - 181	20 - 25
Balljoint stud to knuckle	35 - 40	4.8 - 5.5
Balljoint to control arm	80 - 94	11 - 13
Shock absorber upper nut	44 - 54	6 - 7.5
Rear suspension and axle		
Brake drum nut	80 - 145	11 - 20
Torsion bar outer bushing lock bolt	13 - 18	1.8 - 2.5
Torsion bar outer bracket bolt	43 - 65	6 - 9
4WD vehicles		
Link nut	130 - 166	18 - 23
Companion flange to spindle nut	145 - 181	20 - 25
Rear hub nut	174	24

1 General description

1 The front suspension on FF-1 models is a wishbone type, independent system with torsion bar mounted upper arms and shockabsorbers. The suspension and crossmembers are attached to the body thru rubber cushions to improve riding comfort.

2 On 1300, 1400 and 1600 models the MacPherson strut type

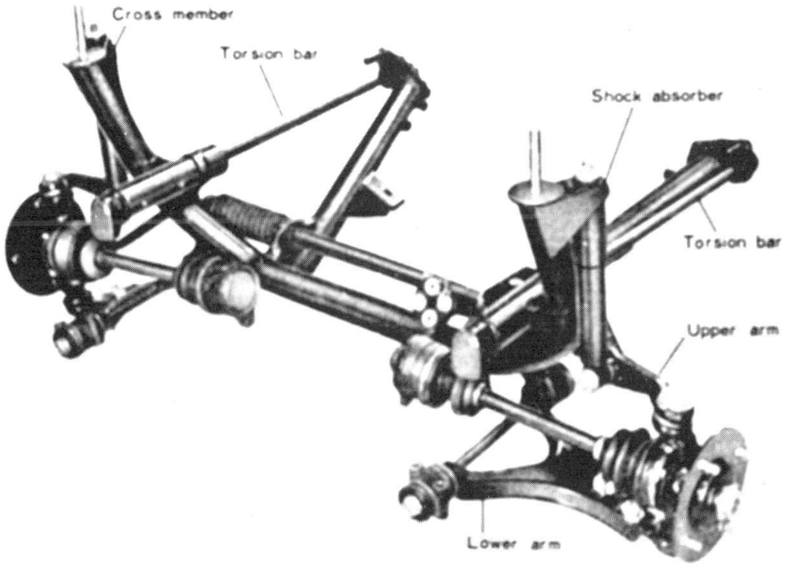

Fig. 11.1. Front suspension - FF - 1, 1100 and 1300G models

1 Nut
2 Spring washer
3 Washer
4 Cap (cushion rubber body mount A)
5 Cushion rubber B (body mount)
6 Cushion rubber A (body mount)
7 Collar A (body mount)
8 Upper arm assembly (rh)
9 Upper arm assembly (lh)
10 Pin (shock absorber)
11 Torsion bar (F.rh)
12 Torsion bar (F.lh)
13 Lock bolt
14 Nut
15 Anchor arm (rh)
16 Anchor arm (lh)
17 Snap-ring
18 Cam (cross member)
19 Nut
20 Spring washer
21 Plate
22 Bushing (lower arm)
23 Cross member assembly (F suspension)
24 Dust seal (upper arm)
25 Plug
26 Bearing (upper arm)
27 Oil seal (upper arm)
28 Dust cover (upper arm)
29 Plate
30 Spacer
31 Lower arm assembly (rh)
32 Lower arm assembly (lh)
33 Bushing (lower arm front)
34 Shaft (lower arm)
35 Bushing (lower arm rear)
36 Bracket (lower arm rh)
37 Bracket (lower arm lh)
38 Spring washer
39 Bolt (10 x 72)
40 Bolt (10 x 36)
41 Bolt (lower arm)
42 Cam (castor/camber)
43 Spring washer
44 Castle nut
45 Cotter pin
46 Nut
47 Shock absorber assembly (front)
48 Washer (shock absorber)
49 Rubber (shock absorber)
50 Rubber (shock absorber)
51 Rubber (shock absorber)
52 Washer (shock absorber)
53 Nut
54 Nut
55 Bolt
56 Spring washer
57 Washer
58 Stopper
59 Cushion rubber
60 Bracket (cross member)

Fig. 11.2. Exploded view of front suspension (FF1 models)

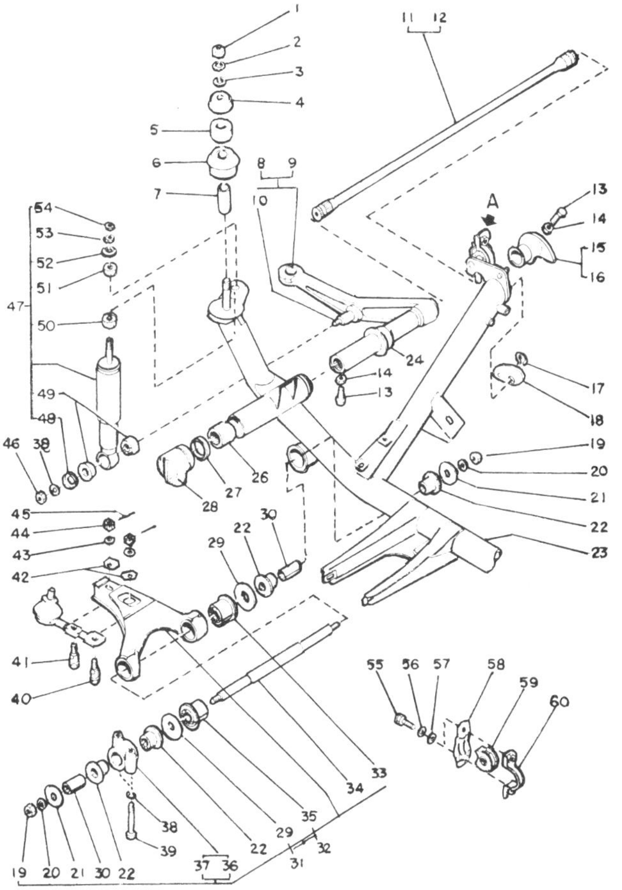

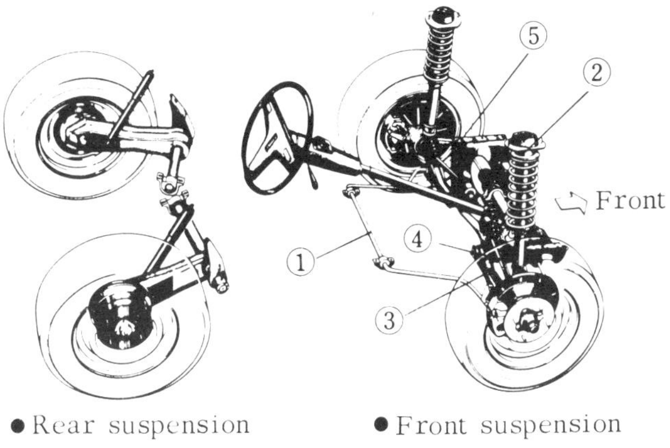

Fig. 11.3. Front and rear suspension - 1300, 1400 and 1600 models

1 Stabilizer
2 Damper strut
3 Transverse link
4 Front axle
5 Front cross member

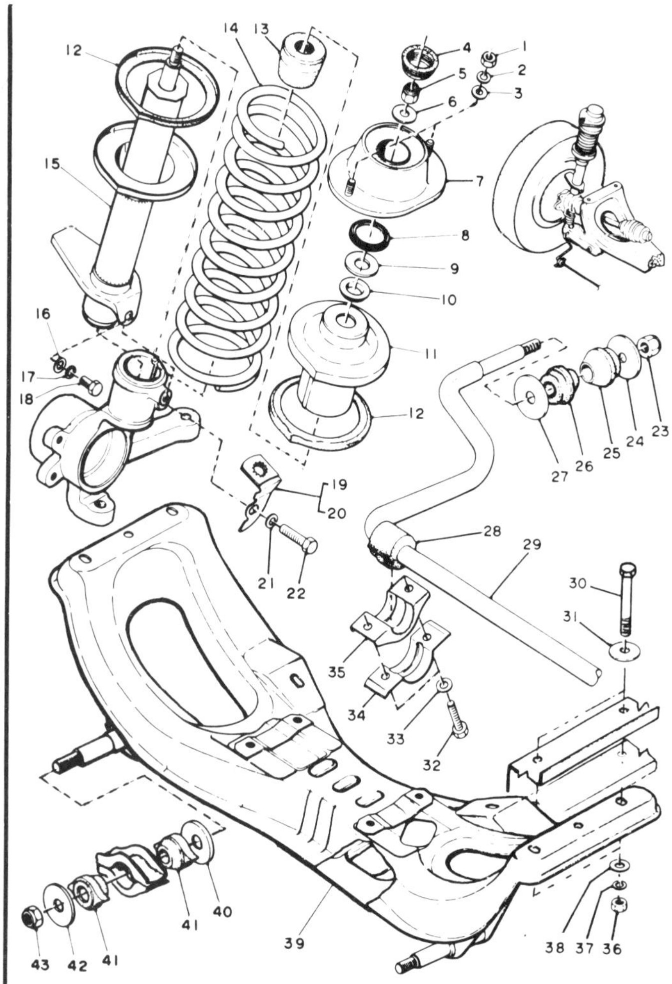

Fig. 11.4. Exploded view of front suspension (1300 and 1400 models 1972 - 74)

1 Nut
2 Spring washer
3 Washer
4 Cap (strut mount)
5 Self locking nut
6 Washer
7 Strut mount
8 Oil seal (strut mount)
9 Washer (thrust bearing)
10 Thrust washer
11 Spring retainer (upper)
12 Rubber seat (coil spring)
13 Helper
14 Coil spring
15 Shock absorber complete
16 Washer
17 Spring washer
18 Bolt
19 Bracket complete (brake hose rh)
20 Bracket complete (brake hose lh)
21 Spring washer
22 Bolt
23 Self locking nut
24 Washer (transverse link inner)
25 Bushing (link outer)
26 Bushing (link outer)
27 Washer (transverse link outer)
28 Bushing (stabilizer)
29 Stabilizer
30 Bolt
31 Washer
32 Bolt (10 x 40)
33 Washer
34 Lock plate
35 Bracket (stabilizer)
36 Nut
37 Spring washer
38 Washer
39 Crossmember complete (F)
40 Washer (transverse link inner)
41 Bushing (inner pivot)
42 Washer (transverse link outer)
43 Self locking nut

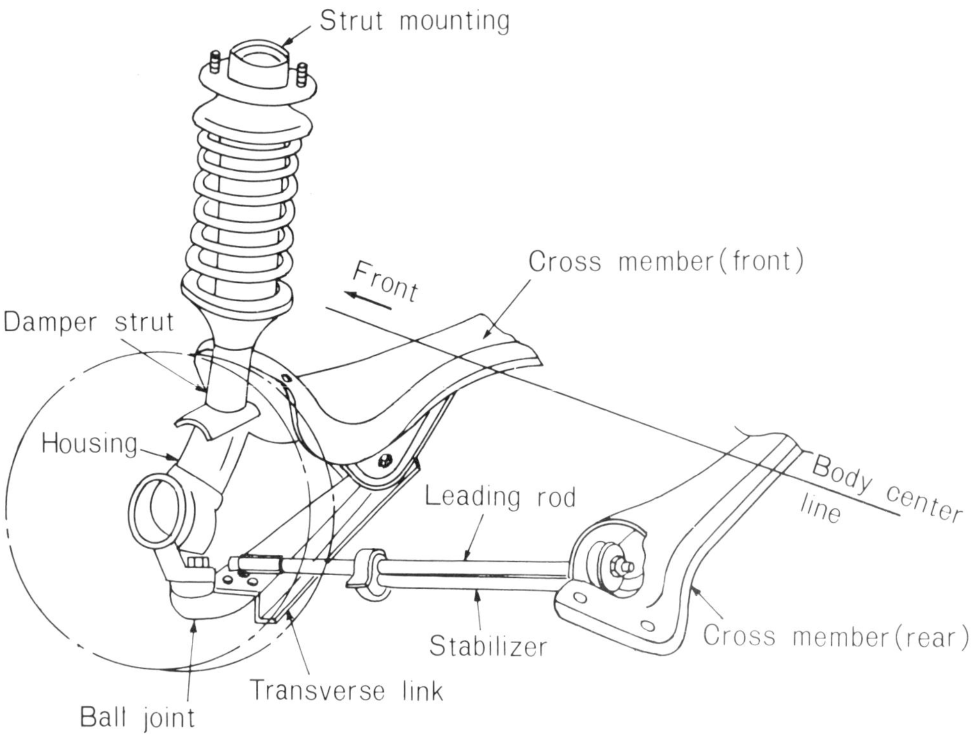

Fig. 11.5. Front suspension on models from 1975

system is used. It consists of independent struts with cylindrical double action shockabsorbers and coil springs mounted on the control arms. The control arms have a maintenance free balljoint riveted at the outer end and the inner end is bolted to the crossmember, thru rubber cushions. The upper end of each strut is secured to the wheel apron, while the lower end is retained by a knuckle housing, bolted to the hub. The stabilizer bar is bolted to the floor of the body and the ends are fastened to the control arms with bushings.

3 On models from 1975, leading rods are added to the suspension system. The leading rod is welded at one end to the control arm and the balljoint is bolted to the control arm instead of being riveted. The ends of the stabilizer bar are connected to the leading rods thru rubber bushings.

4 The rear suspension is basically the same for all models. It is a semi-trailing arm type consisting of a torsion bar and double action shockabsorbers.

2 Front wheel hubs, bearings and steering knuckle - removal, inspection and refitting

FF-1 1100 and 1300G models

1 Chock the rear wheels. Jack up the front of the car and support it on jackstands. Remove the road wheels.

2 Straighten the lockplate and remove the wheel hub nut.

3 Disconnect the tie-rod end from the knuckle arm, refer to Chapter 8, Section 10.

4 Remove the bolts securing the lower arm balljoint and separate the arm from the balljoint. **Note:** When the camber and caster adjusting cams are removed, note the setting number for reassembly, see Fig. 11.20.

5 Separate the upper arm balljoint from the upper arm by straightening the backplate and removing the nut.

6 Remove the hub and knuckle assembly from the splined section of the axle shaft.

7 Separate the hub from the knuckle.

8 Remove the lockplate retaining bolt, washer and lockplate.

9 Remove the inner oil seal from the knuckle, then press out the bearing.

10 Clean the parts and examine them for wear and damage. Check the balljoints for play and their rubber boots for deterioration. If the balljoints have to be renewed, use a balljoint separator to remove them from the knuckle. The two halves of the bearing must be renewed as a set. Always fit new oil seals at reassembly.

Fig. 11.7. Disconnect the lower arm balljoint (FF - 1)

Fig. 11.8. Separating the hub from the knuckle (FF - 1)

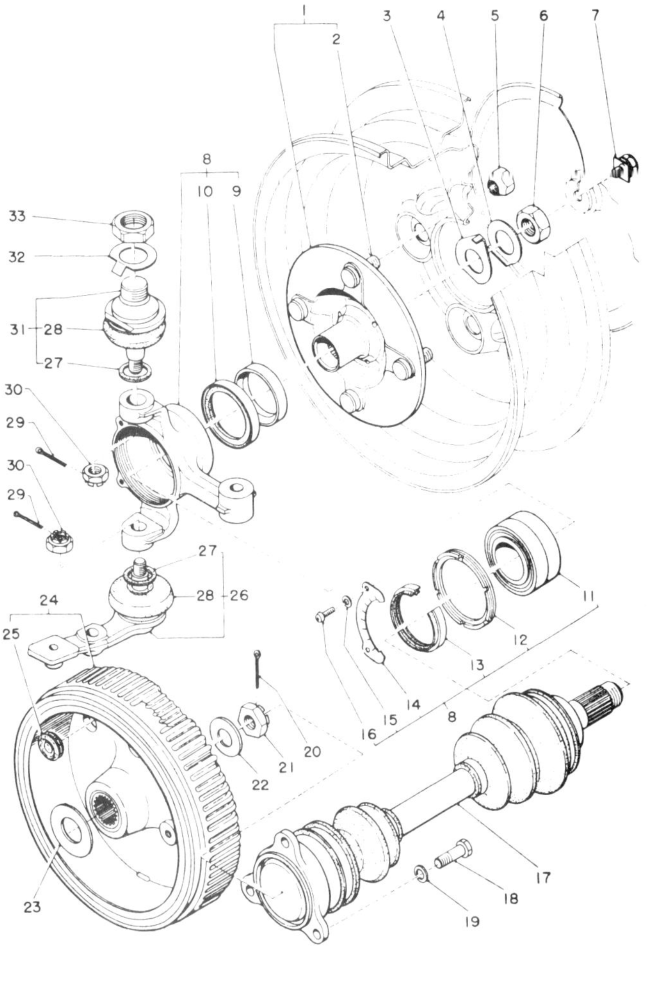

Fig. 11.6. Front wheel hub and knuckle assembly (FF - 1 models)

1 Hub
2 Hub bolt
3 Washer
4 Lock plate
5 Wheel nut
6 Hub nut
7 Bolt (wheel cap)
8 Knuckle assembly
9 Spacer
10 Oil seal
11 Bearing assembly
12 Nut
13 Oil seal
14 Lock plate
15 Spring washer
16 Bolt
17 Axle shaft assembly
18 Bolt
19 Spring washer
20 Cotter pin
21 Castle nut
22 Washer
23 Baffle plate
24 Brake drum
25 Brake adjusting port cover (brake drum)
26 Ball joint assembly (lower)
27 Clip
28 Boot
29 Cotter pin
30 Castle nut
31 Ball joint assembly (upper)
32 Lock plate
33 Nut

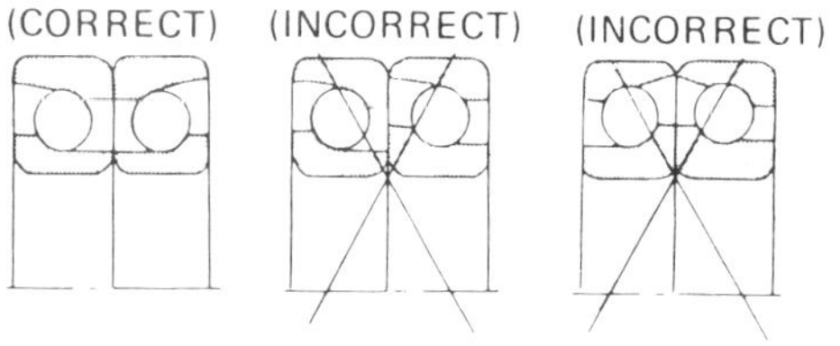

Fig. 11.9. Assemble the two halves of the bearing correctly (FF - 1)

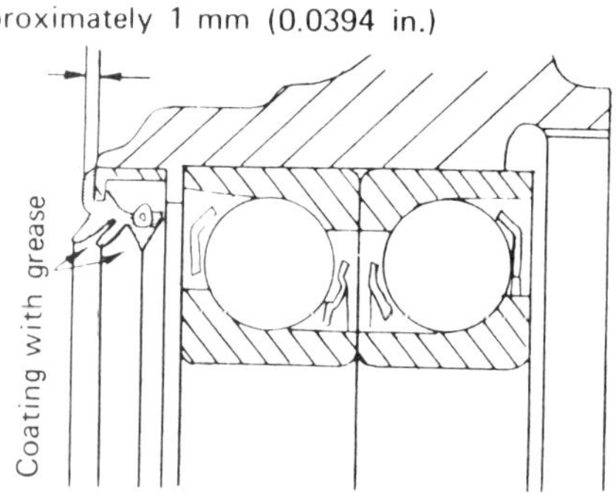

Fig. 11.10. Fitting the outer oil seal (FF - 1)

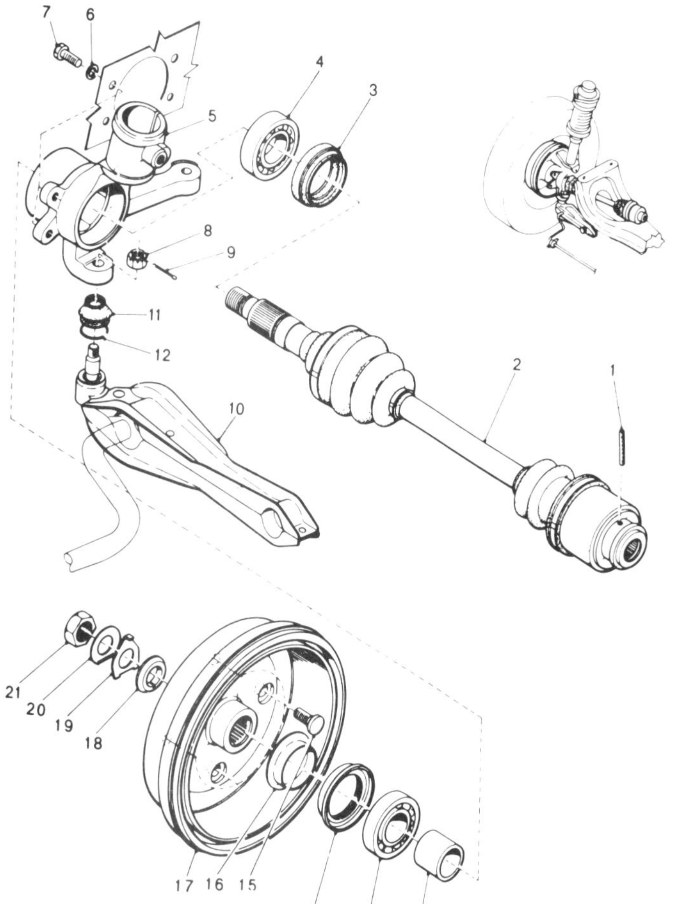

Fig. 11.11. Front hub and knuckle assembly for drum brake (1300, 1400 and 1600 models)

1 *Spring pin*
2 *Axle shaft*
3 *Oil seal (in)*
4 *Bearing*
5 *Housing*
6 *Spring washer*
7 *Bolt*
8 *Castle nut*
9 *Cotter pin*
10 *Transverse link*
11 *Dust seal (ball joint)*
12 *Circlip*
13 *Spacer*
14 *Oil seal (out)*
15 *Hub bolt*
16 *Sleeve*
17 *Brake drum*
18 *Center piece*
19 *Lock washer*
20 *Lock plate*
21 *Nut*

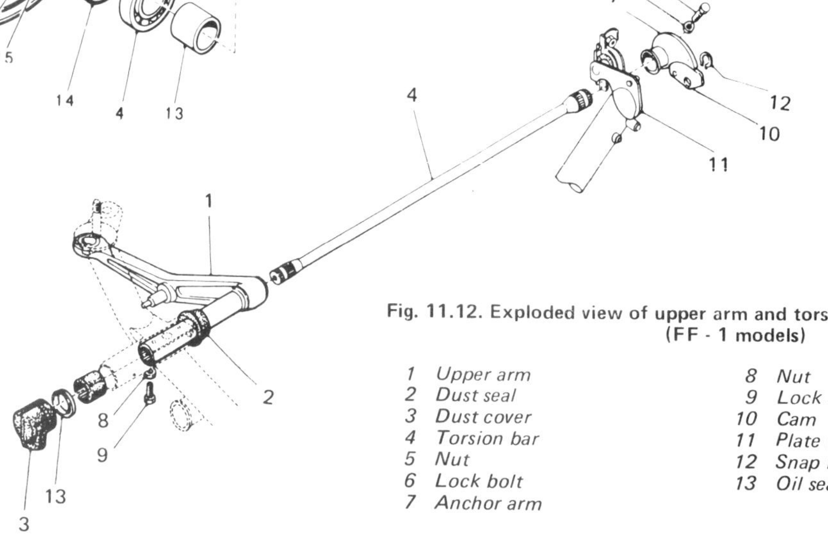

Fig. 11.12. Exploded view of upper arm and torsion bar assembly (FF - 1 models)

1 *Upper arm*
2 *Dust seal*
3 *Dust cover*
4 *Torsion bar*
5 *Nut*
6 *Lock bolt*
7 *Anchor arm*
8 *Nut*
9 *Lock bolt*
10 *Cam*
11 *Plate (cross member)*
12 *Snap ring*
13 *Oil seal*

11 When refitting the bearing, ensure that the two parts are assembled correctly, refer to Fig. 11.9, and pack it with wheel bearing grease.
12 Press the outer oil seal into the knuckle so that it protrudes approximately 1 mm (0.04 in) from the knuckle end surface, see Fig. 11.10.
13 Fit the spacer and bearing nut. Tighten the nut to 115 - 133 lb f ft (16 - 18.5 kg f m), then align the lockplate groove with the groove in the nut, bend over the tab and fit the lockplate bolt.
14 Coat the lip of the inner oil seal with grease and press it into the bearing nut.
15 Refitting of the steering knuckle is the reverse of the removal procedure. When refitting the lower balljoint to the lower arm, refit the camber and caster adjusting cams to the same setting as noted at dismantling. Check the wheel alignment.

1300, 1400 and 1600 models

16 On models with drum brakes remove the backplate as described in Chapter 9, Section 5.
17 On models with disc brakes remove the caliper unit as described in Chapter 9, Section 7.
18 Remove the bolts connecting the damper strut to the knuckle housing.
19 Disconnect the tie-rod balljoints from the knuckle arms, using a balljoint separator, refer to Chapter 8.
20 Carefully pull the knuckle housing downwards to separate the damper strut from the knuckle.
21 Separate the control arm balljoint from the knuckle.
22 Using a puller remove the knuckle from the axle shaft or the disc and hub assembly (disc brakes).
23 Centralize the spacer and insert a brass or copper drift to the surface of the inner race of the bearing and drive the bearing, together with the oil seal, out of the housing. Remove the spacer.
24 Remove the outer race and oil seal in the same way. Discard the oil seals.
25 Clean and inspect the dismantled parts as described in paragraph 10 above. Always fit new oil seals.
26 Refitting is the reverse of the removal procedure. Tighten the bolts and nuts to the torque specified in Specifications at the beginning of this Chapter.

3 Upper control arm and torsion bar (FF-1 models) - removal and refitting

1 Chock the rear wheels. Jack up the front of the car and support it on jackstands. Remove the front road wheels.
2 Fully loosen the road clearance height adjusting cam by removing the end bolt.
3 Remove the shockabsorber upper and lower securing nuts.
4 Remove the upper balljoint nut.
5 Remove the upper arm dust cover and locknut, force the upper arm downwards, to release the tension on the torsion bar, and pull on the anchor to disengage the upper control arm from the torsion bar.
6 If it is necessary to remove the torsion bar, it can be removed from the anchor arm after removing the locking bolt and nut.
7 Refitting is the reverse of the removal procedure. When fitting the torsion bar, align the missing serration gap with the master serration on the anchor arm. After refitting adjust the road clearance height as described in Section 5.

4 Lower control arm (FF-1 models) - removal and refitting

1 Repeat the operations at paragraph 1, Section 3.
2 Separate the lower arm from the crossmember after removing the nut securing the lower arm shaft to the crossmember bracket.
3 Disconnect the lower arm from the balljoint and separate it from the knuckle assembly.
4 Remove the two nuts attaching the lower arm bracket to the body.
5 Refitting is the reverse of removal procedure. Tighten the lower arm bracket to body bolts to 26 - 32 lb f ft (3.5 - 4.5 kg f m) and the shaft seat to 33 - 43 lb f ft (4.5 - 6.0 kg f m).

5 Front end road clearance height (FF-1 models) - adjustment

1 Road clearance height is measured from the center of the lower

Fig. 11.13. Removal of the torsion bar anchor arm (FF - 1 models)

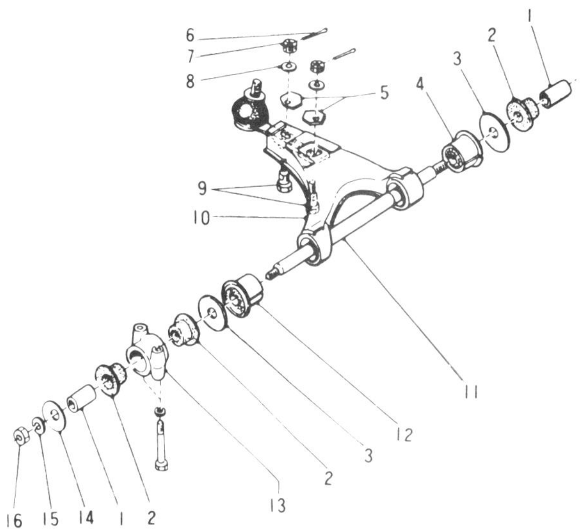

Fig. 11.14. Exploded view of lower control arm (FF - 1 models)

1 *Spacer*
2 *Bushing*
3 *Plate*
4 *Bushing*
5 *Adjusting cam*
6 *Cotter pin*
7 *Castle nut*
8 *Spring washer*
9 *Bolt (ball joint assembly installing)*
10 *Lower arm*
11 *Shaft*
12 *Bushing*
13 *Bracket*
14 *Plate washer*
15 *Spring washer*
16 *Nut*

Fig. 11.15. Removal of lower arm bracket (FF - 1 model)

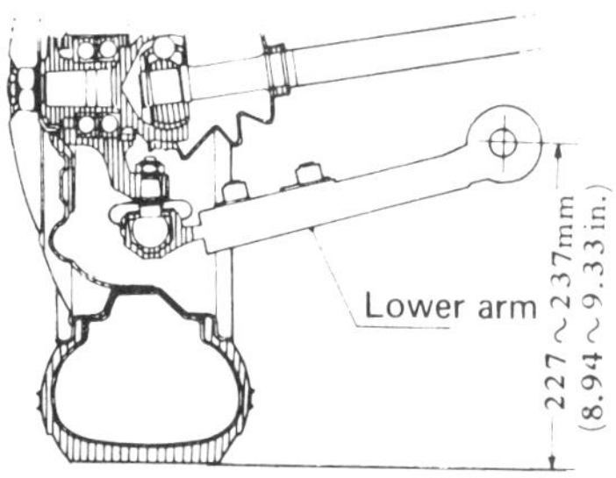

for sedan and station wagon

Fig. 11.16. Standard road clearance - front end (FF - 1 models)

control arm pivot to the ground. Whenever the anchor arm is removed the height must be adjusted.

2 The height is adjusted by turning the adjusting cam on the front of each torsion bar, clockwise to increase the height, counterclockwise to reduce it. The height should be 8.94 - 9.33 in (227 - 237 mm). Turning the cam one notch alters the height position by 0.32 in (8 mm).

3 Access to the cams is through the cooling openings on each side of the front skirt. Use a socket wrench with an extension bar.

6 Rear end road clearance height (FF-1 models) - adjustment

1 Adjustment of the rear road clearance height of the car is by turning the center arm adjusting bolt, built into the center of the crossmember. Access is through a hole in the floor of the trunk.

2 The height is measured at the center of the torsion bar end and should be 13.0 - 13.4 in (330 - 340 mm). Use an 8 mm Allen key on the socket head bolt.

Fig. 11.17. Road clearance adjusting cam (FF-1 models)

7 Shockabsorbers (FF-1) - removal, checking and refitting

1 Jack up the car and support it on jackstands. Remove the road wheels.

2 Fully loosen the road clearance adjusting cam (front) and on station wagons 1971 - 72 loosen the adjusting bolt at the rear also.

3 Remove the shockabsorber upper double nut, washer and rubber bushing.

4 Remove the nut from the damping pin at the bottom mounting and remove the shockabsorber.

5 Inspect the shockabsorber for signs of fluid leaks. If the shockabsorber is leaking it must be renewed.

6 Clean the exterior and examine the shaft for signs of corrosion or distortion, and the body for dents.

7 Check the operation by expanding and contracting it to check that equal resistance is felt on both strokes. If the resistance is weak or uneven the unit must be renewed.

8 Check the rubber bushings and washers for deterioration and wear, renew as necessary.

9 Refitting is the reverse of the removal sequence.

Fig. 11.18. Access to the height adjusting cams is thru the front skirt

8 Camber (FF-1 models) - adjustment

1 When adjusting the camber align the hexagonal cam, as shown in Fig. 11.20, with the camber adjusting reference line. To obtain normal camber set the mark '4' at the reference line. Camber angle at this setting is 1° 50' with the vehicle unloaded.

2 If the cam is turned 3 - 2 - 1, camber becomes minus and if turned 5 - 6, camber becomes plus. Turning one stage corresponds to 30'.

3 Checking camber requires special equipment, this should be left to your Subaru dealer.

9 Caster (FF-1 models) - adjustment

1 When adjusting caster, align the hexogonal cam with the caster

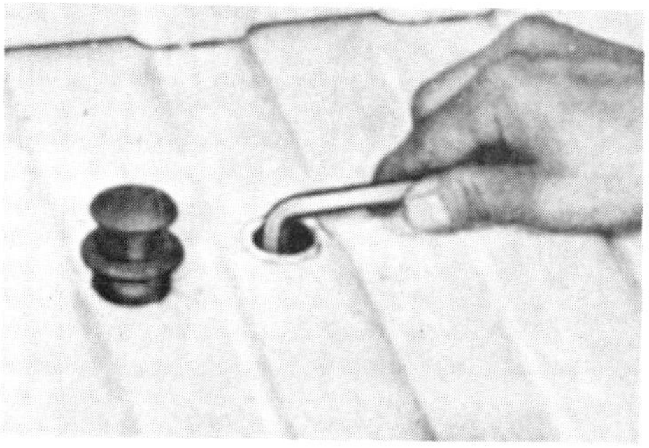

Fig. 11.19. Adjusting the rear end road clearance (FF - 1 models)

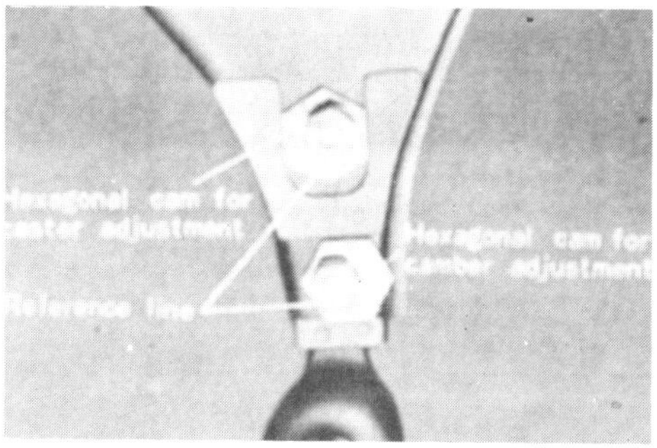

Fig. 11.20. Camber and caster adjusting cams (FF - 1 models)

reference line. To obtain normal caster set the cam mark '3' on the reference line. Caster angle at this setting is 2° when the vehicle is unloaded.

2 If the cam is turned 2 - 1, caster becomes minus and if turned 4 - 5 - 6, caster becomes plus. Turning one stage corresponds to 30'.

3 Checking caster requires special equipment, this should be left to your Subaru dealer.

10 Front suspension damper strut (1972 - 77 models) - removal and refitting

1 Chock the rear wheels, jack up the front of the car and support it securely on jackstands. Remove the front road wheels.

2 Remove the bolts securing the strut to the knuckle and separate the two components.

3 Separate the tie-rod from the knuckles as described in Chapter 8, Section 10.

4 Place a jack under the strut to support it. Working under the hood, remove the nuts attaching the upper end of the strut assembly to the wheel apron. Mark the front of the strut upper end so that it can be refitted in the same position.

5 Lower the jack slowly and remove the strut assembly from under the car.

6 Refitting the strut assembly is the reverse of the removal procedure.

11 Damper strut assembly (1972 - 77 models) - dismantling, inspection and reassembly

1 Unless a coil spring compressor is available it is recommended that you take the strut assembly to your local Subaru dealer for servicing. It is possible to make a suitable tool to compress the spring, but if you do, make sure it is of solid construction, as a spring coming free at the wrong time can be very dangerous. Fig. 11.23 shows the spring compressor supplied by Subaru.

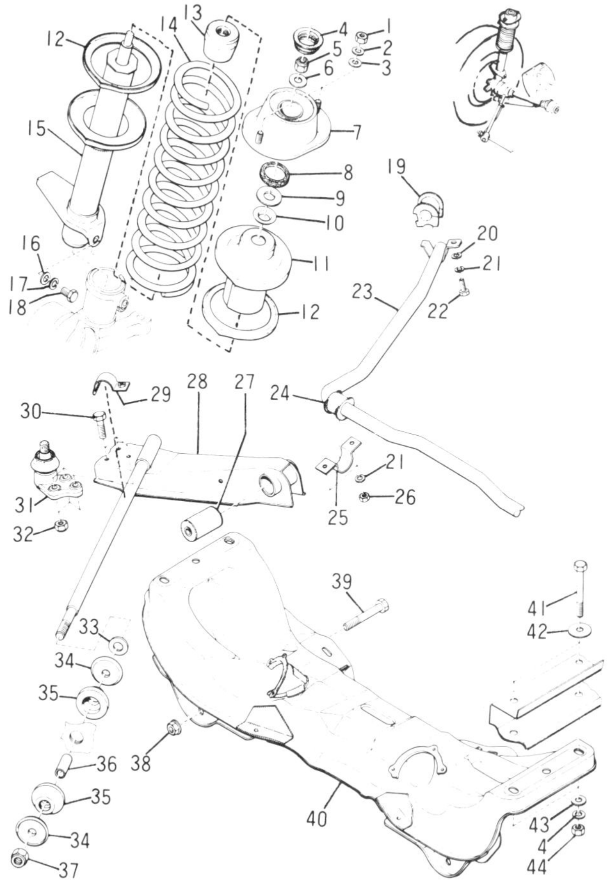

Fig. 11.21. Front suspension components (1400 and 1600 models 1975 - 77)

1 Nut
2 Spring washer
3 Washer
4 Cap (strut mounting)
5 Self-locking nut
6 Washer
7 Strut mounting
8 Oil seal (strut mounting)
9 Washer (thrust bearing)
10 Thrust washer
11 Spring retainer (upper)
12 Rubber seat (coil spring)
13 Helper
14 Coil spring
15 Shock absorber
16 Washer
17 Spring washer
18 Bolt
19 Bushing (stabilizer F)
20 Washer
21 Spring washer
22 Bolt
23 Stabilizer
24 Bushing (stabilizer R)
25 Bracket (stabilizer R)
26 Nut
27 Rubber bushing (in)
28 Transverse link
29 Bracket (stabilizer F)
30 Bolt
31 Ball joint
32 Self locking nut
33 Washer
34 Plate (leading rod)
35 Bushing (leading rod)
36 Pipe (leading rod)
37 Self-locking nut
38 Self-locking nut
39 Bolt
40 Crossmember (F)
41 Bolt
42 Washer
43 Washer
44 Nut

Fig. 11.22. Removing the damper strut upper attaching nuts (Sec. 11)

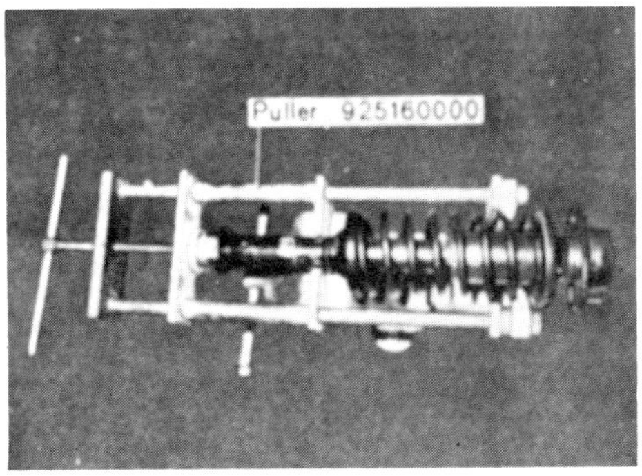

Fig. 11.23. Dismantling the damper strut (Sec. 11)

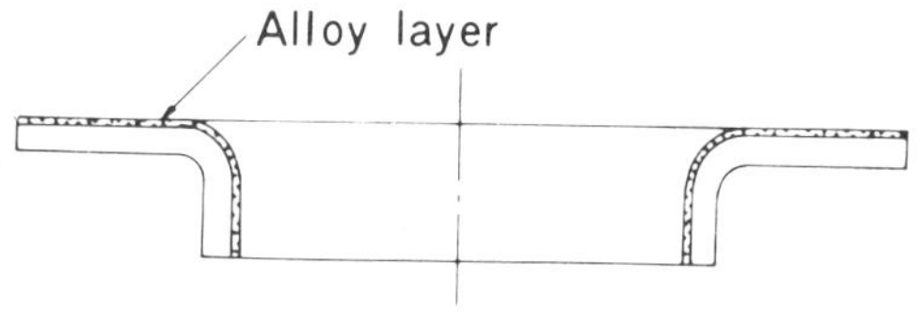

Fig. 11.24. Damper strut thrust washer (Sec. 11)

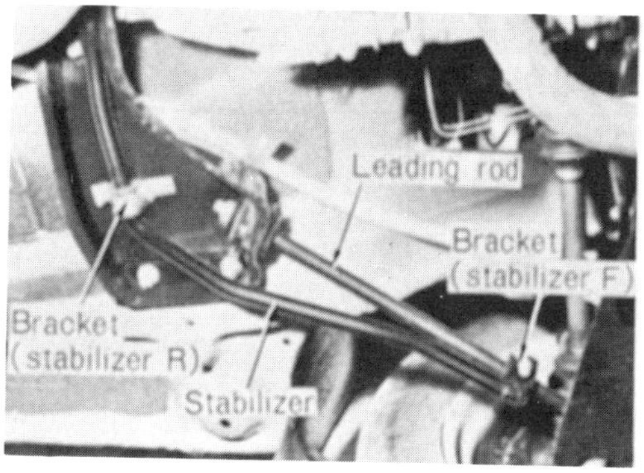

Fig. 11.25. Removing the stabilizer (1975 - 77 models)

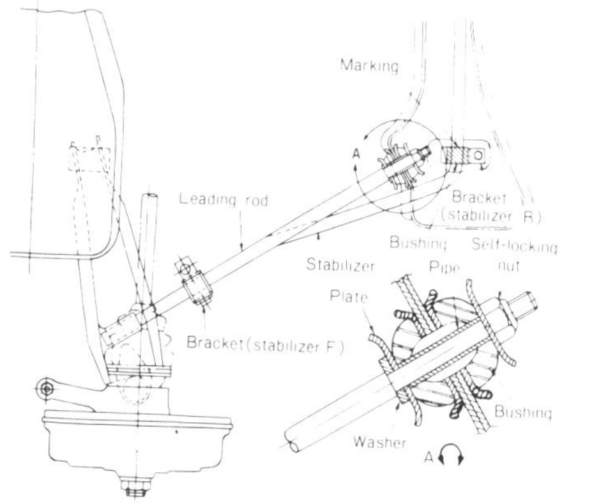

Fig. 11.26. Fitting the stabilizer (1975 - 77 models)

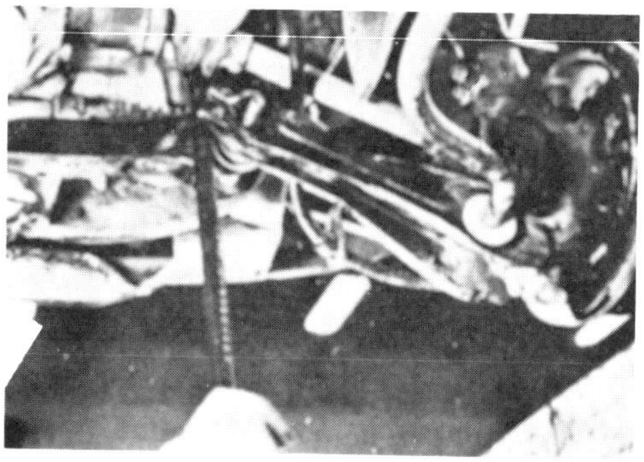

Fig. 11.27. Use a lever to separate the control arm from the crossmember

2 Clean the assembly with kerosene.
3 Fit a coil spring compressor, and compress the spring until it can move freely between the spring seats.
4 Remove the nut connecting the damper to the strut mounting with a box wrench and pull the strut mounting seat off the damper rod.
5 Remove the thrust washers and oil seal, noting the order in which they are removed. Remove the spring upper retainer and the spring.
6 Check the operation of the damper by pushing and pulling the piston rod, if resistance is weak or unequal renew the damper. Examine it for leaks or external damage. Renew as necessary.
7 Examine the spring for chafing or distortion. Check the alloy layer of the thrust washer for peeling or cracks and the coil seal for wear or damage.
8 Refitting is the reverse of the removal procedure. Smear the lip of the oil seal and the surfaces of the thrust washer with grease. Position the thrust washer so that the machined surface faces the spring. Tighten the shockabsorber to upper mounting bracket nut to 44 - 54 lb f ft (6 - 7.50 kg f m).

12 Front suspension stabilizer (1972 - 77 models) - removal and refitting

1972 - 74 models

1 Chock the rear wheels and jack up the front of the car. Support it securely on jackstands. Remove the front wheels.
2 Remove the nuts clamping the bushing to the control arm at the end of the stabilizer.
3 Disconnect the exhaust pipe from the exhaust manifold.
4 Straighten the lockplate and remove the bolts securing the stabilizer bracket to the rear crossmember and remove the stabilizer bracket from the stabilizer.
5 Pull the end of the stabilizer rearwards out of the control arm and remove the stabilizer.

1975 - 77 models

6 Repeat the operations at paragraph 1 above.
7 Remove the bolt at the bracket, stabilizer F in Fig. 11.25, connecting one end of the stabilizer to the leading rod.
8 Remove the nuts attaching the bracket (stabilizer R) to the rear crossmember. Remove the bracket and bushing from the stabilizer.
9 Check the bushings for cracks and deterioration. Examine the curved parts of the stabilizer for cracks. Renew defective parts as necessary.
10 Refitting is the reverse of the removal sequence. On 1975 - 77 models the bushing (stabilizer R) on the rear crossmember should be fitted with the inner end bushing aligned with the mark on the stabilizer. Final tightening of attaching bolts should be carried out with the wheel on the ground and the car unladen.

13 Front suspension control arm (1972 - 77 models) - removal and refitting

1 Chock the rear wheels, jack up the front of the car and support it on jackstands. Remove the front road wheels.
2 Undo the attaching nut and remove the parking brake cable

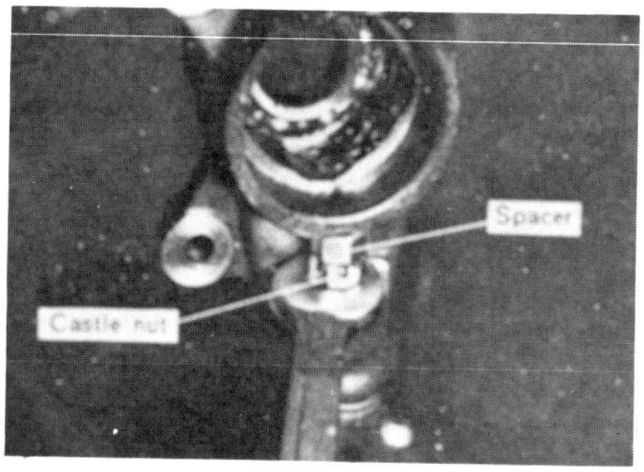

Fig. 11.28. Separating the ball joint from the knuckle

retaining bracket from the control arm.
3 Remove the self-locking nuts securing the control arm to the crossmember and to the stabilizer.
4 Lever the control arm rearwards to free it from the crossmember, then push it forward and pull it off the end of the stabilizer.
5 Remove the cotter pin and castle nut securing the control arm balljoint to the knuckle and separate the balljoint from the knuckle using a suitable balljoint separator. If a balljoint separator is not available position a spacer on top of the castle nut, as shown in Fig 11.28, and as the castle nut is unscrewed the ball stud is pushed out of the knuckle.
6 Check the control arm for damage and distortion. Check that riveted parts are secure. Check the bushing for cracks and deterioration Check the balljoint for wear, if it is defective, the complete control arm will have to be renewed on 1972 - 74 models. Later models have the balljoint bolted to the control arm instead of being riveted and it can be renewed separately. Check the balljoint boot for signs of seepage or of deterioration, renew as necessary. Grease the balljoint and fill the boot with grease before fitting. Refitting is the reverse of removal procedure. Do not apply grease on the taper stud of the balljoint, tighten the balljoint nut to 35 - 39 lb f ft (4.8 - 5.5 kg f m), the control arm to crossmember nut and the stabilizer end nut to 73 - 86 lb f ft (10 - 12 kg f m).

14 Front suspension balljoints - inspection, removal and refitting

1 Chock the rear wheels. Jack up the front of the car and support it on jackstands.
2 While an assistant grips the wheel at the top and bottom and rocks it up and down and back and forward, check for excessive movement at the balljoints. If play is excessive the balljoints must be renewed. Before deciding to renew a balljoint ensure that the play is in the balljoint and is not caused by loose wheel bearings.
3 To renew the balljoints on FF-1 models, remove the knuckle as described in Section 2, then undo the bolts attaching the balljoints to the upper and lower control arms, and remove the balljoints. Refitting is the reverse of the removal procedure.
4 On 1972 - 74 models the control arm balljoint is integral with the control arm and cannot be renewed separately. If the balljoint is defective renew the control arm as described in Section 13.
5 On 1972 - 75 models the balljoint is bolted to the control arm and can be renewed after removing the control arm, as described in Section 13, and removing the attaching bolts.

15 Rear drum/hub and bearing assembly - removal and refitting

1 Apply the parking brake and chock the front wheels. Remove the rear wheel cap and loosen the wheel nuts. Jack up the rear of the car, support it on jackstands and remove the rear wheels.
2 Remove the cotter pin and the drum retaining nut. Using a puller remove the brake drum.
3 Inspect the bearings for wear and damage, do not remove them unless they are defective as they will most likely get damaged during removal.
4 If the bearings have to be renewed press them out with a suitable mandrel. The oil seal is removed by prising it out with a screwdriver. Always fit a new oil seal after each dismantling.
5 When refitting the bearings, press on the outer race as pressing on the inner race may damage the bearing.
6 Pack the drum boss with 0.022 - 0.033 lb (10 - 15 g) of grease.
7 Fit the seal so that the end faces of the drum and seal are flush.
8 Refit the drum and tighten the retaining nut to 80 - 145 lb f ft (11 - 20 kg f m). Lock the nut with a new cotter pin. The torque loading of the retaining nut is important as it determines the loading of the wheel bearings.

16 Rear brake drum, spindle and bearing assembly, 4WD - general description

1 The drive shaft and brake drum are connected through the spindle and companion flange to transmit the drive from the rear differential to the wheels. The spindle is supported by a pair of taper roller bearings which are located inside the housing welded to the trailing

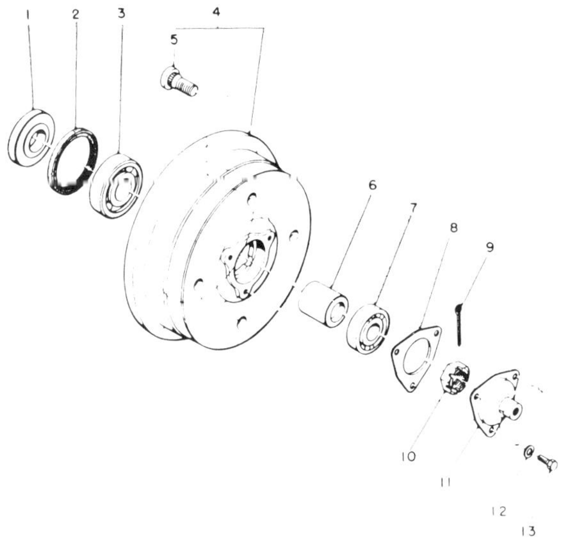

Fig. 11.29. Rear drum/hub assembly (Sec. 15)

1 *Spacer (seal)*
2 *Oil seal*
3 *Bearing (R in)*
4 *Brake drum assembly*
5 *Hub bolt*
6 *Spacer (bearing)*
7 *Bearing (R out)*
8 *Plate (bearing stopper)*
9 *Cotter pin*
10 *Castle nut*
11 *Cap (R drum)*
12 *Spring washer*
13 *Bolt*

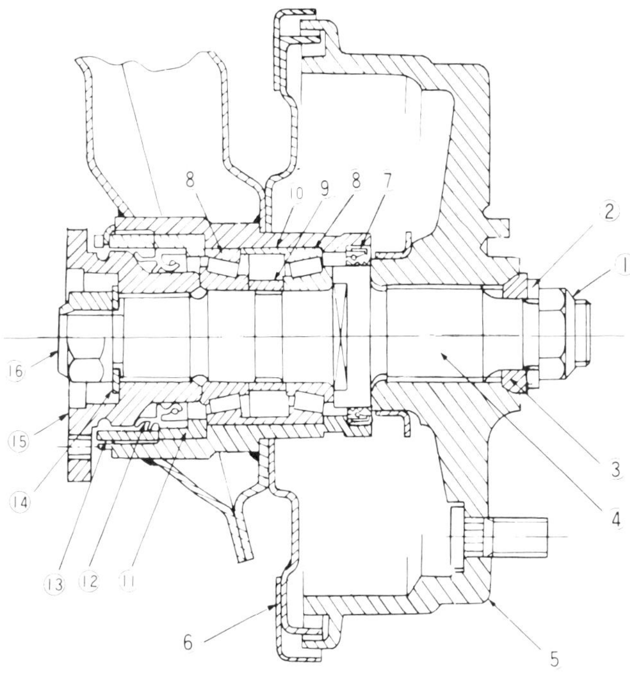

Fig. 11.30. Cross sectional view of rear axle - 4WD

1 *Axle nut*
2 *Conical spring washer*
3 *Center piece*
4 *Spindle*
5 *Brake drum*
6 *Back plate (brake assembly)*
7 *Outer oil seal*
8 *Bearing*
9 *Inner spacer*
10 *Outer spacer*
11 *Collar*
12 *Inner oil seal*
13 *Link nut*
14 *Washer*
15 *Companion flange*
16 *Lock nut*

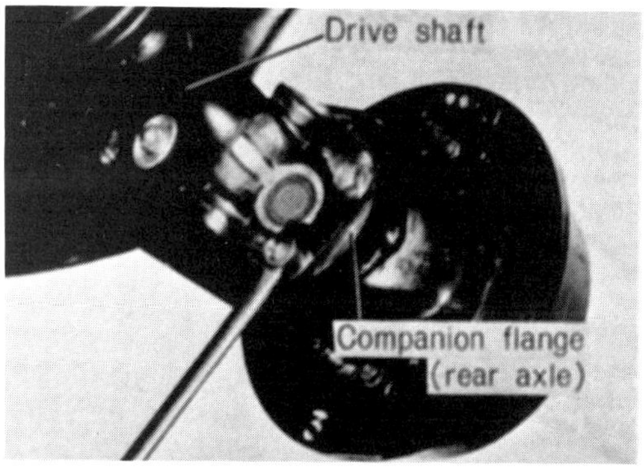

Fig. 11.31. Disconnecting the axle shaft from the rear axle flange (Sec. 17)

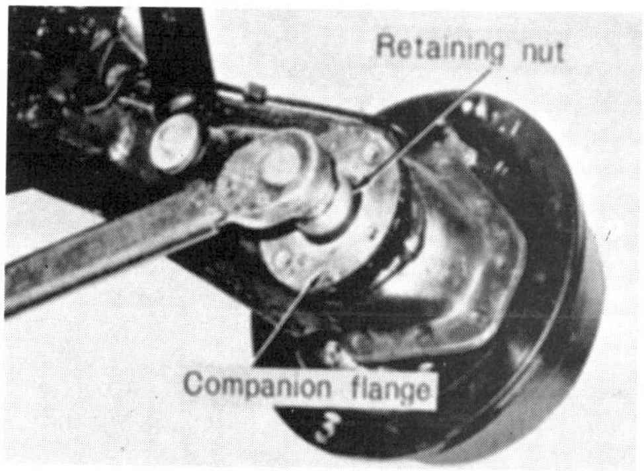

Fig. 11.32. Removing the companion flange retaining nut (Sec. 17)

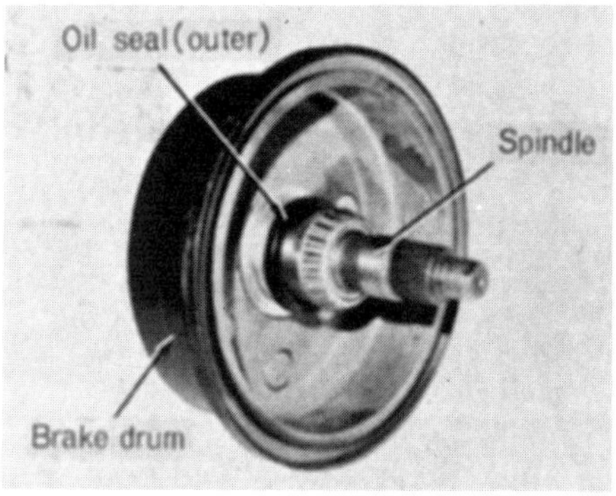

Fig. 11.33. Brake drum and spindle assembly - 4WD

Fig. 11.34. Removing the link nut (Sec. 17)

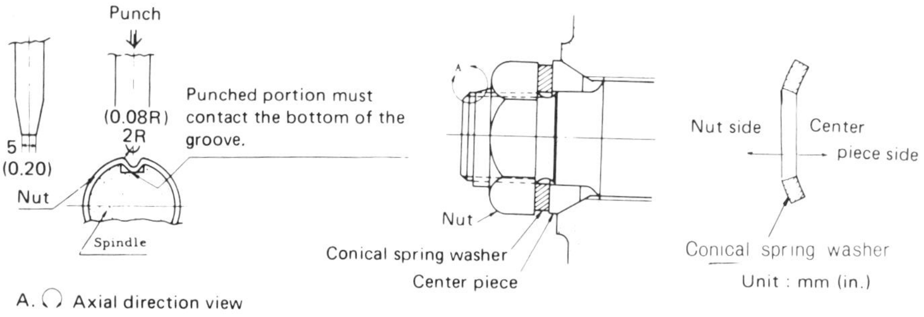

Fig. 11.35. Fitting the brake drum retaining nut (Sec. 17)

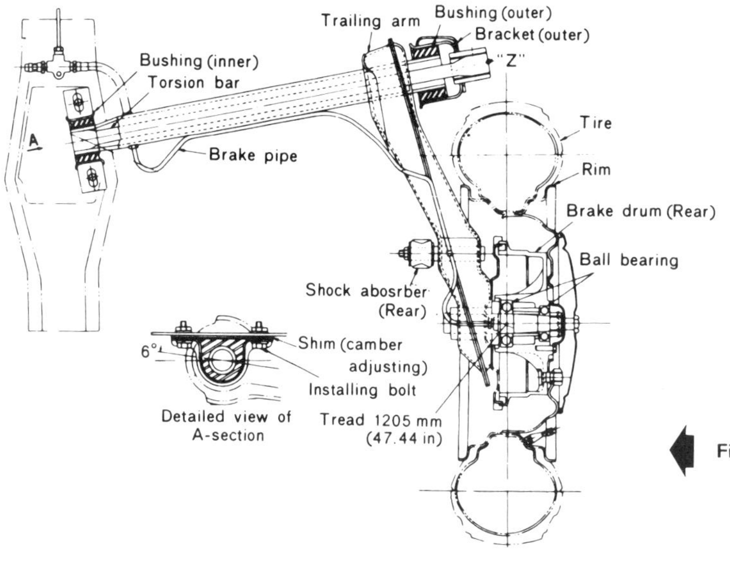

Fig. 11.36. Rear suspension components

arm.

2 No pre-load of the taper roller bearings is required since two spacers are used, for the inner and outer races of the bearings, which eliminates variations of pre-load caused by difference in tightening torque.

17 Rear brake drum and spindle assembly oil seals, 4WD - renewal

1 Apply the parking brake and chock the front wheels. Loosen the rear road wheel nuts. Jack up the rear of the car and support it on jackstands. Remove the rear road wheels.
2 Release the staking on the axle nut and remove the nut.
3 Disconnect the axle shaft from the rear axle companion flange.
4 Have an assistant apply the footbrake while you remove the companion flange to spindle retaining nut and take off the companion flange.
5 Pull the brake drum and spindle out of the housing.
6 Remove the drum retaining nut, separate the drum and spindle and remove the outer oil seal.
7 Unlock the link nut and remove the nut with a peg spanner then take out the inner oil seal.
8 Fitting the new oil seals is the reverse of the removal procedure. Apply 0.21 - 0.28 oz (6 - 8 g) of grease to the outer spacer of the trailing arm housing and fit the spindle. The oil seals must be fitted after the spindle is fitted. Tighten the link nut to 130 - 160 lb f ft (18 - 23 kg f m), the companion flange retaining nut to 145 - 181 lb f ft (20 - 25 kg f m) and the brake drum retaining nut to 174 lb f ft (24 kg f m). After tightening the drum nut stake the flanged part into the groove on the spindle.

18 Rear wheel bearings, 4WD - renewal

1 Renewal of the rear wheel bearings requires special tools. If they are defective, have this work done by your local Subaru dealer.
2 To renew the bearings it is necessary to remove the suspension from the vehicle, as described in Section 19, and you may wish to do this and take the trailing arm housing to the dealer for renewal of the bearings.

19 Rear suspension - removal, dismantling and refitting

1 Apply the parking brake, chock the front wheels and loosen the road wheel nuts. Jack up the rear of the car and support it on jack-stands. Remove the rear wheels.
2 Disconnect the brake hoses from the pipes and plug the end of the pipes.
3 Remove the shockabsorber attaching nut and the inner bushing mounting bolts.
4 Loosen the locking bolt of the outer bushing and remove the outer bracket attaching bolts. On 4WD vehicles disconnect the axle shaft from the spindle companion flange.
5 Remove the suspension from under the car.
6 Pull the outer bracket out of the outer bushing after removing the locking bolt, then pull the torsion bar out of the trailing arm.
7 Clean and examine the parts for wear and damage. If the bushings are defective remove them, using a puller. When fitting new bushings press them in until the end of the outer bushing comes flush with the trailing arm and the collar of the inner bushing comes flush with the trailing arm end.
8 Fit the torsion bars in the trailing arms, the torsion bar marked R on the right and the bar marked L on the left. Incorrect fitting of the torsion bars will result in early failure of the bars. Grease the serrations of the torsion bars. When fitting the bars align the marking on the end of the torsion bar to that of the outer bracket and inner bracket and inner bushing.
9 Refitting the suspension is the reverse of the removal procedure. The wheel alignment must be checked after refitting, refer to Section 21.

20 Rear end road clearance height - adjustment

1 Adjustment of the road clearance height for FF-1 models is described in Section 6.
2 On models from 1972 the specified vehicle height can be approximately established by fitting the torsion bars with the missing tooth gap aligned to the markings on the bushings and the bracket, refer to Section 19.

Fig. 11.37. Removing the inner bushing mounting bolts (Sec. 19)

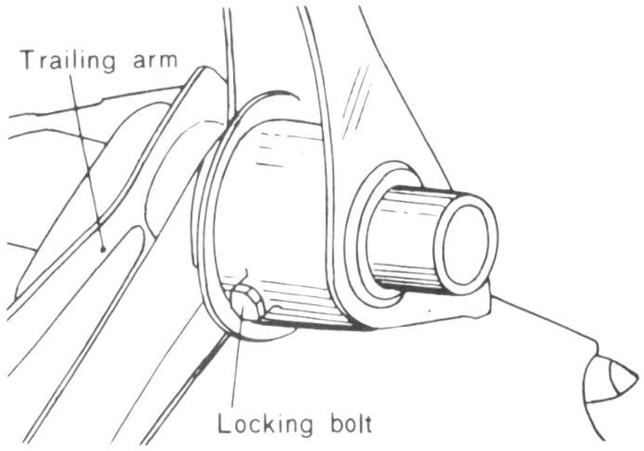

Fig. 11.38. Removing the outer bushing locking bolt (Sec. 19)

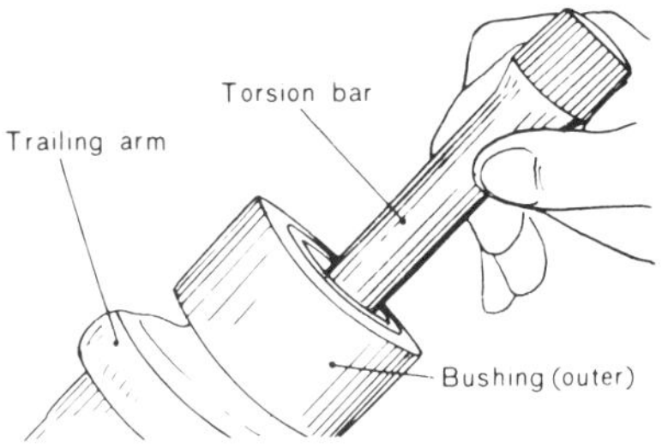

Fig. 11.39. Pulling the torsion bar out of the trailing arm (Sec. 19)

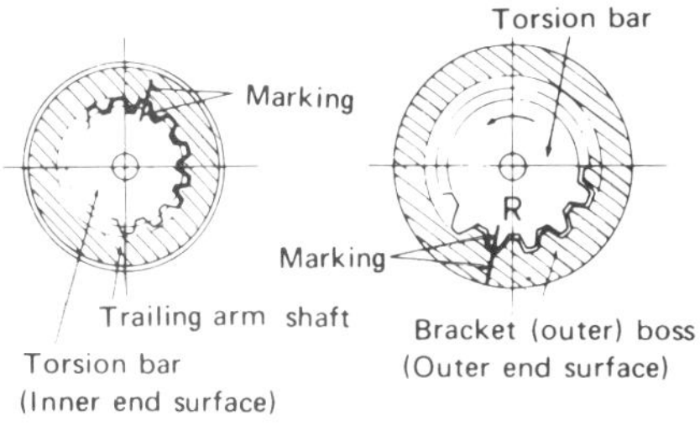

Fig. 11.40. Torsion bar aligning marks

3 The rear road clearance is measured from the trailing arm center line, 'a' in Fig. 11.41, to ground level. The vehicle height can be altered by turning the outer and inner ends of the torsion bar by the same number of teeth in opposite directions. Turning the torsion bar in the direction of the arrow on the end of the bar, see Fig. 11.40, lowers the height and turning it in the opposite direction to the arrow, raises the height.

4 To adjust proceed as follows:

a) Carry out the operations described in Section 19, paragraph 1.
b) Remove the shockabsorber lower attaching nut and separate the shockabsorber from the trailing arm.
c) Loosen the lock bolt on the outer bushing and index mark both ends of the torsion bar and trailing arms.
d) Hold the trailing arm so as not to twist the torsion bar and disengage the serrations.
e) First adjust only the inner end by turning the torsion bar as required, then insert the outer end into the position required by raising and lowering the trailing arm. Altering the torsion bar position by one serration raises or lowers the height by 5 mm (0.2 in).

5 The specified road clearance, ie, the height of point 'a' in Fig. 11.41, from ground level is 11.29 - 11.89 in (287 - 302 mm) for 6.15 - 13 - 4PR tires and 11.06 - 11.66 in (281 - 296 mm) for 145 - SR - 13 tires.

6 Tighten the outer bushing lock bolt, with the wheels on the ground, to 13 - 18 lb f ft (1.8 - 2.5 kg f m).

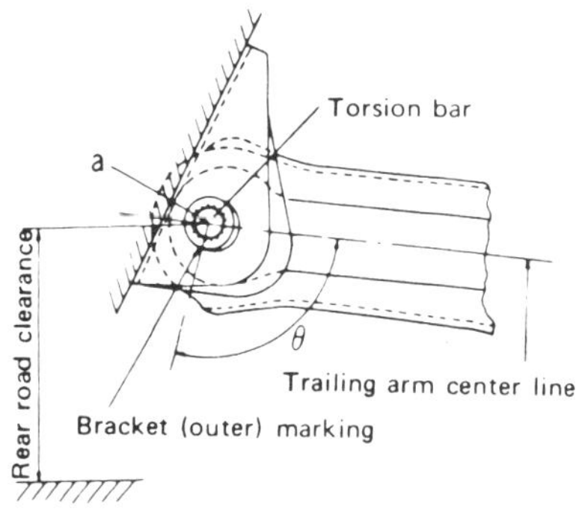

Fig. 11.41. Adjusting road clearance height (Sec. 20)

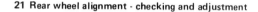

21 Rear wheel alignment - checking and adjustment

1 Frequent checking of the wheel alignment is not necessary under normal running conditions. However the alignment must be checked and adjusted, if necessary, in the event of any of the following:

a) When the tires wear unevenly.
b) If excessively low vehicle height, or uneven height occurs.
c) When any of the rear suspension parts, such as, trailing arm, torsion bar or bushing is renewed.

2 Special equipment is required to check the camber and toe-in, so this is a job for your local Subaru dealer or service station with the necessary equipment.

22 Fault diagnosis

The symptoms dealt with in the following table should be considered in conjunction with those for the steering in Chapter 8 as most symptoms are common to both systems

Symptoms	Reason/s	Remedy
Vibration and wheel wobble	Wear in suspension balljoints	Renew.
	Worn bushings in control arm	Renew.
	Loose wheel bearings	Check and tighten.
	Loose or defective shockabsorbers	Tighten or renew.
	Rear wheel alignment incorrect	Check and adjust as necessary.
Excessive pitching and rolling on corners	Defective shockabsorber and/or broken spring	Renew.

Chapter 12 Bodywork

For modifications, and information applicable to later models, see Supplement at end of manual

Contents

1 General description

1 The body used in Subaru models is of the combined body and underframe integral construction type, having all panels welded. The only exception is the front fenders which are bolted in position. This makes a very strong and torsionally rigid shell whilst acting as a positive location for attachment of the major units.
2 The different body types used on models covered by this manual are: Sedan, Coupe, Hardtop and Station Wagon. Many body parts are interchangeable between the different models. The floor is specially reinforced lengthwise at the central part for safety in the event of a collision. Under the front seat is a crossmember and the rear seat riser is itself a crossmember.
3 From 1974 all models are fitted with energy absorbing bumpers, both front and rear, as additional safety equipment. Also from 1974 on Station Wagons a one piece door is adopted in place of the two piece door on earlier models.

2 Maintenance - body exterior

1 The body is easy to keep clean due to its shape. The general condition of a car's bodywork is the one thing that significantly affects its value. Maintenance is easy but needs to be regular and particular. Neglect, particularly after minor damage, can lead quickly to further deterioration and costly repair bills. It is important also to keep watch on those parts of the car not immediately visible, for instance, the underside, inside all the wheel arches and the engine compartment.
2 The basic maintenance routine for the bodywork is washing - preferably with a lot of water from a hose. This will remove all the solids which may have stuck to the car. It is important to flush these off in such a way as to prevent grit from scratching the finish. The wheel aprons and underbody need washing in the same way to remove any accumulated mud which will retain moisture and rust. Paradoxically the best time to clean the underbody and wheel aprons is in wet weather when the mud is thoroughly wet and soft. In very wet weather the underbody is usually cleaned of large accumulations automatically and this is a good time for inspection.
3 Periodically it is a good idea to have the whole of the underside of the car steam cleaned, engine compartment included, so that a thorough inspection can be carried out to see what minor repairs and renovations are necessary. Steam cleaning is available at many garages and is necessary for removal of accumulations of oily grime which sometimes cakes thick in certain areas near the engine and transmission. The facilities are usually available at commercial vehicle garages but if not there are one or two excellent grease solvents available which can be brush applied. The dirt can then be hosed off.
4 After washing paintwork, wipe it with a chamois leather to give an unspotted clear finish. A coat of protective wax polish will give added protection against chemical pollutants in the air. If the paintwork sheen has dulled or oxidised, use a cleaner/polisher combination to restore the brilliance of the shine. Always check that door and ventilator opening drain holes and pipes are completely clear so that water can drain out.
5 Bright work should be treated the same way as paintwork. Windshields can be kept clear of the smeary film which often appears if detergent is added to the water in the windshield washer. Use a mild one such as washing up liquid. Never use any form of wax or chromium polish on glass.

3 Maintenance - body interior

1 Floor mats should be brushed or vacuum cleaned regularly to keep them free of grit. If they are badly stained remove them from the car for scrubbing or sponging and make quite sure they are dry before replacement. Seats and interior trim panels can be kept clean by a wipe over with a damp cloth. If they do become stained (which can be more apparent on light colored upholstery) use a little liquid detergent and a soft nailbrush to scour the grime out of the grain of the material. Do not forget to keep the roof lining clean in the same way as the upholstery. When using liquid cleaners inside the car do not over-wet the surfaces being cleaned. Excessive damp could get into the seams and padded interior causing stains, offensive odors or even rot. If the inside of the car gets wet accidentally, it is worthwhile taking some trouble

to dry it out properly, particularly where carpets are involved. **DO NOT** leave oil or electric heaters inside the car for this purpose.

4 Minor body damage - repair

See also the photo sequence on pages 198 and 199.

Repair of minor scratches in the bodywork

If the scratch is very superficial and does not penetrate to the metal of the bodywork, repair is very simple. Lightly rub the area of the scratch with a paintwork renovator, or a very fine cutting paste, to remove loose paint from the scratch and to clear the surrounding bodywork of wax polish. Rinse the area with clean water.

Apply touch-up paint to the scratch using a thin paint brush, continue to apply thin layers of paint until the surface of the paint in the scratch is level with the surrounding paintwork. Allow the new paint at least two weeks to harden, then blend it into the surrounding paintwork by rubbing the paintwork in the scratch area with a paintwork renovator or a very fine cutting paste. Finally apply wax polish.

An alternative to painting over the scratch is to use paint patches. Use the same preparation for the affected area; then simply pick a patch of a suitable size to cover the scratch completely. Hold the patch against the scratch and burnish its backing paper; the patch will adhere to the paintwork, freeing itself from the backing paper at the same time. Polish the affected area to blend the patch into the surrounding paintwork. Where a scratch has penetrated right thru to the metal of the bodywork causing the metal to rust, a different repair technique is required. Remove any loose rust from the bottom of the scratch with a penknife, then apply rust inhibiting paint to prevent the formation of rust in the future. Using a rubber or nylon applicator fill the scratch with bodystopper paste. If required, this paste can be mixed with cellulose thinners to provide a very thin paste which is ideal for filling narrow scratches. Before the stopperpaste in the scratch hardens, wrap a piece of smooth cotton rag around the tip of a finger. Dip the finger in cellulose thinners and then quickly sweep it across the surface of the stopperpaste in the scratch; this will ensure that the surface of the stopperpaste is slightly hollowed. The scratch can now be painted over as described earlier in this Section.

Repair of dents in the bodywork

When deep denting of the car's bodywork has taken place, the first task is to pull the dent out, until the affected bodywork almost attains its original shape. There is little point in trying to restore the original shape completely, as the metal in the damaged area will have stretched on impact and cannot be reshaped fully to its original contour. It is better to bring the level of the dent up to a point which is about 3 mm (1/8 in) below the level of the surrounding bodywork. In cases where the dent is very shallow, it is not worth trying to pull it out at all.

If the underside of the dent is accessible, it can be hammered out gently from behind, using a mallet with a wooden or plastic head. Whilst doing this, hold a suitable block of wood firmly against the impact from the hammer blows and thus prevent a large area of bodywork from being 'belled-out.'

Should the dent be in a section of the bodywork which has a double skin or some other factor making it inaccessible from behind a different technique is called for. Drill several small holes thru the metal inside the dent area - particularly in the deeper sections. Then screw long self-tapping screws into the holes just sufficiently for them to gain a purchase in the metal. Now the dent can be pulled out by pulling on the protruding heads of the screws with a pair of pliers.

The next stage of the repair is the removal of the paint from the damaged area, and from an inch or so of the surrounding 'sound' bodywork. This is accomplished most easily by using a wire brush or abrasive pad on a power drill, although it can be done just as effectively by hand using sheets of abrasive paper. To complete the preparations for filling score the surface of the bare metal with a screwdriver or the tang of a file, or alternatively drill small holes in the affected areas. This will provide a really good key for the filler paste.

To complete the repair see the Section on filling and respraying.

Repair of rust holes or gashes in the bodywork

Remove all paint from the affected area and from an inch or so of the surrounding 'sound' bodywork, using an abrasive pad or wire brush on a power drill. If these are not available a few sheets of abrasive paper will do the job just as effectively. With the paint removed you will be able to gauge the severity of the corrosion and therefore decide whether to renew the whole panel (if this is possible) or to repair the affected area. New body panels are not as expensive as most people think and it is often quicker and more satisfactory to fit a new panel than to attempt to repair large areas of corrosion.

Remove all fittings from the affected areas except those which will act as a guide to the original shape of the damaged bodywork (eg, headlamp shells etc.). Then using tin snips or a hacksaw blade, remove all loose metal and any other metal badly affected by corrosion. Hammer the edges of the hole inwards in order to create a slight depression for the filler paste.

Wire brush the affected area to remove the powdery rust from the surface of the remaining metal. Paint the affected area with rust inhibiting paint. If the back of the rusted area is accessible treat this also.

Before filling can take place it will be necessary to block the hole in some way. This can be achieved by the use of one of the following materials: Zinc gauze, Aluminum tape or Polyurethane foam.

Zinc gauze is probably the best material to use for the large hole. Cut a piece to the approximate size and shape of the hole to be filled, then position it in the hole so that its edges are below the level of the surrounding bodywork. It can be retained in position by several blobs of filler paste around its periphery.

Aluminum tape should be used for small or very narrow holes. Pull a piece off the roll and trim it to the appropriate size and shape required, then pull off the backing paper (if used) and stick the tape over the hole; it can be overlapped if the thickness of one piece is insufficient. Burnish down the edges of the tape with the handle of a screwdriver or similar to ensure that the tape is securely attached to the metal underneath.

Polyurethane foam is best used where the hole is situated in a section of bodywork of complex shape, backed by a small box section (eg, where the sill panel meets the rear wheel apron - most cars). The unusual mixing procedure for this foam is as follows. Put equal amounts of fluid from each of the two cans provided into one container. Stir until the mixture begins to thicken, then quickly pour this mixture into the hole, and hold a piece of cardboard over the larger apertures. Almost immediately the polyurethane will begin to expand, squirting out of any holes left unblocked. When the foam hardens it can be cut back to just below the level of the surrounding bodywork with a hacksaw blade.

Bodywork repairs - filling and re-spraying

Before using this Section, see the Sections on dent, deep scratch, rust hole and gash repairs.

Many types of bodyfiller are available, but generally speaking those proprietary kits which contain a tin of filler paste and a tube of resin hardener are best for this type of repair. A wide, flexible plastic or nylon applicator will be found invaluable for imparting a smooth and well contoured finish to the surface of the filler.

Mix up a little filler on a piece of card or board - use the hardener sparingly (follow the maker's instructions on the packet), otherwise the filler will set very rapidly.

Using the applicator, apply the filler paste to the prepared area; draw the applicator across the surface of the filler to achieve the correct contour and to level the filler surface. As soon as a contour that approximates the correct one is achieved, stop working the paste - if you carry on too long the paste will become sticky and begin to 'pick-up' on the applicator. Continue to add thin layers of filler paste at twenty-minute intervals until the level of the filler is just 'proud' of the surrounding bodywork.

Once the filler has hardened, excess can be removed using a plane or file. From then on, progressively finer grades of abrasive paper should be used, starting with a 40 grade production paper and finishing with 400 grade 'wet-and-dry' paper. Always wrap the abrasive paper around a flat rubber, cork or wooden block - otherwise the surface of the filler will not be completely flat. During the smoothing of the filler surface the 'wet-and-dry' paper should be periodically rinsed in water. This will ensure that a very smooth finish is imparted to the filler at the final stage.

At this stage the 'dent' should be surrounded by a ring of bare metal, which in turn should be encircled by the finely 'feathered' edge of the good paintwork. Rinse the repair area with clean water, until all of the dust produced by the rubbing-down operation is gone.

Spray the whole repair area with a light coat of grey primer - this will show up any imperfections in the surface of the filler. Repair these imperfections with fresh filler paste or bodystopper, and once more smooth the surface with abrasive paper. If bodystopper is used, it can be mixed with cellulose thinners to form a really thin paste which is ideal for filling small holes. Repeat this spray and repair procedure until you are satisfied that the surface of the filler, and the feathered edge of the paintwork are perfect. Clean the repair area with clean water and allow to dry fully.

The repair area is now ready for spraying. Paint spraying must be carried out in a warm, dry, windless and dust free atmosphere. This condition can be created artifically if you have access to a large indoor working area, but if you are forced to work in the open, you will have to pick your day very carefully. If you are working indoors, dousing the floor in the work area with water will 'lay' the dust which would otherwise be in the atmosphere. If the repair area is confined to one body panel, mask off the surrounding panels; this will help to minimise the effect of a slight mis-match in colors. Bodywork fittings (eg, chrome strips, door handles etc) will also need to be masked off. Use genuine masking tape and several thicknesses of newspaper for the masking operation.

Before commencing to spray, agitate the aerosol can thoroughly then spray a test area (an old tin or similar) until the technique is mastered. Cover the repair area with a thick coat of primer; the thickness should be built up using several thin layers of paint rather than one thick one. Using 400 grade 'wet-and-dry' paper, rub down the surface of the primer until it is really smooth. While doing this, the work area should be thoroughly doused with water, and the wet-and-dry paper periodically rinsed in water. Allow to dry before spraying on more paint.

Spray on the top coat, again building up the thickness by using several thin layers of paint. Start spraying in the center of the repair area and then, using a circular motion, work outwards until the whole repair area and about 2 inches of the surrounding original paintwork is covered. Remove all masking material 10 to 15 minutes after spraying on the final coat of paint.

Allow the new paint at least 2 weeks to harden fully; then using a paintwork renovator or a very fine cutting paste, blend the edges of the new paint into the existing paintwork. Finally apply wax polish.

5 Major body repairs

1 Where serious damage has occurred or large areas need renewal due to neglect, new sections or panels will need welding in and this is best left to professionals. If the damage is due to impact it will also be necessary to check the alignment of the body structure.

2 If a body is left misaligned it is first of all dangerous as the car will not handle properly - and secondly, uneven stresses will be imposed on the steering, engine and transmission, causing abnormal wear or complete failure. Tire wear will also be excessive.

6 Front bumper - removal and refitting

FF1-1 1100 and 1300G models (1970-71)

1 Remove the two bumper attaching bolts at the front end of the stays and pull the bumper forward off the stays.

2 The side pieces can be separated from the center section by removing the attaching bolts.

3 Refitting is the reverse of removal.

1300 and 1400 models (1972-73)

4 Remove the bolts attaching the bumper stays to the front fenders and remove the bumper complete with stays.

5 Separate the bumper from the stays by removing the attaching bolts.

6 Refitting is the reverse of removal.

1400 and 1600 models (1974-77)

Note: From 1974 all models are equipped with energy absorbing type bumpers. Do not attempt to open them or weld or heat them as they can explode. They must be emptied by drilling a hole to release the contents before being discarded. Use safety glasses when drilling the holes.

7 Remove the two flange nuts attaching the front of each damper (energy absorber) to the body.

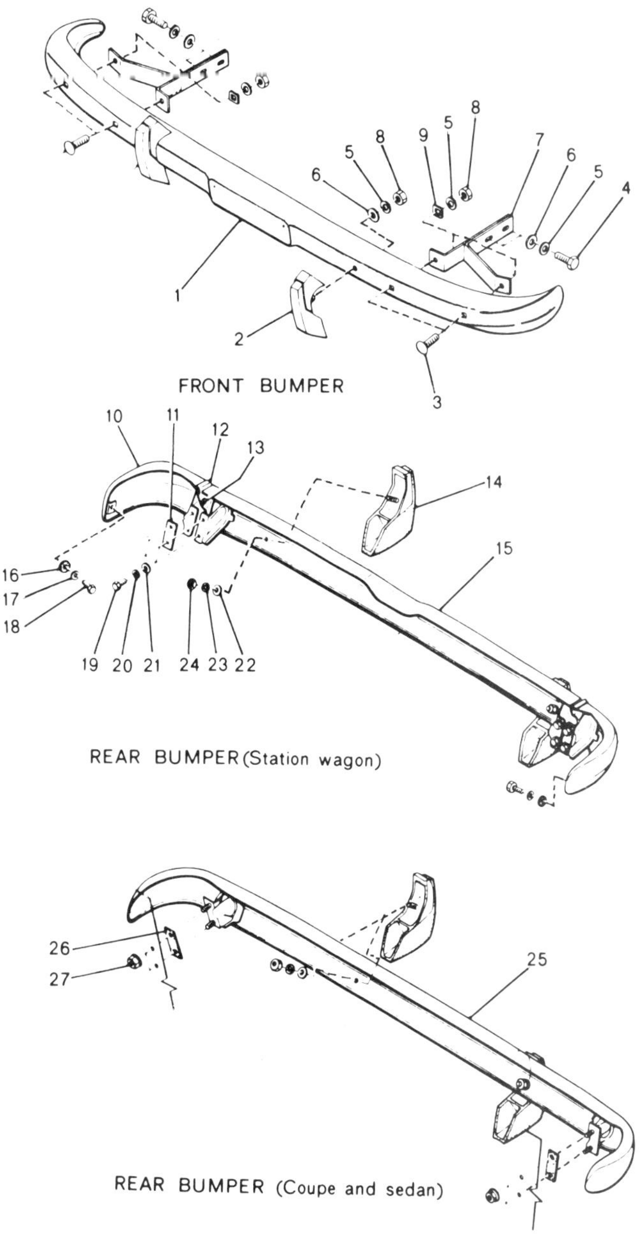

Fig. 12.1. Bumper assemblies - 1972/73 models

1 Front bumper
2 Front bumper guard
3 Bolt
4 Bolt
5 Spring washer
6 Washer
7 Front bumper stay
8 Nut
9 Washer
10 Rear bumper (side)
11 Cushion rubber
12 Bumper cover
13 Screw
14 Rear bumper guard
15 Rear bumper (center)
16 Cushion rubber
17 Washer
18 Bolt
19 Bolt
20 Spring washer
21 Washer
22 Washer
23 Spring washer
24 Nut
25 Rear bumper (SW)
26 Cushion rubber
27 Flange nut

6.8 Remove the front damper rear attaching bolt

Fig. 12.2. Bumper assemblies for all models - 1974/77 (except 4WD)

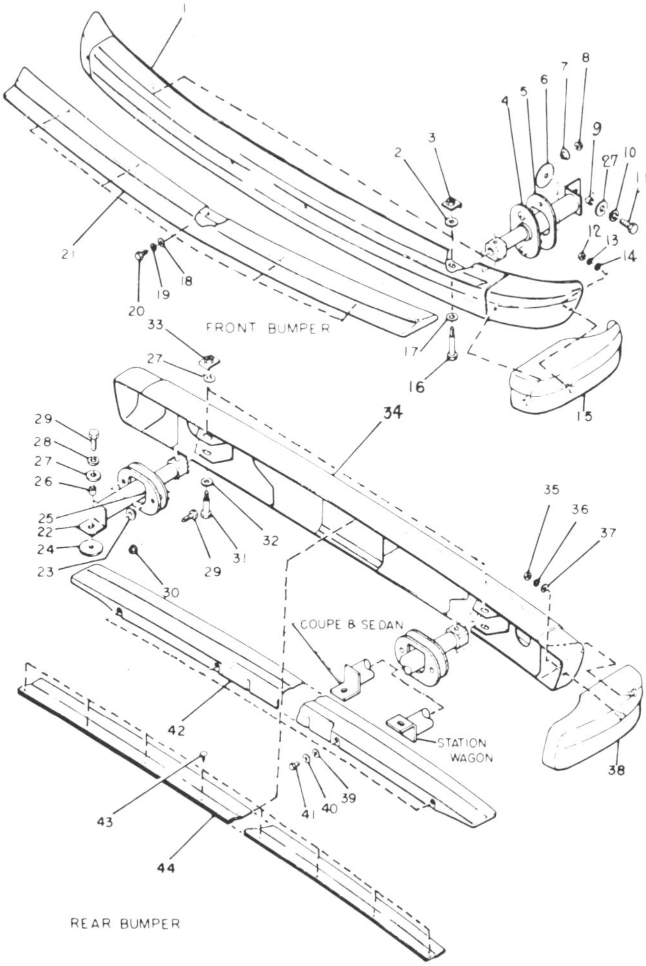

1 *Bumper (front)*
2 *Washer*
3 *Stop nut (bumper)*
4 *Damper*
5 *Cushion rubber*
6 *Cushion rubber*
7 *Spacer*
8 *Flange nut*
9 *Spacer*
10 *Spring washer*
11 *Bolt (cone point)*
12 *Nut*
13 *Spring washer*
14 *Washer*
15 *Bumper side (front)*
16 *Pin (bumper)*
17 *Washer*
18 *Washer*
19 *Spring washer*
20 *Bolt (cross recess)*
21 *Cover (front bumper)*
22 *Damper*
23 *Flange nut*
24 *Cushion rubber*
25 *Cushion rubber*
26 *Spacer*
27 *Washer*
28 *Spring washer*
29 *Bolt (cone point)*
30 *Flange nut*
31 *Pin (bumper)*
32 *Washer*
33 *Stop nut (bumper)*
34 *Bumper (rear)*
35 *Nut*
36 *Spring washer*
37 *Washer*
38 *Bumper side*
39 *Washer*
40 *Washer*
41 *Bolt*
42 *Cover (rear bumper)*
43 *Clip*
44 *Cover (rear bumper)*

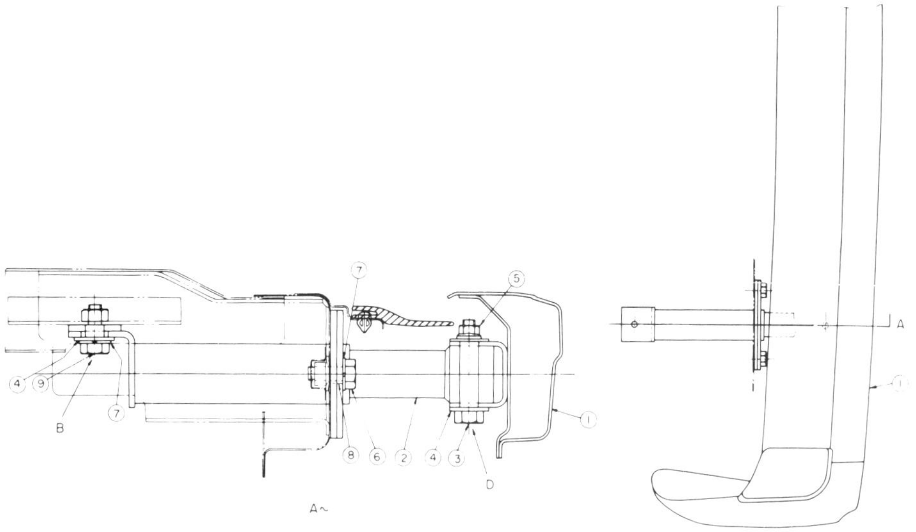

Fig. 12.3. Rear bumper system of Station Wagon (1974/77)

1 *Bumper*
2 *Damper*
3 *Bolt*
4 *Washer*
5 *Flange nut*
6 *Bolt*
7 *Spring washer*
8 *Spacer*
9 *Bolt*

8 Remove the bolt which secures the rear of each damper to the body, and remove the bumper and dampers as an assembly.
9 Separate the bumper from the dampers by removing the attaching bolts.
10 Remove the two bolts at the back of the bumper and separate the end pieces from the center section.
11 When refitting the bumper tighten the flange nut to 15 - 34 ft lb (2.0 - 4.8 kg f m). Temporarily tighten the damper rear attaching bolts, then tighten the flange nuts securing the front of the dampers to 10 - 21 ft lb (1.3 - 3.0 kg f m). Now tighten the rear attaching bolts to 10 - 21 lb f ft (1.3 - 3.0 kg f m).

7 Rear bumpers - removal and refitting

FF-1 1100 and 1300G models (1970-71)

1 Disconnect the license plate lamp wiring harness and pull the lead from the bumper.
2 Working from inside the trunk, remove the six securing bolts and remove the bumper.
3 Refitting is the reverse of removal.

1300 and 1400 models (1972-73) - except Station Wagons

4 Working from inside the trunk, remove the flange nuts and then remove the bumper by pulling it rearwards.
5 Refitting is the reverse of removal.

1970/73 Station Wagons

6 Remove the inner trim panel from both sides of the rear compartment. Remove the flange nuts and bolts attaching the side pieces to the body.
7 Remove the bolts attaching the center section of the bumper to the tailgate and remove the bumper.
8 Refitting is the reverse of removal.

1400 and 1600 models (1974/77) - except Station Wagons

9 Working from inside the trunk remove the damper securing bolts on both sides. Undo the two flange nuts attaching the damper to the rear panel on both sides and remove the bumper assembly. Separate the dampers from the bumper by removing the attaching bolts.
10 Refitting and torque Specifications are the same as described in paragraph 11, Section 6.

1400 and 1600 models (1974-77) - Station Wagons

11 Working from inside the rear compartment remove the damper securing bolts, then remove the bumper attaching bolts.
12 Remove the bolts attaching the dampers to the rear panel and remove the dampers.
13 Refitting is the reverse of removal. Tighten the damper to body bolts to 10 - 21 lb f ft (1.3 - 3.0 kg f m) and the bumper to damper bolts to 15 - 34 lb f ft (2.0 - 4.8 kg f m).

8 Front hood - removal, refitting and adjustment

FF-1 1100 and 1300G models

1 Open the hood and disconnect the hood stay and horn wiring. Remove the hinge bolts and lift off the hood.

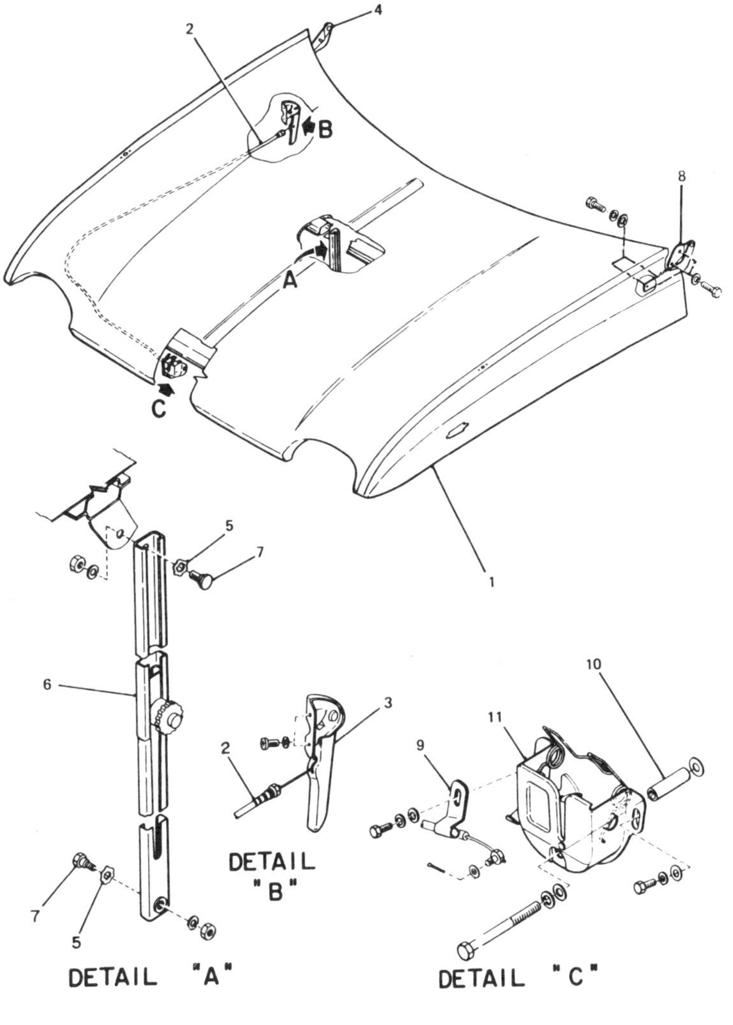

Fig. 12.4. Front hood and lock assembly - FF-1 models

1 Hood assembly (front)
2 Cable (hood lock release)
3 Handle (hood lock release)
4 Hinge (front hood RH)
5 Wavewasher (stay)
6 Stay (front hood)
7 Bolt (stay)
8 Hinge (front hood LH)
9 Clip (hood lock release)
10 Spacer (hood lock)
11 Lock (front hood)

This sequence of photographs deals with the repair of the dent and paintwork damage shown in this photo. The procedure will be similar for the repair of a hole. It should be noted that the procedures given here are simplified – more explicit instructions will be found in the text

In the case of a dent the first job – after removing surrounding trim – is to hammer out the dent where access is possible. This will minimise filling. Here, the large dent having been hammered out, the damaged area is being made slightly concave

Now all paint must be removed from the damaged area, by rubbing with coarse abrasive paper. Alternatively, a wire brush or abrasive pad can be used in a power drill. Where the repair area meets good paintwork, the edge of the paintwork should be 'feathered', using a finer grade of abrasive paper

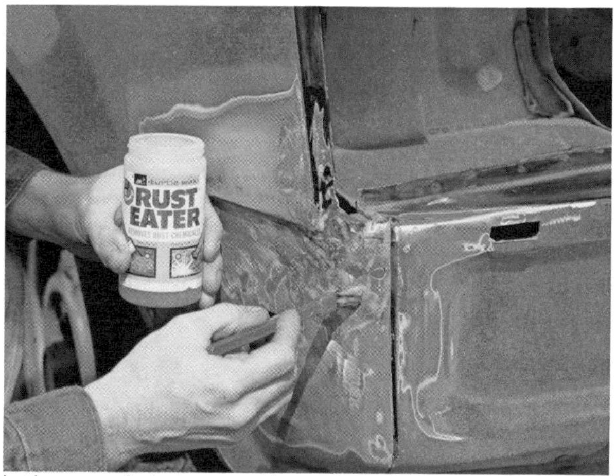

In the case of a hole caused by rusting, all damaged sheet-metal should be cut away before proceeding to this stage. Here, the damaged area is being treated with rust remover and inhibitor before being filled

Mix the body filler according to its manufacturer's instructions. In the case of corrosion damage, it will be necessary to block off any large holes before filling – this can be done with aluminium or plastic mesh, or aluminium tape. Make sure the area is absolutely clean before ...

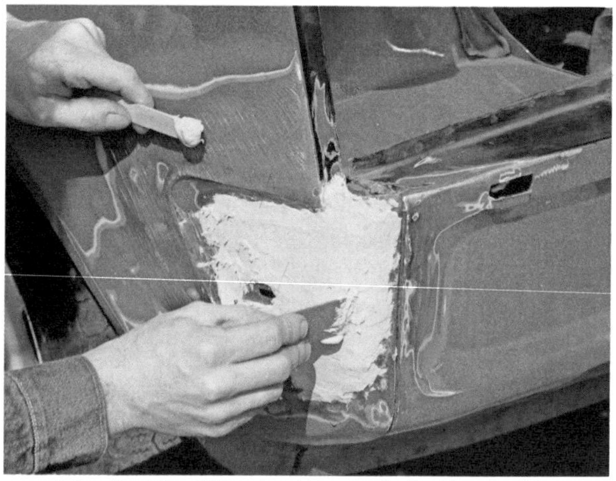

... applying the filler. Filler should be applied with a flexible applicator, as shown, for best results; the wooden spatula being used for confined areas. Apply thin layers of filler at 20-minute intervals, until the surface of the filler is slightly proud of the surrounding bodywork

Initial shaping can be done with a Surform plane or Dreadnought file. Then, using progressively finer grades of wet-and-dry paper, wrapped around a sanding block, and copious amounts of clean water, rub down the filler until really smooth and flat. Again, feather the edges of adjoining paintwork

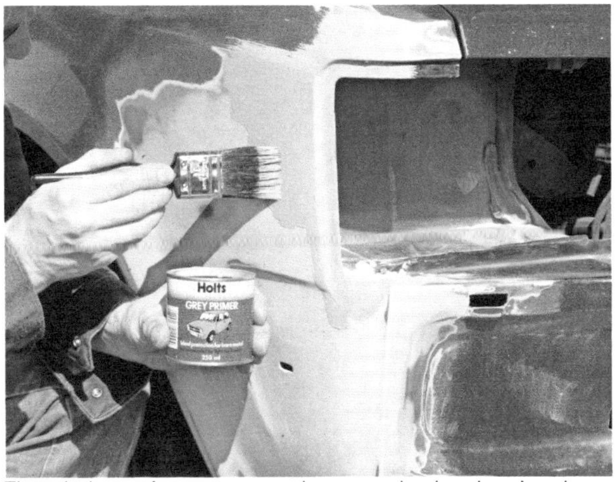

The whole repair area can now be sprayed or brush-painted with primer. If spraying, ensure adjoining areas are protected from over-spray. Note that at least one inch of the surrounding sound paintwork should be coated with primer. Primer has a 'thick' consistency, so will find small imperfections

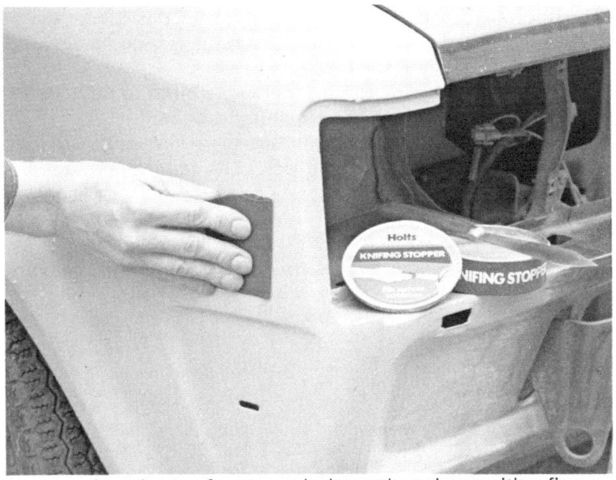

Again, using plenty of water, rub down the primer with a fine grade wet-and-dry paper (400 grade is probably best) until it is really smooth and well blended into the surrounding paintwork. Any remaining imperfections can now be filled by carefully applied knifing stopper paste

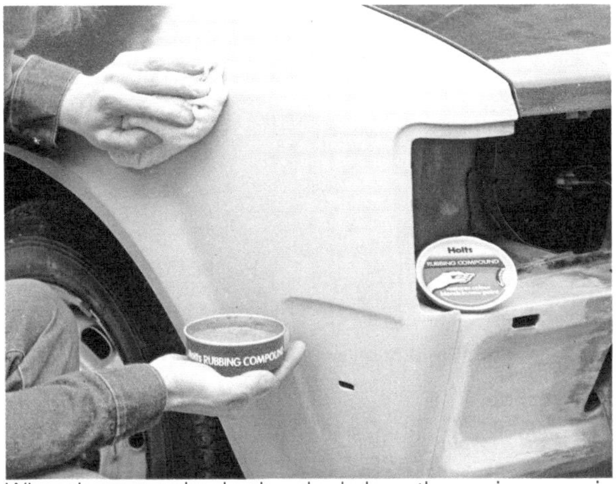

When the stopper has hardened, rub down the repair area again before applying the final coat of primer. Before rubbing down this last coat of primer, ensure the repair area is blemish-free – use more stopper if necessary. To ensure that the surface of the primer is really smooth use some finishing compound

The top coat can now be applied. When working out of doors, pick a dry, warm and wind-free day. Ensure surrounding areas are protected from over-spray. Agitate the aerosol thoroughly, then spray the centre of the repair area, working outwards with a circular motion. Apply the paint as several thin coats

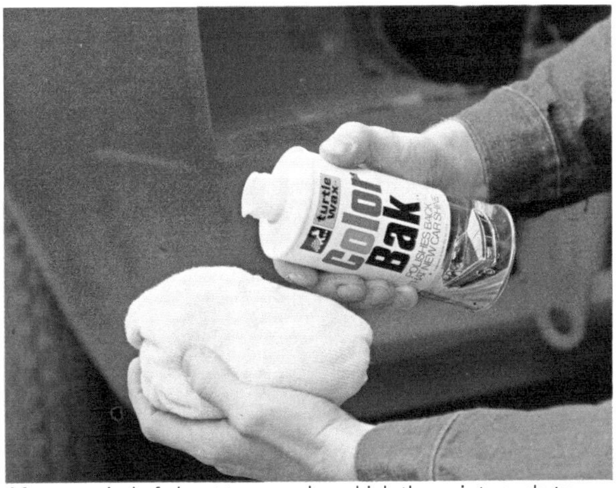

After a period of about two weeks, which the paint needs to harden fully, the surface of the repaired area can be 'cut' with a mild cutting compound prior to wax polishing. When carrying out bodywork repairs, remember that the quality of the finished job is proportional to the time and effort expended

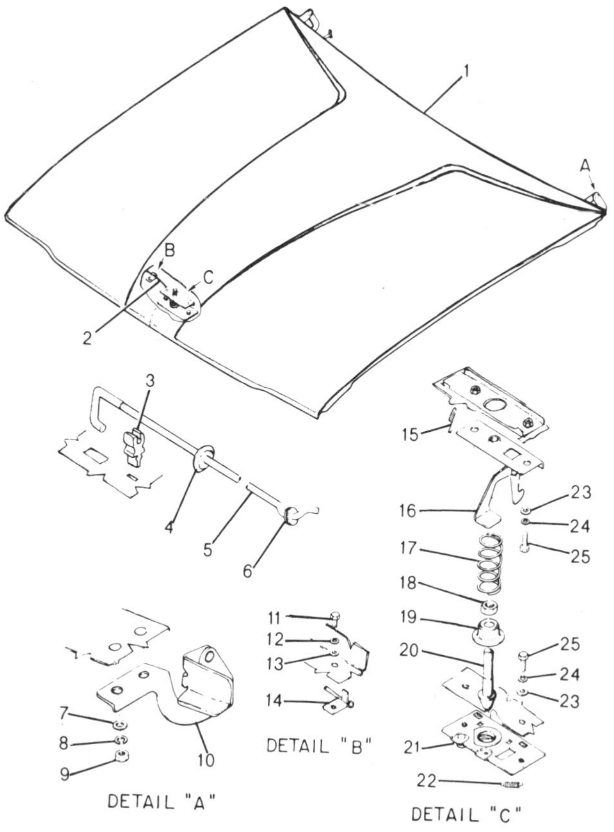

Fig. 12.5. Front hood and lock assembly 1972/77

1 Front hood
2 Release cable
3 Hood stay clip
4 Stopper (hood stay)
5 Hood stay
6 Grommet
7 Washer
8 Spring washer
9 Nut
10 Hinge
11 Screw
12 Spring washer
13 Washer
14 Clip (release cable)
15 Spring
16 Hood lock lever
17 Spring (striker)
18 Nut
19 Retainer
20 Striker
21 Hood lock
22 Spring
23 Washer
24 Spring washer
25 Bolt

Fig. 12.6. Adjusting the front hood striker

2 Refitting is the reverse of removal.
3 Forward and back hood position is adjusted by loosening the hood and hood hinge securing bolts. Up and down adjustment is carried out by loosening the hood lock securing bolts and moving the hood lock up or down as required. The hood lock is adjusted in the same way. When correctly adjusted the hood should make good contact on the stops on the fenders.
Note: If the rear of the hood is too low, it may spring open.

1972-77 models

4 Remove the nuts attaching the hood to the hinges and lift off the hood.
5 When refitting the hood check the operation of the hood lock. Adjust the hood lock by loosening the hood lock securing screws and aligning both centers of the striker and the lock.
6 Adjust the length of the striker, if necessary, by loosening the locknut and turning the striker as required. Tighten the locknut.

9 Trunk lid - renewal, refitting and adjustment

FF-1 1100 and 1300G models

1 Remove the hinge arms to lid bolts and lift off the hood.
2 After refitting adjust the forward and back position of the trunk lid by loosening the hinge to body bolts and moving the lid as necessary, then tighten the bolts.
3 To adjust the lid side to side, loosen the hinge to lid bolts and move the lid as necessary, then tighten the bolts.
4 To adjust the trunk lid lock, loosen the striker bolts and move the striker up or down or loosen the lock bolts and move it sideways as required.

1300, 1400 and 1600 models - 1972-77

5 The trunk lid is adjusted up and down by loosening the bolts

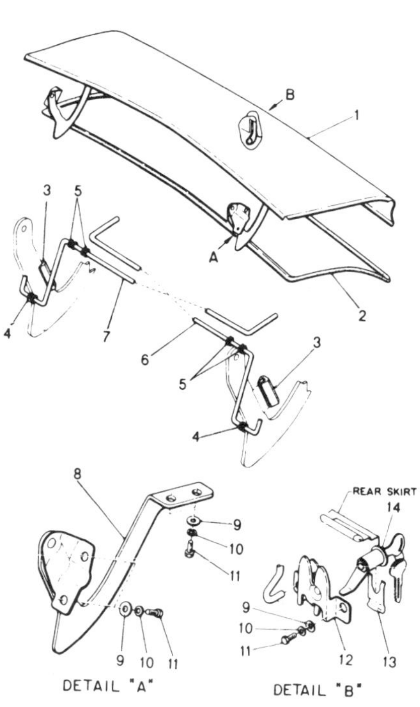

Fig. 12.7. Component parts of trunk lid (1972/77)

1 Trunk lid
2 Weather strip
3 Stopper
4 Roller
5 Bushing
6 Torsion bar (LH)
7 Torsion bar (RH)
8 Hinge
9 Washer
10 Spring washer
11 Bolt
12 Trunk lid lock assembly
13 Clip
14 Key lock assembly

which attach the hinge to the body. Adjustment front to rear is by loosening the bolts attaching the trunk lid to the hinge.
6 The trunk lid is adjusted either left or right by loosening both sets of hinge bolts and moving the lid as required.

10 Door trim panels - removal and refitting

1 Remove the armrest attaching screws from the recessed holes. Lift the armrest and slide it forward to remove it.
2 Press back the window regulator handle retaining spring and pull off the handle.
3 Pull on the inside door handle and remove the cover by undoing the screw.
4 Prise the trim panel off the door with a screwdriver. When prising out the clips take care to avoid damaging the paintwork or trim panel.
5 Refitting is the reverse of the removal procedure. Make sure the clips are located in their recesses, tap the panel fully in with the heel of your hand. Fit the window regulator handle so that when the window is closed the handle is pointing forward.

11 Front door glass - removal and refitting

1 Remove the trim panel as described in Section 10.
2 Remove the glass stoppers (upper), weather strip, stopper (rear) and runchannel.
3 Take out the snap pin which retains the glass-holder and the regulator arm, and remove the regulator arm.
4 Tilt the glass forward and separate the roller of the regulator from the slide rail of the glass holder, then lift the glass upwards and out.
3 Refitting is the reverse of the removal sequence.

12 Front door window regulator - removal and refitting

1 Remove the trim panel and the glass as described in Sections 10

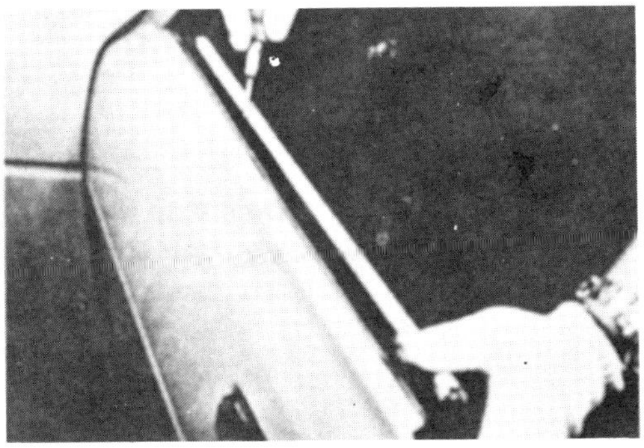

Fig. 12.8. Removing the runchannel

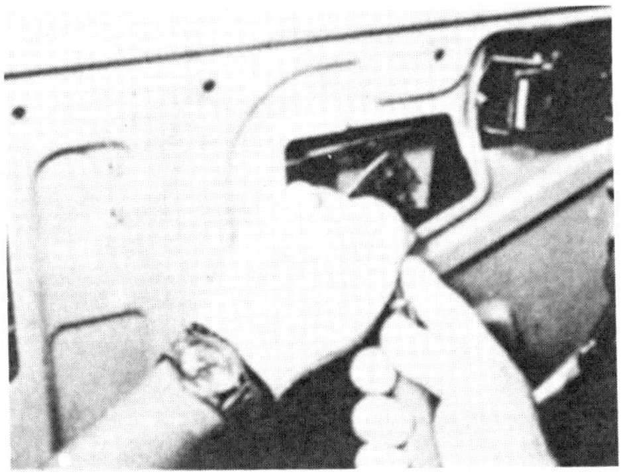

Fig. 12.9. Removing the snap-pin which retains the glass holder and regulator arm

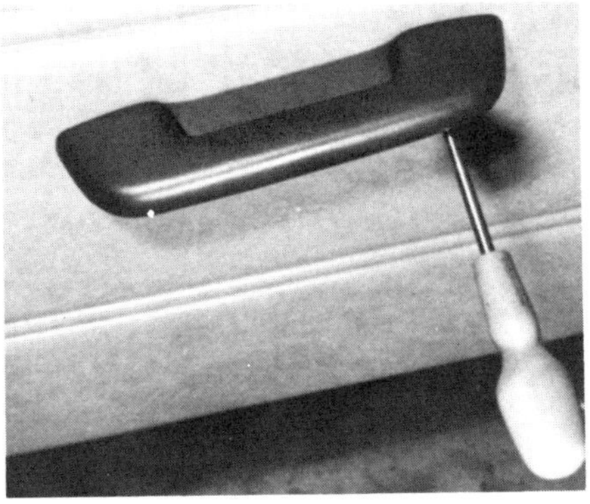

10.1 Removing the armrest attaching screws

10.2a Window regulator handle

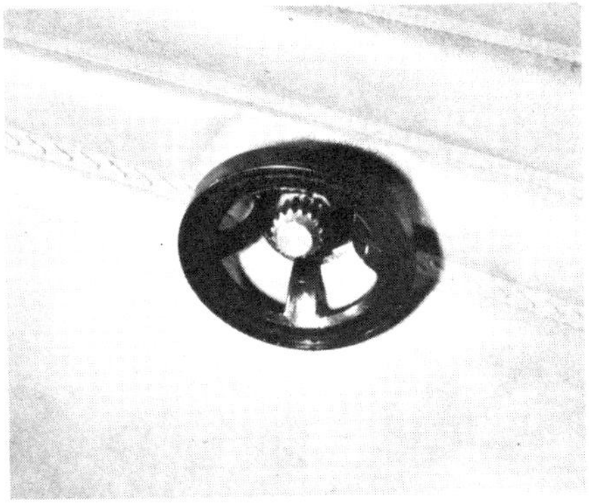

10.2b Spindle for window regulator handle

10.3a Remove the cover retaining screw ...

10.3b ... and take off the door handle cover

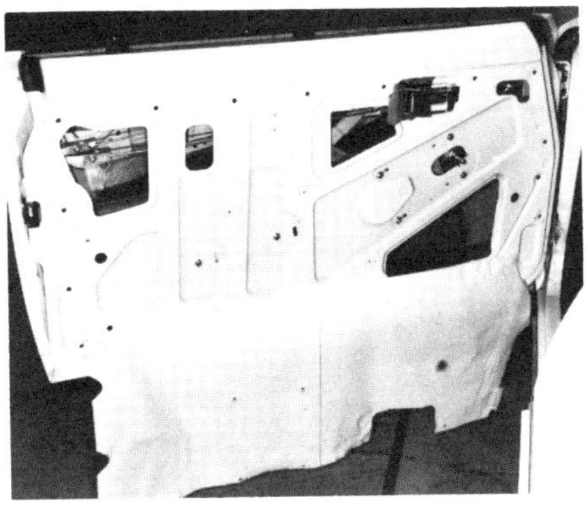

10.4 Door with trim panel removed

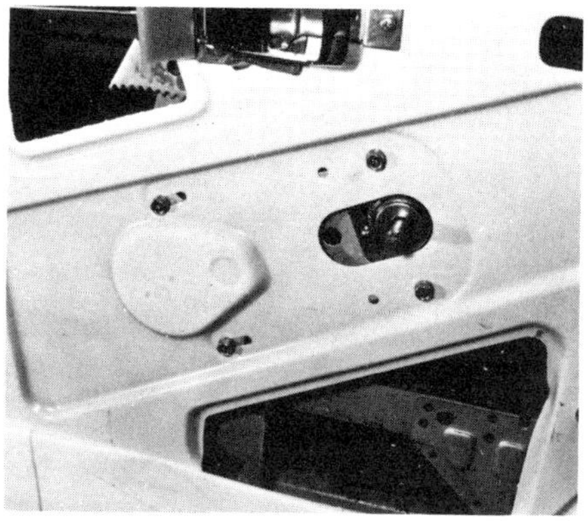

12.2 Remove the window regulator winding mechanism securing bolts

and 11.

2 Remove the regulator winding mechanism securing bolts and the slide rail bolts.

3 Remove the regulator assembly thru the bottom hole in the door inner panel.

4 Refitting is the reverse of removal.

13 Front door interior handle - removal and refitting

1 Remove the trim panel as described in Section 10.

2 Remove the two screws at the connectors and the screws attaching the handle to the inner panel of the door.

3 Disconnect the retaining clip and pull the remote assembly forward out of the door, see Fig. 12.12.

4 Refitting is the reverse of removal. Make sure the retaining clip is securely fitted.

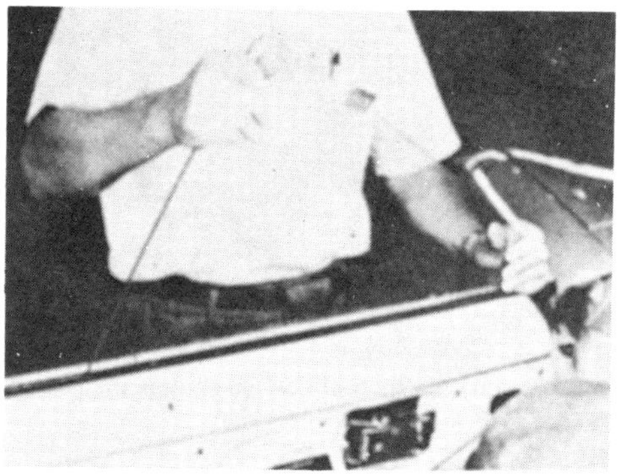

Fig. 12.10. Lifting out the front door glass

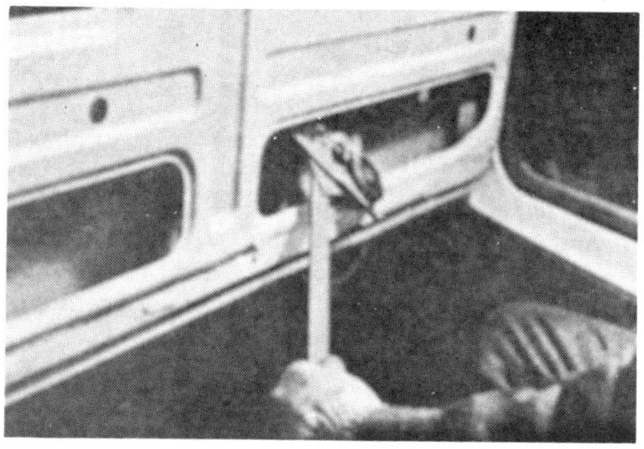

Fig. 12.11. Removing the regulator assembly

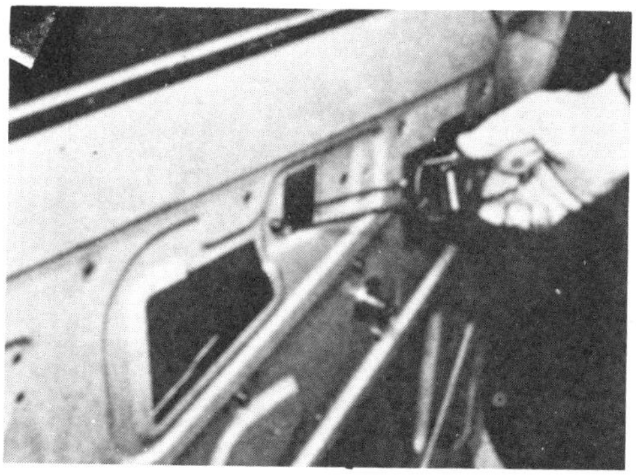

Fig. 12.12. Remove the interior door handle remote assembly

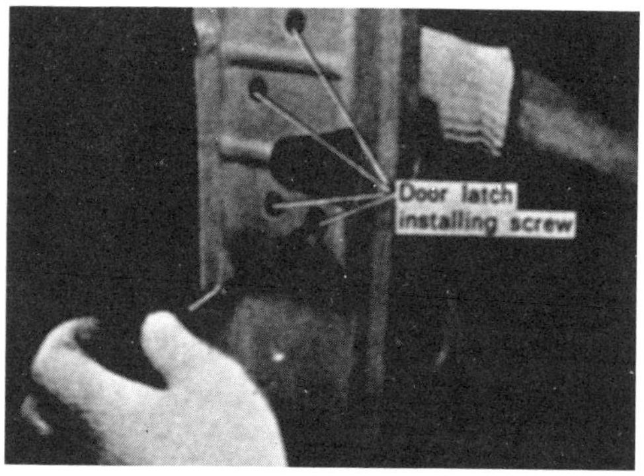

Fig. 12.13. Removing the door latch securing screws

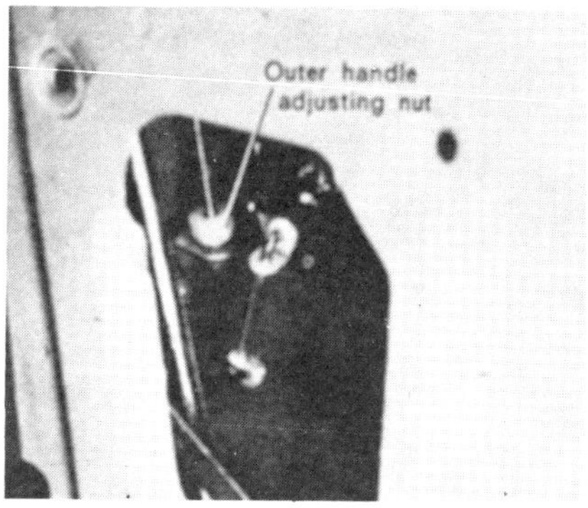

Fig. 12.14. Adjusting the outside door handle

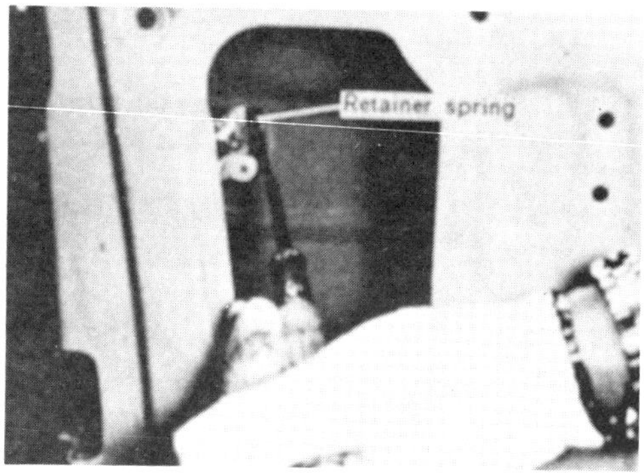

Fig. 12.15. Removing the key lock retainer spring

14 Front door latch - removal and refitting

FF-1 1100 and 1300G models

1 Remove the trim panel as described in Section 10.
2 Remove the interior handle remote control wire connector.
3 Remove the key lock connecting link by lowering the retainer with a pair of pliers.
4 Remove the door lock knob.
5 Remove the three door lock securing screws and withdraw the lock.
6 Refitting is the reverse of the removal sequence.

1972/77 models

7 Remove the trim panel as described in Section 10.
8 Disconnect the wire of the interior handle remote assembly. Remove the rear sash from the lower hole in the door after removing the securing bolts.
9 Disconnect the door latch from the key lock assembly.
10 Undo the four latch securing screws and remove the door latch.
11 Refitting is the reverse of the removal sequence.

15 Front door outside handle - removal and refitting

1 Remove the trim panel and the glass as described in Sections 10 and 11.
2 Disconnect the outside handle and door latch rod.
3 Remove the outside handle securing nuts and the handle is taken off from the outside.
4 Refitting is the reverse of removal. After fitting the handle, adjust it so that the door opens and closes smoothly, by turning the adjusting nut, see Fig. 12.14, as necessary.

16 Front door key lock - removal and refitting

1 Remove the trim panel and disconnect the door latch rod and key lock.
2 Pull the retainer spring out from the back of the key lock.
3 Remove the key lock assembly from the outside.
4 Refitting is the reverse of removal.

17 Front door - removal and refitting

FF-1 1100 and 1300G models

1 Open the door and place a support under the door to take its weight. The help of an assistant should also be enlisted to hold the door.
2 Scribe alignment marks on the hinges and door pillar to assist when refitting the doors.
3 Open the hood and remove the upper hinge securing bolts. To do this loosen the attaching screws at the rear of the front fender and raise the fender up a little.
4 Remove the lower hinge to pillar bolts and lift the door away from the body.

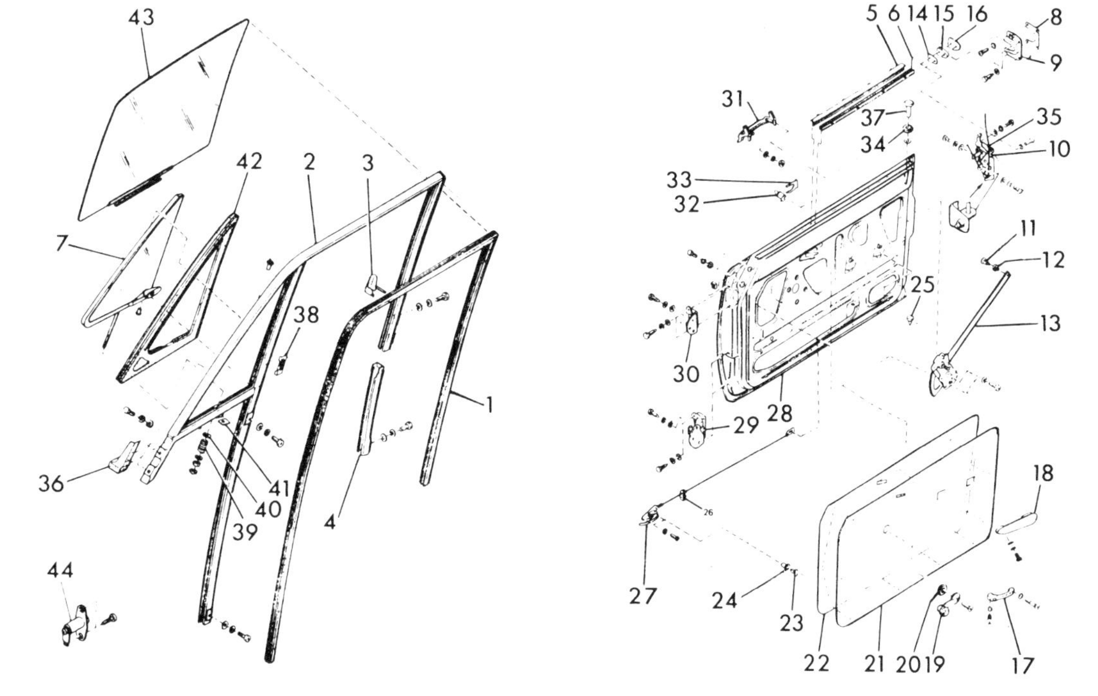

Fig. 12.16. Component parts of front door - FF-1 model

1 *Run channel*
2 *Sash assembly*
3 *Weather strip*
4 *Sash lower*
5 *Weather strip*
6 *Glass channel*
7 *Ventilator*
8 *Spacer*
9 *Striker*
10 *Door lock*
11 *Pin*
12 *Roller*
13 *Regulator*
14 *Spacer A (wedge door lock)*
15 *Wedge assembly (door lock)*
16 *Plate (wedge door lock)*
17 *Pull handle*
18 *Arm rest*
19 *Handle (regulator)*
20 *Escutcheon*
21 *Trim panel*
22 *Sealing cover*
23 *Clip*
24 *Cover (clip)*
25 *Stopper (regulator)*
26 *Holder*
27 *Inner remote control assembly*
28 *Door panel*
29 *Hinge assembly (lower)*
30 *Hinge assembly (upper)*
31 *Door handle (outer)*
32 *Key lock assembly*
33 *Clip*
34 *Cover*
35 *Rod*
36 *Weather strip*
37 *Knob*
38 *Plate*
39 *Spring*
40 *Friction washer (A)*
41 *Friction washer (B)*
42 *Weather strip*
43 *Slide glass assembly*
44 *Door switch*

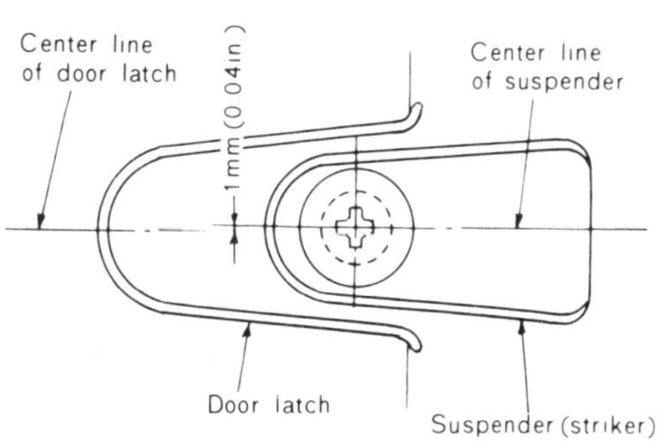

Fig. 12.17. Door striker adjustment

5 Refitting is the reverse of removal procedure. Ensure that the marks made at removal are aligned. Tighten the hinge bolts to 15 - 18 lb f ft (2.0 - 2.6 kg f m).

1972-77 models

6 Repeat the operations at paragraphs 1 and 2 above.
7 Pull aside the carpet which covers the front pillar and remove the hinge securing bolts from the inside of the car.
8 Lift the door away from the car.
9 Refitting is the reverse of removal. Tighten the hinge bolts to 17 - 21 lb f ft (2.3 - 2.9 kg f m).

18 Front door striker - adjustment

1 The door striker is secured to the pillar by three screws.
2 The position of the striker affects the correct closing of the door therefore it must be adjusted correctly.
3 The difference between the center line of the door latch and that of the striker should be 0.04 in (1 mm), see Fig. 12.17. Adjustment is by moving the striker after loosening the securing screws. Make sure the securing screws are fully tightened after each adjustment.

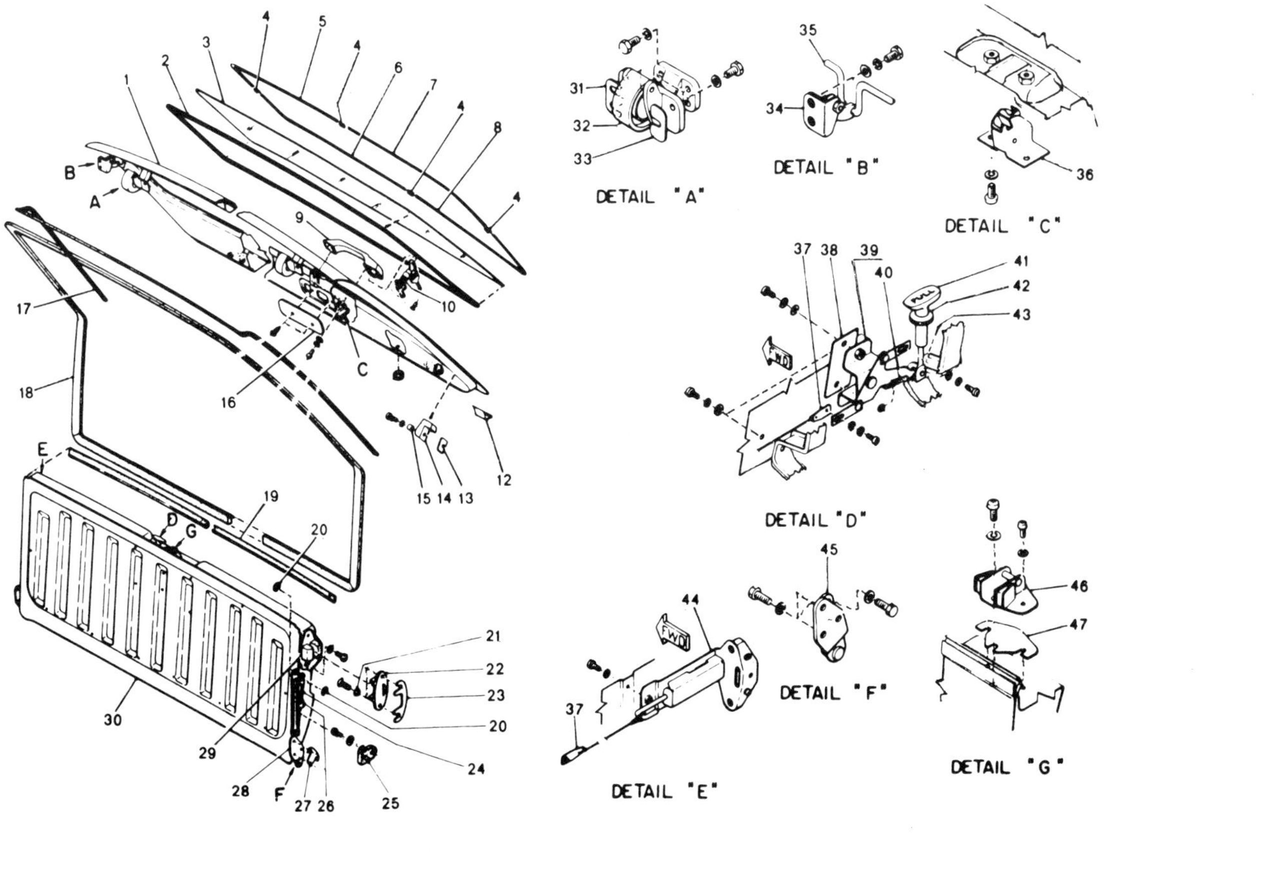

Fig. 12.18. Tailgate assembly - 1972/73 Station Wagon

1 Back door panel
2 Weather strip (upper)
3 Glass
4 Cover (joint)
5 Moulding
6 Moulding
7 Moulding
8 Moulding
9 Back door handle
10 Key lock assembly
11 Drain plug
12 Weather strip
13 Spacer (buffer)
14 Buffer
15 Spacer (buffer)
16 Cover
17 Weather strip (roof end)
18 Weather strip (back door)
19 Weather strip (back door, lower)
20 Retainer clip
21 Lock washer
22 Striker (lower)
23 Spacer (lower striker)
24 Stay (back door, lower)
25 Buffer
26 Back door stay
27 Spacer (back door, lower hinge)
28 Hinge (back door, lower)
29 Door lock assembly
30 Back door panel
31 Spacer
32 Hinge (back door, upper)
33 Spacer
34 Link (back door, upper)
35 Torsion bar
36 Door latch
37 Door lock
38 Washer
39 Lever assembly
40 Return spring
41 Back door knob
42 Grommet
43 Cotter pin
44 Door lock (RH)
45 Spacer
46 Striker (upper)
47 Spacer (upper striker)

19 Rear door - general

Basically the same procedures apply when removing and refitting assemblies of the rear door as for the front door.

20 Tailgate - removal and refitting

1972-73 Station Wagon

1 When removing the upper section of the tailgate insert a pin into the torsion bar bracket as shown in Fig. 12.19, to restrain the torsion bar, and remove the three left and right hinge securing bolts.

Note: The pin must be fitted before removing the hinge bolts to prevent to torsion bar from springing loose and causing damage.

2 If it is necessary to remove the torsion bar, twist the bar enough to free the pin.

3 Withdraw the pin and gradually let the torsion bar return to a free state and then remove the bar.

4 Refitting is the reverse of removal. Of the two torsion bars, the one which has a vynal tube over the end should be fitted first.

5 Hang the bar on the hinge as shown in Fig. 12.20.

Part A - normal position
Part B - - when torsion bar tension is low this position should be used

6 Access to remove the tailgate lower section is by removing the license plate securing screws, and removing the attaching bolts thru the rear holes behind the license plate.

7 Refitting is the reverse of the removal procedure.

1974-77 Station Wagon

8 The 1974-77 Station Wagons are fitted with a one piece tailgate and the removal and refitting procedure is basically the same as for the tailgate upper section on 1972-73 wagons.

21 Tailgate - adjustments

1972-73 Station Wagon

1 Adjust the tailgate stricker on the body so that slight contact is made with the latch. Adjust the striker by loosening the securing screws and locating it in the correct position.

2 Adjustment of the tailgate (lower) to buffer is by fitting shims as necessary. If the tailgate is too loose it may spring open.

3 Adjust the tailgate (lower) stop so that there is no rattle or vibration by loosening the wedge securing screws and moving it as necessary.

4 The tailgate (upper) door striker is fitted on the top side of the lower tailgate. Adjustment is by loosening the securing bolts and moving the striker as necessary. Make sure the securing bolts are tightened after each adjustment.

1974-77 Station Wagons

5 Adjust the tailgate buffer by adding or removing shims so that the tailgate closes tight without rattles or vibration.

6 Adjustment of the striker is by loosening the securing bolts and moving the striker. If necessary the striker may be adjusted with shims.

7 To adjust the push button secure the key cylinder securely with the lock plate, loosen the locknut and adjust so that the clearance between the end of the adjustment screw and the release lever is 0.02 - 0.08 in (0.5 - 2 mm) by turning the adjusting screw, see Fig. 12.21. Lock the adjusting screw with the locknut.

8 If the tailgate does not open when the button is pushed, decrease the clearance, when it cannot be closed, increase the clearance.

22 Front fender - removal and refitting

1 Open the hood.

2 Remove the side sill moulding. Remove the front bumper as described in Section 6.

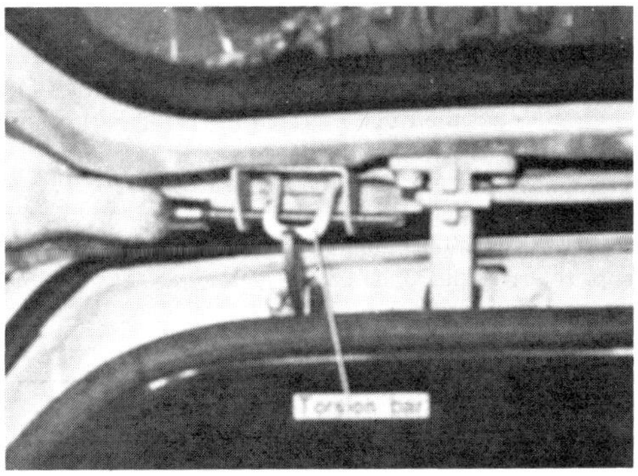

Fig. 12.19. Using a screwdriver to restrain the tailgate torsion bar

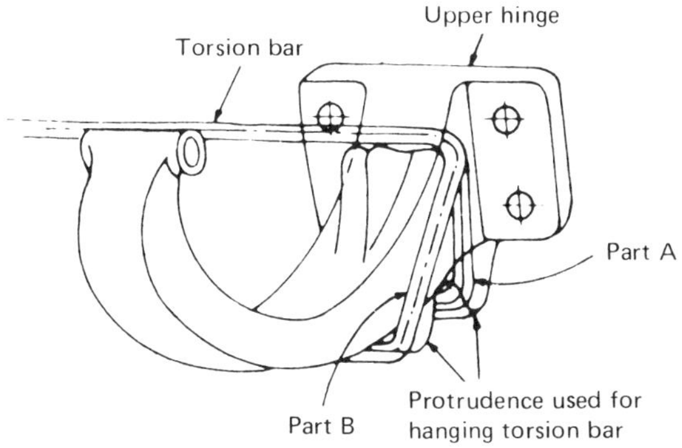

Fig. 12.20. Tailgate torsion bar position

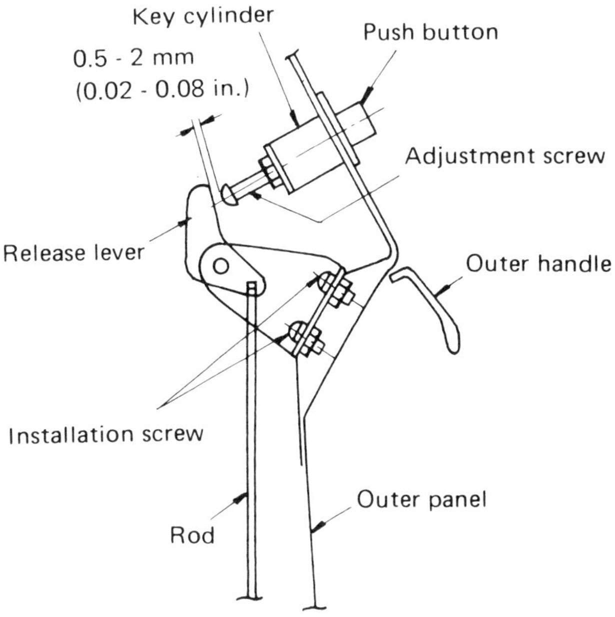

Fig. 12.21. Adjusting the tailgate push button

3 Remove the headlamp cover, the front combination lamp and side marker lamp as described in Chapter 10.
4 Remove the front fender stay.
5 Remove the front fender attaching screws and lift the fender away from the body, taking care not to scratch the body with the edge of the fender.
6 Refitting is the reverse of the removal sequence. Apply a bonding compound on the front apron, front pillar and radiator panel mating faces before repositioning the fender. When tightening the securing screws ensure that the clearance between the hood and fender and between the door pillar and fender is uniform.

23 Instrument panel - removal and refitting

FF-1 1100 and 1300G models

1 Disconnect the battery negative (–) cable. Remove the instrument cluster as described in Chapter 10.
2 Disconnect the wiring harness of the ignition/starter switch.
3 Remove the two screws securing the heater control box cover and take off the cover.
4 Pull out the ashtray and remove the three attaching screws.
5 Remove the radio panel. After removing the four screws securing the radio bracket, disconnect the wiring harness and antenna cable. Disconnect the speaker wire.
6 Disconnect the wiring to the wiper switch and the lighting switch.
7 Remove the nuts attaching the instrument panel to the body at each end.
8 Remove the two bolts attaching the panel to the heater control box.
9 Undo the securing screw and disconnect the defroster duct from the heater control box.

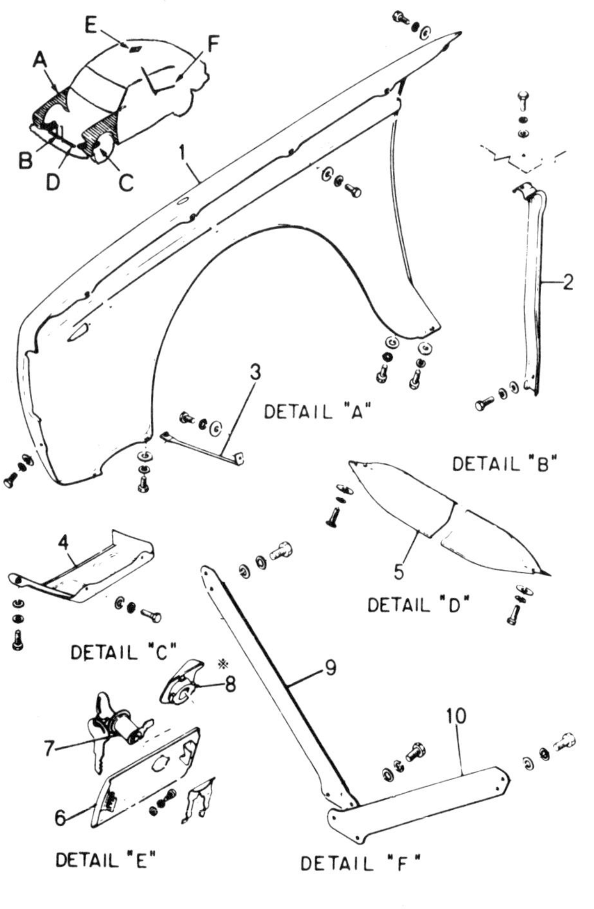

Fig. 12.22. The front fender assembly

1 *Front fender*
2 *Stay (front hood lock)*
3 *Stay (front fender)*
4 *Under cover*
5 *Scoop*
6 *Flap*
7 *Flap key lock*
8 *Flap knob*
9 *Reinforcement*
10 *Reinforcement*

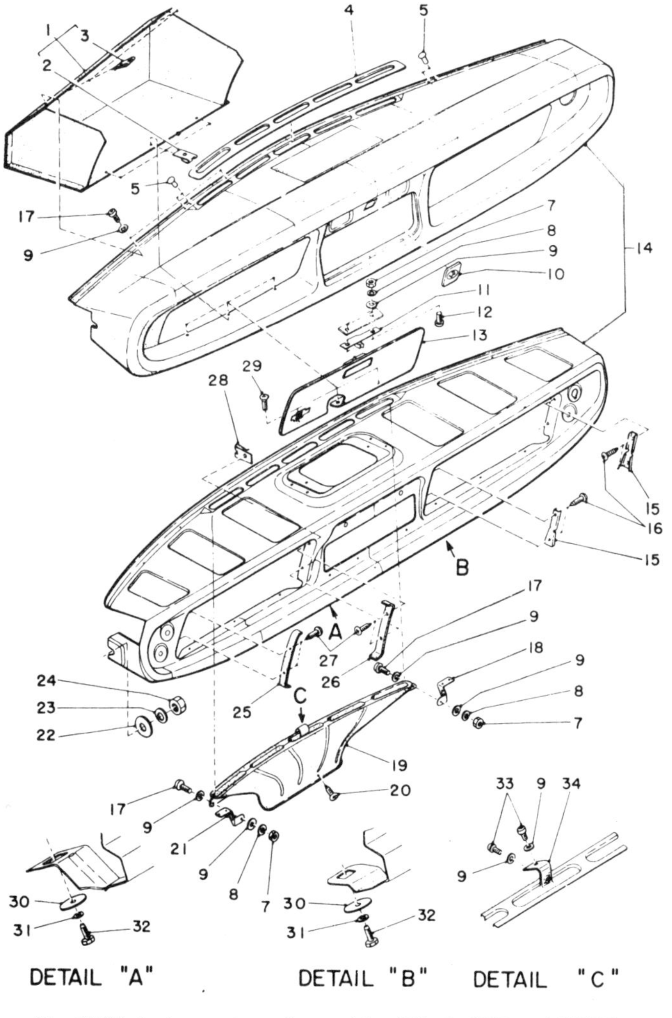

Fig. 12.23. Instrument panel assembly - FF - 1, 1100 and 1300G models

1 *Pocket assembly*
2 *Spring nut*
3 *Nut plate*
4 *Defroster grille*
5 *Rivet*
7 *Nut*
8 *Spring washer*
9 *Washer*
10 *Instrument panel ornament*
11 *Spring*
12 *Pan head screw*
13 *Lid assembly*
14 *Instrument panel assembly*
15 *Meter retainer*
16 *Pan head tapping screw*
17 *Pan head screw*
18 *Heater duct bracket (rh)*
19 *Defroster duct*
20 *Truss head tapping screw*
21 *Heater duct bracket (lh)*
22 *Washer*
23 *Spring washer*
24 *Nut*
25 *Retainer (lh)*
26 *Retainer (rh)*
27 *Tapping screw*
28 *Spring nut*
29 *Screw*
30 *Washer*
31 *Spring washer*
32 *Cone point bolt*
33 *Pan head screw*
34 *Clip*

10 To remove the instrument panel pull it a little to the right and lift it.
11 Refitting is the reverse of the removal procedure.

1300, 1400 and 1600 models

12 Remove the nuts at each end of the instrument panel which attached it to the body.
13 Remove the screws retaining the upper panel of the instrument panel to the body bracket.
14 After removing the bolts attaching the steering stay and steering shaft, remove the nuts securing the lower side of the instrument panel to the steering stay.
15 Disconnect the defroster hoses. On later models disconnect the side ventilation ducts.
16 Disconnect the heater control rod or cable and detach the outer cable clamp.
17 Disconnect the following wiring and cables:

a) Speedometer cable.
b) Tachometer lead (Coupe).
c) Block connector for instrument cluster.
d) Antenna cable.
e) All electrical leads.

18 The instrument panel can now be removed by pulling it forward.
19 Refitting is the reverse of the removal procedure.

24 Windshield glass - removal and refitting

1 If the windshield has been shattered stick adhesive sheeting over the outside of the glass, cover the air vents and remove as much of the broken glass as possible. If the windshield glass is being removed intact an assistant will be required.
2 Remove the metal moulding. Release the rubber weatherstrip by running a blunt screwdriver or similar tool under and around the weatherstrip to break the seal. When the rubber surround is free the glass can be pushed outwards with a steady pressure and the assistant on the outside can remove the glass.

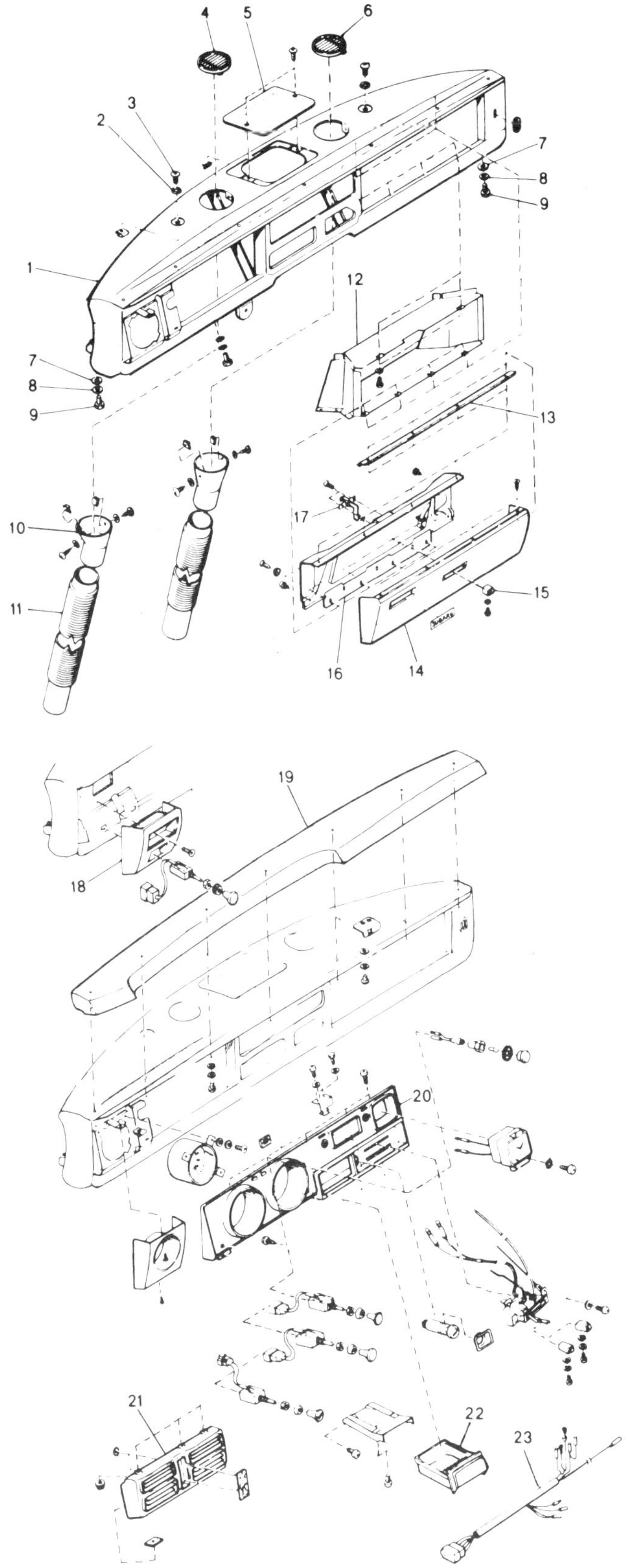

Fig. 12.24. Instrument panel assembly - 1300, 1400 and 1600 models

1 Instrument panel
2 Rosette
3 Screw
4 Defroster grille (l)
5 Speaker grille
6 Defroster grille (r)
7 Washer
8 Spring washer
9 Bolt
10 Defroster duct
11 Defroster hose
12 Pocket
13 Base
14 Cover
15 Knob
16 Plate
17 Lock assembly
18 Side cover
19 Pad
20 Center panel
21 Ventilator grille
22 Ashtray
23 Wiring cord

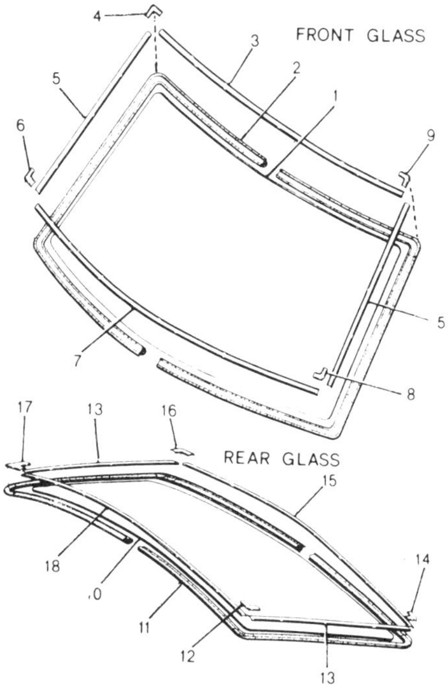

Fig. 12.25. Windshield glass - front and rear

1 Front glass
2 Weatherstrip
3 Moulding
4 Corner patch
5 Moulding
6 Corner patch
7 Moulding
8 Corner patch
9 Corner patch
10 Rear glass
11 Weatherstrip
12 Corner patch
13 Moulding
14 Corner patch
15 Moulding
16 Corner patch
17 Corner patch
18 Moulding

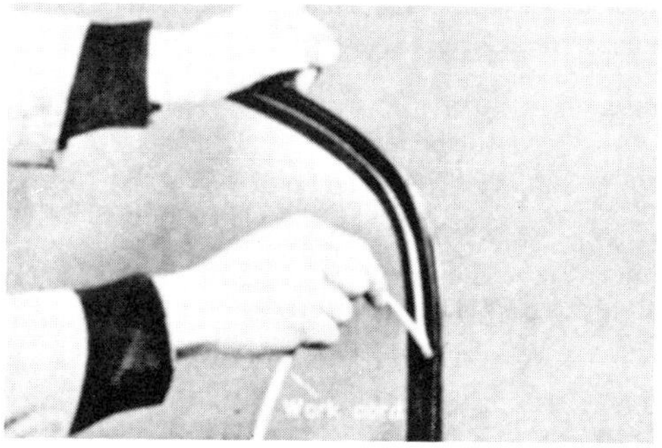

Fig. 12.26. Fitting the cord into the weatherstrip channel

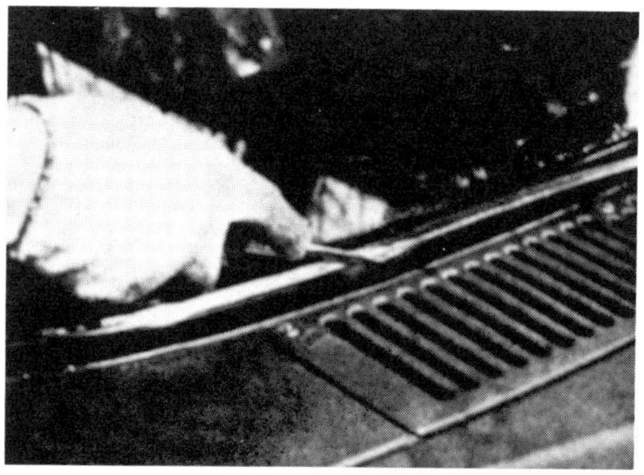

Fig. 12.27. Fitting the windshield metal moulding

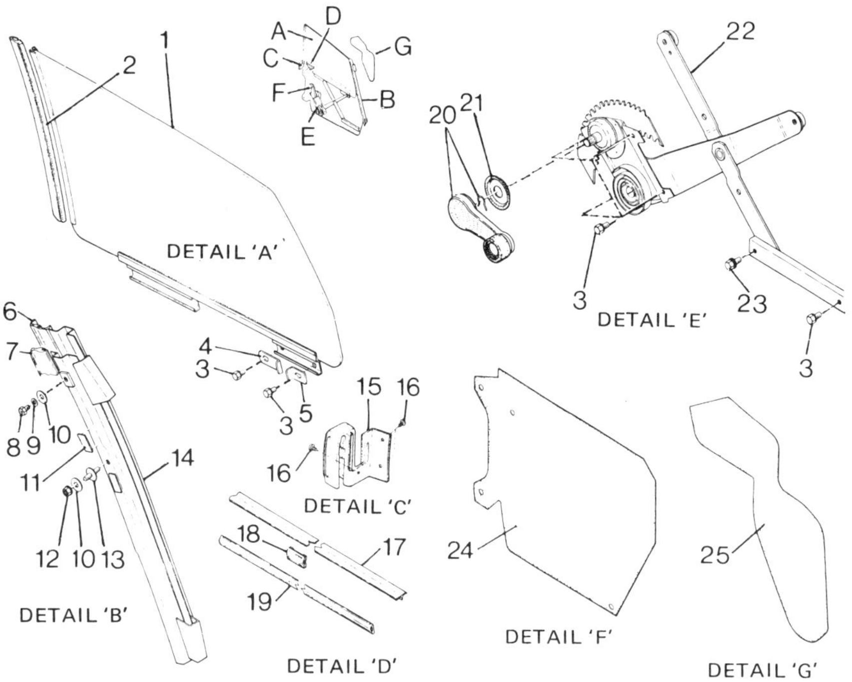

Fig. 12.28. Component parts of side window - Hardtop models

1 Side window glass
2 Weatherstrip
3 Bolt and washer
4 Bracket
5 Bracket
6 Weatherstrip
7 Weatherstrip
8 Bolt
9 Spring washer
10 Washer
11 Stopper
12 Flange nut
13 Bolt
14 Sash
15 Corner patch
16 Tapping screw
17 Weatherstrip (outer)
18 Stopper (glass)
19 Weatherstrip
20 Regulator handle
21 Escutcheon
22 Regulator
23 Bolt and spring washer
24 Sealing cover
25 Sealing cover

3 Fit a new weatherstrip onto the windshield and insert a work cord into the channel in the weatherstrip. Overlap the cord at the top of the glass. After the cord is fitted, coat all round the weatherstrip with gasolene.
4 Apply a thin bead of sealing compound to the face of the weatherstrip that mates with the body.
5 Offer the windshield to the body aperture with the work cord to the interior of the car.
6 Push the windshield into position, and at the same time have the assistant gradually pull the work cord at right angles to the glass. Fit is carried out from the upper center of the glass to the left and right. When the windshield is fitted check that the weatherstrip on the outside of the body is fitted correctly.
7 Fit the metal moulding by raising the groove lip of the weatherstrip to the outside. The fitting of the metal moulding is made easier if the groove is moistened with gasoline.

25 Rear window - removal and refitting

The rear window is removed and refitted using the same procedure as described for the front windshield in Section 24. If it is a heated rear window do not forget to disconnect the electrical wiring.

26 Side window (Hardtop) - removal, refitting and adjusting

1 Remove the attaching screw at the rear end of the rear pillar and remove the pad by moving it to the front.
2 Remove the rear seat cushion and seat back. Disconnect the rear seat outer belt (if fitted).
3 Remove the trim panel and peel off the sealing cover.
4 Pull the stopper and weatherstrip upwards to remove them. Remove the two securing bolts from the guide channel of the side window regulator.
5 Remove the attaching screw from the regulator main arm roller bracket and pull the bracket off the glass holder.
6 Shift the side window glass backwards and, while removing the regulator roller and side glass rail, pull the side glass upwards and out.
7 Refitting is the reverse of the removal sequence. Adjust the glass position by adjusting the three positions, A - B - C in Fig. 12.30 in turn. Always tighten each bolt or nut after adjustment. There is no adjustment at the point marked by an asterisk. Position C can be adjusted by loosening the glass by 2.75 - 3.15 in (70 - 80 mm). After adjustment move the glass up and down and check for smooth operation.

Fig. 12.29. Removing the regulator main arm roller bracket

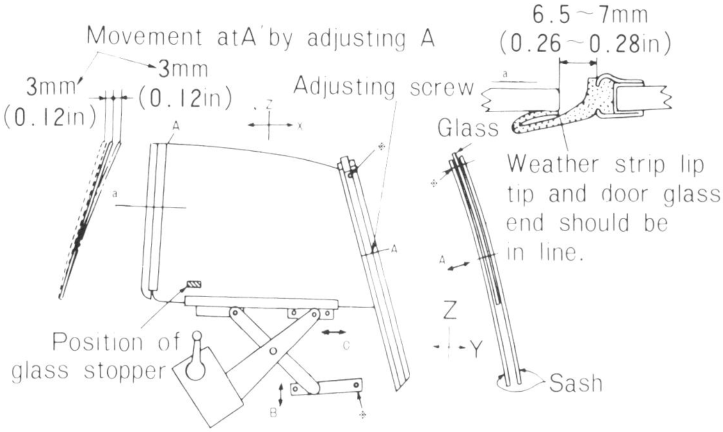

Fig. 12.30a. Adjustment of the side window position

Adjusting position	Adjusting direction (Adjusting allowance)	Direction of glass movement	Purpose
A	Direction Y (2.5 mm (0.10 in.) each to right and left)	Direction Y (3 mm (0.12 in.) each to right and left at top of glass)	Adjustment to fit weather strip against door glass
B	Direction Z (3 mm (0.12 in.) each upward and downward)	 Standard / When B is raised. / When B is lowered.	Adjustment of glass position
C	Direction X (3 mm (0.12 in.) each to front and rear)	Direction X (3 mm (0.12 in.) each to front and rear)	Adjustment to fit rear end line of door glass against front end line of side window glass

Fig. 12.30b. Adjustment of the side window position

Chapter 13 Supplement: Revisions and information on later models

Contents

1 Introduction

This supplement covers amendments and alterations to the Subaru range of vehicles produced from late 1977 onwards and includes information on the 4WD Open MPV introduced in September 1977.

A number of individual components have been the subject of minor changes in design and construction, but unless this affects the operations originally described in the preceding Chapters of this manual, these variations are not referred to.

2 Specifications

Engine

Type	EA71

Compression ratio

All models except Coupe FE	8.5 : 1
Coupe FE	9.3 : 1

Pistons

Diameter:	
Standard production	3.6205 to 3.6216 in (91.960 to 91.990 mm)
0.25 mm oversize	3.6303 to 3.6315 in (92.210 to 92.240 mm)

Crankshaft

Main bearing clearance:	
Front and rear	0.0004 to 0.0016 in (0.010 to 0.040 mm)
Centre	0 to 0.0012 in (0 to 0.03 mm)

Camshaft

Thrust clearance	0.0008 to 0.0035 in (0.020 to 0.090 mm)
Thrust clearance limit	0.008 in (0.20 mm)

Torque wrench settings	**lbf ft**	**kgf m**
Crankcase bolts and nuts (6 mm)	3.3 to 4.0	0.45 to 0.55
Oil pressure switch	16 to 20	2.2 to 2.8
Crankcase plug	46 to 56	6.3 to 7.7
Oil strainer stay	17 to 20	2.3 to 2.7
Oil pan	3.3 to 4.0	0.45 to 0.55
Valve rocker	37 to 43	5.1 to 5.9
Flywheel housing	14 to 20	2.0 to 2.8
Rocker cover	2.2 to 2.9	0.30 to 0.40
Intake manifold	13 to 16	1.8 to 2.2
Spark plug	13 to 17	1.8 to 2.4
Horizontal damper	7 to 10	1.0 to 1.4

Carburetion

Carburetors

Type	**Hitachi DCJ306–12**	
	Primary	**Secondary**
Bore	1.02 in	1.18 in
Venturi diameter	0.32 in	0.28 in
Main jet	112	145
Main air bleed	75	80
Slow jet	52	70
Slow air bleed	170	70
Power jet	35	

Type	**Hitachi DCJ306–13**	
	Primary	**Secondary**
Bore	1.02 in	1.18 in
Venturi diameter	0.32 in	0.28 in
Main jet	106	150
Main air bleed	75	80
Slow jet	48	65
Slow air bleed	170	70
Power jet	45	

Idling speed:

Vehicles for 49 states and Canada	800 to 850 rpm
Vehicles for California	900 rpm

Ignition system

Type	Breakerless

Spark plugs

Type:	
USA models	NGK BP6ES
Canada models	Champion RN-9Y

Coil

Make	Nippon Denso	Hitachi
Type No	0297004450	CIT-53

Distributor

Make	Nippon Denso	Hitachi
Type No:		
USA models	029100-4270	D4H6-01
Canada models	029100-5340	D4H8-02

Ignition control unit

Make	Nippon Denso	Hitachi
Type No	131100-0793	E12-58-1100

Ignition timing (vacuum disconnected)

Vehicles for 49 states and Canada	8° BTDC at 800 rpm
Vehicles for California	8° BTDC at 900 rpm

Transmission

Engine EA71AF, EA71AF2 or EA71AF3

Type	4 forward speeds and 1 reverse

Gear ratios

1st	3.666 : 1
2nd	2.157 : 1
3rd	1.464 : 1
4th	1.029 : 1
Reverse	4.100 : 1

Final reduction gear

Type of gear	Hypoid gear
Reduction ratio	3.700 : 1

Differential gear

Type and number of gears	Straight bevel gears - Pinion 2, side 2
Drive pinion/crown gear backlash	0.0039 to 0.0059 in (0.10 to 0.15 mm)

Transmission mainshaft collar thrust clearance	0 to 0.0079 in (0 to 0.02 mm)

Engine EA71AP, EA71AP2 or EA71AP3

Type	5 forward speeds and 1 reverse
Gear ratios	
1st	3.666 : 1
2nd	2.157 : 1
3rd	1.464 : 1
4th	1.029 : 1
5th	0.780 : 1
Reverse	4.100 : 1
Final reduction gear	
Type of gear	Hypoid gear
Reduction ratio	3.700 : 1
Differential gear	
Type and number of gears	Straight bevel gears - Pinion 2, side 2
Drive pinion/crown gear backlash	0.0039 to 0.0059 in (0.10 to 0.15 mm)
Transmission mainshaft collar thrust clearance	0 to 0.0079 in (0 to 0.02 mm)

Engine EA71EF, EA71EF2 or EA71EF3 (4-wheel drive)

Type	4 forward speeds and 1 reverse
Gear ratios	
1st	4.090 : 1
2nd	2.312 : 1
3rd	1.464 : 1
4th	1.029 : 1
Reverse	4.100 : 1
Reduction gear (front drive)	
Type of gear	Hypoid gear
Reduction ratio	3.889 : 1
Differential gear	
Type and number of gears	Straight bevel gears - Pinion 2, side 2
Reduction gear (rear drive) (4-wheel drive)	
1st reduction:	
Type of gear	Helical gear
Reduction ratio	1.000 : 1
Final reduction:	
Type of gear	Hypoid gear
Reduction ratio	3.900 : 1
Differential gear (rear)	
Type and number of gears	Straight bevel gears - Pinion 2, side 2
Drive pinion/crown gear backlash	0.0039 to 0.0059 in (0.10 to 0.15 mm)
Transmission mainshaft collar thrust clearance	0 to 0.0079 in (0 to 0.02 mm)

Axle shafts, driveshafts and propeller shaft

Rear axle driveshafts (4WD models)

Outer end joint	Double offset joint
Inner end joint	Double offset joint

Electrical system

Battery

Type	N50Z
Capacity	60AH

Alternator

Make and type	Hitachi LT150-21
Nominal output	12V/50A
Rotor coil resistance	4.0 ohms
Stator coil resistance	0.2 ohms

Fuses

Type	Cartridge	
Rating	25A	15A
Number of fuses	2	6
Fusible link:		
Colour code	Green	
Size	0.0013 in^2 (0.85 mm^2)	

Bulbs	Wattage
Headlamp	12V - 50W/40W (Coupe and 4WD - 12V - 37.5W/50W + 37.5W)
Front combination lamp:	
Turn signal lamp	12V - 23W
Clearance lamp	12V - 8W
Rear combination lamp:	
Stop and tail lamp	12V - 23W/8W
Turn signal lamp	12V - 23W
Back-up lamp	12V - 23W
Side marker lamp	12V - 3.8W
Licence plate lamp	12V - 7.5W (Station Wagon and Open MPV: 12V - 3.8W)
Warning and indicator lamps:	
Oil pressure	12V - 3.4W or 12V - 1.4W
Charge	12V - 3.4W or 12V - 1.4W
High beam	12V - 3.4W
Turn signal	12V - 3.4W
Seat belt	12V - 1.4W
Brake fluid level and handbrake	12V - 3.4W
Rear window defogger	12V - 3.4W
Door ajar	12V - 3.4W
Meter illumination	12V - 3.4W and 12V - 1.4W
4WD indicator	12V - 3.4W
Room light	12V - 8W
Trunk light	12V - 5W
Ashtray illumination	12V - 1.4W
Automatic transmission selector	12V - 3.4W
Cigarette lighter	12V - 3W
Clock	12V - 3.4W
Radio	12V - 3.4W

Suspension and axles

Wheel alignment

Front axle	
Toe-in:	
All models except 4WD	0.08 to 0.32 in (2 to 8 mm)
4WD	0.24 to 0.47 in (6 to 12 mm)
Camber:	
Sedan, Hardtop, Coupe	$1^\circ 30' \pm 45'$
Station Wagon	$1^\circ 45' \pm 45'$
4WD	$2^\circ 10' \pm 45'$
Caster:	
Sedan, Hardtop, Coupe	$-50' \pm 45'$
Station Wagon	$-10' \pm 45'$
4WD	$-50' \pm 45'$

Rear axle	
Toe-in:	
Sedan, Hardtop, Coupe	0.04 to 0.20 in (1 to 5 mm)
Station Wagon and 4WD	0.08 to 0.24 in (2 to 6 mm)
Camber:	
Sedan, Hardtop, Coupe	$20' \pm 45'$
Station Wagon	$1^\circ 10' \pm 45'$
4WD	$1^\circ 20' \pm 45'$

3 Engine

Horizontal damper - removal, refitting and adjustment

1 Disconnect the ground cable from the battery negative (—) terminal and remove the spare wheel from the engine compartment.

2 Undo and remove the outer nut, washer and rubber securing the damper threaded rod to the engine bracket. Unscrew the inner nut down the threaded rod as far as it will go.

3 Undo and remove the upper nut and washers securing the cable assembly to the damper. Now unscrew the lower nut as far as it will go down the threaded shaft of the cable assembly.

4 Undo and remove the nut, spring washer and thrust washer securing the damper to the body bracket side pin.

5 Disengage the cable assembly from the damper, then lift the damper off the body bracket side pin and out of the engine bracket.

6 To refit the horizontal damper, engage the forward end with the engine bracket and slide the other end over the body bracket side pin.

7 Refit the rubber, washers, and nut to the side pin and tighten the nut.

8 Refit the rubber, washers and outer nut to the threaded damper rod and tighten the nut until all clearance between the rubber and engine bracket is eliminated. Now screw the inner nut back down the shaft and tighten it.

9 Insert the cable assembly into the damper and refit the upper washer and nut. Hold the cable to prevent it from twisting and tighten the upper nut. Tighten the nut so that the cable is straightened but not strained.

10 Screw the lower nut up the cable and tighten it.

11 With the horizontal damper installed, ensure that there is clearance between the end of the cable and body, and between the cable and starter motor.

12 Refit the spare wheel and reconnect the battery terminal.

Selection of crankshaft main bearings

13 To enable a set of main bearing shells with the correct bearing journal oil clearance to be obtained, the crankshaft centre main bearing is measured using a Plastigage as follows:

(a) Clean the crankcase, crankshaft and main bearings with kerosene and wipe dry. Make absolutely sure that the crankshaft journals and bearings are dry and free of dust.

(b) Fit the bearings in the crankcase halves and set the crankshaft

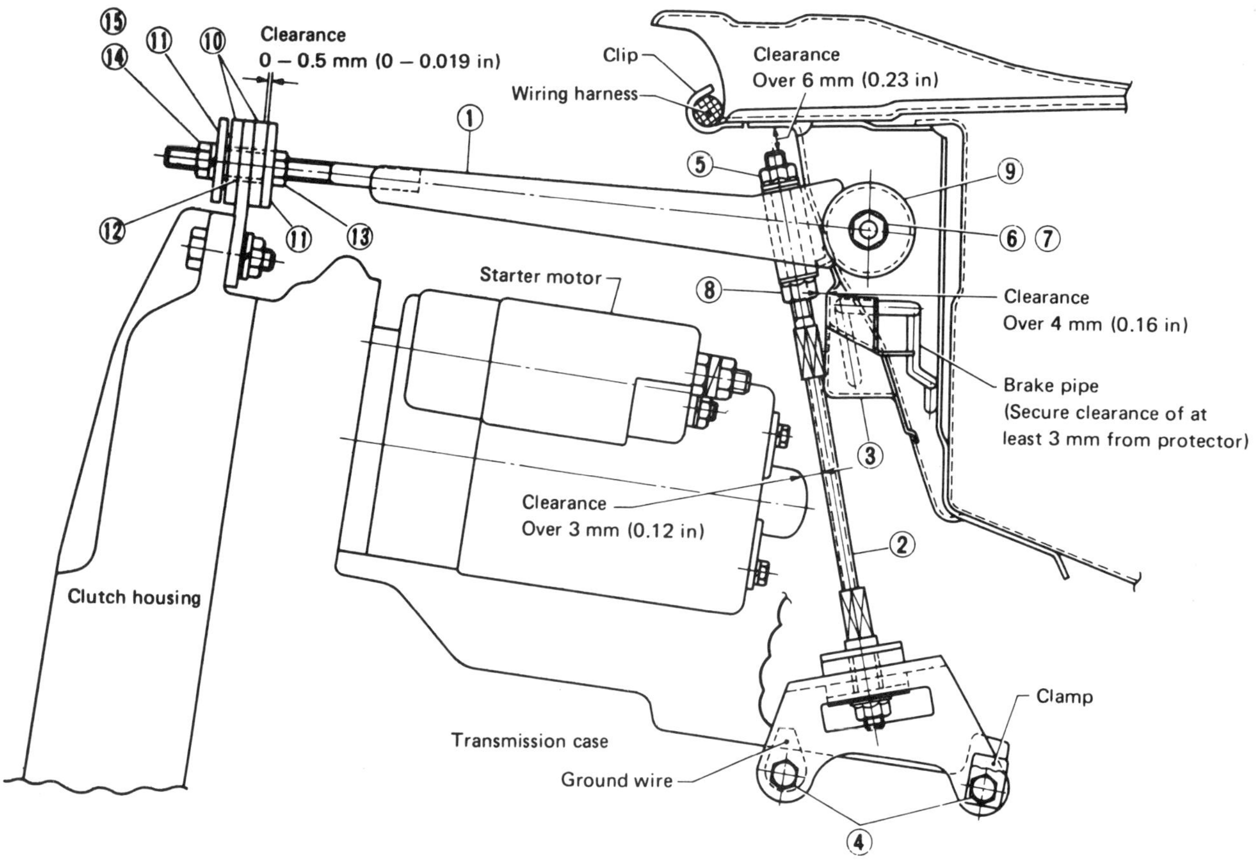

Fig. 13.1. Installation diagram of the horizontal damper (Sec. 3)

1	*Rod assembly*	6	*Nut*	11	*Washer*
2	*Cable unit*	7	*Spring washer*	12	*Sleeve*
3	*Brake pipe protector*	8	*Flange nut*	13	*Nut*
4	*Bolt*	9	*Washer*	14	*Nut*
5	*Flange nut*	10	*Rubber*	15	*Spring washer*

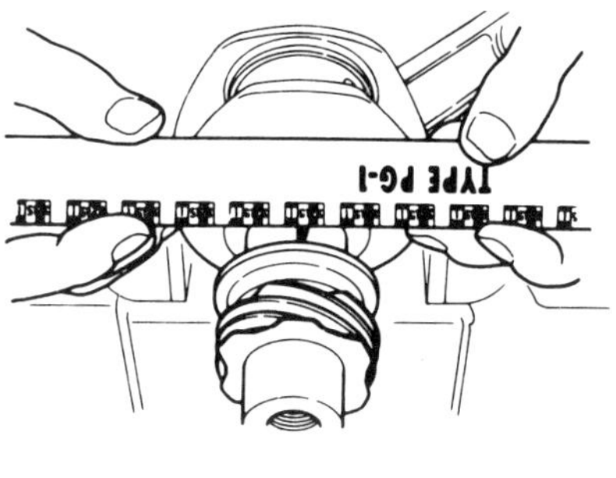

Fig. 13.2. Measuring oil clearance of crankshaft centre journal (Sec. 3)

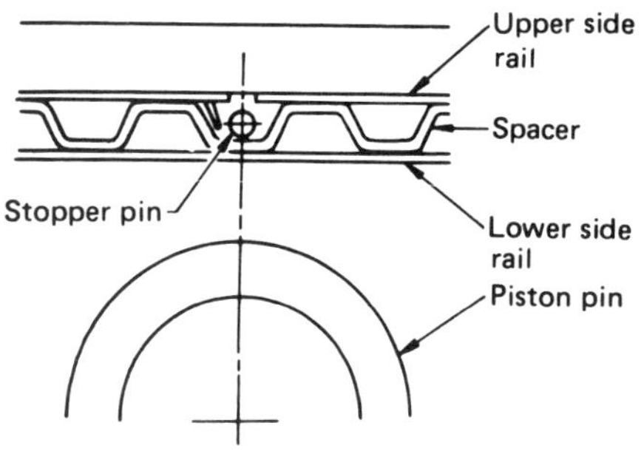

Fig. 13.3. Installation of piston oil ring (Sec. 3)

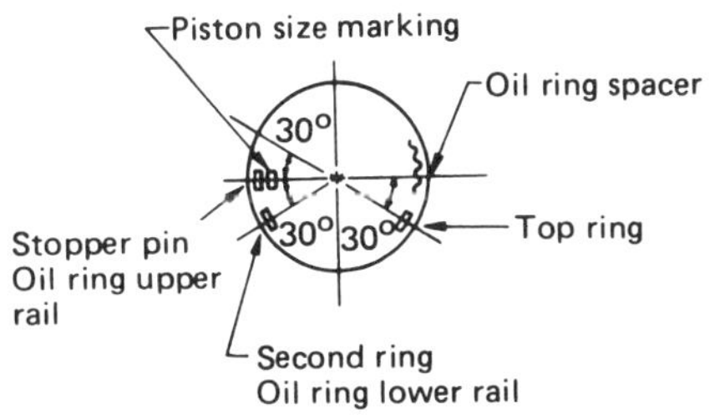

Fig. 13.4. Position of piston rings (Sec. 3)

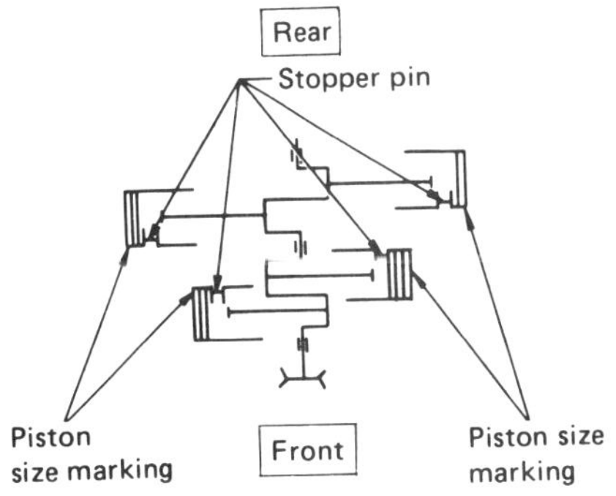

Fig. 13.5. Correct fitting of pistons (Sec. 3)

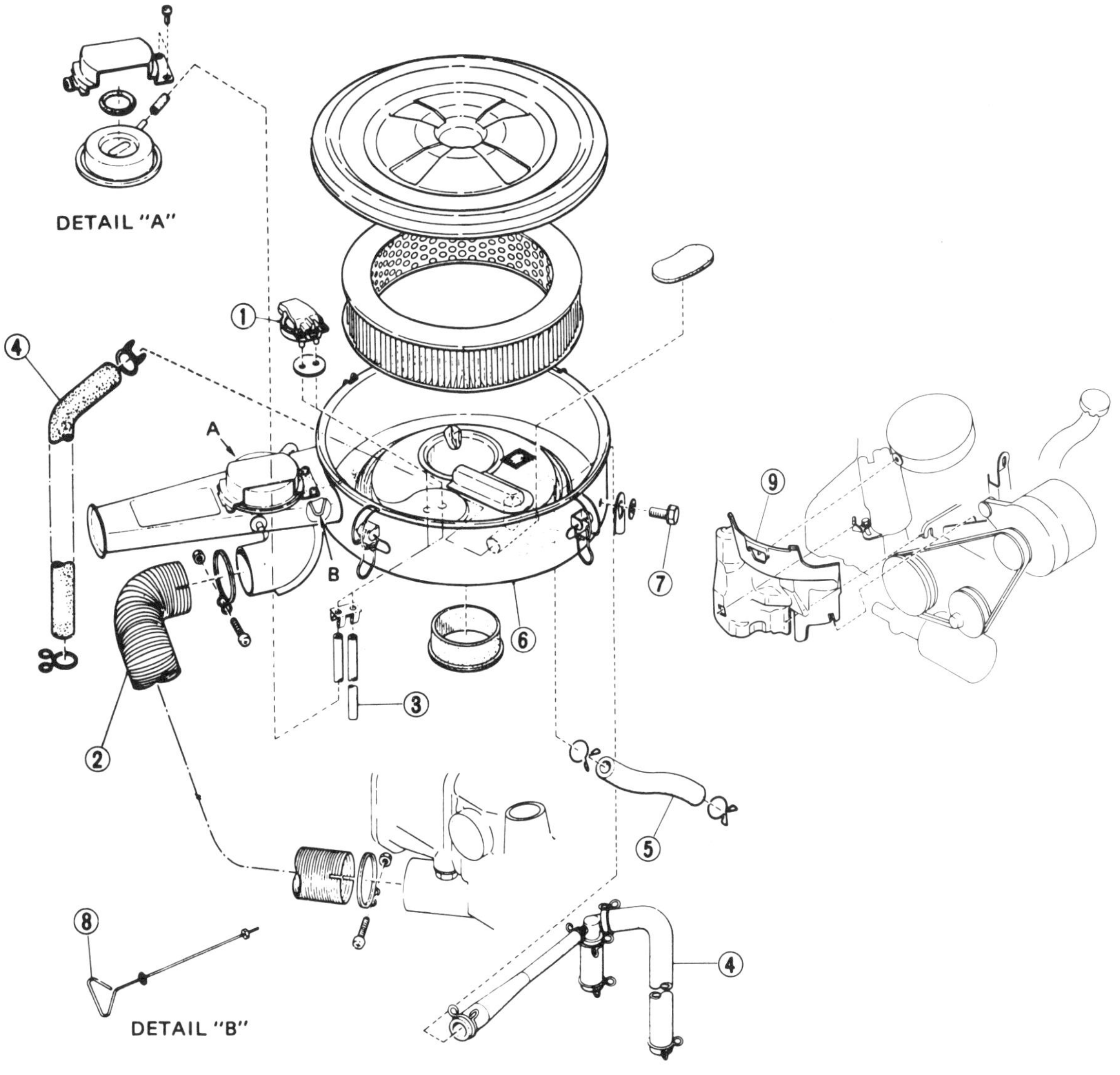

Fig. 13.6. Removing air cleaner (Sec. 4)

1 *Temperature sensor*
2 *Air intake hose*
3 *Temperature sensor hose*
4 *Crankcase ventilation hose*
5 *Air suction hose*
6 *Air cleaner case*
7 *6 mm bolt*
8 *Air cleaner band bolt*
9 *Carburetor shield*

in position.

(c) Cut a piece of Plastigage to the centre main bearing width and place it on the journal parallel with the crankshaft axis. Be careful not to put it on the oil hole or groove. Bolt the crankcase halves together and tighten the nuts to a torque of:

10 mm bolts 29 to 35 lbf ft (4.0 to 4.8 kgf m)
8 mm bolts 17 to 20 lbf ft (2.3 to 2.7 kgf m)
6 mm bolts 3.3 to 4.0 lbf ft (0.45 to 0.55 kgf m)

Do not rotate the crankshaft or turn the crankcase over while doing this work.

14 Remove the bolts, separate the crankcase halves and measure the Plastigage width using the scale printed on the Plastigage cover. From the measurement obtained, the correct main bearing set necessary to satisfy the standard main bearing oil clearance, can be obtained from the chart below:

Measured oil clearance of centre bearing	Bearing set requirement
0 to 0.0012 in (0 to 0.03 mm)	*Standard*
0.0012 to 0.0024 in (0.03 to 0.06 mm)	*0.03 mm undersize*
0.0024 to 0.0031 in (0.06 to 0.08 mm)	*0.05 mm undersize*

Installation of piston rings

15 A stopper pin is fitted to the oil ring groove of each piston to prevent the oil ring rotating in service. When fitting a piston oil ring, ensure that it is installed as shown in Fig. 13.3.

16 When refitting pistons, they must be installed with the stopper pins or piston size markings facing each other (see Fig. 13.5). If this is not done, there is a possibility that the stopper pins may foul the service hole in the crankcase.

4 Carburetion; fuel and emission control systems

Air cleaner - removal and refitting

1 Remove the air cleaner cover from the cleaner case.

2 Pull both sides of the carburetor shield forward first, then slide it upward.

3 Disconnect the connecting hose from the three-way connector.

4 Remove the band securing the air intake hose to the right-hand crankcase ventilation hose.

5 Slacken the hose clip and detach the air intake hose from the air cleaner case.

6 Disconnect the temperature sensor from the intake manifold.

7 Undo and remove the bolt securing the air cleaner case to the support bracket.

8 Slacken the clip securing the air cleaner case to the carburetor and lift off the air cleaner. As the air cleaner is lifted clear, detach the air suction hose from under the air cleaner case.

9 Refitting the air cleaner is the reverse sequence to removal.

Exhaust emission control system

10 To reduce exhaust emission when starting the engine, a timer and two solenoid valves are incorporated into the exhaust emission control system, for California models, described fully in Chapter 3. The timer operates for 130 seconds after starting the engine and causes electric current to be applied to the two solenoids. The solenoids control the operation of the distributor vacuum advance/retard mechanism and by their operation alter the engine ignition timing characteristics after initial start-up.

5 Ignition system

Breakerless ignition

The electronic breakerless ignition system previously fitted to models for California only is now installed on all Subaru vehicles covered by this manual. The system is described fully in Chapter 4.

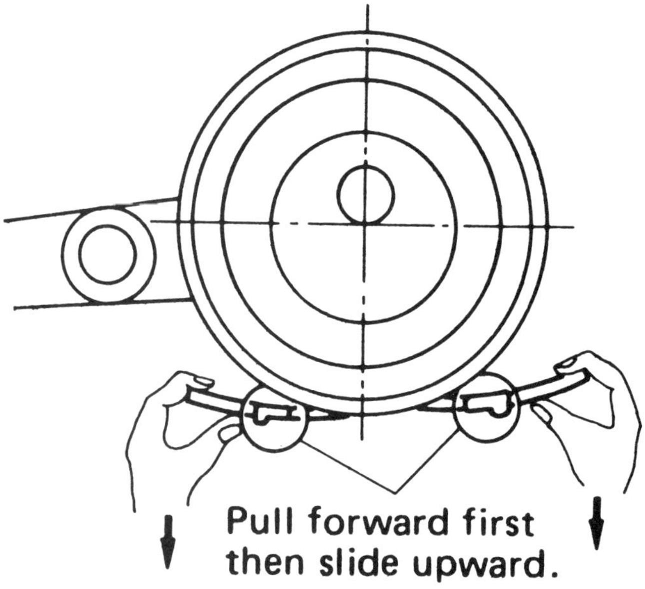
Pull forward first
then slide upward.

Fig. 13.7. Removing carburetor shield (Sec. 4)

6 Axle shafts, driveshafts and propeller shaft

Rear axle driveshafts (4WD) - modifications

1 The rear axle driveshafts fitted to all 4WD models now utilise inboard and outboard double offset joints (DOJ) in place of the universal joint and sliding spline used on earlier models. The overhaul procedures for the DOJ are the same as described in Chapter 7 for the front axle shaft.

Rear axle driveshaft (4WD) - removal and refitting

2 Jack up the rear of the car and support it with jack stands. Remove the rear roadwheel.

3 Support the rear suspension arm on a jack and raise it slightly.

4 Remove the shock absorber lower mounting and detach the shock absorber from the suspension arm.

5 Drive out the spring pin which connects the inner DOJ to the rear differential driveshaft and the outer DOJ to the wheel hub shaft, using a pin punch and hammer. Discard the spring pins and always use new ones when refitting the driveshaft.

6 Lower the jack supporting the suspension arm, slide the outer DOJ off the wheel hub shaft splines and the inner DOJ off the rear differential driveshaft splines. Withdraw the driveshaft out from under the car.

7 Refitting is the reverse sequence to removal, ensuring that the inner and outer DOJ's are installed as shown in Fig. 13.11.

Rear wheel hub shaft and oil seals (4WD) - removal and refitting

8 Remove the rear axle driveshaft as described in the previous Section.

9 Straighten the staked portion of the axle nut, using a chisel and hammer.

10 Undo and remove the axle nut while an assistant applies the footbrake. When removing the axle nut, slacken it initially by an eighth of a turn then retighten it. Do this two or three times before completely removing the nut, to prevent possible damage to the threads caused by the staking.

11 Withdraw the brake drum from the hub.

12 At the rear of the suspension arm, straighten the staked portion of the hub shaft ring nut using a hammer and chisel.

13 Remove the ring nut by carefully tapping it round with a hammer and drift engaged in the slots around the ring nut periphery.

14 Using a soft headed mallet, tap the hub shaft inward and withdraw it from the suspension arm.

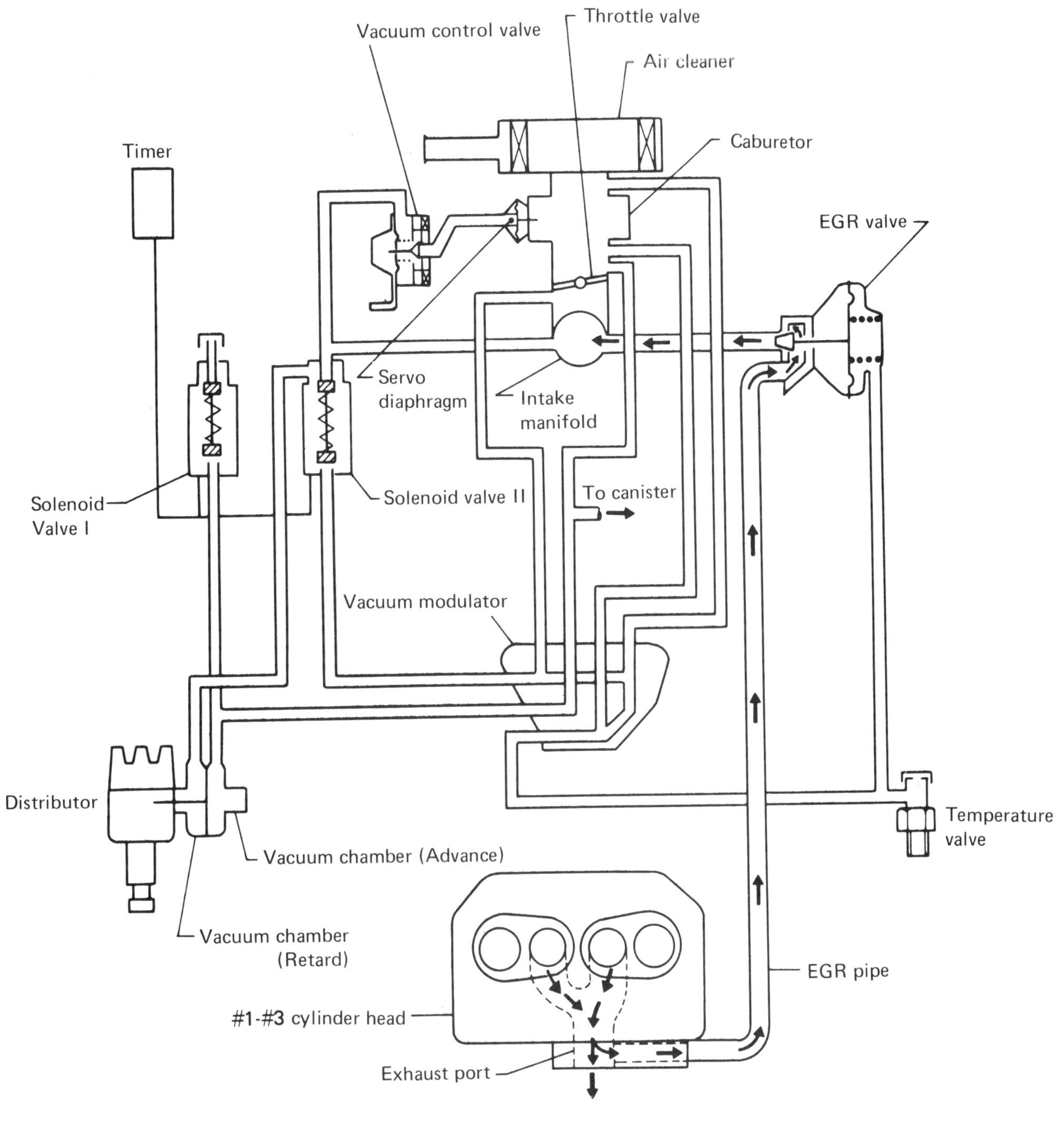

Fig. 13.8. Vacuum circuit layout of exhaust emission control system - manual transmission vehicles for California (except 4WD) (Sec. 4)

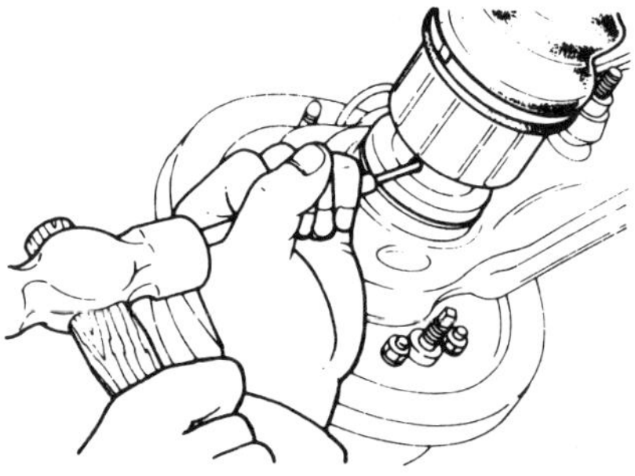

Fig. 13.9. Removing the DOJ retaining spring pin (Sec. 6)

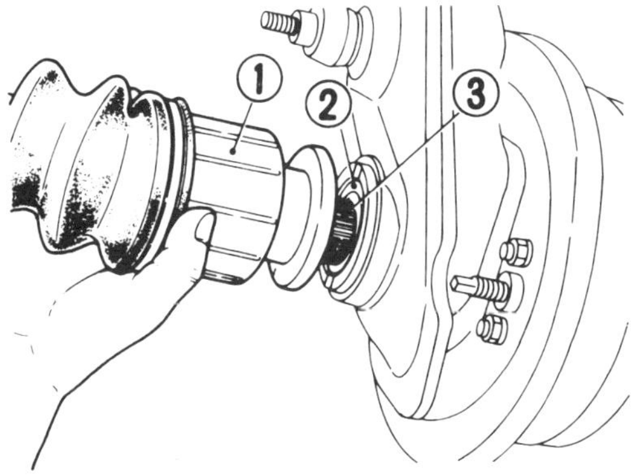

Fig. 13.10. Withdrawing the outer DOJ from the hub shaft (Sec. 6)

1 Outer DOJ
2 Packing
3 Hub shaft

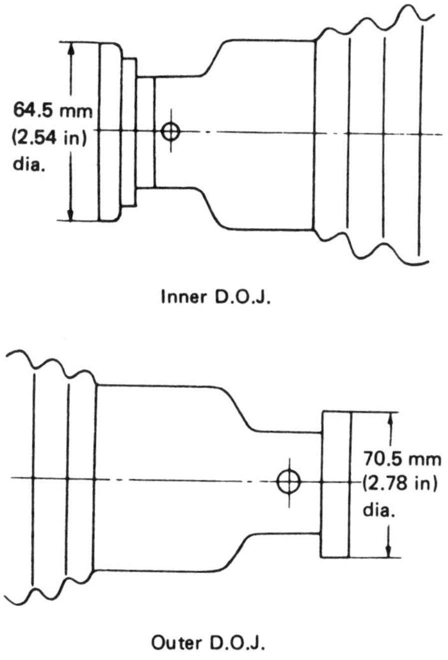

Fig. 13.11. Size comparison of inner and outer DOJ (Sec. 6)

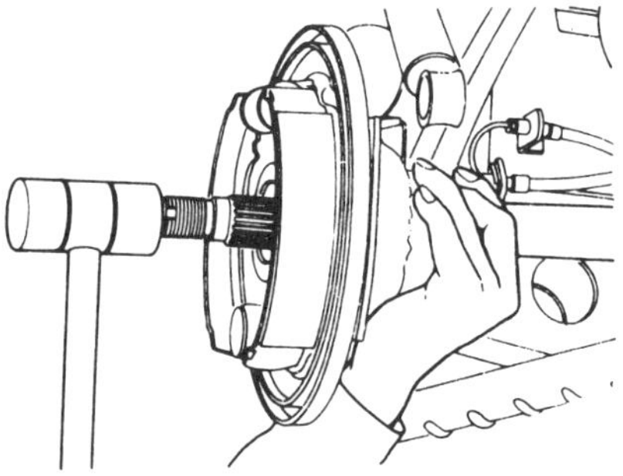

Fig. 13.12. Removing the hub shaft (Sec. 6)

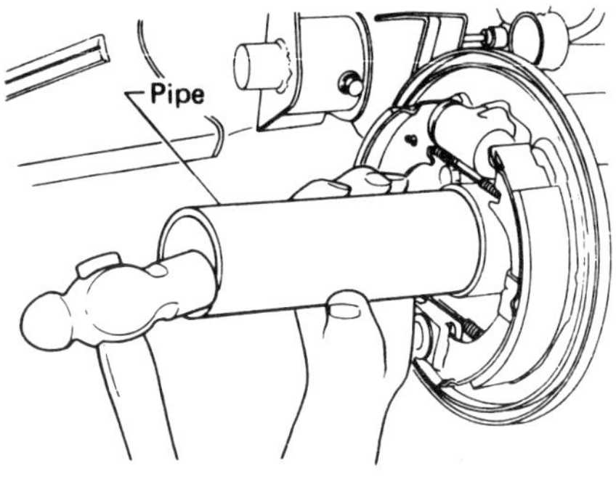

Fig. 13.13. Installation of outer oil seal (Sec. 6)

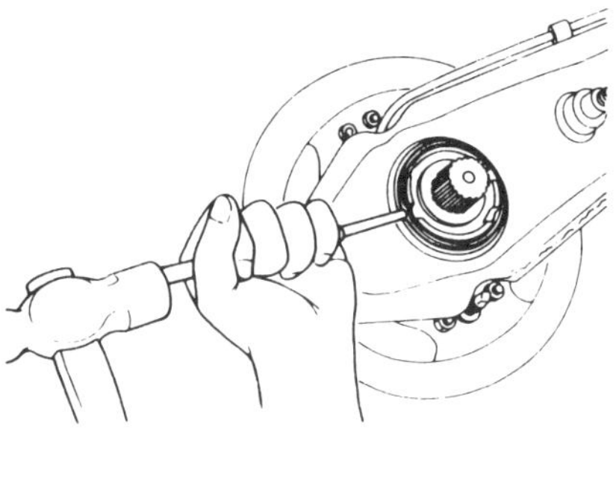

Fig. 13.14. Staking the ring nut (Sec. 6)

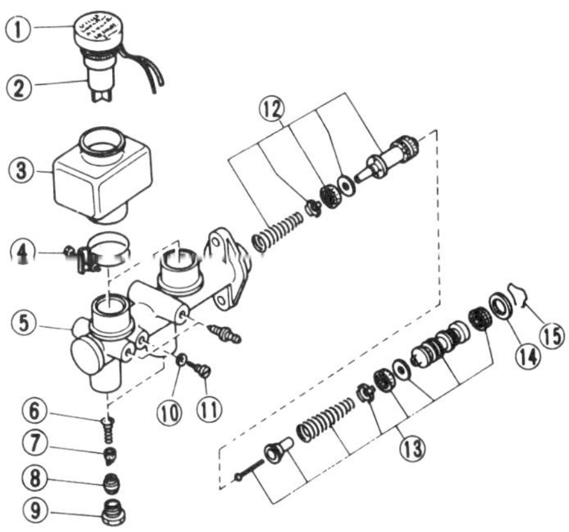

Fig. 13.15. Exploded view of master cylinder incorporating brake fluid level indicator (Sec. 7)

1	*Brake fluid level indicator assembly*	8	*Tube seat*
2	*Filter*	9	*Check valve cap*
3	*Brake fluid reservoir*	10	*Gasket*
4	*Band (reservoir)*	11	*Stopper (secondary piston)*
5	*Cylinder*	12	*Secondary piston assembly*
6	*Check valve spring*	13	*Primary piston assembly*
7	*Check valve*	14	*Washer (piston stop)*
		15	*Ring (piston stop)*

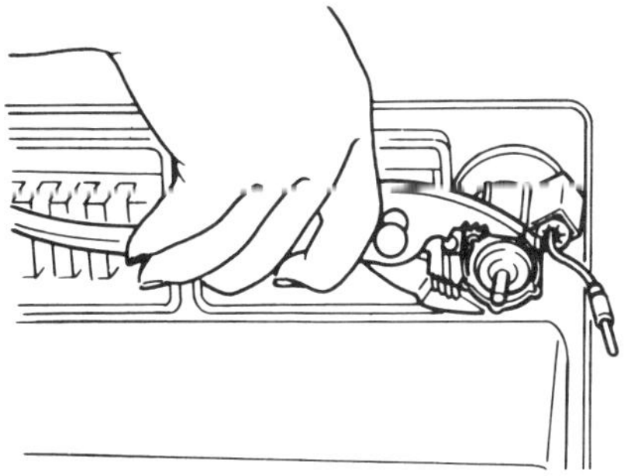

Fig. 13.16. Cigarette lighter removal (Sec. 8)

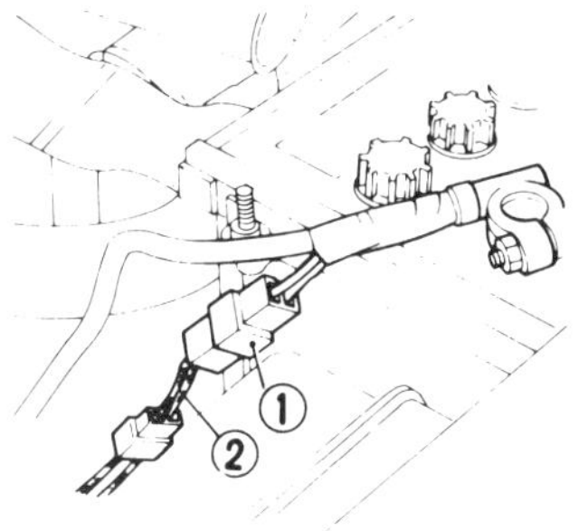

Fig. 13.17. Fusible link location (Sec. 8)

1 *Connector* 2 *Fusible link*

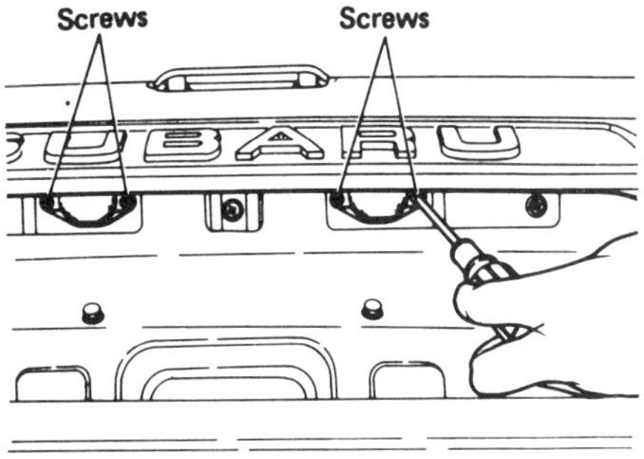

Fig. 13.18. Removing licence plate lamp lens (Sec. 8)

15 Remove the inner oil seal from the ring nut and hook the outer oil seal out of the bearing housing using a screwdriver.

16 To refit the oil seals, install the inner oil seal on the ring nut and install the outer oil seal by tapping it into position using a tube of suitable diameter. Thoroughly lubricate the lips of the oil seals with engine oil.

17 The remainder of the refitting sequence is the reverse of removal, bearing in mind the following points:

- (a) *After fully tightening the new ring nut and axle nut, stake them in position using a small punch*
- (b) *Refit the driveshaft as described in the previous Section*

7 Brakes

Brake fluid level indicator

1 A brake fluid level indicator is now incorporated into the filler cap of the brake master cylinder reservoir. The indicator is connected to a warning light on the dashboard which is illuminated should the fluid level in the master cylinder fall below a predetermined level. The master cylinder remains unchanged and the removal, refitting and overhaul procedures are the same as described in Chapter 9, with the exception that the electrical connection at the filler cap must be disconnected when removing the master cylinder.

8 Electrical system

Cigarette lighter - removal and refitting

1 Remove the center ventilator grille assembly and disconnect the wiring harness for the cigarette lighter and radio.

2 Undo the cigarette lighter socket retaining nut and lift out the socket and lighter.

3 Refitting is the reverse sequence to removal.

Clock - removal and refitting

4 Remove the centre ventilator grille assembly, disconnect the electrical lead to the clock illuminating light, remove the two retaining screws and lift out the clock.

5 Refitting is the reverse sequence to removal.

Fuses

6 The fuse box is now located underneath the left-hand side of the instrument panel. The rating of the fuses and the circuits they protect are shown on the fuse box cover.

Fusible link

7 A fusible link is incorporated in the wiring harness adjacent to the battery positive (+) terminal and protects the complete vehicle electrical system with the exception of the starter motor.

8 When renewing a blown fusible link it is most important that the cause is traced and rectified and that a new fusible link of the correct rating is used (see Specifications).

Licence plate lamp (4WD Open MPV) - bulb renewal

9 Undo and remove the two securing screws, then lift off the lens.

10 Remove the bulb by pulling it out of its socket.

11 Refitting is the reverse sequence to removal.

Headlights

12 Models for certain territories are now equipped with a sealed beam four headlight system. Removal, refitting and adjustment procedures are the same as described in Chapter 10, with the exception that the front grille must first be removed to provide access.

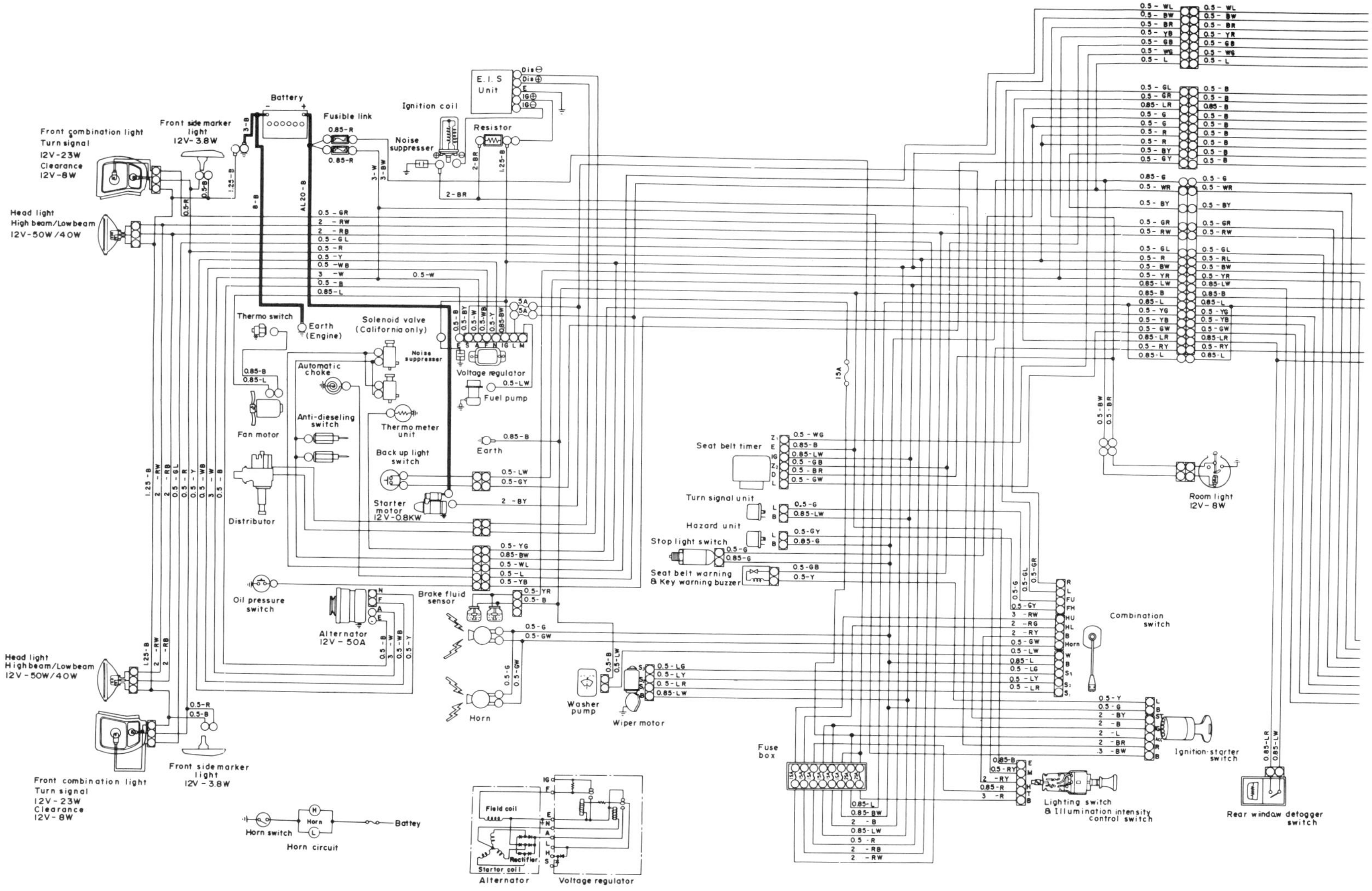

Fig. 13.19. Wiring diagram - Sedan and Coupe (manual transmission) (Sec. 8)

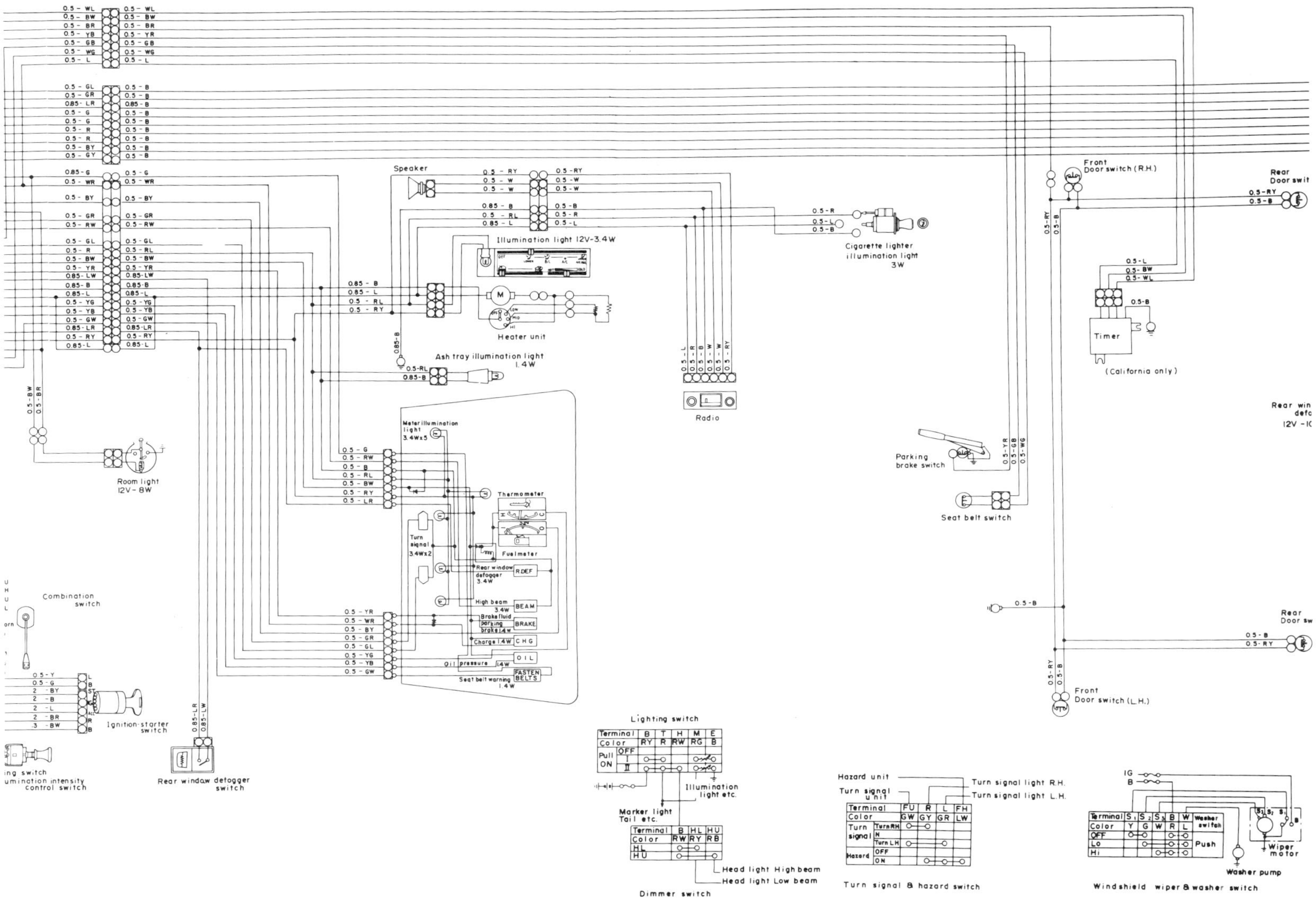
Speaker
Illumination light 12V-3.4W
Cigarette lighter
illumination light
3W
Heater unit
Ash tray illumination light
1.4W
Radio
Room light
12V-8W
Front
Door switch (R.H.)
Rear
Door swit
Timer
(California only)
Rear win
defo
12V -1(
Parking
brake switch
Seat belt switch
Meter illumination
light
3.4Wx5
Thermometer
Fuelmeter
Turn
signal
3.4Wx2
Rear window
defogger
3.4W
R.DEF
High beam
3.4W
BEAM
Brake fluid
parking
brake 1.4W
BRAKE
Charge 1.4W
CHG
Oil pressure 1.4W
OIL
Seat belt warning
1.4W
FASTEN
BELTS
Combination
switch
Ignition-starter
switch
Rear window defogger
switch
ing switch
umination intensity
control switch
Rear
Door sw
Front
Door switch (L.H.)
Lighting switch
Illumination
light etc.
Marker light
Tail etc.
Head light High beam
Head light Low beam
Dimmer switch
Hazard unit
Turn signal
unit
Turn signal light R.H.
Turn signal light L.H.
Turn signal & hazard switch
IG
B
Washer pump
Wiper
motor
Windshield wiper & washer switch

Color Code of Electric Wires					
W	White	R	Red	GB	Green-Black
WR	White-Red	RW	Red-White	L	Blue
WB	White-Black	RB	Red-Black	LW	Blue-White
WG	White-Green	RG	Red-Green	LR	Blue-Red
WL	White-Blue	RL	Red-Blue	LY	Blue-Yellow
Y	Yellow	RY	Red-Yellow	LG	Blue-Green
YW	Yellow-White	G	Green	LB	Blue-Black
YR	Yellow-Red	GW	Green-White	B	Black
YB	Yellow-Black	GY	Green-Yellow	BW	Black-White
YG	Yellow-Green	GR	Green-Red	BY	Black-Yellow
YL	Yellow-Blue	GL	Green-Blue	BR	Black-Red

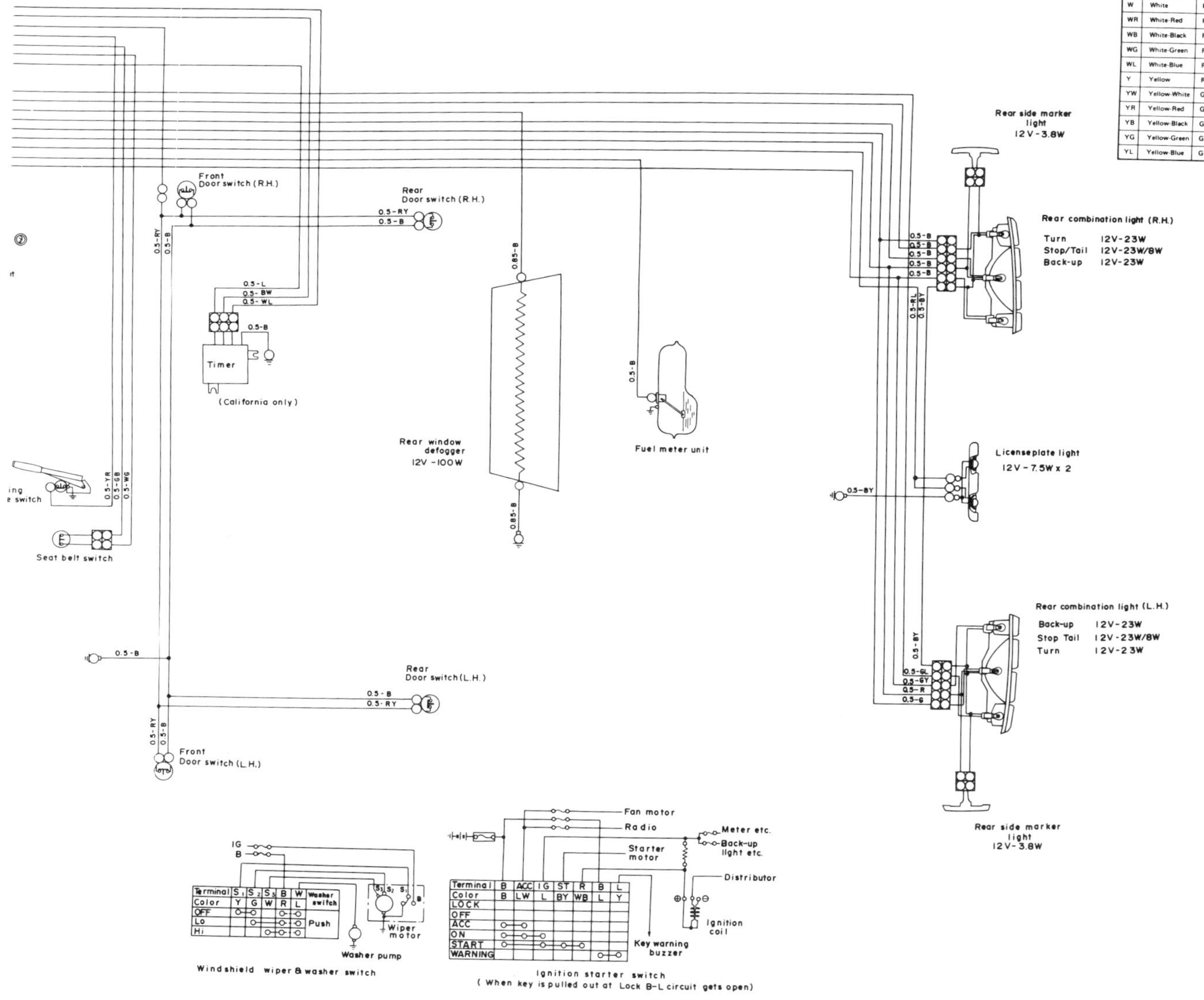

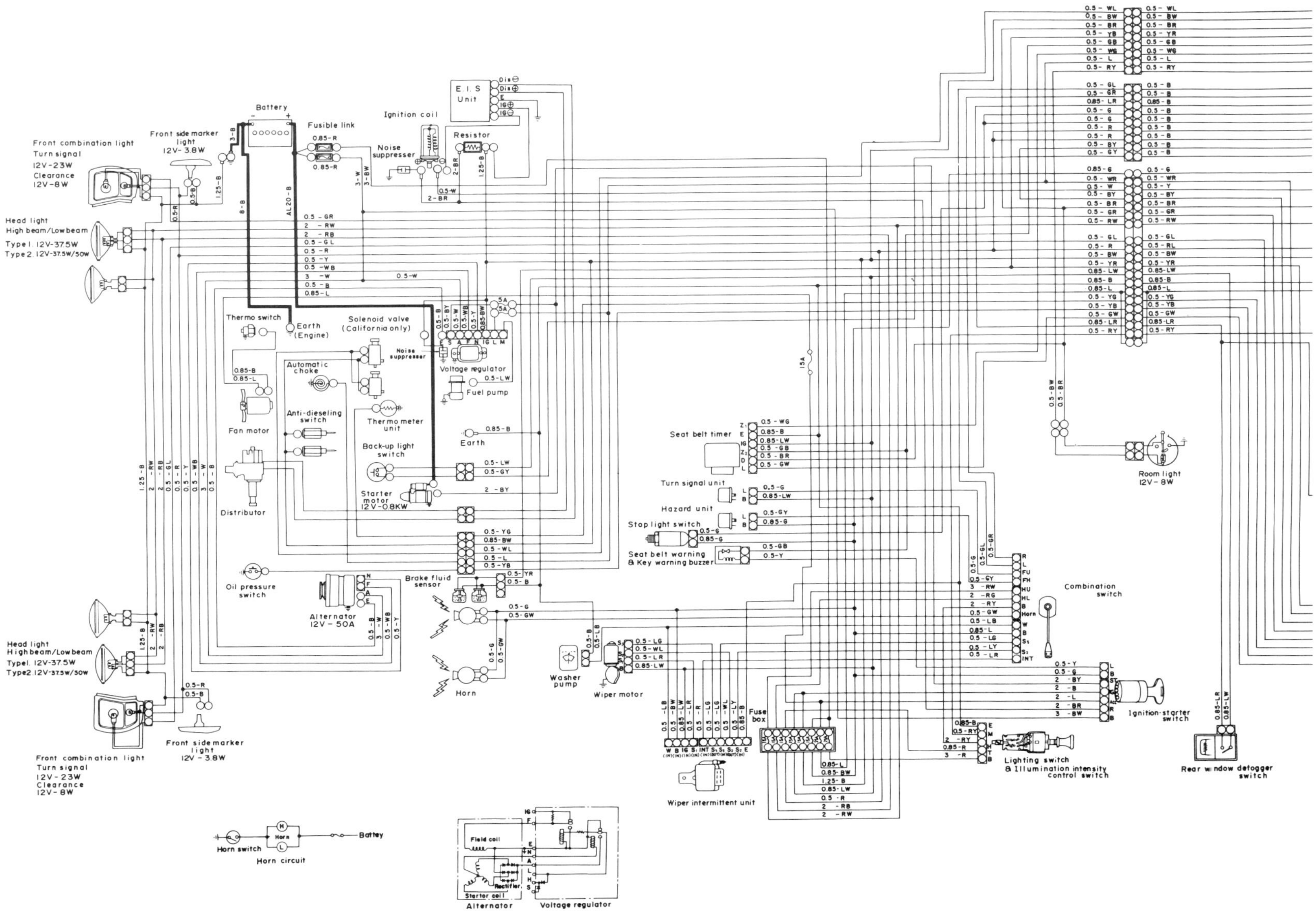

Fig. 13.20. Wiring diagram - Hardtop (manual transmission) (Sec. 8)

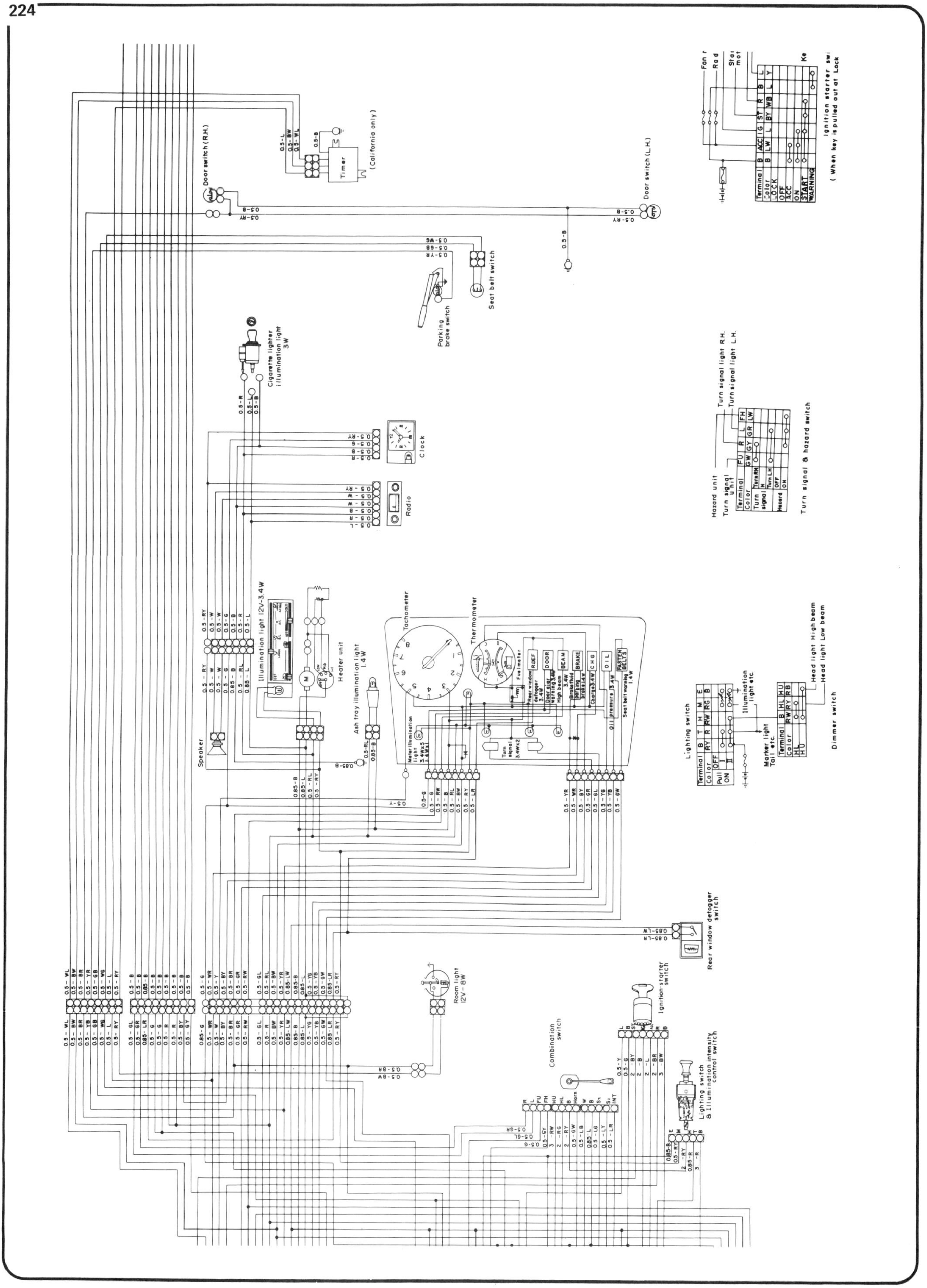
Door switch (R.H.)
Timer
(California only)
Door switch (L.H.)
Seat belt switch
Parking brake switch
Cigarette lighter illumination light 3W
Clock
Radio
Illumination light 12V-3.4W
Heater unit
Ash tray illumination light 1.4W
Speaker
Tachometer
Thermometer
Fuel meter
Rear window defogger switch
Room light 12V-8W
Ignition-starter switch
Combination switch
Lighting switch & illumination intensity control switch
Hazard unit
Turn signal unit
Turn signal light R.H.
Turn signal light L.H.
Turn signal & hazard switch
Lighting switch
Illumination light etc.
Marker light Tail etc.
Head light High beam
Head light Low beam
Dimmer switch
Ignition starter switch
(When key is pulled out at Lock

Color Code of Electric Wires

W	White	R	Red	GB	Green-Black
WR	White-Red	RW	Red-White	L	Blue
WB	White-Black	RB	Red-Black	LW	Blue-White
WG	White-Green	RG	Red-Green	LR	Blue-Red
WL	White-Blue	RL	Red-Blue	LY	Blue-Yellow
Y	Yellow	RY	Red-Yellow	LG	Blue-Green
YW	Yellow-White	G	Green	LB	Blue-Black
YR	Yellow-Red	GW	Green-White	B	Black
YB	Yellow-Black	GY	Green-Yellow	BW	Black-White
YG	Yellow-Green	GR	Green-Red	BY	Black-Yellow
YL	Yellow-Blue	GL	Green-Blue	BR	Black-Red

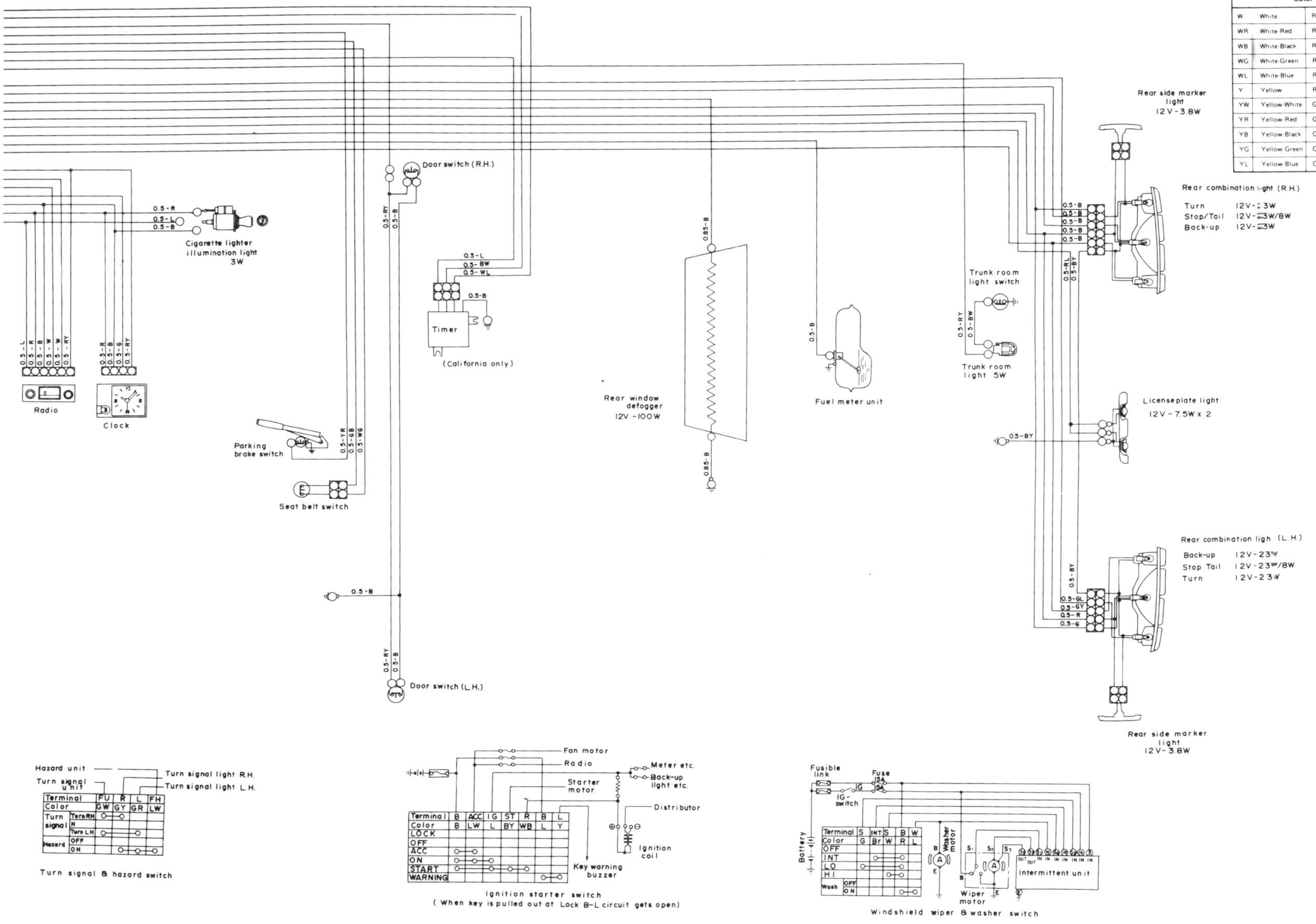

Turn signal & hazard switch

Terminal	FU	R	L	FH
Color	GW	GY	GR	LW
Turn signal Turn RH	○	○		
Turn signal N				
Turn signal Turn LH	○		○	
Hazard OFF				
Hazard ON		○	○	○

Ignition starter switch

Terminal	B	ACC	IG	ST	R	B	L
Color	B	LW	L	BY	WB	L	Y
LOCK							
OFF							
ACC	○	○					
ON	○	○	○				
START	○		○	○	○		
WARNING						○	○

Windshield wiper & washer switch

Terminal	S	INT	S	B	W
Color	G	Br	W	R	L
OFF					
INT	○	○		○	
LO	○		○	○	
HI			○		○
Wash OFF					
Wash ON				○	○

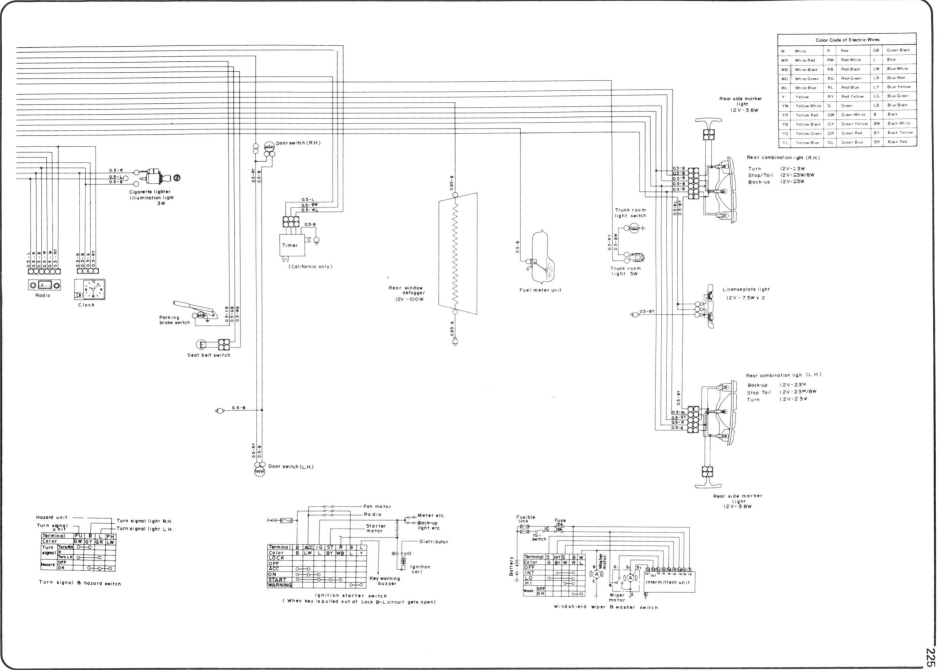

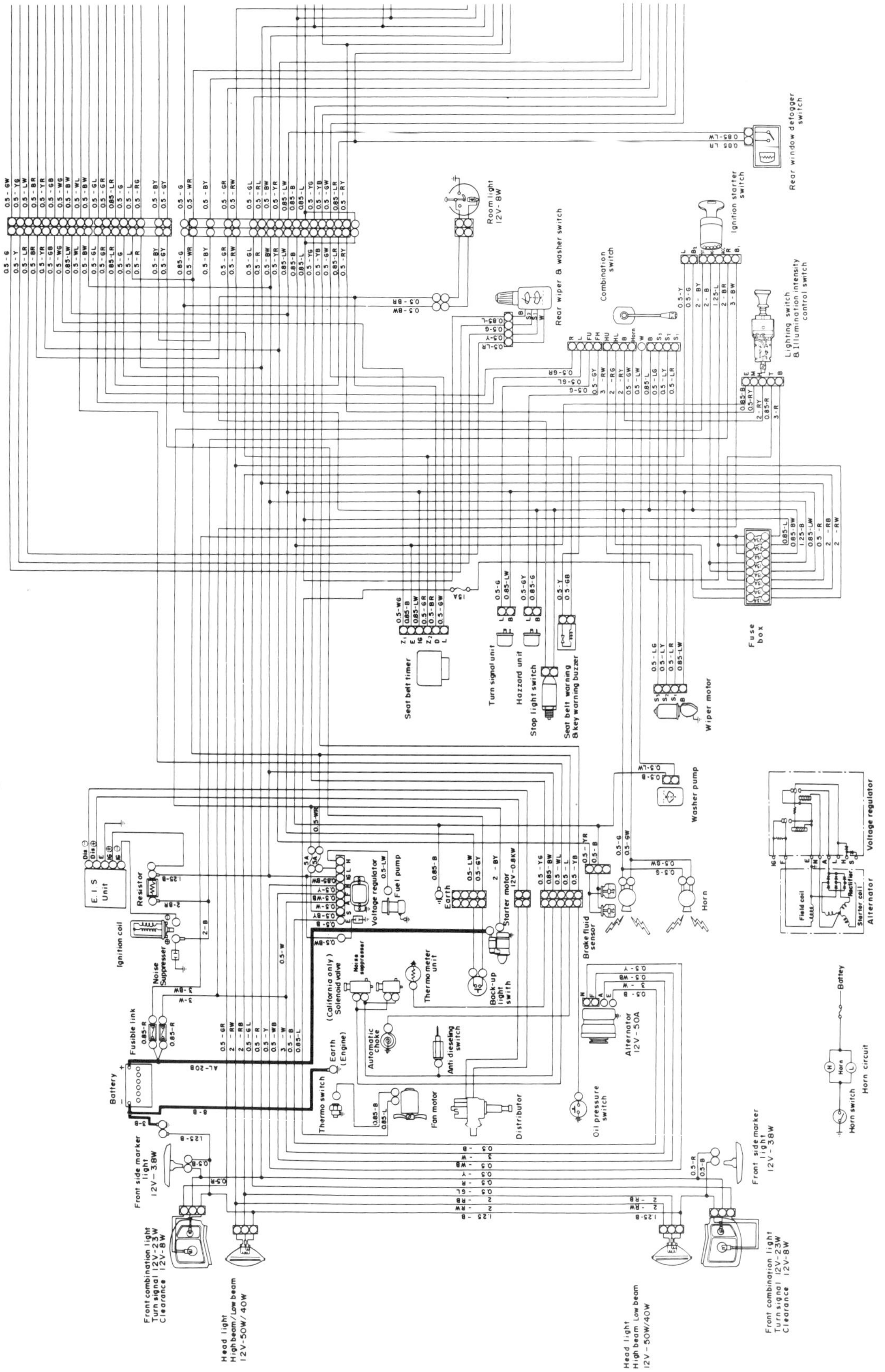

Fig. 13.21. Wiring diagram - Station Wagon (manual transmission) (Sec. 8)

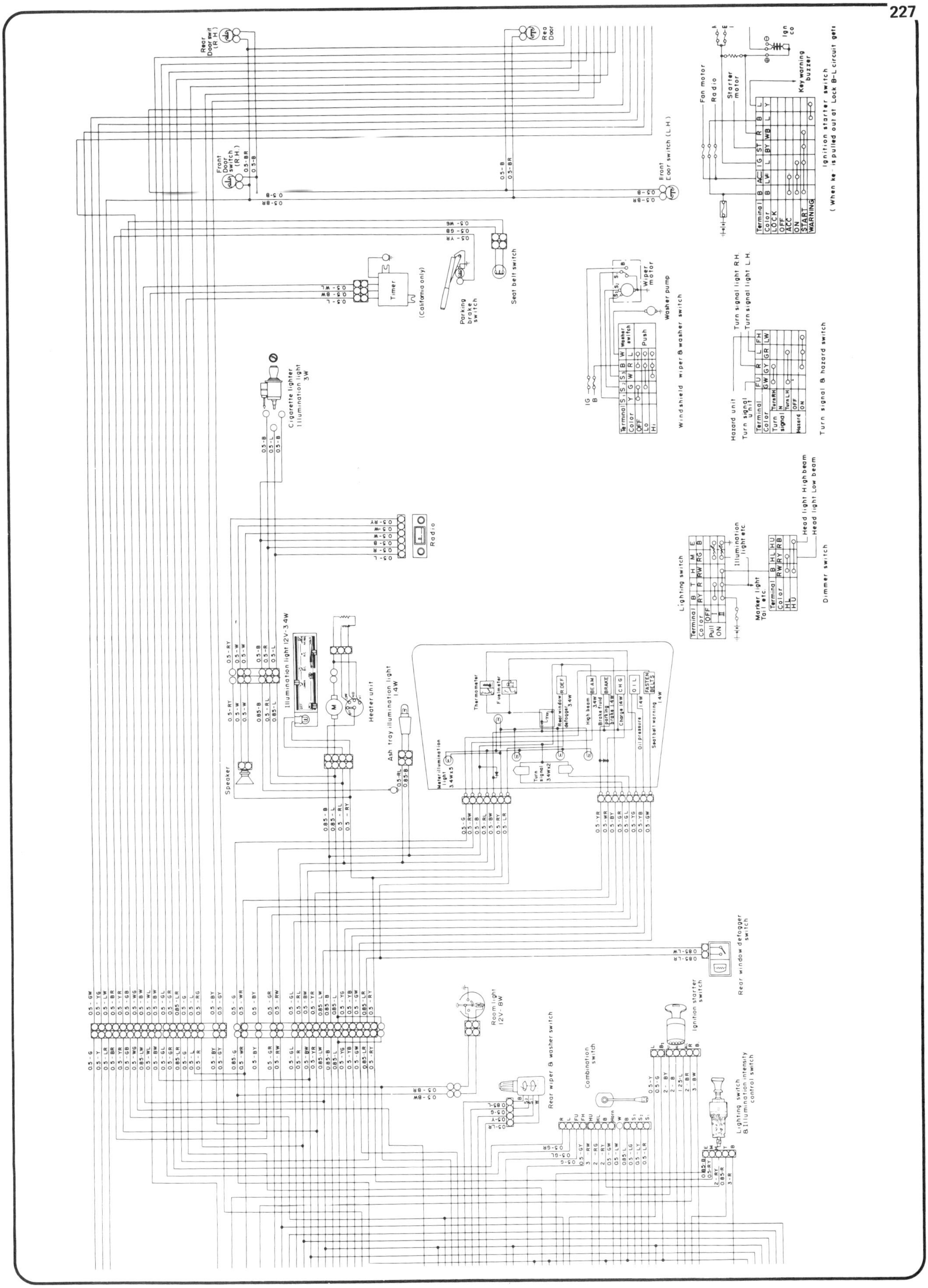

Rear Door switch (R.H.)
Front Door switch (R.H.)
Front Door switch (L.H.)
Seat belt switch
Parking brake switch
Timer
(California only)
Cigarette lighter illumination light 3W
Radio
Illumination light 12V-3.4W
Heater unit
Speaker
Ash tray illumination light 1.4W
Thermometer
Fuel meter
Meter illumination light 3.4W×5
Turn signal 3.4W×2
High beam
Brake fluid
Parking brake 1.4W
Charge 1.4W
Oil pressure 1.4W
Seat belt warning 1.4W
Windshield wiper & washer switch
Wiper motor
Washer pump
Turn signal & hazard switch
Hazard unit
Turn signal unit
Turn signal light RH
Turn signal light LH
Lighting switch
Dimmer switch
Head light High beam
Head light Low beam
Marker light Tail etc.
Illumination light etc.
Ignition starter switch
(When key is pulled out at Lock B-L circuit gets
Fan motor
Radio
Starter motor
Key warning buzzer
Rear window defogger switch
Room light 12V-8W
Rear wiper & washer switch
Combination switch
Lighting switch & Illumination intensity control switch

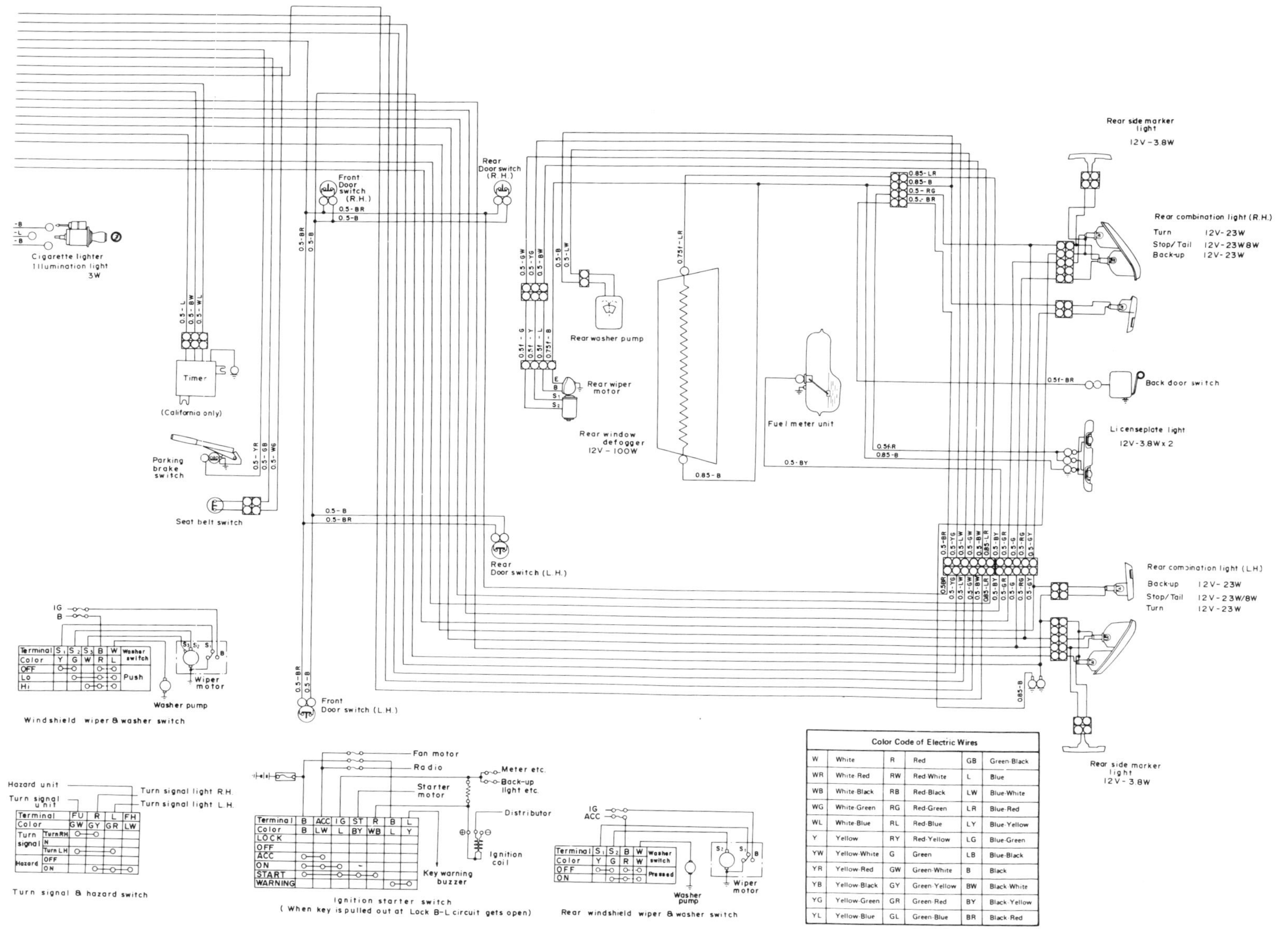

Color Code of Electric Wires

W	White	R	Red	GB	Green-Black
WR	White-Red	RW	Red-White	L	Blue
WB	White-Black	RB	Red-Black	LW	Blue-White
WG	White-Green	RG	Red-Green	LR	Blue-Red
WL	White-Blue	RL	Red-Blue	LY	Blue-Yellow
Y	Yellow	RY	Red-Yellow	LG	Blue-Green
YW	Yellow-White	G	Green	LB	Blue-Black
YR	Yellow-Red	GW	Green-White	B	Black
YB	Yellow-Black	GY	Green-Yellow	BW	Black-White
YG	Yellow-Green	GR	Green-Red	BY	Black-Yellow
YL	Yellow-Blue	GL	Green-Blue	BR	Black-Red

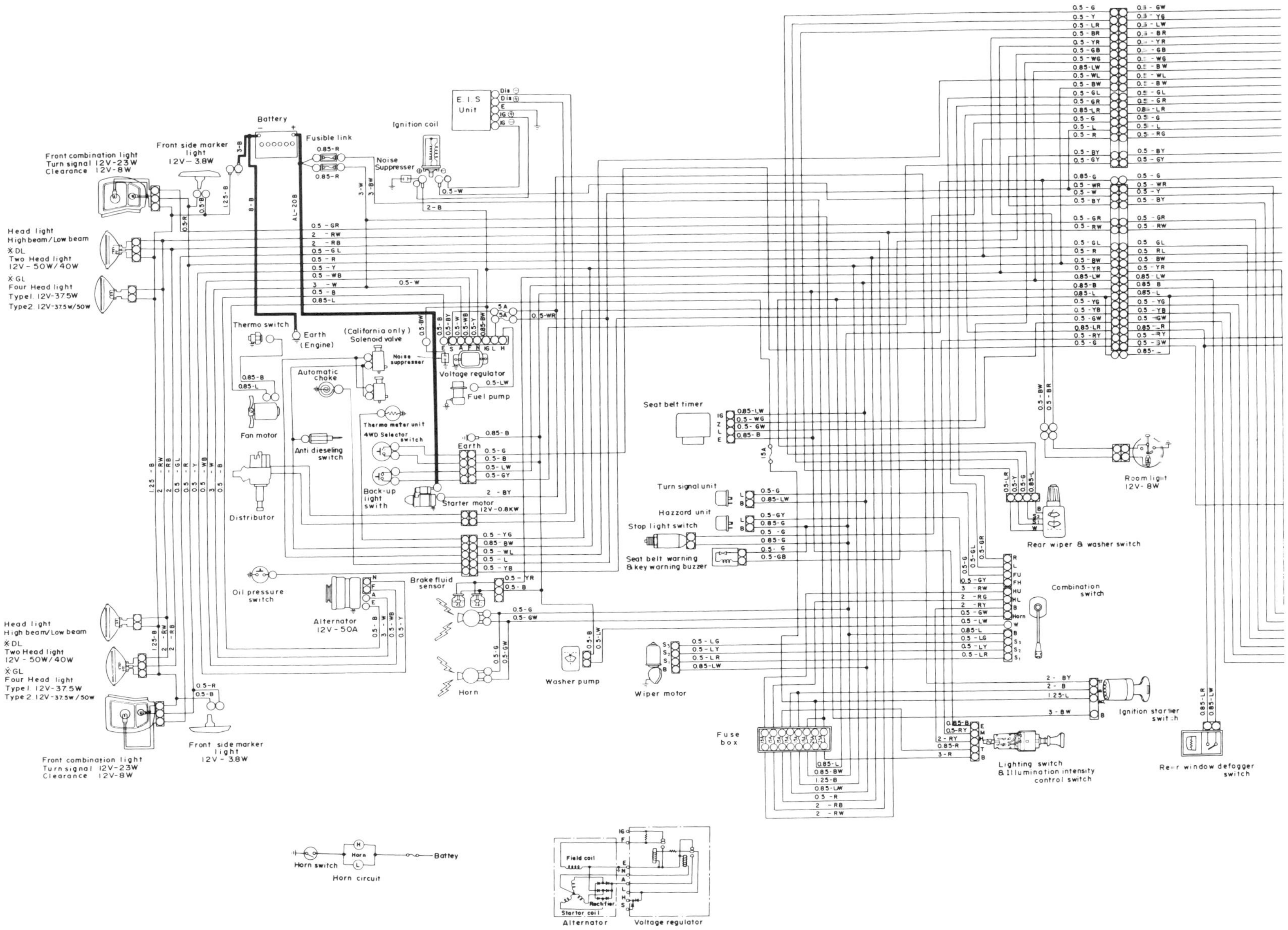

Fig. 13.22. Wiring diagram - 4WD Station Wagon (manual transmission) (Sec. 8)

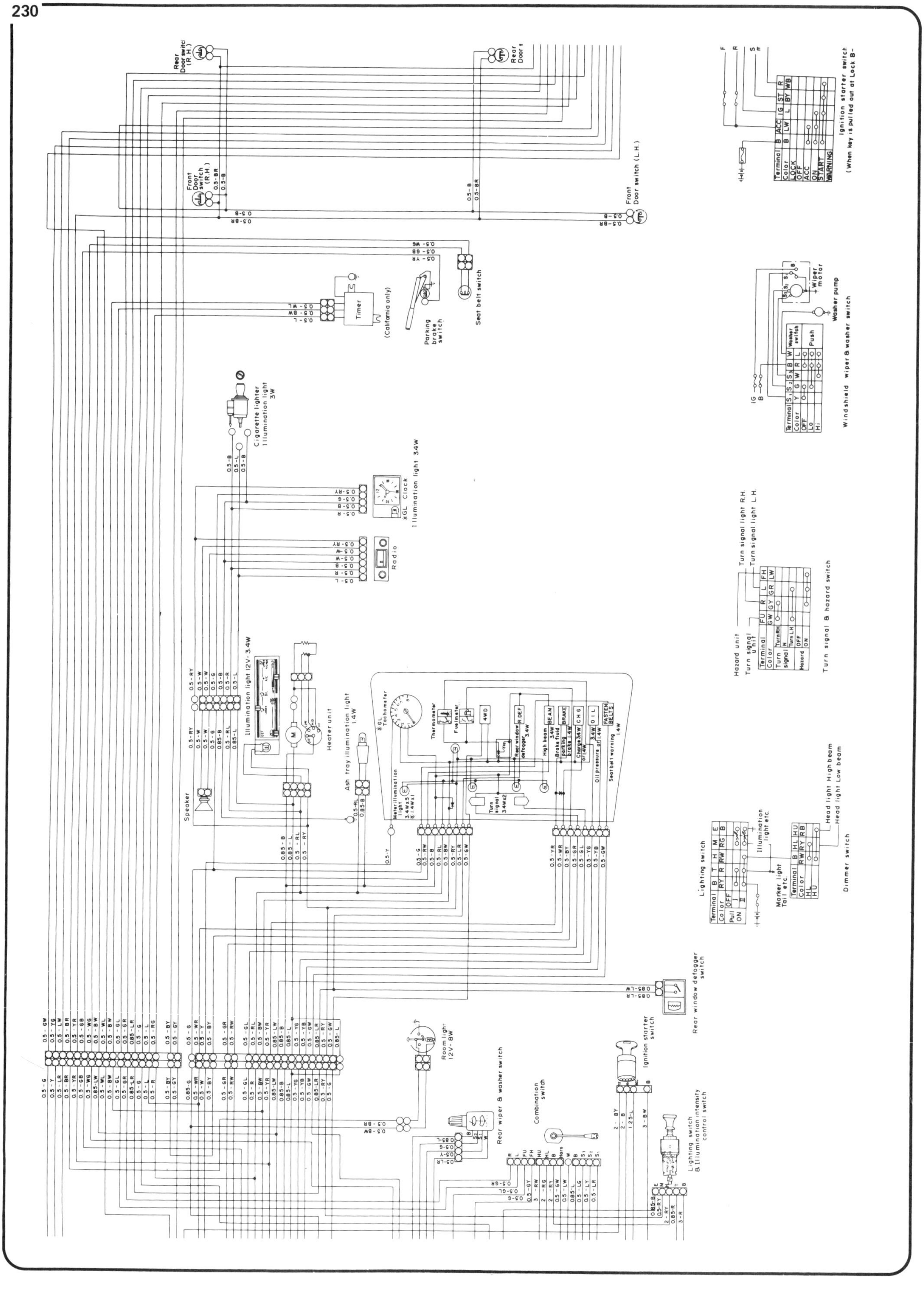
Rear Door switch (R.H.)
Rear Door switch
Front Door switch (R.H.)
Front Door switch (L.H.)
Ignition starter switch
(When key is pulled out at Lock B-)
Timer
(California only)
Parking brake switch
Seat belt switch
Wiper motor
Washer pump
Windshield wiper & washer switch
Cigarette lighter
Illumination light 3W
Clock
Illumination light 3.4W
Radio
Turn signal light RH
Turn signal light L.H.
Hazard unit
Turn signal unit
Turn signal & hazard switch
Illumination light 12V-3.4W
Heater unit
Ash tray illumination light 1.4W
Speaker
Tachometer
Thermometer
Fuel meter
Seat belt warning 1.4W
Lighting switch
Marker light Tail etc.
Illumination light etc.
Head light High beam
Head light Low beam
Dimmer switch
Rear window defogger switch
Room light 12V-8W
Ignition starter switch
Rear wiper & washer switch
Combination switch
Lighting switch & Illumination intensity control switch

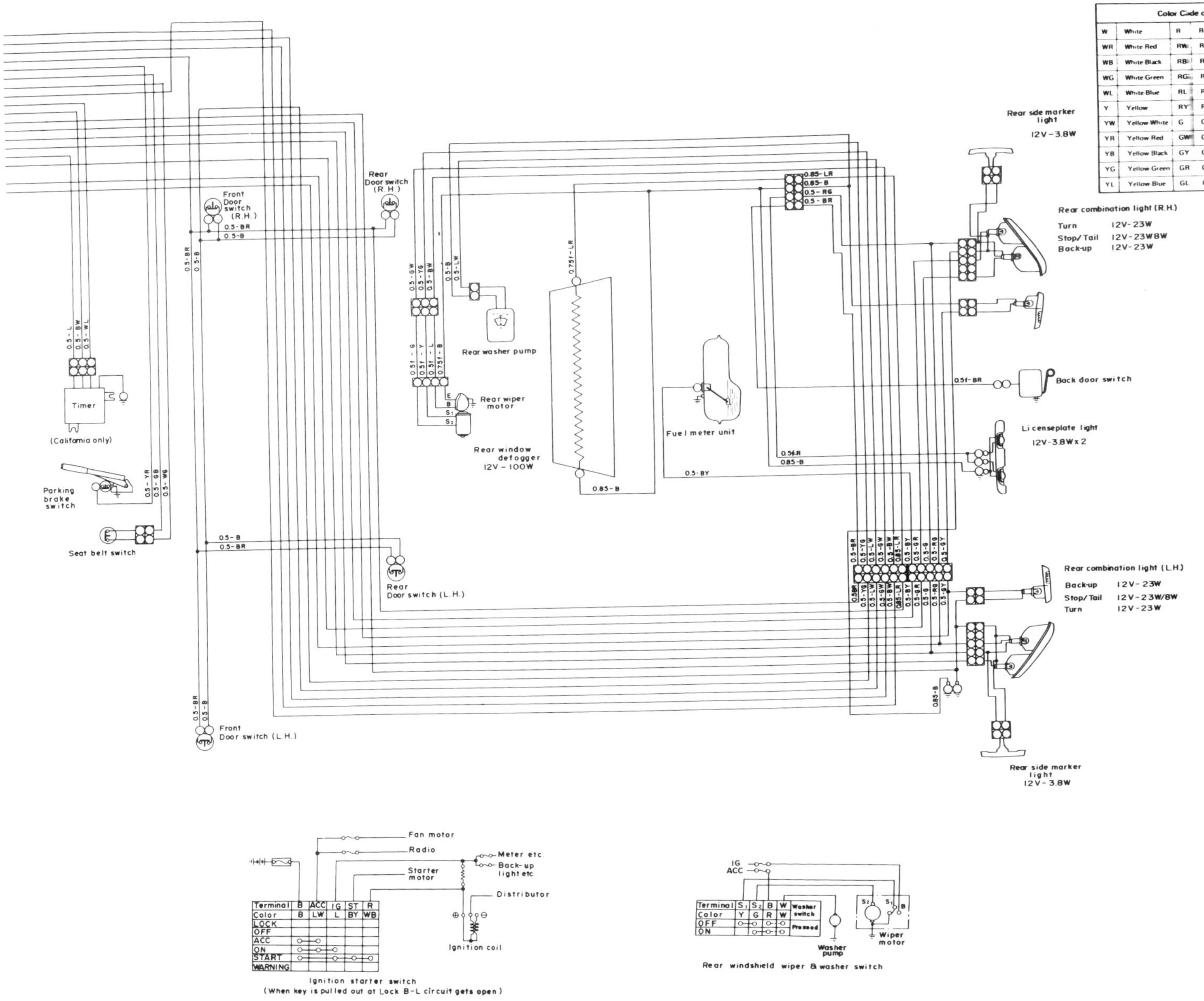

Color Code of Electric Wires

W	White	R	Red	GB	Green-Black
WR	White-Red	RW	Red-White	L	Blue
WB	White-Black	RB	Red-Black	LW	Blue-White
WG	White-Green	RG	Red-Green	LR	Blue-Red
WL	White-Blue	RL	Red-Blue	LY	Blue-Yellow
Y	Yellow	RY	Red-Yellow	LG	Blue-Green
YW	Yellow-White	G	Green	LB	Blue-Black
YR	Yellow-Red	GW	Green-White	B	Black
YB	Yellow-Black	GY	Green-Yellow	BW	Black-White
YG	Yellow-Green	GR	Green-Red	BY	Black-Yellow
YL	Yellow-Blue	GL	Green-Blue	BR	Black-Red

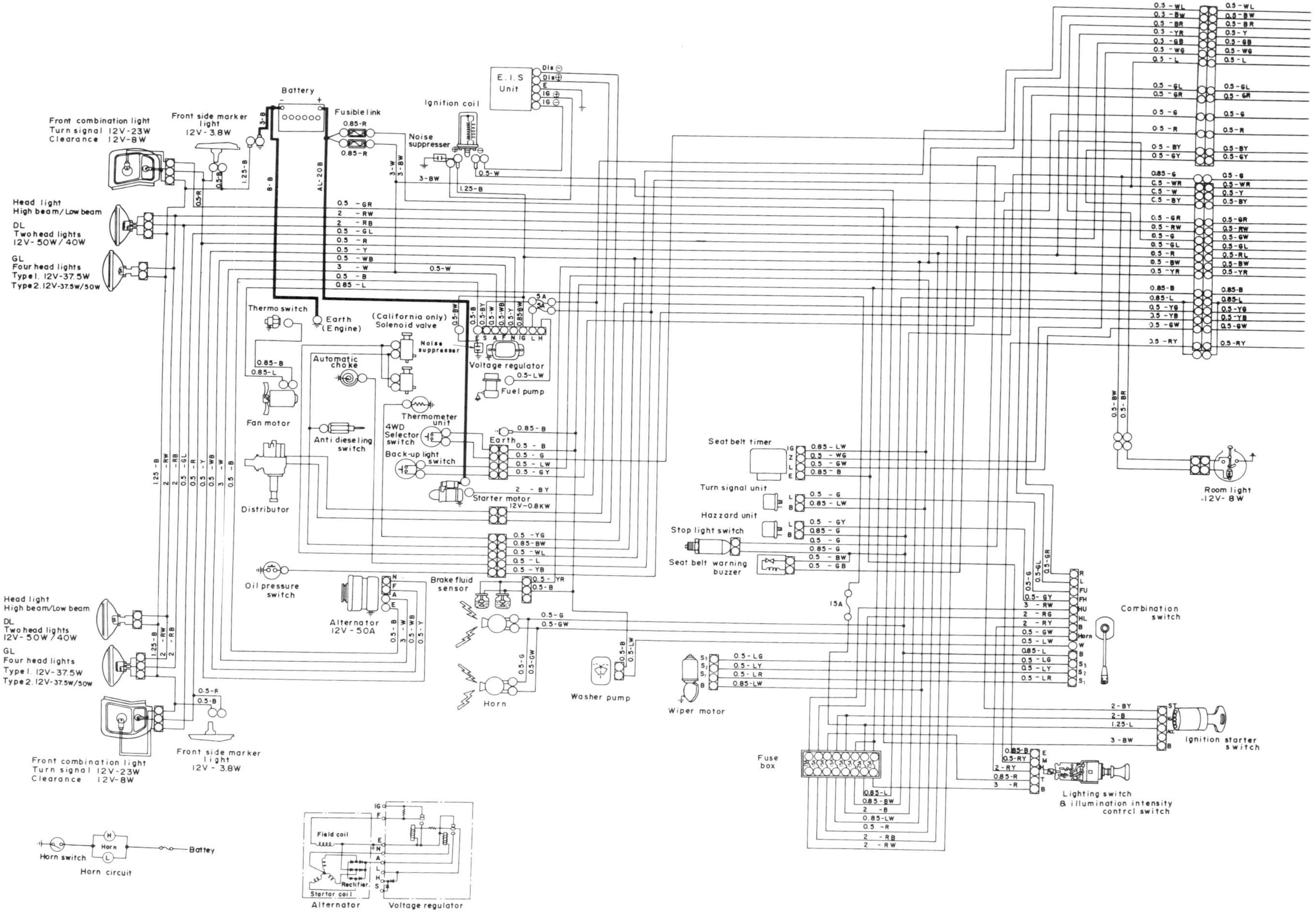

Fig. 13.23. Wiring diagram - 4WD Open MPV (manual transmission) (Sec. 8)

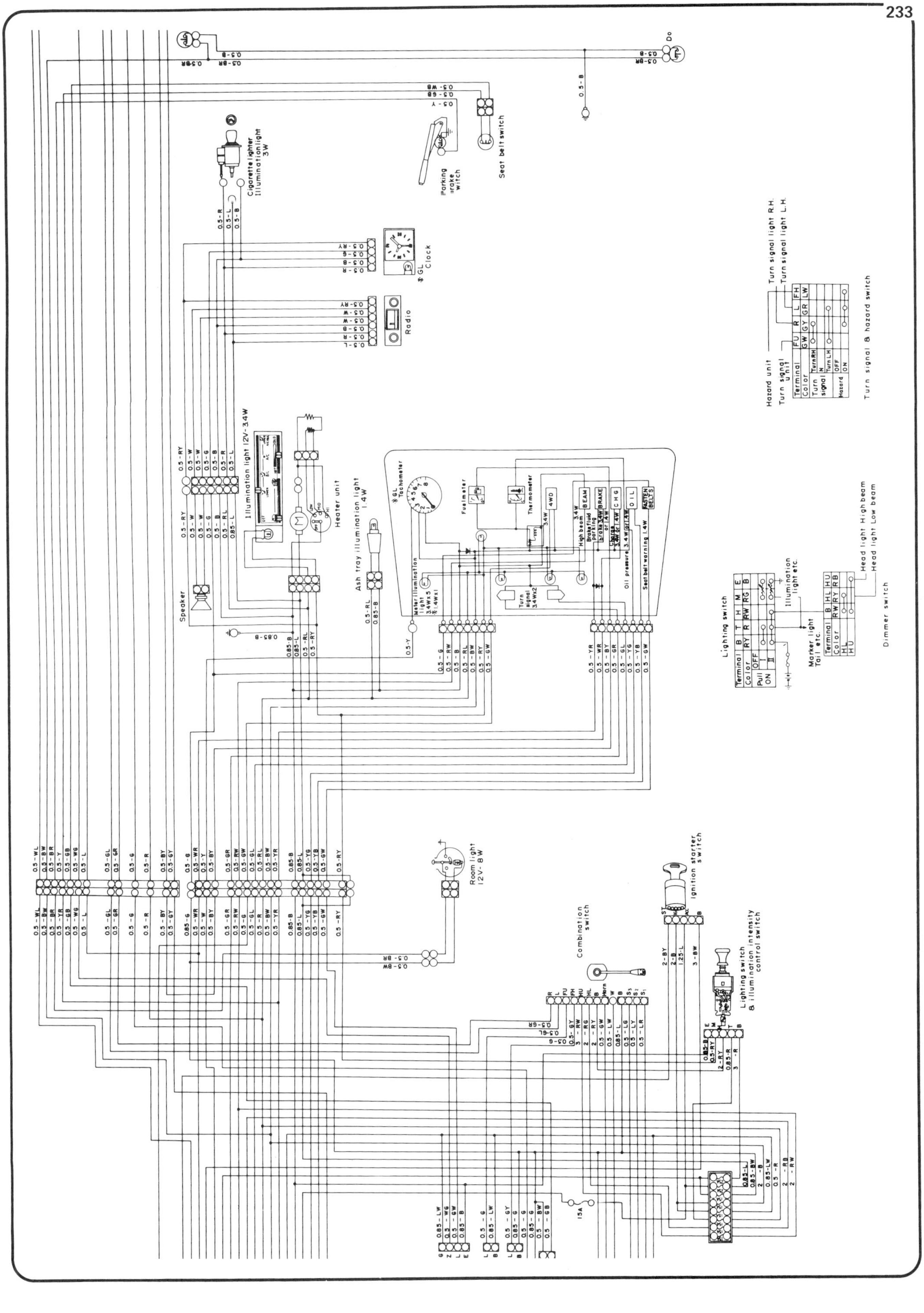
Cigarette lighter Illumination light 3W
Parking brake switch
Seat belt switch
Clock
Radio
Illumination light 12V-3.4W
Heater unit
Speaker
Ash tray illumination light 1.4W
Tachometer
Fuelmeter
Thermometer
Turn signal light R.H.
Turn signal light L.H.
Hazard unit
Turn signal unit
Turn signal & hazard switch
Lighting switch
Illumination light etc.
Marker light Tail etc.
Head light Highbeam
Head light Low beam
Dimmer switch
Room light 12V-8W
Combination switch
Ignition starter switch
Lighting switch & illumination intensity control switch

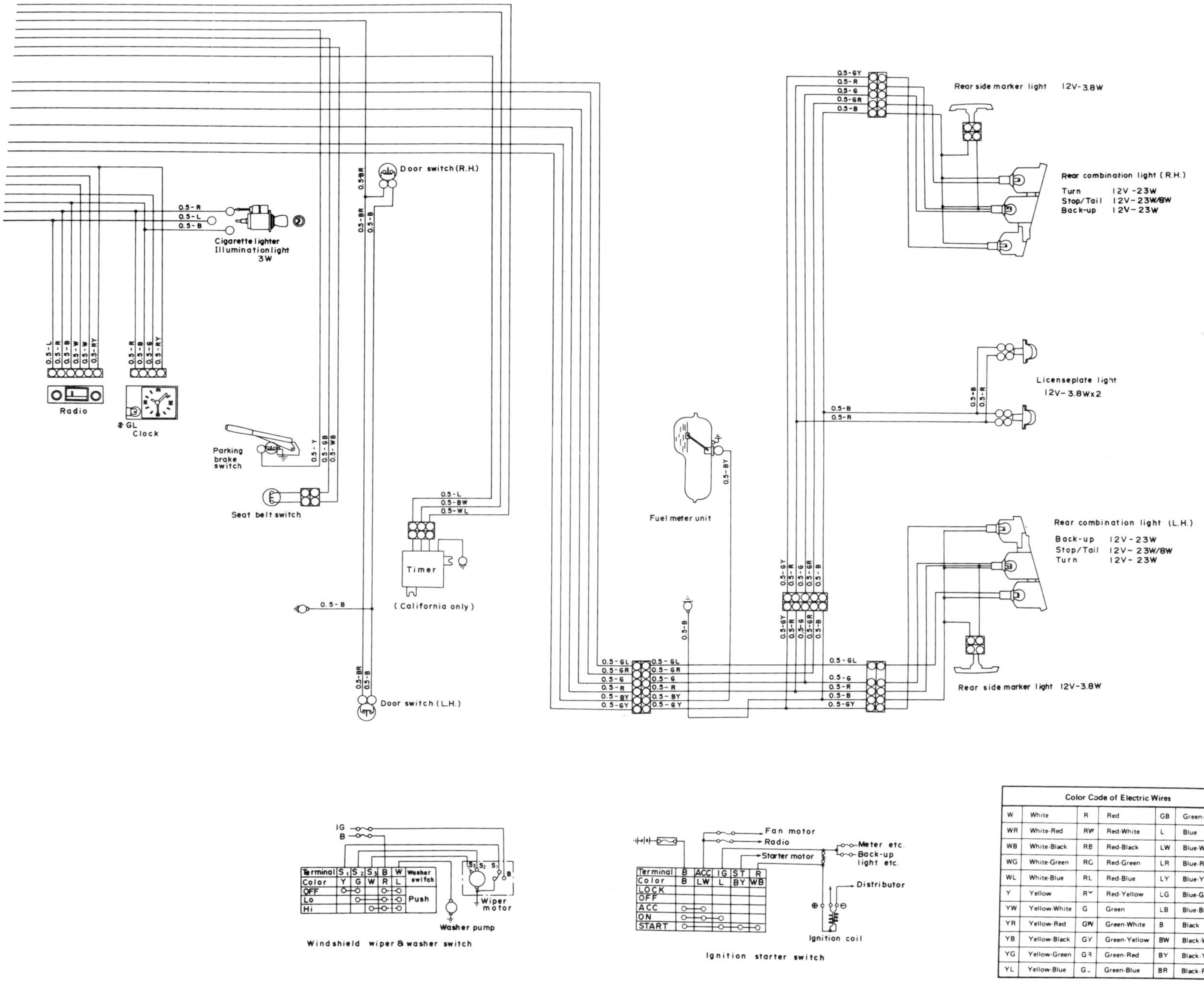

Color Code of Electric Wires

W	White	R	Red	GB	Green-Black
WR	White-Red	RW	Red-White	L	Blue
WB	White-Black	RB	Red-Black	LW	Blue-White
WG	White-Green	RG	Red-Green	LR	Blue-Red
WL	White-Blue	RL	Red-Blue	LY	Blue-Yellow
Y	Yellow	RY	Red-Yellow	LG	Blue-Green
YW	Yellow-White	G	Green	LB	Blue-Black
YR	Yellow-Red	GW	Green-White	B	Black
YB	Yellow-Black	GY	Green-Yellow	BW	Black-White
YG	Yellow-Green	GR	Green-Red	BY	Black-Yellow
YL	Yellow-Blue	GL	Green-Blue	BR	Black-Red

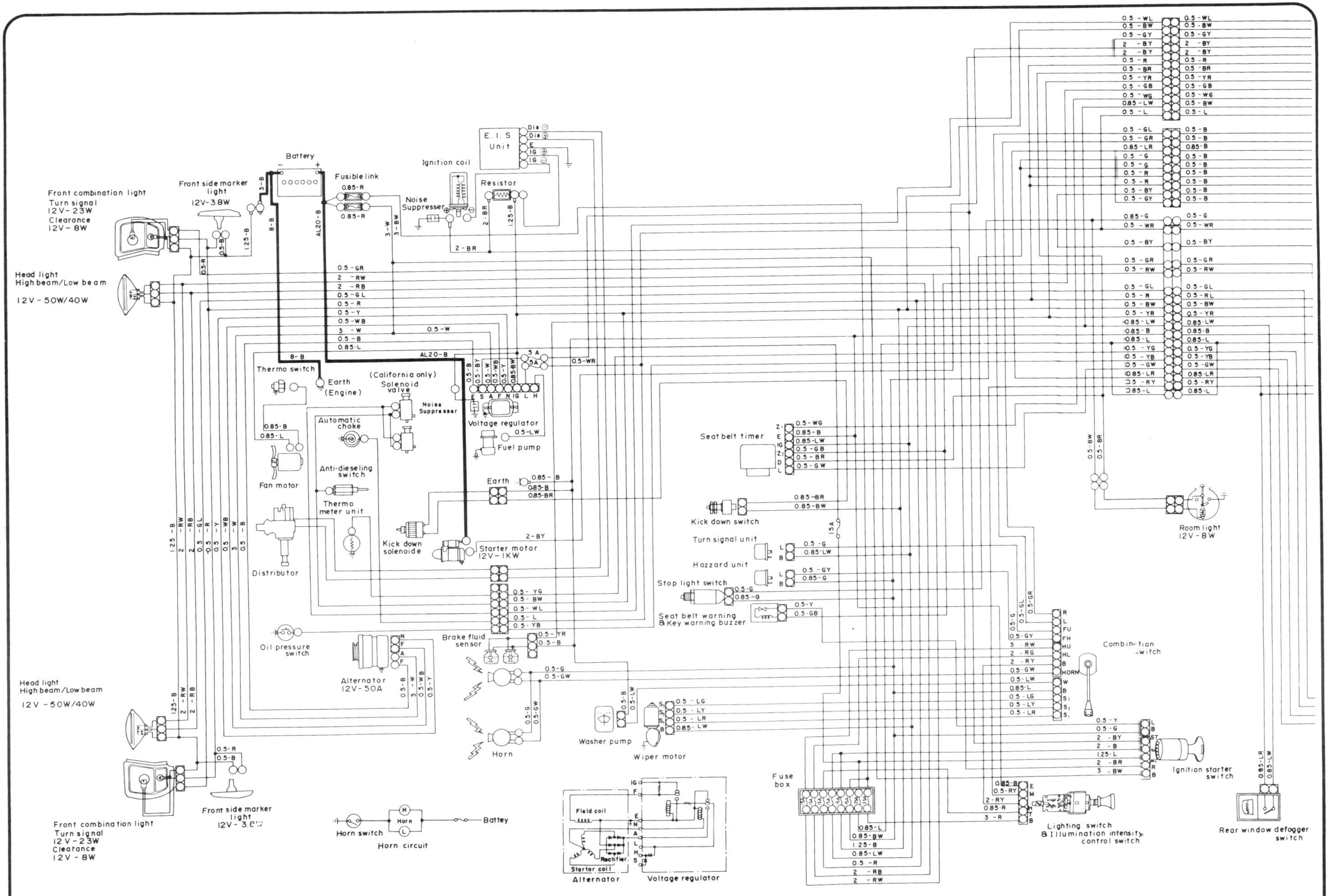

Fig. 13.24. Wiring diagram - Sedan (automatic transmission) (Sec. 8)

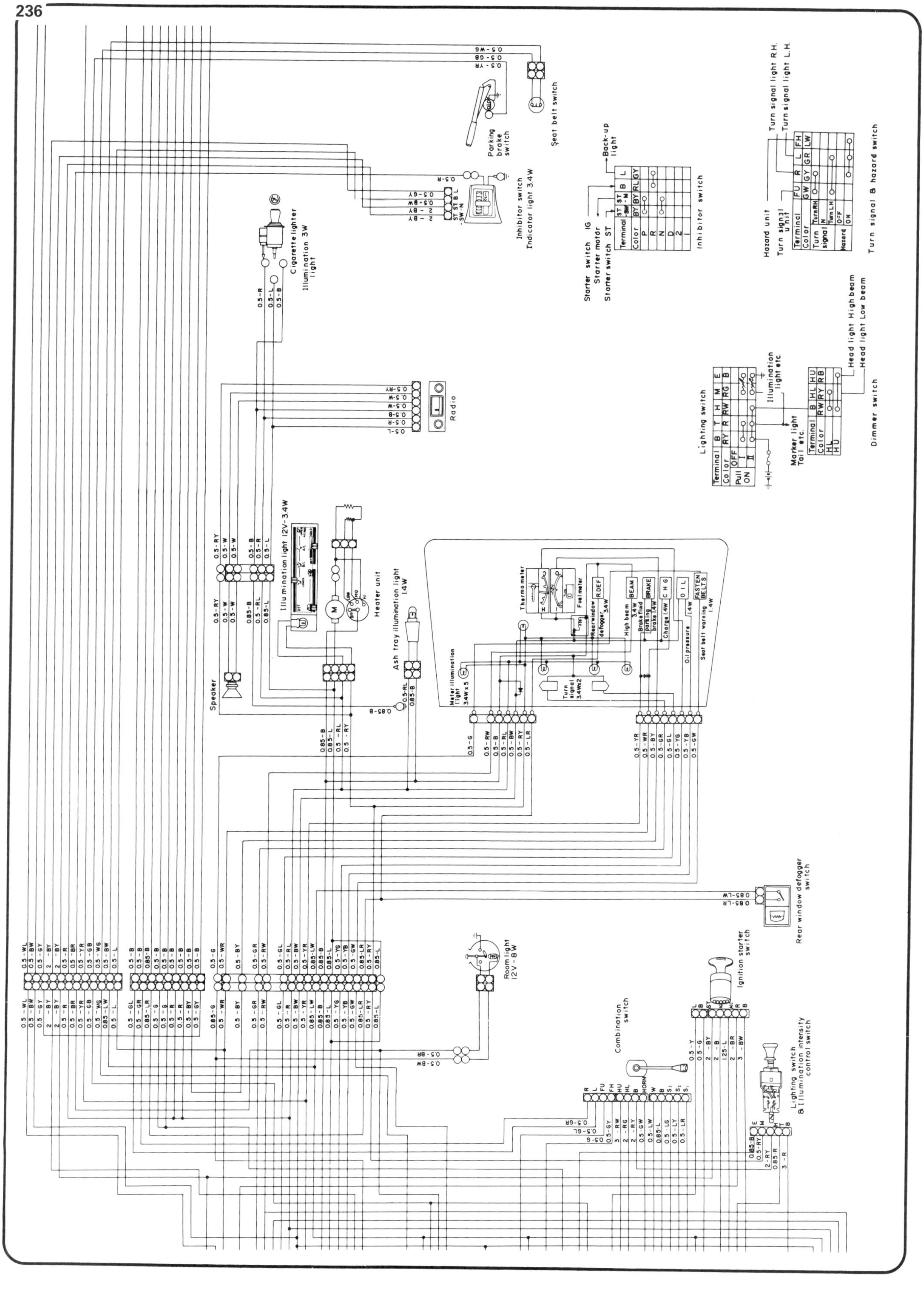

Seat belt switch
Parking brake switch
Inhibitor switch
Indicator light 3.4W
Cigarette lighter
Illumination light 3W
Starter switch IG
Starter motor
Starter switch ST
Back-up light
Inhibitor switch
Hazard unit
Turn signal unit
Turn signal light R.H.
Turn signal light L.H.
Turn signal & hazard switch
Radio
Lighting switch
Illumination light etc
Marker light Tail etc.
Head light High beam
Head light Low beam
Dimmer switch
Speaker
Illumination light 12V-3.4W
Heater unit
Ash tray illumination light 1.4W
Thermometer
Fuel meter
Rear window defogger 3.4W
High beam 3.4W
Brake fluid parking brake 1.4W
Charge 1.4W
Oil pressure 1.4W
Seat belt warning 1.4W
Meter illumination light 3.4W x 5
Turn signal 3.4W x 2
Rear window defogger switch
Room light 12V-8W
Ignition starter switch
Combination switch
Lighting switch & Illumination intensity control switch

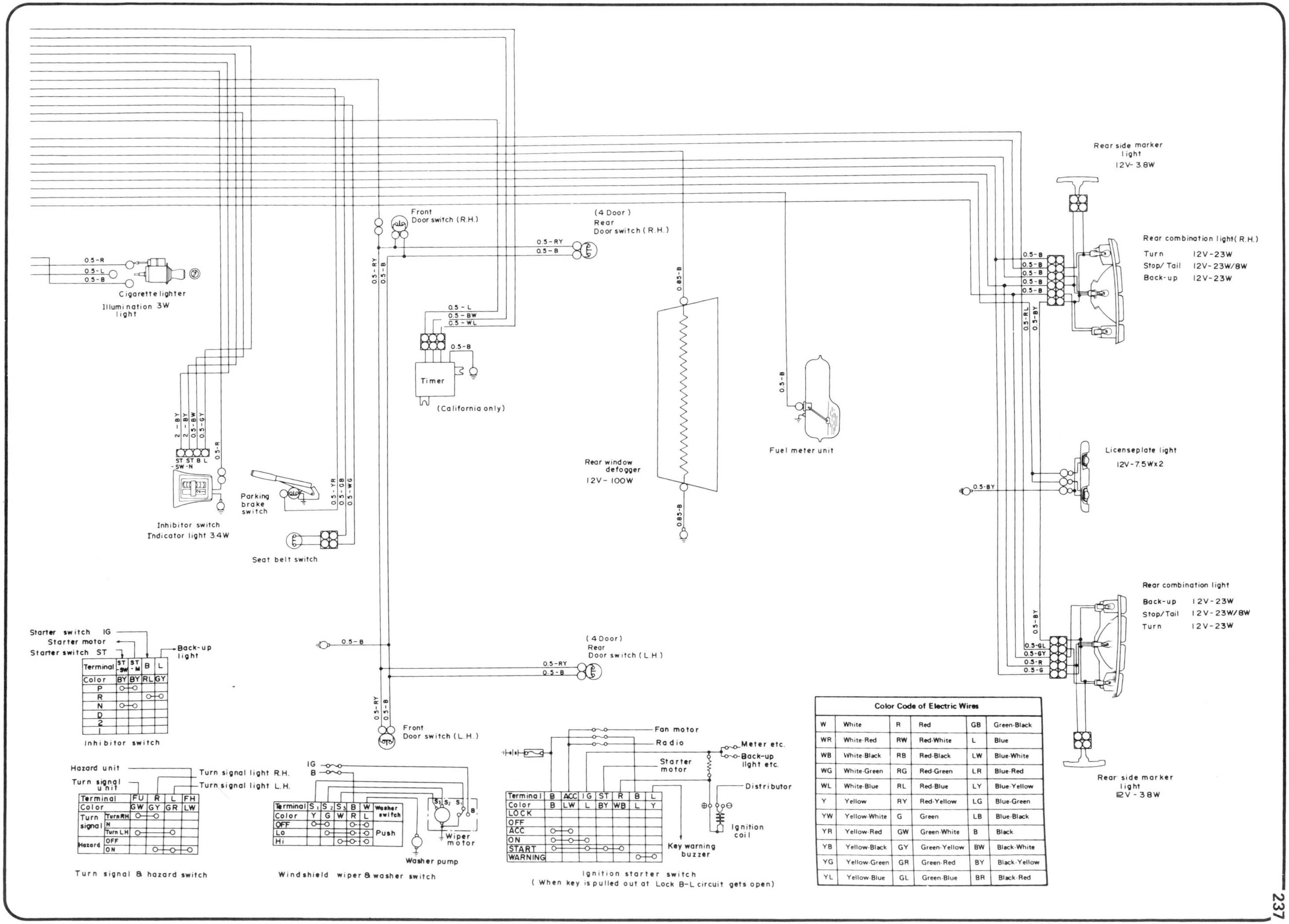

Color Code of Electric Wires

W	White	R	Red	GB	Green-Black
WR	White-Red	RW	Red-White	L	Blue
WB	White-Black	RB	Red-Black	LW	Blue-White
WG	White-Green	RG	Red-Green	LR	Blue-Red
WL	White-Blue	RL	Red-Blue	LY	Blue-Yellow
Y	Yellow	RY	Red-Yellow	LG	Blue-Green
YW	Yellow-White	G	Green	LB	Blue-Black
YR	Yellow-Red	GW	Green-White	B	Black
YB	Yellow-Black	GY	Green-Yellow	BW	Black-White
YG	Yellow-Green	GR	Green-Red	BY	Black-Yellow
YL	Yellow-Blue	GL	Green-Blue	BR	Black-Red

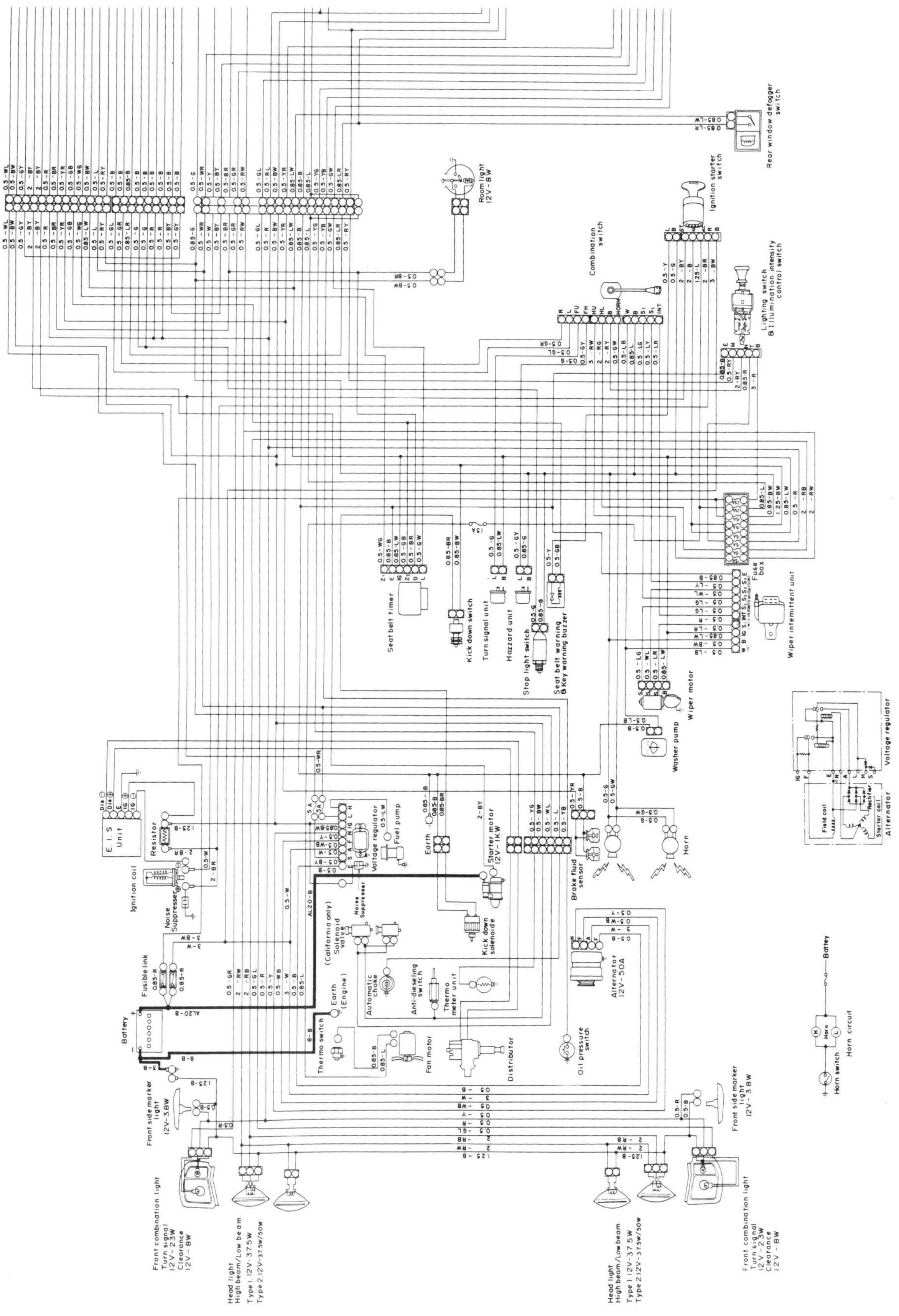

Fig. 13.25. Wiring diagram - Hardtop (automatic transmission) (Sec. 8)

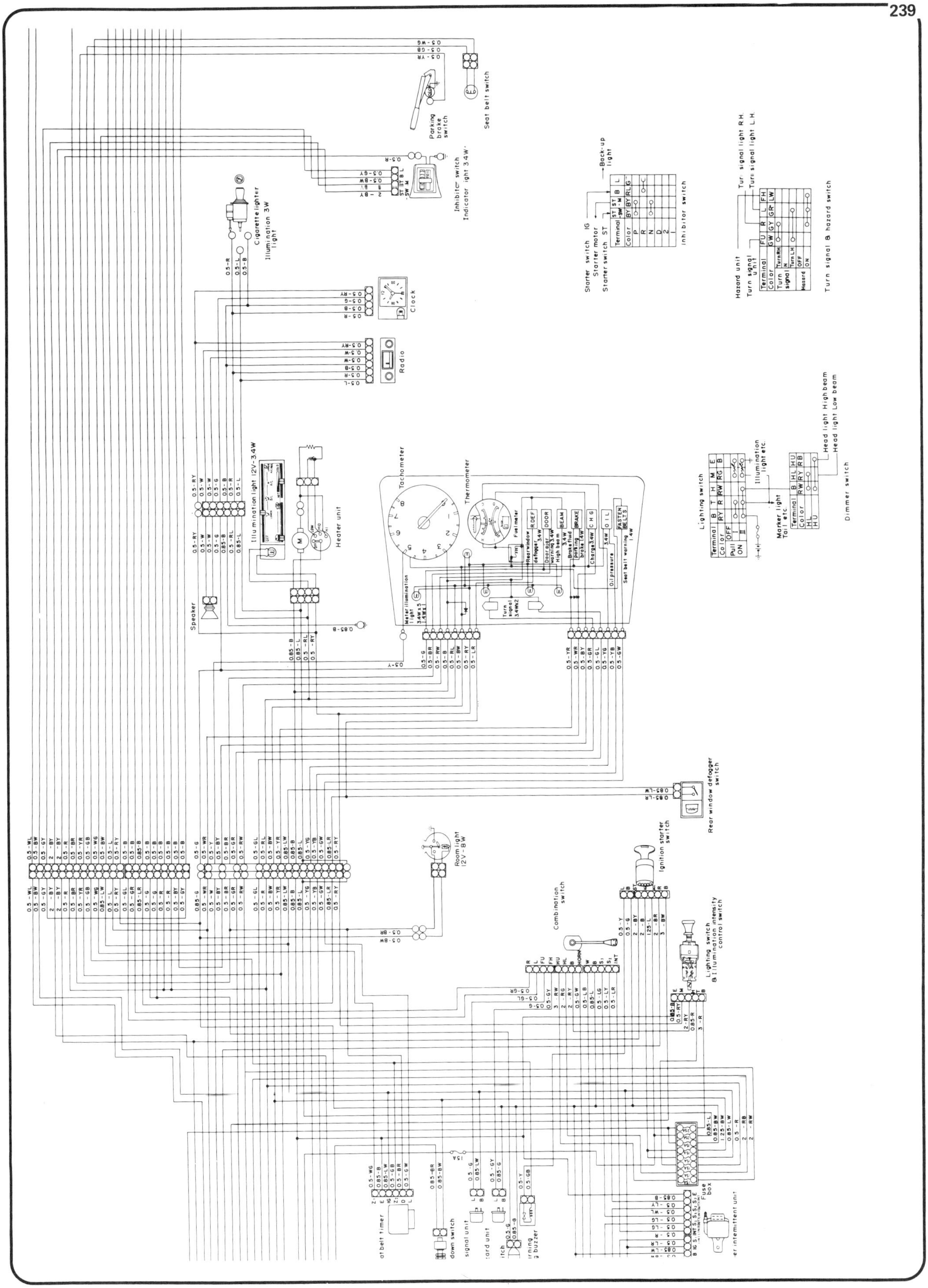

Seat belt switch
Parking brake switch
Inhibitor switch
Indicator light 3.4W
Cigarette lighter
Illumination 3W light
Clock
Radio
Starter switch IG
Starter motor
Starter switch ST
Back-up light
Inhibitor switch
Hazard unit
Turn signal unit
Turn signal light R.H.
Turn signal light L.H.
Turn signal & hazard switch
Illumination light 12V-3.4W
Heater unit
Speaker
Tachometer
Thermometer
Fuel meter
Meter illumination light
Turn signal
Oil pressure
Seat belt warning
Lighting switch
Illumination light etc.
Marker light Tail etc.
Head light High beam
Head light Low beam
Dimmer switch
Rear window defogger switch
Room light 12V-8W
Ignition starter switch
Combination switch
Lighting switch & Illumination intensity control switch
Fuse box

Color Code of Electric Wires

W	White	R	Red	GB	Green Black
WR	White Red	RW	Red White	L	Blue
WB	White Black	RB	Red Black	LW	Blue White
WG	White Green	RG	Red Green	LR	Blue Red
WL	White Blue	RL	Red Blue	LY	Blue Yellow
Y	Yellow	RY	Red Yellow	LG	Blue Green
YW	Yellow White	G	Green	LB	Blue Black
YR	Yellow Red	GW	Green White	B	Black
YB	Yellow Black	GY	Green Yellow	BW	Black White
YG	Yellow Green	GR	Green Red	BY	Black Yellow
YL	Yellow Blue	GL	Green Blue	BR	Black Red

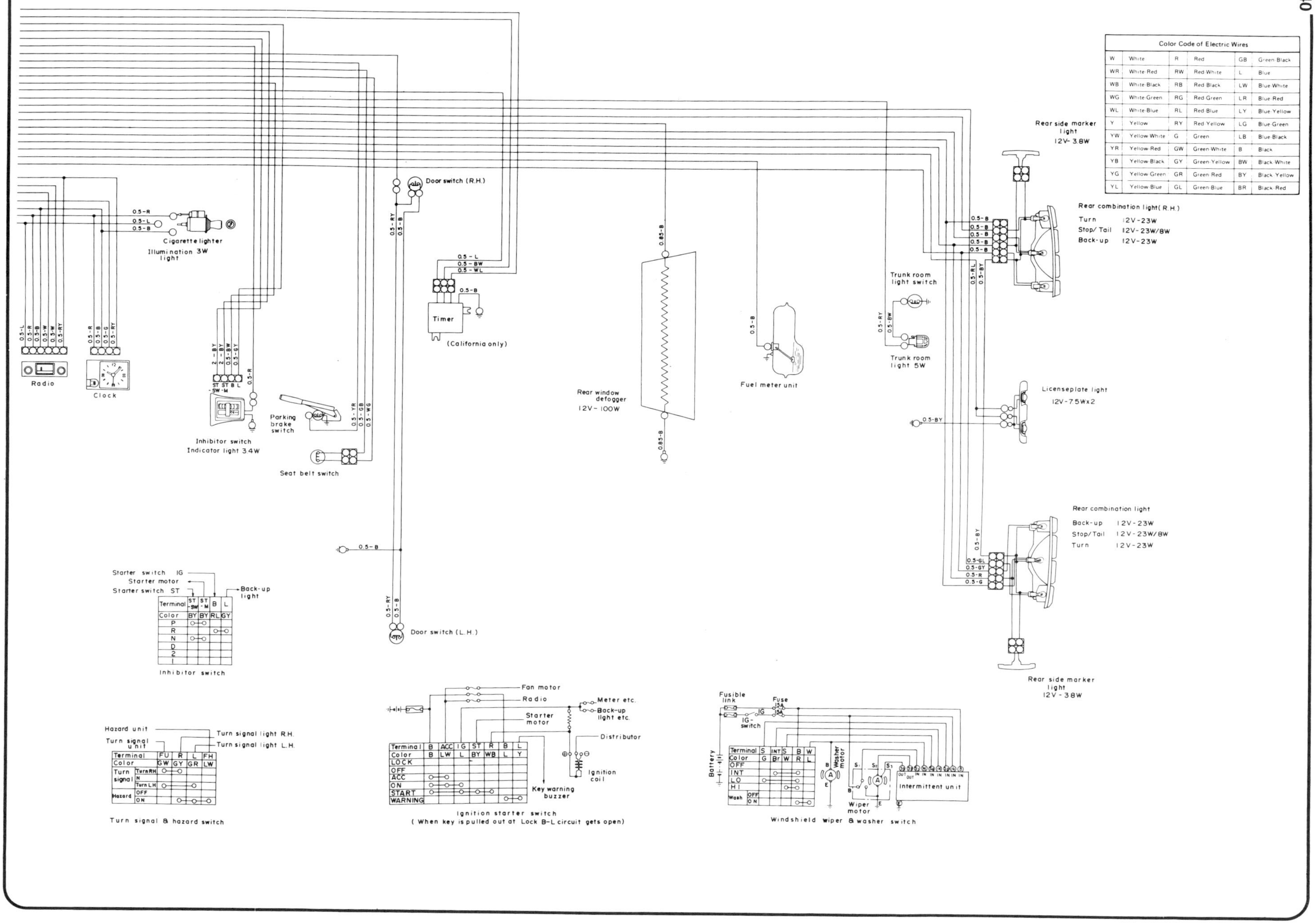

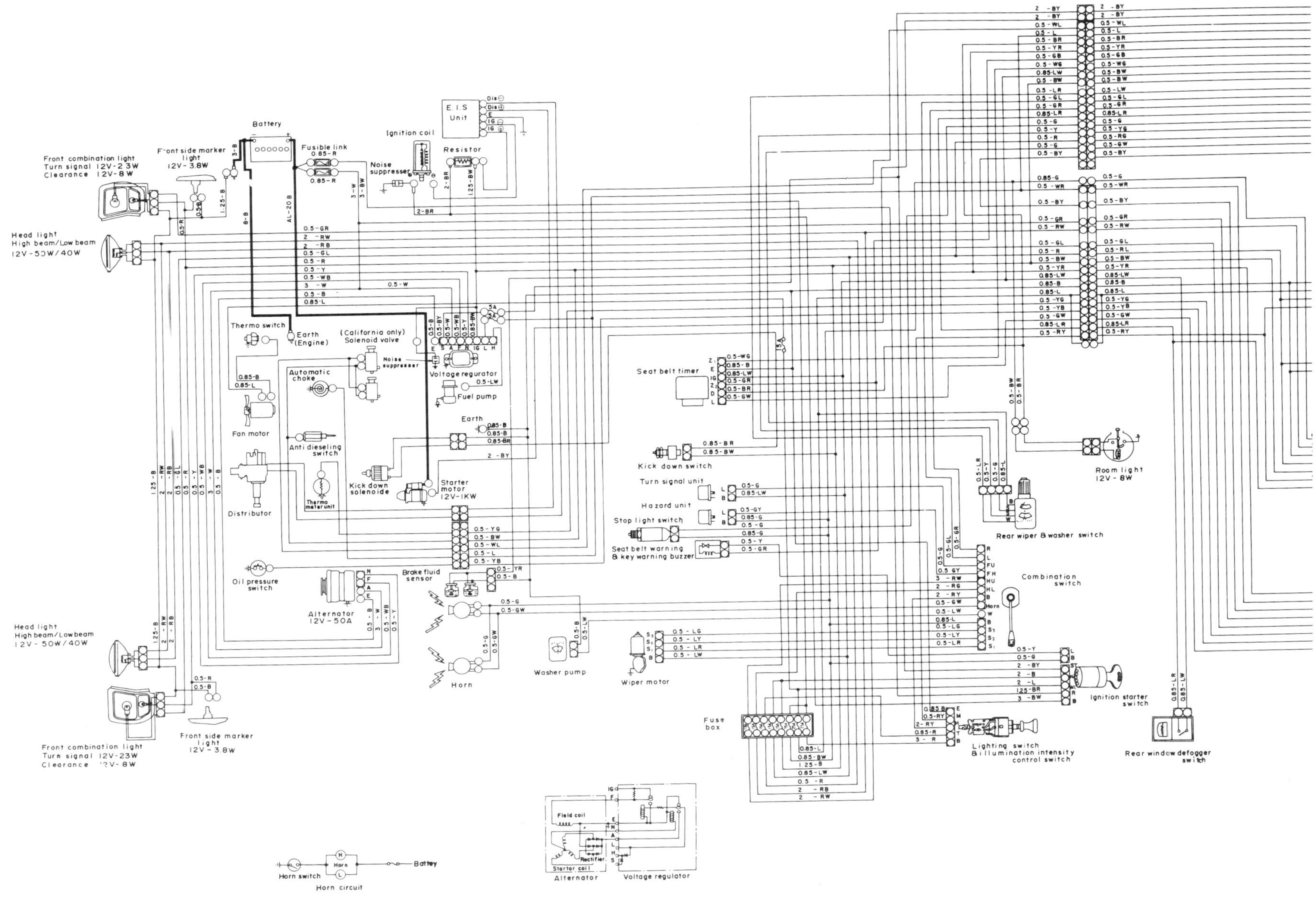

Fig. 13.26. Wiring diagram - Station Wagon (automatic transmission) (Sec. 8)

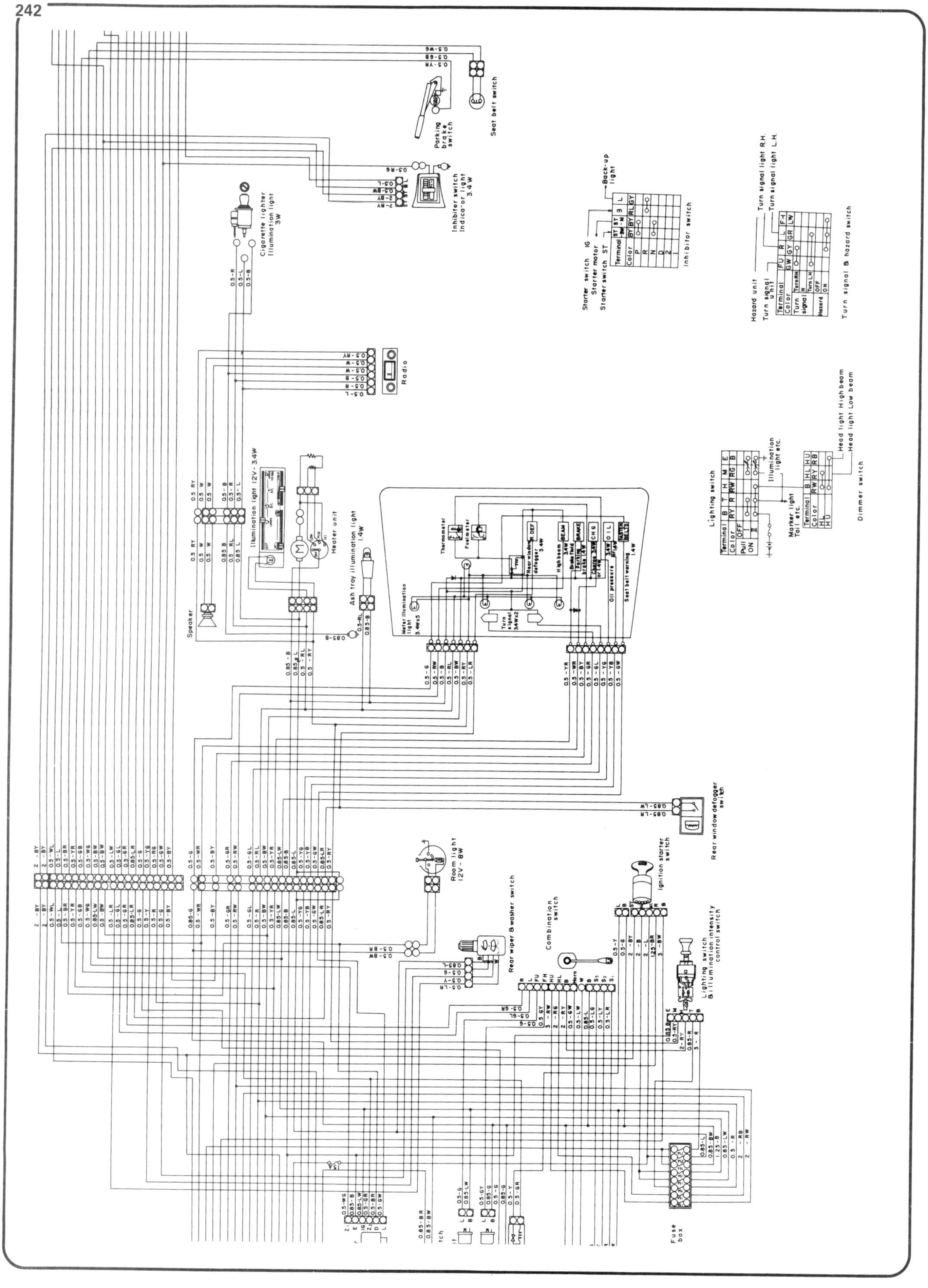
Seat belt switch
Parking brake switch
Inhibiter switch Indica-or light 3.4W
Cigarette lighter Illumination light 3W
Radio
Illumination light 12V-3.4W
Heater unit
Ash tray illumination light 1.4W
Speaker
Room light 12V-8W
Rear window defogger switch
Ignition starter switch
Rear wiper & washer switch
Combination switch
Lighting switch & illumination intensity control switch
Fuse box
Inhibitor switch
Turn signal & hazard switch
Lighting switch
Dimmer switch

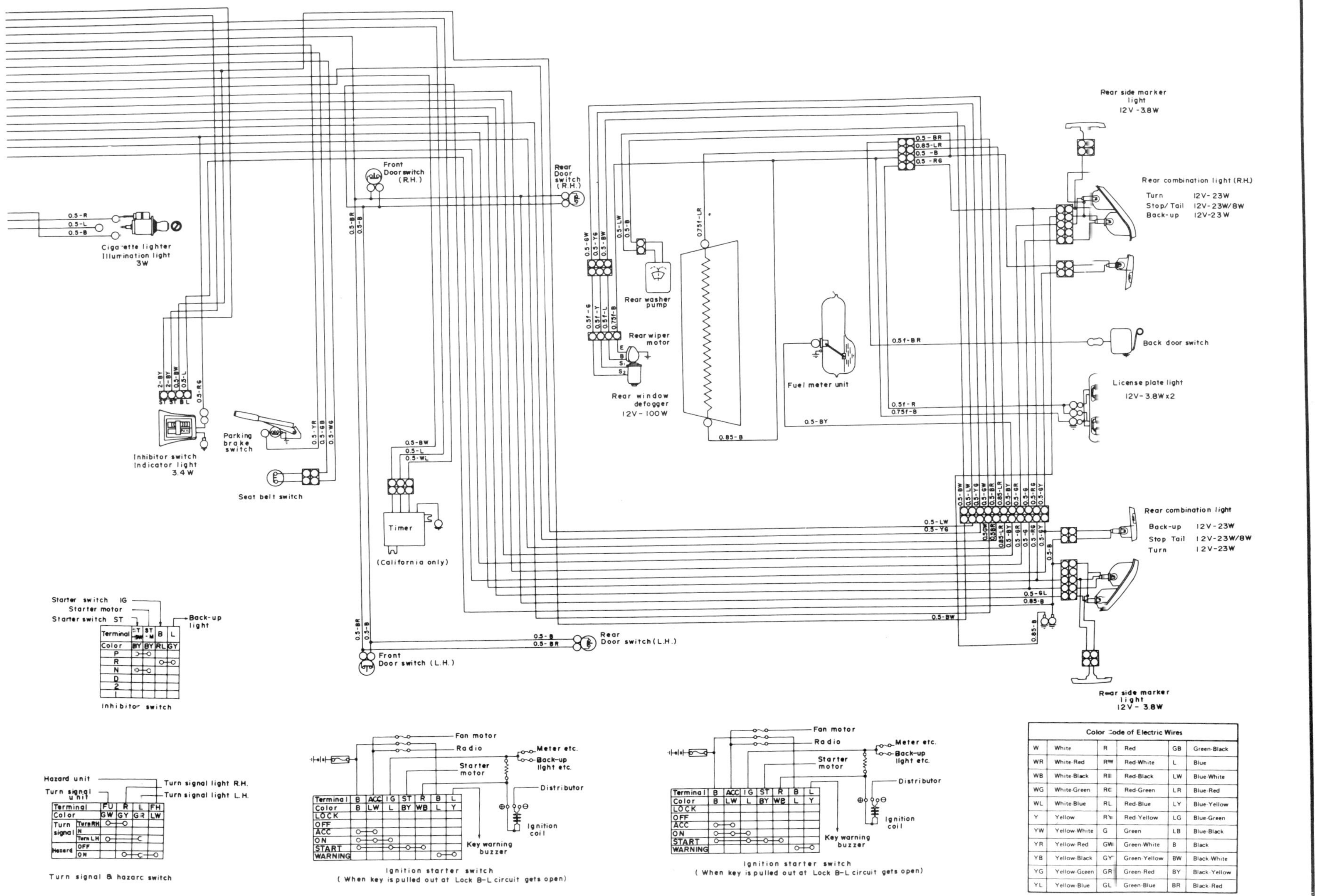

Color Code of Electric Wires

W	White	R	Red	GB	Green-Black
WR	White-Red	RW	Red-White	L	Blue
WB	White-Black	RB	Red-Black	LW	Blue-White
WG	White-Green	RG	Red-Green	LR	Blue-Red
WL	White-Blue	RL	Red-Blue	LY	Blue-Yellow
Y	Yellow	RY	Red-Yellow	LG	Blue-Green
YW	Yellow-White	G	Green	LB	Blue-Black
YR	Yellow-Red	GW	Green-White	B	Black
YB	Yellow-Black	GY	Green-Yellow	BW	Black-White
YG	Yellow-Green	GR	Green-Red	BY	Black-Yellow
YL	Yellow-Blue	GL	Green-Blue	BR	Black-Red

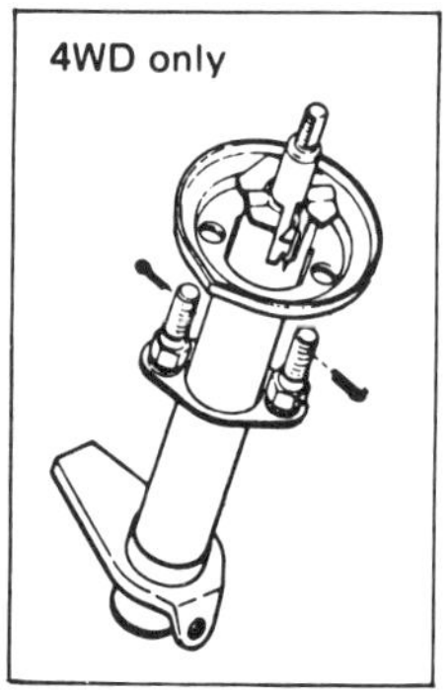

Fig. 13.27. Road clearance height adjusting nuts on front suspension strut (Sec.9)

Fig. 13.28. Measuring point for road clearance height adjustment (Sec. 9)

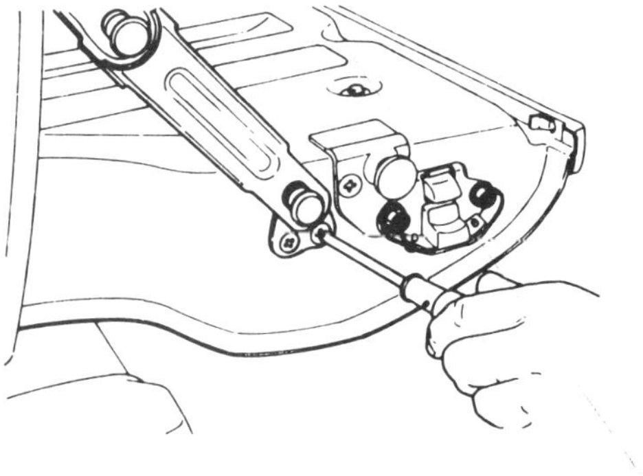

Fig. 13.29. Removing the tailgate stay securing screws (Sec. 10)

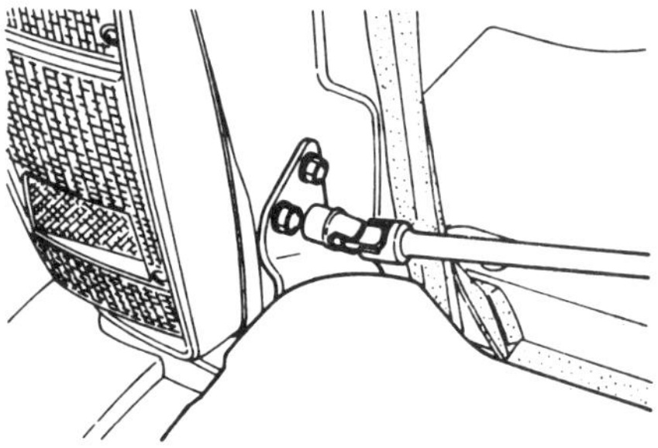

Fig. 13.30. Removing the tailgate hinge securing bolts (Sec. 10)

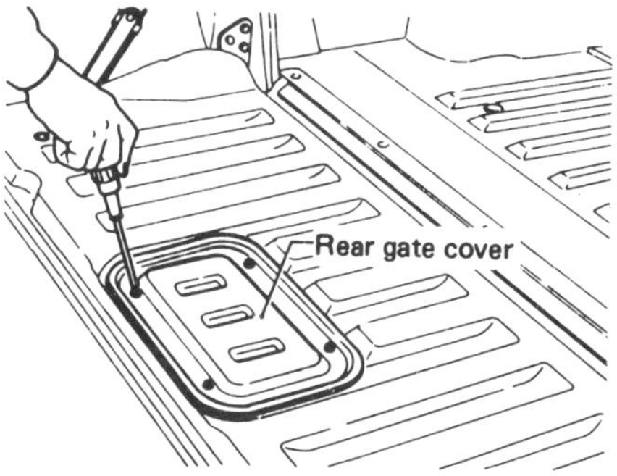

Fig. 13.31. Removing the tailgate inner cover (Sec. 10)

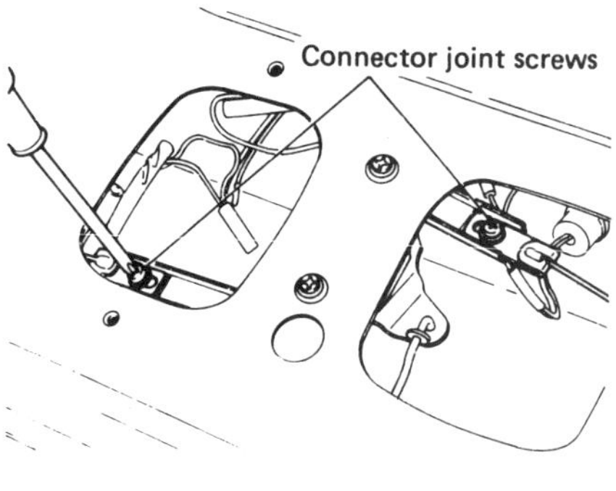

Fig. 13.32. Removing the tailgate lock connector joint screws (Sec. 10)

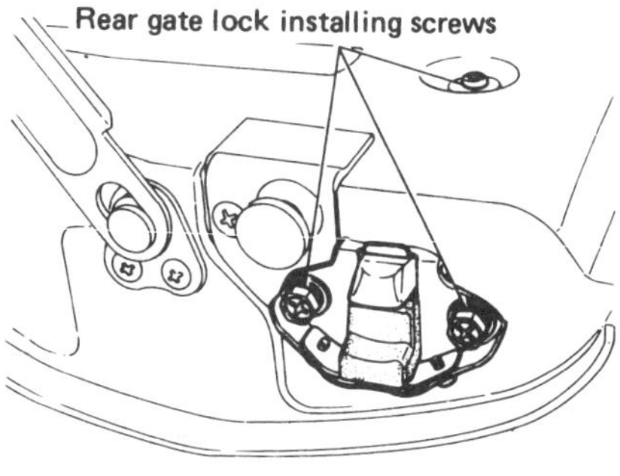

Fig. 13.33. Removing the tailgate lock (Sec. 10)

9 Suspension and axles

Front end road clearance height (4WD) - adjustment

1 The road clearance of the front suspension can be increased or decreased by turning the two adjusting nuts on each front suspension strut.

2 Before making any adjustment make sure that all the tires are correctly inflated and that the car is standing on level ground.

3 Measure the distance between the front end of each transverse link attaching bolt and the ground to give a datum for adjustment.

4 Turn the two nuts on each strut at the same time and by an equal amount until the required height is achieved and the car is level.

10 Bodywork

Rear tailgate (4WD Open MPV) - removal and refitting

1 Disconnect the electrical lead at the connector for the licence plate light.

2 Support the tailgate to prevent it from dropping and then undo and remove the two screws each side securing the stays to the tailgate.

3 Undo and remove the three bolts securing each hinge to the body pillars and then slide out the tailgate.

4 Refitting is the reverse sequence to removal.

Rear tailgate lock, lever and handle (4WD Open MPV) - removal and refitting

5 Open the tailgate, remove the four screws and lift off the inner cover.

6 To remove the tailgate locks, undo and remove the two connector joint screws and the three screws securing each lock to the sides of the tailgate. The locks can now be pulled out.

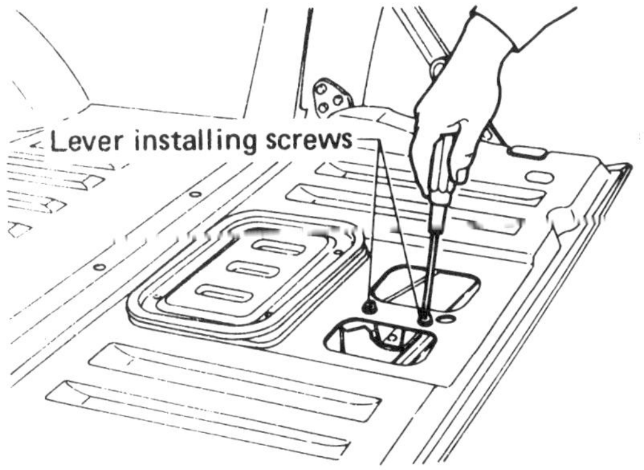

Fig. 13.34. Removing the tailgate lever (Sec. 10)

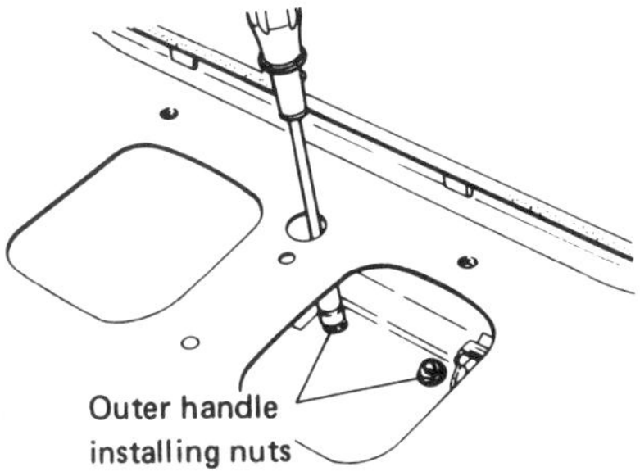

Fig. 13.35. Removing the tailgate outer handle (Sec. 10)

Use of English

As this book has been written in England, it uses the appropriate English component names, phrases, and spelling. Some of these differ from those used in America. Normally, these cause no difficulty, but to make sure, a glossary is printed below. In ordering spare parts remember the parts list will probably use these words:

English	American	English	American
Aerial	Antenna	Layshaft (of gearbox)	Countershaft
Accelerator	Gas pedal	Leading shoe (of brake)	Primary shoe
Alternator	Generator (AC)	Locks	Latches
Anti-roll bar	Stabiliser or sway bar	Motorway	Freeway, turnpike etc
Battery	Energizer	Number plate	License plate
Bodywork	Sheet metal	Paraffin	Kerosene
Bonnet (engine cover)	Hood	Petrol	Gasoline
Boot lid	Trunk lid	Petrol tank	Gas tank
Boot (luggage compartment)	Trunk	'Pinking'	'Pinging'
Bottom gear	1st gear	Propeller shaft	Driveshaft
Bulkhead	Firewall	Quarter light	Quarter window
Cam follower or tappet	Valve lifter or tappet	Retread	Recap
Carburettor	Carburetor	Reverse	Back-up
Catch	Latch	Rocker cover	Valve cover
Choke/venturi	Barrel	Roof rack	Car-top carrier
Circlip	Snap-ring	Saloon	Sedan
Clearance	Lash	Seized	Frozen
Crownwheel	Ring gear (of differential)	Side indicator lights	Side marker lights
Disc (brake)	Rotor/disk	Side light	Parking light
Drop arm	Pitman arm	Silencer	Muffler
Drop head coupe	Convertible	Spanner	Wrench
Dynamo	Generator (DC)	Sill panel (beneath doors)	Rocker panel
Earth (electrical)	Ground	Split cotter (for valve spring cap)	Lock (for valve spring retainer)
Engineer's blue	Prussian blue	Split pin	Cotter pin
Estate car	Station wagon	Steering arm	Spindle arm
Exhaust manifold	Header	Sump	Oil pan
Fast back (Coupe)	Hard top	Tab washer	Tang; lock
Fault finding/diagnosis	Trouble shooting	Tailgate	Liftgate
Float chamber	Float bowl	Tappet	Valve lifter
Free-play	Lash	Thrust bearing	Throw-out bearing
Freewheel	Coast	Top gear	High
Gudgeon pin	Piston pin or wrist pin	Trackrod (of steering)	Tie-rod (or connecting rod)
Gearchange	Shift	Trailing shoe (of brake)	Secondary shoe
Gearbox	Transmission	Transmission	Whole drive line
Halfshaft	Axleshaft	Tyre	Tire
Handbrake	Parking brake	Van	Panel wagon/van
Hood	Soft top	Vice	Vise
Hot spot	Heat riser	Wheel nut	Lug nut
Indicator	Turn signal	Windscreen	Windshield
Interior light	Dome lamp	Wing/mudguard	Fender

Miscellaneous points

An 'oil seal' is fitted to components lubricated by grease!

A 'damper' is a 'shock absorber', it damps out bouncing, and absorbs shocks of bump impact. Both names are correct, and both are used haphazardly.

Note that British drum brakes are different from the Bendix type that is common in America, so different descriptive names result. The shoe end furthest from the hydraulic wheel cylinder is on a pivot; interconnection between the shoes as on Bendix brakes is most uncommon. Therefore the phrase 'Primary' or 'Secondary' shoe does not apply. A shoe is said to be 'Leading' or 'Trailing'. A 'Leading' shoe is one on which a point on the drum, as it rotates forward, reaches the shoe at the end worked by the hydraulic cylinder before the anchor end. The opposite is a 'Trailing' shoe, and this one has no self servo from the wrapping effect of the rotating drum.

Safety First!

Professional motor mechanics are trained in safe working procedures. However enthusiastic you may be about getting on with the job in hand, do take the time to ensure that your safety is not put at risk. A moment's lack of attention can result in an accident, as can failure to observe certain elementary precautions.

There will always be new ways of having accidents, and the following points do not pretend to be a comprehensive list of all dangers; they are intended rather to make you aware of the risks and to encourage a safety-conscious approach to all work you carry out on your vehicle.

Essential DOs and DON'Ts

DON'T rely on a single jack when working underneath the vehicle. Always use reliable additional means of support, such as axle stands, securely placed under a part of the vehicle that you know will not give way.

DON'T attempt to loosen or tighten high-torque nuts (e.g. wheel hub nuts) while the vehicle is on a jack; it may be pulled off.

DON'T start the engine without first ascertaining that the transmission is in neutral (or 'Park' where applicable) and the parking brake applied.

DON'T suddenly remove the filler cap from a hot cooling system – cover it with a cloth and release the pressure gradually first, or you may get scalded by escaping coolant.

DON'T attempt to drain oil until you are sure it has cooled sufficiently to avoid scalding you.

DON'T grasp any part of the engine, exhaust or catalytic converter without first ascertaining that it is sufficiently cool to avoid burning you.

DON'T syphon toxic liquids such as fuel, brake fluid or antifreeze by mouth, or allow them to remain on your skin.

DON'T inhale brake lining dust – it is injurious to health.

DON'T allow any spilt oil or grease to remain on the floor – wipe it up straight away, before someone slips on it.

DON'T use ill-fitting spanners or other tools which may slip and cause injury.

DON'T attempt to lift a heavy component which may be beyond your capability – get assistance.

DON'T rush to finish a job, or take unverified short cuts.

DON'T allow children or animals in or around an unattended vehicle.

DO wear eye protection when using power tools such as drill, sander, bench grinder etc, and when working under the vehicle.

DO use a barrier cream on your hands prior to undertaking dirty jobs – it will protect your skin from infection as well as making the dirt easier to remove afterwards; but make sure your hands aren't left slippery.

DO keep loose clothing (cuffs, tie etc) and long hair well out of the way of moving mechanical parts.

DO remove rings, wristwatch etc, before working on the vehicle – especially the electrical system.

DO ensure that any lifting tackle used has a safe working load rating adequate for the job.

DO keep your work area tidy – it is only too easy to fall over articles left lying around.

DO get someone to check periodically that all is well, when working alone on the vehicle.

DO carry out work in a logical sequence and check that everything is correctly assembled and tightened afterwards.

DO remember that your vehicle's safety affects that of yourself and others. If in doubt on any point, get specialist advice.

IF, in spite of following these precautions, you are unfortunate enough to injure yourself, seek medical attention as soon as possible.

Fire

Remember at all times that petrol (gasoline) is highly flammable. Never smoke, or have any kind of naked flame around, when working on the vehicle. But the risk does not end there – a spark caused by an electrical short-circuit, by two metal surfaces contacting each other, or even by static electricity built up in your body under certain conditions, can ignite petrol vapour, which in a confined space is highly explosive.

Always disconnect the battery earth (ground) terminal before working on any part of the fuel system, and never risk spilling fuel on to a hot engine or exhaust.

It is recommended that a fire extinguisher of a type suitable for fuel and electrical fires is kept handy in the garage or workplace at all times. Never try to extinguish a fuel or electrical fire with water.

Fumes

Certain fumes are highly toxic and can quickly cause unconsciousness and even death if inhaled to any extent. Petrol (gasoline) vapour comes into this category, as do the vapours from certain solvents such as trichloroethylene. Any draining or pouring of such volatile fluids should be done in a well ventilated area.

When using cleaning fluids and solvents, read the instructions carefully. Never use materials from unmarked containers – they may give off poisonous vapours.

Never run the engine of a motor vehicle in an enclosed space such as a garage. Exhaust fumes contain carbon monoxide which is extremely poisonous; if you need to run the engine, always do so in the open air or at least have the rear of the vehicle outside the workplace.

If you are fortunate enough to have the use of an inspection pit, never drain or pour petrol, and never run the engine, while the vehicle is standing over it; the fumes, being heavier than air, will concentrate in the pit with possibly lethal results.

The battery

Never cause a spark, or allow a naked light, near the vehicle's battery. It will normally be giving off a certain amount of hydrogen gas, which is highly explosive.

Always disconnect the battery earth (ground) terminal before working on the fuel or electrical systems.

If possible, loosen the filler plugs or cover when charging the battery from an external source. Do not charge at an excessive rate or the battery may burst.

Take care when topping up and when carrying the battery. The acid electrolyte, even when diluted, is very corrosive and should not be allowed to contact the eyes or skin.

If you ever need to prepare electrolyte yourself, always add the acid slowly to the water, and never the other way round. Protect against splashes by wearing rubber gloves and goggles.

Mains electricity

When using an electric power tool, inspection light etc which works from the mains, always ensure that the appliance is correctly connected to its plug and that, where necessary, it is properly earthed (grounded). Do not use such appliances in damp conditions and, again, beware of creating a spark or applying excessive heat in the vicinity of fuel or fuel vapour.

Ignition HT voltage

A severe electric shock can result from touching certain parts of the ignition system, such as the HT leads, when the engine is running or being cranked, particularly if components are damp or the insulation is defective. Where an electronic ignition system is fitted, the HT voltage is much higher and could prove fatal.

Conversion factors

Length (distance)

Inches (in)	X 25.4	= Millimetres (mm)	X 0.039	= Inches (in)
Feet (ft)	X 0.305	= Metres (m)	X 3.281	= Feet (ft)
Miles	X 1.609	= Kilometres (km)	X 0.621	= Miles

Volume (capacity)

Cubic inches (cu in; in^3)	X 16.387	= Cubic centimetres (cc; cm^3)	X 0.061	= Cubic inches (cu in; in^3)
Imperial pints (Imp pt)	X 0.568	= Litres (l)	X 1.76	= Imperial pints (Imp pt)
Imperial quarts (Imp qt)	X 1.137	= Litres (l)	X 0.88	= Imperial quarts (Imp qt)
Imperial quarts (Imp qt)	X 1.201	= US quarts (US qt)	X 0.833	= Imperial quarts (Imp qt)
US quarts (US qt)	X 0.946	= Litres (l)	X 1.057	= US quarts (US qt)
Imperial gallons (Imp gal)	X 4.546	= Litres (l)	X 0.22	= Imperial gallons (Imp gal)
Imperial gallons (Imp gal)	X 1.201	= US gallons (US gal)	X 0.833	= Imperial gallons (Imp gal)
US gallons (US gal)	X 3.785	= Litres (l)	X 0.264	= US gallons (US gal)

Mass (weight)

Ounces (oz)	X 28.35	= Grams (g)	X 0.035	= Ounces (oz)
Pounds (lb)	X 0.454	= Kilograms (kg)	X 2.205	= Pounds (lb)

Force

Ounces-force (ozf; oz)	X 0.278	= Newtons (N)	X 3.6	= Ounces-force (ozf; oz)
Pounds-force (lbf; lb)	X 4.448	= Newtons (N)	X 0.225	= Pounds-force (lbf; lb)
Newtons (N)	X 0.1	= Kilograms-force (kgf; kg)	X 9.81	= Newtons (N)

Pressure

Pounds-force per square inch (psi; lbf/in^2; lb/in^2)	X 0.070	= Kilograms-force per square centimetre (kgf/cm^2; kg/cm^2)	X 14.223	= Pounds-force per square inch (psi; lbf/in^2; lb/in^2)
Pounds-force per square inch (psi; lbf/in^2; lb/in^2)	X 0.068	= Atmospheres (atm)	X 14.696	= Pounds-force per square inch (psi; lbf/in^2; lb/in^2)
Pounds-force per square inch (psi; lbf/in^2; lb/in^2)	X 0.069	= Bars	X 14.5	= Pounds-force per square inch (psi; lbf/in^2; lb/in^2)
Pounds-force per square inch (psi; lbf/in^2; lb/in^2)	X 6.895	= Kilopascals (kPa)	X 0.145	= Pounds-force per square inch (psi; lbf/in^2; lb/in^2)
Kilopascals (kPa)	X 0.01	= Kilograms-force per square centimetre (kgf/cm^2; kg/cm^2)	X 98.1	= Kilopascals (kPa)

Torque (moment of force)

Pounds-force inches (lbf in; lb in)	X 1.152	= Kilograms-force centimetre (kgf cm; kg cm)	X 0.868	= Pounds-force inches (lbf in; lb in)
Pounds-force inches (lbf in; lb in)	X 0.113	= Newton metres (Nm)	X 8.85	= Pounds-force inches (lbf in; lb in)
Pounds-force inches (lbf in; lb in)	X 0.083	= Pounds-force feet (lbf ft; lb ft)	X 12	= Pounds-force inches (lbf in; lb in)
Pounds-force feet (lbf ft; lb ft)	X 0.138	= Kilograms-force metres (kgf m; kg m)	X 7.233	= Pounds-force feet (lbf ft; lb ft)
Pounds-force feet (lbf ft; lb ft)	X 1.356	= Newton metres (Nm)	X 0.738	= Pounds-force feet (lbf ft; lb ft)
Newton metres (Nm)	X 0.102	= Kilograms-force metres (kgf m; kg m)	X 9.804	= Newton metres (Nm)

Power

Horsepower (hp)	X 745.7	= Watts (W)	X 0.0013	= Horsepower (hp)

Velocity (speed)

Miles per hour (miles/hr; mph)	X 1.609	= Kilometres per hour (km/hr; kph)	X 0.621	= Miles per hour (miles/hr; mph)

*Fuel consumption**

Miles per gallon, Imperial (mpg)	X 0.354	= Kilometres per litre (km/l)	X 2.825	= Miles per gallon, Imperial (mpg)
Miles per gallon, US (mpg)	X 0.425	= Kilometres per litre (km/l)	X 2.352	= Miles per gallon, US (mpg)

Temperature

Degrees Fahrenheit (°F) $= (°C \times \frac{9}{5}) + 32$

Degrees Celsius (Degrees Centigrade; °C) $= (°F - 32) \times \frac{5}{9}$

**It is common practice to convert from miles per gallon (mpg) to litres/100 kilometres (l/100km), where mpg (Imperial) x l/100 km = 282 and mpg (US) x l/100 km = 235*

Index

Printed by
Haynes Publishing Group
Sparkford Yeovil Somerset
England